Management
of Organizational
Behavior

Management of Organizational Behavior

Utilizing Human Resources

Sixth Edition

Paul Hersey

Graduate School of Applied Behavioral Sciences
California American University
Escondido, California

Kenneth H. Blanchard

School of Hotel Administration
Cornell University
Ithaca, NY

PRENTICE HALL, Englewood Cliffs, NJ 07632

Library of Congress Cataloging-in-Publication Data

Hersey, Paul.
    Management of organizational behavior : utilizing human resources
/ Paul Hersey, Kenneth H. Blanchard. — 6th ed.
        p.   cm.
    Includes bibliographical references and index.
    ISBN 0-13-554999-X   0-13-555004-1 {PBK.}
    1. Organizational behavior.   2. Management.   3. Leadership.
I. Blanchard, Kenneth H.   II. Title.
HD58.7.H47   1993
    658.3 — dc20   92-35580
                                                              CIP

Editorial/production supervision and
    interior design: Kristin E. Dackow
Acquisitions editor: Alison Reeves
Prepress buyer: Trudy Pisciotti
Manufacturing buyer: Patrice Fraccio

 ©1993, 1988, 1982, 1977, 1972, 1969 by Prentice-Hall, Inc.
A Simon & Schuster Company
Englewood Cliffs, New Jersey 07632

Printed in the United States of America

10   9   8   7   6   5   4   3   2   1

ISBN 0-13-555004-1 {PBK.}
ISBN 0-13-554999-X

Prentice-Hall International (UK) Limited, *London*
Prentice-Hall of Australia Pty. Limited, *Sydney*
Prentice-Hall Canada Inc., *Toronto*
Prentice-Hall Hispanoamericana, S.A., *Mexico*
Prentice-Hall of India Private Limited, *New Delhi*
Prentice-Hall of Japan, Inc., *Tokyo*
Simon & Schuster Asia Pte. Ltd., *Singapore*
Editora Prentice-Hall do Brasil, Ltda., *Rio de Janeiro*

To

RALPH E. HERSEY, SR., a retired telephone pioneer with over fifty patents for Bell Laboratories, whose work made direct distance dialing a reality. In looking back over his thirty-nine years of work with the telephone industry, he once commented that of all his contributions, the most rewarding aspect to him personally was that he became known as a *developer of people.*

and

the REAR ADMIRAL THEODORE BLANCHARD, USNR, former Naval officer who was decorated with two Silver Stars, the Bronze Star, the Presidential Citation, and a navy Unit Commendation for his courageous and competent World War II leadership in the Pacific. In talking with people who worked for him over the years, he was always described as an inspirational, dedicated, and caring leader who always fought for his people and the "underdog," whether in peace or war time.

Contents

Preface

Almost twenty-five years ago, we introduced our first edition with the following statements which we still believe:

> For a long time management theory has been characterized by a search for universals—a preoccupation with discovering essential elements of all organizations. The discovering of common elements is necessary, but they do not really provide practitioners with "principles" that can be applied with universal success.
>
> In the past decade there has appeared a relative maturity in this field as it begins to focus on "patterned variations"—situational differences. We assume that there are common elements in all organizations, but we also assume differences among them and in particular the managing of their human resources. As the inventory of empirical studies expands, making comparisons and contrasts possible, management theory will continue to emerge. Common elements will be isolated and important variables brought to light.
>
> We believe that management theory is important to all categories of organizations—business, government, military, medicine,

education, "voluntary" organizations such as the church, and even the home. We thus have drawn our illustrations and cases from a variety of these organizations and incorporated concepts from many disciplines. Our purpose is to identify a framework which may be helpful in integrating independent approaches from these various disciplines to the understanding of human behavior and management theory.

The focus of this book is on behavior within organizations and not between organizations. Our belief is that an organization is a unique living organism whose basic component is the individual and this individual is our fundamental unit of study. Thus, our concentration is on the interaction of people, motivation, and leadership.

Though this book is an outgrowth of the insights of many earlier writers, we hope it will make some contribution to management theory.

The response to our first five editions has been very gratifying and encouraging. Individuals and organizations not only in the United States but throughout the world have made use of the behavioral science concepts, tools, and techniques to improve performance. Our goal of writing a readable book that would make the behavioral sciences come alive for operating managers, parents, teachers, and students alike appears to have been accomplished through this broad-based acceptance.

In writing this sixth edition, as in the previous editions, we have assumed the serious responsibility of preparing you for the real world through a quality research-based approach to the behavioral sciences. Our purpose is to equip you for the real world, not the fantasy world — a real world, where each of us has to understand the challenges of managing human organizations in a highly competitive environment. This is why our primary emphasis is on practical applied behavioral science concepts, tools, and techniques.

After writing an earlier edition of *Management of Organizational Behavior,* we went our separate ways and crystallized our different approaches to the field of applied behavioral sciences. We are excited about once again working together to produce this latest edition of *Management of Organizational Behavior.*

The emphasis of Paul's work and his colleagues at the Center for Leadership Studies has been the refinement of Situational Leadership and the expansion of its applications to various organizational settings as well as to the selling process. These efforts culminated in the writing of *The Situational Leader* and *Situational Selling,* both of which continue to have a significant impact on many of the changes and improvements found in this edition.

The major thrust of Ken's work and his colleagues at Blanchard Training and Development has been on taking some of the basic concepts associated with performance management and Situational Leadership and organizing them into the One Minute Management system. The international best seller, *The One Minute Manager,* which he co-authored with Spencer Johnson, and the follow-up books *Putting the One Minute Manager to Work,* written with Bob Lorber, and *Leadership and the One Minute Manager* with Drea and Patricia Zigarmi, were the result of these efforts. The concepts presented in these books are again highlighted in this revision.

All of the continuing developments in our thinking and the varied research and consulting activities of our respective organizations are reflected in this edition. Each chapter has been carefully revised and updated. We trust that this sixth edition will make an important contribution to your personal and professional growth and development.

We owe much to colleagues and associates without whose guidance, encouragement, and inspiration the first edition of this book—much less the sixth—would never have been written. In particular, we are indebted to Harry Evarts, Ted Hellebrandt, Norman Martin, Don McCarty, Bob Melendes, Walter Pauk, Warren Ramshaw, and Franklin Williams.

We wish to make special mention of Chris Argyris, William J. Reddin, and Edgar A. Schein. Their contributions to the field of applied behavioral science have been most valuable to us in the course of preparing this book, and we hereby express our appreciation to them.

The comments and suggestions provided by students, managers, teachers, researchers, consultants, and reviewers have been tremendously important to us as we have prepared this revision. Special assistance has been provided by Elizabeth Linquist, Ron Brown, Lori Paris, Gail Johnson, Gustav Pansegrow, Douglas Long, Bo Gyllenpalm, Lance Doyle, Joan Johnson, Mary Viancourt.

John R. Thuerer of The College of Idaho, Richard I. Lester of the Department of the Air Force Air University, Ned B. Lovell of Stetson University, Charles R. Nuckles of Concordia College—St. Paul, Charles K. Lingren of South Dakota State University, and Donald L. Eversole of Wayland Baptist University.

We also want to make note of the contributions of Ron Campbell of the Center for Leadership Studies, for his thoughtful review of the manuscript, and those of Robert Nelson of Blanchard Training and Development, for drafting chapters 17 and 18.

Special thanks are also due to Kristin Dackow, Alison Reeves, and Garret White of Prentice Hall for their hard work and dedication to the development, design, and production of this Sixth Edition.

We appreciate the interest of all who have made the applied behavioral sciences highly relevant to your daily leadership and management roles.

We also wish to express our special appreciation to our friend and colleague for two decades, Dewey E. Johnson, Professor of Management, California State University-Fresno, who assisted us in the preparation of this edition as well as the previous edition.

Finally, to Suzanne and Margie, our wives, for their continued patience, support, and interest in the progress of our work.

Paul Hersey

Kenneth H. Blanchard

Management
of Organizational
Behavior

1

Management:
An Applied Behavioral Sciences Approach

This is a tremendously exciting period for both the understanding and practice of leadership and management. Now, as perhaps never before, there is a growing awareness that the success of our organizations is directly dependent on the effective use of human resources based on the applied behavioral sciences.[1] As we consider the challenging problems in the management of organizations—business, government, not-for-profit, school, military, and family—we realize that the real test of our abilities as leaders and managers is how effectively we can establish and maintain human organizations.

To meet these challenges we need special tools and the skills to use these tools. This is what this book is all about. It not only presents fundamental behavioral science concepts and theories, but also suggests proven simple-to-use tools based on the behavioral sciences.

Some concepts in the behavioral sciences by themselves are well intended, but fall short of the mark. They give you good ideas to think about, but they do not always tell you how or when to put these ideas into practice in the management of human organizations. It is said that success in life is ". . . twenty percent timing and eighty percent just showing up."[2] We have all seen people who just "show up" in leadership and management situations. But we believe that success is much more than just "showing up." We believe it is the knowledge and application of tested behavioral science concepts plus the "timing" skills to get things done. This book will not only help you to acquire the knowledge, but also to develop the skills necessary to be a high-performing leader.

Leading, the influencing of the behavior of others, must not be thought of as a single event. Leadership and management are full-time responsibilities that must be practiced every hour of every day. Each minute must be spent wisely. Of course, this is not easy. Leadership and management, because they involve the complexities of people, almost defy description and understanding. We have all known courageous men and women who have provided the vision and energy to make things happen in very difficult situations. But even after decades of research, we are still unable to identify with certainty the specific causal factors that determine leadership and management success at a specific time and place. This is because real-life situations are never static. They are in a constant state of change, with many factors or variables interacting at the same time. Because of this, the behavioral sciences, unlike the physical sciences, deal in probabilities. Our purpose then is to help increase the odds in your favor, not to suggest rules. In the arena of behavioral sciences, there are no rules.

What has long been needed is an approach to leadership and management that is both conceptually sound and practical in application. We have found through our research and writing, our conversations with thousands of managers throughout the world, our consulting and seminars that most people want an easy-to-grasp approach that is broad enough in scope to permit its application to a number of organizations and situations. Such an approach would promote a common understanding and language that would make it possible for managers to work together and act upon the problems they experience in managing their human resources. In developing these ideas and skills, we wanted to build upon the considerable legacy of the behavioral sciences by using a common language so managers could easily master the key ideas and skills. Situational Leadership provides such a common language to help solve performance problems. It provides a valuable language that can be used on the job, in the home, and in every leadership situation. It provides a common language we can use to diagnose leadership problems, to adapt behavior to solve these problems, and to communicate solutions.

Rather than reacting to problems in an emotional way, Situational Leadership provides a vehicle for talking about performance problems in a rational way that focuses on the key issues involved. We also wanted to present an approach that has face validity and that is based on empirical evidence. The acceptance that we have received for more than twenty-five years has indicated to us that this approach is easily understood, accepted, and implemented at all levels of organizations. It is a fundamental approach to the management of organizational behavior.

A LOOK BACK

The transformation of American society since the turn of the century has been breathtaking. We have progressed from a basically agrarian society to a dynamic industrial society, with a higher level of education and standard of living than was ever thought possible. In addition, our scientific and technical advancement staggers the imagination.

This progress has not been without its seamy side. At a time when we should be rejoicing in a golden age of plenty, we find ourselves wallowing in conflict—conflict between nations, conflict between races, conflict between management and workers, even conflict between neighbors. These problems that we face cannot be solved by scientific and technical skills alone; they will require social skills. Many of our most critical problems are not in the world of *things,* but in the world of *people.* Our greatest failure as human beings has been the inability to secure cooperation and understanding with others. Shortly after World War II, Elton Mayo recognized this problem when he reflected that "the consequences for society of the unbalance between the development of technical and of social skills have been disastrous."[3]

SUCCESSFUL VERSUS UNSUCCESSFUL SCIENCES

In seeking reasons for this unbalance, Mayo suggested that a significant part of the problem might be traced to the difference between what he called "the successful sciences" (chemistry, physics, and physiology) and "the unsuccessful sciences" (psychology, sociology, and political science). He labeled the former "successful" because in studying these sciences, both theory and practice are provided. Pure knowledge is limited in value unless it can be applied in real situations. The implication of these profound conclusions is that in learning about chemistry or physics, students or practitioners are given direct experience in using their new technical skills in the laboratory, but on the other hand, according to Mayo, the unsuccessful sciences

> do not seem to equip students with a single social skill that is usable in ordinary human situations ... no continuous and direct contact with the social facts is contrived for the student. He learns from books, spending endless hours in libraries; he reconsiders ancient formulae, uncontrolled by the steady development of experimental skills, the equivalent of the clinic or indeed of the laboratory.[4]

Change

Early contributions in the behavioral sciences, as Mayo suggests, seemed to provide knowledge without effecting changes in behavior. But an organization's survival depends on change. Therefore, this book will focus on four levels of change in people: (1) knowledge changes; (2) attitudinal changes; (3) behavioral changes; and (4) group or organizational performance changes.[5] The time relationship and the relative difficulty involved in making each of these levels of change when force or compliance is not a factor are illustrated in Figure 1-1.

Changes in knowledge are the easiest to make, followed by changes in attitudes. Attitude structures differ from knowledge structures in that they are emotionally charged in a positive or a negative way. Changes in behavior are significantly more difficult and time consuming than either of the two previous levels. But the implementation of group or organizational performance change is perhaps the most difficult and time consuming. Our survival may, in fact, be dependent upon how well the behavioral sciences are able to resolve conflict through understanding and implementing change.

FIGURE 1-1 Time and difficulty involved in making various changes

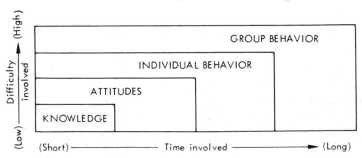

MANAGEMENT DEFINED

It is obvious after reviewing the literature that there are almost as many definitions of management as there are writers in the field. A common thread that appears in these definitions is the manager's requirement to accomplish organizational goals or objectives.[6] We shall define management as the process of *working with and through individuals and groups and other resources to accomplish organizational goals.*

This definition, it should be noted, makes no mention of business or industrial organizations. Management, as defined, applies to organizations whether they are businesses, educational institutions, hospitals, political or military organizations, or even families. To be successful, these organizations require their management personnel to have interpersonal skills. The achievement of organizational objectives through leadership is management. Thus, everyone is a manager in at least certain activities.

Distinction Between Management and Leadership

Management and leadership are often thought of as one and the same thing. We feel, however, that there is an important distinction between the two concepts.

In essence, leadership is a broader concept than management. Management is thought of as a special kind of leadership in which the achievement of organizational goals is paramount. The key difference between the two concepts, therefore, lies in the word *organization.* Leadership occurs any time one attempts to *influence the behavior* of an individual or group, regardless of the reason. It may be for one's own goals or for those of others, and they may or may not be congruent with organizational goals.

THREE COMPETENCIES OF LEADERSHIP

In leading or influencing, there are three general skills or competencies: (a) diagnosing—being able to understand the situation you are trying to influence; (b) adapting—being able to adapt your behavior and the other resources you have available to meet the contingencies of the situation; and (c) communicating—being able to communicate in a way that people can easily understand and accept. We will discuss each of these competencies in greater detail in subsequent chapters, but for now here is a brief summary of each.

- Diagnosing is a *cognitive*–or cerebral–competency. It is understanding what the situation is now and knowing what you can reasonably expect it to be in the future. The discrepancy between the two is the *problem* to be solved. This is what the other competencies are aimed at changing.
- Adapting is a *behavioral* competency. It involves adapting your behaviors and other resources in a way that helps to close the gap between the current situation and what you want to achieve.
- Communicating is a *process* competency. Even if you are able to understand the situation, even if you are able to adopt behavior and resources to meet the situation, you need to communicate effectively. If you can't communicate in a way that people can understand and accept, the whole process will not have the impact you would like it to have.[7]

MANAGEMENT PROCESS

The managerial functions of *planning, organizing, motivating,* and *controlling* are considered central to a discussion of management by many authors. These functions that comprise the management process—a step-by-step way of doing something—are relevant regardless of the type of organization or level of management with which one is concerned. As Harold Koontz and Cyril O'Donnell have said: "Acting in their managerial capacity, presidents, department heads, foremen, supervisors, college deans, bishops, and heads of governmental agencies all do the same thing. As managers they are all engaged, in part, in getting things done with and through people. As a manager, each must, at one time or another, carry out all the duties characteristic of managers."[8] In today's world, even a well-run household uses these managerial functions.

Planning involves setting *goals* and *objectives* for the organization and developing "work maps" showing how these goals and objectives are to be accomplished. Once plans have been made, organizing becomes meaningful. This involves bringing together resources—people, capital, and equipment—in the most effective way to accomplish the goals. Organizing, therefore, involves an integration of resources.

Along with planning and organizing, motivating plays a large part in determining the level of performance of employees, which, in turn, influences how effectively the organizational goals will be met. Motivating is sometimes included as part of directing, along with communicating and leading.

In his research on motivation, William James of Harvard found

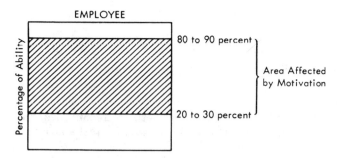

FIGURE 1-2 **The potential influence of motivation on performance**

that hourly employees could maintain their jobs (that is, not be fired) by working at approximately 20 to 30 percent of their ability. His study also showed that employees work at close to 80 to 90 percent of their ability if highly motivated. Both the minimum level at which employees might work and yet keep their jobs and the level at which they could be expected to perform with proper motivation are illustrated in Figure 1-2.

This illustration shows us that if motivation is low, employees' performance will suffer as much as if their ability were low. For this reason, motivating is an extremely important function of management.

Another function of management is controlling. This involves feedback of results and follow-up to compare accomplishments with plans and to make appropriate adjustments where outcomes have deviated from expectations.

Although these management functions are stated separately, and as presented seem to have a specific sequence, one must remember that they are interrelated, as illustrated in Figure 1-3. While these functions are interrelated, at any one time one or more may be of primary importance.

FIGURE 1-3
Interrelated management
functions

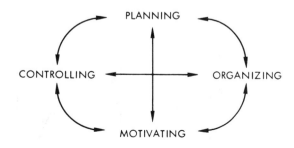

SKILLS OF A MANAGER

It is generally agreed that there are at least three areas of skill necessary for carrying out the process of management: technical, human, and conceptual.

- *Technical skill*—Ability to use knowledge, methods, techniques, and equipment necessary for the performance of specific tasks acquired from experience, education, and training.
- *Human skill*—Ability and judgment in working with and through people, including an understanding of motivation and an application of effective leadership.
- *Conceptual skill*—Ability to understand the complexities of the overall organization and where one's own operation fits into the organization. This knowledge permits one to act according to the objectives of the total organization rather than only on the basis of the goals and needs of one's own immediate group.[9]

The appropriate mix of these skills varies as an individual advances in management from supervisory to top-management positions. This is illustrated in Figure 1-4.

To be effective, less technical skill tends to be needed as one advances from lower to higher levels in the organization, but more conceptual skill is necessary. Supervisors at lower levels need considerable technical skill because they are often required to train and develop technicians and other employees in their sections. At the other extreme, executives in a business organization do not need to know how to perform all the specific tasks at the operational level. However, they should be able to see how all these functions are interrelated in accomplishing the goals of the total organization.

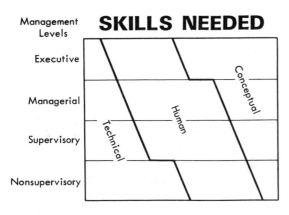

SKILLS NEEDED

FIGURE 1-4
Management skills necessary at various levels of an organization

While the amount of technical and conceptual skills needed at these different levels of management varies, *the common denominator that appears to be crucial at all levels is human skill.*

Emphasis on Human Skills

The emphasis on human skills was considered important in the past, but it is of primary importance today. For example, one of the great entrepreneurs, John D. Rockefeller, stated: "I will pay more for the ability to deal with people than any other ability under the sun."[10] These words of Rockefeller are often echoed. According to a report by the American Management Association, an overwhelming majority of the two hundred managers who participated in a survey agreed that the most important single skill of an executive is effective relationship skill.[11] In this survey, management rated this ability more vital than intelligence, decisiveness, knowledge, or job skills.

ORGANIZATIONS AS SOCIAL SYSTEMS

Although the emphasis in this text will be on human skills development, we must recognize that the organizations in which most managers operate are social systems comprised of many interrelated subsystems, only one of which is a human/social system. The others could include an administrative/structural subsystem, an informational/decision-making subsystem, and an economic/technological subsystem.[12]

The focus of the administrative/structural subsystem is on authority, structure, and responsibility within the organization: "who does what for whom" and "who tells whom to do what, how, when, where, and why." The informational/decision-making subsystem emphasizes key decisions and their informational needs to keep the system going. The main concern of the economic/technological subsystem is the work to be done and the cost effectiveness of that work within the specific goals of the organization.

Although the focus of the human/social system is on the motivation and needs of the members of the organization and on the leadership provided or required (the major emphasis of this book), it should be emphasized that within a systems approach there is a clear understanding that changes in one subsystem affect changes in other parts of the total system. As illustrated in Figure 1-5, if the total system is healthy and functioning well, each of its parts or subsystems is effectively interacting with the others. Therefore, an organization over a sustained period of time cannot afford to overemphasize the impor-

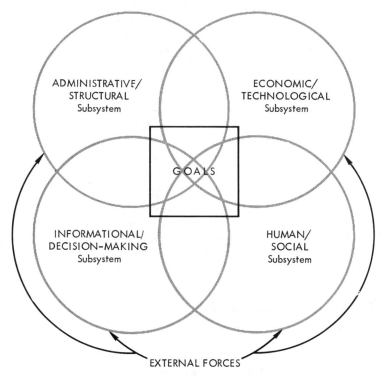

FIGURE 1-5 The interrelated subsystems of an organization

tance of one subsystem at the expense of the others. At the same time, the internal management of the organization cannot ignore the needs and pressures from the external environment.

Managerial Roles in a Social System

According to Ichak Adizes,[13] four managerial roles must be performed if an organization is to be run effectively. These four roles are *producing, implementing, innovating,* and *integrating.* Each of these managerial roles is clearly related to one of the four social subsystems of an organization.

A manager in the role of *producing* is expected to achieve results equal to or better than the competition. "The principal qualification for an achiever is the possession of a functional knowledge of his field, whether marketing, engineering, accounting, or any other discipline."[14] The role of producing emphasizes activities in the economic/technological subsystem.

Being individually productive and having technical skills do not necessarily enable a manager to produce results in working with a group of people. As we stated earlier, a manager should have more than just technical skill. Managers should be more than individual producers. They should be able to administer the people with whom they work and to see that these people also produce results. In this *implementing* role, managers schedule, coordinate, control, and discipline. If managers are implementers, they see to it that the system works as it has been designed to work. Implementing emphasizes the administrative/structural subsystem.

While producing and implementing are important, in a changing environment managers must use their judgment and have the discretion to change goals and change the systems by which goals are implemented. In this role, managers must be organizational entrepreneurs and innovators since, unlike administrators who are given plans to carry out and decisions to implement, entrepreneurs have to generate their own plan of action. They have to be self-starters. This *innovating* role stresses the informational/decision-making subsystem.

According to Adizes, the three roles of producing, implementing, and innovating in combination are insufficient for adequate managerial functioning. He contends, "Many an organization that had been managed by an excellent achiever-administrator-entrepreneur (usually their founder) nosedived when this key individual died or for some reason was replaced. For an organization to be continuously successful, an additional role must be performed . . . integrating."[15]

Integrating is the process by which individual strategies are merged into a group strategy; individual risks become group risks; individual goals are harmonized into group goals; ultimately, individual entrepreneurship emerges as group entrepreneurship. "When a group can operate on its own with a clear direction in mind and can choose its own direction over time without depending on any one individual for a successful operation, then we know that the integrating role has been performed adequately. It requires an individual who is sensitive to people's needs. Such an individual unifies the whole organization behind goals and strategies."[16] Integrating emphasizes the human/social system.

Adizes contends that whenever one of the four managerial roles is not performed in an organization, a certain style of mismanagement can be observed. And yet, Adizes argues that

few managers fill perfectly all four of these roles and thus exhibit no mismanagement style since they are at once excellent technicians, administrators, entrepreneurs, and integrators. Thus, to discuss the

role of THE manager, as is done in management literature, is a theoretical mistake. *No one manager can manage alone.* It takes several to
perform the process adequately, several people to perform roles which
seem to be in conflict, but really are complementary. There should be
individuals who possess the entrepreneurial and integrating qualities
which can guide a united organization to new directions. There should
be administrators who can translate these new actions into operative
systems which should produce results. And there should be performers
who can put the system into action and set an example for efficient
operation.[17]

While all the roles seem to be necessary for running an effective
organization, Adizes argues that if any one of the four roles can be
truly indispensable for any executive, it is integration. If managers do
not perform the other roles themselves, there may be others to supply
them; but they have to be able to integrate in order to allow the other
functions to work in a positive fashion. If this people-part of the
managerial role is not fulfilled, the entrepreneur will become a "crisis
maker," the administrator a "bureaucrat," and the producer a "loner."

INGREDIENTS FOR EFFECTIVE HUMAN SKILLS

If one accepts the fact that human skill development is important, one
may ask what kind of expertise managers and leaders need to be
effective in their ability to have an impact on the behavior of other
people. We feel that managers need three levels of expertise.

Understanding Past Behavior

First, managers need to understand why people behave as they do. If
you are going to get things done through other people, you have to
know why other people engage in behavior that is characteristic of
them. So, understanding past behavior is the first area that managers
need to examine.

What motivates people? What produces the patterns of behavior
that are characteristic of individuals or groups? This is where most of
the literature focuses. Most of what has been written in the behavioral sciences focuses on why people behave as they do. In both
popular and scholarly books and periodicals, there are literally hundreds of different classifications that are useful in communicating the
patterns of behavior that describe individuals and groups interacting
with other people. We can say a person is schizophrenic or is paranoid
or is a task leader or a team leader, and so on. All these are useful

classifications for communicating to others why an individual or group is behaving in certain ways.

Predicting Future Behavior

Although understanding past behavior is important for developing effective human skills, it is not enough by itself. If you are supervising other people, it is essential that you understand why they did what they did yesterday, but perhaps even more important is being able to predict how they are going to behave today, tomorrow, next week, and next month under similar as well as changing environmental conditions. Therefore, the second level of expertise that managers need is predicting future behavior.

Directing, Changing, and Controlling Behavior

If you are going to be effective in your role as a manager or leader, you need to do more than just understand and predict behavior. You need to develop skills in directing, changing, and controlling behavior. You must also accept the responsibility for *influencing* the behavior of others in accomplishing tasks and reaching goals.

These skills determine whether leadership attempts will be successful or unsuccessful, effective or ineffective. Understanding what motivates people, predicting how they will behave in response to your leadership attempts, and directing their future behavior are all necessary for effective leadership.

Note that the first two skills are passive in nature. Understanding and predicting do not require actions involving other people. The key to obtaining results is directing, changing, and controlling the efforts of people in the accomplishment of organizational goals. That's where the manager translates thoughts and intentions into end results.

Controlling People

People who hear the word *control* often ask, "Does that mean that we have to manipulate others?" Words that suggest control and manipulation sometimes have a negative connotation to many people. However, when you accept the role of leader, you also accept with it the responsibility of having an impact on the behavior of other people—for influencing the behavior of others toward achieving results. That's true whether you're at work striving to gain the commitment of your people or at home attempting to assist your children in developing their basic values.

It's also important to remember that words are simply packages of ideas and, as such, are often misinterpreted. If manipulation means taking unfair advantage, being deceitful, and influencing others for self-interest, then it has a negative connotation. On the other hand, if manipulation means using influence and strategies skillfully and managing people fairly for mutually rewarding and productive purposes, it's an appropriate and necessary means for goal accomplishment.

If you are still concerned about words such as *control* or *manipulation*, think instead of training or facilitating. Whatever words you choose, your overall effectiveness depends upon *understanding, predicting,* and *influencing* the behavior of other people.

A Hammer Won't Always Do the Job

For every job there is an appropriate tool. Hammers are great for pounding nails. You could also use a hammer to cut a two by four, but it would leave a lot of rough edges. For that particular job there is a better tool. To build effectively you need a variety of tools and the knowledge of how to use them.

The same is true for leadership and management. It is unrealistic to think that a single tool is all that's needed to manage effectively. If all you have is a hammer, then all you will see are nails. Many people fall into the trap of relying on the latest fad to solve all their management problems. They seem to develop an unrealistic assumption of what this will do for them. Many useful management tools have developed over the years. But you should know what to expect from them and, just as importantly, what not to expect. You need to understand and be able to use different tools when leading and managing people.[18]

Learning to Apply Behavioral Science Theory

Learning to apply behavioral sciences is much like learning anything; for example, how do you learn to hit a baseball? You learn to hit a baseball by getting up there and attempting to hit—by practice, by doing what you are attempting to learn. There is no way you are going to learn to hit a baseball by merely reading books (even those by people considered to be experts in the field) or by watching (in person or on slow-motion film) great hitters. All that will do is give you conceptual knowledge of how to hit a baseball.

Psychologists define learning as a change in behavior—being able to do something different from what you were able to do before. So, in reading and watching others, all we can get is, perhaps, a change in our knowledge or a change in our attitude. But if we actually want to learn something, we have to "try on," or practice, that which we want to learn to make it part of our relevant behavior.

Another thing to keep in mind in terms of learning is how you feel about learning something new. How did you feel the first time you ever tried to hit a baseball? If you were like most people, you felt anxious, nervous, and uncomfortable. This is the way most of us feel any time we attempt to do something new—something significantly different from the things we are already comfortable doing within our behavioral patterns.

It's the same with learning to use behavioral science. Much of what you read in this book may have an impact on your knowledge and attitudes, but this book becomes relevant only if you are willing to "try on" some new behaviors. If you are, we think you should recognize that the first time you "try on" a new pattern of behavior in terms of attempting to implement behavioral science theory, you are going to feel ill at ease and uncomfortable. It is this "unfreezing" that we have to go through if we want to learn.

Another caution is to be patient—give the new behavior time to work. If you are up at bat attempting to hit a baseball for the first time, what is the probability that you will get a base hit from the first ball the pitcher delivers? The probability is low. It is not any different in learning behavioral science theory. The first time you attempt to behave differently based on theory, we can predict that you probably would have been more effective using your old style of behavior rather than the new (although in the long run the new style may have a higher probability of success). This is why so often practitioners who go through a training experience in which they learn new knowledge as well as attitudes find that in "trying on" some new behavior for the first time, it doesn't work. As a result, they begin to respond negatively to the whole training experience, saying such things as, "How can we accept these things?" "They are not usable." "They do not work in the real world." It is this kind of attitude that has hindered managers from attempting to make behavioral science theory a reality in terms of managing more effectively. All of us have to recognize that, just like hitting a baseball, it takes practice. The first few times up, the probability of success is quite low. But the more we practice, the more we attempt to get relevant feedback, the more we can predict that the probability of success will increase.

APPLIED BEHAVIORAL SCIENCES

If managers are able to understand, predict, and direct change and to control behavior, they are essentially applied behavioral scientists.

What Is a Behavioral Scientist?

One way to answer this question is to say that a behavioral scientist attempts to bring together, from a variety of disciplines, those concepts, theories, and research that may be useful to people in making decisions about the behavior of individuals and groups. This means that a behavioral scientist integrates concepts and theories and the results of empirical studies from the areas of cultural anthropology, economics, political science, psychology, sociology, and social psychology. At the same time, a behavioral scientist also borrows from other areas such as engineering, physics, quantitative analysis, and statistics. For example, force field analysis, developed by Kurt Lewin, which we will be talking about later in this book, is directly related to concepts in physics. So, perhaps the best way to look at the field is to say that a behavioral scientist attempts to integrate all of those areas or disciplines that can be useful to practitioners in better understanding, predicting, and having an impact on the behavior of individuals and groups.

The emphasis in this book will be on the applied behavioral sciences: those concepts from the behavioral sciences that can have an impact on making managers more effective—whether they be managers, supervisors, teachers, or parents. The hope is to apply behavioral science concepts in such a way as to move them from being strictly theoretical and descriptive to being more applied and prescriptive. In doing that, though, it should be remembered that applied behavioral science is not an exact science such as physics, chemistry, and biology. There are no principles or universal truths when it comes to management. People are difficult to predict. All that the behavioral sciences can give you are ways to increase your behavioral batting average. In other words, the behavioral sciences are probability sciences; there aren't any principles of management, only books titled *Principles of Management.*

THE DESIGN OF THIS BOOK

In the chapters that follow, we will attempt to help you better understand the field of applied behavioral science. As we noted in *Organizational Change Through Effective Leadership,* with Robert H. Guest:

> ... by sharing the insights of those who have studied organizational change and linking their observations, however briefly, to an evolving situation, we hope that managers out on the firing line might come to realize that there are available, in the organizational behavior literature, concepts and frameworks that might help them to do a better job.

We believe that these behavioral science contributions might assist managers, in a variety of institutional settings, to sharpen their diagnostic skills and to develop appropriate change strategies. They might, in short, go beyond the intuitive, beyond seat-of-the-pants experience, to sense better the probabilities that one course of action will work and another will not.[19]

Chapters 2 and 3 on motivation are designed to provide information to help you understand and predict the how and why people behave as they do. Chapters 4 through 12 trace the development of modern leadership theory and introduce Situational Leadership. Chapters 13 through 19 focus on applied behavioral science with special attention to One Minute Management and its relationship to Situational Leadership (chapters 17 and 18).

Chapter 20 attempts to integrate all of the concepts on understanding, predicting, and controlling behavior into a common framework that we believe will be helpful to you in increasing organizational productivity. We think you will find the remaining chapters of your journey through this book interesting, informative, and, most important, of practical value.

NOTES

1. J. J. Sullivan, "Human Nature, Organizations, and Management Theory," *Academy of Management Review,* 11 (July 1985), pp. 534–549. See also T. J. Hutton, "Human Resources or Management Resources?" *Personnel Administrator,* 32 (January 1987), pp. 66 ff.; A. Fowler, "When Chief Executives Discover Human Resource Management," *Personnel Management,* 19 (January 1987), p. 3; Randolph M. Hale, "Managing Human Resources," *Enterprise,* June 1985, pp. 6–9; Perry Pascarella, "The New Science of Management," *Industry Week,* January 6, 1986, pp. 45–50.
2. Woody Allen as quoted in Paul Hersey, *The Situational Leader* (Escondido, Calif.: Center for Leadership Studies, 1984), p. 13.
3. Elton Mayo, *The Social Problems of an Industrial Civilization* (Boston: Harvard Business School, 1945), p. 23.
4. *Ibid.,* p. 20.
5. R. J. House discusses similar concepts in *Management Development: Design, Implementation and Evaluation* (Ann Arbor: Bureau of Industrial Relations, University of Michigan, 1967).
6. See Kenneth H. Blanchard and Robert Lorber, *Putting the One-Minute Manager to Work* (New York: Berkeley Publishing Group, 1987); John R. Schermerhorn, Jr., *Management for Productivity,* 2nd ed. (New York: Wiley, 1989).
7. Hersey, *The Situational Leader.*
8. Harold Koontz and Cyril O'Donnell, *Principles of Management,* 5th ed. (New York: McGraw-Hill, 1972), p. 20.
9. These descriptions were adapted from a classification developed by Robert L. Katz, "Skills of an Effective Administrator," *Harvard Business Review,* January–February 1955, pp. 33–42.
10. John D. Rockefeller as quoted in Garret L. Bergen and William V. Haney, *Organizational Relations and Management Action* (New York: McGraw-Hill, 1966), p. 3.
11. Data as reported in Bergen and Haney, *Organizational Relations and Management Action.*

12. Paul Hersey and Douglas Scott identify these components of an internal social system in "A Systems Approach to Educational Organizations: Do We Manage or Administer?" OCLEA (a publication of the Ontario Council for Leadership in Educational Administration, Toronto, Canada), pp. 3–5. Much of the material for that article was adapted from lectures given by Boris Yavitz, Dean, School of Business Administration, Columbia University.

13. Ichak Adizes, *How to Solve the Mismanagement Crisis* (Los Angeles: MDOR Institute, 1980). Also see Adizes, "Mismanagement Styles," *California Management Review,* 19, No. 2 (Winter 1976).

14. Adizes, "Mismanagement Styles," p. 6.

15. *Ibid.*

16. *Ibid.*

17. *Ibid.,* p. 18.

18. Adapted from Hersey, *The Situational Leader,* pp. 20–22.

19. Robert H. Guest, Paul Hersey, and Kenneth H. Blanchard, *Organizational Change Through Effective Leadership* (Englewood Cliffs, N.J.: Prentice Hall, 1986), p. 222.

2

Motivation and Behavior

The study of motivation and behavior is a search for answers to perplexing questions about human nature. Recognizing the importance of the human element in organizations, we will attempt in this chapter to develop a theoretical framework that may help managers to understand human behavior, not only to determine the "whys" of past behavior, but to some extent to predict, to change, and even to control future behavior.

BEHAVIOR

Behavior is basically goal-oriented. In other words, our behavior is generally motivated by a desire to attain some goal. The specific goal is not always consciously known by the individual. All of us may wonder at times, "Why did I do that?" The reason for our action is not always apparent to the conscious mind. The drives that motivate distinctive individual behavioral patterns ("personality") are to a considerable degree subconscious and, therefore, not easily accessible for examination and evaluation.

Sigmund Freud was one of the first to recognize the importance of subconscious motivation. He believed that people are not always aware of everything they want; hence, much of their behavior is affected by subconscious motives or needs. In fact, Freud's research convinced him that an analogy could be drawn between the motivation of most people and the structure of an iceberg. A significant segment of human motivation appears below the surface, where it is not always evident to the individual. Therefore, many times only a small portion of one's motivation is clearly visible or conscious to oneself.[1] This may be due to an individual's lack of effort to gain self-insight. Yet, even with professional help—for example, psychotherapy—understanding oneself may be a difficult process, yielding varying degrees of success.

The basic unit of behavior is an *activity*. In fact, all behavior is a series of activities. As human beings we are always doing something: walking, talking, eating, sleeping, working, and the like. In many instances we are doing more than one activity at a time, such as talking with someone as we walk or drive to work. At any given moment we may decide to change from one activity or combination of activities and begin to do something else. This raises some important questions. Why do people engage in one activity and not another? Why do they change activities? How can we as managers understand, predict, and even control what activity or activities a person may engage in at a given moment? To predict behavior, managers must know which motives or needs of people evoke a certain action at a particular time.

Motives

People differ not only in their ability to do, but also in their will to do, or *motivation*. The motivation of people depends on the strength of their motives. *Motives* are sometimes defined as needs, wants, drives, or impulses within the individual. Motives are directed toward goals which may be conscious or subconscious.

Motives are the "whys" of behavior. They arouse and maintain activity and determine the general direction of the behavior of an individual. In essence, motives or needs are the mainsprings of action. In our discussions we shall use these two terms—*motives* and *needs*—interchangeably. In this context, the term *need* should *not* be associated with urgency or any pressing desire for something. It simply means something within an individual that prompts that person to action.

Goals

Goals are *outside* an individual; they are sometimes referred to as "hoped for" rewards toward which motives are directed. These goals are often called *incentives* by psychologists. However, we prefer not to use this term since many people in our society tend to equate incentives with tangible financial rewards, such as increased pay, although most of us would agree that there are many intangible rewards, such as praise or power, which are just as important in evoking behavior. Managers who are successful in motivating employees are often providing an environment in which appropriate goals (incentives) are available for need satisfaction.

Motive Strength

We have said that motives, or needs, are the reasons underlying behavior. All individuals have many hundreds of needs. All of these needs compete for their behavior. What, then, determines which of these motives a person will attempt to satisfy through activity? The need with the *greatest strength* at a particular moment leads to activity, as illustrated in Figure 2-1. Satisfied needs decrease in strength and normally do not motivate individuals to seek goals to satisfy them.

In Figure 2-1 Motive B is the highest strength need and, therefore, it is this need that determines behavior. What can happen to change this situation?

Changes in Motive Strength

A motive tends to decrease in strength if it is either satisfied or blocked from satisfaction.

Need satisfaction. When a need is satisfied, according to Abraham Maslow, it is no longer a motivator of behavior.[2] High-strength needs that are satisfied are sometimes referred to as "satis-

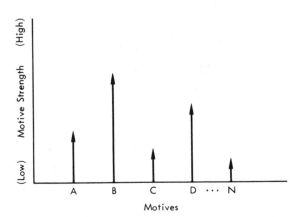

FIGURE 2-1
The most prepotent motive determines behavior (Motive B in this illustration)

ficed"—that is, the need has been satisfied to the extent that some competing need is now more potent. If a high-strength need is thirst, drinking tends to lower the strength of this need, and other needs may now become more potent.

Blocking need satisfaction.   The satisfaction of a need may be blocked. While a reduction in need strength sometimes follows, it does not always occur initially. Instead, there may be a tendency for the person to engage in *coping behavior*. This is an attempt to overcome the obstacle by trial-and-error problem solving. The person may try a variety of behaviors to find one that will accomplish the goal or will reduce tension created by blockage, as illustrated in Figure 2-2.

Initially, this coping behavior may be quite rational. Perhaps the person may even make several attempts in direction 1 before going to direction 2, and make several attempts in direction 2 before moving in direction 3, where some degree of perceived success and goal attainment is finally achieved.

If people continue to strive for something without success, they may substitute goals that can satisfy the need. For example, if Mary has a strong desire to be a CPA, but continually receives average grades in accounting, she may be willing eventually to settle for another career in business.

Cognitive dissonance.   Blocked motives and continually unsuccessful rational coping behavior may lead to forms of irrational coping behavior. Leon Festinger analyzes this phenomenon.[3] His theory of

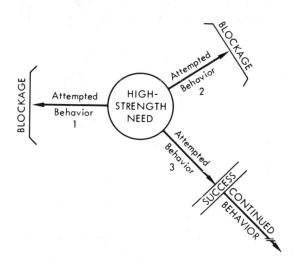

FIGURE 2-2
Coping behavior when blockage occurs in attempting to accomplish a particular goal

cognitive dissonance deals primarily with the relationships that exist between perceptions people have about themselves and their environment. When individual perceptions have nothing to do with each other, they are considered irrelevant to each other. If one supports the other, they are said to be in a consonant relationship. Dissonance is created when two perceptions that are relevant to each other are in conflict. This creates tension, which is psychologically uncomfortable, and causes the individual to try to modify one of the incompatible knowledges so as to reduce the tension or dissonance. In a sense, that person engages in coping behavior to regain a condition of consonance or equilibrium. For example, Festinger has done research that shows that "heavy smokers are less likely to believe that there is a relationship between smoking and lung cancer than nonsmokers."[4] In other words, if they cannot give up smoking, they can at least remain skeptical about research that reports harmful effects. The same phenomenon is at work when a person goes out fishing all day, doesn't catch anything, and remarks about the beautiful weather.

Frustration. The blocking or thwarting of goal attainment is referred to as *frustration*. This phenomenon is defined in terms of the condition of the individual, rather than in terms of the external environment. A person may be frustrated by an imaginary barrier and may fail to be frustrated by a real barrier.

As previously discussed, rational coping behavior can lead to alternative goal setting or decreasing need strength. Irrational behavior may occur in several forms when blockage to goal accomplishment continues and frustration develops. Frustration may increase to the extent that the individual engages in aggressive behavior.

Aggression can lead to destructive behavior such as hostility and striking out. Freud was one of the first to demonstrate that hostility or rage can be exhibited by an individual in a variety of ways.[5] If possible, individuals will direct their hostility against the object or the person that they feel is the cause of frustration. Angry workers may try to hurt their boss through gossip and other malicious behavior. Often, however, people cannot attack the cause of their frustration directly, and they may look for a scapegoat as a target for their hostility. Scapegoats may be other workers, family members, or innocent pets.

As Norman R. F. Maier has said, aggression is only one way in which frustration can be shown.[6] Other forms of frustrated behavior — such as rationalization, regression, fixation, and resignation — may develop if pressures continue and/or increase.

Rationalization simply means making excuses. For example, an individual might blame someone else for an inability to accomplish a given goal—"It was my boss's fault that I didn't get a raise." Or the person may downgrade the desirability of that particular goal—"I didn't want to do that anyway."

Regression is essentially not acting one's age. "Frustrated people tend to give up constructive attempts at solving their problems and regress to more primitive and childish behavior."[7] A person who cannot start the car and proceeds to kick it is demonstrating regressive behavior; so too is a manager who throws a temper tantrum when annoyed and frustrated. Barker, Dembo, and Lewin showed experimentally that when children are exposed to mild frustration, their play may resemble that of a child two or more years younger.[8]

Fixation occurs when a person continues to exhibit the same behavior pattern over and over again, although experience has shown that it can accomplish nothing. Thus, "frustration can freeze old and habitual responses and prevent the use of new and more effectual ones."[9] Maier has shown that although habits are normally broken when they bring no satisfaction or lead to punishment, a fixation actually becomes stronger under these circumstances.[10] In fact, he argued that it is possible to change a habit into a fixation by too much punishment. This phenomenon is seen in children who blindly continue to behave objectionably after being severely punished. Thus, Maier concluded that punishment can have two effects on behavior: It may either eliminate the undesirable behavior or lead to fixation and other symptoms of frustration as well. It follows that punishment may be a dangerous management tool, since its effects are difficult to predict. According to J. A. C. Brown, common symptoms of fixation in industry are "the inability to accept change, the blind and stubborn refusal to accept new facts when experience has shown the old ones to be untenable, and the type of behavior exemplified by the manager who continues to increase penalties" even when this is only making conditions worse.[11]

Resignation or apathy occurs after prolonged frustration when people lose hope of accomplishing their goal(s) in a particular situation and withdraw from reality and the source of their frustration. This phenomenon is characteristic of people in boring, routine jobs where often they resign themselves to the fact that there is little hope for improvement within their environments.

A manager should remember that aggression, rationalization, regression, fixation, and resignation are all symptoms of frustration and may be indications that problems exist.

Increasing motive strength. Behavior may change if an existing need increases in strength to the extent that it is now the high-strength motive. The strength of some needs tends to appear in a cyclical pattern. For example, the need for food tends to recur regard-

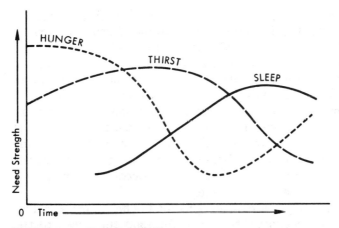

FIGURE 2-3 Multiple needs

less of how well it has been satisfied at a given moment. One can increase or delay the speed of this cyclical pattern by affecting the environment. For example, a person's need for food may not be high strength unless the immediate environment is changed such that the senses are exposed to the sight and the aroma of tempting food.

People have a variety of needs at any given time. They may be hungry, thirsty, and tired, but the need with the highest strength will determine what they do. For example, they may eat, drink, and sleep, in that order, as shown in Figure 2-3.[12] All of these tend to be cyclical over time.

CATEGORIES OF ACTIVITIES

Activities resulting from high-strength needs can generally be classified into two categories—goal directed activity and goal activity. These concepts are important to practitioners because of their differing influence on need strength, which can be useful in understanding human behavior.

Goal-directed activity, in essence, is motivated behavior directed at reaching a goal. If one's strongest need at a given moment is hunger, various activities such as looking for a place to eat, buying food, or preparing food would be considered goal-directed activities. On the other hand, *goal activity* is engaging in the goal itself. In the case of hunger, food is the goal and eating, therefore, is the goal activity.

An important distinction between these two classes of activities is their effect on the strength of the need. In goal-directed activity, the strength of the need tends to increase as one engages in the activity until the goal is reached or frustration sets in. As discussed earlier, frustration develops when one is continually blocked from reaching a goal. If the frustration becomes intense enough, the strength of the need for that goal may decrease until it is no longer potent enough to affect behavior—a person gives up.

The strength of the need tends to increase as one engages in goal-directed activity; however, once goal activity begins, the strength of the need tends to decrease as one engages in it. For example, as one eats more and more, the strength of the need for food declines for that particular time. At the point when another need becomes more potent than the present need, behavior changes.

On Thanksgiving Day, for example, as food is being prepared all morning (goal-directed activity), the need for food increases to the point of almost not being able to wait until the meal is on the table. As we begin to eat (goal activity), the strength of this need diminishes to the point where other needs become more important. As we leave the table, our need for food seems to be well satisfied. Our activity changes to that of watching football. This need for passive recreation has now become most potent, and we find ourselves in front of the television set. But gradually this need decreases, too. After several games, even though the competition is fierce, the need for passive recreation may also decline to the extent that other needs become more important— perhaps the need for fresh air and a walk or, better still, another piece of pumpkin pie. Several hours before, we had sworn not to eat for a week, but now that pie looks very good. So once again hunger is the strongest need. Thus, it should be remembered that we never completely satiate a need. We satisfy it for only a period of time.

MOTIVES, GOALS, AND ACTIVITIES

The relationship among motives, goals, and activity can be shown in a simplified fashion, as illustrated in Figure 2-4.

FIGURE 2-4   Relationship among motives, goals, and activities

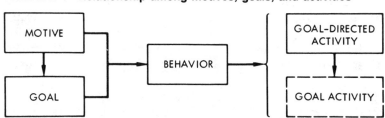

The strongest motive produces behavior that is either goal-directed or goal activity. Since not all goals are attainable, individuals do not always reach goal activity, regardless of the strength of the motive. Thus, goal activity is indicated by a dashed line.

An example of a tangible goal being used to influence behavior is illustrated in Figure 2-5.

With a broad goal such as food, it should be recognized that the type of food that satisfies the hunger motive varies from situation to situation. If individuals are starving, they may eat anything; at other times, they may realign their goals and only a steak will satisfy their hunger motive.

A similar illustration could be given for an intangible goal. If individuals have a need for recognition—a need to be viewed as contributing, productive people—praise is one incentive that will help satisfy this need. In a work situation, if their need for recognition is strong enough, being praised by their manager or supervisor may be an effective incentive in influencing people to continue to do good work.

In analyzing these two examples, it should be remembered that if you want to influence another person's behavior, you must first understand what motives or needs are most important to that person at that time. A goal, to be effective, must be appropriate to the need structure of the person involved.

A question that may be considered at this point is whether it is better to engage in goal-directed activity or in goal activity. Actually, maintenance at either level exclusively creates problems. If one stays at goal-directed activity too long, frustration will occur to the extent that the person may give up or other patterns of irrational behavior may be evoked. On the other hand, if one engages exclusively in goal activity and the goal is not challenging, a lack of interest and apathy will develop, with motivation again tending to decrease. A more appropriate and effective pattern might be a continuous cycling function between goal-directed activity and goal activity, as shown in Figure 2-6.

FIGURE 2-5   Use of a tangible goal

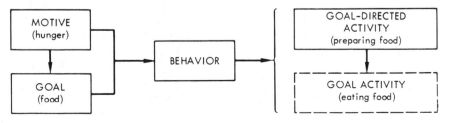

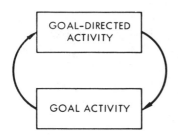

FIGURE 2-6
Cycling function of goal-directed activity and goal activity

A goal that is appropriate for a six-year-old may not be a meaningful goal for the same child at seven. Once the child becomes proficient in attaining a particular goal, it becomes appropriate for the parent to provide an opportunity for the child to evaluate and set new goals. In the same light, what is an appropriate goal for a new employee may not be meaningful for an employee who has been with a corporation six months or a year. There also may be distinctions between employees who have been with an organization for only a few years and those who have been with it for longer periods of time.

This cycling process between goal-directed activity and goal activity is a continuous challenge for the parent or the manager. As employees increase in their ability to accomplish goals, it is appropriate that the manager reevaluate and provide an environment that allows continual realignment of goals and an opportunity for growth and development. The learning and developing process is not a phenomenon that should be confined to only one stage of a person's life. In this process, the role of managers is not always that of setting goals for their workers. Instead, effectiveness may be increased by providing an environment in which co-workers can play a role in setting their own goals. Research indicates that commitment increases when people are involved in their own goal setting. If individuals are involved, they will tend to engage in much more goal-directed activity before they become frustrated and give up. On the other hand, if their manager sets the goals for them, they are likely to give up more easily because they perceive these goals as their manager's and not as their own.

Goals should be set high enough so that a person has to stretch to reach them, but low enough so that they can be attained. Thus, goals must be realistic before a person will make a real effort to achieve them. As J. Sterling-Livingston so aptly states:

[Followers] will not be motivated to reach high levels of productivity unless they consider the boss' high expectations realistic and achievable. If they are encouraged to strive for unattainable goals, they eventually give up trying and settle for results that are lower than they are capable of achieving. The experience of a large electrical manufacturing company demonstrates this; the company discovered that production actually declined if production quotas were set too high, because the workers simply stopped trying to meet them. In other words, the practice of "dangling the carrot just beyond the donkey's reach," endorsed by many managers, is not a good motivational device.[13]

David C. McClelland and John W. Atkinson[14] have demonstrated in their research that the degree of motivation and effort rises until the probability of success reaches 50 percent, then begins to fall even though the probability of success continues to increase. This relationship can be depicted in the form of a bell-shaped curve, as illustrated in Figure 2-7.

As Figure 2-7 suggests, people are not highly motivated if a goal is seen as almost impossible or virtually certain to achieve.

Another problem with goals is that so often final goals are set and the person is judged only in terms of success in relation to these goals. For example, a team has an established completion date for its work on a new marketing plan, a project that is scheduled to take four months. Suppose after the first month the project is only five percent completed. The usual result is that the vice-president for marketing would become upset and start micromanaging the team. If this continues to occur, there is a high probability that the team may stop trying. Progress on the marketing plan, instead of accelerating, may

FIGURE 2-7
The relationship of motivation to probability of success

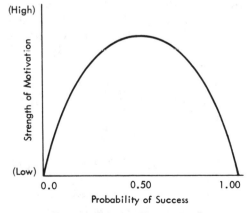

Source: This figure was adapted from J. Sterling Livingston, "Pygmalion in Management," Harvard Business Review, September/October 1988, p. 127.

get worse. An alternative for the marketing vice-president is to set interim goals—realistic goals that move toward the final goal. Now this moderate change in the marketing plan allows positive reinforcement to be used, rather than reprimand.

EXPECTANCY THEORY

We have already discussed the strength of needs. What additional factors affect the strength of needs? Victor Vroom[15] has suggested an approach in his expectancy theory of motivation that attempts to answer this question. Furthermore, his theory is consistent with our previous assertion that felt needs cause human behavior.

In simplified form, felt needs cause behavior, and this motivated behavior in a work setting is increased if a person perceives a positive relationship between effort and performance. Motivated behavior is further increased if there is a positive relationship between good performance and outcomes or rewards, particularly if the outcomes or rewards are valued. Thus, there are three relationships that enhance motivated behavior: a positive relationship between effort and performance, a positive relationship between good performance and rewards, and the delivery or achievement of valued outcomes or rewards. Let's look at an example. A new manager perceives that a 60-hour workweek is vital to good job performance. Further, the manager also perceives that good job performance will probably result in an early promotion that carries with it a badly needed 10 percent raise. If this sequence of events happens, both the manager's willingness to work hard and confidence in the behavior pattern will be reinforced. "Success breeds success!" However, should one or more steps in the sequence be proven wrong—for example, performance does not improve, promotion is denied, or pay raise falls short of expectations—motivation, willingness, and confidence will decline.

This linkage between effort and performance and between performance and valued outcomes is important not only to our understanding of motivation[16] but also to our understanding of a number of leadership theories, especially the Path-Goal Theory discussed in Chapter 5.

EXPECTANCY AND AVAILABILITY

We have already discussed the strength of needs. Two important factors that affect need strength are expectancy and availability. Although these two concepts are interrelated, expectancy tends to affect motives, or needs, and availability tends to affect the perception of goals.

Expectancy is the perceived probability of satisfying a particular need of an individual based on past experience. Although expectancy is the technical term used by psychologists, it refers directly to the sum of the past experience. Experience can be either actual or vicarious. Vicarious experience comes from sources the person considers legitimate such as parents, peer groups, teachers, and books or periodicals. To illustrate the effect that past experience can have on behavior, let us look at an example. Suppose a boy's father was a basketball star and the boy wants to follow in his footsteps. Initially, his expectancy may be high and, therefore, the strength of the need is high. If he is cut from the eighth-grade team, it is difficult to determine whether this failure will discourage the boy. Since a single failure is usually not enough to discourage a person (in fact, it sometimes results in increased activity), little change in his expectancy is anticipated. But if he continues to get cut from a team year after year, eventually this motive will no longer be as strong or of such high priority. In fact, after enough unsuccessful experiences, he may give up completely on his goal.

Availability reflects the perceived limitations of the environment. It is determined by how accessible the goals that can satisfy a given need are perceived by an individual. For example, if the electricity goes off in a storm, one cannot watch television or read. These goal activities are no longer possible because of the limitations of the environment. One may have a high desire to read, but if there is no suitable substitute for the type of illumination required, that person will soon be frustrated in any attempts to satisfy this desire and will settle for something else, such as sleeping.

Consequently, availability is an environmental variable. Yet it should be stressed that it is not important whether the goals to satisfy a need are really available. It is the perception, or the interpretation of reality, that affects one's actual behavior. In other words, reality is what a person perceives.

An example of how perception can affect behavior was dramatically illustrated in an experiment with a fish. A pike was placed in an aquarium with many minnows swimming around it. After the fish became accustomed to the plentiful supply of food, a sheet of glass was placed between the pike and the minnows. When the pike became hungry, it tried to reach the minnows, but it continually hit its head on the glass. At first, the strength of the need for food increased and the pike tried harder than ever to get the minnows. But finally its repeated failure of goal attainment resulted in enough frustration that the fish no longer attempted to eat the minnows. In fact, when the glass partition was finally removed, the minnows again swam all around the pike, but no further goal-directed activity took place. Eventually, the pike died of starvation while in the midst of plenty of food. In both cases, the fish operated according to the way it perceived reality and not on the basis of reality itself.

The expanded diagram of a motivating situation including expectancy and availability is presented in Figure 2-8.

Motives, needs within an individual, are directed toward goals that are aspirations in the environment. These are interpreted by the individual as being available or unavailable. This affects expectancy. If expectancy is high, motive strength will increase. This tends to be a cyclical pattern moving in the direction of the prominent arrows. But to some extent these are interacting variables indicated by the secondary arrows. For example, experience may affect the way we perceive our feelings of availability. The presence of goals in the environment may affect the given strength of motives and so forth.

PERSONALITY DEVELOPMENT

As individuals mature, they develop habit patterns, or conditioned responses, to various stimuli. The sum of these habit patterns, as perceived by others, determines their *personality*.

habit *a*, habit *b*, habit *c*, . . . , habit *n* = *personality*

As individuals begin to behave in a similar fashion under similar conditions, this behavior is what others learn to recognize as them — as their personality. They expect and can even predict certain kinds of behavior from these people.

Changing Personality

Many psychologists contend that basic personality structures are developed quite early in life. In fact, some claim that few personality changes can be made after age seven or eight. Using a model similar

FIGURE 2-8 Expanded diagram of a motivating situation

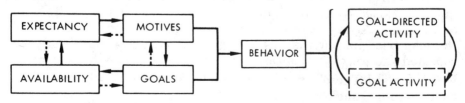

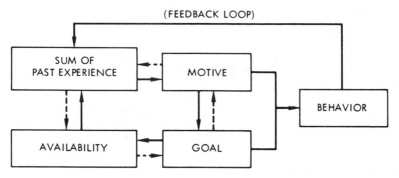

FIGURE 2-9 Feedback model

to the one in Figure 2-8, we can begin to understand why it tends to become more difficult to make changes in personality as people grow older.

Note that in this model we are using *sum of past experience* in place of the term *expectancy* used in the earlier model. These terms can be used interchangeably.

When an individual behaves in a motivating situation, that behavior becomes a new input to that person's inventory of past experience, as the feedback loop in Figure 2-9 indicates. The earlier in life that this input occurs, the greater its potential effect on future behavior. The reason is that early in life, this behavior represents a larger portion of the total past experience of a young person than the same behavior input will later in life. In addition, the longer behavior is reinforced, the more patterned it becomes and the more difficult it is to change.

HIERARCHY OF NEEDS

We have argued that the behavior of individuals at a particular moment is usually determined by their strongest need. It would seem significant, therefore, for managers to have some understanding about the needs that are commonly most important to people.

An interesting framework that helps explain the strength of certain needs was developed by Abraham Maslow.[17] According to Maslow, there seems to be a hierarchy into which human needs arrange themselves, as illustrated in Figure 2-10.

The *physiological* needs are shown at the top of the hierarchy because they tend to have the highest strength until they are somewhat satisfied. These are the basic human needs to sustain life itself—food, clothing, shelter. Until these basic needs are satisfied to the

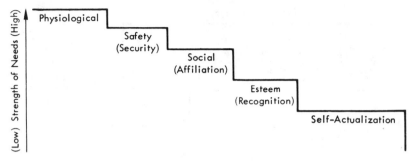

FIGURE 2-10 Maslow's hierarchy of needs

degree needed for the sufficient operation of the body, the majority of a person's activity will probably be at this level, and the other needs will provide little motivation.

But what happens to a person's motivation when these basic needs begin to be fulfilled? Instead of physiological needs, other levels of needs become important, and these motivate and dominate the behavior of the individual. And when these needs are somewhat satiated, other needs emerge, and so on down the hierarchy.

Once physiological needs become gratified, the *safety,* or *security,* needs become predominant, as illustrated in Figure 2-11. These needs are essentially the need to be free of the fear of physical danger and deprivation of the basic physiological needs. In other words, this is a need for self-preservation. In addition to the here and now, there is a concern for the future. Will people be able to maintain their property and/or job so they can provide food and shelter tomorrow and the next day? If an individual's safety or security is in danger, other things seem unimportant.

Once physiological and safety needs are fairly well satisfied, *social,* or *affiliation,* will emerge as dominant in the need structure, as illustrated in Figure 2-12. Since people are social beings, they have a need to belong to and be accepted by various groups. When social

FIGURE 2-11 Safety need when dominant in the need structure

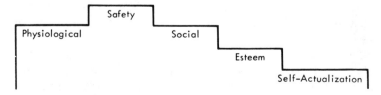

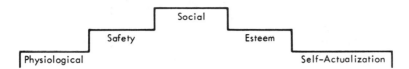

FIGURE 2-12   Social need when dominant in the need structure

needs become dominant, a person will strive for meaningful relations with others.

After individuals begin to satisfy their need to belong, they generally want to be more than just a member of their group. They then feel the need for *esteem*—both self-esteem and recognition from others, as seen in Figure 2-13. Most people have a need for a high evaluation of themselves that is firmly based in reality—recognition and respect from others. Satisfaction of these esteem needs produces feelings of self-confidence, prestige, power, and control. People begin to feel that they are useful and have some effect on their environment. There are other occasions, though, when persons are unable to satisfy their need for esteem through constructive behavior. When this need is dominant, an individual may resort to disruptive or immature behavior to satisfy the desire for attention—a child may throw a temper tantrum, employees may engage in work restriction or arguments with their co-workers or manager. Thus, recognition is not always obtained through mature or adaptive behavior. It is sometimes garnered by disruptive and irresponsible actions. In fact, some of the social problems we have today may have their roots in the frustration of esteem needs.

Once esteem needs begin to be adequately satisfied, the *self-actualization* needs become more prepotent, as shown in Figure 2-14. Self-actualization is the need to maximize one's potential, whatever it may be. A musician must play music, a poet must write, a general must win battles, a professor must teach. As Maslow expressed it, "What a man *can* be, he *must* be." Thus, self-actualization is the desire to become what one is capable of becoming. Individuals satisfy this

FIGURE 2-13   Esteem need when dominant in the need structure

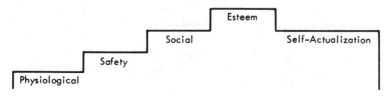

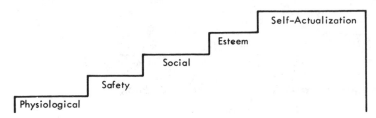

FIGURE 2-14 Self-actualization needs when dominant in the need structure

need in different ways. In one person it may be expressed in the desire to be an ideal mother; in another it may be expressed in managing an organization; in another it may be expressed athletically; in still another by playing the piano.

In combat, a soldier may rush a machine-gun nest in an attempt to destroy it, knowing full well that chances for survival are low. This courageous act is not done for affiliation or recognition, but rather for what the soldier thinks is important. In this case, you may consider the soldier to have self-actualized—to be maximizing the potential of what is important at this time.

The way self-actualization is expressed can change over the life cycle. For example, a self-actualized athlete may eventually look for other areas in which to maximize potential as physical attributes change over time or as horizons broaden. In addition, the hierarchy does not necessarily follow the pattern described by Maslow. It was not his intent to say that this hierarchy applies universally. Maslow felt this was a *typical* pattern that operates most of the time. He realized, however, that there were numerous exceptions to this general tendency. For example, the Indian leader Mahatma Gandhi frequently sacrificed his physiological and safety needs for the satisfaction of other needs when India was striving for independence from Great Britain. In his historic fasts, Gandhi went weeks without nourishment to protest governmental injustices. He was operating at the self-actualization level while some of his other needs were unsatisfied.

In discussing the preponderance of one category of need over another, we have been careful to use such terms as "if one level of needs has been somewhat gratified, then other needs emerge as dominant." This was done because we did not want to give the impression that one level of needs has to be completely satisfied before the next level emerges as the most important. In reality, most people in our society tend to be partially satisfied and partially unsatisfied at each level, with greater satisfaction tending to occur at the physiological and safety levels than at the social, esteem, and self-actualization

FIGURE 2-15
Need structure when physiological and safety are high strength needs

levels. In contrast, people in an emerging society, where much of the behavior engaged in tends to be directed toward satisfying physiological and safety needs, still operate to some extent at other levels. Therefore, Maslow's hierarchy of needs is not intended to be an all-or-nothing framework, but rather one that may be useful in predicting behavior on a high or a low probability basis. Figure 2-15 attempts to portray need structure in an emerging nation.

Many people in our society today might be characterized by very strong social or affiliation needs, relatively strong esteem and safety needs, with self-actualization and physiological needs much less important, as shown in Figure 2-16.

Some people, however, can be characterized as having satisfied to a large extent the physiological, safety, and social needs, and their behavior tends to be dominated by esteem and self-actualizing activities, as shown in Figure 2-17. This will tend to become more characteristic if standards of living and levels of education continue to rise.

These are intended only as examples. For different individuals, varying configurations may be appropriate. In reality, they would fluctuate tremendously from one individual or group to another.

Clare W. Graves[18] developed a theory that seems to be compatible with Maslow's hierarchy of needs. Graves contends that human beings exist at different "levels of existence." "At any given level, an individual exhibits the behavior and values characteristic of people at that level; a person who is centralized at a lower level cannot even

FIGURE 2-16
Need structure when social needs are high strength and self-actualization and physiological needs are much less important

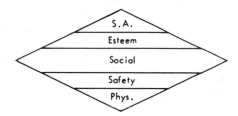

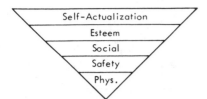

FIGURE 2-17
Need structure when esteem and self-actualization needs are high strength needs

understand people who are at a higher level."[19] According to Graves, "most people have been confined to lower [subsistence] levels of existence where they were motivated by needs shared with other animals. Now, Western man appears ready to move up to a higher [being] level of existence, a distinctly human level. When this happens there will likely be a dramatic transformation of human institutions."[20]

MOTIVATIONAL RESEARCH

Having discussed Maslow's hierarchy of needs, we can now examine what researchers say about some of our motives and the incentives that tend to satisfy them.

Physiological Needs

The satisfaction of physiological needs (shelter, food, clothing) is usually associated in our society with *money*. It is obvious that most people are not interested in dollars as such, but only as a means to be used to satisfy other motives. Thus, it is what money can buy, not money itself, that satisfies one's physiological needs. To suggest that money as a tool is useful *only* to satisfy physiological needs would be shortsighted because money can play a role in the satisfaction of needs at every level. Extensive studies of the impact of money have found that money is so complicated an incentive that it is entangled with all kinds of needs besides physiological ones, and its importance is difficult to ascertain. It is clear that the ability of a given amount of money to satisfy *seems* to diminish as one moves from physiological and safety needs to other needs on the hierarchy. In many cases, money can buy the satisfaction of physiological and safety needs and even social needs if, for example, it provides entry into a desired group, such as a country club. But as one becomes concerned about esteem, recognition, and eventually self-actualization, money becomes a less appropriate tool to satisfy these needs and, therefore, less effective. The more individuals become involved with esteem and self-actualization needs, the more they will have to earn their satisfaction directly, and thus the less important money will be in their attainment.

Safety (Security) Needs

We mentioned earlier that motives are not always apparent to the individual. Although some motives appear above the surface, many are largely subconscious and are not obvious or easy to identify. According to Saul W. Gellerman, security needs appear in both forms.[21]

The conscious security needs are quite evident and very common among most people. We all have a desire to remain free from the hazards of life – accidents, wars, diseases, and economic instability. Therefore, individuals and organizations are interested in providing some assurance that these catastrophes will be avoided if possible. Gellerman suggests that many organizations tend to overemphasize the security motive by providing elaborate programs of fringe benefits, such as health, accident, and life insurance and retirement plans. Such emphasis on security may make people more docile and predictable, but it does not mean they will be more productive. In fact, if creativity or initiative is necessary in their jobs, an overemphasis on security can thwart desired behavior.

Although concern for security can affect major decisions, such as remaining in or leaving an organization, Gellerman indicates it is not likely to be an individual's dominant motive. Conscious security needs usually play a background role, often inhibiting or restraining impulses rather than initiating outward behavior. For example, if a particular course of action, such as disregarding a rule or expressing an unpopular position, might endanger one's job, then security considerations motivate a person *not* to take this course of action. Organizations can influence these security needs either positively – through pension plans, insurance programs, and the like – or negatively, by arousing fears of being fired or laid off, demoted, or passed over. In both cases, the effect can be to make behavior too cautious and conservative.

Peter F. Drucker suggests that one's attitude toward security is important to consider in choosing a job.[22] He raises some interesting questions: Do you belong in a job calling primarily for faithfulness in the performance of routine work and promising security? Do you find real satisfaction in the precision, order, and system of a clearly laid-out job? Do you prefer the security not only of knowing what your work is today and what it is going to be tomorrow, but also security in your job, in your relationship to the people above, below, and next to you? Or do you belong in a job that offers a challenge to imagination and ingenuity – with the attendant penalty for failure? Are you one of those people who tends to grow impatient with anything that looks like a "routine" job? The answers to these questions are not always easy even though we all understand ourselves to some degree. But the answers are involved with how important the security motive is for that particular individual.

To reiterate, security needs can be conscious or subconscious. A strong subconscious orientation toward security is often developed early in childhood. Gellerman discusses several ways in which it can be implanted. A common way is through identification with security-minded parents who are willing to accept whatever fate comes along. This often occurs in depressed economic areas where the prospects for improvement are poor.[23]

The world seems uncertain and uncontrollable to people raised in a security-minded home. As a result, such people may not feel they are competent enough to be able to influence their environment.

The security-minded people we have been describing are often very likable. They are not competitive and, therefore, do not put people on the defensive. Others tend to expect little of them and thus are seldom critical of their work. This combined with the fact that they are pleasant to have around, often enables them to obtain a secure, nonthreatening position in an organization.

Subconscious security motives may also develop in children through interaction with overprotective parents. Such parents are constantly trying to shield their children from heartache, disappointment, or failure. The supportive attitude of these parents in many instances permits their children to have their own way. Conflict is avoided at all costs. As a result, these children are given a distorted picture of reality and gain little insight into what they can expect of other people and what others will expect of them. In some cases, they become unrealistic in their optimism about life. Even in the face of disaster, when they should feel threatened, they seem to believe that all is well until it is too late.

When such security-minded people leave home after high school to seek their way in the world, they quickly wake up to reality. Often they find themselves unequipped to handle the hardships of life because they have *not* been permitted the opportunity to develop the capacity to handle frustration, tension, and anxiety. As a result, even a minor setback may throw them for a loop. Drucker suggests that getting fired from their first job might be the best thing that could happen to such young people. He feels that getting fired from the first job is the least painful and least damaging way to learn how to take a setback, and that this is a lesson well worth learning. If people learn how to recover from seeming disaster when they are young, they will be better equipped to handle worse fate as they get older.

To many people, the security motive carries with it a negative connotation. A strong security need is frowned upon, for some reason, as if it were less respectable than other motives. This seems unjust, especially since nearly everyone has some conscious and subconscious security motives. Life is never so simple or clear-cut that one does not maintain some concern for security. In addition, many segments of our society often cater to these needs to the exclusion of such important needs as affiliation and self-actualization. We have already mentioned how industry concentrates on security needs by providing elaborate fringe benefits. Unions have a similar effect with their emphasis on seniority, and the government does much the same thing with welfare and other similar support programs.

Social (Affiliation) Needs

After the physiological and safety needs have become somewhat satisfied, the social needs may become predominant. Since people are social animals, most individuals like to interact and be with others in situations where they feel they belong and are accepted. While this is a common need, it tends to be stronger for some people than for others and stronger in certain situations. In other words, even such a commonplace social need as belongingness is, upon examination, quite complex.

In working toward a better understanding of our need to belong, Stanley Schachter of the University of Minnesota has made a significant contribution.[24] His efforts, in particular, have been directed toward studying the desire to socialize as an end in itself—that is, when people interact simply because they enjoy it. In some of these situations, no apparent reward such as money or protection was gained from this affiliation.

Schachter found that it was not always simply good fellowship that motivated affiliation. In many instances, people seek affiliation because they desire to have their beliefs confirmed. People who have similar beliefs tend to seek each other out, especially if a strongly held belief has been shattered. In this case, they tend to assemble and try to reach some common understanding about what happened and what they should believe (even if it is the same as before). In this instance, the need for affiliation was prompted by a desire to make one's life *seem* a little more under control. When alone, the world seems "out of whack," but if one can find an environment in which others hold the same beliefs, it somehow makes order out of chaos. This attitude hints at some of the problems inherent in any change.

In pursuing this question further, it was found that when people are excited, confused, or unhappy, they do not seek out just anyone— they tend to want to be with others "in the same boat." Misery does not just love company, it loves other miserable company. These conclusions suggest that the strong informal work groups that Elton Mayo found developing in the factory system might have been a reaction to the boredom, insignificance, and lack of competence that the workers felt.[25] As a result, workers congregated because of mutual feelings of being beaten by the system.

In observing loners and rate-busters in similar factory situations, it became apparent that there is not some universal need for affiliation as an end in itself. It was found, however, that these exceptions to the affiliation tendency were special types of people. They tended not to join informal work groups because they felt either suspicious or contemptuous of them or else secure and competent enough to fend for themselves.

Management is often suspicious of informal groups that develop at work because of the potential power these groups have to lower productivity. Schachter found that such work-restricting groups were sometimes formed as a reaction to the insignificance and impotence that workers tend to feel when they have no control over their working environment. Such environments develop when the work is routine, tedious, and oversimplified. This situation is made worse when, at the same time, the workers are closely supervised and controlled but have no clear channels of communication with management.

In this type of environment, workers who cannot tolerate this lack of control over their environment depend on the informal group for support of unfulfilled needs such as affiliation or achievement. Work restriction follows not from an inherent dislike for management but as a means to preserve the identification of individuals within the group and the group itself. Rate-busters are not tolerated because they weaken the group and its power with management, and to weaken the group destroys the only dignity, security, and significance the workers feel they have.

Lowering productivity is not always the result of informal work groups. In fact, informal groups can be a tremendous asset to management if their internal organization is understood and fully utilized. The productivity of a work group seems to depend on how the group members see their own goals in relation to the goals of the organization. For example, if they perceive their own goals as being in conflict with the goals of the organization, then productivity will tend to be low. However, if these workers see their own goals as being the same as the goals of the organization or as being satisfied as a direct result of accomplishing organizational goals, then productivity will tend to be high. Work restriction is therefore not a necessary aspect of informal work groups.

Esteem Needs

The need for esteem or recognition appears in a number of forms. In this section we shall discuss two motives related to esteem—prestige and power.

Prestige. The prestige motive is becoming more evident in our society today, especially as we move toward a middle-class society. People with a concern for prestige want to "keep up with the Joneses"; in fact, given the choice, they would like to stay ahead of the Joneses. Vance Packard[26] and David Riesman[27] probably had the greatest impact in exposing prestige motivation. Packard wrote about the status seekers and their motives, while Riesman unveiled "other-directed" individuals who were part of "the lonely crowd."

What exactly is prestige? Gellerman describes it as "a sort of unwritten definition of the kinds of conduct that other people are expected to show in one's presence; what degree of respect or disrespect, formality or informality, reserve or frankness."[28] Prestige seems to have an effect on how comfortably or conveniently one can expect to get along in life.

Prestige is something intangible bestowed upon an individual by society. In fact, at birth children inherit the status of their parents. In some cases, this is enough to carry them through life on "a prestige-covered wave."

People seek prestige throughout their lives in various ways. Many tend to seek only the material symbols of status, while others strive for personal achievement or self-actualization, which might command prestige in itself. Regardless of the way it is expressed, there seems to be a widespread need for people to have their importance clarified and, in fact, set at a level that each feels is deserved. As discussed earlier, people normally want to have a high evaluation of themselves that is firmly based in reality as manifested by the recognition and respect accorded them by others.

Power. The resource that enables a person to induce compliance from or to influence others is *power.* It is a person's influence potential. There tend to be two kinds of power—position and personal. Individuals who are able to induce compliance from others because of their position in the organization have *position* power; individuals who derive their influence from their personality and behavior have *personal* power. Some people are endowed with both position and personal power. Others seem to have no power at all.

Alfred Adler, a one-time colleague of Freud, became very interested in this power motive.[29] By power, Adler essentially meant the ability to manipulate or control the activities of others to suit one's own purposes. He found that this ability starts at an early age when children as babies realize that if they cry they influence their parents' behavior. Children's position as babies gives them considerable power over their parents.

According to Adler, this manipulative ability is inherently pleasurable. Children, for example, often have a hard time adjusting to the continuing reduction in their position power. In fact, they might spend a significant amount of time as adults trying to recapture the power they had as children. However, Adler did not feel that children seek power for its own sake as often as they do out of necessity. Power, for children, is often a life-and-death matter because they are helpless and need to count on their parents' availability. Parents are a child's lifeline. Thus, power acquires an importance in children that they somehow never lose, even though they are later able to fend for themselves.

After childhood, the power motive again becomes very potent in individuals who feel somehow inadequate in winning the respect and recognition of others. These people go out of their way to seek attention to overcome this weakness, which is often felt but not recognized. In this connection, Adler introduced two interesting and now well-known concepts in his discussion—*inferiority complex* and *compensation.*

A person with an inferiority complex has underlying fears of inadequacy, which may or may not have some basis in reality. In some cases, individuals compensate for this inferiority complex by exerting extreme efforts to achieve goals or objectives that (they feel) inadequacy would deny. In many cases, extreme effort seems to be an overcompensation for something not clearly perceived, although felt. Once accurately perceived, the frame of reference can be realigned with reality and can result in more realistic behavior.

Adler found another interesting thing. If children do not encounter too much tension as they mature, their need for power gradually transforms itself into a desire to perfect their social relationships. They want to be able to interact with others without fear or suspicion in an open and trusting atmosphere. Thus, individuals often move from the *task* aspect of power, wanting to structure and manipulate their environment and the people in it, to a concern for *relationships,* developing trust and respect for others. This transformation is often delayed with individuals who have had tension-filled childhoods and have not learned to trust. In these cases, the power motive would not only persist but might even become stronger. Thus, Adler, like Freud, felt that the personality of an individual is developed early in life and is often a result of the kind of past experiences the child had with adults in the world. We will discuss power in much greater detail in Chapter 9.

Self-actualization Needs

Of all the needs discussed by Maslow, the one that social and behavioral scientists know least about is self-actualization. Perhaps this is because people satisfy this need in different ways. Thus, self-actualization is a difficult need to pin down and identify.

Although little research has been done on the concept of self-actualization, extensive research has been done on two motives that we feel are related to it—*competence* and *achievement.*

Competence. According to Robert W. White, one of the mainsprings of action in a human being is a desire for competence.[30] Competence implies control over environmental factors—both physical and social. People with this motive do not wish to wait passively for things to happen; they want to be able to manipulate their environment and make things happen.

The competence motive can be identified in young children as they move from the early stage of wanting to touch and handle everything in reach to the later stage of wanting not only to touch but to take things apart and put them back together again. Children begin to learn their way around their world. They become aware of what they can and cannot do. This is not in terms of what they are allowed to do but in terms of what they are able to do. During these early years, children develop a feeling of competence.

This feeling of competence is closely related to the concept of expectancy discussed earlier. Whether children have a strong or weak sense of competence depends on their successes and failures in the past. If their successes overshadow their failures, then their feeling of competence will tend to be high. They will have a positive outlook toward life, seeing almost every new situation as an interesting challenge that they can overcome. If, however, their failures carry the day, their outlook will be more negative and their expectancy for satisfying various needs may become low. Since expectancy tends to influence motives, people with low feelings of competence will not often be motivated to seek new challenges or take risks. These people would rather let their environment control them than attempt to change it.

According to White, the competence motive reveals itself in adults as a desire for job mastery and professional growth. The job is one arena where people can match their ability and skills against their environment in a contest that is challenging, but not overwhelming. In jobs where such a contest is possible, the competence motive in an individual can be expressed freely, and significant personal rewards can be gained. But in routine, closely supervised jobs, this contest is often impossible. Such situations make the worker dependent on the system and, therefore, completely frustrate people with high competence needs.

Achievement. Over the years, behavioral scientists have observed that some people have an intense need to achieve; others, perhaps the majority, do not seem to be as concerned about achievement. This phenomenon has fascinated David C. McClelland. For more than thirty years, he and his associates at Harvard University have been studying this urge to achieve.[31]

McClelland's research has led him to believe that the need for achievement is a distinct human motive that can be distinguished from other needs. More important, he believes the achievement motive can be isolated and assessed in any group.

What are some of the characteristics of people with a high need for achievement? McClelland illustrates some of these characteristics in describing a laboratory experiment. Participants were asked to throw rings over a peg from any distance they chose. Most people tended to throw at random—now close, now far away; but individuals with a high need for achievement seemed to measure carefully where they were most likely to get a sense of mastery—not too close to make the task ridiculously easy or too far away to make it impossible. They set moderately difficult, but potentially achievable goals. In biology, this is known as the *overload principle.* In weight lifting, for example, strength cannot be increased by tasks that can be performed easily or that cannot be performed without injury to the organism. Strength can be increased by lifting weights that are difficult, but realistic enough to stretch the muscles.

Do people with a high need for achievement behave like this all the time? No. Only if they can influence the outcome. Achievement-motivated people are not gamblers. They prefer to work on a problem rather than leave the outcome to chance.

With managers, setting moderately difficult but potentially achievable goals may be translated into an attitude toward risks. Many people tend to be extreme in their attitude toward risks, either favoring wild speculative gambling or minimizing their exposure to losses. Gamblers seem to choose the big risk because the outcome is beyond their power and, therefore, they can easily rationalize away their personal responsibility if they lose. The conservative individual chooses tiny risks where the gain is small but secure, perhaps because there is little danger of anything going wrong for which that person might be blamed. Achievement-motivated people take the middle ground, preferring a moderate degree of risk because they feel their efforts and abilities will probably influence the outcome. In business, this aggressive realism is the mark of the successful entrepreneur.

Another characteristic of achievement-motivated people is that they seem to be more concerned with personal achievement than with the rewards of success. They do not reject rewards, but the rewards are not as essential as the accomplishment itself. They get a bigger kick out of winning or solving a difficult problem than they get from any money or praise they receive. Money, to achievement-motivated people, is valuable primarily as a measurement of their performance. It provides them with a means of assessing their progress and comparing their achievements with those of other people. They normally do not seek money for status or economic security.

A desire by people with a high need for achievement to seek situations in which they get concrete feedback on how well they are doing is closely related to this concern for personal accomplishment. Consequently, achievement-motivated people are often found in sales jobs or as owners and managers of their own businesses. In addition to concrete feedback, the nature of the feedback is important to achievement-motivated people. They respond favorably to information about their work. They are not interested in comments about their personal characteristics, such as how cooperative or helpful they are. Affiliation-motivated people might want social or attitudinal feedback. Achievement-motivated people might want task-relevant feedback. They want to know the score.

Why do achievement-motivated people behave as they do? McClelland claims it is because they habitually spend time thinking about doing things better. In fact, he has found that wherever people start to think in achievement terms, things start to happen. Examples can be cited. College students with a high need for achievement will generally get better grades than equally bright students with weaker achievement needs. Achievement-motivated people tend to get more raises and are promoted faster because they are constantly trying to think of better ways of doing things. Companies with many such people grow faster and are more profitable. McClelland has even extended his analysis to countries where he related the presence of a large percentage of achievement-motivated individuals to the national economic growth.

McClelland has found that achievement-motivated people are more likely to be developed in families in which parents hold different expectations for their children than do other parents. More importantly, these parents expect their children to start showing some independence between the ages of six and eight, making choices and doing things without help, such as knowing the way around the neighborhood and taking care of themselves around the house. Other parents tend either to expect this too early, before children are ready, or to smother the development of the personality of these children. One extreme seems to foster passive, defeatist attitudes as children feel unwanted at home and incompetent away from home. They are just not ready for that kind of independence so early. The other extreme yields either overprotected or overdisciplined children. These children become very dependent on their parents and find it difficult to break away and make their own decisions.

Given all we know about the need for achievement, can this motive be taught and developed in people? McClelland is convinced that this can be done. In fact, he has also developed training programs for business people that are designed to increase their achievement motivation. He is also in the process of developing similar programs for other segments of the population. These programs could have tremendous implications for training and developing human resources.

Achievement-motivated people can be the backbone of most organizations, but what can we say about their potential as managers? As we know, people with a high need for achievement get ahead because as individuals they are producers—they get things done. However, when they are promoted—when their success depends not only on their own work but on the activities of others—they may be less effective. Since they are highly task-oriented and work to their capacity, they tend to expect others to do the same. As a result, they sometimes lack the human skills and patience necessary for being effective managers of people who are competent but have a higher need for affiliation than they do. In this situation, their overemphasis on producing frustrates these people and prevents them from maximizing their own potential. Thus, while achievement-motivated people are needed in organizations, they do not always make the best managers unless they develop their human skills. As was pointed out in chapter 1, being a good producer is not sufficient to make an effective manager.

Money Motive

As stated earlier, money is a very complicated motive that is entangled in such a way with all kinds of needs besides physiological needs that its importance is often difficult to ascertain. For example, in some cases, money can provide individuals with certain material things, such as fancy sports cars, from which they gain a feeling of affiliation (join a sports car club), recognition (status symbol), and even self-actualization (become outstanding sports car drivers). Consequently, we delayed our discussion of the money motive until other basic concepts were clarified.

From extensive research on incentive pay schemes, William F. Whyte found that money, the old reliable motivational tool, is not as almighty as it is supposed to be, particularly for production workers.[32] For each of these workers, another key factor, as Mayo discovered, is their work group. Using the ratio of high-producing rate-busters to low-producing restrictors as an index, Whyte estimates that only about 10 percent of the production workers in the United States will ignore group pressure and produce as much as possible in response to an incentive plan. It seems that while workers are interested in advancing their own financial position, there are many other considerations—such as the opinions of their fellow workers, their comfort and enjoyment on the job, and their long-range security—that prevent them from making a direct, automatic, positive response to an incentive plan.

According to Gellerman, the most subtle and most important characteristic of money is its power as a symbol. Its most obvious symbolic power is its market value. It is what money can buy, not money itself, that gives it value. But money's symbolic power is not limited to its market value. Since money has no intrinsic meaning of its own, it can symbolize almost any need an individual wants it to represent. In other words, money can mean whatever people want it to mean.[33]

Bushardt, Toso, and Schnake suggest that: "While money is one of the most powerful motivational tools, its use must be tailored to each employee's values."[34] One approach to this "tailoring" is through the use of expectancy theory discussed earlier in this chapter. These authors suggest that for money to motivate, three considerations must be met. One, the employee must have a high "net" preference for money. This concept of "net" is important because frequently long hours are part of higher pay. The positive motivating effects of more pay must be greater than the negative effects of undesirable hours. Second, there needs to be a direct relationship between money and performance that the employee can perceive. If performance increases, then pay should increase and vice versa. Third, there needs to be a direct relationship between effort and performance. If effort increases, performance should increase.

There are many problems with implementing such a system, including the difficulties of assessing employee perceptions, measuring performance, establishing a pay system tied to performance, and so forth. Both the costs and the benefits in this approach need to be determined; it has a sound motivational base.

WHAT DO WORKERS WANT FROM THEIR JOBS?

In talking about motives, it is important to remember that people have many needs, all of which are continually competing for their behavior. No one person has exactly the same mixture or strength of these needs. There are some people who are driven mainly by money, others who are concerned primarily with security, and so on. While we must recognize individual differences, this does not mean that, as managers, we cannot make some predictions about which motives seem to be currently more prominent among our employees than others. According to Maslow, these are prepotent motives—those that are still *not* satisfied. An important question for managers to ask is: What do workers really want from their jobs? The answer, as we will see in the following paragraphs, will vary. First, let's go back to research reported in 1949.

What Do Workers Want?—1949

Research has been conducted among employees in American industry in an attempt to answer this question. In one such study[35] supervisors were asked to try to put themselves in a *worker's* shoes by ranking in order of importance a series of items that describe things workers may want from their jobs. It was emphasized that in ranking the items the supervisors should *not* think in terms of what they want but what they think a worker wants. In addition to the supervisors, the workers themselves were asked to rank these same items in terms of what *they* wanted most from their jobs. The results are given in Table 2-1 (1 = highest and 10 = lowest in importance).

As is evident from the results, the supervisors in this study generally ranked good wages, job security, promotion, and good working conditions as the things workers want most from their jobs. On the other hand, workers felt that what they wanted most was full appreciation for work done, feeling "in" on things, and sympathetic understanding of personal problems—all incentives that seem to be related to affiliation and recognition motives. It is interesting to note that things that workers indicated they wanted most from their jobs were rated by their supervisors as least important. This study suggested

TABLE 2-1 What Do Workers Want from Their Jobs?

	SUPERVISORS	WORKERS
Good working conditions	4	9
Feeling "in" on things	10	2
Tactful disciplining	7	10
Full appreciation for work done	8	1
Management loyalty to workers	6	8
Good wages	1	5
Promotion and growth with company	3	7
Sympathetic understanding of personal problems	9	3
Job security	2	4
Interesting work	5	6

very little sensitivity by supervisors as to what things were really most important to workers. Supervisors seemed to think that incentives directed to satisfying physiological and safety motives tended to be most important to their workers. Since these supervisors perceived their workers as having these motives, they acted, undoubtedly, as if these were their true motives. Therefore, these supervisors probably used the old reliable incentives–money, fringe benefits, and security–to motivate workers.

We have replicated this study periodically over the last several decades as part of management training programs and have found similar results in the perceptions of managers. The only real changes seem to be that workers, over the last five to ten years, were increasing in their desire for "promotion and growth with the company" and "interesting work" (both motivators in Herzberg's framework). We say *were* increasing because with the economic decline of the 1980s and 1990s, "good wages" and "job security" once again were becoming high-strength needs for workers. It is important that managers know the tremendous discrepancies that seemed to exist in the past between what they thought workers wanted from their jobs and what workers said they actually wanted. It is also important that they realize what effect an economic or other change has on these priorities.

What Do Workers Want?—Sex Differences in Work Values

Beutell and Brenner[36] have examined the questions: What do men and women want from their jobs? Are there sex differences in work values? Based on their research, work values in general showed a high degree of similarity between men and women. This substantial consistency was not only true in this study, but also in other similar studies. Table 2-2 lists some of the work values studied, together with a ranking of these values.

There were, however, some items in which women scored significantly higher than men, and vice versa. Women scored higher than men on these items: feeling of accomplishment, respect, pleasant work environment, development of knowledge and skills, intellectual stimulation, independence, use of educational background, originality and creativity, social contribution, respect from supervisor, and cultural and esthetic interests.

Men scored higher than women in the importance of job security, income, advancement to high administrative responsibility, leisure time off the job, working on problems of central importance to the organization, and taking risks.

Few of the participants ranked career as the primary source of

TABLE 2-2 Work Values of Men and Women

HOW IMPORTANT IS IT TO YOU TO HAVE A JOB WHICH:	Men Rank	Women Rank
1. Provides a feeling of accomplishment	1	1
2. Provides job security	2	2
3. Provides opportunity to earn a high income	3	5
4. Permits advancement to high administrative responsibility	4	6
5. Is respected by other people	5	3
6. Rewards good performance with recognition	6	8
7. Provides comfortable working conditions	7	4
8. Encourages continued development of knowledge and skills	8	7
9. Is intellectually stimulating	9	9

life satisfaction. This may indicate a trend toward an increasing desire for a more balanced life.

What Do Workers Want?—Recent Findings

Studies are continuing on the important question of worker values. Table 2-3, which summarizes a variety of studies, reinforces the need for managers to assess the needs of their employees and to be sensitive to these needs.

SUMMARIZING MOTIVES AND BEHAVIOR

In summarizing what we know about motives, it is important to remember that people have many needs, all of which are continually competing for their behavior. No one person has exactly the same mixture or strength of these needs. There are some people who are driven mainly by money, others who are concerned primarily with security, and so on. While we must recognize individual differences, this does not mean that we, as managers, cannot make some predictions about which motives seem to be more prominent among our employees than others. According to Maslow, these are the prepotent motives—those that are still *not* satisfied. If we are to understand, predict, and control future behavior, we must know what our employees really want from their jobs. While it is interesting to learn what employees in other organizations seem to want from their jobs, our primary efforts should be an attention on and a concern for our followers.

TABLE 2-3 What Do Workers Want From Their Jobs?—Recent Findings

JOB REWARD	Supervisors[a]	Truckers[b]	Social Workers[c]	Doctors[d]	Nurses[e]
Advancement	3	5			
Autonomy			1	1	
Caring Boss					3
Company Philosophy	1			5	
Fringe Benefits	5				6
Improved Communication with Boss					2
Job Status				2	
Monetary Compensation	2	1	3	3	1
More Responsibility	4				
Non-Isolation		2			
Team Work with Co-Workers	6				
Work Recognition					4
Work Schedule		3	2		
Working Conditions		4		4	5

[a]John S. McClenahen, "It's No Fun Working Here Anymore," *Industry Week*, 240 (1991), pp. 20–22.

[b]John D. Schultz, "Truckers Look to Returning Troops as Partial Solution to Driver Crises," *Traffic World*, 225 (1991), pp. 24–26.

[c]Beverly B. Butler, "Job Satisfaction: Management's Continuing Challenges," *Social Work*, 35 (1990), pp. 112–16.

[d]Suzanne B. Cashman, CindyLou Parks, Arlene Ash, David Hemingway, and William J. Bicknell, "Physician Satisfaction in a Major Chain of Investor Owned Walk-in Centers," *Health Care Management Review*, 15 (1990), pp. 47–57.

[e]Barbara B. Gray. "Are California Nurses Happy?" *California Nursing*, 13 (1991), pp. 12–17.

In assessing needs, managers have to know their people to understand what motivates them; they cannot just make assumptions. Even if managers ask employees how they feel about something, this does not necessarily result in accurate feedback. The primary reason is that individuals act on the basis of their perceptions or interpretation of reality and *not* on the basis of reality itself. In fact, one of the reasons that we study the behavioral sciences is that they give us ways to get our perceptions closer and closer to reality. The closer we get our perceptions to a given reality, the higher the probability that we can have some impact on that particular piece of reality. Therefore, by bringing their perceptions closer and closer to reality—what their people really want—managers can often increase their effectiveness. As we continue our study and practice of the behavioral sciences in the following chapters, our ability to understand, predict, and to control people, individually and in groups, will develop.

NOTES

1. Sigmund Freud, *The Ego and the Id* (London: Hogarth Press, 1927). See also *New Introductory Lectures on Psychoanalysis* (New York: Norton, 1933).
2. Abraham H. Maslow, *Motivation and Personality* (New York: Harper & Row, 1954). See also Maslow, *Motivation and Personality*, 2nd ed. (New York: Harper & Row, 1970).
3. Leon Festinger, *A Theory of Cognitive Dissonance* (Stanford, Calif.: Stanford University Press, 1957); Stephen Kaplan, *Cognition and Environment: Functioning in an Uncertain World* (New York: Praeger, 1982).
4. Festinger, *A Theory of Cognitive Dissonance,* p. 155.
5. Freud, *The Ego and the Id.*
6. Norman R. F. Maier, *Frustration* (Ann Arbor: University of Michigan Press, 1961).
7. J. A. C. Brown, *The Social Psychology of Industry* (Baltimore: Penguin Books, 1954), p. 252.
8. H. Barker, T. Dembo, and K. Lewin, *Frustration and Aggression* (Iowa City: University of Iowa Press, 1942).
9. Brown, *The Social Psychology,* p. 253.
10. Maier, *Frustration.*
11. Brown, *The Social Psychology,* p. 254.
12. Dewey E. Johnson, *Concepts of Air Force Leadership* (Washington, D.C.: Air Force ROTC, 1970), p. 209.
13. Livingston, "Pygmalion in Management," pp. 81–89.
14. See John W. Atkinson, "Motivational Determinants of Risk-Taking Behavior, *Psychological Review,* 64, No. 6 (1957), 365; C. N. Cofer and M. H. Appley, *Motivation: Theory and Research* (New York: Wiley, 1964).
15. Victor, H. Vroom, "Leader," in M. D. Dunnette (ed.), *Handbook of Industrial and Organizational Psychology* (Chicago: Rand McNally, 1976), pp. 1527–51.
16. Martin L. Maehr and Larry A. Braskampt, *The Motivation Factor: A Theory of Personal Investment* (Lexington, Mass.: Health, 1986).
17. Maslow, *Motivation and Personality.*
18. Clare W. Graves, "Human Nature Prepares for a Momentous Leap," *The Futurist,* April 1974, pp. 72–87.
19. *Ibid.,* p. 72.
20. *Ibid.*
21. Saul W. Gellerman, *Motivation and Productivity* (New York: American Management Association, 1963). See also Gellerman, *Management by Motivation* (New York: American Management Association, 1968); Frederick Herzberg, *Motivating People,* in P. Mali (ed.) *Management Handbook* (New York: Wiley, 1981); Michael LeBoeuf, *The Productivity Challenge: How to Make It Work for America and You* (New York: McGraw-Hill, 1982).
22. Peter F. Drucker, "How to Be an Employee," *Psychology Today,* March 1968, a reprint from *Fortune* magazine; G. J. Gorn and R. N. Kanungo, "Job Involvement and Motivation: Are Intrinsically Motivated Managers More Job Involved?" *Organizational Behavior and Hu-*

    man Performance 26 (1980), pp. 265–77; W. R. Nord, "Job Satisfaction Reconsidered," *American Psychologist,* 32 (1977), pp. 1026–35; Craig Pinder, *Work Motivation: Theory, Issues, and Applications* (Glenview, Ill.: Scott, Foresman, 1984).

23. Gellerman, *Motivation and Productivity,* pp. 154–55.
24. Stanley Schachter, *The Psychology of Affiliation* (Stanford, Calif.: Stanford University Press, 1959).
25. Elton Mayo, *The Social Problems of an Industrial Civilization* (Boston: Harvard Business School, 1945); see also Mayo, *The Human Problems of an Industrial Civilization* (New York: Macmillan, 1933).
26. Vance Packard, *The Status Seekers* (New York: David McKay, 1959).
27. David Reisman, *The Lonely Crowd* (New Haven, Conn.: Yale University Press, 1950).
28. Gellerman, *Motivation and Productivity,* p. 151.
29. Alfred Adler, *Social Interest* (London: Faber & Faber, 1938). See also H. L. Ansbacher and R. R. Ansbacher, eds., *The Individual Psychology of Alfred Adler* (New York: Basic Books, 1956).
30. Robert W. White, "Motivation Reconsidered: The Concept of Competence," *Psychological Review,* No. 5 (1959).
31. David C. McClelland, J. W. Atkinson, R. A. Clark, and E. L. Lowell, *The Achievement Motive* (New York: Appleton-Century-Crofts, 1953); and *The Achieving Society* (Princeton, N.J.: D. Van Nostrand, 1961); John William Atkinson, *Motivation and Achievement* (New York: Halsted Press, 1974). See also Craig Pinder, "Concerning the Application of Human Motivation Theories in Organizational Settings," *Academy of Management Review,* 21 (1977), pp. 384–397.
32. William F. Whyte, ed., *Money and Motivation* (New York: Harper & Row, 1955).
33. Gellerman, *Motivation and Productivity,* pp. 160–69.
34. Stephen C. Bushardt, Roberto Toso, and M. E. Schnake, "Can Money Motivate?" in Timpe A. Dale, ed., *Motivation of Personnel* (New York: KEND Publishing, 1986), pp. 50–53.
35. Lawrence Lindahl, "What Makes a Good Job?" *Personnel,* 25 (January 1949).
36. Nicholas J. Beutell and O. C. Brenner, "Sex Differences in Work Values," *Journal of Vocational Behavior,* 28 (1986), pp. 29–41.

3

Motivating Environment

In 1924, efficiency experts at the Hawthorne, Illinois, plant of the Western Electric Company designed a research program to study the effects of illumination on productivity. At first, nothing about this program seemed exceptional enough to arouse any unusual interest. After all, efficiency experts had long been trying to find the ideal mix of physical conditions, working hours, and working methods that would stimulate workers to produce at maximum capacity. Yet by the time these studies were completed (a decade later), there was little doubt that the work at Hawthorne would stand the test of time as one of the most exciting and important research projects ever done in an industrial setting. For it was at Western Electric's Hawthorne plant that the Human Relations Movement began to gather momentum, and one of its early advocates, Elton Mayo of the Harvard Graduate School of Business Administration, gained recognition.[1]

HAWTHORNE STUDIES

Elton Mayo

In the initial study at Hawthorne, efficiency experts assumed that increases in illumination would result in higher output. Two groups of employees were selected: an *experimental,* or *test group,* which worked under varying degrees of light; and a *control group,* which worked under normal illumination conditions in the plant. As lighting power was increased, the output of the test group went up as anticipated. Unexpectedly, however, the output of the control group went up also—without any increase in light.

Determined to explain these and other surprising test results, the efficiency experts decided to expand their research at Hawthorne. They felt that in addition to technical and physical changes, some of the behavioral considerations should be explored, so Mayo and his associates were called in to help.

Mayo and his team started their experiments with a group of women who assembled telephone relays and, like the efficiency experts, the Harvard staff uncovered astonishing results. For more than a year and a half during this experiment, Mayo's researchers improved the working conditions of the women by implementing such innovations as scheduled rest periods, company lunches, and shorter work weeks. Baffled by the results, the researchers suddenly decided to take everything away from the women, returning the working conditions to the exact way they had been at the beginning of the experiment. This radical change was expected to have a tremendous negative psychological impact on the women and to reduce their output. Instead, their output jumped to a new *all-time high.* Why?

The answers to this question were *not* found in the production aspects of the experiment (changes in plant and physical working conditions), but in the *human* aspects. As a result of the attention lavished upon them by experimenters, the women felt that they were an important part of the company. They no longer viewed themselves as isolated individuals, working together only in the sense that they were physically close to each other. Instead, they had become participating members of a congenial, cohesive work group. The relationships that developed elicited feelings of affiliation, competence, and achievement. These needs, which had long gone unsatisfied at the workplace, were now being fulfilled. The women worked harder and more effectively than previously.

Realizing that they had uncovered an interesting phenomenon, the Harvard team extended their research by interviewing more than twenty thousand employees from every department in the company. Interviews were designed to help researchers find out what the workers thought about their jobs, their working conditions, their supervisors, their company, and anything that bothered them, and how these feelings might be related to their productivity. After several interview sessions, Mayo's group found that a structured question-and-answer-type interview was useless for eliciting the information they wanted. Instead, the workers wanted to talk freely about what *they* thought was important. So the predetermined questions were discarded and the interviewer allowed the workers to say what they wanted to say.

The interviews proved valuable in a number of ways. First they were therapeutic; the workers got an opportunity to express themselves. Many felt this was the best thing the company had ever done. The result was a wholesale change in attitude. Since many of their suggestions were being implemented, the workers began to feel that management viewed them as important, both as individuals and as a group; they were now participating in the operation and future of the company and not just performing unchallenging, unappreciated tasks.

Second, the implications of the Hawthorne studies signaled the need for management to study and understand relationships among people. In these studies, as well as in the many that followed, the most significant factor affecting organizational productivity was found to be the interpersonal relationships that are developed on the job, not just pay and working conditions. Mayo found that when informal groups identified with management, as they did at Hawthorne through the interview program, productivity rose. The increased productivity seemed to reflect the workers' feelings of competence—a sense of mastery over the job and work environment. Mayo also discovered that when the group felt that their own goals were in opposition to those of management, as often happened in situations where workers were closely supervised and had no significant control over the job or environment, productivity remained at low levels or was even lowered.

These findings were important because they helped answer many of the questions that had puzzled management about why some groups seemed to be high producers while others hovered at a minimal level of output. The findings also encouraged management to involve workers in planning, organizing, and controlling their own work in an effort to secure their positive cooperation.

Mayo saw the development of informal groups as an indictment of a society that treated human beings as insensitive machines that were concerned only with economic self-interest. As a result, workers had been expected to look at work merely as an impersonal exchange of money for labor. Work in American industry, according to Mayo, meant humiliation—the performance of routine, tedious, and oversimplified tasks in an environment over which one had no control. This environment denied satisfaction of esteem and self-actualization needs on the job. Instead, only physiological and safety needs were satisfied. The lack of avenues for satisfying other needs led to tension, anxiety, and frustration in people. Such feelings of helplessness were called *anomie* by Mayo. This condition was characterized by workers feeling unimportant, confused, and unattached—victims of their own environment.

While anomie was a creation of the total society, Mayo felt its most extreme application was found in industrial settings where management held certain negative assumptions about the nature of people. According to Mayo, too many managers assumed that society consisted of a horde of unorganized individuals whose only concern was self-preservation or self-interest. It was assumed that people were primarily dominated by physiological and safety needs, wanting to make as much money as they could for as little work as possible. Thus, management organized work on the basic assumption that workers, on the whole, were a contemptible lot. Mayo called this assumption the Rabble Hypothesis. He deplored the authoritarian, task-oriented management practices that it created.

THEORY X AND THEORY Y

Douglas McGregor

The work of Mayo and particularly his idea of the Rabble Hypothesis may have paved the way for the development of the now classic "Theory X–Theory Y" by Douglas McGregor.[2] According to McGregor, the traditional organization—with its centralized decision making, hierarchical pyramid, and external control of work—is based upon certain assumptions about human nature and human motivation (see Table 3-1). These assumptions, which McGregor called Theory X, are very similar to the view of people defined by Mayo in the Rabble Hypothesis. Theory X assumes that most people prefer to be directed, are not interested in assuming responsibility, and want safety above all. Accompanying this philosophy is the belief that people are motivated by money, fringe benefits, and the threat of punishment.

Managers who accept Theory X assumptions attempt to struc ture, control, and closely supervise their employees. These managers feel that external control is clearly appropriate for dealing with unreliable and irresponsible people.

After describing Theory X, McGregor questioned whether this view of human nature is correct and if management practices based upon it are appropriate in many situations today: Are not people in a democratic society, with its increasing level of education and standard of living, capable of more responsible behavior? Drawing heavily on Maslow's hierarchy of needs, McGregor concluded that Theory X assumptions about human nature, when universally applied, are often inaccurate and that management approaches that develop from

TABLE 3-1 List of Assumptions about Human Nature that Underlie McGregor's Theory X and Theory Y

THEORY X	THEORY Y
1. Work is inherently distasteful to most people.	1. Work is as natural as play, if the conditions are favorable.
2. Most people are not ambitious, have little desire for responsibility, and prefer to be directed.	2. Self-control is often indispensable in achieving organizational goals.
3. Most people have little capacity for creativity in solving organizational problems.	3. The capacity for creativity in solving organizational problems is widely distributed in the population.
4. Motivation occurs only at the physiological and safety levels.	4. Motivation occurs at the social, esteem, and self-actualization levels, as well as at the physiological and security levels.
5. Most people must be closely controlled and often coerced to achieve organizational objectives.	5. People can be self-directed and creative at work if properly motivated.

these assumptions may fail to motivate many individuals to work toward organizational goals. Management by direction and control may not succeed, according to McGregor, because it is a questionable method for motivating people whose physiological and safety needs are reasonably satisfied and whose social, esteem, and self-actualization needs are becoming predominant.

McGregor felt that management needed practices based on a more accurate understanding of human nature and motivation. As a result of his feeling, McGregor developed an alternate theory of human behavior called Theory Y. This theory assumes that people are *not*, by nature, lazy and unreliable. It postulates that people *can be* basically self-directed and creative at work if properly motivated. Therefore, it should be an essential task of management to unleash this potential in individuals. Properly motivated people can achieve their own goals *best* by directing *their own* efforts toward accomplishing organizational goals.

The impression that one might get from this discussion of Theory X–Theory Y is that managers who accept Theory X assumptions about human nature usually direct, control, and closely supervise people, while Theory Y managers are supportive and facilitating. We want to caution against drawing this conclusion because it could lead to the trap of thinking that Theory X is "bad" and Theory Y is "good" and that everyone is independent and self-motivated rather than, as McGregor implies, that most people have the *potential* to be independent and self-motivated. This assumption of the potential self-motivation of people necessitates a recognition of the difference between attitude and behavior.

Theory X and Theory Y are attitudes, or predispositions, toward people. Thus, although the "best" assumptions for a manager to have may be Theory Y, it may not be appropriate to behave consistently with those assumptions all the time. Managers may have Theory Y assumptions about human nature, but they may find it necessary to behave in a very directive, controlling manner (as if they had Theory X assumptions) with some people in the short run to help them "grow up" in a developmental sense, until they are truly Theory Y acting people.

Chris Argyris recognizes the difference between attitude and behavior when he identifies and discusses behavior patterns A and B in addition to Theory X and Y.[3] Pattern A represents the interpersonal behavior, group dynamics, and organizational norms that Argyris has found in his research to be associated with Theory X; pattern B represents the same phenomena found to be associated with Theory Y. In pattern A, individuals do not own up to feelings, are not open, reject experimenting, and do not help others to engage in these behaviors. Their behavior tends to be characterized by close supervision and a high degree of structure. On the other hand, pattern B finds individuals owning up to feelings, open, experimenting, and helping others to engage in these behaviors. Their behavior tends to be more supportive and facilitating. The result is norms of trust, concern, and individuality.

As Argyris emphasizes, "although XA and YB are *usually* associated with each other in everyday life, they do not have to be. Under certain conditions, pattern A could go with Theory Y or pattern B with Theory X."[4] Thus, XA and YB are the most frequent combinations, but some managers, at times, may be XB or YA. Although XB managers have negative assumptions about people, they seem to behave in supportive and facilitating ways. We have found that this XB combination tends to occur for two reasons. These managers (although they think most people are lazy and unreliable) engage in supportive and facilitating behaviors either because they have been told or have learned from experience that such behavior will increase productivity or because they work for people who have created a supportive environment and if they want to maintain their jobs they are expected to behave accordingly. On the other hand, YA managers (although they think people are generally independent and self-motivated) control and closely supervise people either because they work for controlling people who demand similar behavior from them or because they find it necessary to behave in a directive, controlling manner for a period of time. When they use pattern A behavior, these managers usually are attempting to help people develop the skills and abilities necessary for self-direction and thus are creating an environment in which they can become YB managers.

The latter type of Y manager attempts to help employees develop by exposing them to progressively less external control, allowing them to assume more and more self-control. Employees are able to achieve the satisfaction of social, esteem, and self-actualization needs within this kind of environment—one that is often neglected on the job. To the extent that the job does not provide satisfaction at every level, today's employee will usually look elsewhere for significant need satisfaction. This helps explain some of the current problems management is facing in such areas as turnover and absenteeism. McGregor argues that this does not have to be the case.

Management is interested in work, and McGregor feels that work is as natural and can be as satisfying for people as play. After all, both work and play are physical and mental activities; consequently, there is no inherent difference between work and play. In reality, however, particularly under Theory X management, a distinct difference in need satisfaction is discernible. Whereas play is internally controlled by the individuals (they decide what they want to do), work is externally controlled by others (people have no control over their jobs). Thus, management and its assumptions about the nature of people have built in a difference between work and play that seems unnatural. As a result, people are stifled at work, hence look for excuses to spend more and more time away from the job in order to satisfy their esteem and self-actualization needs (provided they have enough money to satisfy their physiological and safety needs). Because of their conditioning to Theory X management, most employees consider work a *necessary evil* rather than a source of personal challenge and satisfaction.

Does work really have to be a necessary evil? No—especially in organizations where cohesive work teams have developed and where the team's goals parallel organizational goals. In such organizations there is high productivity and people come to work gladly because work is inherently satisfying.

HUMAN GROUP

George C. Homans

Management is often suspicious of strong informal work groups because of their potential power to control the behavior of their members and, as a result, the level of productivity. Where do these groups get their power to control behavior? George C. Homans developed a model of social systems that may be useful in answering this question.[5]

There are three elements in a social system. *Activities* are the tasks that people perform. *Interactions* are the behaviors that occur between people in performing these tasks. And *sentiments* are the attitudes that develop between individuals and within groups. Homans argues that while these concepts are separate, they are closely related. In fact, as Figure 3-1 illustrates, they are mutually dependent upon each other. A change in any one of these three elements will produce some change in the other two.

In an organization, certain activities, interactions, and sentiments are essential, or required from its members if it is to survive. In other words, jobs (activities) have to be done that require people to work together (interactions). These jobs must be sufficiently satisfying (sentiments) for people to continue doing them. As people interact on their jobs, they develop sentiments toward each other. As people increase interaction with each other, it is important that positive sentiments be developed. The more positive the sentiment, the more people will tend to interact with each other. It can become an upward-spiraling process until some equilibrium is reached. As this upward-spiraling process continues, there is a tendency for the group members to become more alike in their activities and sentiments—in what they do and how they feel about things. As this happens, the group tends to develop expectations or norms that specify how people in the group "might" tend to behave under specific circumstances. For example, a group of workers might have a norm that "you should not talk to Mary or help her any more than necessary." If the group is cohesive enough—that is, the group is attractive to its members and they are reluctant to leave it—then it will have little trouble in getting members to conform. People who deviate significantly from group norms

FIGURE 3-1
The mutual dependence of activities, interactions, and sentiments

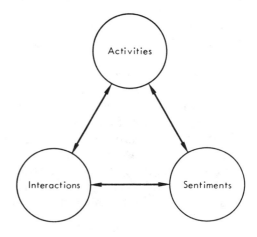

usually incur sanctions from the group. "The group has at its disposal a variety of penalties, ranging from gentle kidding to harsh ostracism, for pressuring deviant members into line."[6] Group members may react in several ways. They may decide to go ahead and continue to deviate from group norms. If the resulting pressure from their peers becomes too great, they may leave the group.

The influence group pressures can have in achieving conformity in the perceptions and behavior of people is well documented. For example, S. E. Asch conducted a classic experiment in which groups of eight college men were each asked to match the length of a line with one of three unequal lines.[7] Seven members of each group were privately told to give the same incorrect answer. The uninstructed member was the last one asked to give his answer and was thus confronted with the dilemma of either reporting what he saw as being correct or reporting what all the others had said in order to be congruent with the group. Asch reported that "one-third of all the estimates were errors identical with or in the direction of the distorted estimates of the majority."[8] If pressure can cause distorted behavior in this kind of exercise, imagine what peer group pressure can induce with more subjective judgments.

It should be reiterated that strong informal work groups do not have to be a detriment to organizations. In fact, as Mayo discovered at Hawthorne, these groups can become powerful driving forces in accomplishing organizational goals if they see their own goals as being satisfied by working for organizational goals.

INCREASING INTERPERSONAL COMPETENCE

Chris Argyris

Even though management based on the assumptions of Theory X is perhaps no longer widely appropriate, in the opinion of McGregor and others, it is still widely practiced. Consequently, a large majority of the people in the United States today are treated as immature human beings in their working environments. In attempting to analyze this situation, Chris Argyris,[9] compared bureaucratic-pyramidal values (the organizational counterpart to Theory X assumptions about people) that still dominate most organizations with a more humanistic-democratic value system (the organizational counterpart to Theory Y assumptions about people), as illustrated in Table 3-2.[10]

According to Argyris, bureaucratic or pyramidal values lead to poor, shallow, and mistrustful relationships. Because these relation-

TABLE 3-2 Two Different Value Systems as Seen by Chris Argyris

BUREAUCRATIC-PYRAMIDAL VALUE SYSTEM	HUMANISTIC-DEMOCRATIC VALUE SYSTEM
1. Important human relationships—the crucial ones—are those related to achieving the organization's objectives, i.e., getting the job done. 2. Effectiveness in human relationships increases as behavior becomes more rational, logical, and clearly communicated; but effectiveness decreases as behavior becomes more emotional. 3. Human relationships are most effectively motivated by carefully defined direction, authority, and control, as well as appropriate rewards and penalties that emphasize rational behavior and achievement of the objective.	1. The important human relationships are not only those related to achieving the organization's objectives but those related to maintaining the organization's internal system and adapting to the environment as well. 2. Human relationships increase in effectiveness as *all* the relevant behavior (rational and interpersonal) becomes conscious, discussible, and controllable. 3. In addition to direction, controls, and rewards and penalties, human relationships are most effectively influenced through authentic relationships, internal commitment, psychological success, and the process of confirmation.

Used by permission of the publisher from *Interpersonal Competence and Organizational Effectiveness*, 1962. © Richard D. Irwin. All rights reserved.

ships do not permit the natural and free expression of feelings, they are phony or nonauthentic and result in decreased interpersonal competence. "Without interpersonal competence or a 'psychologically safe' environment, the organization is a breeding ground for mistrust, intergroup conflict, rigidity, and so on, which in turn lead to a decrease in organizational success in problem solving."[11]

If, on the other hand, humanistic or democratic values are adhered to in an organization, Argyris claims that trusting, authentic relationships will develop among people and will result in increased interpersonal competence, intergroup cooperation, flexibility, and the like and should result in increases in organizational effectiveness. In this kind of environment people are treated as human beings, both organizational members and the organization itself are given an opportunity to develop to the fullest potential, and there is an attempt to make work exciting and challenging. Implicit in "living" these values is "treating each human being as a person with a complex set of needs, *all* of which are important in his work and in his life . . . and providing opportunities for people in organizations to influence the way in which they relate to work, the organization, and the environment."[12]

Argyris' Immaturity-Maturity Theory

The fact that bureaucratic-pyramidal values still dominate most organizations, according to Argyris, has produced many of our current organizational problems. While at Yale, he examined industrial organizations to determine what effect management practices have had on individual behavior and personal growth within the work environment.[13]

According to Argyris, seven changes should take place in the personality of individuals if they are to develop into mature people over the years.

First, individuals move from a passive state as infants to a state of increasing activity as adults. Second, individuals develop from a state of dependency upon others as infants to a state of relative independence as adults. Third, individuals behave in only a few ways as infants, but as adults they are capable of behaving in many ways. Fourth, individuals have erratic, casual, and shallow interests as infants, but develop deeper and stronger interests as adults. Fifth, the time perspective of children is very short, involving only the present, but as they mature, their time perspective increases to include the past and the future. Sixth, individuals as infants are subordinate to everyone, but they move to equal or superior positions with others as adults. Seventh, as children, individuals lack an awareness of a "self," but as adults they are not only aware of, but they are able to control "self." Argyris suggests that these changes reside on a continuum and that the "healthy" personality develops along the continuum from "immaturity" to "maturity" (see Table 3-3).

These changes are only general tendencies, but they give some light on the matter of maturity. Norms of the individual's culture and personality inhibit and limit maximum expression and growth of the adult, yet the tendency is to move toward the "maturity" end of the continuum with age. Argyris would be the first to admit that few, if any, develop to full maturity.

TABLE 3-3 Argyris' Immaturity-Maturity Continuum

IMMATURITY ⟶ MATURITY	
Passive	Active
Dependence	Independence
Behave in a few ways	Capable of behaving in many ways
Erratic shallow interests	Deeper and stronger interests
Short time perspective	Long time perspective (past and future)
Subordinate position	Equal or superordinate position
Lack of awareness of self	Awareness and control over self

In examining the widespread worker apathy and lack of effort in industry, Argyris questions whether these problems are simply the result of individual laziness. He suggests that this is *not* the case. Argyris contends that, in many cases, when people join the work force, they are kept from maturing by the management practices utilized in their organizations. In these organizations, they are given minimal control over their environment and are encouraged to be passive, dependent, and subordinate; therefore, they behave immaturely. The worker in many organizations is expected to act in immature ways rather than as a mature adult. This does not occur only in industrial settings. In fact, one can even see it happening in many school systems, where most high school students are subject to more rules and restrictions and generally treated less maturely than their younger counterparts in elementary school.

According to Argyris, keeping people immature is built into the very nature of the formal organization. He argues that because organizations are usually created to achieve goals or objectives that can best be met collectively, the formal organization is often the architect's conception of how these objectives may be achieved. In this sense, the individual is fitted to the job. The design comes first. This design is based upon four concepts of scientific management: task specialization, chain of command, unity of direction, and span of control. Management tries to increase and enhance organizational and administrative efficiency and productivity by making workers "interchangeable parts."

Basic to these concepts is that power and authority should rest in the hands of a few at the top of the organization, and thus those at the lower end of the chain of command are strictly controlled by management or the system itself. Task specialization often results in the oversimplification of the job so that it becomes repetitive, routine, and unchallenging. This implies directive, task-oriented leadership where decisions about the work are made by the manager, with the workers only carrying out those decisions. This type of leadership evokes managerial controls such as budgets, some incentive systems, time-and-motion studies, and standard operating procedures which can restrict the initiative and creativity of workers.

Theory into Practice

Argyris feels that these concepts of formal organization lead to assumptions about human nature that are incompatible with the proper development of maturity in human personality. He sees a definite incongruity between the needs of a mature personality and the formal organizations as they now exist. Since he implies that the classical

theory of management (based on Theory X assumptions) usually prevails, management creates childlike roles for workers that frustrate
natural development.

An example of how work is often designed at this extremely low
level was dramatically illustrated by the successful use of developmentally disabled workers in such jobs. Argyris cites two instances,
one in a knitting mill and the other in a radio manufacturing corporation, in which developmentally disabled people were successfully employed on unskilled jobs. In both cases, the managers praised these
workers for their excellent performance. In fact, a manager in the
radio corporation reported that these workers:

> . . . proved to be exceptionally well-behaved, particularly obedient, and
> strictly honest and trustworthy. They carried out work required of them
> to such a degree of efficiency that *we were surprised they were classed as
> subnormals for their age.* Their attendance was good, and their behavior
> was, if anything, certainly better than that of any other employee of the
> same age.[14]

Disturbed by what he finds in many organizations, Argyris, as
did McGregor, challenges management to provide a work climate in
which everyone has a chance to grow and mature as individuals, as
members of a group by satisfying their own needs, while working for
the success of the organization. Implicit here is the belief that people
can be basically self-directed and creative at work if properly motivated, and, therefore, management based on the assumptions of Theory Y will be more profitable for the individual and the organization.

More and more companies are starting to listen to the challenge
that Argyris is directing at management. For example, the president
of a large company asked Argyris to show him how to better motivate
his workers. Together, they went into one of his production plants
where a product similar to a radio was being assembled. There were
twelve women involved in assembling the product, each doing a small
segment of the job, as designed by an industrial engineer. The group
also had a foreman, an inspector, and a packer.

Argyris proposed a one-year experiment during which each of
the women would assemble the total product in a manner of her own
choice. At the same time, each woman would inspect, sign her name to
the product, pack it, and handle any correspondence involving complaints about it. The women were assured that they would receive no
cut in pay if production dropped, but would receive more pay if
production increased.

Once the experiment began, production dropped 70 percent during the first month. By the end of six weeks it was even worse. The

women were upset—morale was down. This continued until the eighth week, when production started to rise. By the end of the fifteenth week production was higher than it had ever been before. And this was without an inspector, a packer, or an industrial engineer. More important than increased productivity, costs due to errors and waste decreased 94 percent; letters of complaint dropped 96 percent.

Experiments such as this are being duplicated in numerous other situations.[15] It is being found over and over again that broadening individual responsibility is beneficial to both the workers and the company. Giving people the opportunity to grow and develop on the job helps them satisfy more than just physiological and safety needs, which, in turn, motivates them and allows them to use more of their potential in accomplishing organizational goals. Although all workers do *not* want to accept more responsibility or deal with the added problems responsibility inevitably brings, Argyris contends that the number of employees whose motivation can be improved by increasing and upgrading their responsibility is much larger than most managers would suspect.

MOTIVATION-HYGIENE THEORY

Frederick Herzberg

We have noted that needs such as esteem and self-actualization seem to become more important as people develop. One of the most interesting series of studies that concentrates heavily on these areas was directed by Frederick Herzberg.[16] Out of these studies has developed a theory of work motivation that has broad implications for management and its efforts toward effective utilization of human resources.

Herzberg, in developing his motivation-hygiene theory, seemed to sense that scholars such as McGregor and Argyris were touching on something important. Knowledge about human nature, motives, and needs could be invaluable to organizations and individuals:

> To industry, the payoff for a study of job attitudes would be increased productivity, decreased absenteeism, and smoother working relations. To the individual, an understanding of the forces that lead to improved morale would bring greater happiness and greater self-realization.[17]

Herzberg set out to collect data on job attitudes from which assumptions about human behavior could be made. The motivation-hygiene theory resulted from the analysis of an initial study by Herzberg and his colleagues at the Psychological Service of Pittsburgh. This study involved extensive interviews with some two hundred engineers and accountants from eleven industries in the Pittsburgh area. In the interviews, they were asked about what kinds of things on their job made them unhappy or dissatisfied and what things made them happy or satisfied.

In analyzing the data from these interviews, Herzberg concluded that people have two different categories of needs that are essentially independent of each other and affect behavior in different ways. He found that when people felt dissatisfied with their jobs, they were concerned about the environment in which they were working. On the other hand, when people felt good about their jobs, this had to do with the work itself. Herzberg called the first category of needs *hygiene* or *maintenance* factors: hygiene because they describe people's environment and serve the primary function of preventing job dissatisfaction; maintenance because they are never completely satisfied—they have to continue to be maintained. He called the second category of needs *motivators* since they seemed to be effective in motivating people to superior performance. Table 3-4 presents a summary of motivation and hygiene factors.

Hygiene Factors

Company policies and administration, supervision, working conditions, interpersonal relations, money, status, and security may be thought of as maintenance factors. These are not an intrinsic part of a job, but they are related to the conditions under which a job is performed. Herzberg related his original use of the word *hygiene* to its medical meaning (preventive and environmental). He found that hygiene factors produced no growth in worker output capacity; they only prevented losses in worker performance due to work restrictions. This is why, more recently, Herzberg has been calling these maintenance factors.

TABLE 3-4   Motivation and Hygiene Factors

MOTIVATORS	HYGIENE FACTORS
The Job Itself	*Environment*
Achievement	Policies and administration
Recognition for accomplishment	Supervision
Challenging work	Working conditions
Increased responsibility	Interpersonal relations
Growth and development	Money, status, security

Motivators

Factors that involve feelings of achievement, professional growth, and recognition that one can experience in a job that offers challenge and scope are referred to by Herzberg as motivators. Herzberg used this term because these factors seem capable of having a positive effect on job satisfaction, often resulting in an increase in one's total output capacity.

In recent years motivation-hygiene research has been extended well beyond scientists and accountants to include every area of an organization, from top management to hourly employees. For example, in an extensive study at Texas Instruments, Scott Meyers concluded that Herzberg's motivation-hygiene theory "is easily translatable to supervisory action at all levels of responsibility. It is a framework on which supervisors can evaluate and put into perspective the constant barrage of 'helpful hints' to which they are subjected, and hence serves to increase their feelings of competence, self-confidence, and autonomy."[18]

Perhaps an example will further differentiate between hygiene factors and motivators and help explain the reason for classifying needs as Herzberg has done.

Let us assume that an employee is highly motivated and is working at 90 percent capacity. The person has a good working relationship with the supervisor, is well satisfied with pay and working conditions, and is part of a congenial work group. Suppose the supervisor is suddenly transferred and replaced by a person who is difficult to work with, or suppose the employee finds out that someone whose work seems inferior is receiving more pay. How will these factors affect this individual's behavior? Since we know performance or productivity depends on both ability and motivation, these unsatisfied hygiene needs (supervision and money) may lead to restriction of output. This decline in productivity may be intentional or the employee may not be consciously aware of holding back. In either case, productivity will be lowered, as illustrated in Figure 3-2.

In our illustration, even if the worker's salary is adjusted well above expectations and the former supervisor returns, productivity will probably increase only to its original level.

Conversely, let us take the same employee and assume that dissatisfaction has not occurred; work is at 90 percent capacity. Suppose the person is given an opportunity to develop and satisfy motivational needs in an environment where there is freedom to exercise some initiative and creativity, to make decisions, to handle problems, and to take responsibility. What effect will this situation have on this individual? If the employee is able to fulfill the supervisor's expecta-

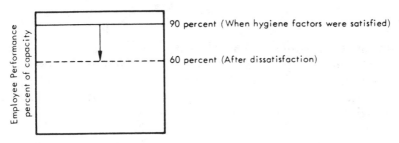

FIGURE 3-2 Effect of dissatisfying hygiene factors

tions in performing these new responsibilities, that person may still work at 90 percent capacity, but may have developed and grown in ability and may be capable now of more productivity, as illustrated in Figure 3-3. Capacity has increased.

Hygiene factors, when satisfied, tend to eliminate dissatisfaction and work restriction, but they do little to motivate an individual to superior performance or increased capacity. Enhancement of the motivators, however, will permit an individual to grow and develop, often increasing ability. Thus, hygiene factors affect an individual's willingness and motivators affect an individual's ability.

The Relationship of Herzberg to Maslow

In terms of Hersey and Blanchard's motivating situation framework discussed in chapter 2, Maslow is helpful in identifying needs or motives and Herzberg provides us with insights into the goals and incentives that tend to satisfy these needs, as illustrated in Figure 3-4.

Thus, in a motivating situation, if you know what are the high-

FIGURE 3-3 Effect of satisfying motivators

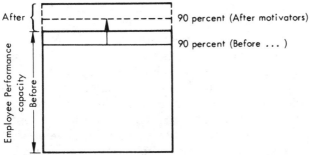

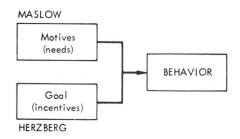

FIGURE 3-4
The relationship of Maslow and
Herzberg to motivation situation

strength needs (Maslow) of the individuals you want to influence, then you should be able to determine what goals (Herzberg) you could provide in the environment to motivate those individuals. At the same time, if you know what goals these people want to satisfy, you can predict what their high-strength needs are. That is possible because it has been found that money and benefits tend to satisfy needs at the physiological and security levels; interpersonal relations and supervision are examples of hygiene factors that tend to satisfy social needs; increased responsibility, challenging work, and growth and development are motivators that tend to satisfy needs at the esteem and self-actualization levels. Figure 3-5 shows the relationship we feel exists between the Maslow and Herzberg frameworks.

We feel that the physiological, safety, social, and part of the esteem needs are all hygiene factors. The esteem needs are divided because there are some distinct differences between status per se and recognition. Status tends to be a function of the position one occupies. One may have gained this position through family ties and thus this position may not be a reflection of personal achievement or earned recognition. Recognition is gained through competence and achieve-

FIGURE 3-5   The relationship between Herzberg's motivation-hygiene theory
and Maslow's hierachy of needs

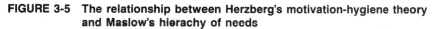
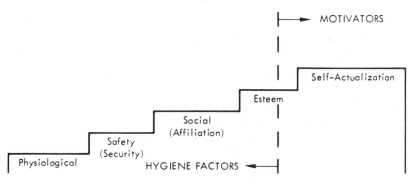

ment. It is earned and granted by others. Consequently, status is classified with physiological, safety, and social needs as a hygiene factor, while recognition is classified with esteem as a motivator.

It appears to us that McClelland's[19] concept of achievement motivation is also related to Herzberg's motivation-hygiene theory. People with high achievement motivation tend to be interested in the motivators (the job itself). Achievement-motivated people want task-relevant feedback. They want to know how well they are doing on their job. On the other hand, people with low achievement motivation are more concerned about the environment. They want to know how people feel about them rather than how well they are doing.

JOB ENRICHMENT

Prior to Herzberg's work, many other behavioral scientists were concerned with worker motivation. For several years there was an emphasis on what was termed "job enlargement" or "job rotation." This was purported to be an answer to the overspecialization that had characterized many industrial organizations. The assumption was that workers could gain more satisfaction at work if their jobs were enlarged; that is, if the number or variety of their tasks was increased.

Herzberg makes some astute observations about this trend. He claims that doing a snippet of this and a snippet of that does not necessarily result in motivation. Washing dishes, then silverware, and then pots and pans does no more to satisfy and provide an opportunity to grow than washing only dishes. What we really need to do with work, Herzberg suggests, is to *enrich* the job. By job enrichment is meant the deliberate upgrading of responsibility, scope, and challenge in work.

Example of Job Enrichment

An example of job enrichment may be illustrated by the experience an industrial relations superintendent had with a group of janitors. After a transfer to a new plant, the superintendent learned that the position responsibilities included supervising fifteen janitors in a plant maintenance crew. There was no foreman over this crew. Reviewing the files one day, the superintendent noticed that there was a history of complaints about housekeeping around the plant. After talking to others and observing, it took the superintendent little time to confirm these reports. The janitors seemed to be lazy, unreliable, and generally unmotivated. They were walking examples of Theory X assumptions about human nature.

Determined to do something about the behavior of the janitors, the superintendent called a group meeting, discussed some of the problems, and asked the janitors, since they were the experts, for ideas. "Does anyone have a suggestion?" There was dead silence. The superintendent sat down and said nothing. This lasted for almost twenty minutes. Finally, one janitor spoke up, related a problem, and made a suggestion. Soon others joined in and suddenly the janitors were involved in a lively discussion while the superintendent listened and jotted down their ideas. At the conclusion of the meeting, the suggestions were summarized with tacit acceptance by all, including the superintendent.

After the meeting, the superintendent referred any housekeeping problems to the janitors, individually or as a group. For example, when any cleaning equipment or material salespersons came to the plant, the superintendent did not talk to them—the janitors did. In fact, regular meetings continued to be held in which problems and ideas were discussed.

All of this had a tremendous influence on the behavior of the crew. They developed a cohesive productive team that took pride in its work. Even their appearance changed. Once a grubby lot, now they appeared at work in clean, pressed work clothes. All over the plant, people were amazed at how clean and well kept everything had become. The superintendent was continually stopped by supervisors in the plant and asked, "What have you done to those lazy, good-for-nothing janitors, given them pep pills?" Even the superintendent could not believe what had happened. It was not uncommon to see one or two janitors running floor tests to see which wax or cleaner did the best job. Since they had to make all the decisions, including committing funds for their supplies, they wanted to know which were the best. Such activities, while taking time, did not detract from their work. In fact, the crew worked harder and more efficiently than ever before in their lives. This example illustrates several positive aspects of job enrichment. The tasks were redesigned so the janitors were responsible for the housekeeping of the plant— what is called horizontal job expansion. In addition, the janitors were given responsibility for making decisions regarding equipment, supplies, and methods—what is called vertical job expansion—previously reserved to higher management. Both horizontal and vertical job expansion are required to gain the greatest improvement in motivation and satisfaction.[20]

This example also illustrates that even at low levels in an organization, people can respond in responsible and productive ways to a work environment in which they are given an opportunity to grow and mature. People begin to satisfy their esteem and self-actualization needs by participating in the planning, organizing, motivating, and controlling of their own tasks.

A Problem of Placement

It should be pointed out that the problem of motivation is not always a question of enriching jobs. As Chris Argyris dramatically showed in the successful use of developmentally disabled workers on the assembly line, some organizations have a tendency to hire people with ability far in excess of the demands of the work.

An example of overhiring happened in the start-up operation of a large plant. As in the case of most new plants, one of the first work groups to be assembled was security. The supervisor of plant security set as hiring criteria a high school education and three years of police or plant protection experience as minimal requirements for applicants. Being the first large industrial plant in a relatively agricultural area, the company was able to hire people not at the minimum level, but well over these standards.

When these people began their jobs—which consisted simply of checking badges on the way in and lunch pails on the way out—boredom, apathy, and lack of motivation soon characterized their performance. This resulted in a high rate of turnover. When the problem was reevaluated, the reverse of the hiring procedures was found to be appropriate. Those applicants with a high school education were considered overqualified. Those with police or security experience were also considered overqualified. Rather than experienced workers, applicants with fourth- and fifth-grade educations, and thus lower job expectations, were hired for these positions. Their performance was found to be much superior, and the turnover, absenteeism, and tardiness rates were cut to a minimum. Why? For these workers, a new uniform, a badge, and some power were important, but they also found the job as one incorporating opportunities for more responsibility and challenging work.[21]

MOTIVATION AND SATISFACTION

Edward E. Lawler, III, a researcher, educator, and consultant, has examined the relationship between motivation and satisfaction because some managers may think these may be similar if not synonymous terms. Lawler disagrees.

They are, in fact, very different. Motivation is influenced by forward-looking perceptions concerning the relationship between performance and rewards, while satisfaction refers to people's feelings about the rewards they have received. Thus satisfaction is a consequence of past events while motivation is a consequence of their expectations about the future.[22]

Managers should be aware of this important difference. Attempts to improve future performance by focusing on past rewards and benefits demonstrates a lack of understanding of the character of satisfaction. Satisfaction is past-oriented; motivation is future-oriented. Managers wanting to improve future performance should use the concepts and techniques discussed in these pages to enhance motivation.

TRANSACTIONAL ANALYSIS

Eric Berne

If it is true that we cannot always anticipate the reaction of people to a management intervention, how can we better predict the kind of responses our interventions may evoke from people? *Transactional analysis* (TA) may help us in this area.

TA is a method of analyzing and understanding behavior that was developed by Eric Berne[23] and in more recent years has been popularized in the writings of Thomas Harris,[24] Muriel James and Dorothy Jongeward,[25] and Abe Wagner.[26] In particular, Jongeward[27] and Wagner[28] have shown how the concepts of TA can be applied to organizations and related to the work of other theorists, such as McGregor and Likert. Their work has been very helpful to us in writing this section on transactional analysis.

TA, as we view it, is an outgrowth of earlier Freudian psychology. Sigmund Freud[29] was the first to suggest that there are three sources within the human personality that stimulate, monitor, and control behavior. The Freudian *id, ego,* and *superego* are important concepts, but their definitions are difficult for practitioners to understand or apply without extensive training in psychotherapy. Thus, one of the major contributions of TA theorists is that they have, in a sense, borrowed from Freud but have put some of his concepts into a language that everyone can understand and, without being trained psychiatrists, can use for diagnostic purposes in understanding why people behave as they do.

Ego States

According to TA, a *transaction* is a stimulus plus a response. For example, if you say to one of your staff, "You really did a fine job on that project, Don." that's a stimulus; if he says, "Thanks," that's a response. Thus, transactions take place between people. They can also take place between the "people" in our heads. If we have a sudden impulse to say something to someone, we may mentally hear a voice telling us not to say it and then a second voice agreeing. These people in our heads are called *ego states.*

The personality of a person is the collection of behavior patterns developed over time that other people begin to recognize as that person. These behavior patterns are evoked in differing degrees from three ego states—Parent, Adult, and Child. These terms are capitalized so as not to be confused with their lower-cased counterparts. Thus, a parent (mother or father) has Parent, Adult, and Child ego states; and a child (son or daughter) also has Parent, Adult, and Child ego states. These ego states have nothing to do with chronological age, only psychological age.

As Berne states, "Although we cannot directly observe these ego states, we can observe behavior and from this infer which of the three ego states is operating at that moment.[30] The three ego states are usually diagrammed as shown in Figure 3-6.

The *Parent* ego state is a result of the "messages" (conditioning) people receive from their parents, older sisters and brothers, school teachers, Sunday school teachers, and other authority figures during their early childhood. These messages can be thought of as recorded on "little cassette tapes" in people's heads. They're in place, stored up, and ready to go. All you have to do is push the right button and you get the message—almost like dialing a number on the telephone. Push

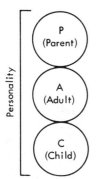

FIGURE 3-6
The Parent, Adult, and Child (P-A-C) subsystems

another button and you get a different message. After the message is given, the tape is rewound and ready to go again. For instance, if a father's son was eating his dinner and was playing with his food, a common Parent tape such as the following might be played: "Stop playing with your food, Garth, and clean up your plate. People are starving all over the world, so you're going to eat everything." Now where did the father learn to say that? He probably learned it from his mother and father, who learned it from their parents. And now he's playing it on his kids. This is a Parent tape. Many of us were taught when we were young that it's good to clean our plate and bad to leave food on our plate. In fact, many of us probably still feel guilty today if we leave food on our plate.

Thus, a person is operating from Parent ego state when "old tapes" from childhood are mentally played back. These recordings say such things as "it's right!" "it's wrong!" "it's bad!" "it's good!" "you should!" "you shouldn't!" Thus, our Parent ego state is the *evaluative* part of us that evokes value-laden behavior. But remember, this value-laden behavior is not necessarily "real value"—it's "learned value." In our example with Garth not cleaning his plate, it might have been more appropriate had his father said, "Don't feel you have to eat everything on your plate if you are really not hungry"—particularly if Garth were a little overweight. Thus, cleaning up one's plate is a "learned value" because, in a real sense, whether or not Garth eats all the food on his plate won't impact starving children around the world; it will only impact the size of the garbage.

There are two kinds of Parent ego states: *Nurturing Parent* and *Critical Parent.* The Nurturing Parent is that part of a person that is understanding and caring about other people. While behavior coming from the Nurturing Parent may set limits on and provide direction for people's behavior, it will not put these people down and make them feel not okay as individuals. The Critical Parent makes people feel that they, not just their behavior, are not okay. Thus, Critical Parent behavior attacks people's personalities as well as their behavior. When people are in their Critical Parent ego state, they are very evaluative and judgmental. They are always ready to respond with a "should" or "ought" to almost anything people tell them. People with a heavy Critical Parent ego state "should" on other people as well as "should" on themselves.

The *Adult* ego state evokes behavior that could be described simply as logical, reasonable, rational, and unemotional. Behavior from the Adult ego state is characterized by problem-solving analysis and rational decision making. People operating from the Adult ego state are taking the emotional content of their Child ego state and the value-laden content of their Parent ego state and checking them out in the reality of the external world. These people are examining alternatives, probabilities, and values prior to engaging in behavior.

As suggested, the *Child* ego state is associated with behaviors that appear when a person is responding emotionally. A person's Child contains the "natural" impulses and attitudes learned from child experiences. There are several forms of the Child ego state that various authors discuss.[31] In our work we use two kinds of Child ego states: *Happy Child* and *Destructive Child.*

People behaving from their Happy Child are doing things because they want to, but their behavior is not disruptive to others or destructive to the environment. People in their Destructive Child are also doing things because they feel like it, but their behavior is either disruptive to others or destructive to themselves or their environment. In understanding the difference between these two types of the Child state, it helps to remember that behavior by itself is not happy or destructive. Whether a person's behavior is coming from the Happy Child or the Destructive Child depends on the transaction or feedback from others. For example, if George is a draftsman and is singing while he works, he may be in his Happy Child. But if one of his co-workers, Helen, tells him she's having trouble working because of his singing and he keeps on singing, he has moved from Happy Child to Destructive Child.

One form of the Destructive Child ego state is the *Rebellious Child.* When people are in this ego state, they aren't going to listen to anyone who tells them what to do. They either rebel openly by being very negative or rebel subtly by forgetting, being confused, or putting off doing something that someone wants them to do. Persons behaving from Rebellious Child will not do anything an authority figure asks them to do even if it makes sense.

Another destructive Child ego state is *Compliant Child.* When people are in this ego state, they do what others want. Complying with the wishes of others is okay if the person really wants to or if it makes sense to do it. When that is the case, Compliant Child would be classified as a form of Happy Child because the behavior would not be considered disruptive to others or destructive to themselves or their environment. However, Compliant Child can hurt the development of people who comply unquestionably all the time, even when it makes no sense to them. These people tend to remain dependent instead of becoming independent. When this occurs, Compliant Child becomes a form of Destructive Child.

It is healthy for people to have a functioning Child ego state that is spontaneous, emotional, and sometimes dependent. However, as managers, we want to discourage too much development of our people's Compliant or Rebellious forms of Destructive Child. In later chapters we will talk about when and how people develop a Rebellious or Compliant Child ego state and how to discourage behaviors evoked from these two forms of Child ego state.

Behavior coming from the Adult ego state is very different from behavior evoked from the Child ego state. Child ego state behavior is behavior that's often almost a stimulus-response relationship. Something happens and the person responds almost immediately. What happens is not processed intellectually. It almost goes in one ear, picks up speed, and goes out the other ear. With Adult ego state behavior, when something happens, there is not an immediate response. A response follows only conscious evaluation and thought.

A Healthy Personality

All people behave from these three ego states at different times. A healthy person has a personality that maintains a balance among all three; particularly, according to Abe Wagner,[32] Nurturing *Parent, Adult,* and Happy *Child.* This means that these people are able, at times, to let the Adult ego state take over and think very rationally and engage in problem solving. At other times, these people are able to free the Child ego state and let their hair down, have fun, and be spontaneous and emotional. At still other times, healthy people are able to defer to the Parent ego state and learn from experience; they do not have to reinvent the wheel every time. They develop values that aid in the speed and effectiveness of decision making.

While a balance among all three ego states seems to be most healthy, some people seem dominated at times by one or two ego states. This is especially a problem when the Adult ego state is not in the "executive position" and a person's personality is being dominated by the Critical Parent or the Destructive Child. When this occurs in people, it poses problems for their managers in the world of work.

More specifically, Child-dominated people who are mainly coming from Destructive Child do not engage in much rational problem solving. They learned in their early years that they could get things by screaming, hollering, and being emotional. It's very difficult to reason with them in many situations. Instead of solving their own problems, these people want their managers or some other person to tell them what to do, where to do it, and how to do it—or what's right, what's wrong, what's good, and what's bad.

Parent-dominated people, who are mainly coming from Critical Parent, also do not engage in much rational problem solving because they already know what's right and what's wrong. They seem to have an answer for everything. These people we would characterize with the comment, "Look! Don't confuse me with the facts. I've already made up my mind." It really doesn't matter how much real information anyone brings to these people—they've already decided "it's good," "it's bad," "you should," or "you shouldn't."

Even Adult-dominated people can be troublesome, because they can be very boring people with whom to work. They are often "work-aholics." They don't seem to act like other people. They are never able to let down their hair and have fun. Thus, a balance between the three ego states makes for a healthy person.

Life Position

In the process of growing up, people make basic assumptions about their own self-worth, as well as about the worth of significant people in their environment, that may or may not be generalized to other people later in life. Harris[33] calls the combination of an assumption about oneself and another person a *life position.* Life positions tend to be more permanent than ego states. They are learned throughout life by way of reinforcements for, and responses to, expressed needs. These assumptions are described in terms of "okayness." Thus, individuals assume that they are either OK or not OK, or that as people they do not possess value or worth. Further, other individuals are assumed to be either OK or not OK.

Four possible relationships result from these life positions: (1) neither person has value ("I'm not OK, you're not OK"); (2) you have value, but I do not have value ("I'm not OK, you're OK"); (3) I have value, but you do not ("I'm OK, you're not OK"); and (4) we both have value ("I'm OK, you're OK").

"I'm not OK, you're not OK" people tend to feel bad about themselves and see the whole world as miserable. People with this life position usually give up. They don't trust other people and have no confidence in themselves.

People with an *"I'm not OK, you're OK"* life position often come from their Compliant Child ego state. They feel that others are more capable and generally have fewer problems than they themselves do. They tend to think that they always get the short end of the stick. This is the most common life position for people who have a high deference for authority. They see their world as "I don't have any control or much power, but those people (folks with authority or position power) seem to have all the power and rewards and punishments."

People who feel *"I'm OK, you're not OK"* often come from their Critical Parent ego state. They tend to be down on other people for at least two reasons. First, they often regard other people as sources of criticism. They feel that if they're not exactly perfect or right, people will be excessively critical of them. Second, they want to break away or rebel from some authority figure and become more independent, but they're either not sure how to go about this or they have had unpleasant experiences in attempting it in the past.

This is a life position in which the person has had a few "zaps" along the road and feels, "I've got a lot of self-confidence and autonomy but I sure don't want to be open, honest, and sharing with others in my environment or I'll get punished." With this life position, listening often tends to stop even when someone is still trying to communicate with this person. Harris found in his work that people with an *"I'm OK, you're not OK"* life position, while acting self-confident and under control, really were hiding "not OK" feelings about themselves. The way they play out their "not OK" feelings often is expressed in the need for power and control.

"I'm OK, you're OK" is suggested as the healthy life position. People with these feelings express confidence in themselves as well as trust and confidence in other people in their environment. Their behavior tends to come from their Nurturing Parent, Adult, and Happy Child ego states, while seldom being evoked from their Destructive Child or Critical Parent.

Transactions Between People

TA may be used to explain why people behave in specific patterns—patterns that frequently seem to be repeated throughout their lives (life scripts). In this form of analysis, the basic observational unit is called a *transaction*. Transactions are exchanges between people that consist of no less than one stimulus and one response. This analysis enables people to identify patterns of transactions between themselves and others. Ultimately, this can help us determine which ego state is most heavily influencing our behavior and the behavior of other people with whom we interact.

Two types of transactions may be useful for managers to know: *open* (complementary) and *blocked* (crossed).[34] There are many combinations of open transactions; however, the basic principle to remember is that the ego state that is addressed is the one that responds. Therefore, the response to the stimulus is the expected or predictable one. When this occurs, communication can continue. (This in no way suggests effective communication or indicates any openness between individuals, for, in fact, the content of the communication may be a distortion of true data.) Open transactions are Adult to Adult, Child to Child, Parent to Child, and Parent to Parent. Not all open transactions are beneficial. What we want to strive for in our relationships are OK open transactions–Happy Child to Happy Child. Nurturing Parent to Happy Child, Adult to Adult, and Nurturing Parent to Nurturing Parent. Not OK open transactions involve any of the less healthy ego states–for example, Critical Parent, Rebellious Child, or Compliant Child (when complying does not make sense to the person's Adult ego state.) Examples of both OK and not OK open transactions are shown in Figure 3-7.

As illustrated in Transaction 1, if a manager says to one of her staff members from her Nurturing Parent, "I want you to be more careful in writing your reports because I found a number of typographical and grammatical errors in this report," and her staff member responds from this Compliant Child, "OK, Mrs. Jones, I didn't notice all those mistakes," then we have a completed communication in which information has been easily shared and everyone still feels OK about themselves. If, however, as illustrated in Transaction 2, this manager was coming from her Critical Parent and said something like, "How can you be so stupid? The last report you gave me had all kinds of typographical and grammatical errors. I don't see how you can possibly do your job if you don't know how to write a decent report," and her staff member responded from Compliant Child back to his manager's Critical Parent by meekly saying, "I'm sorry, I'll try not to make those mistakes next time," we have a completed communication in which information is shared with a minimum effort. But the staff member feels put down by his boss and does not feel OK.

A blocked transaction is one that results in the closing, at least temporarily, of communications. Unlike open transactions, the response is either inappropriate or unexpected, as well as being out of context with what the sender of the stimulus had originally intended. This occurs when a person responds with an ego state different from the one the other person was addressing. In other words, it occurs when the stimulus from one ego state to another ego state is responded to as if the source were some other ego state, such that the

FIGURE 3-7 Two types of open transactions

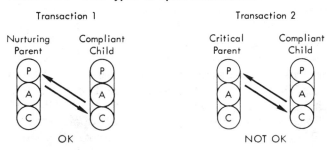

Transaction 1

Nurturing Parent   Compliant Child

OK

Transaction 2

Critical Parent   Compliant Child

NOT OK

sender feels misunderstood, confused, or even threatened. When this occurs, sharing and listening stop, at least temporarily. For example, if Alan asks a co-worker a question from his Adult ego state "What time is it, John?" he would expect John to respond from his Adult ego state and share information with him; that is, tell him what time it is. If, however, John responds from his Critical Parent and answers, "Don't ask so many questions," then a blocked transaction has taken place, as illustrated in Figure 3-8.

The example in Figure 3-8 illustrates that in a blocked transaction the lines of communication get crossed and stop effective communication (although talking may continue).

Blocked transactions can either be helpful or destructive to the development of people. The preceding example was a destructive transaction because the Critical Parent response to Alan's Adult question leaves Alan with not OK feelings. Destructive blocked transactions occur between people when either responds to the other from the Critical Parent or the Rebellious or Compliant Destructive Child.

When people argue or fight, a destructive blocked transaction is usually involved. For example, if a manager makes a statement in a Critical Parent manner ("I don't think you should hire that person for your staff assistant. There will be nothing but trouble.") directed toward the staff member's Compliant (happy) Child and the staff member responds from the Rebellious (destructive) Child ("You have no right to tell me who I can hire for my staff assistant.") to the boss's Child, the lines of communication get blocked and the manager and the subordinate stop listening (although talking or yelling may continue). Now the interaction becomes a win-lose power struggle. Manager and staff member seem to be talking past each other, matching "oughts and shoulds" with the other's "oughts and shoulds." If, in this example, the boss wins—and bosses usually do—the win has a cost. It forces the staff member to become Destructive (compliant) Child and teaches the staff member to either go "underground" with feelings in the future, plot how to get out from under the command of

FIGURE 3-8   A blocked transaction

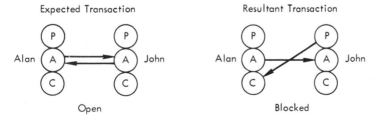

the boss, or become compliant and do what others say because "I'm not OK."

In some situations, we may find blocked transactions useful in helping people to switch out of the less healthy Rebellious Child, Compliant Child, and Critical Parent ego states into their Adult, Nurturing Parent, or Happy Child. This will become clear as we integrate concepts from TA with other theories in later chapters.

By analyzing open and blocked transactions, it is possible to determine the various strengths of the three ego states. This in turn provides an indication of which life position the individual has selected. We can thus gather data on individuals in a way that will help to predict future patterns of behavior.

Ulterior transactions, like blocked transactions, are generally not desired. "An ulterior transaction happens when someone appears to be sending one kind of message but is secretly sending another. Thus, the real message is disguised.[35] An example of an ulterior transaction is when Alice says to her boss, "I'd be happy to add up all those figures, Mr. Johnson. It looks like it would be a real challenge."

In this example of an ulterior transaction (see Figure 3-9), Alice is not talking straight about her needs but is sending her message in a disguised way. She appears to be giving Mr. Johnson factual information in an Adult to Adult transaction. Actually, she is probably annoyed about all of the routine, boring tasks that she's continually asked to do. Perhaps she would like to ask Mr. Johnson directly if there's a way that she could expand her responsibilities and take on more exciting tasks. "It should be challenging to add up all those figures" may be a plea for more challenging work from Alice's Child to Mr. Johnson's Parent.

Strokes

It is important to recognize one more thing about transactions. "Strokes" are being exchanged *whenever* two people are transacting. According to Jongeward and Seyer,[36] in TA language:

> The term "stroke" refers to giving some kind of recognition to a person. This may or may *not* involve physical touching. As we grow from

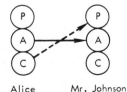

FIGURE 3-9
Ulterior transaction

Alice   Mr. Johnson

infancy into child and adulthood, we do not entirely lose our need for stroking. Part of our original need for physical stroking seems to be satisfied with symbolic stroking. We no longer need constant cuddling, but we need attention. When we receive a stroke, we choose to feel either good or bad. If we chose to feel good, we think of the stroke as a "warm fuzzy" or "positive" stroke. On the flip side, if we choose to feel bad, we can think of it as a "cold prickly" or "negative" stroke.

If it is true that people have a basic need for strokes, they will work hard to get them. For example, ignored people will engage in all sorts of creative activities to get strokes. Often, such people quickly learn at work that they can get strokes from their boss by

- fighting with co-workers.
- doing sloppy work.
- injuring themselves.

A person who carries out one of these actions is likely to get a cold prickly (negative) stroke. But given a choice between no strokes or negative strokes, most people will opt for negative strokes. To such a person, any kind of stroke is better than no stroke at all; a cold prickly is better than nothing. The same is true for children who live in a stroke-deprived home.

Psychological Game Analysis

When people don't get enough strokes at work, they will try a variety of things, some harmful, to make up their "stroke deficit." To do that, they may play *psychological games.*[37] A psychological game is a set of transactions with the following characteristics:

- Transactions tend to be repeated.
- They make sense on a superficial or social level.
- One or more of the transactions is ulterior.
- A set of transactions ends with a predictable payoff—a negative feeling. Payoffs usually reinforce the decision made in childhood about oneself or about others. They reflect feelings of not okayness, as we shall see.

Let's look at an example of a psychological game called *Yes, But:*

Doug: "I need your help again, Ken. I just don't seem to be very excited about my job. I really can't remember a job that really 'turned me on.' "

Ken: "Why don't you go to a career-planning center and take some of those tests to find out what you might really be interested in?"

Doug: "Yes, I've thought of doing that, but they cost quite a bit of money and our budget is a little tight right now."

Ken: "Why don't you talk to your boss and see if there's any opportunity to enlarge or expand your job?"

Doug: "Yes, that's possible, but he's awfully busy and is hard to get to see."

Ken: "I know! Why don't you try to get a teaching job? You could go over and see . . . ?"

Doug: "Yes, but teaching jobs are really hard to find these days."

Ken: (Silent)

Let's examine how each of the characteristics of a psychological game is present in this example:[38]

- *Repeated transactions:* Doug and Ken have played this game before. Note Doug's opening line, "I need your help *again,* Ken."
- *Transactions make sense:* Outwardly, it seems Doug is honestly asking Ken for help. Ken's suggestions are reasonable and Doug's replies also seem to make sense.
- *Ulterior transactions:* Notice that Doug consistently rejects all of Ken's advice. At one level, Doug seems to be giving reasons why Ken's advice won't work. But he is also simultaneously sending an ulterior message that says, "Nobody's going to tell me what to do." Doug may still be rebelling against the advice his parent figures gave him when he was young. He operates from a belief that authority figures are not OK.
- *Predictable payoff:* According to TA theory, the game of *Yes, But* is often played by people whose parents either dominated them or didn't give them reasonable answers. So they tend to take a stand against parental figures. They play *Yes, But* to prove to themselves that nobody can tell them anything they don't already know. The feeling of power they get becomes a payoff for playing the game, which they seek over and over again. They prove once more that "Parents can't tell me anything."[39]

SCRIPT ANALYSIS

As we have pointed out, the life positions (I'm OK, you're OK, etc.) that people act out tend to vary according to the situation. The life position that people take and the games that they learn to play are part of what TA calls a "script":

> In everyday language, a script is the text of a play, motion picture, or radio or TV program. In TA, a person's life is compared to a play and the script is the text of that play. A person's psychological script is a life plan—a drama he or she writes and then feels compelled to live out.

These plans may be positive, negative, or circular—endless repetition headed nowhere.[40]

All people have a script. People develop their scripts based on their experiences as a child. The most important influence on how one's script develops is through interactions with parents or other authority figures. These interactions in turn lead us to make certain decisions, formulate our life positions, play psychological games, and start the drama of our script.

Jongeward and Seyer[41] cite an excellent example of script development and its impact on later life:

As Edwin was growing up, he was frequently put down and compared to his older brother, Sid. He constantly heard things like:

- "Well, Edwin, you only got 60% on this test, but gee, that's pretty good for you, considering your ability."
- "Edwin! You spilled the soda all over my new chair. What's wrong with you? Why are you always doing such dumb things? Don't you have a brain in your head?"
- "Edwin is not as bright as Sid, you know, so don't expect much from him"
- "What a stupid thing to do, Edwin. Sid would never have done a thing like that."

Given this background, what psychological position do you think Edwin usually took as a child? Edwin most likely took an I'm not OK position on many occasions as a child. He often felt not OK about himself because of all the negative things he heard from his parents. He probably felt his parents (and others) were not OK because of the cruel way they spoke to him.

Assuming that Edwin believed what he heard about himself, imagine him as a high school student. Do you think he liked school? Do you think he was a good student? Given his predominant psychological position, Edwin would probably dislike school and be a poor student. (Occasionally, however, a person like Edwin takes an "I'll show you" stance and knocks himself out trying to be perfect at everything, yet rarely satisfied with how he's doing.)

Now imagine Edwin on the job later in life. He is talking to one of his co-workers about a report he is working on. Which one of these things would he be most likely to say? (a) "I feel concerned about the progress I've made on this project" or (b) "I'm just a bungling idiot, I misplaced that report again! I'll never learn, will I?" Undoubtedly, he would have taken (b).

Do you think it is clear that Edwin was born with inferior mental capacity? Edwin might have a good brain and the potential to become a brilliant executive. But he has come to believe that he *is* stupid. Consequently, Edwin may have unconsciously (and compulsively) arranged things to strengthen this script.

We must remember that all of us have scripts. And, like Edwin, without being aware of it, we often arrange our environment so that our script prevails. Sometimes managers have to deal with the scripts that people bring with them to the world of work. In later chapters we will be discussing some concepts that may be useful to managers in helping people write new scripts.

SUMMARY AND CONCLUSION

We have tried through the material presented to examine what is known today about understanding and motivating employees. The attempt has been to review theoretical literature, empirical research, and case examples with the intention of integrating these sources into frameworks that may be useful to managers for analyzing and understanding behavior. In reflecting upon the theories we have discussed, we can easily isolate two polar positions. At one extreme (and most people still think it is the most common extreme) are organizations that are dominated by Theory X assumptions about human nature, bureaucratic-pyramidal values, and Pattern A behavior. As a result, these organizations tend to be managed by Critical Parent managers with I'm OK, you're not OK life positions, who think people are only motivated by physiological and safety needs and satisfied hygiene factors. The subordinates in these organizations tend to be passive, dependent, and childlike, with "I'm not OK, you're not OK" or "I'm not OK, you're OK" feelings.

At the other extreme are the "ideal" organizations with their Theory Y assumptions about human nature, humanistic-democratic values, and pattern B behavior. As a result, these organizations tend to be managed by people with a good balance of Parent-Adult-Child (P.-A.-C.), "I'm OK, you're OK" feelings and a sense that people are also motivated by affiliation, esteem, and self-actualization needs as job-related "motivators." The style(s) of these managers fosters similar feelings among subordinates and evokes Adult problem-solving behavior. Although the differences between these two extremes and the suggested movement are obvious, as Argyris argues, the journey from XA to YB is not an "easy road to haul." To prepare for this journey, analyzing and understanding are necessary, but real skills are also needed in directing, changing, and controlling behavior. Beginning with chapter 4, a framework for applying leader behavior may help get us "on the road."

NOTES

1. For detailed descriptions of this research, see F. J. Roethlisberger and W. J. Dickson, *Management and the Worker* (Cambridge: Harvard University Press, 1939); T. N. Whitehead, *The Industrial Worker*, 2 vols. (Cambridge: Harvard University Press, 1938); Elton Mayo, *The Human Problems of an Industrial Civilization* (New York: Macmillan, 1933); Elton Mayo, *The Human Problems of an Industrial Civilization* (Salem, N.H.: Ayer Company, 1977). See also R. E. Dutton, "On Alix Carev's Radical Criticism of the Hawthorne Studies: Comment," *Academy of Management Journal*, 14 (September 1971), pp. 394–96; Randolph M. Hale, "Managing Human Resources: Challenge for the Future," *Enterprise*, June 1985, pp. 6–9.

2. Douglas McGregor, *The Human Side of Enterprise* (New York: McGraw-Hill, 1960). See also McGregor, *Leadership and Motivation* (Boston: MIT Press, 1966); Craig C. Pinder, *Work Motivation: Theory, Issues, and Applications* (Glenview, Ill.: Scott, Foresman, 1984).

3. Chris Argyris, *Management and Organizational Development: The Path from XA to YB* (New York: McGraw-Hill, 1971); Walter E. Natemeyer, ed., *Classics of Organizational Behavior* (Oak Park, Ill.: Moore Publishers, 1978); David R. Hampton, *Organizational Behavior and the Practice of Management* (Glenview, Ill.: Scott, Foresman, 1986).

4. Argyris, *Management and Organizational Development*, p. 12.

5. George C. Homans, *The Human Group* (New York: Harcourt, Brace & World, 1950).

6. Anthony G. Athos and Robert E. Coffey, *Behavior in Organization: A Multidimensional View* (Englewood Cliffs, N.J.: Prentice Hall, 1968), p. 101.

7. S. E. Asch, "Effects of Group Pressure upon the Modification and Distortion of Judgments," in *Groups, Leadership and Men*, ed. Harold Guetzkow (New York: Russell and Russell, 1963), pp. 177–90. Also in Dorwin Cartwright and Alvin Zander, *Group Dynamics*, 2nd ed. (Evanston, Ill.: Row, Peterson, 1960), pp. 189–200.

8. *Ibid.*

9. Chris Argyris, *Interpersonal Competence and Organizational Effectiveness* (Homewood, Ill.: Irwin, Dorsey Press, 1962).

10. *Ibid.*, p. 43.

11. *Ibid.*

12. *Ibid.*

13. Chris Argyris, *Personality and Organization* (New York: Harper & Row, 1957); *Interpersonal Competence and Organizational Effectiveness* (Homewood, Ill.: Irwin, Dorsey Press, 1962); and *Integrating the Individual and the Organization* (New York: Wiley, 1964).

14. N. Breman, *The Making of a Moron* (New York: Sheed & Ward, 1953).

15. For other examples of successful interventions, see Argyris, *Intervention Theory and Method: A Behavioral Science View* (Reading, Mass.: Addison-Wesley, 1970); Robert W. Nay, *Behavioral Intervention: Contemporary Strategies* (New York: Gardner Press, 1976).

16. Frederick Herzberg, Bernard Mausner, and Barbara Snyderman, *The Motivation to Work* (New York: Wiley, 1959); and Herzberg, *Work and the Nature of Man* (New York: World Publishing, 1966). See also R. M. Steers and L. W. Porter *Motivation and Work Behavior*, 2nd ed. (New York: McGraw-Hill, 1979); A. J. Stewart (ed.), *Motivation and Society* (San Francisco: Jossey-Bass, 1982); Terence R. Mitchell, "Motivation: New Directions for Theory, Research and Practice," *Academy of Management Review*, January 1982, pp. 80–88.

17. Herzberg, Mausner and Snyderman, *The Motivation to Work*, p. ix.

18. Scott M. Meyers, "Who Are Your Motivated Workers?" in David R. Hampton, *Behavioral Concepts in Management* (Belmont, Calif.: Dickenson Publishing, 1968). p. 64. Originally published in *Harvard Business Review*, January–February 1964, pp. 73–88.

19. David C. McClelland, J. W. Atkinson, R. A. Clark, and E. L. Lowell, *The Achievement Motive* (New York: Appleton-Century-Crofts, 1953); and *The Achieving Society* (Princeton, N.J.: D. Van Nostrand, 1961).

20. Edward E. Lawler, III, *High Involvement Management* (San Francisco: Jossey-Bass, 1990), p. 32.

21. A. J. Marrow, D. G. Bowers, and S. E. Seashore, eds., *Strategies of Organizational Change* (New York: Harper & Row, 1967).

22. Lawler, *High Involvement Management*, p. 32.

23. Eric Berne, *Games People Play* (New York: Grove Press, 1964).
24. Thomas Harris, *I'm OK – You're OK: A Practical Guide in Transactional Analysis* (New York: Harper & Row, 1969).
25. Muriel James and Dorothy Jongeward, *Born to Win* (Reading, Mass.: Addison-Wesley, 1971).
26. Abe Wagner, *The Transactional Manager: How to Solve Your People Problems with T.A.* (Englewood Cliffs, N.J.: Prentice Hall, 1981). See also Muriel James and Louis Savary, *A New Self: Self Therapy with Transactional Analysis* (Reading, Mass.: Addison-Wesley, 1977).
27. Dorothy Jongeward, *Everybody Wins: Transactional Analysis Applied to Organizations* (Reading, Mass.: Addison-Wesley, 1973). See also Dorothy Jongeward and Muriel James, *Born to Win* (NAL, 1978); Dorothy Jongeward and Muriel James, *Born to Win: Transactional Analysis with Gestalt Experiments* (Reading, Mass.: Addison-Wesley, 1971); Dorothy Jongeward and Dru Scott, *Women as Winners: Transactional Analysis for Personal Growth* (Reading, Mass.: Addison-Wesley; *Transactional Analysis Bulletin: Selected Articles from Volume 1–9,* (San Francisco: TA Press, 1976).
28. Wagner, *The Transactional Manager.*
29. Sigmund Freud, *The Ego and the Id* (London: Hogarth Press, 1927).
30. Eric Berne, *Principles of Group Treatment* (New York: Oxford University Press, 1964), p. 281.
31. The most popular classification of child ego states is Natural Child, Adaptive Child, and Little Professor.
32. Abe Wagner was very helpful in the writing of this particular section.
33. Harris, *I'm OK – You're OK.*
34. The work of Dorothy Jongeward and Abe Wagner was very helpful in this section. See Dorothy Jongeward and Phillip C. Seyer, *Choosing Success: Transactional Analysis on the Job* (New York: Wiley, 1978), and Wagner, *The Transactional Manager.*
35. Jongeward and Seyer, *Choosing Success,* p. 21.
36. *Ibid.,* p. 26.
37. *Ibid.,* pp. 28–29.
38. This information was adapted from Jongeward and Seyer, *Choosing Success,* p. 28.
39. *Ibid.*
40. *Ibid.,* p. 34.
41. *Ibid.,* pp. 35–36.

4

Leadership:
Trait and Attitudinal Approaches

The successful organization has one major attribute that sets it apart from unsuccessful organizations: dynamic and effective leadership. Peter F. Drucker points out that managers (business leaders) are the basic and scarcest resource of any business enterprise.[1]

On all sides there is a continual search for persons who have the necessary ability to lead effectively. This shortage of effective leadership is not confined to business, but is evident in the lack of able administrators in government, education, foundations, churches, and every other form of organization. Thus, when we decry the scarcity of leadership talent in our society, we are not talking about a lack of people to fill administrative positions. What we are agonizing over is a scarcity of people who are willing to assume significant leadership roles in our society and who can get the job done effectively.

LEADERSHIP DEFINED

According to George R. Terry, "Leadership is the activity of influencing people to strive willingly for group objectives."[2] Robert Tannenbaum, Irving R. Weschler, and Fred Massarik define leadership as "interpersonal influence exercised in a situation and directed, through the communication process, toward the attainment of a specialized goal or goals."[3] Harold Koontz and Cyril O'Donnell state that "leadership is *influencing* people to follow in the achievement of a common goal."[4]

A review of other writers reveals that most management writers agree that leadership is *the process of influencing the activities of an individual or a group in efforts toward goal achievement in a given situation.* From this definition of leadership, it follows that the leadership process is a function of the *leader,* the *follower,* and other *situational* variables—$L = f(l,f,s)$.

It is important to note that this definition makes no mention of any particular type of organization. In any situation in which someone is trying to influence the behavior of another individual or group, leadership is occurring. Thus, everyone attempts leadership at one time or another, whether activities are centered on a business, educational institution, hospital, political organization, or family.

It should also be remembered that when this definition mentions leader and follower, one should not assume that we are talking only about a hierarchical relationship such as suggested by manager–co-worker. Any time an individual is attempting to influence the behavior of someone else, that individual is the *potential leader* and the person subject to the influence attempt is the *potential follower,* no matter whether that person is the boss, a colleague (associate), a subordinate, a friend, a relative, or a group.

LEGACIES OF THE PAST

Perhaps it is appropriate, before we look at trait, attitudinal, and situational approaches to leadership, to recognize and give credit to the many distinguished authors and researchers who have contributed to the rich legacy of modern leadership. Without the forward-looking visionaries of past generations (some of whom are listed in Table 4-1), we would not have the insights that we have today. And, as we review the contributions of these visionaries from the perspective of the present, we should not be to hasty to criticize their efforts and their different approaches. They probably were applicable in their time.

In this book we will take these insights, these visions from the past, and move with them to greater understanding that will help you to create and to accomplish a more productive future. We want to help you "lead your best" during the remaining years in the decade of the 1990s and as you move on into the twenty-first century.

TABLE 4-1   Significant Milestones in the Development of Motivation and
            Leadership

CONTRIBUTOR	THEORY	REFERENCE DATE*
Taylor	Scientific Management	1911
Mayo	Hawthorne Studies	1933
Barnard	Executive Functions	1938
Stogdill	Ohio State Studies	1948
Holmans	Human Group	1950
Maslow	Hierarchy of Needs	1954
McGregor	Theory X-Y	1957
Tannenbaum-Schmidt	Continuum of Leader Behavior	1957
Blake-Mouton	Managerial Grid	1964
McClelland	Achievement Theory	1965
Herzberg	Motivation-Hygiene	1966
Likert	Systems 1-4	1967
Fiedler	Contingency Model	1967
Argyris	Maturity-Immaturity	1964
Reddin	3-D Managment Style	1967
Hersey-Blanchard	Situational Leadership	1969
Vroom-Yetten	Contingency Model	1973
House-Mitchell	Path-Goal	1974
Vroom	Expectancy Theory	1976
House	Charismatic Leadership	1977
Burns	Transformational Leadership	1978
Kerr-Jermier	Substitutes for Leadership	1978
McCall-Lombardo	Fatal Leadership Flaws	1983
Bennis-Nanus	Leadership Competencies	1985
Tichy-Devanna	Transformational Leadership	1986
Manz	Super Leadership	1989
Yukl	Integrating Model	1989
Covey	Principle Centered Leadership	1991

*These dates correspond to the publication of significant research on the model or theory.

SCHOOLS OF ORGANIZATIONAL THEORY

We have defined leadership as the process of influencing the activities
of an individual or a group in efforts toward goal achievement in a
given situation. In essence, leadership involves accomplishing goals
with and through people. Therefore, a leader must be concerned about
tasks and human relationships. Although using different terminology, Chester I. Barnard identified these same leadership concerns in
his classic work *The Functions of the Executive,* in the late 1930s.[5]
These leadership concerns seem to be a reflection of two of the earliest

schools of thought in organizational theory—scientific management
and human relations.

Scientific Management Movement

Frederick Winslow Taylor

In the early 1900s one of the most widely read theorists on administration was Frederick Winslow Taylor. The basis for his *scientific
management* was technological in nature. It was felt that the best way
to increase output was to improve the techniques, or methods, used by
workers. Consequently, he has been interpreted as considering people
as instruments or machines to be manipulated by their leaders. Accepting this assumption, other theorists of the scientific management
movement proposed that an organization as rationally planned and
executed as possible be developed to create more efficiency in administration and consequently increase production. Management was to be
divorced from human affairs and emotions. The result was that the
workers had to adjust to the management and not the management to
the workers.

To accomplish this plan, Taylor initiated time-and-motion
studies to analyze work tasks to improve performance in every aspect
of the organization. Once jobs had been reorganized with efficiency in
mind, the economic self-interest of the workers could be satisfied
through various incentive work plans (piece rates and such).

The function of the leader under scientific management or classical theory was obviously to set up and enforce performance criteria to
meet organizational goals. The main focus of a leader was on the
needs of the organization and not on the needs of the individual.[6]

Human Relations Movement

Elton Mayo

In the 1920s and early 1930s, the trend started by Taylor was to be
replaced at center stage by the *human relations* movement, initiated
by Elton Mayo and his associates. These theorists argued that in
addition to finding the best technological methods to improve output,
it was beneficial to management to look into human affairs. It was
claimed that the real power centers within an organization were the
interpersonal relations that developed within the working unit. The
study of these human relations was the most important consideration
for management and the analysis of organization. The organization
was to be developed around the workers and had to take into consideration human feelings and attitudes.[7]

The function of the leader under human relations theory was to facilitate cooperative goal attainment among followers while providing opportunities for their personal growth and development. The main focus, contrary to scientific management theory, was on individual needs and not on the needs of the organization.

In essence, then, the scientific management movement emphasized a concern for task (output), while the human relations movement stressed a concern for relationships (people). The recognition of these two concerns has characterized the writings on leadership ever since the conflict between the scientific management and the human relations schools of thought became apparent.

Looking specifically at leadership, we find that basic approaches to leadership have moved through three rather dominant phases: trait, attitudinal, and situational.

TRAIT APPROACH TO LEADERSHIP

Prior to 1945, the most common approach to the study of leadership concentrated on leadership traits per se, suggesting that there were certain characteristics, such as physical energy or friendliness, that were essential for effective leadership. These inherent personal qualities, like intelligence, were felt to be transferable from one situation to another. Since all individuals did not have these qualities, only those who had them would be considered potential leaders. Consequently, this approach seemed to question the value of training individuals to assume leadership positions. It implied that if we could discover how to identify and measure these leadership qualities (which are inborn in the individual), we should be able to screen leaders from nonleaders. Leadership training would then be helpful only to those with inherent leadership traits.

A review of the research literature using this trait approach to leadership has revealed few significant or consistent findings.[8] As Eugene E. Jennings concluded, "Fifty years of study have failed to produce one personality trait or set of qualities that can be used to discriminate leaders and nonleaders."[9]

This is not to say that certain traits may hinder or facilitate leadership; the key is that no set of traits has been identified that clearly predicts success or failure. As Yukl has observed,

> The old assumption that "leaders are born" has been discredited completely, and the premise that certain leader traits are absolutely necessary for effective leadership has never been substantiated in several decades of trait research. Today there is a more balanced viewpoint

about traits. It is now recognized that certain traits increase the likelihood that a leader will be effective, but they do not guarantee effectiveness, and the relative importance of different traits is dependent upon the nature of the leadership situation.[10]

What are some traits and skills found to be most characteristic of successful leaders? Yukl has offered some suggestions, shown in Table 4-2.

Trait research is still continuing. Warren Bennis completed a five-year study of ninety outstanding leaders and their followers. On the basis of this research, he identified four common traits or areas of competence shared by all ninety leaders.[11]

1. *Management of attention*—The ability to communicate a sense of outcome, goal, or direction that attracts followers.
2. *Management of meaning*—The ability to create and communicate meaning with clarity and understanding.
3. *Management of trust*—The ability to be reliable and consistent so people can count on them.
4. *Management of self*—The ability to know one's self and to use one's skills within limits of strengths and weaknesses.

Bennis suggests leaders empower their organizations to create an environment where people feel significant, learning and competence matter, people are part of the community or team, and work is

TABLE 4-2 Traits and Skills Found Most Frequently to Be Characteristic of Successful Leaders

TRAITS	SKILLS
Adaptable to situations	Clever (intelligent)
Alert to social environment	Conceptually skilled
Ambitious and achievement-oriented	Creative
Assertive	Diplomatic and tactful
Cooperative	Fluent in speaking
Decisive	Knowledgeable about group task
Dependable	Organized (administrative ability)
Dominant (desire to influence others)	Persuasive
Energetic (high activity level)	Socially skilled
Persistent	
Self-confident	
Tolerant of stress	
Willing to assume responsibility	

Source: Gary A. Yukl, *Leadership in Organizations*, © Second Edition, 1989, p. 176. Reprinted with permission of Prentice Hall, Inc., Englewood Cliffs, New Jersey.

exciting. Leaders should also create an environment where quality matters and dedication to work energizes effort.[12]

As Yukl indicated, there may be negative traits that hinder a person from reaching leadership potential. In one such study, Geier[13] found three traits that kept group members from competing for a leadership role. These three traits were, in order of importance, the perception of being uninformed, of being nonparticipants, or of being extremely rigid. Why were these traits so critical? Because the other group members believed members who were uninformed, disinterested, or overly rigid would hinder the group's accomplishment of its goals. As an aside, isn't our educational system designed to make students more informed, more motivated, and less rigid? We think so.

McCall and Lombardo have examined differences between executives who went all the way to the top and those who were expected to go to the top but were "derailed" just before reaching their goal. Both winners and losers were a patchwork of strengths and weaknesses, but those who fell short seemed to have one or more of what McCall and Lombardo call "fatal flaws."

1. Insensitive to others: abrasive, intimidating, bullying style
2. Cold, aloof, arrogant
3. Betrayal of trust
4. Overly ambitious: thinking of next job, playing politics
5. Specific performance problems with the business
6. Overmanaging—unable to delegate or build a team
7. Unable to staff effectively
8. Unable to think strategically
9. Unable to adapt to boss with different style
10. Overdependent on advocate or mentor.[14]

While the most frequent cause for derailment was insensitivity to others, the one "unforgivable sin" was betrayal of trust—not following through on promises or double-dealing.[15]

Kirkpatrick and Locke in the *Academy of Management Executive* reinforce the views of Bennis, Yukl and others:

> Recent research, using a variety of methods, has made it clear that successful leaders are not like other people. The evidence indicates that there are certain core traits which contribute to business leaders' success. . . . Leaders do not have to be great men or women by being intellectual geniuses or omniscient prophets to succeed, but they do need to have the "right stuff" and this stuff is not equally present in all people.[16]

Table 4-3 lists the traits Kirkpatrick and Locke say *do* matter.

TABLE 4-3   Leadership Traits that Do Matter

Drive: Achievement, ambition, energy, tenacity, initiative
Leadership motivation (personalized vs. socialized)
Honesty and Integrity
Self-confidence (including emotional stability)
Cognitive ability
Knowledge of the business
Other traits (weaker suppport): charisma, creative/originality, flexibility

Source: Shelley A. Kirkpatrick and Edwin A. Locke, "Leadership: Do Traits Matter?" *Academy of Management Executive,* 5, no. 2 (1991), p. 49.

In summary, empirical research studies[17] suggest that leadership is a dynamic process, varying from situation to situation with changes in the leader, the followers, and the situation. Because of this, while there may be helping or hindering traits in a given situation, there is no universal set of traits that will ensure leadership success. The lack of validation of trait approaches led to other investigations of leadership. Among the most prominent areas were the attitudinal approaches.

ATTITUDINAL APPROACHES

The main period of the attitudinal approaches to leadership occurred between 1945, with the Ohio State and Michigan studies, and the mid-1960s, with the development of the Managerial Grid.[18]

By attitudinal approaches, we mean approaches that use paper and pencil instruments such as questionnaires to measure attitudes or predispositions toward leader behavior. For example, the dimensions of the Managerial Grid, Concern for Production, and Concern for People are *attitudinal.* Concern may be defined as a predisposition or feeling toward or against production and people. In contrast, Situational Leadership uses the *observed* behavior dimensions of task behavior and relationship behavior. Situational Leadership thus describes how people are actually behaving. In this section, we will look specifically at three attitudinal approaches to leadership: the Ohio State Studies; the Michigan Studies, including Rensis Likert's work; and the Managerial Grid.

Ohio State Leadership Studies

The leadership studies initiated in 1945 by the Bureau of Business Research at Ohio State University attempted to identify various dimensions of leader behavior.[19] The researchers, directed by Ralph

Stogdill, defining leadership as the behavior of an individual when directing the activities of a group toward goal attainment, eventually narrowed the description of leader behavior to two dimensions: *Initiating Structure* and *Consideration*. Initiating Structure refers to "the leader's behavior in delineating the relationship between himself and members of the work group and in endeavoring to establish well-defined patterns of organization, channels of communication, and methods of procedure."[20] On the other hand, Consideration refers to "behavior indicative of friendship, mutual trust, respect, and warmth in the relationship between the leader and the members of his staff."[21]

To gather data about the behavior of leaders, the Ohio State staff developed the Leader Behavior Description Questionnaire (LBDQ), an instrument designed to describe *how* leaders carry out their activities.[22] The LBDQ contains fifteen items pertaining to Consideration and an equal number for Initiating Structure. Respondents judge the frequency with which their leader engages in each form of behavior by checking one of five descriptions—always, often, occasionally, seldom, or never—as it relates to each particular item of the LBDQ. Thus, Consideration and Initiating Structure are dimensions of observed behavior as perceived by others. Examples of items used in the LBDQ for both these dimensions follow in Table 4-4.

Although the major emphasis in the Ohio State Leadership Studies was on *observed behavior,* the staff did develop the Leader Opinion Questionnaire (LOQ) to gather data about the self-perceptions that leaders have about their own leadership style. The LBDQ was completed by leaders' follower(s), supervisor(s), or associates (peers), but the LOQ was scored by the leaders themselves.

In studying leader behavior, the Ohio State staff found that Initiating Structure and Consideration were separate and distinct dimensions. A high score on one dimension does not necessitate a low score on the other. The behavior of a leader could be described as any mix of both dimensions. Thus, it was during these studies that leader behavior was first plotted on two separate axes rather than on a single continuum. Four quadrants were developed to show various combina-

TABLE 4-4 Examples of LBDQ Items

CONSIDERATION	INITIATING STRUCTURE
The leader finds time to listen to group members.	The leader assigns group members to particular tasks.
The leader is willing to make changes.	The leader asks the group members to follow standard rules and regulations.
The leader is friendly and approachable.	The leader lets group members know what is expected of them.

tions of Initiating Structure (task behavior) and Consideration (relationship behavior), as illustrated in Figure 4-1.

Michigan Leadership Studies

In the early studies by the Survey Research Center at the University of Michigan, there was an attempt to approach the study of leadership by locating clusters of characteristics that seemed to be related to each other and various indicators of effectiveness. The studies identified two concepts, which they called *employee orientation* and *production orientation.*

Leaders who are described as employee-oriented emphasize the relationships aspect of their job. They feel that every employee is important and take interest in everyone, accepting their individuality and personal needs. Production-oriented leaders emphasize production and the technical aspects of the job; employees are seen as tools to accomplish the goals of the organization. These two orientations parallel the democratic (relationship) and authoritarian (task) concepts of the leader behavior continuum of the Tannenbaum–Schmidt model presented in Chapter 6.

Group Dynamics Studies

Dorwin Cartwright and Alvin Zander, summarizing the findings of numerous studies at the Research Center for Group Dynamics, claim that group objectives fall into one of two categories: (1) the achievement of some specific group goal; or (2) the maintenance or strengthening of the group itself.[22]

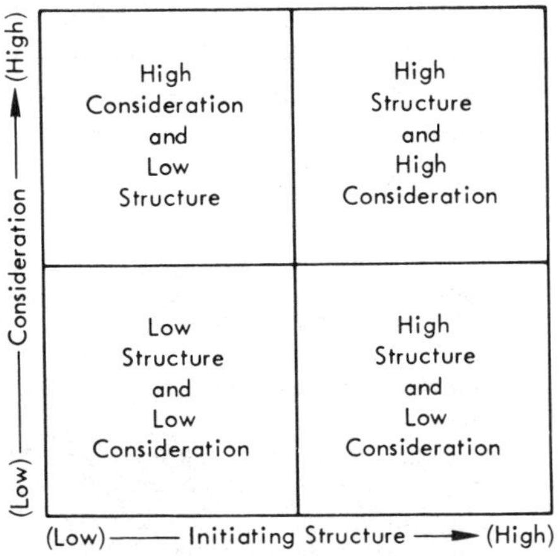

FIGURE 4-1
The Ohio State leadership quadrants

According to Cartwright and Zander, the type of behavior involved in goal achievement is illustrated by these examples: the manager "initiates action . . . keeps members' attention on the goal . . . clarifies the issue and develops a procedural plan."[23]

On the other hand, typical behaviors for group maintenance are characterized by a manager who "keeps interpersonal relations pleasant . . . arbitrates disputes . . . provides encouragement . . . gives the minority a chance to be heard . . . stimulates self-direction . . . and increases the interdependence among members."[24]

Goal achievement seems to coincide with the task concepts discussed earlier (production orientation), while group maintenance parallels the relationship concepts (employee orientation).

Research findings in recent years indicate that leadership styles vary considerably from leader to leader. Some leaders emphasize the task and can be described as authoritarian leaders; others stress interpersonal relationships and may be viewed as democratic leaders. Still others seem to be both task-oriented and relationship-oriented. There are even some individuals in leadership positions who are not concerned about either. No dominant style appears. Instead, various combinations are evident. Thus, task and relationship are not either/or leadership styles. They are separate and distinct dimensions that can be plotted on two separate axes.

Rensis Likert's Management Systems

Using the earlier Michigan studies as a starting place, Rensis Likert did some extensive research to discover the general pattern of management used by high-producing managers in contrast to the pattern used by the other managers. He found that "supervisors with the best records of performance focus their primary attention on the human aspects of their employees' problems and on endeavoring to build effective work groups with high performance goals."[25] These supervisors were called "employee-centered." Other supervisors who kept constant pressure on production were called "job-centered" and were found more often to have low-producing sections. Figure 4-2 presents the findings from one study.

Likert also discovered that high-producing supervisors "make clear to their employees what the objectives are and what needs to be accomplished and then give them freedom to do the job."[26] Thus, he found that general rather than close supervision tended to be associated with high productivity. This relationship, found in a study of clerical workers, is illustrated in Figure 4-3. The Figure shows that nine out of ten high-producing sections are led by first-line supervisors who use general supervision, while eight out of twelve low-

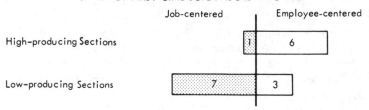

NUMBER OF FIRST-LINE SUPERVISORS WHO ARE

FIGURE 4-2 Employee-centered supervisors are higher producers than job-centered supervisors

Rensis Likert, **New Patterns of Management** *(New York: McGraw-Hill, 1961).*

producing sections are led by supervisors who use close supervision. Note that general supervision does not always result in high production or close supervision in low production. However, general supervision under the conditions described in this study has a higher probability of resulting in high production than does close supervision.

Likert's continuing research together with his colleagues at the Institute for Social Research at the University of Michigan emphasized the need to consider both human resources and capital resources as assets requiring proper management attention. He found that most managers when asked what they would do if they suddenly lost half of their plant, equipment, or capital resources were quick to answer that they would depend upon insurance or borrowed money to keep them in business. Yet when these same managers are asked what they would do if they suddenly lost half of their human resources—managers, supervisors, and hourly employees—they were at a loss for words. There is no insurance against outflows of human resources. Recruiting, training, and developing large numbers of new personnel into a working team takes years. In a competitive environment, this is

FIGURE 4-3 Low-producing sections are more closely supervised than high-producing sections

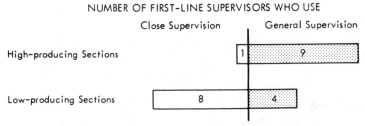

Rensis Likert, **New Patterns of Management** *(New York: McGraw-Hill, 1961).*

almost an impossible task. Organizations are now realizing that their most important assets are human resources and that the managing of these resources is one of their most crucial tasks.

As a result of behavioral research studies of numerous organizations, Likert implemented organizational change programs in various industrial settings. These programs were intended to help organizations move from Theory X to Theory Y assumptions, from fostering immature behavior to encouraging and developing mature behavior, from emphasizing only hygiene factors to recognizing and implementing motivators.

Likert in his studies found that the prevailing management styles of organizations can be depicted on a continuum from System 1 through System 4. These systems might be described as follows:[27]

System 1—Management is seen as having no confidence or trust in employees since they are seldom involved in any aspect of the decision-making process. The bulk of the decisions and the goal setting of the organization are made at the top and issued down the chain of command. Employees are forced to work with fear, threats, punishment, and occasional rewards. Need satisfaction is at the physiological and safety levels. The limited management-employee interaction that does take place is usually with fear and mistrust. Although the control process is highly concentrated in top management, an informal organization generally develops in opposition to the goals of the formal organization.

System 2—Management is seen as having condescending confidence and trust in employees, such as a master has toward the servants. The bulk of the decisions and goal setting of the organization are made at the top, but many decisions are made within a prescribed framework at lower levels. Rewards and some actual or potential punishment are used to motivate workers. Any interaction takes place with some condescension by management and fear and caution by employees. Although the control process is still concentrated in top management, some is delegated to middle and lower levels. An informal organization usually develops, but it does not always resist formal organizational goals.

System 3—Management is seen as having substantial, but not complete confidence and trust in employees. Broad policy and general decisions are kept at the top, but employees are permitted to make more specific decisions at lower levels. Communication flows both up and down the hierarchy. Rewards, occasional punishment, and some involvement are used to motivate workers. There is a moderate amount of interaction, often with a fair amount of confidence and trust. Significant aspects of the control process are delegated downward, with a feeling of responsibility at both higher and lower levels. An informal organization may develop, but it may either support or partially resist goals of the organization.

System 4—Management is seen as having complete confidence and trust in employees. Decision making is widely dispersed throughout the organization, although well integrated. Communication flows not only up and down the hierarchy, but among peers. Workers are motivated by participation and involvement in developing economic rewards, setting goals, improving methods, and appraising progress toward goals. There is extensive friendly management-employee interaction, with a high degree of confidence and trust. There is widespread responsibility for the control process, with the lower units fully involved. The informal and formal organizations are often one and the same. Thus, all social forces support efforts to achieve stated organizational goals.

In summary, System 1 is a task-oriented, highly structured authoritarian management style; System 4 is a relationship-oriented management style based on teamwork, mutual trust, and confidence. Systems 2 and 3 are intermediate stages between two extremes, which approximate closely Theory X and Theory Y assumptions.

To expedite the analysis of a company's present behavior, Likert's group developed an instrument that enables members to evaluate their organization in terms of its management system. This instrument is designed to gather data about a number of operating characteristics of an organization. These characteristics include leadership, motivation, communication, decision making, interaction and influence, goal setting, and the control process used by the organization. Sample items from this instrument are presented in Table 4-5. The complete instrument includes more than twenty such items. Various forms of this instrument have been adapted to be situation specific. For example, a version for school systems is now available with forms for the school board, superintendent, central staff, principals, teachers, parents, and students.

In testing this instrument, Likert asked hundreds of managers from many different organizations to indicate where the *most* productive department, division, or organization they have known would fall between System 1 and System 4. Then these same managers were asked to repeat this process and indicate the position of the *least* productive department, division, or organization they have known. While the ratings of the most and the least productive departments varied among managers, almost without exception each manager rated the high-producing unit closer to System 4 than the low-producing department. In summary, Likert has found that the closer the

TABLE 4-5 Examples of Items from Likert's Table of Organizational and Performance Characteristics of Different Management Systems

Organizational Variable	System 1	System 2	System 3	System 4
Leadership processes used				
Extent to which superiors have confidence and trust in subordinates	Have no confidence and trust in subordinates	Have condescending confidence and trust, such as master has to servant	Substantial but not complete confidence and trust; still wishes to keep control of decisions	Complete confidence and trust in all matters
Character of motivational forces				
Manner in which motives are used	Fear, threats, punishment, and occasional rewards	Rewards and some actual or potential punishment	Rewards, occasional punishment, and some involvement	Economic rewards based on compensation system developed through participation; group participation and involvement in setting goals, improving methods, appraising progress toward goals, etc.
Character of interaction-influence process				
Amount and character of interaction	Little interaction and always with fear and distrust	Little interaction and usually with some condescension by superiors; fear and caution by subordinates	Moderate interaction, often with fair amount of confidence and trust	Extensive, friendly interaction with high degree of confidence and trust

Source: Rensis Likert, *The Human Organization* (New York: McGraw-Hill, 1967), pp. 197–211.

management style of an organization approaches System 4, the more likely it will be to have a continuous record of high productivity. Similarly, the closer this style reflects System 1, the more likely it is to have a sustained record of low productivity.

Likert has also used this instrument not only to measure what individuals believe are the present characteristics of their organization, but also to find out what they would like these characteristics to be. Data generated from this use of the instrument with managers of well-known companies have indicated a large discrepancy between the management system they feel their company is now using and the management system they feel would be most appropriate. System 4 is seen as being most appropriate, but few see their companies presently utilizing this approach. These implications have led to attempts by some organizations to adapt their management system to approximate more closely System 4. Changes of this kind are not easy. They involve a massive reeducation of all concerned, from the top management to the hourly workers.

Theory into Practice

One instance of a successful change in the management style of an organization occurred with a leading firm in the pajama industry.[28] After being unprofitable for several years, this company was purchased by another corporation. At the time of the transaction, the purchased company was using a management style falling between System 1 and System 2. Some major changes were soon implemented by the new owners. The changes that were put into effect included extensive modifications in how the work was organized, improved maintenance of machinery, and a training program involving managers and workers at every level. Managers and supervisors were exposed in depth to the philosophy and understanding of management approaching System 4. All of these changes were supported by the top management of the purchasing company.

Although productivity dropped in the first several months after the initiation of the change program, productivity increased by almost 30 percent within two years. Although it is not possible to calculate exactly how much of the increased productivity resulted from the change in management system, it was obvious to the researchers that the impact was considerable. In addition to increases in productivity, manufacturing costs decreased 20 percent, turnover was cut almost in half, and morale rose considerably (reflecting a more friendly attitude of workers toward the organization). The company's image in the community was enhanced, and for the first time in years the company began to show a profit.

The implication throughout Likert's writings is that the ideal and most productive leader behavior for industry is employee-centered or democratic. Yet, his own findings raise questions as to whether there can be an ideal or single normatively good style of leader behavior that can apply in all leadership situations. Referring back to figures 4-2 and 4-3, one of the eight job-centered supervisors and one of the nine supervisors using close supervision had high-producing sections; also, three of the nine employee-centered supervisors and four of the thirteen supervisors who used general supervision had low-producing sections. In other words, in almost 35 percent of the low-producing sections, the suggested ideal type of leader behavior produced undesirable results and almost 15 percent of the high-producing sections were supervised by the suggested "undesirable" style.

Similar findings and interpretations were made by Halpin and Winer in a study of the relationship between aircraft commanders' leadership patterns and the proficiency rating of their crews.[29] Using the LBDQ, they found that eight of ten commanders with high-proficiency ratings were described as using above average Consideration and Initiating Structure and that six of seven commanders with low ratings were seen as below average in Consideration and Initiating Structure. As Likert did, Halpin and Winer reported only that the leaders above average in both Consideration and Initiating Structure are likely to be effective and did not discuss the two high-proficiency, low-Consideration, low-Initiating Structure commanders and the one low-producing, high-Initiating Structure, high-Consideration commander.

Evidence suggesting that a single ideal or normative style of leader behavior is unrealistic was provided when a study was done in an industrial setting in Nigeria.[30] The results were almost the exact opposite of Likert's findings. In that country, the tendency was for job-centered supervisors who provide close supervision to have high-producing sections and for employee-centered supervisors who provide general supervision to have low-producing sections. Thus, a single normative leadership style does not take into consideration cultural differences, particularly customs and traditions as well as the level of education, the standard of living, or industrial experience. These are examples of cultural differences in the followers and the situations that are important in determining the appropriate leadership style to be used. Therefore, based on the definition of leadership process as a function of the leader, the followers, and other situational variables, *a single ideal type of leader behavior seems unrealistic.*

Managerial Grid

Robert R. Blake and Jane S. Mouton

In discussing the Ohio State, Michigan, and Likert leadership studies, we concentrated on two theoretical concepts—one emphasizing *task* accomplishment and the other stressing the development of personal *relationships.* Robert R. Blake and Jane S. Mouton have modified these concepts in their Managerial Grid and have used them extensively in organization and management development programs.[31]

In the Managerial Grid, five different types of leadership based on concern for production (task) and concern for people (relationship) are located in four quadrants (see Figure 4-4) similar to those identified by the Ohio State studies.

Concern for production is illustrated on the horizontal axis. Production becomes more important to the leader as the rating advances on the horizontal scale. A leader with a rating of nine on the horizontal axis has a maximum concern for production.

Concern for people is illustrated on the vertical axis. People become more important to leaders as their ratings progress up the vertical axis. A leader with a rating of nine on the vertical axis has maximum concern for people.

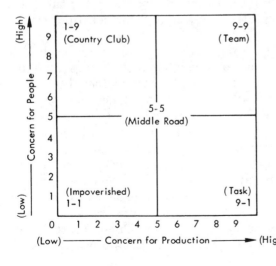

FIGURE 4-4
Blake and Mouton's
Managerial Grid leadership
styles[32]

The five leadership styles are described as follows:

Impoverished. Exertion of minimum effort to get required work done is appropriate to sustain organization membership.

Country Club. Thoughtful attention to needs of people for satisfying relationships leads to a comfortable, friendly organization atmosphere and work tempo.

Task. Efficiency in operations results from arranging conditions of work in such a way that human elements interfere to a minimum degree.

Middle-of-the-Road. Adequate organization performance is possible through balancing the necessity to get out the work while maintaining morale of people at a satisfactory level.

Team. Work accomplishment is from committed people; interdependence through a "common stake" in organization purpose leads to relationships of trust and respect.[33]

In essence, we feel the Managerial Grid has given popular terminology to five points within the four quadrants of the Ohio State studies. However, we want to point out one significant difference between the two frameworks. "Concern for" is a predisposition about something, or an attitudinal dimension. Therefore, the Managerial Grid tends to be an attitudinal model that measures the values and feelings of a manager, while the Ohio State framework attempts to include behavioral concepts (items) as well as attitudinal items.

IS THERE A BEST STYLE OF LEADERSHIP?

While some researchers such as Blake, Mouton, and McGregor have argued that there is "one best" style of leadership—a style that maximizes productivity and satisfaction, and growth and development in all situations, further research in the last several decades has clearly supported the contention that there is no one best leadership style.[34] Successful and effective leaders are able to adapt their style to fit the requirements of the situation. For example, John Scully, CEO of Apple Computer, compares leading to sailing, "One has to make a lot of navigational decisions and then continually trim sails and do a lot of things to adjust to currents and winds."[35] To amplify this idea, it is necessary to place the current state of leadership theory into perspective.

First, *all* leadership theories, like the vast majority of behavioral science theories (one is attempted to say *all*), have not been conclusively validated by scientific research. As Robbins has observed,

". . . simple and universal principles [of organizational behavior] are avoided because there exist no simple and universal truths or principles that consistently explain organizational behavior."[36] But just because research does not conclusively validate a behavioral science theory does not necessarily make it invalid. If this were not true, there probably wouldn't be any organizational behavior theories (or books such as this one based on the behavioral sciences). For example, as both Miner and Robbins suggested in their different appraisal of Maslow's Hierarchy of Needs, ". . . remember that there is a difference between finding 'insufficient evidence' for a theory and labeling it 'invalid.' It is clear that the available research does not support the Maslow theory to any significant degree. *This does not imply that the theory is wrong, merely that it has not been supported*" (emphasis added).[37]

The lack of solid scientific evidence supporting *all* leadership theories may be because leadership "theories" are, at this point, sets of empirical generalizations and have not developed into scientifically testable theories. This does not make them "wrong," merely that they have not been supported.[38]

Perhaps the problem is that we have been expecting too much from so-called leadership "theories." They really are not "theories" at all but, as we have suggested, descriptions of concepts, procedures, actions, and outcomes that exist. This is why we refer to Situational Leadership as a model.

The primary reason why there is no "one best way" of leadership is that leadership is basically situational, or contingent. All of the leadership theories of House, Fiedler, Kerr, Reddin, Vroom-Yetten, Yukl—to name a few—are situational and represent, together with Situational Leadership, the mainstream of leadership thought. As Robbins has stated, ". . . OB [organizational behavior] concepts are founded on situational conditions; that is, if X, then Y, but only under conditions specified in Z (the contingency variables). . . ."[39] In other words, the effectiveness of a particular leadership style is contingent upon the situation in which it is utilized. As several researchers have noted, one of the most important contributions of Situational Leadership is its attention to the situational nature of leadership.[40]

It is also important to know that effective managers not only have the diagnostic ability to determine the most appropriate leadership style, but they also have the ability to correctly apply that style. As Owens has observed:

These managers expressed a virtual consensus that, based on their actual experience, each situation they handled demanded a different leadership style. No single style could suffice under the day-to-day, even minute-by-minute, varying conditions of different personalities and moods among their employees, routine process vs. changing or sudden deadlines, new and ever-changing government regulations and paperwork, ambiguous roles of workers, wide ranges in job complexity from simple to innovation-demanding, changes in organizational structure and markets and task technologies and so on. Contingency theory has come to mean, therefore, that the effective manager has, and knows how to use, many leadership styles as each is appropriate to a particular situation.[41]

We believe that Owens has correctly described the situational nature of leadership and that no "one best way" approach can adequately describe what leaders must do to cope with the challenges facing them. Perhaps Ralph Stogdill, author of the *Handbook of Leadership* and a distinguished leadership researcher for more than forty years, has said it best: "The most effective leaders appear to exhibit a degree of versatility and flexibility that enables them to adapt their behavior to the changing and contradictory demands made on them."[42]

What are some of these "changing and contradictory demands"? How do they influence leadership? How does a potential leader diagnose the situation to determine the high probability leadership style to use? These and many other important issues will be the subjects for chapter 5 and the following chapters.

NOTES

1. Peter F. Drucker, *The Practice of Management* (New York: Harper & Row, 1954). See also Allen L. Appell, *A Practical Approach to Human Behavior in Business* (Columbus: Merrill, 1984).
2. George R. Terry, *Principles of Management,* 3rd ed. (Homewood, Ill.: Irwin, 1960), p. 493.
3. Robert Tannenbaum, Irwin R. Weschler, and Fred Massarik, *Leadership and Organization: A Behavioral Science Approach* (New York: McGraw-Hill, 1959).
4. Harold Koontz and Cyril O'Donnell, *Principles of Management,* 2nd ed. (New York: McGraw-Hill, 1959), p. 435.
5. Chester I. Barnard, *The Functions of the Executive* (Cambridge, Mass.: Harvard University Press, 1938).
6. Frederick W. Taylor, *The Principles of Scientific Management* (New York: Harper & Brothers, 1911).
7. Elton Mayo, *The Social Problems of an Industrial Civilization* (Boston: Harvard Business School, 1945), p. 23.
8. Cecil A. Gibb, "Leadership," in *Handbook of Social Psychology,* Gardner Lindzey, ed. (Cambridge, Mass.: Addison-Wesley, 1954). See also Roger M. Stogdill, "Personal Factors Associated with Leadership: A Survey of Literature," *Journal of Psychology,* 25 (1948), pp. 35–71.
9. Eugene E. Jennings, "The Anatomy of Leadership," *Management of Personnel Quarterly,* 1, No. 1 (Autumn 1961). See also A. G. Jago, "Leadership: Perspectives in Theory and Research," *Management Science,* March 1982, pp. 315–36.

10. Gary A. Yukl, *Leadership in Organizations,* 2nd ed. (Englewood Cliffs, N. J.: Prentice Hall, 1989), p. 176.
11. Warren Bennis, "The 4 Competencies of Leadership," *Training and Development Journal,* August 1984, pp. 15–19. See also Warren Bennis and Bert Nanus, *Leaders: The Strategies for Taking Charge* (New York: Harper & Row, 1986).
12. *Ibid.*
13. John G. Geier, "A Trait Approach to the Study of Leadership in Small Groups," *Journal of Communications,* December 1967.
14. Morgan W. McCall, Jr. and Michael M. Lombardo, "What Makes a Top Executive?" *Psychology Today,* February 1983, pp. 26–31.
15. *Ibid.*
16. Shelley A. Kirkpatrick and Edwin A. Locke, "Leadership: Do Traits Matter?" *Academy of Management Executive,* 5, no. 2 (1991), pp. 49, 59.
17. See cited research by Bennis, McCall, Owens, Yukl, and others.
18. Robert R. Blake and Jane S. Mouton, *The Managerial Grid III,* 3rd ed. (Houston, Tex.: Gulf Publishing, 1984). See also Robert R. Blake and Jane S. Mouton, "The Managerial Grid III," *Personnel Psychology,* 39 (Spring 1986), pp. 238–40.
19. Ralph M. Stogdill and Alvin Coons, eds., *Leader Behavior: Its Description and Measurement,* Research Monograph No. 88 (Columbus: Bureau of Business Research, Ohio State University, 1957). See also Fred E. Fiedler and M. M. Chemers, "Improving Leadership Effectiveness," *Personnel Psychology,* 38 (Spring 1985), pp. 220–22.
20. *Ibid.*
21. Andrew W. Halpin, *The Leadership Behavior of School Superintendents* (Chicago: Midwest Administration Center, University of Chicago, 1959), p. 4.
22. Dorwin Cartwright and Alvin Zander, eds., *Group Dynamics: Research and Theory,* 2nd ed. (Evanston, Ill.: Row, Peterson, 1960). See also Patrick R. Penland, *Group Dynamics and Individual Development* (New York: Dekker, 1974); R. H. Guest, *Work Teams and Team Building* (New York: Pergamon, 1986).
23. Cartwright and Zander, *Group Dynamics* p. 496. See also *Group Plannings and Problems–Solving Methods in Engineering Management,* ed. by Shirley A. Olsen (New York: Wiley, 1982).
24. Cartwright and Zander, *Group Dynamics.*
25. Rensis Likert, *New Patterns of Management* (New York: McGraw-Hill, 1961), p. 7.
26. *Ibid.,* p. 9.
27. Adapted from Table 2-1, Table of Organizational and Performance Characteristics of Different Management Systems, in Rensis Likert, *The Human Organization* (New York: McGraw-Hill, 1967), pp. 3–10.
28. L. Coch and J. R. P. French, Jr., "Overcoming Resistance to Change," *Human Relations,* 1, No. 4 (1948), pp. 512–32.
29. Andrew W. Halpin and Ben J. Winer, *The Leadership Behavior of Airplane Commanders* (Columbus: Ohio State Research Foundation, 1952).
30. Paul Hersey, unpublished research project, 1965.
31. Robert R. Blake and Jane S. Mouton, *The Managerial Grid* (Houston, Tex.: Gulf Publishing, 1964). See also R. R. Blake and J. S. Mouton, "The Managerial Grid III," *Personnel Psychology;* R. R. Blake and J. S. Mouton, *The Versatile Manager: A Grid Profile* (Homewood, Ill.: Irwin, 1982); R. R. Blake and J. S. Mouton, *The Secretary Grid: A Program for Increasing Office Synergy* (New York: AMACOM, 1983); Robert Blake et al., *The Academic Administration Grid: A Guide to Developing Effective Management Teams* (San Francisco: Jossey-Bass, 1981).
32. *Ibid.*
33. Robert Blake et al., "Breakthrough in Organizational Development," *Harvard Business Review,* November–December 1964, p. 136.
34. See research by Bennis, Kerr, Yukl, House, Robbins, Tannenbaum and Schmidt, Fiedler, Reddin, Bass, Vroom.
35. Quoted in Harry Levinson, "You Won't Recognize Me: Predictions About Change in Top Management Characteristics." *The Academy of Management Executive,* Vol. II, No. 2:124, 1988.

36. Stephen P. Robbins, *Organizational Behavior: Concepts Controversies, and Applications,* 4th ed. (Englewood Cliffs, N. J.: Prentice Hall, 1989), pp. 11–12.
37. *Ibid,* p. 136.
38. John B. Miner, *Theories of Organizational Behavior* (Hinsdale, Ill.: Dryden Press, 1980).
39. Robbins, *Organizational Behavior,* p. 12.
40. Yukl, *Leadership in Organizations,* p. 144.
41. James Owens, "A Reappraisal of Leadership Theory and Training," *Personnel Administrator,* 26 (November 1981), p. 81.
42. Ralph M. Stogdill, "Historical Trends in Leadership Theory and Research," *Journal of Contemporary Business,* Autumn 1974, p. 7.

5

Leadership:
Situational Approaches

The focus in situational approaches to leadership is on observed behavior, not on any hypothetical inborn or acquired ability or potential for leadership. The emphasis is on the behavior of leaders and their group members (followers) and various situations. With this emphasis on behavior and environment, more encouragement is given to the possibility of training individuals in adapting styles of leader behavior to varying situations. Therefore, it is believed that most people can increase their effectiveness in leadership roles through education, training, and development. From observations of the frequency (or infrequency) of certain leader behavior in numerous types of situations, models can be developed to help leaders make some predictions about the most appropriate leader behavior for their present situation. For these reasons, in this chapter we will talk in terms of leader behavior rather than leadership traits, thus emphasizing the situational approach to leadership.

SITUATIONAL APPROACHES TO LEADERSHIP

As we noted in the last chapter, current organizational behavior theory views leadership as well as other organizational behavior concepts and theories as situational, or contingent in nature. While

we cited Robbins, his views are not unique. Schriesheim, Tolliver, and Behling have noted, ". . . the literature supports the basic notion that a situational view is necessary to portray accurately the complexities of the leadership process."[1] Vroom concurs, "I do not see any form of leadership as optimal for all situations. The contribution of a leader's actions to the effectiveness of his organization cannot be determined without considering the nature of the situation in which that behavior is displayed."[2]

Earlier we identified the three main components of the leadership process as the leader, the follower, and the situation. Situational approaches to leadership examine the interplay among these variables in order to find causal relationships that will lead to predictability of behavior. You will find a common thread among the situational approaches that we will elaborate upon in this and in subsequent chapters. This common thread is that all situational approaches require the leader to behave in a flexible manner, to be able to diagnose the leadership style appropriate to the situation, and to be able to apply the appropriate style.

While there are many situational models and theories, we will focus on six that have received wide attention in leadership research: the Tannenbaum and Schmidt Continuum of Leader Behavior, Fiedler's Contingency Model, the House–Mitchell Path-Goal Theory, the Stinson-Johnson Model, Vroom–Yetten Contingency Model, and the Hersey–Blanchard Tri-Dimensional Leader Effectiveness Model.[3]

TANNENBAUM–SCHMIDT CONTINUUM OF LEADER BEHAVIOR

Robert Tannenbaum and Warren H. Schmidt's 1957 *Harvard Business Review* article "How to Choose a Leadership Pattern" was one of the initial and certainly one of the most significant situational approaches to leadership.[4] In this model the leader selects one of seven possible leader behaviors depending upon the forces among the leader, follower, and situation. As Figure 5-1 indicates, the range of continuum of choices is between democratic or relationship-oriented behaviors and authoritarian or task-oriented behaviors. You will remember that these are dimensions from the Michigan and Ohio State studies, respectively.

Past writers have felt that concern for task tends to be represented by authoritarian leader behavior, while a concern for relationships is represented by democratic leader behavior. This feeling was popular because it was generally agreed that leaders influence their followers in either of two ways: (1) they can tell their followers what to do and how to do it; or (2) they can share their leadership respon-

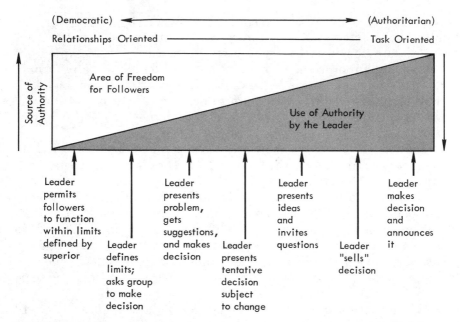

FIGURE 5-1   The Tannenbaum and Schmidt Continuum of leader behavior

sibilities with their followers by involving them in the planning and execution of the task. The former is the traditional authoritarian style, which emphasizes task concerns. The latter is the more non-directive democratic style, which stresses the concern for human relationships.

The differences in the two styles of leader behavior are based on the assumptions leaders make about the source of their power or authority and human nature. The authoritarian style of leader behavior is often based on the assumption that the power of leaders is derived from the position they occupy and that people are innately lazy and unreliable (Theory X). The democratic style assumes that the power of leaders is granted by the group they are to lead and that people can be basically self-directed and creative at work if properly motivated (Theory Y). As a result, in the authoritarian style, all policies are determined by the leader; in the democratic style, policies are open for group discussion and decision.

There are, of course, a wide variety of styles of leader behavior between these two extremes. Robert Tannenbaum and Warren H. Schmidt depicted a broad range of styles as a continuum moving from authoritarian, or manager-centered, leader behavior at one end to democratic, or follower-centered, leader behavior at the other end,[5] as illustrated in Figure 5-1. Tannenbaum and Schmidt now refer to these two extremes as manager power and influence and non-manager power and influence.

Leaders whose behavior is observed to be at the authoritarian end of the continuum tend to be task-oriented and use their power to influence their followers; leaders whose behavior appears to be at the democratic end tend to be group-oriented and thus give their followers considerable freedom in their work. Often this continuum is extended beyond democratic leader behavior to include a *laissez-faire* style.[6] This style of behavior permits the members of the group to do whatever they want to do. No policies or procedures are established. Everyone is left alone. No one attempts to influence anyone else. As is evident, this is not included in the continuum of leader behavior illustrated in Figure 5-1. This was done because it was felt that in reality, a *laissez-faire* atmosphere represents an absence of formal leadership. The formal leadership role has been abdicated and, therefore, any leadership that is being exhibited is informal and emergent.

It is interesting to note that in the 1973 reprint of their article in the *Harvard Business Review,* Tannenbaum and Schmidt commented that the interrelationships among leader, follower, and situation were becoming increasingly complex.[7] With this complexity it becomes more difficult to identify causes and effects, particularly when more forces outside the traditional situation are exerting influence. As the world becomes more international, as more stakeholders come into play, and as more traditional customs, practices and authorities are eroded, the leadership process becomes more difficult. Warren Bennis's "Where Have All the Leaders Gone?" is one astute commentary on this phenomenon.[8]

FIEDLER'S LEADERSHIP CONTINGENCY MODEL

Widely respected as the Father of the Contingency Theory of Leadership, Fred Fiedler has developed the Leadership Contingency Model. He suggests that three major situational variables seem to determine whether a given situation is favorable to leaders: (1) their personal relations with the members of their group (leader-member relations); (2) the degree of structure in the task that their group has been assigned to perform (task structure); and (3) the power and authority that their position provides (position power).[9] Leader-member relations seem to parallel the relationship concepts discussed earlier, while task structure and position power, which measure very closely related aspects of a situation, seem to be associated with task concepts. Fiedler defines the *favorableness of a situation* as "the degree to which the situation enables the leader to exert his influence over his group."[10]

In this model, eight possible combinations of these three situational variables can occur. As a leadership situation varies from high to low on these variables, it will fall into one of the eight combinations (situations). The most favorable situation for leaders to influence their group is one in which they are well liked by the members (good leader-member relations), have a powerful position (high position power), and are directing a well-defined job (high task structure); for example, a well-liked general making an inspection in an army camp. On the other hand, the most unfavorable situation for leaders is one in which they are disliked, have little position power, and face an unstructured task—such as an unpopular head of a voluntary hospital fund-raising committee.

Having developed this model for classifying group situations, Fiedler has attempted to determine what the most effective leadership style—task-oriented or relationship-oriented—seems to be for each of the eight situations. In a reexamination of old leadership studies and an analysis of new studies, Fiedler has concluded that:

1. *Task-oriented* leaders tend to perform best in group situations that are either very favorable or very unfavorable to the leader.
2. *Relationship-oriented* leaders tend to perform best in situations that are intermediate in favorableness.

These conclusions are summarized in Figure 5-2.[11]

Although Fiedler's model is useful to a leader, he seems to be reverting to a single continuum of leader behavior, suggesting that there are only two basic leader behavior styles, task-oriented and relationship-oriented. Most evidence indicates that leader behavior must be plotted on two separate axes rather than on a single continuum. Thus, a leader who is high on task behavior is not necessarily

FIGURE 5-2 Leadership styles Fiedler concludes are appropriate for various group situations

Source: Adapted from Fred E. Fiedler, A Theory of Leadership Effectiveness (New York: McGraw-Hill, 1967), p. 14.

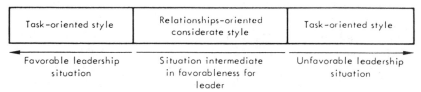

high or low on relationship behavior. Any combination of the two dimensions may occur.

HOUSE-MITCHELL PATH-GOAL THEORY

The Path-Goal model builds upon two concepts that we have looked at earlier—the Ohio State leadership studies and the expectancy model of motivation.[12] You will recall that the expectancy model focused on the effort-performance and the performance–goal satisfaction (reward) linkages.[13]

You will also remember that the key dimensions of the Ohio State model are initiating structure and consideration and that the model suggested that the most effective leaders would be high on both the initiating structure and the consideration dimensions.

Robert House did much of his leadership research at Ohio State University and was interested in explaining the contradictions in the Ohio State model; for example, the situations where initiating structure, consideration, or certain combinations of the two variables were not the most effective. In other words, he was interested in those situations where initiating structure was most appropriate and those situations where consideration was most appropriate. Furthermore, he was interested in explaining *why* a certain style of leadership was effective.

Before we go further, it is important to state why this theory is called the Path-Goal Theory. House and Mitchell explain it in this manner:

> According to this theory, leaders are effective because of their impact on [followers'] motivation, ability to perform effectively and satisfactions. The theory is called Path-Goal because its major concern is how the leader influences the [followers'] perceptions of their work goals, personal goals and paths to goal attainment. The theory suggests that a leader's behavior is motivating or satisfying to the degree that the behavior increases [followers'] goal attainment and clarifies the paths to these goals.[14]

How does the Path-Goal Theory relate to the expectancy model and the Ohio State Leadership Model? The expectancy model tells us that "... people are satisfied with their job if they think it leads to things that are highly valued, and they work hard if they believe that effort leads to things that are highly valued."[15] Leadership is related to this because "... subordinates are motivated by leader behavior to the extent that this behavior influences expectancies ..."[16] Leaders do this best according to Path-Goal Theory when they supply what is missing from the situation. For example, in an unstructured task situation, leaders may increase job satisfaction by supplying more structure, more leader directiveness. This can be seen in Figure 5-3.

In this Figure, task structure is the contingency variable. Job satisfaction is highest in a situation that is *unstructured*—for example, a basic research lab. When leader directiveness is high, job satisfaction would be low if leader directiveness is low. In a *structured* task situation—for example, an assembly line, job satisfaction would be highest when leader directiveness is low. Job satisfaction would be lowest when leader directiveness is high. Why is this so?

House and Mitchell propose that if followers are performing highly structured tasks, the most effective leader behavior style is one that is high on supportive (relationship) behavior and low on structuring (task) behavior. This proposition is based on the assumption that highly structured tasks are inherently less satisfying and a source of frustration and stress for followers. Leaders should help reduce the frustration and mitigate the dissatisfying nature of highly structured tasks by using relationship behavior. Further, it is assumed that if followers' tasks are highly structured, the required activities are clear to followers and leader task behavior (providing direction and instruction) is not needed.

If followers are performing relatively unstructured tasks, the Path-Goal Theory proposes that a leadership style high on task behavior and low on relationship behavior will be most effective. It is assumed that required activities and performance expectations are

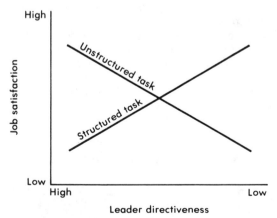

FIGURE 5-3
Path-Goal Theory (House and Mitchell): Hypothetical relationship between directive leadership and job follower satisfaction with task structure as a contingency factor

Source: R. J. House and T. R. Mitchell, "Path-Goal Theory of Leadership," Journal of Contemporary Business, Autumn 1974, p. 86.

unclear and leader task behavior is needed to provide direction and role structuring. Unstructured tasks, however, are assumed to be more challenging, more intrinsically satisfying, and less frustrating and stressful. Under these conditions, leader relationship behavior is not needed.[17]

STINSON–JOHNSON MODEL

Research by John E. Stinson and Thomas W. Johnson[18] has suggested that the relationship between leader behavior and task structure is somewhat more complex than was proposed by House. Stinson and Johnson found that although leader relationship behavior is more important if followers are performing highly structured tasks, the amount of task behavior the leader should use depends on the nature of the followers as well as the type of task the followers are performing.

Specifically, they propose that high leader task behavior is most effective if:

1. Followers' tasks are highly structured *and* followers have strong needs for achievement and independence and a high level of education and/or experience (that is, followers are overqualified for the job).
2. Followers' tasks are unstructured *and* followers have weak needs for achievement and independence and a low level of task relevant education and/or experience (that is, followers are underqualified for the job).

Low task behavior by the leader is most effective if:

1. Followers' tasks are highly structured *and* followers share weak needs for achievement and independence but an adequate level of task-relevant education and/or experience.
2. Followers' tasks are unstructured *and* followers have strong needs for achievement and independence and a high level of education and/or experience.

Figure 5-4 shows the high probability leader behavior style for different combinations of task structure and follower capacity. Follower capacity refers to the degree of achievement motivation, need for independence, and task-relevant education and experience.

As Figure 5-4 suggests, a high task–low relationship tends to be an effective leadership style if a manager is supervising an unstructured task being performed by followers with low capacity; high task–

TASK STRUCTURE		
	Low	High
Follower Capacity — High	Low Relationship Low Task	High Task High Relationship
Follower Capacity — Low	High Task Low Relationship	High Relationship Low Task

FIGURE 5-4 Stinson and Johnson's model of the relationship between leadership style and different combinations of task structure and follower capacity

high relationship style seems to be appropriate for high-capacity followers performing a structured task; high relationship–low task behavior tends to be effective with low-capacity followers performing a highly structured task; and finally, low relationship–low task behavior seems appropriate for high capacity followers performing an unstructured task.

The Stinson and Johnson model provides further evidence that follower characteristics—in this example, their needs for achievement and independence and their relevant education and/or experience—effect the most desirable leadership style.

VROOM–YETTEN CONTINGENCY MODEL

The Contingency Model developed by Victor Vroom and Phillip Yetten is based on a model commonly used by researchers who take a contingency approach to leadership. This model, shown in Figure 5-5[19] is based on the assumption that situational variables interacting with personal attributes or characteristics of the leader result in leader behavior that can affect organizational effectiveness. This change in the organization—because the organization is part of the situation—can, in turn, affect the next leadership intervention.

Because Figure 5-5 blends several of the ideas we have and will be considering in our discussion of leadership, it is important that we pause to look at it in some detail. Figure 5-5 assumes that situational variables [1] such as followers, time, and job demands interacting with personal attributes [2] of the leader such as experience and/or communication skills result in leader behavior [3] such as a directive style of leadership to influence organizational effectiveness [4] which is also influenced by other situational variables [1a] outside the control of the

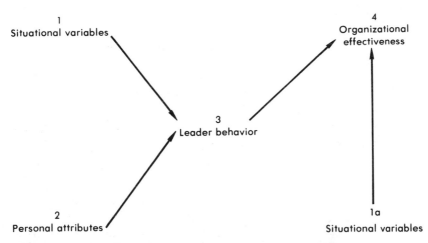

1
Situational variables

4
Organizational
effectiveness

3
Leader behavior

2
Personal attributes

1a
Situational variables

**FIGURE 5-5   Schematic representation of important variables used in leadership
research**

leader; for example, world economic conditions, actions of competitors,
government legislation. We will look in greater detail at situational
variables in a subsequent chapter. Before we leave Figure 5-5, you
will note that it draws upon not only the situational approach to
leadership, but also upon some of the personal attributes cited in the
trait approach that we considered earlier.

How does the Vroom–Yetten Contingency Model Work? Assume
that you have decided to let your group participate in making a
decision. You can use Figure 5-6 (Vroom–Yetten Decision Model), as a
guide, by asking questions A through F in sequence. Table 5-1, Types
of Managerial Decision Styles in the Vroom–Yetten Model, describes
the five different types of decision styles possible in this model. Let's
try an example.

As we suggested in discussing Figure 5-5, the manager should
first diagnose the situational variable. Table 5-2, Problem Attributes
Used in the Vroom–Yetten Model, is very useful for this purpose and
has been found to have a high success rate in improving decision
quality. After asking these seven questions, the manager should refer
to Figure 5-6 and work through this decision tree from left to right
asking the questions. When the response indicates a type of decision,
for example AI, then the manager should turn to Table 5-1 for a
description of the appropriate decision style.

This model is a contingency model because the leader's possible
behaviors are contingent upon the interaction between the questions
and the leader's assessment of the situation in developing a response
to the questions. Perhaps you recognized that the questions used the

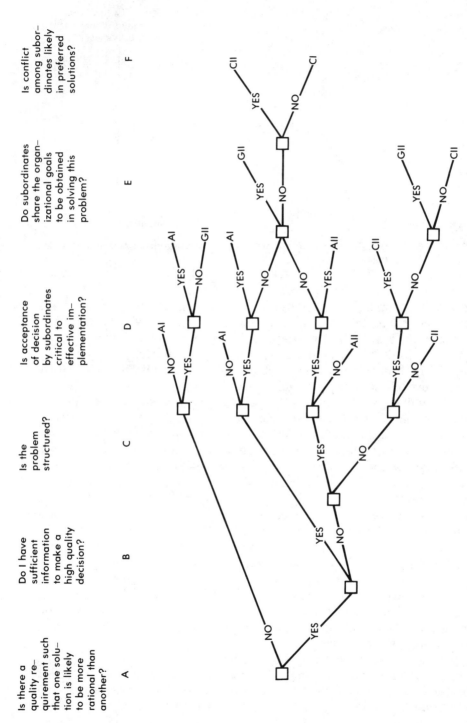

FIGURE 5-6   Vroom–Yetten decision model

Source: Victor H. Vroom, Journal of Contemporary Business, Autumn 1974.

TABLE 5-1 Types of Managerial Decision Styles in the Vroom–Yetten Model

AI You solve the problem or make the decision yourself, using information available to you at the time.

AII You obtain the necessary information from your [follower(s)], then decide on the solution to the problem yourself. You may or may not tell your [followers] what the problem is in getting information from them. The role played by your [followers] in making the decision is clearly one of providing the necessary information to you, rather than generating or evaluating alternative solutions.

CI You share the problem with relevant [followers] individually, getting their ideas and suggestions without bringing them together as a group. Then *you* make the decision that may or may not reflect your [followers'] influence.

CII You share the problem with your [followers] as a group, collectively obtaining their ideas and suggestions. Then *you* make the decision that may or may not reflect your [followers'] influence.

GII You share a problem with your [followers] as a group. Together you generate and evaluate alternatives and attempt to reach agreement (consensus) on a solution. Your role is much like that of chairman. You do not try to influence the group to adopt "your" solution and you are willing to accept and implement any solution that has the support of the entire group.

Source: Victor H. Vroom, *Journal of Contemporary Business,* Autumn 1974.

TABLE 5-2 Problem Attributes Used in the Vroom–Yetten Model

PROBLEMS ATTRIBUTES	DIAGNOSTIC QUESTIONS
A. The importance of the quality of the decision.	Is there a quality requirement such that one solution is likely to be more rational than another?
B. The extent to which the leader possesses sufficient information/expertise to make a high-quality decision.	Do I have sufficient information to make a high-quality decision?
C. The extent to which the problem is structured.	Is the problem structured?
D. The extent to which acceptance or commitment on the part of [followers] is critical to the effective implementation of the decision.	Is acceptance of the decision by [followers] critical to effective implementation?
E. The prior probability that the leader's autocratic decision will receive acceptance by subordinates.	If I were to make the decision by myself, it is reasonably certain that it would be accepted by my [followers]?
F. The extent to which [followers] are motivated to attain the organizational goals as represented in the objectives explicit in the statement of the problem?	Do [followers] share the organizational goals to be obtained in solving the problem
G. The extent to which [followers] are likely to be in conflict over preferred solutions.	Is conflict among [followers] likely in preferred solutions?

Source: Victor H. Vroom, *Journal of Contemporary Business,* Autumn 1974.

quality and acceptance aspects of decision making popularized by Norman R. R. Maier. The first three questions concern the quality or technical accuracy of the decision, and the last four concern the acceptance of the decision by the group members. The questions are designed to eliminate alternatives that would jeopardize the quality or the acceptance of the decision, as appropriate.

The Vroom–Yetten approach is important for several reasons. One is that it is widely respected among researchers in leadership behavior. Another reason is that the authors believe that leaders have the ability to vary their styles to fit the situation. This point is critical to acceptance of situational approaches to leadership. A third reason is that they believe that people can be developed into more effective leaders.

HERSEY–BLANCHARD TRI-DIMENSIONAL LEADER EFFECTIVENESS MODEL

In the leadership models developed by Paul Hersey and Kenneth H. Blanchard in their research efforts, the terms *task behavior* and *relationship behavior* are used to describe concepts similar to Initiating Structure and Consideration of the Ohio State studies. The four basic leader behavior quadrants are labeled: high task and low relationship; high task and high relationship; high relationship and low task; and low relationship and low task (see Figure 5-7)

These four basic styles depict essentially different leadership styles. The *leadership style* of an individual is the behavior pattern

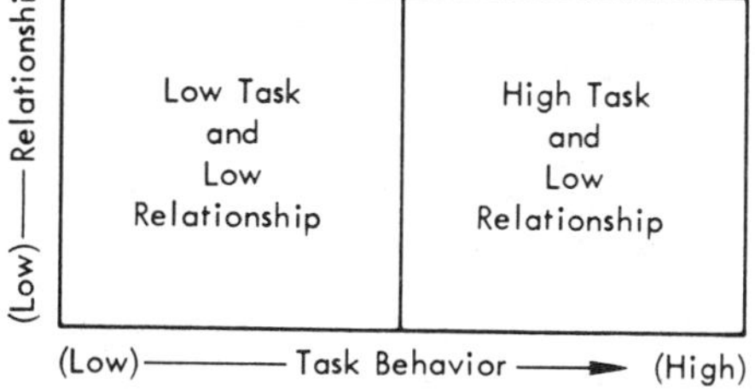

FIGURE 5-7
A two-dimensional model: Basic leader behavior styles suggested by Hersey–Blanchard

that a person exhibits when attempting to influence the activities of others as perceived by those others. This may be very different from the leader's perception of leadership behavior, which we shall define as *self-perception;* rather than style. A person's leadership style involves some combination of task behavior and relationship behavior. The two types of behavior—task and relationship—which are central to the concept of leadership style, are defined as follows:

> *Task behavior*—The extent to which leaders are likely to organize and define the roles of the members of their group (followers); to explain what activities each is to do and when, where, and how tasks are to be accomplished; characterized by endeavoring to establish well-defined patterns of organization, channels of communication, and ways of getting jobs accomplished.
>
> *Relationship behavior*—The extent to which leaders are likely to maintain personal relationships between themselves and members of their group (followers) by opening up channels of communication, providing socioemotional support, "psychological strokes," and facilitating behaviors.[20]

Effectiveness Dimension

Recognizing that the effectiveness of leaders depends on how their leadership style interrelates with the situation in which they operate, an effectiveness dimension should be added to the two-dimensional model. This is illustrated in Figure 5-8.

In his 3-D Management Style Theory, William J. Reddin was the first to add an effectiveness dimension to the task concern and rela-

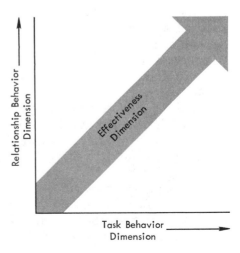

FIGURE 5-8
Adding an effectiveness dimension to the Hersey–Blanchard dimensions of task and relationship

tionship concern dimensions of earlier attitudinal models such as the Managerial Grid.[21] Reddin, whose pioneer work influenced us greatly in the development of our Tri-Dimensional Leader Effectiveness Model presented in this book, felt that a useful theoretical model "must allow that a variety of styles may be effective or ineffective depending on the situation."[22]

By adding an effectiveness dimension to the task behavior and relationship behavior dimensions of the earlier Ohio State leadership model, we are attempting in the Tri-Dimensional Leader Effectiveness Model to integrate the concepts of leader style with situational demands of a specific environment. When the style of a leader is appropriate to a given situation, it is termed *effective*; when the style is inappropriate to a given situation, it is termed *ineffective*.

If the effectiveness of a leader behavior style depends on the situation in which it is used, it follows that any of the basic styles may be effective or ineffective, depending on the situation. The difference between the effective and ineffective styles is often not the actual behavior of the leader, but the appropriateness of this behavior to the environment in which it is used. In reality, the third dimension is the environment. It is the interaction of the basic style with the environment that results in a degree of effectiveness or ineffectiveness. We call the third dimension *effectiveness* because in most organizational settings various performance criteria are used to measure the degree of effectiveness or ineffectiveness of a manager or leader. But the authors feel it is important to keep in mind that the third dimension is the environment in which the leader is operating. One might think of the leader's basic style as a particular stimulus, and it is the response to this stimulus that can be considered effective or ineffective. This is an important point because theorists and practitioners who argue that there is one best style of leadership are making value judgments about the stimulus, while those taking a situational approach to leadership are evaluating the response or the results rather than the stimulus. This concept is illustrated in the diagram of the Hersey–Blanchard Tri-Dimensional Leader Effectiveness Model presented in Figure 5-9.

Although effectiveness appears to be an either/or situation in this model, in reality it should be represented as a continuum. Any given style in a particular situation could fall somewhere on this continuum, from extremely effective to extremely ineffective. Effectiveness, therefore, is a matter of degree, and there could be an infinite number of two-dimensional models on the effectiveness dimension rather than only three. To illustrate this fact, the effectiveness dimension has been divided into quartiles, ranging on the effective side from +1 to +4 and on the ineffective side from −1 to −4.

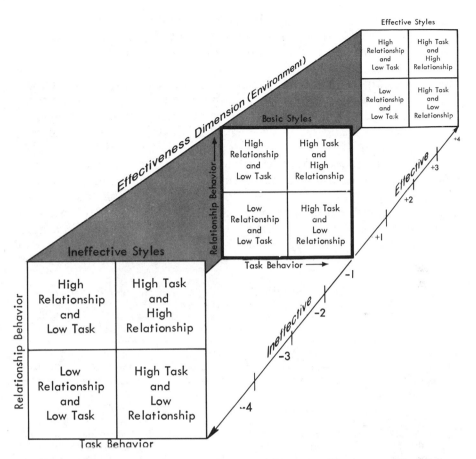

FIGURE 5-9 **Hersey–Blanchard Tri-Dimensional Leader Effectiveness Model**

Let's use an example to illustrate this model. A department head has been given an important promotion from one department to another, much larger department. What will be her high probability primary leadership style? Most likely it will be the one that earned her the valued promotion–in this case, a high relationship–low task style. Will this style be effective in the new situation? It could be extremely effective (upper-right, two-dimensional model) or extremely ineffective (lower-left, two-dimensional model) or somewhere in between (middle, two-dimensional model). The effectiveness of a given leadership style will be contingent or will depend upon its relevance to the situation.

The four effective, the four neutral, and the four ineffective styles are, in essence, how appropriate a leader's basic style is to a given situation as seen by the leader's followers, superiors, or associates. Table 5-3 describes briefly one of many different ways each style might be perceived as effective or ineffective by others.[23]

A model such as the Tri-Dimensional Leader Effectiveness Model is distinctive because it does not depict a single ideal leader behavior style that is suggested as being appropriate in all situations. For example, the high task and high relationship style is appropriate only in certain situations. In basically crisis-oriented organizations, such as the military or the fire department, there is considerable evidence that the most appropriate style would be high task and low relationship, since under combat, fire, or emergency conditions success often depends on immediate response to orders. Time demands do not permit talking things over or explaining decisions. But once the crisis is over, other styles might become appropriate. For example, although the fire chief may have to initiate a high level of structure at

TABLE 5-3 How the Basic Leader Behavior Styles May Be Seen by Others When They Are Effective or Ineffective

BASIC STYLES	EFFECTIVE	INEFFECTIVE
High Task and Low Relationship Behavior	Seen as having well-defined methods for accomplishing goals that are helpful to the followers.	Seen as imposing methods on others; sometimes seen as unpleasant and interested only in short-run output.
High Task and High Relationship Behavior	Seen as satisfying the needs of the group for setting goals and organizing work, but also providing high levels of socioemotional support.	Seen as initiating more structure than is needed by the group and often appears not to be genuine in interpersonal relationships.
High Relationship and Low Task Behavior	Seen as having implicit trust in people and as being primarily concerned with faciltating their goal accomplishment.	Seen as primarily interested in harmony; sometimes seen as unwilling to accomplish a task if it risks disrupting a relationship or losing "good person" image.
Low Relationship and Low Task Behavior	Seen as appropriately delegating to followers decisions about how the work should be done and providing little socioemotional support where little is needed by the group.	Seen as providing little structure or socioemotional support when needed by members of the group.

the scene of a fire, upon returning to the firehouse it may be appropriate for the chief to engage in other styles while the staff is participating in ancillary functions such as maintaining the equipment or studying new firefighting techniques.

Instrumentation

To gather data about the behavior of leaders, the Leader Effectiveness and Adaptability Description (LEAD)[24] instruments were developed for use in training settings. The LEAD-Self contains twelve leadership situations in which respondents are asked to select from four alternative actions—a high task–low relationship behavior, a high task–high relationship behavior, a high relationship–low task behavior, and a low relationship–low task behavior—the style they felt would most closely describe their own behavior in that type of situation. An example of a situation-action combination used in the LEAD-Self is shown in Table 5-4.

The LEAD-Self was designed to measure self-perception of three aspects of leader behavior: (1) style; (2) style range; and (3) style adaptability. Style and style range are determined by four style scores, and the style adaptability (effectiveness score) is determined by one normative score. The LEAD-Self was originally designed as a training instrument and should be properly used only in training situations and not, as some researchers have done, as a research instrument. The length of the scale (twelve items) and time requirement (ten minutes) clearly reflect the intended function.[25]

We have also developed the LEAD-Other to gather leadership-style information in training situations. The LEAD-Self is scored by leaders themselves, but the LEAD-Other is completed by leaders' follower(s), superior(s), or associates (peers). We will discuss both these instruments in more detail in Chapter 12.

TABLE 5-4   Sample Item from Lead-Self Instrument

SITUATION	ALTERNATIVE ACTIONS
Your followers, usually able to take responsibility, are not responding to your recent redefinition of standards.	A. Allow group involvement in redefining standards, but don't push. B. Redefine standards and supervise carefully. C. Avoid confrontation by not applying pressure. D. Incorporate group recommendations, but see that new standards are met.

WHAT ABOUT CONSISTENCY?

What is consistent leadership behavior? Consistent leadership is not using the same leadership style all of the time, but using the style appropriate for the followers' level of readiness in such a way that followers understand *why* they are getting a certain behavior, a certain style from the leader. Inconsistent leadership is using the *same* style in *every* situation. Therefore, if a manager uses a supportive high relationship–low task style with a staff member when that person is performing well and also when that staff member is performing poorly, that manager would be inconsistent, not consistent. Managers are consistent if they direct their followers and even sometimes discipline them when they are performing poorly, but support and reward them when they are performing well. Managers are inconsistent if they smile and respond supportively when their followers are not doing their job as well as when they are.

To be *really* consistent (in our terms) managers must behave the same way in similar situations for all parties concerned. Thus, a consistent manager would not discipline one follower when that person makes a costly mistake, but not another staff member, and vice versa. It is also important for managers to lead their followers the *same way* in *similar circumstances* even when it is *inconvenient—* when they don't have time or when they don't feel like it.

Some managers are consistent only when it is convenient. They may praise and support their people when they feel like it and redirect and supervise their activities when they have time. This leads to problems. Parents are probably the worst in this regard. For example, suppose Wendy and Walt get upset when their children argue with each other and are willing to clamp down on them when it happens. However, there are exceptions to their consistency in this area. If they are rushing off to a dinner party, they will generally not deal with the children's fighting. Or if they are in the supermarket with the kids, they will frequently permit behavior they would normally not allow because they are uncomfortable disciplining the children in public. Since children are continually testing the boundaries or limits of their behavior (they want to know what they can do and cannot do), Walt and Wendy's kids soon learn that they should not fight with each other except when "Mom and Dad are in a hurry to go out or when we're in a store." Thus, unless parents and managers are willing to be consistent even when it is inconvenient, they may actually be encouraging misbehavior.

Another thing that frequently happens is instead of using appropriate leader behavior matched with follower readiness, performance, and demonstrated ability, privileges are based upon chronological age or gender. For example, a parent may permit an irresponsible 17-year-old son to stay out until 2:00 A.M. but not permit a very responsible 15-year-old daughter to stay out until midnight.

ATTITUDE VERSUS BEHAVIOR

One of the ideas behind the old definition of consistency was the belief that your behavior as a manager *must* be consistent with your attitudes. This was a problem with some people who were heavily involved with the human relations or sensitivity-training movement. They believed that if you care about people and have positive assumptions about them, you should also treat them in high relationship ways and seldom in directive or controlling ways.

We feel that much of this problem stemmed from the failure of some theorists and practitioners to distinguish between an attitudinal model and a behavioral model. For example, in examining the dimensions of the Managerial Grid (concern for production and concern for people) and Reddin's 3-D Management Style Theory (task orientation and relationship orientation), one can see that these appear to be *attitudinal* dimensions. Concern or orientation is a feeling or an emotion toward something. The same can be said about McGregor's Theory X and Theory Y assumptions about human nature. Theory X describes negative feelings about the nature of people, and Theory Y describes positive feelings. These are all models that describe attitudes and feelings.

On the other hand, the dimensions of the Hersey–Blanchard Tri-Dimensional Leader Effectiveness model (task behavior and relationship behavior) are dimensions of *observed* behavior. Thus, the Tri-Dimensional Leader Effectiveness model describes *how* people behave, while the Managerial Grid, the 3-D Management Style Theory, and Theory X–Theory Y describe *attitudes* or *predispositions* toward production and people.[26]

Although attitudinal models and the Tri-Dimensional Leader Effectiveness model examine different aspects of leadership, they are not incompatible. A conflict develops only when behavioral assumptions are drawn from analysis of the attitudinal dimension of models such as the Managerial Grid and theories such as Theory X–Theory Y. First of all, it is very difficult to predict behavior from attitudes and values. In fact, it has been found that you can actually do better the other way around. You can do a much better job of predicting values or attitudes from behavior. If you want to know what's in a person's heart, look at what that person does. Look at the person's behavior.

For example, assume that a person has a very high concern for conditions in the ghetto—for poverty. Does that tell you what that person's going to do about it? No. You may have one person who has a high concern for conditions in the ghetto and poverty who engages in the following behavior: "Don't even talk to me about it. I don't want to go on that side of town." In other words, the person engages in avoidance or withdrawal behavior (low relationship behavior and low task behavior). You may have another person who has a very high concern for conditions in the ghetto and poverty, who goes down into the ghetto and begins to tell people what to do, how to do it, when to do it, and where to do it (high task behavior and low relationship behavior). You may have another person who has high concern for conditions in the ghetto and poverty who would go down to the ghetto areas saying, "Gee, I'm sorry you have problems. Do you want to talk to me about it? Let's discuss it. Gosh, I'm sympathetic" (high relationship behavior and low task behavior). Finally, you might get someone else who has a high concern for conditions in the ghetto and poverty who would try to provide high amounts of both task behavior and relationship behavior.

What we're suggesting is that the same value set can evoke a variety of behaviors. You cannot easily predict behaviors from values. A look at one of the simplest models in the behavioral sciences may help to emphasize our point of view. The model is the S–O–R (a stimulus directed toward an organism produces some response). The trap that many of the humanistic trainers fall into is to suggest that we assess the effectiveness of management by looking at the stimulus, or the leadership style. In other words, they say there are good styles and bad styles. What we are saying is that if you are going to assess performance, you don't evaluate the stimulus, you assess the results— the response. It's here that we need to make assessments in terms of performance. This is exactly what we suggest. There is no best leadership style, or stimulus. Any leadership style can be effective or ineffective depending on the response that style gets in a particular situation. We also have to look at the impact the leaders have on the human resources. It's not enough to have a tremendous amount of productivity for the next six months and then have your people get upset and leave and join your competitors in other organizations. You've also got to be concerned about what impact you are having on the human resources, on developing their competency and their commitment. So when we talk about response, or results, we're talking about output and impact on the human resources.

There is another reason to be careful about making behavioral assumptions from attitudinal measures. Although high *concern* for both production and people (9-9 attitude) and positive Theory Y assumptions about human nature are basic ingredients for effective managers, it may be appropriate for managers to engage in a variety of behaviors as they face different problems in their environment. Therefore, the high task–high relationship style often associated with the Managerial Grid 9-9 Team style or the participative high relationship–low task behavior that is often argued as consistent with Theory Y may not always be appropriate.

For example, if a manager's employees can take responsibility for themselves, the appropriate style of leadership for working with them may be low task and low relationship. In this case, the manager delegates to those employees the responsibility of planning, organizing, and controlling their own operation. The manager plays a background role, providing socioemotional support only when necessary. In using this style appropriately, the manager would not be "impoverished" (low concern for both people and production). In fact, delegating to competent and confident people is the best way a manager can demonstrate a 9-9 attitude and Theory Y assumptions about human nature. The same is true for using a directive high task–low relationship style. Sometimes the best way you can show your concern for people and production (9-9) is to direct, control and closely supervise their behavior when they are insecure and don't have the skills yet to perform their job.

In summary, empirical studies tend to show that there is no normative (best) style of leadership.[27] Effective leaders adapt their leader behavior to meet the needs of their followers and the particular environment. If their followers are different, they must be treated differently. Therefore, effectiveness depends on the *leader,* the *follower*(s), and other *situational* variables: $E=f(l, f, s)$. Anyone who is interested in success as a leader must give serious thought to these behavioral and environmental considerations.

We have now discussed a number of approaches to the study of leader behavior, concluding with the Hersey–Blanchard Tri-Dimensional Leader Effectiveness model. In Chapter 6 we will discuss the effectiveness dimension in this model.

NOTES

1. Chester A. Schriesheim, James M. Tolliver, and Orlando C. Behling, "Leadership Theory: Some Implications for Managers," *MSU Business Topics,* 22:2 (Summer 1978), pp. 34–40, in William E. Rosenbach and Robert L. Taylor, eds., *Contemporary Issues in Leadership* (Boulder, Colo. Westview Press, 1984), p. 128.
2. Victor Vroom, "Can Leaders Learn to Lead?" *Organizational Dynamics,* 4 (Winter 1976). See also R. Tannenbaum and W. H. Schmidt, "How to Choose a Leadership Pattern," *Harvard Business Review,* July–August 1986, p. 129.
3. These models and theories are frequently cited in management and organizational behavior texts.

4. Robert Tannenbaum and Warren H. Schmidt, "How to Choose a Leadership Pattern," *Harvard Business Review,* May–June 1973. This is an update of their original 1957 article, one of the landmarks in leadership research.

5. *Ibid.*

6. K. Lewin, R. Lippitt and R. White identified *laissez-faire* as a third form of leadership style. See Lewin, Lippitt, and White, "Leader Behavior and Member Reaction in Three 'Social Climates,'" in *Group Dynamics: Research and Theory,* 2nd ed., Dorwin Cartwright and Alvin Zander, eds. (Evanston, Ill.: Row, Peterson, 1960).

7. Tannenbaum and Schmidt, "How to Choose a Leadership Pattern," *Harvard Business Review,* May–June 1973.

8. Warren G. Bennis, "Where Have All The Leaders Gone?" *Technology Review,* 758:9 (March–April 1977), pp. 3–12.

9. Fred E. Fiedler, *A Theory of Leadership Effectiveness* (New York: McGraw-Hill, 1967). See also Fred E. Fiedler and P. M. Bons, "Changes in Organizational Leadership and the Behavior of Relationship- and Task-motivated Leaders," *Administrative Science Quarterly,* 21 (September 1976), pp. 453–473; Fred E. Fiedler and M. M. Chemers, "Improving Leadership Effectiveness," *Personnel Psychology,* 38 (Spring 1985), pp. 220–222; Fred E. Fiedler and M. M. Chemers, *Improving Leadership Effectiveness: The Leader Match Concept* (New York: Wiley, 1984).

10. F. Fiedler, *A Theory of Leadership Effectiveness,* p. 13.

11. See also N. H. Snyder, "Leadership: The Essential Quality for Transforming United States Business," *Advanced Management Journal,* 51 (Spring 1986), pp. 15–18.

12. See Chapter 3.

13. See Chapter 3.

14. R. J. House and T. R. Mitchell, "Path-Goal Theory of Leadership," *Journal of Contemporary Business,* Autumn 1974, p. 81. See also Mark J. Knoll and Charles D. Pringle, "Path-Goal Theory and the Task Design Literature: A Tenuous Linkage," *Akron Business and Economic Review,* 17, No. 4 (Winter 1986), pp. 75–83.

15. House and Mitchell, "Path-Goal Theory of Leadership."

16. *Ibid.*

17. Robert J. House, "A Path-Goal Theory of Leader Effectiveness," *Administrative Science Quarterly,* 16 (1971), pp. 321–38. See also House and G. Dressler, "The Path-Goal Theory of Leadership: Some Post Hoc and a Priori Tests," in J. G. Hunt and L. L. Larson, eds., *Contingency Approaches to Leadership* (Carbondale, Ill.: Southern Illinois University Press, 1974), pp. 29–55.

18. John E. Stinson and Thomas W. Johnson, "The Path-Goal Theory of Leadership: A Partial Test and Suggested Refinement," *Academy of Management Journal,* 18, No. 2 (June 1975), pp. 242–52.

19. Victor H. Vroom and Philip W. Yetten, *Leadership and Decision-Making* (Pittsburgh: University of Pittsburgh Press, 1973), p. 198.

20. Since our model is an outgrowth of the Ohio State Leadership Studies, these definitions have been adapted from their definitions of "Initiating Structure" (task) and "Consideration" (relationship): R. M. Stogdill and Alvin E. Coons, eds., *Leader Behavior: Its Description and Measurement,* Research monograph no. 88 (Columbus: Bureau of Business Research, Ohio State University, 1957), pp. 42–43.

21. William J. Reddin, "The 3-D Management Style Theory," *Training and Development Journal,* April 1967, pp. 8–17; see also *Managerial Effectiveness* (New York: McGraw-Hill, 1970).

22. Reddin, "The 3-D Management Style Theory," p. 13.

23. Parts of this table were adapted from the managerial style descriptions of William J. Reddin, *The 3-D Management Style Theory,* Theory Paper #2—Managerial Styles (Fredericton, N. B., Canada: Social Science Systems, 1967), pp. 5–6.

24. The first publication on the LEAD (formerly known as the Leader Adaptability and Style Inventory [LASI]) appeared as Paul Hersey and Kenneth H. Blanchard, "So You Want to Know Your Leadership Style?" *Training and Development Journal,* February 1974. LEAD instruments are distributed through Center for Leadership Studies, Escondido, Calif.

25. Instrument is available from Center for Leadership Studies, Escondido, Calif.

26. Fiedler in his Contingency Model of Leadership Effectiveness (Fiedler, *A Theory of* *ship Effectiveness*) also tends to make behavioral assumptions from data gathered fr attitudinal measure of leadership style. A leader is asked to evaluate his least preferred worker (LPC) on a series of semantic differential type scales. Leaders are classified as high or low LPC depending on the favorableness with which they rate their LPC.

27. See cited research by Owens, House, Bennis, Kerr, and others.

6

Determining Effectiveness

One of the most important issues facing the applied behavioral sciences is that of human productivity—the quality and quantity of work. Productivity concerns both effectiveness (the attainment of goals) and efficiency (resource costs, including those human resource costs affecting the quality of life).

Our focus in this chapter will be primarily on effectiveness because, as Peter Drucker, a founding father of management theory, has written, "Effectiveness is the foundation of success—efficiency is a minimum condition for survival *after* success has been achieved. Efficiency is concerned with doing things right. Effectiveness is doing the right things."[1]

MANAGEMENT EFFECTIVENESS VERSUS LEADERSHIP EFFECTIVENESS

The most important aspect of the Hersey–Blanchard Tri-Dimensional Leader Effectiveness Model is that it adds *effectiveness* to the task and relationship dimensions of earlier leadership models. For this reason, it seems appropriate to examine closely the concept of effectiveness.

In discussing effectiveness, it is important once again to distinguish between *management* and *leadership*. As we discussed in Chapter 1, leadership is a broader concept than management. Management is thought of as a special kind of leadership in which the accomplishment of organizational goals is paramount. Leadership is simply an attempt to influence, for whatever reason. Influence and leadership may be used interchangeably. It should be noted that not all of your leadership behavior is directed toward accomplishing organizational goals. In fact, many times when you are trying to influence someone else you are not even part of an organization. For example, when you are trying to get some friends to go someplace with you, you are not engaging in management, but you certainly are attempting leadership. If they agree to go, you are an effective leader, but not an effective manager. Even within an organizational setting, managers may attempt to engage in leadership rather than management since they are trying to accomplish personal goals, not organizational ones. For example, a vice-president may have a strong personal goal to become the company president. In attempting to achieve this goal, this executive may not be concerned with organizational goals at all, but only with undermining the plans of the president and other executives who may be contenders for the job. The vice-president may accomplish this personal goal and, in that sense, be a successful leader. However, this individual cannot be considered an effective manager because these actions were probably disruptive to the effective operation of the firm. *Parkinson's Law*[2] suggests a clear example of a person's personal goals being placed before organizational goals. His law states that in bureaucracies, managers often tend to try to build up their own departments by adding unnecessary personnel, more equipment, or expanded facilities. Although this tendency may increase the prestige and importance of these managers, it often leads to "an organizational environment which not only is inefficient but stifling and frustrating to the individuals who must cope with [it]."[3] Thus, in discussing effectiveness, we must recognize the differences between *individual goals, organizational goals, leadership,* and *management.*

SUCCESSFUL LEADERSHIP VERSUS EFFECTIVE LEADERSHIP

If an individual attempts to have some effect on the behavior of another, we call this *attempted* leadership. The response to this leadership attempt can be successful or unsuccessful. Since a basic responsibility of managers in any type of organization is to get work done with and through people, their success is measured by the output or productivity of the group they lead. With this thought in mind, Bernard M. Bass suggests a clear distinction between *successful* and *effective* leadership or management.[4]

Suppose manager A attempts to influence individual B to do a certain job. A's attempt will be considered successful or unsuccessful depending on the extent to which B accomplishes the job. It is not really an either/or situation. A's success could be depicted on a continuum (Figure 6-1) ranging from very successful to very unsuccessful, with gray areas in between that would be difficult to ascertain as either.

Let us assume that A's leadership is successful. In other words, B's response to A's leadership stimulus falls on the successful side of the continuum. This still does not tell the whole story of effectiveness.

If A's leader style is not compatible with the expectations of B, and if B is antagonized and does the job only because of A's position power, then we can say that A has been successful, but not effective. B has responded as A intended because A has control of rewards and punishment—not because B's needs are being accomplished by satisfying the goals of the manager or the organization.

On the other hand, if A's attempted leadership leads to a successful response, and B does the job because it's personally rewarding, then we consider A as having not only position power, but also personal power. B respects A and is willing to cooperate, realizing that A's request is consistent with some personal goals. In fact, B sees these personal goals as being accomplished by this activity. This is what is meant by effective leadership, keeping in mind that effectiveness also appears as a continuum that can range from very effective to very ineffective, as illustrated in Figure 6-2.[5]

Success has to do with how the individual or the group behaves. On the other hand, effectiveness describes the internal state, or predisposition of an individual or a group, and thus is attitudinal in

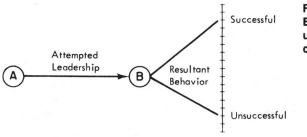

FIGURE 6-1
Bass's successful and unsuccessful leadership continuum

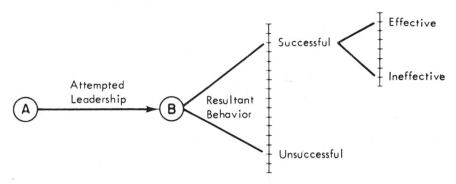

FIGURE 6-2 Bass's successful and effective leadership continuums

nature. If individuals are interested only in success, they tend to emphasize their position power and use close supervision. However, if they are effective, they will also depend on personal power and be characterized by more general supervision. Position power tends to be delegated down through the organization, while personal power is generated upward from below through follower acceptance.

Fred Luthans, a professor of management at the University of Nebraska, conducted a four-year observational study to determine what *successful* managers (those who were rapidly promoted), had in common with *effective* managers (those who had satisfied, committed employees and high-performing departments).[6] The study reported that successful managers spent more of their time and effort networking with others inside and outside the organization. Politicking and socializing occupied most of their time, with less time spent on the traditional activities of managing—planning, decision making, and controlling. In contrast, the effective managers spent most of their time in communication, i.e. exchanging information and paperwork, and in human resource management (Figure 6-3). These activities contributed most to the quality and quantity of their high-performing departments.

Less than 10 percent of the managers in the study sample were found to be in the top third of successful managers as well as the top third of effective managers. These managers were able to achieve a balanced approach in their activities; they networked and got the right job done. The study concluded that more attention needs to be paid to designing systems to reward and support the effective managers, not those with the most successful political and social skills. By rewarding effectiveness, organizations will increase their abilities to compete and excel in rapidly changing market and environmental conditions.

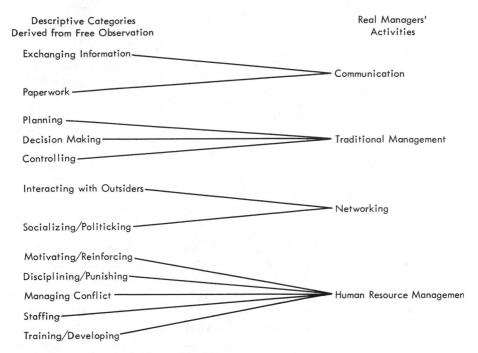

Descriptive Categories
Derived from Free Observation

Real Managers'
Activities

Exchanging Information
Paperwork
Planning
Decision Making
Controlling
Interacting with Outsiders
Socializing/Politicking
Motivating/Reinforcing
Disciplining/Punishing
Managing Conflict
Staffing
Training/Developing

Communication
Traditional Management
Networking
Human Resource Managemen

FIGURE 6-3 The Activities of Real Managers

In the management of organizations, the difference between successful and effective often explains why many supervisors can get a satisfactory level of output only when they are right there looking over a worker's shoulder. But as soon as they leave, output declines and often such things as horseplay and scrap loss increase.

This same phenomenon occurs in organizations which rely on phone conversations with service representatives for order placement. By monitoring incoming calls, the supervisor can rapidly determine if service representatives are answering calls quickly, correctly, and in a friendly fashion. If the representatives perceive the monitoring in a negative fashion and view the supervisor as ineffective, their performance can deteriorate when the monitoring is stopped. A supervisor who uses the monitoring as a tool to assist the representatives in achieving department goals and who rewards positive improvements in call answering and order placement will find that performance stabilizes or improves even when the monitoring is discontinued. The supervisor has used effective leadership to help the representatives meet department and corporate goals.

The phenomenon described applies not only to educational and business organizations, but also to less formal organizations such as the family. If parents are successful and effective, have both position and personal power, their children accept family goals as their own. Consequently, if the husband and wife leave for the weekend, the children behave no differently than if their parents were there. If, however, the parents continually use close supervision and the children view their own goals as being stifled by their parents' goals, the parents have only position power. They maintain order because of the rewards and the punishments they control. If these parents went away on a trip leaving the children behind, upon returning they might be greeted by havoc and chaos.

In summary, managers could be successful, but ineffective, having only a short-lived influence over the behavior of others. On the other hand, if managers are both successful and effective, their influence tends to lead to long-run productivity and organizational development. This really is what leadership and management are all about. In the words of *The Wall Street Journal,* "The first job of the manager is to make the organization perform."[7]

It should be pointed out that this *successful versus effective framework is a way of evaluating the response to a specific behavioral event and not of evaluating performance over time.* Long-term evaluation is not a result of a single leadership event, but a summation of many different leadership events. The evaluation of a leader or an organization over time will be discussed in the following section.

WHAT DETERMINES ORGANIZATIONAL EFFECTIVENESS?

In discussing effectiveness we have concentrated on evaluating the results of individual leaders or managers. These results are significant, but perhaps the most important aspect of effectiveness is its relationship to an entire organization. Here we are concerned not only with the outcome of a given leadership attempt, but with the effectiveness of the organizational unit over a period of time. Rensis Likert identifies three variables—causal, intervening, and end result—which are useful in discussing effectiveness over time.[8]

Causal Variables

Causal variables are those factors that influence the course of developments within an organization and its results or accomplishments. These independent variables can be altered by the organization and its management; they are not beyond the control of the organization, as are general business conditions. Leadership strategies, skills, and behavior; management's decisions; and the policies and structure of the organization are examples of causal variables.

Intervening Variables

Leadership strategies, skills, behavior, and other causal variables affect the human resources or intervening variables in an organization. According to Likert,[9] intervening variables represent the current condition of the internal state of the organization. They are reflected in the commitment to objectives, motivation, and morale of members and their skills in leadership, communications, conflict resolution, decision making, and problem solving.

Output or End-Result Variables

Output or end-result variables are the dependent variables that reflect the achievements of the organization. In evaluating effectiveness, perhaps more than 90 percent of managers in organizations look at measures of output alone. Thus, the effectiveness of managers is often determined by net profits; the effectiveness of college professors may be determined by the number of articles and books they have published; and the effectiveness of basketball coaches may be determined by their win-loss records.

Many researchers talk about effectiveness by emphasizing similar output variables. Fred E. Fiedler, for example, in his studies evaluated "leader effectiveness in terms of group performance on the group's primary assigned task."[10] William J. Reddin, in discussing management styles, thinks in similar terms about effectiveness. He argues that the effectiveness of a manager should be measured "objectively by his profit center performance"—maximum output, market share, or other similar criteria.[11]

We might visualize the relationship between the three classes of variables as stimuli (causal variables) acting upon the organism (intervening variables) and creating certain responses (output variables), as illustrated in Figure 6-4.[12]

The level or condition of the intervening variables is produced largely by the causal variables and in turn has influence upon the end-result variables. Attempts by members of the organization to improve the intervening variables by endeavoring to alter these variables directly will be much less successful usually than efforts directed toward modifying them through altering the causal variables. Similarly, efforts to improve the end-result variables by attempting to modify the intervening variables usually will be less effective than changing the causal variables.

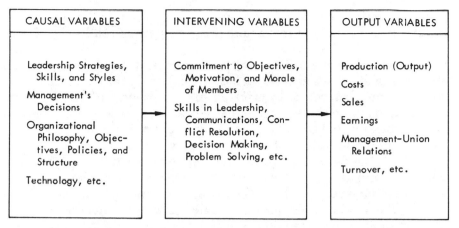

CAUSAL VARIABLES	INTERVENING VARIABLES	OUTPUT VARIABLES
Leadership Strategies, Skills, and Styles Management's Decisions Organizational Philosophy, Objectives, Policies, and Structure Technology, etc.	Commitment to Objectives, Motivation, and Morale of Members Skills in Leadership, Communications, Conflict Resolution, Decision Making, Problem Solving, etc.	Production (Output) Costs Sales Earnings Management–Union Relations Turnover, etc.

FIGURE 6-4 Relationship among Likert's causal, intervening, and output variables

Long-Term Goals versus Short-Term Goals

Intervening variables are concerned with building and developing the organization, and they tend to be long-term goals. This is the part of effectiveness that many managers overlook because it emphasizes long-term potential as well as short-term performance. This oversight is understandable because most managers tend to be promoted on the basis of short-term output variables, such as increased production and earnings, without concern for long-run potential and organizational development. This creates an organizational dilemma.

Organizational Dilemma

One of the major problems in industry today is that there is a shortage of effective managers. Therefore, it is not uncommon for managers to be promoted in six months or a year if they are "producers." Since the basis on which top management promotes is often short-run output, managers attempt to achieve high levels of productivity and often overemphasize tasks, placing extreme pressure on everyone, even when it is inappropriate.

We probably all have had some experience with coming into an office or a home and raising the roof with people. The immediate or short-run effect is probably increased activity. We also know that if this style is inappropriate for those concerned and if it continues over a long period of time, the morale of the organization will deteriorate. Some indications of deterioration of these intervening variables at work may be turnover, absenteeism, increased accidents, scrap loss, and numerous grievances. Not only the number of grievances, but the nature of grievances is important. Are grievances really significant problems or do they reflect pent-up emotions due to anxieties and frustration? Are they settled at the complaint stage between the employee and the manager or are they pushed up the hierarchy to be settled at higher levels or by arbitration? The organizational dilemma is that in many instances, a manager who places pressure on everyone and produces in the short run is promoted out of this situation before the disruptive aspects of the intervening variables catch up.

There tends to be a time lag between declining intervening variables and significant restriction of output by employees under such a management climate. Employees tend to feel things will get better. Thus, when high-pressure managers are promoted rapidly, they often stay "one step ahead of the wolf."

The real problem is faced by the next manager. Although productivity records are high, this manager has inherited many problems. Merely the introduction of a new manager may be enough to collapse the slowly deteriorating intervening variables. A tremendous drop in morale and motivation leading almost immediately to a significant decrease in output can occur. Change by its very nature is frightening; to a group whose intervening variables are declining, it can be devastating. Regardless of this new manager's style, the present expectations of the followers may be so distorted that much time and patience will be needed to close the now apparent "credibility gap" between the goals of the organization and the personal goals of the group. No matter how effective this manager may be in the long run, senior management in reviewing a productivity drop may give the manager only a few months to improve performance. But as Likert's studies indicate, rebuilding a group's intervening variables in a small organization may take one to three years, and in a large organization it may extend to seven years.

This dilemma is not restricted to business organizations. It is very common in school systems where superintendents and other top administrators can get promoted to better, higher paying jobs in other systems if they are innovative and implement a number of new programs in their systems. One such superintendent brought a small town national prominence by putting every new and innovative idea being discussed in education into a school. In this process, there was almost no involvement or participation by the teachers, or community administrator(s), in the decision making that went into these programs. After two years, the superintendent, because of these innovations, was promoted to a larger system with a $15,000-a-year raise. A new superintendent was appointed in the "old" system, but almost before the new superintendent unpacked turmoil hit the system with tremendous teacher turnover, a faculty union, and a defeated bond issue. As things became unglued, people were heard saying that they wished the old superintendent were back. And yet, in reality, it was the old superintendent's style that deteriorated the intervening variables and caused the current problems.

Most people tend to evaluate coaches on win-and-loss records. Let's look at an example. Charlie, a high school coach, has had several good seasons. He knows if he has one more good season he will have a job offer with a better salary at a more prestigious school. Under these conditions, he may decide to concentrate on the short-run potential of the team. He may play only his seniors and he may have an impressive record at the end of the season. Short-run output goals have been maximized, but the intervening variables of the team have been neglected. If Charlie leaves this school and accepts another job, a new coach will find himself with a tremendous rebuilding job. But because developing the freshmen and sophomores and rebuilding a good team take time and much work, the team could have a few poor seasons in the interim. When the alumni and fans see the team losing, they soon forget that old adage "It's not whether you win or lose, it's how you play the game." They immediately consider the new coach a bum. After all, "We had some great seasons with good old Charlie." They don't realize that the previous coach concentrated only on short-run winning at the expense of building for the future. The problem is that the effectiveness of a new coach is judged immediately on the same games-won basis as his predecessor. The new coach may be doing an excellent job of rebuilding and may have a winning season in two or three years, but the probability of the coach being given the opportunity to build a future winner is low.

Problems don't occur just when leaders concentrate on output. For example, in the classic World War II movie about the Air Force, *Twelve O'Clock High,* Frank Savage (played by Gregory Peck) is asked suddenly to take over a bomber group from a commanding officer whom everyone loves and respects. However, his overidentification with his men and concern about his human resources have resulted in an outfit that is not producing and is hurting the war effort.[13]

Thus, it should be clear that we do not think this is an either/or process. It is often a matter of determining how much to concentrate on each—output and intervening variables. Let's look at a basketball example. Suppose a women's team has good potential, with a large number of experienced senior players, but as the season progresses it does not look as if it is going to be an extremely good year. There comes a point in this season when the coach must make a basic decision. Will she continue to play her experienced seniors and hope to win a majority of her final games, or should she forget about concentrating on winning the last games and play her sophomores and juniors to give them experience, in hopes of developing and building a winning team for future years? The choice is between short- and long-term goals. If the accepted goal is building the team for the future, then the coach should be evaluated on these terms and not entirely on the season's win-loss record. The art of achieving a balance is essential to effective leadership.

Although intervening variables do not appear on win-loss records, balance sheets, sales reports, or accounting ledgers, we feel that these long-term considerations are just as important to an organization as short-term output variables. Therefore, although difficult to measure, intervening variables should not be overlooked in determining organizational effectiveness. One of the instruments used by Likert to measure these variables was discussed in Chapter 4.

In summary, we feel that effectiveness is actually determined by whatever the manager and the organization decide are their goals and objectives, but they should remember that *effectiveness is a function of*:

1. Output variables (productivity/performance).
2. Intervening variables (the condition of the human resources).
3. Short-range goals.
4. Long-range goals.

FORCE FIELD ANALYSIS

Kurt Lewin

Force field analysis, a technique developed by Kurt Lewin for diagnosing situations, may be useful in looking at the variables involved in determining effectiveness.[14]

Lewin assumes that in any situation there are both driving and restraining forces that influence any change that may occur. *Driving forces* are those forces affecting a situation that are pushing in a particular direction; they tend to initiate a change and keep it going. In terms of improving productivity in a work group, encouragement from a supervisor, incentive earnings, and competition may be examples of driving forces. *Restraining forces* are forces acting to restrain or decrease the driving forces. Apathy, hostility, and poor maintenance of equipment may be examples of restraining forces against increased production. Equilibrium is reached when the sum of the driving forces equals the sum of the restraining forces. In our example, equilibrium represents the present level of productivity, as shown in Figure 6-5.[15]

This equilibrium, or present level of productivity, can be raised or lowered by changes in the relationship between the driving and the restraining forces. For illustration, let us look again at the dilemma of the new manager who takes over a work group in which productivity is high, but whose predecessor drained the human resources (intervening variables). The former manager had upset the equilibrium by increasing the driving forces (that is, being autocratic and keeping continual pressure on workers) and thus achieving increases in output in the short run. By doing this, however, new restraining forces developed, such as increased hostility and antagonism; and at the time of the former manager's departure, the restraining forces were beginning to increase and the results manifested themselves in turnover, absenteeism, and other restraining forces, which lowered productivity shortly after the new manager arrived. Now a new equilibrium at a significantly lower productivity is faced by the new manager.

Now just assume that our new manager decides not to increase the driving forces, but to reduce the restraining forces. The manager may do this by taking time away from the usual production operation and engaging in problem solving and in training and development. In the short run, output will tend to be lowered still further. However, if commitment to objectives and technical know-how of the group are increased in the long run, they may become new driving forces, and, along with the elimination of the hostility and apathy that were

FIGURE 6-5 Driving and restraining forces in equilibrium

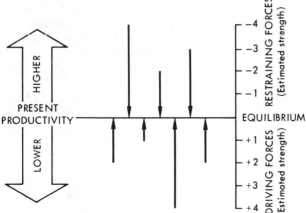

restraining forces, will now tend to move the balance to a higher level of output.

Managers are often in a position in which they must consider not only output, but also intervening variables, not only short-term, but also long-term goals in diagnosing these interrelationships. Force field analysis is a useful framework for this.

INTEGRATION OF GOALS AND EFFECTIVENESS

The extent that individuals and groups perceive their own goals as being satisfied by the accomplishment of organizational goals is the degree of integration of goals. When organizational goals are shared by all, this is what McGregor calls a true "integration of goals."[16]

To illustrate this concept, we can divide an organization into two groups, management and employees. The respective goals of these two groups and the resultant attainment of the goals of the organization to which they belong are illustrated in Figure 6-6.[17]

In this instance, the goals of management are somewhat compatible with the goals of the organization, but are not exactly the same. On the other hand, the goals of the employees are almost at odds with those of the organization. The result of the interaction between the goals of management and the goals of employees is a compromise, and actual performance is a combination of both. It is at this approximate point that the degree of attainment of the goals of the organization can be pictured. This situation can be much worse when there is little accomplishment of organizational goals, as illustrated in Figure 6-7.

FIGURE 6-6
Directions of goals of management, employees, and the organization—
moderate **organizational accomplishment**

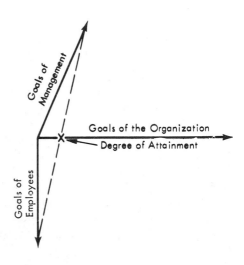

FIGURE 6-7
Little organizational accomplishment

In this situation, there seems to be a general disregard for the welfare of the organization. Both managers and workers see their own goals conflicting with those of the organization. Consequently, both morale and performance will tend to be low and organizational accomplishment will be negligible. In some cases, the organizational goals can be so opposed that no positive progress is obtained.

The result often is substantial losses, or draining off of assets (see Figure 6-8). In fact, organizations are going out of business every day for these very reasons.

The hope in an organization is to create a climate in which one of two things occurs. The individuals in the organization (both managers and employees) either perceive their goals as being the same as the goals of the organization or, although different, see their own goals being satisfied as a direct result of working for the goals of the organization. Consequently, the closer we can get the individual's

FIGURE 6-8
No positive organizational accomplishment

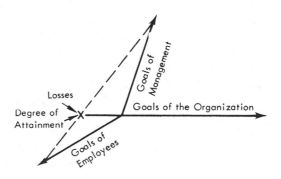

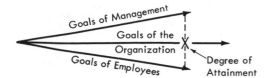

FIGURE 6-9
An integration of the goals of management, subordinates, and the organization—*high* organizational accomplishment

goals and objectives to the organization's goals, the greater will be the organizational performance, as illustrated in Figure 6-9.

One of the ways in which effective leaders bridge the gap between the individual's and the organization's goals is by creating a loyalty to themselves among their followers. They do this by being an influential spokesperson for their followers with higher management.[18] These leaders have little difficulty communicating organizational goals to followers, and these followers find it easy to associate the acceptance of these goals with accomplishment of their own need satisfaction.

PARTICIPATION AND EFFECTIVENESS

In an organizational setting, it is urged that the criteria for an individual's or a group's performance should be mutually decided in advance. In making these decisions, managers and their employees should consider output and intervening variables, short- and long-range goals. This process has two advantages. First, it will permit employees to participate in determining the basis on which their efforts will be judged. Second, involving employees in the planning process will increase their commitment to the goals and objectives established. Research evidence seems to support this contention.

One of the classic studies in this area was done by Coch and French in an American factory.[19] They found that when managers and employees discussed proposed technological changes, productivity increased and resistance to change decreased when these procedures were initiated. Other studies have shown similar results.[20] These studies suggest that involving employees in decision making tends to be effective in our society. Once again, we must remember that the success of using participative management depends on the situation. Although this approach tends to be effective in some industrial settings in America, it may not be appropriate in other cultures.

This argument was illustrated clearly when French, Israel, and As attempted to replicate the original Coch and French experiment in a Norwegian factory.[21] In this setting, they found no significant difference in productivity between work groups in which participative management was used and those in which it was *not* used. In other words, increased participation in decision making did not have the same positive influence on factory workers in Norway as it did in America. Similar to Hersey's replication of one of Likert's studies in Nigeria, this Norwegian study suggests that cultural differences in the followers and the situation may be important in determining the appropriate leadership style.

Management by Objectives

We realize that it is not an easy task to integrate the goals and objectives of all individuals with the goals of the organization. Yet it is not an impossible task. A participative approach to this problem, which has been used successfully in some organizations in our culture, is a process called *Management by Objectives* (MBO). The concepts behind MBO were introduced by Peter Drucker[22] in the early 1950s and have become popularized throughout the world, particularly through the efforts of George Odiorne[23] and John Humble.[24] Through their work and the efforts of others,[25] managers in all kinds of organizational settings, whether they be industrial, educational, governmental, or military, are attempting to run their organizations with the MBO process as a basic underlying management concept.

Management by objectives is basically:

A process whereby the senior and the junior managers of an enterprise jointly identify its common goals, define each individual's major areas of responsibility in terms of the results expected of him, and use these measures as guides for operating the unit and assessing the contribution of each of its members.[26]

This process in some cases has been successfully carried beyond the managerial level to include hourly employees. The concept rests on a philosophy of management that emphasizes an integration between external control (by managers) and self-control (by employees). It can apply to any manager or individual no matter what level or function, and to any organization, regardless of size.

The smooth functioning of this system is an agreement between a manager and an employee about that employee's own or group performance goals during a stated time period. These goals can emphasize either output variables or intervening variables or some combination of both. The important thing is that goals are jointly established and agreed upon in advance. This is then followed by a review of performance in relation to accepted goals at the end of the time period. Both the employee and the manager participate in this review and in any other evaluation that takes place. It has been found that objectives that are formulated with each person participating seem to gain more acceptance than those imposed by an authority figure in the organization. Consultation and participation in this area tend to establish personal risk for the attainment of the formulated objective by those who actually perform the task.

Prior to setting individual objectives, the common goals of the entire organization should be clarified, and, at this time, any appropriate changes in the organizational structure should be made: changes in titles, duties, relationships, authority, responsibility, span of control, and so forth.

Throughout the time period, what is to be accomplished by the entire organization should be compared with what is actually being accomplished; necessary adjustments should be made and inappropriate goals discarded. At the end of the time period, a final mutual review of objectives and performance takes place. If there is a discrepancy between the two, efforts are initiated to determine what steps can be taken to overcome these problems. This sets the stage for the determination of objectives for the next time period.

The entire cycle of management by objectives is represented graphically in Figure 6-10.[27]

Many companies have found MBO to be a useful adjunct to achieving corporate effectiveness, but years of use have highlighted some of its shortcomings. Employees may react to the implementation of an MBO program with distrust and skepticism; they may question why managers are interested in their input after years of giving orders.

After implementation, the MBO system can generate excessive documentation and paperwork for participants. Goals of improved communication and planning can be lost in the shuffle of papers. Related to this is the problem of overemphasizing the grading and evaluating of employee performance in achieving MBO goals. MBO needs to focus on helping employees assist each other in improved performance.

Another problem of the MBO system can develop when managers set meaningless or easily achieved goals. Goals must be carefully monitored with an eye on overall corporate goals and objectives. Problems can also develop when the feedback process is slow and managers are unable to change or adapt their goals to meet rapidly changing conditions.

Management by objectives may become a powerful tool in gaining mutual commitment and high productivity for an organization in which management realizes this type of involvement of employees is appropriate for its situation. However, the system must be developed, implemented, and managed with an understanding of the problems it can generate.

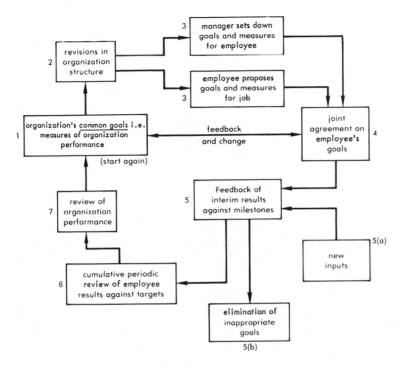

FIGURE 6-10 The cycle of management by objectives

STYLE AND EFFECTIVENESS

Examples of research that supports the argument that all of the basic leader behavior styles may be effective or ineffective depending on the situation are readily available.

A. K. Korman gathered some of the most convincing evidence that dispels the idea of a single best style of leader behavior.[28] Korman attempted to review all studies that examined the relationships between the Ohio State behavior dimensions of Initiating Structure (task) and Consideration (relationship) and various measures of effectiveness, including group productivity, salary, performance under stress, administrative reputation, work group grievances, absenteeism, and turnover. In all, more than twenty-five studies were reviewed. In every case the two dimensions were measured by either the Leadership Opinion Questionnaire or the Leader Behavior Description Questionnaire. The former is used to assess how leaders think they should behave in a given situation; the latter measures follower perceptions of leader behavior. Korman concluded that:

> Despite the fact that "Consideration" and "Initiating Structure" have become almost bywords in American industrial psychology, it seems

apparent that very little is now known as to how these variables may predict work group performance and the conditions which affect such predictions. At the current time, we cannot even say whether they have any predictive significance at all.[29]

Thus, Korman found that Consideration and Initiating Structure had no significant predictive value in terms of effectiveness. This suggests that since situations differ, so must leader style.

Fred Fiedler, in testing his contingency model of leadership in more than fifty studies covering a span of sixteen years (1951–1967), concluded that both directive, task-oriented leaders and nondirective, human relations–oriented leaders are effective under some conditions. As Fiedler argues:

> While one can never say that something is impossible, and while someone may well discover the all-purpose leadership style or behavior at some future time, our own data and those which have come out of sound research by other investigators do not promise such miraculous cures.[30]

A number of other investigators besides Korman and Fiedler have also shown that *different leadership situations require different leader styles.*[31] In summary, the evidence is clear that there is no single all-purpose leader behavior style that is effective in all situations.

While our basic conclusion in this chapter is that the type of leader behavior needed depends on the situation, this conclusion leaves many questions unanswered for a specific individual in a leadership role. Such individuals may be personally interested in how leadership depends on the situation and how they can find some practical value in theory. To accommodate this type of concern, in Chapter 7 we will discuss the environmental variables that may help a leader or a manager to make effective decisions in problematic leadership situations.

NOTES

1. Peter F. Drucker, *Management: Tasks, Responsibilities, Practices* (New York: Harper & Row, Pub., 1973), p. 45.
2. C. Northcote Parkinson, *Parkinson's Law* (Boston: Houghton Mifflin, 1957).
3. Fred J. Carvell, *Human Relations in Business* (Toronto: Macmillan, 1970), p. 182.
4. Suggested by Bernard M. Bass in *Leadership, Psychology, and Organizational Behavior* (New York: Harper & Brothers, 1960).
5. *Ibid.*
6. Fred Luthans, "Successful vs. Effective Real Managers," The Academy of Management *Executive*, 11, no. 2 (May 1988), pp. 127–32.
7. *Wall Street Journal*, January 9, 1978, p. 12.
8. Rensis Likert, *The Human Organization* (New York: McGraw-Hill, 1967), pp. 26–29.
9. Rensis Likert, *New Patterns of Management* (New York: McGraw-Hill, 1961), p. 2.
10. Fred E. Fiedler, *A Theory of Leadership Effectiveness* (New York: McGraw-Hill, 1967), p. 9.
11. William J. Reddin, "The 3-D Management Style Theory," *Training and Development Journal*, April 1967. This is one of the critical differences between Reddin's 3-D Management

Style Theory and the Tri-Dimensional Leader Effectiveness Model. Reddin in his model seems to consider only output variables in determining effectiveness, while in the Tri-Dimensional Leader Effectiveness Model both intervening variables and output variables are considered.

12. Adapted from Likert, *The Human Organization,* pp. 47–77.

13. This classic film is an excellent illustration of the concepts of motivation, Situational Leadership, and improving organizational performance.

14. Kurt Lewin, "Frontiers in Group Dynamics: Concept, Method, and Reality in Social Science; Social Equilibria and Social Change," *Human Relations,* 1, no. 1 (June 1947), pp. 5–41.

15. *Ibid.*

16. Douglas McGregor, *The Human Side of Enterprise* (New York: McGraw-Hill, 1960). See also McGregor, *Leadership and Motivation* (Boston: MIT Press, 1966).

17. In reality, the schematics presented in the following pages are simplifications of vector analyses and therefore would be more accurately portrayed as parallelograms.

18. Saul W. Gellerman, *Motivation and Productivity* (New York: American Management Association, 1963), p. 265. See also Gellerman, *Management by Motivation* (New York: American Management Association, 1968).

19. L. Coch and J. R. P. French, "Overcoming Resistance to Change," in Dorwin Cartwright and Alvin Zander, eds., *Group Dynamics: Research and Theory,* 2nd ed. (Evanston, Ill.: Row, Peterson, 1960).

20. See Kurt Lewin, "Group Decision and Social Change," In G. Swanson, T. Newcomb, and E. Hartley, eds., *Readings in Social Psychology* (New York: Henry Holt, 1952), pp. 459–73; K. Lewin, R. Lippitt, and R. White, "Leader Behavior and Member Reaction in Three 'Social Climates,'" in Cartwright and Zander, *Group Dynamics: Research and Theory;* and N. Morse and E. Reimer, "The Experimental Change of a Major Organizational Variable," *Journal of Abnormal Social Psychology,* 52 (1956), pp. 120–29.

21. John R. P. French, Jr., Joachim Israel, and Dagfinn Ås, "An Experiment on Participation in a Norwegian Factory," *Human Relations,* 13 (1960), pp. 3–19.

22. Peter F. Drucker, *The Practice of Management* (New York: Harper and Row, 1964).

23. George S. Odiorne, *Management by Objectives: A System of Managerial Leadership* (New York: Pitman Publishing, 1965); Odiorne, *The Human Side of Management* (San Diego, Calif.: University Associates, 1987); Odiorne et al., *Executive Skills: A Management Objectives Approach* (Dubuque, Iowa: Brown, 1980); Odiorne, *MBO II: A System of Managerial Leadership for the 80's* (Belmont, Calif.: Pitman, Learning, 1979); Odiorne, "The Managerial Bait-and-Switch Game," *Personnel,* 63, No. 3 (March 1986), pp. 32–37.

24. John W. Humble, *Management by Objectives* (London: Industrial Education and Research Foundation, 1967); Humble, *Management Objectives in Action* (New York: McGraw-Hill, 1970).

25. See also J. D. Batten, *Beyond Management by Objectives* (New York: American Management Association, 1966); Ernest C. Miller, *Objectives and Standards Approach to Planning and Control,* AMA Research Study '74 (New York: American Management Association, 1966); and William J. Reddin, *Effective Management by Objectives: The 3-D Method of MBO* (New York: McGraw-Hill, 1971).

26. Odiorne, *Management by Objectives,* pp. 55–56.

27. *Ibid.,* p. 78.

28. A. K. Korman, "'Consideration, Initiating Structure,' and Organizational Criteria—A Review," *Personnel Psychology: A Journal of Applied Research,* 19, No. 4 (Winter 1966), pp. 349–61.

29. *Ibid.,* p. 360.

30. Fiedler, *A Theory of Leadership Effectiveness,* p. 247.

31. See C. A. Gibb, "Leadership," in *Handbook of Social Psychology,* Gardner Lindzey, ed. (Cambridge, Mass.: Addison-Wesley, 1964); A. P. Hare, *Handbook of Small Group Research* (New York: Wiley, 1965); and D. C. Pelz, "Leadership within a Hierarchical Organization," *Journal of Social Issues,* 7 (1961), pp. 49–55. See also J. R. Nicholls, "Congruent Leadership," *Leadership and Organization Review Journal,* 7, no. 1 (1986), pp. 27–31; John H. Zenger, "Leadership: Management's Better Half," *Training,* 22, no. 12 (December 1985), pp. 44ff. See also previously cited research by Bennis, Schriesheim, Yukl, Kerr, and many others.

7

Diagnosing the Environment

The situational approach to leadership is built on the concept that effectiveness results from a leader's using a behavioral style that is appropriate to the demands of the environment. The key for managers or leaders is learning to diagnose their environment, the first of the three important leadership competencies. You will recall from Chapter 1 that the remaining two are adapting and communicating.

ENVIRONMENTAL VARIABLES

The environment in an organization consists of the leader, that leader's follower(s), supervisor(s), associates, organization, job demands, and other things like time.[1] This list is not all-inclusive, but it contains some of the interacting components that tend to be important to a leader.[2] As illustrated in Figure 7-1, the environment a leader faces may have some other situational variables that are unique to it, as well as an external environment that has an impact on it.

Except for job demands, each of these environmental variables can be viewed as having two major components—style and expectations. Thus, our list of variables is expanded to include the following:

Leader's style   Leader's expectations
Followers' styles   Followers' expectations
Supervisors' styles   Supervisors' expectations
Associates' styles   Associates' expectations
Organization's style   Organization's expectations
Job demands

Style Defined

As discussed in Chapter 5, the style of leaders is the consistent behavior patterns that they use when they are working with and through other people, as perceived by those people. These patterns emerge in people as they begin to respond in the same fashion under

FIGURE 7-1 Interacting components of an organizational setting

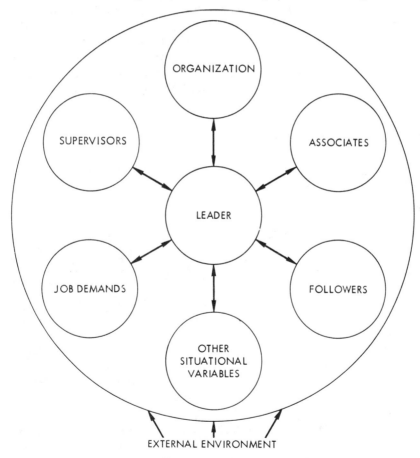

similar conditions; they develop habits of action that become some-what predictable to those who work with them.

Some writers, including the authors of this text, have used style and personality interchangeably. In Chapter 10 we will distinguish between these two terms.

Expectations Defined

Expectations are the perceptions of appropriate behavior for one's own role or position or one's perception of the roles of others within the organization. In other words, the expectations of individuals define for them what they should do under various circumstances in their particular job and how they think others—their supervisors, peers, and followers—should behave in relation to their positions. To say that a person has *shared expectations* with another person means that each of the individuals involved perceives accurately and accepts a personal role and the role of the other. If expectations are to be compatible, it is important to share common goals and objectives. While two individuals may have differing styles because their roles require different styles of behavior, it is imperative for an organization's effectiveness that they perceive and accept the institution's goals and objectives as their own.

The task of diagnosing a leader environment is very complex when we realize that the leader is the pivotal point around which all of the other environmental variables interact, as shown in Figure 7-1. In a sense, all these variables are communicating role expectations to the leader.

STYLE AND EXPECTATIONS

The behavior of managers in an organization, as Jacob W. Getzels suggests, results from the interaction of style and expectations.[3] Some managerial positions or roles are structured greatly by expectations; that is, they allow people occupying that position very little room to express their individual style. The behavior of an army sergeant, for example, may be said to conform almost completely to role expectations. Little innovative behavior is tolerated. In supervising highly structured, routine jobs based on Theory X assumptions about human nature, the behavior required by a manager is almost predetermined, that is, close supervision.

On the other hand, some managerial positions have fewer formal expectations, allowing for more individual latitude in expressing one's style of operating. The behavior of a research and development manager, for example, is derived extensively from that person's style, as innovation and creativity are encouraged. It seems that as a manager moves from supervising an unstructured job to working with people on a more structured job, style tends to play a more important role than expectations.

The difference between these two positions in terms of style and expectations is illustrated in Figure 7-2.[4] For example, style is a larger component of the R&D manager's job than of that of the army sergeant.

While the mix varies from job to job, behavior in an organization remains a function of both style and expectations and involves some combination of task and relationship behaviors.

Leader's Style and Expectations

One of the most important elements of a leadership situation is the style of the leader(s). Leaders develop their style over a period of time from experience, education, and training. Tannenbaum and Schmidt suggest there are at least four internal forces that influence a manager's leadership style: value system, confidence in employees, leadership inclinations, and feelings of security in an uncertain situation.[5]

A manager's value system consists of the answers to such questions as: How strongly does a manager feel that individuals should have a share in making the decisions that affect them or how convinced is the manager that the person who is paid to assume responsibility should personally carry the burden of decision making? The strength of a manager's convictions on questions such as these will tend to affect that manager's leadership style, particularly in terms of the amount of direction or support that manager is willing to provide for staff members.

Confidence in employees is often influenced by the manager's Theory X or Theory Y assumptions about human nature. In other

FIGURE 7-2
Style and expectations as related to two different positions or roles

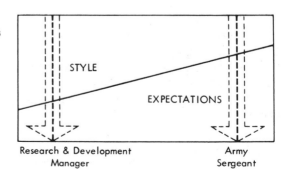

Research & Development
Manager

Army
Sergeant

words, the amount of control or freedom a manager gives to staff members depends on whether that manager believes that people are basically lazy, unreliable, or irresponsible or that people can be creative and self-motivated in an environment if properly motivated. In addition, a manager's confidence in employees also depends on feelings about the knowledge and competence of staff members in a particular area of responsibility.

A manager's own inclinations have an impact on leadership style; thus, some managers are much more comfortable being directive (controlling and supervising). Other managers operate more comfortably in a team management situation in which they are providing some direction and/or facilitating the interactions of team members. Still other managers are at ease in delegating and letting staff members run with the ball on specific problems and issues.

Feelings of security in an uncertain situation have a definite impact on the manager's willingness to release control over decision making to other people in an uncertain environment. What might be involved here is the manager's tolerance for ambiguity.

While it is important to recognize that managers have different leadership styles, it is also important to remember that style is not how leaders *think* they behave in a situation, but how others (most importantly, their followers) perceive their behavior. This is often a difficult concept for leaders to understand. For example, if Jane's followers think that she is a hard-nosed, task-oriented leader, this is very valuable information for her to know. In fact, it makes little difference whether *she* thinks she is a relationship-oriented, democratic leader because her followers will behave according to how *they* perceive her behavior. In this case, the followers will treat Jane as if she were a hard-nosed, task-oriented leader. Thus, leaders have to learn how they are coming across to others. Yet this kind of information is difficult to obtain. People are often reluctant to be honest with one another on this subject, especially in a supervisor-employee relationship.

One method that has been developed to help individuals learn how others perceive their behavior is sensitivity, or T-group, training. This method was developed at Bethel, Maine, in 1947 by Leland P. Bradford, Kenneth D. Benne, and others.[6] It is based on the assumption that a number of individuals meeting in an unstructured situation in an open climate will develop working relations with each other and will learn a great deal about themselves, as perceived by the other group members.

The training process relies primarily and almost exclusively on the behavior experienced by the participants; i.e., the *group itself* becomes the focus of inquiry. . . . In short, the participants learn to analyze and become more sensitive to the processes of human interaction and acquire concepts to order and control these phenomena.[7]

Although the main objective of T-group training was originally personal growth or self-insight, the process has been used extensively to implement organizational improvement or change.[8] It has some critics as well as advocates among organizations that have experimented with these techniques.

A central problem according to some is that sensitivity training is designed to change individuals, not necessarily to change the environment in which they work. When individuals attempt to use what they have learned, they often find their co-workers unwilling to accept it or, even worse, what they have learned may not be appropriate for their back-home situation.

All leaders have expectations about the way they should behave in a certain situation. How they actually behave often depends on these expectations. The resulting behavior, however, is sometimes modified by the impact of how they interpret the expectations of other persons in their environment, such as their supervisor or followers.

Followers' Styles and Expectations

The styles of followers are an important consideration for leaders in appraising their situation. In fact, as Fillmore Sanford has indicated, there is some justification for regarding the followers "as the most crucial factor in any leadership event."[9] Followers in any situation are vital, not only because individually they accept or reject the leader, but because as a group they actually determine whatever personal power that leader will have. If the follower decides not to follow, it really doesn't matter what the other elements in the situation are.

This is important at all levels of management. Victor H. Vroom has uncovered evidence that the effectiveness of a leader is dependent to a great extent on the style of the individual workers.[10]

Place a group with strong independence drives under a supervisor who needs to keep his men under his thumb, and the result is very likely to be trouble. Similarly, if you take docile men who are accustomed to obedience and respect for their supervisors and place them under a supervisor who tries to make them manage their own work, they are likely to wonder uneasily whether he really knows what he is doing.[11]

It has been argued that a leader can permit followers greater freedom if the following essential conditions exist:

- If the [followers] have relatively high needs for independence.
- If the [followers] have a readiness to assume responsibility for decision making.
- If they have a relatively high tolerance for ambiguity.
- If they are interested in the problem and feel it is important.
- If they understand and identify with the goals of the organization.
- If they have the necessary knowledge and experience to deal with the problem.
- If they have learned to expect to share in decision making.[12]

Therefore, even though managers would prefer to change their followers' styles, they may find that they must adapt, at least temporarily, to the followers' present behavior. For example, a supervisor who wants followers to take more responsibility and to operate under general rather than close supervision cannot expect this kind of change to take place overnight. The supervisor's current behavior, at least to some extent, must be compatible with the present expectations of the group, with planned change taking place over a long-term period. We have seen numerous examples of the need for this kind of diagnosis in schools where humanistic teachers have tried to turn over significant responsibility to students without recognizing that many of these students expect teachers to tell them what to do. This rapid change in style often produces irresponsibility rather than more student initiative.

Leaders should know the expectations that followers have about the way they should behave in certain situations. This is especially important if leaders are new in their position. Their predecessor's leader behavior style is still a powerful influence. If this style is different from the one they plan to use, this may create an immediate problem.[13] Leaders must either change their style to coincide with followers' expectations or change follower expectations. Since the style of leaders often has been developed over a long period of time, it can be difficult for them to make any drastic changes in the short run. It may, therefore, be more effective if leaders concentrate on changing the expectations of their followers. In other words, in some cases they may be able to convince their followers that their style, although not what they, as followers, would normally expect, if accepted, will be adequate.

Supervisor's Style and Expectations

Another element of the environment is the leadership style of one's supervisor. By "supervisor" we mean the leader's leader. Just about everyone has a supervisor of one kind or another. Most managers give considerable attention to supervising followers, but some do not pay enough attention to being a follower themselves. Yet meeting the supervisor's expectations is often an important factor affecting one's style, particularly if one's supervisor is located in close proximity. If a supervisor is very task-oriented, for example, the supervisor might expect follower(s) to operate in the same manner. Relationship-oriented behavior might be evaluated as inappropriate, without even considering results. This has become evident when first-line supervisors are sent to training programs to improve their human relations skills. Upon returning to the company, they try to implement some of these new ideas in working with their people. Yet, because the supervisor has not accepted these concepts, he or she becomes impatient with the first-line supervisor's newfound concern for people: "Joe, cut out all that talking with the workers and get the work done." With such reactions, it would not take this first-line supervisor long to revert to the previous style, and in the future, it will be much more difficult to implement any behavioral change.

It is important for managers to know their supervisor's expectations, particularly if these managers want to advance in the organization. If they are predisposed toward promotion, they may tend to adhere to the customs and mores (styles and expectations) of the group to which they aspire to join rather than those of their peer group.[14] Consequently, their supervisors' expectations may become more important to them than those of the other groups with which they interact—their followers or associates.

The importance of the expectations of one's supervisor and the effect it can have on leadership style was vividly illustrated by Robert H. Guest in a case analysis of organizational change.[15] He examined a large assembly plant of an automobile company, Plant Y, and contrasted the situation under two different leaders.

Under Stewart, the plant manager, working relationships at Plant Y were dominated by hostility and mistrust. His high task style was characterized by continual attempts to increase the driving forces pushing for productivity. As a result, the prevailing atmosphere was that of one emergency following on the heels of another, and the governing motivation for employee activity was fear—fear of being chewed out right on the assembly line, fear of being held responsible for happenings in which one had no clear authority, fear of losing one's job. Consequently, of the six plants in this division of the corporation, Plant Y had the poorest performance record, and it was getting worse.

Stewart was replaced by Cooley, who seemed like an extremely effective leader. Over the next three years dramatic changes took place. In various cost and performance measures used to rate the six plants, Plant Y was now truly the leader; and the atmosphere of interpersonal cooperation and personal satisfaction had improved impressively over the situation under Stewart. These changes, moreover, were effected through an insignificant number of dismissals and reassignments. Using a much higher relationship style, Cooley succeeded in turning Plant Y around.

On the surface, the big difference was style of leadership. Cooley was a good leader. Stewart was not. But Guest points out clearly in his analysis that leadership style was only one of two important factors. The other was that while Stewart received daily orders from division headquarters to correct specific situations, Cooley was left alone. Cooley was allowed to lead; Stewart was told how to lead.[16] In other words, when productivity in Plant Y began to decline during changeover from wartime to peacetime operations, Stewart's supervisors expected him to get productivity back on the upswing by taking control of the reins, and they put tremendous pressure on him to do just that. Guest suggests that these expectations forced Stewart to operate in a very crisis-oriented, autocratic way. However, when Cooley was given charge as plant manager, a hands-off policy was initiated by his supervisors. The fact that the expectations of top management had changed gave Cooley an opportunity to operate in a completely different style.

Associates' Styles and Expectations

A leader's associates, or peers, are those individuals who have similar positions within the organization. For example, the associates of a vice-president for production are the other vice-presidents in the company; the associates of a teacher would be other teachers. Yet not all associates are significant for leaders; only those they interact with regularly are going to have impact on their style and effectiveness.

The styles and expectations of one's associates are important when a leader has frequent interactions with them, such as a situation that involves trading and bargaining for resources.[17]

We mentioned managers who have a strong drive to advance in an organization. Some people, however, are satisfied with their present positions. For these people, the expectations of their associates may be more important in influencing their behavior than those of their supervisors. College professors tend to be good examples. Often they are more concerned about the opinions of other professors or colleagues in their area of expertise than they are in the opinions of administrators.

Organization's Style and Expectations

The style and expectations of an organization are determined by the history and tradition of the organization, as well as by the organizational goals and objectives that reflect the style and expectations of present top management.

Over a period of time, an organization, much like an individual, becomes characterized by certain modes of behavior that are perceived as its style. The development of an organizational style, or corporate image, has been referred to as the process of institutionalization.[18] In this process, the organization is infused with a system of values that reflects its history and the people who have played vital roles in its formation and growth. Thus, it is difficult to understand Ford Motor Company without knowing the impact that Henry Ford had on its formation. Some organizations, for example, hold to the notion that the desirable executive is one who is dynamic, imaginative, decisive, and persuasive. Other organizations put more emphasis on the importance of the executive's ability to work effectively with people—human relations skills.[19]

Members of the organization soon become conscious of the value system operating within the institution and guide their actions from many expectations derived from these values. The organization's expectations are most often expressed in forms of policies, operating procedures, and controls, as well as in informal customs and mores developed over time.

Organizational goals. The goals of an organization usually consist of some combination of output and intervening variables. As we discussed earlier, output variables are those short-run goals that can easily be measured, such as net profits, annual earnings, and win-loss records. On the other hand, intervening variables consist of those long-run goals reflecting the internal condition of the organization that *cannot* easily be measured, such as its capacity for effective interaction, communication, and decision making.

OTHER SITUATIONAL VARIABLES

Job Demands

Another important element of a leadership situation is the demands of the job that the leader's group has been assigned to perform. Fiedler[20] called this situation variable *task structure*—the degree of structure in the task that the group has been asked to do. He found that a task that has specific instructions on what leaders and their followers should do requires a different leadership style than an unstructured task with no prescribed operating procedure.[21] Research findings indicate that highly structured jobs that need directions seem to require high task behavior, while unstructured jobs that do not need directions seem to favor relationship-oriented behavior.[22]

The *amount of interaction* the job requires of employees is an important consideration for managers in analyzing their work environment. Victor H. Vroom and Floyd C. Mann studied this aspect of a job in a large trucking company.[23] They investigated two groups of workers. One group was involved in the packaging operation and the other consisted of truck drivers and their dispatchers. The nature of the work in the packaging operation required that the men work closely together in small groups. Cooperation and teamwork were required not only among the workers, but also between the workers and their supervisors. In this situation, the workers preferred and worked better under employee-centered supervisors. The truck drivers, on the other hand, usually worked alone, having little contact with other people. These men did not depend on others for accomplishing their task, except for the dispatchers from whom they needed accurate information. Since the truck drivers generally worked alone, they were not concerned about harmony, but were concerned about the structure of the job in terms of where and when they were to deliver or pick up. In this situation, they preferred task-oriented supervisors.

Another important aspect of job demands that managers should consider is the type of control system being used. In our work, we have identified three types of control systems, as shown in Figure 7-3.

As illustrated, Type I shows the simplest and most structured of the control systems. The supervisor controls the activities of three separate functions and the horizontal arrows show the work moving in an assembly-line fashion to completion.

FIGURE 7-3   Three fundamental types of control systems

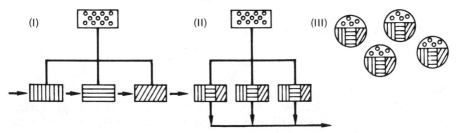

Type II depicts an organization in which work has been "enlarged." The supervisor still controls the activities of three people, but now all three functions are combined in each job and the three employees see end-product results (vertical arrows).

Type III is the least structured organization model ("enriched"), with each employee having the advantage of Type II plus decision-making responsibility, reserved only for the supervisor in Types I and II.

In an example of producing booklets, under a Type I control system, employee A is responsible for reproduction, B for distribution, and C for word processing. The boss is responsible for coordination, end results, and customer relations.

In Type II, job enlargement takes place, and the boss is now responsible for directing the activities of three people who prepare, reproduce and distribute their own work. Here, some motivational considerations come into play. The supervisor is motivated by relating directly to the customers (or persons needing booklets). The employees' motivation comes closer to being served in Type II since they can now see a new dimension of their work, and psychologically they come closer to the customer.

In Type III, all four members of the group act as separate decision-making and functional units, having the advantages reserved for only the manager in Types I and II: contact with the customer and control of the work.

Time

Another important element in the environment of a leader is the *time available for decision making*. If a manager's office burst into flames, he could not seek opinions and suggestions from his followers or use other methods of involvement to determine the best way to leave the building. The leader must make an immediate decision and point the way. Therefore, short-time demands, such as in an emergency, tend to require task-oriented behavior. On the other hand, if time is not a major factor in the situation, there is more opportunity for the leader to select from a broader range of leadership styles, depending on the other situational variables.

One could probably enumerate many more variables. For example, even the physical stature of a leader can affect the kind of style that leader can use. Take the example of the foreman in the steel mill who is six feet six inches tall and weighs over two hundred fifty pounds. He may be able to use a different style than a foreman five feet four inches tall weighing ninety-eight pounds, since their followers' expectations about their behavior will probably be influenced by their leader's physical appearance. Gender may be similar. For example, some men may respond and interact very differently with a female supervisor, associate, or follower than a male, and vice versa. This undoubtedly is influenced by the amount of past experience one has had in working with members of the opposite sex. But it certainly may be a situational variable worth examining in a leadership environment.

The kinds of environmental variables we have been discussing tend to be important whether one is concerned about an educational, an informal, or a business organization. But specific organizations may have additional variables unique to themselves that must be evaluated before determining effectiveness.

External Environment

Years ago, managers didn't worry much about the external environment because it didn't seem to affect them or their decisions. Today, this is no longer true. Organizations are continually influenced by external variables. Reality dictates that organizations do not exist in a vacuum, but are continually affected in numerous ways by changes in the society.

In the last several decades we have been bombarded by numerous movements that have challenged many of our society's core beliefs and practices. Consider the implications for organizations of such social developments as the youth revolution and its distrust and contempt for the "establishment"; the civil rights movement and the opening of wider opportunities in organizations for all minority groups; the ecology and consumer movements and their demands on organizations from the outside; and the increasing widespread concern for the quality of working life and its relationship to worker productivity, participation, and satisfaction.[24]

> These and other societal changes make effective leadership in the future a more challenging task, requiring even greater sensitivity and flexibility than was ever needed before. Today's manager is more likely to deal with employees who resent being treated as subordinates, who may be highly critical of any organizational system, who expect to be consulted and to exert influence, and who often stand on the edge of alienation from the institution that needs their loyalty and commitment. In addition, he is frequently confronted by a highly turbulent, unpredictable environment.[25]

DEVELOPING STRATEGIES

Changing Style

One of the most difficult changes to make is a complete change in the style of a person, and yet industry invests many millions of dollars annually for training and development programs that concentrate on changing the style of its leaders. As Fiedler suggests:

> A person's leadership style reflects the individual's basic motivational and need structure. At best it takes one, two, or three years of intensive psychotherapy to effect lasting changes in personality structure. It is difficult to see how we can change in more than a few cases an equally important set of core values in a few hours of lectures and role playing or even in the course of a more intensive training program of one or two weeks.[26]

Fiedler's point is well taken. It is indeed difficult to effect changes in the styles of managers overnight. While not completely hopeless, it is a slow and expensive process that requires creative planning and patience. In fact, Likert found that it takes from three to seven years, depending on the size and complexity of the organization, to implement a new management theory effectively.

> Haste is self-defeating because of the anxieties and stresses it creates. There is no substitute for ample time to enable the members of an organization to reach the level of skillful and easy, habitual use of the new leadership.[27]

What generally happens in present training and development programs is that managers are encouraged to adopt certain normative behavior styles. In our culture, these styles are usually high relationship–low task or high task–high relationship styles. Although we agree that there is a growing tendency for these two styles to be more effective than the high task–low relationship or low relationship–low task styles, we recognize that this is not universally the case even in our own culture. In fact, it is often not the case even within a single work group. Most people might respond favorably to the high relationship styles, but a few might react in a negative manner, taking advantage of what they consider a soft touch. As a result, certain individuals will have to be handled in a different way. Perhaps they will respond only to close supervision (a high task–low relationship style). Thus, it is unrealistic to think that any of these styles can be successfully applied everywhere. In addition to considering application, it is questionable whether every leader can adapt to one normative style.

Most training and development programs do not recognize these two considerations. Consequently, a foreman who has been operating as a task-oriented, authoritarian leader for many years is encouraged to change style—get in step with the times. Upon returning from the training program, the foreman will probably try to utilize some of the new relationship-oriented techniques. The problem is that the style the foreman has used for a long time is not compatible with the new concepts. As long as things are running smoothly, there is no difficulty in using them. However, the minute an important issue or a crisis develops, the foreman tends to revert to the old basic style and becomes inconsistent, vacillating between the new relationship-oriented style and the old task-oriented style, which has the force of habit behind it.

This idea was supported in a study that the General Electric Company conducted at one of its turbine and generator plants.[28] In this study the leadership styles of about ninety foremen were analyzed and rated as "democratic," "authoritarian," or "mixed." In discussing the findings, Saul W. Gellerman reported that:

> The lowest morale in the plant was found among those men whose foremen were rated *between* the democratic and authoritarian extremes. The GE research team felt that these foremen may have varied inconsistently in their tactics, permissive at one moment and hardfisted the next, in a way that left their men frustrated and unable to anticipate how they could be treated. The naturally autocratic supervisor who is exposed to human relations training may behave in exactly such a manner . . . a pattern which will probably make him even harder to work for than he was before being "enlightened."[29]

In summary, changing the style of managers is a difficult process and one that takes considerable time. Expecting miracles overnight will only lead to frustration and uneasiness for both managers and their employees. Consequently, we recommend that change in overall management style in an organization should be planned and implemented on a long-term basis so that expectations can be realistic for all involved.

Changes in Expectations versus Changes in Style

Using the feedback model discussed in chapter 2 (see Figure 7-4), we can begin to explain why it is so difficult to make changes in leader style in a short period of time.

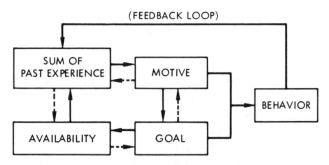

FIGURE 7-4 Feedback model

As discussed earlier, when a person behaves in a motivating situation, that behavior becomes a new input to the individual's inventory of past experience. The earlier in life that this input occurs, the greater its potential effect on future behavior. At that time, this behavior represents a larger portion of the individual's total past experience than the same behavior input will later in life. In addition, the longer a behavior is reinforced, the more patterned it becomes and the more difficult it is to change. That is why it is easier to make personality changes early in life. As a person gets older, more time and new experiences are necessary to effect a change in behavior.

As discussed in chapter 1, changes in behavior are much more difficult and time consuming than changes in knowledge and attitudes if force is not a factor. Since changes in expectations, in reality, are changes in knowledge and attitudes, these can be implemented more rapidly than changes in style. In fact, changes in expectations may be accomplished merely by having leaders sit down and clarify what their behavior will be with the individuals involved. Once they understand their leader's style, followers can more easily adjust their expectations to it. This is easier than attempting the tedious task of changing the basic style of leader.

Team Building: Selection of Key Employees

It is important to point out that it is not always necessary for supervisors and employees within an organization to have similar styles. People do not have to have the same personalities to be compatible. What is necessary is that they share perceptions of each other's roles and have common goals and objectives. It is often more appropriate for a manager to recruit key executives who can compensate for areas in which they have shortcomings than to surround themselves with aides who are all alike. And yet there are large companies today that have created problems for themselves by using a testing and selection process that eliminates personalities not congruent with the norm. The usual process is to measure the values and styles of the top management and then select new people who are compatible with those patterns. The assumption is that if those people got to the top, their values and styles must be what are needed to be successful in the organization. When these norms become part of the screening process, what the organization is saying is that there is a best style, at least for this organization.

One of the reasons that hiring "likes" became popular is that it led to a more harmonious organization. For example, if we have the same set of values and behave in similar ways, will we tend to get along? Yes, because we will tend to be compatible. There will probably not be much conflict or confrontation. On the surface, this kind of screening appears to be very positive. Yet we have found that this approach can lead to organizational or management inbreeding, which tends to stifle creativity and innovation. To be effective in the long run, we feel that organizations need an open dialogue in which there is a certain amount of conflict, confrontation, and differing points of view to encourage new ideas and patterns of behavior so that the organization will not lose its ability to adjust to external competition. Organizations that have had these problems almost have been forced to break their prior policy of promoting only from within and have had to hire some key people from the outside who can encourage open dialogue.

What is often needed in organizations is more emphasis on team building in which people are hired who complement rather than replicate a manager's style. For example, Henry Ford, who was considered a paternalistic leader, placed in key positions in the organization men who supplemented him rather than duplicated his style. Henry Bennett, for one, acted as a hatchet man, clearing deadwood from the organization (high task). Another executive acted as a confidant to Henry (high relationship). While these styles differed considerably, Ford's success during that time was based on compatibility of expectations; each understood the other's role and was committed to common goals and objectives.

Other examples could be cited. This kind of team building is common in sports such as football. Assistant coaches not only may have differential task roles—that is, line coach, backfield coach, and so forth—but may have different behavioral roles with the players. The same is true with principals and vice-principals, and so on.

Changing Situational Variables

Recognizing some of the limitations of training and development programs that concentrate only on changing leadership styles, Fiedler has suggested that "it would seem more promising at this time to teach the individual to recognize the conditions under which he can perform best and to modify the situation to suit his leadership style."[30] This philosophy, which he calls "organizational engineering," is based on the following assumption: "It is almost always easier to change a man's work environment than it is to change his personality or his style of relating to others."[31] Although we basically agree with Fiedler's assumption, we want to make it clear that we feel changes in both are difficult but possible. In many cases, the best strategy might be to attempt to make some changes in both the style of leaders and the situation, rather than concentrating on one or the other.

Fiedler is helpful, however, in suggesting ways in which a leadership situation can be modified to fit the leader's style. These suggestions are based on his Leadership Contingency Model, which we discussed in Chapter 5. As you will recall, Fiedler feels there are three major situational variables that seem to determine whether a given situation is favorable or unfavorable to leaders: (1) *leader-member relations*—their personal relations with the members of their group; (2) *position power*—the power and authority that their position provides; and (3) *task structure*—the degree of structure (routine versus challenging) in the task that the group has been assigned to perform. The changes in each of these variables that Fiedler recommends can be expressed in task or relationship terms; each change tends to favor either a task-oriented or a relationship-oriented leader, as illustrated in Table 7-1.[32]

With changes such as these, Fiedler suggests that the situational variables confronting leaders can be modified to fit their style. He recognized, however, as we have been arguing, that the success of organizational engineering depends on training individuals to be able to diagnose their own leadership style and the other situational variables. Only when they have accurately interpreted these variables can they determine whether any changes are necessary. If changes are needed, leaders do not necessarily have to initiate any in their own particular situation. They might prefer to transfer to a situation

TABLE 7-1 Changes in the Leadership Situation Expressed in Terms of Task and Relationship

VARIABLE BEING CHANGED	CHANGE MADE	
	STYLE FAVORS	
	Task	*Relationship*
Leader-Member Relations	Leaders could be given: 1. Followers who are quite different from them in a number of ways. 2. Followers who are notorious for their conflict.	Leaders could be given: 1. Followers who are very similar to them in attitude, opinion, technical background, race, etc. 2. Followers who generally get along well with their superiors.
Position Power of the Leader	Leaders could be given: 1. High rank and corresponding recognition, i.e., a vice-presidency. 2. Followers who are two or three ranks below them. 3. Followers who are dependent upon their leader for guidance and instruction. 4. Final authority in making all decisions for the group. 5. All information about organizational plans, thus making them expert in their group.	Leaders could be given: 1. Little rank (office) or official recognition. 2. Followers who are equal to them in rank. 3. Followers who are experts in their field and are independent of their leader. 4. No authority in making decisions for the group. 5. No more information about organizational plans than their followers get, placing the followers on an equal "footing" with the leaders.
Task Structure	Leaders could be given: 1. A structured production task that has specific instructions on what they and their followers should do.	Leaders could be given: 1. An unstructured policy-making task that has no prescribed operating procedures.

that better fits their style. In this new environment, no immediate changes may be necessary.

DIAGNOSING THE ENVIRONMENT—A CASE

Any of the situational elements we have discussed may be analyzed in terms of task and relationship. Let us take the case of Steve, a general foreman who has been offered a promotion to superintendent in an-

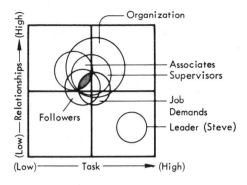

FIGURE 7-5
An example of all the environmental variables being analyzed together in terms of task and relationship

other plant. In his present position, which he has held for fifteen years, Steve has been extremely effective as a task-oriented manager responsible for the operation of several assembly-line processes.

Steve's first impulse is to accept this promotion in status and salary and move his family to the new location. But, instead, he feels it is important first to visit the plant and to talk with some of the people with whom he will be working. In talking with these people, Steve may gain some insight into some of the important dimensions of this new position. An analysis of all these variables in terms of task and relationship could be summarized together, as illustrated in Figure 7-5.[33]

If Steve, using diagnostic skills, makes this type of analysis, he has gone a long way toward gathering the necessary information he needs for effectively determining his appropriate actions.

The circle designated for the leader represents Steve's primary leadership style, which has been reinforced over the past fifteen years. The other circles represent the expectations of all the other environmental variables in terms of what is considered appropriate behavior for a foreman. In this plant, all of the situational variables seem to demand a high task–high relationship or high relationship–low task superintendent. Unfortunately, Steve's style does not seem appropriate for any of the situational variables, for he tends to be a high task–low relationship manager. Thus, if he accepts the job and makes no changes, there is a high probability that Steve will be ineffective. At this point, he has to make a decision. Several alternatives are available to him.

1. He can attempt to change his style of behavior, thus permitting him to work effectively with the various situational variables in the new environment.

2. He can attempt to change some or all of the situational elements. For example, he can attempt to change the behavior and the expectations of his followers through training and development programs and/or coaching and counseling.

3. He can attempt to make *some* changes in both his own range of behavior and some or all of the situational elements, thus attempting in the long run to have the two move toward each other rather than concentrating only on changing one or the other.

4. He can reject the job and seek another superintendent's position in an environment in which his range of behavior is more compatible with the demands of the other situational elements.

5. He can remain in his present position, where he knows he has been effective and will probably continue to be.

Reddin,[34] in doing a similar analysis, would attempt to find an area where the expectations of the organization, supervisors, associates, followers, and job demands intersected. It is within this area that he would suggest that a leader would probably have to behave to maximize effectiveness. While that averaging process, perhaps, could be used for a case such as Steve's in which the expectations of all the other situational variables are grouped closely together, it would not be useful in other situations.

When the expectations of various key variables do not intersect, it is not possible to use a generalized style, but will require that leaders use different styles with each of the important situational variables in their environment. Thus, Dorothy, a sales manager, may have to treat her supervisor differently from the way she treats any of her followers or associates. Even among the salespeople who report to her, she will probably have to treat some differently from others.

Although these examples have been written from the point of view of an individual, this type of analysis is just as important from an organization's point of view. It is vital that the people placed in key positions throughout the organization have the prerequisites for carrying out the organizational goals effectively. Management must realize that it does not follow that a person will be effective in one position merely because the person has been effective in another situation. Laurence J. Peter writes about such assumptions. The Peter Principle is stated as follows: "In a hierarchy every employee tends to rise to his level of incompetence."[35]

Anti–Peter Principle Vaccine

The dilemma expressed by Peter is not necessarily a self-fulfilling prophecy or principle. There are several ways an organization can develop an immunity to the problem. One method is appropriate training and development before upward mobility takes place. This training may often include, prior to movement, the delegation of some responsibility, so that the person has had an opportunity for some real experience that approximates the new position. Another part of the solution is careful selection of those whose personality and expectations are appropriate for the new job, instead of having upward mobility depend only on good performance at the preceding level.

HOW CAN MANAGERS LEARN TO DEAL WITH ALL THESE ENVIRONMENTAL VARIABLES?

It is our feeling that it would be an impossible task for managers to attempt to look at all the interacting influence variables discussed in this chapter every time they had to make a leadership decision. As a result, in the next chapter we are going to zero in on what we think is the key variable—the relationship between the leader and the follower.

Why do we say that the relationship between the leader and the follower is the key variable for diagnosing a situation? The main reason is that our work confirms Sanford's[36] work. We have found that if the follower decides not to follow, it really doesn't matter what the boss thinks, what the nature of the work is, how much time is involved, or what the other situational variables are.

NOTES

1. These environmental variables have been adapted from a list of situational elements discussed by William J. Reddin in *The 3-D Management Style Theory,* Theory Paper #5 – Diagnostic Skill (Fredericton, N.B., Canada: Social Science Systems, 1967), p. 2.
2. Robert Tannenbaum and Warren H. Schmidt indicate that the appropriate leadership style that should be used in a given situation is the function of factors in the leader, the follower, and the situation. What constitutes the situation can vary in different environmental settings. See Tannenbaum and Schmidt, "How to Choose a Leadership Pattern," *Harvard Business Review,* March–April, 1957.
3. The introductory section here was adapted from a model that discusses the interaction of personality and expectations. See Jacob W. Getzels and Egon G. Guba, "Social Behavior and the Administrative Process," *The School Review,* 65, No. 4 (Winter 1957), pp. 423–41. See also Getzels "Administration as a Social Process," in Andrew W. Halpin, ed., *Administrative Theory in Education* (Chicago: Midwest Administration Center, University of Chicago, 1958).
4. Adapted from Getzels, p. 158.
5. Tannenbaum and Schmidt, "How to Choose a Leadership Pattern."
6. Leland P. Bradford, Jack R. Gibb, and Kenneth D. Benne, *T-Group Theory and Laboratory Method* (New York: Wiley, 1964).
7. Warren G. Bennis, *Changing Organizations* (New York: McGraw-Hill, 1966), p. 120; Warren G. Bennis, *The Planning of Change* (New York: Harper & Row, 1985); D. G. Bowers,

"Organizational Development: Promises, Performances, Possibilities," *Organizational Dynamics,* Spring 1976, pp. 50–62.

8. See Chris Argyris, "T-Groups for Organization Effectiveness," *Harvard Business Review,* 42 (1964), pp. 60–74; Edgar H. Schein and Warren G. Bennis, *Personal and Organizational Change through Group Methods* (New York: Wiley 1965); Robert R. Blake et al., "Breakthrough in Organization Development," *Harvard Business Review,* November–December 1964; and Chris Argyris, *Interpersonal Competence and Organizational Effectiveness* (Homewood, Ill.: Dorsey Press, 1962). See also E. H. Schein, *Organizational Psychology,* 2nd ed. (Englewood Cliffs, N.J.: Prentice-Hall, 1977); Robert R. Blake and Jane S. Mouton, *Consultation: A Comprehensive Approach to Individual and Organization Development* (Reading, Mass.: Addison-Wesley, 1983).

9. Fillmore H. Sanford, *Authoritarianism, and Leadership* (Philadelphia: Institute for Research in Human Relations, 1950).

10. Victor H. Vroom, *Some Personality Determinants of the Effects of Participation* (Englewood Cliffs, N.J.: Prentice Hall, 1960).

11. Saul W. Gellerman, *Motivation and Productivity* (New York: American Management Association, 1963).

12. Tannenbaum and Schmidt, "How to Choose a Leadership Pattern."

13. Reddin, *The 3-D Management Style Theory,* Theory Paper #5–Diagnostic Skill, p. 4.

14. William E. Henry, "The Business Executive: The Psychodynamics of a Social Role," *The American Journal of Sociology,* 54, no. 4 (January 1949), pp. 286–91.

15. Robert H. Guest, *Organizational Change: The Effect of Successful Leadership* (Homewood, Ill.: Irwin, Dorsey Press, 1964). See also Robert Guest, Paul Hersey, and Kenneth Blanchard, *Organizational Change through Effective Leadership,* 2nd ed. (Englewood Cliffs, N. J.: Prentice Hall 1986).

16. *Ibid.*

17. Reddin, *The 3-D Management Style Theory,* Theory Paper #5–Diagnostic Skill, p. 4.

18. Waino W. Suojanen, *The Dynamics of Management* (New York: Holt, Rinehart & Winston, 1966).

19. Tannenbaum and Schmidt, "How to Choose a Leadership Pattern."

20. Fred E. Fiedler, *A Theory of Leadership Effectiveness* (New York: McGraw-Hill, 1967).

21. *Ibid.*

22. Edwin P. Hollander, *Leadership Dynamics: A Practical Guide to Effective Relationships* (New York: Free Press, 1978).

23. Victor H. Vroom and Floyd C. Mann, "Leader Authoritarianism and Employee Attitudes," *Personnel Psychology,* 13, no. 2 (1960).

24. Robert Tannenbaum, and Warren H. Schmidt, "How to Choose a Leadership Pattern," *Harvard Business Review,* May–June 1973.

25. *Ibid.*

26. Fiedler, *A Theory of Leadership Effectiveness,* p. 248.

27. Rensis Likert, *New Patterns of Management* (New York: McGraw-Hill, 1961), p. 248.

28. *Leadership Style and Employee Morale* (New York: General Electric Company, Public and Employee Relations Services, 1959).

29. Gellerman, *Motivation and Productivity,* p. 43.

30. Fiedler, *A Theory of Leadership Effectiveness,* p. 255.

31. *Ibid.*

32. This table was adapted from Fiedler's discussion in *A Theory of Leadership Effectiveness,* pp. 255–56.

33. Adapted from Reddin, Theory Paper #6–Style Flex, p. 6.

34. Reddin, Theory Paper #6–Style Flex.

35. Laurence J. Peter and Raymond Hull, *The Peter Principle: Why Things Go Wrong* (New York: Morrow, 1969).

36. Fillmore H. Sanford, *Authoritarianism and Leadership* (Philadelphia: Institute for Research in Human Relations, 1950).

8

Situational Leadership®

The importance of a leader's *diagnostic ability* cannot be over-emphasized. Edgar H. Schein expresses it well when he contends that *the successful manager must be a good diagnostician and must value a spirit of inquiry.* If the abilities and motives of the people under the manager are so variable, he or she must have the sensitivity and diagnostic ability to be able to sense and appreciate the differences.[1] In other words, managers must be able to identify clues in an environment. Yet even with good diagnostic skills, leaders may still not be effective unless they can *adapt* their leadership style to meet the demands of their environment. This is the second of the three important leadership competencies discussed in Chapter 1. "He must have the personal flexibility and range of skills necessary to vary his own behavior. If the needs and motives of his [followers] are different, they must be treated differently."[2]

It is easier said than done to tell practicing managers that they should use behavioral science theory and research to develop the necessary diagnostic skills to maximize effectiveness. First, much of the research currently published in the field of applied behavioral sciences is not even understood by practitioners, and often appears in final form to be more an attempt to impress other researchers than to help managers to be more effective. Second, even if practitioners could understand the research, many would argue that it is impractical to consider every situational variable in every decision.

As a result, one of the major focuses of our work has been the development of a practical model that can be used by managers, salespeople, teachers, or parents to make the moment-by-moment decisions necessary to effectively influence other people. The result: Situational Leadership.

This approach uses as its basic data the perceptions and observations made by managers—parents in the home or supervisors on the job—on a day-to-day basis in their own environments.

Situational Leadership was developed by Paul Hersey and Kenneth H. Blanchard at the Center for Leadership Studies in the late 1960s.[3] Until 1982, Hersey and Blanchard worked together to continually refine Situational Leadership. After that time, Blanchard and his colleagues at Blanchard Training and Development (BTD) began to modify the original Situational Leadership model and developed diagnostic instruments and training materials to support their approach (called SLII®) in training seminars and presentations. The best description of this approach to Situational Leadership can be found in *Leadership and the One Minute Manager.*[4]

The Situational Leadership model used in this book will reflect the present thinking of Paul Hersey and the Center for Leadership Studies and will not include any changes to the model made by Ken Blanchard in SLII®.

SITUATIONAL LEADERSHIP

The Center For Leadership Studies

Situational Leadership is based on an interplay among (1) the amount of guidance and direction (task behavior) a leader gives; (2) the amount of socioemotional support (relationship behavior) a leader provides; and (3) the readiness level that followers exhibit in performing a specific task, function or objective. This concept was developed to help people attempting leadership, regardless of their role, to be more effective in their daily interactions with others. It provides leaders with some understanding of the relationship between an effective style of leadership and the level of readiness of their followers.

Thus, while all the situational variables (leader, follower(s), senior management, associates, organization, job demands, and time) are important, the emphasis in Situational Leadership will be on the behavior of a leader in relation to followers. As Fillmore H. Sanford has indicated, there is some justification for regarding the followers "as the most crucial factor in any leadership event."[5] Followers in any situation are vital, not only because individually they accept or reject the leader, but because as a group they actually determine whatever personal power the leader may have.

It may be appropriate at this point to note the difference between a model and a theory. A theory attempts to explain *why* things happen as they do. As such, it is not designed to recreate events. A model, on the other hand, is a pattern of already existing events that can be learned and therefore repeated. For example, in trying to imagine why Henry Ford was motivated to mass-produce automobiles, you would be dealing with a theory. However, if you recorded the procedures and sequences necessary for mass production, you would have a model of the process.

Situational Leadership is a model, *not* a theory. Its concepts, procedures, actions, and outcomes are based upon tested methodologies that are practical and easy to apply.

It was emphasized in chapter 4 that when discussing leader-follower relationships, we are not necessarily talking about a hierarchical relationship: that is, manager-employee. The same caution will hold during our discussion of Situational Leadership. *Thus, any reference to leader(s) or follower(s) in this model should imply potential leader and potential follower.* As a result, although our examples may suggest a hierarchical relationship, the concepts presented in Situational Leadership should have application no matter whether you are attempting to influence the behavior of an employee, your supervisor, an associate, a friend, a relative, or a group.

Basic Concept of Situational Leadership

According to Situational Leadership, there is no one best way to influence people. Which leadership style a person should use with individuals or groups depends on the readiness level of the people the leader is attempting to influence, as illustrated in Figure 8-1.

Before we look at the application of the Situational Leadership model, it is important that we understand leadership styles as they are used in the model and the idea of follower readiness.

Our earlier discussion of different leadership theories in chapters 4 and 5 introduced us to our definition of leadership style—behavior by the leader as perceived by the follower(s). We also saw the ways that classifying leader behaviors developed, including the identification of task and relationship behavior.[6]

> *Task behavior* is defined as the extent to which the leader engages in spelling out the duties and responsibilities of an individual or group.

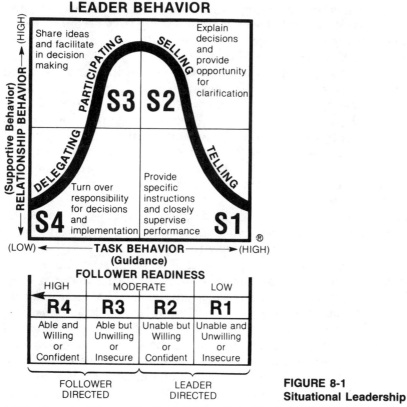

FIGURE 8-1
Situational Leadership

Adapted from Paul Hersey, Situational Selling (Escondido, Calif.: Center for Leadership Studies, 1985), p. 19.

These behaviors include telling people what to do, how to do it, when to do it, where to do it, and who is to do it.

An example of high amounts of task behavior might be the last time you asked someone for directions. The person was probably very precise and clear about telling you what streets to take and what turns to make. You were told where to start and where to finish. It is important to notice that being directive does not mean being nasty or short-tempered. The person helping you might have been very pleasant toward you, but the actions and statements were aimed at completing the task—that of helping you find your way. Task behavior is characterized by one-way communication from the leader to the follower. The person was not so much concerned with your feelings, but with how to help you achieve your goal.

Relationship behavior is defined as the extent to which the leader engages in two-way or multi-way communication. The behaviors include listening, facilitating, and supportive behaviors.[7]

An example of high amounts of relationship behavior might be when you reach an impasse with an assignment. You basically know how to do the assignment, but need some encouragement to get you over the hump. The listening, encouraging, and facilitating a leader does in this example is an illustration of relationship behavior.

Task behavior and relationship behavior are separate and distinct dimensions. They can be placed on separate axes of a two-dimensional graph, and the four quadrants can be used to identify four basic leadership styles.[8] Figure 8-2 illustrates these styles. You will note that task behavior is plotted from low to high on the horizontal axis while relationship behavior is plotted from low to high on the vertical axis. This makes it possible to describe leader behavior in four ways or styles.

As we discussed in Chapter 5, the four quadrants shown in Figure 8-2 can be used as the basis for assessing effective leader behavior. No one style is effective in all situations. *Each* style is appropriate and effective depending on the situation.

FIGURE 8-2
Leadership styles

EFFECTIVE LEADER BEHAVIOR

Adapted from Paul Hersey, Situational Selling *(Escondido, Calif.: Center for Leadership Studies, 1985), p. 20.*

The following descriptions apply to the four styles:

- Style 1 (S1): This leadership style is characterized by above-average amounts of task behavior and below-average amounts of relationship behavior.
- Style 2 (S2): This leadership style is characterized by above-average amounts of both task and relationship behavior.
- Style 3 (S3): This style is characterized by above-average amounts of relationship behavior and below-average amounts of task behavior.
- Style 4 (S4): This style is characterized by below-average amounts of both relationship behavior and task behavior.

The important information presented by this model is in the operational *definitions* of task behavior and relationship behavior presented earlier. In leadership situations involving the family, schools, or other settings, different words may be more appropriate than *task* and *relationship*—for example, *guidance* and *supportive* behavior or *directive* behavior and *facilitating* behavior—but the underlying definitions remain the same.

Readiness of the Followers or Group

In Chapter 7 we looked at the situation—the complex pattern of conditions that exist within a given environment. We have noted that there is no one best style of leadership; it depends upon the situation within which the attempt to influence takes place. The more that leaders can adapt their behaviors to the situation, the more effective their attempts to influence become. The situation, in turn, is influenced, as we have noted, by the various conditions that are present.

Some of the primary factors in the situation that influence leader effectiveness include the following:

- Leader
- Followers
- Supervisor
- Key associates
- Organization
- Job demands
- Decision time.

These variables do not operate in isolation. They are interactive. For example, Style 1 is often referred to as "crisis leadership" because it is appropriate in times of crisis. The important thing to remember is that we should use it to *respond* to crises, not to create them. *If we treat an organization as if it is in crisis, that's what we get . . . crisis. If we treat people like children, they will often begin to behave like children.* This is one of the most important concepts in the field of applied behavioral sciences—the concept of the *self-fulfilling prophecy.* In working with others and helping them develop, leaders should have positive assumptions about followers' potential. Effective leaders believe that people have the potential to grow and that, given an opportunity, can and will respond.[9]

We need to remind ourselves that the relationship between leaders and followers is the crucial variable in the leadership situation. If the followers decide not to follow, it doesn't matter what the supervisor or key associates think or what the job demands may be. *There is no leadership without someone following.*

In order to maximize the leader-follower relationship, the leader must first determine the task-specific outcomes the followers are to accomplish—on an individual and group basis. Without creating clarity on outcomes, objectives, subtasks, milestones, and so on, the leader has no basis for determining follower readiness or the specific behavioral style to use for that level of readiness.

Readiness Defined

Readiness in Situational Leadership is defined as the extent to which a follower has the ability and willingness to accomplish a specific task. People tend to be at different levels of readiness depending on the *task* they are being asked to do. Readiness is *not* a personal characteristic; it is not an evaluation of a person's traits, values, age, and so on. *Readiness is how ready a person is to perform a particular task.* This concept of readiness has to do with specific situations—not with any *total* sense of readiness. All persons tend to be more or less ready in relation to a specific task, function, or objective that a leader is attempting to accomplish through their efforts. Thus, a salesperson may be very responsible in securing new sales, but very casual about completing the paper work necessary to close on a sale. As a result, it is appropriate for the manager to leave the salesperson alone in terms of closing on sales, but to supervise closely in terms of paper work until the salesperson can start to do well in that area too.

In addition to assessing the level of readiness of individuals within a group, a leader may have to assess the readiness level of the group as a group, particularly if the group interacts frequently together in the same work area, as happens with students in the classroom. Thus, a teacher may find that a class as a group may be at one level of readiness in a particular area, but a student within that group may be at a different level. When the teacher is one-to-one with that student, the teacher may have to behave very differently than when working with the class as a group. In reality, the teacher may find a number of students at various readiness levels. For example, the teacher may have one student who is not doing the assigned work regularly; and when the work *is* turned in, it is poorly organized and not very academic. With that student, the teacher may have to initiate some structure and supervise closely. Another student, however, may be doing good work, but is insecure and shy. With that student, the teacher may not have to engage in much task behavior in terms of schoolwork, but may need to be supportive, to engage in two-way communication, and to help facilitate the student's interaction with others in the class. Still another student may be competent and confident in the schoolwork and thus can be left alone. So leaders have to understand that they may have to behave differently one-on-one with members of their group from the way they do with the group as a whole.

The two major components of readiness are *ability* and *willingness.*[10]

> *Ability* is the knowledge, experience, and skill that an individual or group brings to a particular task or activity.

When considering the ability level of others, it is very important to be *task specific.* A person who has a Ph.D. in music and twenty years of professional experience playing the piano may be of little help in the design of a new jet engine. It is essential to focus on the specific outcome desired and to consider the ability of the followers in light of that outcome.

> *Willingness* is the extent to which an individual or group has the confidence, commitment, and motivation to accomplish a specific task.

Willingness is only one word that describes the issue. Sometimes, it isn't so much that people are really unwilling, it's just that they've never done a specific task before. Perhaps they don't have any experience with it, so they're insecure or afraid. Generally, *if it is an issue of never having done something, the problem is insecurity.* The term *unwilling* might be most appropriate when, for one reason or another, the individuals have slipped, or lost some of their commitment and motivation. It might imply that they are regressing.

Even though the concepts of ability and willingness are different, it is important to remember that they are an *interacting influence system.* This means that *a significant change in one will affect the whole.* The extent to which followers bring willingness into a specific situation affects the use of their present ability. And it affects the

HIGH	MODERATE		LOW
R4	**R3**	**R2**	**R1**
Able and Willing or Confident	Able but Unwilling or Insecure	Unable but Willing or Confident	Unable and Unwilling or Insecure

FIGURE 8-3 Continuum of follower readiness

Adapted from Paul Hersey, Situational Selling *(Escondido, Calif.: Center for Leadership Studies, 1985), p. 27.*

extent to which they will grow and develop competence and ability. Similarly, the amount of knowledge, experience, and skill brought to a specific task will often affect competence, commitment, and motivation.

Readiness levels are the different combinations of ability and willingness that people bring to each task. (See Figure 8-3.)

The continuum of follower readiness can be divided into four levels.[11] Each represents a different combination of follower ability and willingness or confidence:

- Readiness Level One (R1)
  Unable and unwilling
  The follower is unable and lacks commitment and motivation.

  or

  Unable and insecure
  The follower is unable and lacks confidence.
- Readiness Level Two (R2)
  Unable but willing
  The follower lacks ability, but is motivated and making an effort.

  or

  Unable but confident
  The follower lacks ability, but is confident as long as the leader is there to provide guidance.
- Readiness Level Three (R3)
  Able but unwilling
  The follower has the ability to perform the task, but is not willing to use that ability.

  or

  Able but insecure
  The follower has the ability to perform the task, but is insecure or apprehensive about doing it alone.

- Readiness Level Four (R4)
  Able and willing
  The follower has the ability to perform and is committed.

or

  Able and confident
  The follower has the ability to perform and is confident about doing it.

Note: Some people have difficulty understanding the development of followers from R1 to R2 to R3. How can one go from being insecure to confident and then become insecure again? The important thing to remember is that at the lower levels of readiness, the leader is providing the direction—the what, where, when, and how. Therefore, the decisions are *leader directed.* At the higher levels of readiness, *followers* become responsible for task direction, and the decisions are *follower directed. This transition from leader directed to self directed may result in apprehension or insecurity.*

As followers move from low levels of readiness to higher levels, the combinations of task and relationship behavior appropriate to the situation begin to change.

The curved line through the four leadership styles shown in Figure 8-1 represents the high probability combination of task behavior and relationship behavior. These combinations correspond to the readiness levels directly below. To use the model, identify a point on the readiness continuum that represents follower readiness to perform a specific task. Then construct a perpendicular line from that point to a point where it intersects with the curved line representing leader behavior. This point indicates the most appropriate amount of task behavior and relationship behavior for that specific situation.

In selecting the high probability combination of task behavior and relationship behavior, it isn't necessary to be exact. As you move away from the optimal combination, the probability of success gradually falls off, slowly at first and then more rapidly the farther away you move. Because of this, you don't need a direct hit—a close approximation keeps the probability of success high.

Selecting Appropriate Styles

*Match of Readiness Level 1 with Leadership
Style 1—Telling*

For a follower or group that is at Readiness Level 1 for a specific task, it is appropriate to provide high amounts of guidance, but little supportive behavior. A word that describes this specific leadership style is *telling*—telling the followers what to do, where to do it, and how to do it. This style is appropriate when an individual or group is low in ability and willingness and needs direction. Other one-word descriptors for this leadership style include *guiding, directing,* or *structuring.*

Match of Readiness Level 2 with Leadership Style 2—Selling

The next range of readiness is Readiness Level 2. This is an individual or group that is still unable, but they're trying. They're willing or confident. The high probability styles are combinations of high amounts of both task and relationship behavior. The task behavior is appropriate because people are still unable. But since they're trying, it is important to be supportive of their motivation and commitment.

This style is *selling.* It is different from *telling* in that the leader is not only providing the guidance, but is also providing the opportunity for dialogue and for clarification, in order to help the person "buy in" psychologically to what the leader wants. If a leader simply says "go stand by the door and keep people from coming through," that is *telling.* On the other hand, if the leader suggests "I'd sure appreciate it if you would be willing to stand by the door to guide people around the classroom because people coming through here have been disruptive," this would be an example of *selling.* The follower can ask questions and get clarification, even though the leader has provided the guidance.

The definition of task behavior includes providing the *what, how, when, where,* and *who.* The reason that *why* isn't included is that efforts to explain *why* bridge both task and relationship behaviors. One of the differences between *telling* and *selling* is the explanation of *why.* Other words for this leadership style include *explaining, persuading,* or *clarifying.*

Match of Readiness Level 3 with Leadership Style 3—Participating

Readiness Level 3 would include a person or group that's able, but they've just developed this ability and haven't had an opportunity to gain confidence in doing it on their own. An example is the fledgling salesperson who goes out on a sales call for the first time without the sales manager.

Readiness Level 3 could also be a person or group that was able and willing, but for one reason or another is slipping in terms of motivation. Perhaps they're upset, mad at the supervisor, or just tired of performing this behavior and, therefore, are becoming *unwilling.*

In either case, the appropriate behavior would be high amounts of two-way communication and supportive behavior, but low amounts of guidance. Since they have already shown that they are able to perform the task, it isn't necessary to provide high amounts of what to do, where to do it, or how to do it. Discussion and supportive and facilitating behaviors would tend to be more appropriate for solving the problem or soothing the apprehension.

In *participating*, the leader's major role becomes encouraging and communicating. Other descriptors for this style of leadership include *collaborating*, *facilitating*, or *committing*. Each of these implies high relationship, low task behaviors.

Match of Readiness Level 4 with Leadership Style 4–Delegating

Readiness Level 4 is where the individual or group is both ready and willing, or ready and confident. They've had enough opportunity to practice, and they feel comfortable without the leader providing direction.

It is unnecessary to provide direction about where, what, when, or how because the followers already have the ability. Similarly, above-average amounts of encouraging and supportive behaviors aren't necessary because they are confident, committed, and motivated. The appropriate style involves giving them the ball and letting them run with it.

This style is called *delegating*. Other words for this leadership style include *observing* or *monitoring*. Remember – some relationship behavior is still needed, but it tends to be less than average. It is still appropriate to monitor the pulse of what's going on, but it is important to give these followers an opportunity to take responsibility and implement on their own.

One point to remember is that when an individual or group is developing, the issue is usually one of insecurity; when they are regressing, the issue is usually one of unwillingness. We will go into these ideas in greater detail in subsequent chapters.

It should be clear that the appropriate leadership style for all four of the readiness designations – low (R1), low to moderate (R2), moderate to high (R3), and high (R4) – correspond to the following leadership style designations: *telling* (S1), *selling* (S2), *participating* (S3), and *delegating* (S4). That is, low readiness needs a *telling* style, low to moderate readiness needs a *selling* style, and so on. These combinations are shown in Table 8-1.

Situational Leadership not only suggests the high probability leadership style for various readiness levels, but it also indicates the

TABLE 8-1 Leadership Styles Appropriate for Various Readiness Levels

READINESS LEVEL	APPROPRIATE STYLE
R1 *Low Readiness* Unable and unwilling or insecure	*S1* *Telling* High task Low relationship behavior
R2 *Low to Moderate Readiness* Unable, but willing or confident	*S2* *Selling* High task High relationship behavior
R3 *Moderate to High Readiness* Able, but unwilling or insecure	*S3* *Participating* High relationship Low task behavior
R4 *High Readiness* Able/competent and willing/confident	*S4* *Delegating* Low relationship Low task behavior

probability of success of the other style configurations if a leader is unable to use the desired style. The probability of success of each style for the four readiness levels, depending on how far the style is from the high probability style along the prescriptive curve in the style of leader portion of the model, tends to be as follows:

- R1   S1 high, S2 2nd, S3 3rd, S4 low probability
- R2   S2 high, S1 2nd, S3 3rd, S4 low probability
- R3   S3 high, S2 2nd, S4 3rd, S1 low probability
- R4   S4 high, S3 2nd, S2 3rd, S1 low probability

In Situational Leadership, who has the problem? The *follower.* The follower can get any behavior desired depending upon the *follower's* behavior. The follower's behavior determines the leader's behavior. What a marvelous thing we now have available to use at home, at the office, in any kind of interpersonal situation. For example, how much easier parenting would be if children were to realize that it is not Mom and Dad who determine and control the children's behavior; it is *they* who control their own behavior.

Another important consideration: Why is it that a leadership style that may not be our "natural" style is frequently our most *effective* style? This is because we have worked at these learned styles, we have practiced and practiced those behaviors, and we have worked at them with some expert help. We have also paid attention to the details of applying these learned styles. We do not put the same amount of skill practice into our "natural" style(s) as we do our learned styles. As a consequence, they are not as effective.

One last thought: Situational Leadership is not a prescription with hard-and-fast rules. In the behavioral sciences, there are no rules. Situational Leadership as a major contribution to the behavioral sciences is attempting to improve the odds. In so doing, managers will be able to achieve the productivity of human resources they have been seeking.

APPLICATION OF SITUATIONAL LEADERSHIP

In using Situational Leadership, it is useful to keep in mind that there is no "one best way" to influence others. Rather, any leader behavior may be more or less effective depending on the readiness level of the person you are attempting to influence. Shown in Figure 8-4 is a more comprehensive version of the Situational Leadership Model that brings together our discussion of the past several pages. It will provide you with a quick reference to assist in (1) diagnosing the level of readiness; (2) adapting by selecting high probability leadership styles; and (3) communicating these styles effectively to influence behavior. Implicit in Situational Leadership is the idea that a leader should help followers grow in readiness as far as they are able and willing to go. This development of followers should be done by adjusting leadership behavior through the four styles along the leadership curve in Figure 8-4.

Situational Leadership contends that strong direction (task behavior) with followers with low readiness is appropriate if they are to become productive. Similarly, it suggests that an increase in readiness on the part of people who are somewhat unready should be rewarded by increased positive reinforcement and socioemotional support (relationship behavior). Finally, as followers reach high levels of readiness, the leader should respond by not only continuing to decrease control over their activities, but also by continuing to decrease relationship behavior as well. With people with high readiness, the need for socioemotional support is no longer as important as the need for greater freedom. At this stage, one of the ways leaders can prove their confidence and trust in these people is to leave them more and more on their own. It is not that there is less mutual trust and

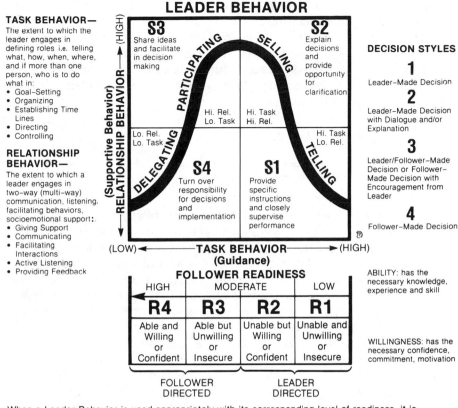

TASK BEHAVIOR—
The extent to which the
leader engages in
defining roles i.e. telling
what, how, when, where,
and if more than one
person, who is to do
what in:
• Goal–Setting
• Organizing
• Establishing Time
  Lines
• Directing
• Controlling

**RELATIONSHIP
BEHAVIOR—**
The extent to which a
leader engages in
two–way (multi–way)
communication, listening,
facilitating behaviors,
socioemotional support:
• Giving Support
• Communicating
• Facilitating
  Interactions
• Active Listening
• Providing Feedback

LEADER BEHAVIOR

(Supportive Behavior)
RELATIONSHIP BEHAVIOR
(HIGH)

S3
Share ideas
and facilitate
in decision
making

PARTICIPATING

Hi. Rel.
Lo. Task

Lo. Rel.
Lo. Task

DELEGATING

S4
Turn over
responsibility
for decisions
and
implementation

S2
Explain
decisions
and
provide
opportunity
for
clarification

SELLING

Hi. Task
Hi. Rel.

Hi. Task
Lo. Rel.

TELLING

S1
Provide
specific
instructions
and closely
supervise
performance

(LOW) ◄──── **TASK BEHAVIOR** ────► (HIGH)
(Guidance)

DECISION STYLES

1
Leader–Made Decision

2
Leader–Made Decision
with Dialogue and/or
Explanation

3
Leader/Follower–Made
Decision or Follower–
Made Decision with
Encouragement from
Leader

4
Follower–Made Decision

FOLLOWER READINESS

HIGH	MODERATE		LOW
R4	**R3**	**R2**	**R1**
Able and Willing or Confident	Able but Unwilling or Insecure	Unable but Willing or Confident	Unable and Unwilling or Insecure

FOLLOWER
DIRECTED

LEADER
DIRECTED

ABILITY: has the
necessary knowledge,
experience and skill

WILLINGNESS: has the
necessary confidence,
commitment, motivation

When a Leader Behavior is used appropriately with its corresponding level of readiness, it is
termed a High Probability Match. The following are descriptors that can be useful when using
Situational Leadership for specific applications:

S1	S2	S3	S4
Telling	Selling	Participating	Delegating
Guiding	Explaining	Encouraging	Observing
Directing	Clarifying	Collaborating	Monitoring
Establishing	Persuading	Committing	Fulfilling

FIGURE 8-4   Expanded Situational Leadership Model

Paul Hersey, Situational Selling *(Escondido, Calif.: Center for Leadership Studies, 1985), p. 32.*

friendship between leader and follower—in fact, there is more—but it
takes less supportive behavior on the leader's part to prove this to
them.

Regardless of the level of readiness of an individual or group,
change may occur. Whenever a follower's performance begins to slip—
for whatever reason—and ability or motivation decreases, the leader
should reassess the readiness level of this follower and move back-

ward through the leadership curve, providing appropriate socioemotional support and direction.

These developmental and regressive processes will be discussed in depth in chapters 10 and 11. At this point, though, it is important to emphasize that Situational Leadership focuses on the appropriateness or effectiveness of leadership styles according to the task-relevant readiness of the followers.

Determining Appropriate Style

To determine what leadership style you should use with a person in a given situation, you must make several decisions.

What objective(s) do we want to accomplish? First, you must decide what areas of an individual's or a group's activities you would like to influence. Specifically, what objective(s) do you want to accomplish? In the world of work, those areas would vary according to a group's responsibilities. For example, sales managers may have responsibilities in sales, administration (paperwork), service, and group development. Therefore, before managers can begin to determine the appropriate leadership style to use with a group, they must decide what aspect of that group's job they want to influence.

If the organization's goal was "to ship 100 percent of customer orders within 24 hours of order receipt," we would say it is too general a goal and needs to be broken up into specific tasks that can be assigned to a group. The vice-president for customer services of an international supplier of multipurpose pumps, identifies the specific tasks needed to accomplish the goal. Developed in association with a customer service unit, it works like this:

1. The goal is summarized using trigger words, e.g. *prompt service.*
2. Tasks to accomplish the goal are identified by the people involved.
   a. Answering the phone.
   b. Completing the order form.
   c. Completing the packing order.
   d. Shipping the order.
   e. Adjusting service problems.

What is the readiness of the situation? The sales manager must then diagnose the readiness of the group to accomplish these tasks. The key issue is: "How ready or receptive is the group to accomplish these tasks?" If the group is at a high level of readiness, only a low amount of leadership intervention will be required. If, on the other hand, the group is at a low level of readiness, considerable leadership intervention may be required.

What leadership action should be taken? The next step is deciding which of the four leadership styles (see Table 8-1) would be appropriate for the team. Suppose the manager has determined that the group's readiness level, in terms of accomplishing all of these tasks, is high—that is, the group is able and willing (R4). Using Table 8-1, the manager would know that when working with this group, a *delegating* (S4) style (low task–low relationship behavior) should be used. Some members of the group may be lower in readiness than the group as a whole with respect to specific tasks. For example, a team member may be R3 (able but insecure) with regard to responding to service problems on a new line of equipment. The manager would use an S3 (high relationship–low task) leadership style to build the member's confidence and self-esteem.

What was the result of the leadership intervention? This step requires assessment to determine if results match expectations. As will be discussed in chapter 10, individuals and groups learn a little bit at a time. Development involves positively reinforcing successive approximations as the individual or group approaches the desired level of performance. Therefore, after a leadership intervention, the manager must assess the result through rechecking the objectives, rediagnosing readiness, and ascertaining if further leadership is indicated.

What follow-up, if any, is required? If there is a gap between present performance and desired performance of the individual or group, then follow-up is required in the form of additional leadership interventions, and the cycle starts again. In a dynamic environment such as the leadership environment, follow-up is almost a certainty. Leadership under modern competitive conditions means moving targets. Tasks, readiness, and results are all changing; follow-up is a must. Paul Hersey summarizes this reality by observing, "Leading is a full-time job that must be practiced every hour of every day."

Components of Readiness

It has been argued that the key to effective leadership is to identify the *readiness level* of the individual or group you are attempting to influence and then bring to bear the appropriate leadership style. If that is true, how can managers get a better handle on what readiness actually means?

In examining the components of readiness, several comments should be made. First, according to David C. McClelland's research,[12] achievement-motivated people have certain characteristics in common, including the capacity to set high but obtainable goals, the concern for personal achievement rather than the rewards of success, and the desire for task-relevant feedback (how well am I doing?) rather than for attitudinal feedback (how well do you like me?). Of these characteristics we are most interested, in terms of task-relevant readiness, in the capacity to set high but attainable goals.

Second, in terms of education and/or experience, we are contending that there is no conceptual difference between the two. One can gain task-relevant readiness through education or experience or some combination of both. The only difference between the two is that when we are talking about education, we are referring to formal classroom experiences, and experience involves what is learned on one's own or on the job.

Third, in our recent work, we have argued that education and/or experience affects ability and that achievement motivation affects willingness. As a result, we are suggesting that the concept of readiness consists of two dimensions: ability and willingness.

Ability (job readiness) is related to the ability to do something. It has to do with knowledge and demonstrated skill. Individuals who have high job readiness in a particular area have the knowledge, skill, and experience to perform certain tasks without direction from others. A person high in job readiness might say: "My talent really lies in that aspect of my job. I can work on my own in that area without much help from my boss."

Willingness (psychological readiness) is related to the willingness, or motivation, to do something. It has to do with confidence and commitment. Individuals who have high psychological readiness in a particular area or responsibility think that responsibility is important and have self-confidence and good feelings about themselves in that aspect of their job. They do not need extensive encouragement to get them to do things in that area. A comment from a person high in psychological readiness might be: "I really enjoy that aspect of my job. My boss doesn't have to get after me or provide any encouragement for me to do work in that area."

To recap the previous discussion:

Ability is a function of:

- *Knowledge*—knowledge of the task.
- *Experience*—experience with or related to the task.
- *Skill or performance*—demonstrated skill and/or performance in successfully completing similar tasks.

Willingness is a function of:

- *Confidence*—the person's feeling that, "I can do it."
- *Commitment*—the person's feeling that, "I will do it."
- *Motivation*—the person's feeling of, "I want to do it."

The high probability leadership style is one that is appropriate to the person's readiness level regarding that specific task. Very few people are likely to be at the extremes of a readiness continuum; most individuals fall somewhere in between.

Writing Effective Task Statements

A well-formulated task statement contributes greatly toward the assessment of individual readiness. In contrast, the leader will find that vague and weakly formulated task statements make it difficult to accurately assess task readiness, and can lead to unnecessary friction and conflict.

Gustav Pansegrouw, president of P-E Corporate Services, a management consulting firm, has found the following technique for writing task statements very useful, particularly from the follower's perspective.[13]

A key task for a customer order clerk may be stated as follows:

"To answer the phone promptly."

Using this task statement as a guide, the manager may assess the clerk's task readiness level as R2, willing but unable.

Using the same task statement as a guide, the clerk may assess the task readiness level as R4, willing and able.

This difference in task readiness assessment between manager and clerk is usually the result of different meanings attached to the word "promptly." Each person might have a different interpretation of what "promptly" means.

If the task is formulated in the following way:

"To answer the phone on the first ring."

both persons would have a much clearer understanding of the task. With such a specific statement of the task as a guide, it becomes much easier to assess task-relevant readiness. The probability of agreement between both parties' assessments also increases.

The major difference between the two task statements just presented is that the second one contains a *clearly defined and measur-*

able performance standard for the task. The expected performance is thus an *integral part* of the task.

Of all the aspects of accomplishing tasks, individual readiness is the most critical. At any given time, each person is at a variety of task-specific readiness levels, depending on the task that must be performed. It is not that an individual is high or low in readiness, but that each person tends to be approximately ready according to a specific task.

It should be remembered that although readiness is a useful concept for making diagnostic judgments, other situational variables—the supervisor's style (if close by), a crisis or time bind, the nature of the work—can be of equal or greater importance. Yet, the readiness concept is a solid bench mark for choosing the appropriate style with an individual or group at a particular time.

Direction of Readiness Change

Recent research at the Center for Leadership Studies has indicated that it is useful to measure not only a follower's general level of readiness, such as R1 or R2, but the *direction* of this readiness. The primary reason is that there are important differences in leader behavior if the follower's readiness is increasing, decreasing, or static.

For example, place yourself in the role of leader in each of three situations. Recall that one aspect of your role as leader is to diagnose the follower's ability and willingness to respond to your efforts to implement a specific goal. In other words, how receptive is the follower in each of these situations to your leadership efforts?

Situation 1

The follower's confidence, commitment, and motivation are low and are continuing to decline. Knowledge, experience, and skill remain marginal.

Situation 2

The follower's knowledge, skill, and experience are increasing from an entry level while confidence, commitment, and motivation remain low.

Situation 3

Ability and willingness remain low; the follower is unable and insecure.

After reading the three situations, you can diagnose the appropriate readiness level by looking for the key elements of ability and willingness. Remember that ability has the three components of knowledge, experience, and skill, while willingness has the three components of confidence, commitment, and motivation. One convenient way of assessing these components is to use a scale from $+++$ for a high level of readiness to $---$ for a low level of readiness.

Suppose you have made the correct diagnosis that the follower is R1–unable, unwilling, and insecure regarding the goal. You now want to diagnose the *direction* of the follower's readiness. Based on the information in each situation, do any of the elements seem to be increasing, decreasing, or remaining static?

In Situation 1 the follower is declining in readiness; in Situation 2 the follower is increasing in readiness; while in Situation 3 the follower remains static or unchanged in readiness.

What is the implication of this analysis to your leadership efforts? Although in *each* situation the follower's general level of readiness is R1, does this mean that your leadership interventions should be the same? Probably not. Situation 1 suggests action to correct regressive behavior; Situation 2 suggests continuing developmental behavior; and Situation 3 suggests initiating developmental behavior. Each of these potential leadership interventions will be discussed further in chapters 10 and 11.

Instruments to Measure Readiness

To help managers and their followers make valid judgments about follower readiness, the Center for Leadership Studies has developed two different Readiness Scale instruments: the *Manager Rating Scale* and the *Self-Rating Scale*.[14] Both leadership instruments measure Job Readiness (ability) and Psychological Readiness (willingness) on five behavioral dimensions.

In the Manager Rating Scale, for example, the manager selects one to five of the staff member's major objectives or responsibilities and writes them on the form. Then, with respect to *each* major objective or responsibility, the manager rates the staff member on five Job Readiness dimensions and five Psychological Readiness dimensions, basing the rating on observations of the staff member's behavior. Two of the five items from the Job Readiness Dimension and two of the five items from the Psychological Readiness Dimension are illustrated in Figure 8-5. The ten items used on the complete form were selected after a pilot study from a pool of more than thirty indicators of both dimensions. The reader will note that behavioral indicators, e.g. "Has experience relevant to the job" and "Does not have experience relevant to the job," were also developed and are opposite ends of the eight-point rating scale.

Your name _____ Today's date _____

Your staff member's name _____

In performing the objective _____ this person

JOB READINESS DIMENSIONS									
1. Past job experience	Has experience relevant to the job				Does not have experience relevant to the job				
	8	7	6	5	4	3	2	1	
2. Job Knowledge	Possesses necessary job knowledge				Does not have necessary job knowledge				
	8	7	6	5	4	3	2	1	

PSYCHOLOGICAL READINESS DIMENSIONS									
1. Willingness to take responsibility	Is very eager				Is very reluctant				
	8	7	6	5	4	3	2	1	
2. Achievement motivation	Has a high desire to achieve				Has little desire to achieve				
	8	7	6	5	4	3	2	1	

FIGURE 8-5 Representative sections from Readiness Scale: Manager Rating Scale

In more recent work, the Center for Leadership Studies developed a Readiness Style Match rating form that measures readiness using only one scale for each dimension—one measuring *ability* and the other measuring *willingness*.[15] In this instrument, a person's ability (knowledge, skill, and experience) is thought of as a matter of degree. That is, an individual's ability does not change drastically from one moment to the next. At any given moment, an individual has a little, some, quite a bit, or a great deal of ability.

Willingness (confidence, commitment, and motivation), however, is different. A person's motivation can, and often does, fluctuate from one moment to another. Therefore, a person is seldom, on occasion, often, or usually willing to take responsibility in a particular area.

The use of both a *Manager's Rating Form* and a *Staff Member Form* of the *Readiness Style Match* is necessary to initiate a program combining *Situational Leadership* with *Contracting for Leadership Style*.[16] We will discuss that process in some detail in chapter 12.

Components of Leadership Style

Once managers have identified the readiness level of the individual or group they are attempting to influence, the key to effective leadership then is to bring to bear the *appropriate leadership style*. If that is true, how can managers get a better handle on the behaviors that comprise each of the four leadership styles?

Instruments to measure leader behavior. To help managers and their staff members make better judgments about leadership style, the Center for Leadership Studies has developed two different *Leadership Scale* instruments: *Leadership Scale: Perception by Manager* and *Leadership Scale: Perception by Staff Member*.[17] Both leadership instruments measure task and relationship behavior on five behavioral dimensions. The five task behavior dimensions and five relationship behavior dimensions are listed in Table 8-2.

After the five dimensions were established for both leader behaviors, behavioral indicators of the extremes of each of these dimensions were identified to help managers and their staff members differentiate between high and low amounts of each leader behavior. For example, with the task-behavior dimension "organizing" on the Staff Member Form, the end points of a rating scale were chosen to be "organizes the work situation for me" and "lets me organize the work situation." For the relationship-behavior dimension "providing feedback," the end points of the rating scale were chosen to be "frequently provides feedback on my accomplishments" and "leaves it up to me to evaluate accomplishments."

TABLE 8-2 Task Behavior and Relationship Behavior Dimensions and Their Behavior Indicators

TASK-BEHAVIOR DIMENSIONS	BEHAVIORAL INDICATOR
	The extent to which a leader . . .
Goal setting	Specifies the goals people are to accomplish.
Organizing	Organizes the work situation for people.
Setting time lines	Sets time lines for people.
Directing	Provides specific directions.
Controlling	Specifies and requires regular reporting on progress.

RELATIONSHIP-BEHAVIOR DIMENSIONS	BEHAVIORAL INDICATOR
	The extent to which a leader . . .
Giving support	Provides support and encouragement.
Communicating	Involves people in "give-and-take" discussions about work activities.
Facilitating interactions	Facilitates people's interactions with others.
Active listening	Seeks out and listens to people's opinions and concerns.
Providing feedback	Provides feedback on people's accomplishments.

In the Readiness Style Match instrument discussed earlier, each of the four basic leadership styles are described, rather than the separate behavioral dimensions that make up each style. The descriptions of the four leader behaviors follow:

- Telling (S1)–Provide specific instructions and closely supervise performance
- Selling (S2)–Explain decisions and provide opportunity for clarification
- Participating (S3)–Share ideas and facilitate in making decisions
- Delegating (S4)–Turn over responsibility for decisions and implementation.

The advantage of using the readiness *Style Match* is that it permits managers and their staff members to rate leadership style and readiness on the same instrument. Figure 8-6 shows that integration. This figure provides a good summary of the key components involved in Situational Leadership.

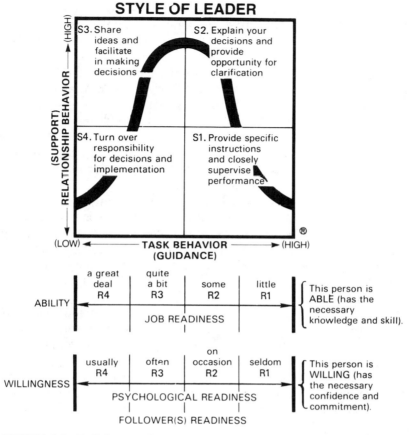

STYLE OF LEADER

S3. Share ideas and facilitate in making decisions

S2. Explain your decisions and provide opportunity for clarification

S4. Turn over responsibility for decisions and implementation

S1. Provide specific instructions and closely supervise performance

(HIGH) — RELATIONSHIP BEHAVIOR — (SUPPORT)

(LOW) ◄— TASK BEHAVIOR —► (HIGH)
(GUIDANCE)

	a great deal R4	quite a bit R3	some R2	little R1	
ABILITY		JOB READINESS			This person is ABLE (has the necessary knowledge and skill).

	usually R4	often R3	on occasion R2	seldom R1	
WILLINGNESS		PSYCHOLOGICAL READINESS			This person is WILLING (has the necessary confidence and commitment).

FOLLOWER(S) READINESS

FIGURE 8-6   Defining readiness and the four basic leadership styles

SITUATIONAL LEADERSHIP AND VARIOUS ORGANIZATIONAL SETTINGS

We have found that Situational Leadership has application in every kind of organizational setting, whether it be business and industry, education, government, military, or even the family. The concepts apply in any situation in which people are trying to influence the behavior of other people.

The only problem we have found in working in various organizational settings is that some of the language has to be adapted to fit specific vocabularies. For example, we found that in training non-working spouses, when we talked about task and relationship behavior, that did not ring any bells for them. We soon realized that in working in such family settings, it was much easier for parents and children to identify with "directive" behavior than with task behavior and to identify with "supportive" behavior than with relationship behavior.

On the other hand, when working with trainers and facilitators who have had a lot of personal growth experience and, therefore, are high on human relation quotients, even directive behavior will often tend to be a negative stimulus. Therefore, in working with these people we have found the word *guidance* is a good substitute for *directive behavior.* We want to emphasize that in utilizing various labels for the two basic leader behaviors—task behavior and relationship behavior—we are not changing the definitions at all. Task behavior is essentially the extent to which a leader engages in one-way communication by explaining what each staff member is to do as well as when, where, and how tasks are to be accomplished. Relationship behavior, even when we call it supportive behavior, is still the extent to which a leader engages in two-way communication by providing socioemotional support, "psychological strokes," and facilitating behaviors.

The reason it is important to modify the use of various words is that a key concept in all behavioral sciences is communication. If you're going to help people grow and develop, you have to learn to put frameworks, concepts, and research results into terminology that is acceptable to the groups you are attempting to influence. This has to be done if you want to have the highest probability of gaining acceptance and, therefore, affecting their growth.

Parent-Child Relationships

We have found tremendous application of Situational Leadership to the family and the parent-child relationship. The book *A Situational Approach to Parenting*[18] is devoted completely to applying Situational Leadership to the family setting.

We suggest that when working with children (while they will need "different strokes even for the same folks"), there is a general pattern and movement in leadership style over their developmental years. Thus, when working with children who are low in readiness on a particular task, a directive parent style has the highest probability of success. This is especially true during the first few years of children's lives when they are unable to control much of their own environment. This whole developmental process will be discussed in more depth in chapter 10.

Ineffective Parent Styles

One of the useful aspects of Situational Leadership is that one can begin to predict not only the leadership styles with the highest probability of effectiveness, but also which styles tend to be ineffective in what circumstances. For instance, we can take four examples of parents who tend to use a single leadership style during the child's entire developmental period.

First, let us look at the parent who uses a high directive–low supportive style (S1) with their children throughout the developmental years; that is, "As long as you're living in this house, you'll be home at ten o'clock and abide by the rules I've set." Two predictions might be made. The first one is that the children might pack their bags and leave home at the earliest opportunity. If this does not occur, they may succumb to their parents' authority and become very passive, dependent individuals throughout their lives, always needing someone to tell them what to do and when to do it.

A high probability result of a parent using exclusively a style of high directive–high supportive behavior (S2) might be called the "mama's boy" or "daddy's little girl" syndrome. Even when the children get older, they may chronologically be adults, but they are still psychologically dependent on their parent(s) to make decisions for them. Since most of the direction for their behavior and socioemotional support has been provided by their parent(s), these young people are unable to provide it for themselves.

What happens when parents are unfailingly supportive and never structure or direct any of their children's activities? The response to this high supportive–low directive style (S3) may be called a "spoiled brat" syndrome, for the children develop into individuals who have little regard for rules and little consideration for the rights of others.

As we mentioned in Chapter 5, some people might question why it is inappropriate to use the same leadership style all the time—"after all, we've been told that consistency is good." This advice might have been given in the past, but, as we argue, according to Situational Leadership, consistency is *not* using the same style all the time. Instead, consistency is using the same style for all similar situations, but varying the style appropriately as the situation changes. Parents are consistent if they tend to discipline their children when they are behaving inappropriately and reward them when they are behaving appropriately. Parents are inconsistent if they smile and engage in other supportive behavior when their children are bad as well as when they are good.

This discussion of consistency urges parents to remember that children are often at different levels of readiness in various aspects of their lives. Thus, parental style must vary as children's activities change.

Management of Research and Development Personnel

In working with highly trained and emotionally stable people, an effective leader behavior style in many cases is low relationship–low task behavior.[19] This was dramatically demonstrated in a military setting. Normally, in basically crisis-oriented organizations such as the military or the fire department, the most appropriate style tends to be high task (S1), since under combat or fire conditions success often depends on immediate response to orders. Time demands do not permit talking things over or explaining decisions. For success, behavior must be almost automatic. Although a high task style may be effective for a combat officer, it is often ineffective in working with research and development personnel within the military. This was pointed out when line officers trained at West Point were sent to command outposts in the American advanced-warning system. The scientific and technical personnel involved, living in close quarters in an Arctic region, did not respond favorably to the high levels of task behavior of the combat-trained officers. The levels of education, research experience, and readiness of these people were such that they did not need their commanding officer to initiate a great deal of structure in their work. In fact, they tended to resent it. Other experiences with scientific and research-oriented personnel indicate that many of these people also desire or need a limited amount of socioemotional support.

Educational Setting

Educational settings provide us with numerous examples of Situational Leadership in operation.[20]

Teacher-student relationship. In an educational setting, Situational Leadership is being used in studying the teacher-student relationship.

For example, Paul Hersey and two colleagues in Brazil, Arrigo L. Angelini and Sofia Caracushansky,[21] conducted a study applying Situational Leadership to teaching. In the study, an attempt was made to compare the learning effectiveness scores between (1) students who attended a course in which a conventional teacher-student relationship prevailed (control subgroups); and (2) students who attended a course in which Situational Leadership was applied by the same teacher (experimental subgroups). In the control group classes, lectures prevailed, but group discussions, audiovisual aids, and other participative resources were also used. In the experimental classes, the readiness level of students (willingness and ability to direct their own learning and provide their own reinforcement) was developed over time by a systematic shift in teaching style. The teacher's style started at S1 (high task–low relationship–teacher in front of the class lecturing); then moved to S2 (high task–high relationship behavior–group discussions in a circular design with the teacher directing the conversation); then to S3 (high relationship–low task–group discussions with the teacher participating as a supportive, but nondirective group member); and finally to S4 (low relationship–low task–the group continuing to discuss with the teacher involved only when asked by the class). The development of student readiness was a slow process at first, with gradual decreases in teacher direction and increases in teacher encouragement. As the students demonstrated their ability not only to assume more and more responsibility for directing their own learning, but also to provide their own reinforcement (self-gratification), decreases in teacher socioemotional support accompanied continual decreases in teacher direction.

In two experiments with this design, the experimental classes showed not only higher performance on content exams, but were also observed to have a higher level of enthusiasm, morale, and motivation, as well as less tardiness and absenteeism.

Administrator–governing board relationship. An important area for the top administrator (college president or superintendent) in an educational institution is the relationship this person maintains with the governing board. Since these boards have the ultimate power to remove college presidents or superintendents when they lose confidence in their leadership, these administrators often tend to use a high relationship style (S3), providing only a limited amount of structure for these decision-making groups.[22] In fact, they sometimes seem to shy away from directing the activities of their board for fear of arousing their criticism. Situational Leadership questions this behavior.

Although the members of the governing board are often responsible, well-educated individuals, they tend to have little work experience in an educational setting. For example, in a survey of college trustees in New York State, it was found that less than 10 percent of the trustees serving on these boards had any teaching or administrative experience in an educational institution.[23] In fact, the large majority of the 1,269 trustees sampled were employed primarily in industry, insurance and banking, merchandising and transportation, and medicine and law. Virtually half acted as corporation officials with the rank of treasurer, director, or above. In addition to their involvement in other than educational institutions, these trustees tended to be overcommitted and were probably unable to give the time to university problems they would have liked to give. In fact, the most frequent dissatisfaction expressed by trustees was the lack of time to devote to the board.

The relative inexperience of the trustees and the heavy commitment elsewhere suggest that it may be appropriate for college presidents to combine with their high relationship behavior an increase of task behavior in working with their trustees. In fact, the responsibility for defining the role of trustees and organizing their work should fall on the college president. Henry Wriston, former president of Brown University, said it well:

> It may seem strange, at first thought, that this should be a president's duty. A moment's reflection makes it clear that it can evolve on no other person. Trustees are unpaid; they have no method of analyzing talents and making assignments. The president is in a position to do so.[24]

Administrator–faculty relationship. In working with experienced faculty, the low relationship–low task style (S4) characterized by a decentralized organization structure and delegation of responsibility to individuals may be appropriate. The level of education and experience of these people is often such that they do not need their department chairperson to initiate much structure. Sometimes they tend to resent it. In addition, some faculty desire or need only a limited amount of socioemotional support (relationship behavior).

Often an effective leader style in working with faculty tends to be low relationship–low task, but certain deviations may be necessary. For example, during the early stages of a school year or a curriculum change, a certain amount of structure as to the specific areas to be taught, by whom, when, and where must be established. Once these requirements and limitations are understood by the faculty, the administrator may move rapidly back to low relationship–low task style appropriate for working with experienced, responsible, self-motivated faculty.

Other deviations may be necessary. For example, a new, inexperienced teacher might need more direction and socioemotional support until gaining experience in the classroom.

UNDERSTANDING EARLIER RESEARCH

Determining the Effectiveness of Participation

An analysis of studies in participation[25] in terms of Situational Leadership also suggests some interesting things about the appropriate use of participation. Situational Leadership suggests that the higher the level of task-relevant readiness of an individual or group, the higher the probability that participation will be an effective management technology. The less task-relevant readiness, the lower the probability that participation will be a useful management practice.

Involvement and participation in decision making with people at extremely low levels of readiness might be characterized by a pooling of ignorance, or the blind leading the blind; therefore, directive leadership might have a higher probability of success. At the other end of the readiness continuum (extremely high levels of task-relevant readiness), some of these people tend to resist engaging in "group think." They would prefer the individual with the highest level of expertise in an area to make the decisions there. "Bill, how do you think we should go on this? It's your area." Thus, according to Situational Leadership, participation as a management technique has a higher probability of success as one moves from low to moderate levels of readiness, and then begins to plateau in potential effectiveness as one's followers become high in task-relevant readiness, as illustrated in Figure 8-7.

One further point about participation. Although participation tends to satisfy affiliation and esteem needs by giving people a chance to feel in on things and be recognized as important in the decision-making process, it should be remembered that self-actualization may not result from participation. The high-level need satisfaction most often occurs in a work environment where people are given a job that

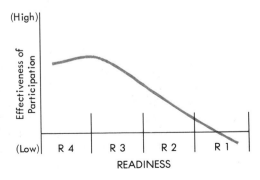

FIGURE 8-7
Participation as an effective management technique

allows them an opportunity for achievement, growth and development, and challenge.

The Influence of Cultural Change[26]

The scientific and technical advancements in United States society since the turn of the century almost stagger the imagination. As a result, we have become a dynamic, industrial society with a higher level of education and standard of living then ever thought possible. This phenomenon is beginning to have a pronounced effect on much of the work force utilized by organizations.

Today, many employees enjoy a higher standard of living and tend to be better educated and more sophisticated than ever before. As a result, these workers have increased potential for self-direction and self-control. Consistent with these changes in readiness, a large majority of our population, in Maslow's terms, now have their basic physiological and safety-security needs fairly well satisfied. Management can no longer depend on the satisfaction of these needs—through pay, incentive plans, hospitalization, and so on—as primary motivating factors that influence industrial employees. In our society today, there is almost a built-in expectation in people that physiological and safety needs will be fulfilled. In fact, most people do not generally have to worry about where their next meal will come from or whether they will be protected from the elements of physical danger. They are now more susceptible to motivation from other needs: people want to belong, to be recognized as "somebody," and to have a chance to develop to their fullest potential. As William H. Haney has said:

> The managerial practice, therefore, should be geared to the subordinate's *current level of [readiness] with the overall goal of helping him to develop, to require progressively less external control, and to gain more and more self-control.* And why would a man want this? Because under these conditions he achieves satisfaction on the job at the levels, primarily the ego and self-fulfillment levels, at which he is the most motivatable.[27]

This concept is illustrated in Figure 8-8.

This shift in the readiness level and need disposition of our general population helps us to understand why the findings of many studies of the relationship between leadership styles and productivity, such as those conducted by Likert and Halpin, seem to cluster around styles 2 and 3, but not at the extremes (1 and 4).

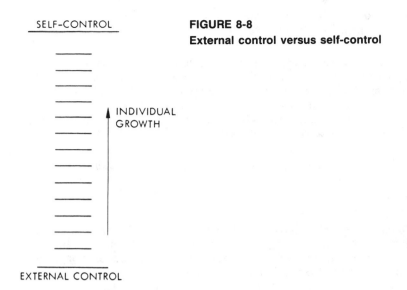

SELF-CONTROL

INDIVIDUAL
GROWTH

EXTERNAL CONTROL

FIGURE 8-8
External control versus self-control

DOES SITUATIONAL LEADERSHIP WORK?

The widespread acceptance of Situational Leadership for more than two decades as a concept with face validity is well documented. Practicing managers, parents, teachers, and administrators throughout the world say it has given them a practical, easy-to-use approach for determining what they should do in challenging situations. It has been a major factor in training and development programs for more than 400 of the Fortune 500 companies, such as Bank of America, Caterpillar, IBM, Mobil Oil, Union 76, and Xerox. It has been widely accepted in all of the military services and numerous fast-growing entrepreneurial companies. More than one million leaders receive Situational Leadership development per year. While research studies have attempted to validate Situational Leadership from various directions, the real question that managers, teachers, parents, and administrators ask is: Does Situational Leadership work? We would like to present just two of the many studies that attempt to answer this question.

Some years ago, the Information Systems Group (ISG) of Xerox, responsible for copier/duplicator products, made a major commitment to Situational Leadership as a training concept. Situational Leadership now is a cornerstone of ISG's building-block training strategy and is taught to middle-level as well as new first-level managers. As Gumpert and Hambleton indicate:

> Despite the model's intuitive appeal and quick acceptance by our managers, because of the training resources required, ISG management development had to answer a critical question: Are managers who use the model correctly in their interactions with employees more effective than those who do not? After all, if they are no more effective, there would be no point to training in Situational Leadership.[28]

Sixty-five managers in sales, service, administration, and staff functions participated in the study. These managers completed three types of forms.[29]

- A *manager questionnaire,* which was constructed to provide demographic data, such as age, sex, years of service, and so on. The questionnaire also asked for perceptions of the managers' job performance and use of Situational Leadership.
- A *professional [readiness] scale,* which was used to determine a [follower's] level of [readiness] for a set of major job objectives. Each manager assessed one to four employees.
- A *manager rating form,* which allowed the managers to assess their own leadership styles and their [followers'] job performance for each major job objective. The following job performance rating scale, identical to Xerox's appraisal scale, was used:

RATING	PERFORMANCE DESCRIPTION
5	Exceptional
4	Consistently exceeds expected level
3	Expected level
2	Meets minimal requirements
1	Unsatisfactory

To test the validity of Situational Leadership, data were collected for two predictions:

- Highly effective managers will indicate more knowledge and use of Situational Leadership than less effective managers.
- Employee job performance will be higher when managers apply Situational Leadership correctly than when they apply it incorrectly.[30]

The study led to these conclusions:

- Highly effective managers indicate greater knowledge and use of Situational Leadership than less effective ones.

- All managers in the study reported using Situational Leadership at least some of the time. This finding demonstrates that training in this area has had substantial on-the-job impact.

- On the average, managers who apply the model correctly rate their [followers'] job performance higher than managers who do not. The data in this area are highly supportive of the Hersey–Blanchard model of leadership effectiveness.[31]

Gumpert and Hambleton conclude:

Stated simply, highly effective managers knew more about Situational Leadership and used it more than less effective managers. Data supporting this came from the managers themselves. Also, there is strong evidence suggesting that when Situational Leadership was applied correctly, subordinate job performance was judged higher, and the gains in job performance were practically and statistically significant.[32]

Research was conducted on the impact of the interactive video Situational Leadership program on managers of a large firm that was undergoing major changes and internal restructuring. The sample of 161 managers who had received the training nine to eighteen months prior to the research completed a questionnaire booklet that included four sections: (1) an appraisal of training course content; (2) a test of skill and knowledge retention; (3) a report of a critical incident involving use of the training; and (4) an open-ended opportunity to provide feedback.

The results indicated that Situational Leadership was highly effective. Managers offered favorable appraisals of the course; they demonstrated an impressive level of mastery (retention) of course skills; and they reported successful outcomes as a consequence of using the skills on the job. The findings lend support to the claim that managerial training can improve managerial performance, even under conditions of change in the work place.[33]

CHANGING LEADERSHIP STYLE APPROPRIATELY

If managers are currently using a style that is appropriate for the level of readiness of their group, one of the indicators that they can use in determining when and to what degree they should shift their style is performance, or results.[34] How well is their group performing in their present activities? If performance is increasing, it would be appropriate for managers to shift their style to the left along the curvilinear function of the Situational Leadership model. This would indicate that task-relevant readiness is increasing. If performance results are on the decline, it gives managers a clue that they may need to shift their leader behavior to the right along the curvilinear function. In the next chapter, we will discuss specifically the implications and implementation of these processes.

NOTES

1. Edgar H. Schein, *Organizational Psychology* (Englewood Cliffs, N. J.: Prentice Hall, 1965), p. 61.
2. *Ibid.*
3. Situational Leadership was first published by Paul Hersey and Kenneth H. Blanchard as "Life Cycle Theory of Leadership" in *Training and Development Journal,* May 1969.
4. Kenneth Blanchard, Patricia Zigarmi and Drea Zigarmi. *Leadership and the One Minute Manager.* (New York: William Morrow & Co., Inc. 1985). For further information on SLII® contact Blanchard Training and Development, Inc., 125 State Place, Escondido, CA 92029.
5. Fillmore H. Sanford, *Authoritarianism and Leadership* (Philadelphia: Institute for Research in Human Relations, 1950).
6. The following section has been adopted from Paul Hersey, *Situational Selling* (Escondido, Calif.: Center for Leadership Studies, 1985), p. 19 and following.
7. *Ibid.*
8. *Ibid.*
9. *Ibid.,* p. 22.
10. *Ibid.,* pp. 25–26.
11. *Ibid.,* pp. 28–31.
12. David C. McClelland, J. W. Atkinson, R. A. Clark and E. L. Lowell, *The Achievement Motive* (New York: Appleton-Century-Crofts, 1953); and *The Achieving Society* (Princeton, N. J.: D. Van Nostrand, 1961).
13. Contributed by Gustav Pansegrouw, P-E Corporate Services.
14. These two instruments, originally using the term "maturity," were developed by Ronald K. Hambleton, Kenneth H. Blanchard, and Paul Hersey through a grant from Xerox Corporation. We are grateful to Xerox Corporation not only for providing financial support for the instrument development project but also for allowing us to involve many of their managers and employees in our development and validation work. In particular, we would like to acknowledge Audian Dunham, Warren Rothman, and Ray Gumpert for their assistance, encouragement, and constructive criticism of our work. The instruments are available through the Center for Leadership Studies, Escondido, Calif.
15. These instruments, originally using the term "maturity," were developed by Paul Hersey, Kenneth H. Blanchard, and Joseph Keilty. Information on these instruments is available through Center for Leadership Studies, Escondido, Calif.
16. The *Integration of Situational Leadership with Contracting for Leadership Styles* was first published as Paul Hersey, Kenneth H. Blanchard, and Ronald K. Hambleton, "Contracting for Leadership Style: A Process and Instrumentation for Building Effective Work Relationships" in *The Proceedings of OD78,* San Francisco, Calif., sponsored by University Associates/LRC. This presentation is available through the Center for Leadership Studies, Escondido, Calif.
17. The initial versions of these leadership scales were developed by Paul Hersey, Kenneth H. Blanchard, and Ronald K. Hambleton. Information on these instruments is available through the Center for Leadership Studies, Escondido, Calif.
18. Paul Hersey and Kenneth H. Blanchard, *The Family Game* (Escondido, Calif.: Center for Leadership Studies, 1979).

19. See Paul Hersey and Kenneth H. Blanchard, "Managing Research and Development Personnel: An Application of Leadership Theory," *Research Management,* September 1969.
20. See Kenneth H. Blanchard and Paul Hersey, "A Leadership Theory for Educational Administrators," *Education,* Spring 1970.
21. Arrigo L. Angelini, Paul Hersey and Sofia Caracushansky, "The Situational Leadership Theory Applied to Teaching: A Research on Learning Effectiveness," Sao Paulo, Brazil.
22. Kenneth H. Blanchard, "College Boards of Trustees: A Need for Directive Leadership," *Academy of Management Journal,* December 1967.
23. F. H. Stutz, R. G. Morrow, and K. H. Blanchard, "Report of a Survey," in *College and University Trustees and Trusteeship: Recommendations and Report of a Survey* (Ithaca: New York State Regents Advisory Committee on Educational Leadership, 1966).
24. Henry M. Wriston, *Academic Procession* (New York: Columbia University Press, 1959), p. 78.
25. A classic study in the area of participation is Victor H. Vroom, *Some Personality Determinants of the Effects of Participation* (Englewood Cliffs, N. J.: Prentice Hall, 1960).
26. See Paul Hersey and Kenneth H. Blanchard, "Cultural Changes: Their Influence on Organizational Structure and Management Behavior," *Training and Development Journal,* October 1970.
27. William H. Haney, *Communication and Organizational Behavior: Text and Cases,* rev. ed. (Homewood, Ill.: Irwin, 1967), p. 20.
28. Raymond A. Gumpert and Ronald K. Hambleton, "Situational Leadership: How Xerox Managers Fine-Tune Managerial Styles to Employee Maturity and Task Needs," *Management Review,* December 1979, p. 9.
29. *Ibid.,* p. 11.
30. *Ibid.*
31. *Ibid.,* p. 12.
32. *Ibid.*
33. Research summary available from Center for Leadership Studies, Escondido, Calif.
34. Suggestion made by Fred Finch at the Faculty Club, University of Massachusetts, Fall 1974. Fred is now a consultant with Blanchard Training and Development.

9

Situational Leadership, Perception, and the Impact of Power

The concepts of leadership and power have generated lively interest, debate, and occasionally confusion throughout the evolution of management thought. The concept of power is closely related to the concept of leadership, for power is one of the means by which a leader influences the behavior of followers.[1] Given this integral relationship between leadership and power, leaders must not only assess their leader behavior in order to understand how they actually influence other people, but they must also examine their possession and use of power.[2]

POWER DEFINED

We earlier defined leadership as an attempt to influence another individual or group and concluded that leadership is an influence process. How do you influence? Through power. Power is influence potential—the resource that enables a leader to gain compliance or commitment from others. Despite its critical importance, power is a subject that is often avoided. This is because power can have its seamy side, and many people want to wish it away and pretend it is not there. But power is a real-world issue. Leaders who understand and know how to use power are more effective than those who do not or will not use power. It is important to understand that to successfully influence the behavior of others, the leader should understand the impact of power on the various leadership styles. In today's world, many sources of power within organizations have been legislated, negotiated, or policied away. Since leaders now have less power to draw from, it is more important to be effective in the use of what is available. Since power bases drive your leadership styles, using them appropriately can enhance your effectiveness as a leader.[3]

In spite of the widespread usage of the term *power* in the management literature, there is considerable confusion over its definition. Power and other concepts, such as influence and authority, are often definitionally indistinct among scholars.[4] Russell[5] defined power as "the production of intended effects." Bierstedt[6] defined power as "the ability to employ force." Wrong[7] limited power to the intended, successful control of others. French[8] defined the power that person A has over person B as "equal to the maximum force which A can induce on B minus the maximum force which B can mobilize in the opposing direction." For Dahl,[9] "A has power over B to the extent that A can get B to do something that B would otherwise not do."

Rogers[10] attempted to clear up the terminological confusion by defining power as "the potential for influence." Thus, power is a resource which may or may not be used. The use of power resulting in a change in the probability that a person or group will adopt the desired behavioral change is defined as "influence." Accepting Rogers's definition, we make this distinction between leadership and power. As was suggested in Chapter 4, leadership is defined as the process of influencing the activities of an individual or a group in efforts toward goal accomplishment in a given situation. Therefore, leadership is simply any attempt to influence, while power is well described as a leader's *influence potential*. It is the resource that enables a leader to induce compliance from or to influence others.

POWER: AN ERODING CONCEPT

If power is defined as influence potential, how does one describe authority? Authority is a particular type of power that has its origin in the position that a leader occupies. Thus, authority is the power that is legitimatized by virtue of an individual's formal role in a social organization.

Hundreds of years ago, the kings and queens had all the power; the serfs had none. After all, their positions gave them ultimate authority. For years, it was almost a similar case with managers.

They could make all the decisions. If they didn't like the way you looked or the way you combed your hair, they could fire you, and workers could do very little to stop such arbitrary action. Today, that is no longer the case. What does that mean in terms of a leader's influence potential?

First of all, managers must realize that power is not infinite. There is only so much power around. If someone else has it, you don't. If your power is legislated or negotiated away, it is no longer there. The amount of power available does not expand in different situations. As James A. Lee argues, "Leader power is what is left after subtracting all [follower] power (i.e., collective, legal, economic independence, and expertise), power removed from their grasp by the nature of the task (i.e., a machine-paced assembly line, lack of proximity, and physical barriers), and that removed by power sources outside their organizational unit (organizational policies, intrusions from their boss, and public sentiment)."[11] Thus, today's manager only has a limited amount of power.

Second, if managers have only a portion of the total power available, they must learn ways to use the power they have in realistic and meaningful ways. In addition, where managers used to rely on the power of their position, they now have to look for other bases, or sources, of power.

POSITION POWER AND PERSONAL POWER

One of the characteristics of leadership is that leaders exercise power. Amitai Etzioni discusses the difference between *position power* and *personal power*. His distinction springs from his concept of power as the ability to induce or influence behavior. He claims that power is derived from an organizational office, personal influence, or both. Individuals who are able to induce other individuals to do a certain job because of their position in the organization are considered to have position power; individuals who derive their power from their followers are considered to have personal power. Some individuals can have both position power and personal power.[12]

Where do managers get the position power that is available to them? Although Etzioni would argue that it comes from the organizational office of a manager, we feel it comes from above and, therefore, is not inherent in the office. Managers occupying positions in an organization may have more or less position power than their predecessor or someone else in a similar position in the same organization. It is not a matter of the office having power, but rather the extent to which those people to whom managers report are willing to delegate authority and responsibility down to them. So position power tends to flow down in an organization. This is not to say that leaders do not have any impact on how much position power they accrue. They certainly do. The confidence and trust they develop with the people above them will often determine the willingness of upper management to delegate down to them. And remember, it is not just a downward delegation; their supervisor can take it back. We have all seen this occur on occasions when managers still have the same responsibilities, but all of a sudden their authority (reward system and sanctions) to get the job done in the way they once did is taken away.

Personal power is the extent to which followers respect, feel good about, and are committed to their leader, and see their own goals as being satisfied by the goals of their leader. In other words, personal power is the extent to which people are willing to follow a leader. As a result, personal power in an organizational setting comes from below—the followers. Thus, we must be careful when we say that some leaders are charismatic or have personal power that flows from them. If that were true, we would have to be able to say that managers with personal power could take over any department and have the same commitment and rapport they had in their last department. We know that is not true. Although managers certainly can influence the amount of personal power they have by the way they treat their people, it is a volatile kind of power. It can be taken away rapidly by followers. Make a few dramatic mistakes and see how many people are willing to follow. Personal power is a day-to-day phenomenon—it can be earned and it can be taken away.

Etzioni suggested that the best situation for leaders is when they have both personal power and position power. But in some cases it is not possible to build a relationship on both. Then the question becomes whether it is more important to have personal power or position power. Happiness and human relations have been culturally reinforced over the past several decades. With this emphasis, most people would pick personal power as being the most important. But there may be another side of the coin.

In his sixteenth-century treatise *The Prince,* Machiavelli presents an interesting viewpoint when he raises the question of whether it is better to have a relationship based on love (personal power) or fear (position power).[13] Machiavelli, as does Etzioni, contends that it is best to be both loved and feared. If, however, one cannot have both, he suggests that a relationship based on love alone tends to be volatile, short-lived, and easily terminated when there is no fear of retaliation. On the other hand, Machiavelli contends that a relationship based on fear tends to be longer lasting, in that the individual must be willing to incur the sanction (pay the price) before terminating the relationship. This is a difficult concept for many people to accept, and yet one of the most difficult roles for leaders—whether they be a supervisor, teacher, or parent—is disciplining someone about whom they care. Yet to be effective, leaders sometimes have to sacrifice short-term friendship for long-term respect if they are interested in the growth and development of the people with whom they are working. Machiavelli warns, however, that one should be careful that fear does not lead to hatred. For hatred often evokes overt behavior in terms of retaliation, undermining, and attempts to overthrow.

In summary, *position power* is the extent to which the leader has rewards, punishments and sanctions to bring to bear in reference to followers.[14] It tends to come from above in the organization. Position power can be thought of as the authority to use the rewards and sanctions that are delegated down. But one must be careful. Just because you have position power today does not mean that you will have it tomorrow. People above you can delegate it, but they can also take it back. It doesn't mean you don't have any impact on how much you receive. That is the result of the trust and confidence you build with your people.

Personal power is defined as the extent to which leaders gain the confidence and trust of those people that they're attempting to influence. It's the cohesiveness, commitment, and rapport between leaders and followers. It is also impacted by the extent to which followers see their own goals as being the same, similar to, or at least dependent upon the accomplishment of the leader's goals.

While position power comes from above in the organization, personal power flows from the followers. Personal power is not inherent in the leader. It has to be earned from the followers on a day-to-day basis. Just because you've got it today, doesn't mean you've got it tomorrow. This country re-elected Richard Nixon with a landslide victory in 1972 and just a few months later took back its commitment. Personal power is not within the leader, but comes from the people the leader is attempting to influence.

Although personal and position power are unique and distinct, they are an interacting influence system: one directly affects the other. Often followers are affected by their perception of the leader's ability to provide rewards, punishments and sanctions, and influence up the organization. Also, the extent to which people above you in the organization are willing to delegate position power is often dependent on their perception of the followers' commitment to you. *So it is not sufficient just to have either position or personal power alone—you need to work at gaining both.*

Supervisor/Associates

SELLING

Leadership = Influence

MANAGING

FIGURE 9-1
Selling up/Managing down   Staff members/Followers

Source: Paul Hersey, Situational Selling *(Escondido, Calif.:*
Center for Leadership Studies, 1985), p. 15.

Selling Within Your Own Organization[15]

It is important to keep in mind that no matter where you are within your organization, you are trying to influence people. If you are managing, you can use both position power and personal power to influence the people who report directly to you. However, when attempting to influence your supervisor, senior executives, and associates, you must depend almost exclusively on personal power. Therefore, you are selling. When you have little or no position power, you must learn to develop rapport through personal power, because it is through this trust and confidence that an effective relationship can be built. Figure 9-1 illustrates this important idea. Keep in mind that power is a real-world issue. People who understand and know how to use power are more effective than those who do not or will not. Recognition of the fact that all managers are in the business of selling is an important aspect of this understanding.

ADDITIONAL BASES OF POWER

While position power and personal power are important and useful in examining power, they are limited because you are always forced to divide "the pie" into just two pieces.

Natemeyer cites a number of other attempts to classify bases of power.[16] Peabody[17] classified the statements of respondents in a police department, a welfare office, and an elementary school into four categories. These were power of legitimacy (laws, rules, policies); of position; of competence (professional and technical expertise); and of person.

A study by Filley and Grimes[18] identified eleven reasons why an individual would seek a decision from another on various work-related matters in a professional organization. These reasons, from most frequently to least frequently mentioned, were responsibility and function (the person is responsible for the particular matter); formal authority (the person is in a position to make decisions generally); control of resources (the person controls money, information, and so on); collegial (a group of peers has the right to be consulted); manipulation (the person can get the decision made in the manner desired); default or avoidance (the person is available and will deal with the problem); bureaucratic rules (the rules specify the person to consult); traditional rules (custom, tradition, or seniority specify the person to consult); equity (the person is a fair decision maker); friendship (the person is personally liked); and expertise (the person has superior knowledge of the subject).

Many other power base classification systems have been developed,[19] but the framework devised by French and Raven[20] appears to be the most widely accepted. They propose that there are five different bases of power: coercive power, expert power, legitimate power, referent power, and reward power.

Later, Raven collaborating with Kruglanski,[21] identified a sixth power base—information power. Then, in 1979,[22] Hersey and Goldsmith proposed a seventh basis of power—connection power. These seven bases of power, identified as potential means of successfully influencing the behavior of others, are shown in Figure 9-2.

The Perception of Power[23]

You will note that in the following discussion of power bases, we use the word *perceived* in such instances as: coercive power—the perceived ability to provide sanctions. We do this because the key issue in the

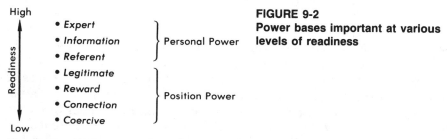

FIGURE 9-2
Power bases important at various levels of readiness

Source: Paul Hersey, Situational Selling *(Escondido, Calif.: Center for Leadership Studies, 1985), p. 114.*

concept of power is that it is not based on the reality of how much power the manager has but rather on the followers' perception of that power. *Truth and reality evoke no behavior. All behavior is based on people's perception and interpretation of truth and reality.* For example, when a couple has a fight, it does not matter whether the cause was real or imagined—it was just as much of a fight. It is the perception others hold about power that gives people the ability to influence.

We operate using psychological maps. The caution that one must make is that no matter how hard we work or how detailed our psychological maps, the map is not the territory. But the closer and closer we match our psychological map to the territory, the higher the probability that we will effectively be able to operate within that territory. We have to remember, however, that the map is not the territory—no matter how much information and specificity we have in terms of our psychological map.

Get the Data Out[24]

With power, people must not only perceive you as having it, they must see you as able and willing to use it. Because power is a matter of perception, it is important that you get out the data. It's not enough to have access to power. You have to let people know you're willing to use it. You can't hide your light under a bushel. Information has no value in a data bank. It has value only when you get it out to the end user in a fashion that can be understood and accepted. It means simply that, if you don't blow your own horn, somebody else will use it as a spitoon! Some leaders *have* plenty of power, but are unwilling to *use* it.

Consider a father examining his son's report card and suffering mild cardiac tremors as he sees a solid column of *D* grades. Outraged that a product of his genes could so disgrace the family, he confronts his son and says, "Dave, this just won't do. I can't tolerate these grades, and if you don't show me an immediate turn-around, you're going to be grounded!"

Six weeks later, Dave brings home another report card. This time the *D* grades are written in red ink with exclamation points. The father says, "David, get in here! I'm really upset, and now you have no choice at all. Hit those books hard or you're definitely going to be grounded!

Next time it's the same except that the teacher has added some pointed remarks about Dave's inattentive behavior in class. Dave's father turns crimson, crumples his beer can, and shouts, "David Ralph, this is it . . . last chance city . . . you're in real trouble with the old man now!"

What has Dave learned? That his father, who has the ability to ground him, won't use the power! Because of his Dad's reluctance to follow through with his threatened punishments, Dave knows that all he has to do is take heat for six minutes and he's off the hook for six weeks!

Power is a matter of perception—use it or lose it!

Readiness, Styles, and Power Bases[25]

The relationship between readiness, the appropriate style, and the power base that drives that style will be explained from the aspects of managing and leading.

Coercive Power—The Perceived Ability to Provide Sanctions or Consequences for Nonperformance

Followers at readiness level R1 need guidance. It is important to remember that too much supportive behavior with people who are not performing may be perceived as permissive or as rewarding the lack of performance. Without some coercive power to drive the *telling* style, attempts to influence may be like water off a duck's back. Followers need to know that if they do not respond, there may be some costs, sanctions, or other consequences. These may take the form of a reprimand, cut in pay, transfer, demotion, or even dismissal.

Managers often erode their coercive power by not following through. They may have the ability to impose sanctions, but for one reason or another are unwilling to do so. This can result in a loss of power.

Another way to erode coercive power is by not differentiating in the use of sanctions based upon performance. If people feel they will be punished regardless of performance, coercive power has little impact.

It is even possible to "talk" coercive power away. A manager begins a performance appraisal interview with a low performer by saying, "Now, look, both of us know that you've been here over twenty years and I can't get rid of you. . . ." In just a few words, the manager has stripped away any coercive power the follower might have perceived.

Connection Power—The Perceived Association with Influential Persons or Organizations

Connection power is an important driver for *telling* and *selling* leadership styles. Usually followers at R1 and R2 want to avoid the sanction or gain the favor they associate with powerful connections. The important issue is not whether there is a real connection, but whether there is a perception of a real connection.

For example, a first-level supervisor may be regarded as having limited power. But, if that supervisor is married to a relative of the company president, the perceived connection may provide added influence with others in the organization.

Reward Power—The Perceived Ability to Provide Things That People Would Like to Have

Reward power is enhanced if managers are seen as having the ability to give appropriate rewards. Followers who are unable but willing are more likely to try on new behaviors if they feel increases in performance will be rewarded. Rewards may include raises, bonuses, promotions, or transfers to more desirable positions. They may also include intangibles such as a pat on the back or feedback on accomplishment. In the final analysis, managers get what they reward.

A significant amount of reward power has been legislated, negotiated, and policied away. We find that this is true in the classroom as well as in almost every organization. Yet, using managers as an example, the managers themselves often erode the power that remains by making promises they don't keep. For example:

Salesperson: "I did it! I made the 15 percent over quota with room to spare. When am I going to get that 10 percent bonus?"

Sales Mgr: "I'm sorry, but economic conditions are such that we'll have to postpone it for a while. But don't worry, if you keep up the good work, I promise I'll make it up to you."

Other managers erode their reward power by hoping for *A* but rewarding *B*. An example might be an organization that gives all salespeople a 10 percent cost-of-living adjustment and yet the difference between reward for *average* sales and *outstanding* sales is only 1 or 2 percent. In this case, "hanging around" for another year is significantly rewarded. This often results in high performers losing their motivation and commitment or looking outside the company for opportunities.

Legitimate Power—The Perception That It Is Appropriate for the Leader to Make Decisions Due to Title or Position in the Organization

Legitimate power can be a useful driver for the *selling* and *participating* styles. Followers who are both unable and unwilling could care less about whether someone's title is "manager," "regional manager," or "vice-president." By the same token, followers high in readiness are far less impressed with title or position than they are with expertise or information that the leader has to offer. But followers in the moderate ranges of readiness can often be influenced if they feel it is appropriate for a person in *that* position or with *that* title to make *that* decision. For example, a salesperson commenting to a peer about the department's recent reorganization: ". . . Pat should be making those kinds of decisions . . . that's what the Sales Manager gets paid to do."

Referent Power—The Perceived
Attractiveness of Interacting
with Another Person

In attempting to influence people who have the ability, but are insecure or unwilling, high relationship behavior is necessary. If people have a confidence problem, the manager needs to *encourage*. If they have a motivation problem, the manager needs to *discuss* and *problem solve*. In either case, if the manager has not taken time to build rapport, attempts to participate may be perceived as adversarial rather than helpful. Confidence, trust, and rapport are important in influencing people. If a follower feels that the manager will provide encouragement and help when it is needed, it can make an important difference in the success of the influence attempt.

Referent power is based on the manager's personal traits. A manager high in referent power is generally liked and admired by others because of personality. It is this liking for, admiration for, and identification with the manager that influences others.

Information Power—The Perceived Access
to—Or Possession of—Useful Information

The styles that tend to effectively influence followers at above average readiness levels, R3 and R4, are *participating and delegating*. Information Power is helpful in driving these styles. This power source has grown in importance during the high-tech explosion, with the emphasis on data storage and data retrieval.

Information power is based on perceived access to data. This is different from expert power, which is the *understanding* of or ability to *use* data. For example, in a recent study, it was found that secretaries in a major corporate office had a significant amount of information power, but little expert power in some technical areas. They were able to help gain or prevent access to information, but in a few technical areas had little expertise themselves.

Expert Power—The Perception that the
Leader Has Relevant Education, Experience,
and Expertise

Followers who are competent and confident require little direction or supportive behavior. They are able and willing to perform on their own. The driver for influencing these followers is expert power. With followers who are able and willing, leaders are more effective if they possess the expertise, skill, and knowledge that followers respect and regard as important.

IS THERE A BEST TYPE OF POWER?

The French and Raven initial classification system motivated a number of scholars to try to answer the following question: Given the wide variety of power bases available to the leader, which type of power should be emphasized in order to maximize effectiveness? In any attempt to answer this question, it is important to remember the definition of effectiveness. As stated in chapter 6, organizational effectiveness, as well as leader effectiveness, is a function of both output variables and intervening variables. Natemeyer[26] reviewed the various studies that attempted to investigate the relationship between work group effectiveness and the degree to which a leader utilizes various power bases.

Student[27] studied forty production groups in two plants of a company that manufactured home appliances. Employees rated the extent to which they complied with their foremen due to each of the five French and Raven power bases. Legitimate power was found to be the strongest reason for compliance, followed by expert power, reward power, referent power, and last, coercive power.

Student also related the foreman's power base utilization (as perceived by the workers) to a number of measures of performance. He found that legitimate power, while most important among the reasons for compliance, was not related to the performance of the work groups. Reward and coercive power were positively related to some performance measures (suggestions submitted, supply cost performance), but negatively related to others (average earnings, maintenance cost performance). Expert and referent power were significantly and positively related to four and five measures of performance, and thus emerged as the most effective base of supervisory power. Student explains these results by suggesting that expert and referent power are qualitatively different from legitimate, reward, and coercive power. Expert and referent power are considered idiosyncratic in character and dependent on an individual's unique role behavior, while legitimate, reward, and coercive power are organizationally determined and designed to be equal for supervisors at the same hierarchical level. Implicit in Student's conclusions is the contention that followers are more responsive to and satisfied with a leader whose influence attempts are not based entirely on position-based power (that is, legitimate, reward, and coercive).

Similar results were obtained in a study by Bachman, Smith, and Slesinger.[28] Data were obtained from thirty-six branch offices of a national sales organization. Each office was managed by a single office supervisor. Employees were asked to rank each of the five power bases according to the extent to which it was a reason for compliance. These results were then correlated with satisfaction and performance measures. Legitimate and expert power again emerged as numbers 1 and 2 in importance, followed by referent, reward, and coercive power.

In those offices in which referent and expert power predominated, performance and satisfaction were high. In those offices in which reward power was high, performance tended to be poor and there was marked dissatisfaction. Coercive and legitimate bases of power were associated with dissatisfaction, but they were unrelated to performance.

The findings of Student and Bachman and others were included in a comparative study of five organizations by Bachman, Bowers, and Marcus.[29] In addition to the appliance firm and the sales organization, other organizations examined were twelve liberal arts colleges, forty agencies of a life insurance company, and twenty-one work groups of a large Midwestern utility company. A ranking procedure was used to ascertain the strength of the supervisors' power bases in the colleges and the utility company, while an independent rating procedure for each power base was used with the life insurance agencies.

Expert and legitimate power were again the most important reasons for complying with supervisors in all three organizations. Expert power was most important and legitimate power, second, in the colleges and insurance agencies, while the order was reversed in the utility company. Referent power was third in importance in the colleges, fourth in the insurance agencies, and fifth in the utility companies. Reward power was third in importance in the utility company and the agencies, and fourth in the colleges. Finally, coercive power was least important in the colleges and the insurance agencies, and fourth in the utility company.

Expert and referent power were again strongly and positively related to satisfaction in these three additional organizations, while reward and legitimate power were not strongly related to the satisfaction measures. Coercive power was consistently related to dissatisfaction. Performance data were obtained from the insurance agencies, but not from the colleges or utility company. Expert and reward power were positively related to insurance agency performance measures, while coercive, legitimate, and referent power yielded insignificant correlations.

Ivancevich and Donnelly[30] studied salespersons' perceptions of their managers' power bases in thirty-one branches of a large firm that produces food products. The employees were asked to rank the power bases in order of importance for compliance. Expert power was most important, followed by legitimate, reward, referent, and coercive power. Referent and expert power were positively related to performance, while reward, legitimate, and coercive power showed no relationship.

Burke and Wilcox[31] conducted a study of leader power bases and follower satisfaction in six offices of a large public utility company. Using a 1 to 5 ranking method, expert power emerged as most important, followed by legitimate, coercive, referent, and reward power. Referent and expert power were associated with greatest satisfaction; legitimate and reward power were intermediate; and coercive power was associated with least satisfaction.

Jamieson and Thomas[32] conducted a study of power in the classroom. Data were collected from high school, undergraduate, and graduate students on their teachers' bases of power, and results were correlated with several measures of student satisfaction. For the high school students, legitimate power was most important, followed by coercive, expert, referent, and reward power. The undergraduate students viewed coercive power as most important, followed by legitimate, expert, reward, and referent power. The graduate students perceived expert power as the strongest, followed by legitimate, reward, coercive, and referent power. Coercive power was strongly and negatively associated with satisfaction among all three groups, while the other four power bases yielded insignificant results.

In summarizing his review of the most important research that has been done relating supervisory power bases to follower satisfaction and performance, Natemeyer[33] made the following general conclusion. While expert and legitimate power bases appear to be the most important reason for compliance, and expert and referent power bases tend to be often strongly and consistently related to follower performance and satisfaction measures, the results are not clear enough to generalize about a *best* power base. In fact, the results suggest that the appropriate power base is largely affected by situational variables. In other words, leaders may need various power bases, depending on the situation.[34]

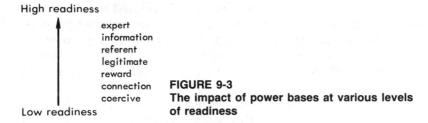

High readiness

expert
information
referent
legitimate
reward
connection
coercive

Low readiness

FIGURE 9-3
The impact of power bases at various levels of readiness

Power Bases and Readiness Level

Hersey and Natemeyer[35] suggest that there appears to be a direct relationship between the level of readiness of individuals and groups and the kind of power bases that have a high probability of gaining compliance from those people. Situational Leadership views readiness as the ability and willingness of individuals or groups to take responsibility for directing their own behavior in a particular situation. Thus, it must be reemphasized that readiness is a task-specific concept and depends on what the leader is attempting to accomplish.

As people move from lower to higher levels of readiness, their competence and confidence to do things increase. The seven power bases appear to have significant impact on the behavior of people at various levels of readiness, as seen in Figure 9-3.

INTEGRATING POWER BASES, READINESS LEVEL, AND LEADERSHIP STYLE THROUGH SITUATIONAL LEADERSHIP

Situational Leadership can provide the basis for understanding the potential impact of each power base. It is our contention that the readiness of the follower not only dictates which style of leadership will have the highest probability of success, but that the readiness of the follower also determines the power base that the leader should use in order to induce compliance or influence behavior.

The Situational Use of Power

Even if the leader is using the appropriate leadership style for a given readiness level, that style may not be maximizing the leader's probability of success if it does not reflect the appropriate power base. Therefore, just as an effective leader should vary leadership style according to the readiness level of the follower, it may be appropriate to vary the use of power in a similar manner. The power bases that may influence people's behavior at various levels of readiness are pictured in Figure 9-4.

Figure 9-4 shows a relationship only between power bases and readiness level. There also appears to be a direct relationship between the kind of power bases a person has and the corresponding leadership style that will be effective for that person in influencing the behavior of others at various readiness levels.

Coercive power. A follower low in readiness generally needs strong directive behavior in order to become productive. To engage effectively in this *telling* style, coercive power is often necessary. The behavior of people at low levels of readiness seems to be influenced by the awareness that costs will be incurred if they do not learn and follow the rules of the game. Thus, if people are *unable and unwilling,* sanctions—the perceived power to fire, transfer, demote, and so on— may be an important way that a leader can induce compliance from them. The leader's coercive power may motivate the followers to avoid the punishment or "cost" by doing what the leader tells them to do.

Connection power. As a follower begins to move from *readiness level* R1 to R2, directive behavior is still needed, but increases in supportive behavior are also important. The *telling* and *selling* leadership styles appropriate for these levels of readiness may become more effective if the leader has connection power. The possession of this power base may induce compliance because a follower at these readiness levels tends to aim at avoiding punishments or gaining rewards available through the powerful connection.

Reward power. A follower at a low to moderate level of readiness often needs high amounts of supportive behavior and directive behavior. This *selling* style is often enhanced by reward power. Since individuals at this readiness level are *willing* to "try on" new behavior, the leader needs to be perceived as having access to rewards in order to gain compliance and reinforce growth in the desired direction.

FIGURE 9-4
Power bases necessary to influence people's behavior at various levels of readiness

READINESS LEVEL		
High	Moderate	Low
R4	R3	R2	R1
Expert	Referent	Reward	Coercive
	Information	Legitimate	Connection

Legitimate power. The leadership styles that tend to influence effectively those at both *moderate levels of readiness* (R2 and R3) are *selling* and *participating.* To engage effectively in these styles, legitimate power seems to be helpful. By the time a follower reaches these moderate levels of readiness, the power of the leader has become legitimized. That is, the leader is able to induce compliance or influence behavior by virtue of the leader's position in the organizational hierarchy.

Referent power. A follower at a moderate to high level of readiness tends to need little direction, but still requires a high level of communication and support from the leader. This *participating* style may be effectively utilized if the leader has referent power. This source of power is based on good personal relations with the follower. With people who are *able but unwilling or insecure,* this power base tends to be an important means of instilling confidence and providing encouragement, recognition, and other supportive behavior. When that occurs, followers will generally respond in a positive way, permitting the leader to influence them because they like, admire, or identify with the leader.

Information power. The leadership styles that tend to motivate followers effectively at *above-average readiness levels* (R3 and R4) are *participating* and *delegating.* Information power seems to be helpful in using these styles. People at these levels of readiness look to the leader for information to maintain or improve performance. The transition from moderate to high readiness may be facilitated if the follower knows that the leader is available to clarify or explain issues and provide access to pertinent data, reports, and correspondence when needed. Through this information power, the leader is able to influence those people who are both willing and able.

Expert power. A follower who develops to a high level of readiness often requires little direction or support. This follower is *able and willing* to perform the tasks required and tends to respond most readily to a *delegating* leadership style and expert power. Thus, a leader may gain respect from and influence most readily a person who has both competence and confidence by possessing expertise, skill, and knowledge that this follower recognizes as important.

An easy way to think about sources of power in terms of making diagnostic judgments is to draw a triangle, as shown in Figure 9-5, around the three power bases necessary to influence below-average, moderate, and above-average levels of readiness.

A way to examine the high-probability power base for a specific

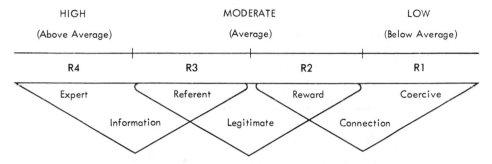

FIGURE 9-5 **Power bases necessary to influence people at various readiness levels**

readiness level is to draw inverted triangles, as shown in Figure 9-6. Note that R1 and R4, the extreme readiness levels, include only two power bases instead of three.

Developing Sources of Power

Although these seven power bases are potentially available to any leader as a means of influencing the behavior of others, it is important to note that there is significant variance in the powers that leaders may actually possess. Some leaders have a great deal of power while others have very little. Part of the variance in actual power is due to the organization and the leader's position in the organization (position power), and part is due to individual differences among the leaders themselves (personal power), as shown in Figure 9-7.

The power bases that are most relevant at the below-average levels of readiness tend to be those that the organization or others can bestow upon the leader. The power bases that influence people who are above average in readiness must, to a large degree, be earned from

FIGURE 9-6 **Power bases necessary to influence people's behavior at *specific* levels of readiness**

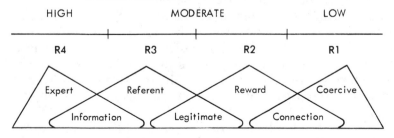

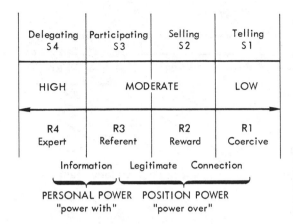

FIGURE 9-7
Summary of relationships between power bases, readiness level, and leadership style

the people the leader is attempting to influence. Therefore, we suggest that position power and the phrase *power over* are most descriptive with coercive, connection, reward, and legitimate power bases; and we suggest that personal power and the phrase *power with* more accurately describe the effect on behavior from referent, information, and expert power.

Sources of Power

Just as some leaders start off with little power in the beginning and gradually build and develop various power sources, other leaders gradually let their power bases erode and lose them. Why does this happen? Before we answer this question, managers need to understand where position and personal power sources come from.

As we discussed earlier, position power can be thought of simply as the authority that is delegated down in an organization. It is important to remember that just because a manager has position power today, it doesn't mean that the manager will have it tomorrow. Not only can the people above delegate the authority to provide rewards and sanctions, they can also take that authority away. So managers must remember that position power is volatile.

This is not to suggest that managers do not have some impact on how much coercive, connection, reward, and legitimate power they get. Of course they do. The extent to which they develop rapport, confidence, and trust between themselves and senior management will determine how willing those above will be to delegate power. But position power is something that a manager has to earn on a day-to-day basis.

The same can be said about personal power, except the reward, information, and expert power that managers possess depend on the confidence and trust these managers generate from the people they are attempting to influence. For example, people might think that some leaders have charisma and other leaders don't. Leaders don't have charisma; followers *give* leaders charisma. We have all seen that phenomenon with elected officials. They are often carried into office because of their charisma, but when their actions do not gain general approval, they may lose their charisma overnight. Again, this is not to say that managers do not have some impact on how much personal power they get, but it's something that they have to earn on a day-to-day basis.

It should be remembered that position power and personal power bases together constitute an interaction-influence system. That is, power does not develop in a vacuum. Each power base tends to affect each of the other power bases. Thus, it has been found that the extent to which people are willing to grant personal power to a manager depends a great deal on their perception of a leader's ability to provide rewards, punishment, or sanctions (position power). At the same time, the willingness of managers above a leader to delegate position power is often determined by the extent to which they perceive that leader as being liked and respected and having information and expertise (personal power) with their people. Keep in mind that we did not say how much personal power or position power affects whether leaders will be delegated authority or treated with respect. As we have noted before, it is the *perception* that others have of those power bases that is crucial. So, the key word, perhaps, in the whole area of the behavioral sciences is *perception.*

Eroding Sources of Power

Since leaders have only a limited amount of power available to them, one would hope for their sake that they would hold on to whatever power bases they have. And, yet, some leaders who often start off with significant power gradually lose their power bases and let them erode. The key to avoiding such erosion is using your power bases (in the eyes of others). For example, a leader could have a significant amount of coercive power, but gradually lose it by threatening. If a leader continually threatens followers with some kind of punishment, but never delivers the punishment, the people will start to think that the leader really does not have any coercive power. Similarly, leaders can lose their reward power if everyone gets the same reward whether they perform or not, or just because they have seniority in industry, or are older in the family. Some parents establish age requirements when kids can get to do things. "When you're thirteen, you'll be able to stay out past ten o'clock. When you're sixteen, you'll be able to stay home alone." The problem with using age as a factor in determining when people can do things is that all they have to do is get older. When that is done, reward power as a parent or a leader is lost. What is happening is that people are getting rewards for being older, not for being more ready to take responsibility.

Connection power can be eroded when people begin to see that the sponsor or connection does not make any disciplinary interventions or provide any favors or sanctions. In other words, to be maintained, connection power needs occasional interventions from the sponsor.

Managers can lose their legitimate power by not making decisions that people think they ought to make, given their position. Erosion of this power base can also occur if a manager continually makes decisions that are not fruitful. After awhile, their staff members will no longer look to them to make decisions even if they have the title of Senior Research Scientist or Department Chairman.

This process also works with referent power. When you give "strokes" to those who are performing and the same strokes to those who are not performing, you begin to erode your referent power. If people do not have to earn strokes, then you no longer have referent power.

Leaders also have to be careful about eroding their information and expert power. This is particularly a concern if you give away expertise and information to people whose goals are not organizational goals. If you give away too much information and knowledge, eventually they will not need you. The only way you can get around this is to continually develop new information and new expertise so that they have to come back to the source.

If leaders let their power bases erode, they will also reduce the effectiveness of their leadership attempts. For example, an effective *telling* (S1) leadership style depends on having some coercive power. If leaders are not seen as being able to deliver punishments and sanctions, their use of that style is limited.

The same can be said about a *selling* (S2) style. Without some control over rewards, leaders are seen as not able to reinforce or reward increased performance as people grow and develop their skills.

A *participating* (S3) style won't work if people don't like and respect a manager. If a manager has let reward power erode because the manager hasn't been responsive to people, then a participative, high relationship style is going to be seen not as a reward, but as a punishment. It's like a manager who has ignored and left a staff member alone for a long time, then, suddenly, when that person's family life begins to deteriorate, the manager tries to "fill the void." Since the manager has eroded available referent power, these supportive leadership attempts are not seen as rewards, but as sanctions and punishments. Time with the boss is not seen as a positive situation.

If a manager is supervising highly competent and motivated people, that manager needs to have some expert power to make any kind of significant intervention with these people. If the manager has eroded information and expert power, the possibility of influencing these people in any significant way will be very limited.

Willingness to Take a Power Role

As we just noted, a person desiring a leadership role must also be willing to assume the responsibilities of that role. This means gaining and exercising power. Managing, supervising, and leading are all influencing behaviors. If a person is unwilling or unable to exercise power, any attempt to manage, supervise, or lead is doomed to failure.

Katherine Benzinger has provided some special insights into the process of gaining and using power.[36] We will spend the next few paragraphs summarizing her important contributions.

Benzinger defines power as "the ability to get your way."[37] She notes that there are important differences between personal and organizational power. In the former, a person has freedom of choice as far as who to influence and the size of the group(s) is much smaller. In the latter, a person is not free to choose co-workers and supervisors, and there are many more people in the group. These differences are very significant, particularly in the way men and women approach these differences.

Men, Benzinger observes, have been trained since childhood—particularly in athletic groups—to develop trust and respect among fellow group members, even those they may personally dislike. Women, on the other hand, have been socialized to use personal power. When confronted with an unpleasant situation, they may choose to either avoid the threatening person or accommodate.

We have equated leadership with influence, but as Benzinger has correctly concluded, accommodation does not influence. Therefore, "The first difference between personal and organizational power is: in seeking organizational power, you must consciously try to build the trust and respect of your co-workers."[38]

As was just noted, women have a tendency when faced with a difficult situation to rely on past experience; that is, to seek a family-sized group such as their own staff or peer group as a power base. If they had control of their own staff, women believe, they would be perceived as competent and doing an effective job. But this neglects contextual power—power external to one's immediate staff. Men assume that they have control of their immediate staff, and place their primary focus of power on persons *external* to their unit or department. This brings up the second difference between personal and organizational power. "The second difference is the need to develop influence with a large number of people."[39]

Do You Want Power?

Benzinger suggests that "If . . . you want to climb a career ladder or influence your organization significantly, you must not only understand power, you must seek it actively and skillfully. . . . To protect yourself from frustration and burn-out, you must therefore decide consciously whether you want power and are willingly to do what it takes to acquire it."[40] She suggests two guidelines that relate to our previous discussion.

1. Earning power requires a very substantial time commitment. If you are not willing to invest the time, perhaps gaining power is not right for you.
2. Gaining power in organizations requires confrontation. If you are not willing to play "King of the Mountain" to get on top and stay on top, then you may not wish to seek power.[41]

Once you have decided to acquire power, you may wish to consider Benzinger's twelve-step strategy:

1. Learn and use your organization's language and symbols.
2. Learn and use your organization's priorities.
3. Learn the power lines.
4. Determine who has power and get to know these people.
5. Develop your professional knowledge.
6. Develop your power skills.
7. Be proactive.
8. Assume authority.
9. Take risks.
10. Beat your own drum.
11. Meet [your supervisor's] needs.
12. Take care of yourself.[42]

Benzinger concludes this list with a worthwhile personal note, ". . . you may discover that being powerful is not as exhausting as some people might have you believe. What's more you might discover having power is fun—it gets things you want done."[43]

THE POWER PERCEPTION PROFILE

To provide leaders with feedback on their power bases so that they can determine which power bases they already have and which they need to develop, Hersey and Natemeyer developed the Power Perception Profile.[44] There are two versions of this instrument: one measures self-perception of power and the other determines an individual's perception of another's power.

Development of the Power Perception Profile

The Power Perception Profile contains twenty-one forced-choice pairs of reasons often given by people when asked why they do things that a leader suggests or wants them to do. Each statement reflects one of the seven sources of power just discussed. In the following pair of statements, referent power is represented by the first statement and coercive power is depicted by the second statement.

> I like this person and want to do things that will please.
>
> This person can administer sanctions and punishments to those who do not cooperate.

Respondents are asked to allocate three points between each set of two alternative choices. They are asked to base their judgments on the relative importance of each alternative, judging either their perception of why people comply with their wishes (self-perception) or why they comply with a particular leader's wishes (other perception).

Respondents are asked to allocate the points between the first item and the second item based on perceived importance in any of the following ways:

3	2	1	0
0	1	2	3

After completing the Power Perception Profile, respondents are able to obtain a score of the relative strength of each of the seven bases of power. This score represents the perception of influence for themselves or some other leader.

One of the shortcomings of most forced-choice instruments is that they provide comparisons only between items or categories, but they do not offer any perspective on the overall scope of the concepts. In other words, a leader might score high or low on a certain power base when compared with each of the other power bases, but no indication is given of how that power base score compares with the score another leader might receive. For example, even if a leader's score on coercive power is low in relation to the other six power bases, the leader may be relatively high in coercive power when compared with other leaders the respondent has known. To correct this deficiency, the Power Perception Profile goes one step further than most forced-choice questionnaires and asks respondents to compare the leader with other leaders they have known, in reference to each of the seven power bases.

Uses of the Power Perception Profile

The Power Perception Profile can be used to gather data in actual organizational settings or any learning environment—for example, student or training groups.

In learning groups, the instrument is particularly helpful in groups that have developed some history—that is, they have spent a considerable amount of time interacting with each other analyzing or solving cases, participating in simulations or other training exercises, and so on. In this kind of situation, it is recommended that the group fill out one instrument together, using a particular member as the subject and arriving at a consensus on each of the items on the instrument. During each discussion, the person whose power bases are being examined should play a nonparticipant role. That person should not ask any questions or attempt to clarify, justify, or explain actions. An appropriate response might be, "Could you tell me more about that?" or "I'd like to hear more on that point." Then, at the end of the group's assessment, the person whose power bases were being examined is given an opportunity to respond to the group's discussion. This process is repeated until every participant has had a turn to get feedback from the group.

If the Power Perception Profile is being used to gather data in an organization, each organizational member from whom perceptions are desired should fill out a separate instrument. In this case, it is strongly suggested that the leaders not collect the data themselves. Instead, a third party who has the trust and confidence of all involved—such as a representative from personnel or human resources—should administer the questionnaire. It is also important to assure respondents that only generalized data will be shared with the leader, not the scores from any particular instrument. These suggestions are important because if leaders collect their own data, even if the instruments are anonymous, there is a tendency for some respondents to answer according to what they feel the leaders do or do not want to hear. Thus, to help establish a valid data base, leaders may want to have their data gathered by a third party.

Another value of understanding power bases is important to mention. If you understand which power bases tend to influence a group of people, you have some insight into who should be given a particular project assignment or responsibility. The person you assign to a particular task should have the power bases and be comfortable in using the appropriate leadership styles that are required in a particular setting. If someone really wants an assignment and doesn't have the appropriate power bases, it's a problem of self-development. You can work out a program to build that power base or appropriate style. What all this means is that we can increase the probability of success of a particular manager if we understand the territory—if we know what power bases and corresponding leadership styles are needed to influence the people involved in the new situation effectively. That's the whole concept of team building. We will be talking about this in much greater depth in later chapters.

CONCLUSIONS

As has been emphasized throughout this chapter, whether or not a leader is maximizing effectiveness is not a question of style alone. It is also a question of what power bases are available to that leader and whether or not these power bases are consistent with the readiness levels of the individual or group that the leader is trying to influence. As managers consider these relationships, it appears that dynamic and growing organizations gradually move away from reliance on power bases that emphasize "power over" and move toward the utilization of power bases that aim at gaining "power with." It is important to keep in mind that many times this change, by necessity, will be evolutionary rather than revolutionary.

In the next chapter, we will show how leaders can develop their people from lower levels of readiness to higher levels. After all, the growth and development of people is the key to the long-term effectiveness of an organization.

NOTES

1. R. M. Stogdill, *Handbook of Leadership* (New York: Free Press, 1974).
2. Many of the concepts in this chapter were first published in Paul Hersey, Kenneth H. Blanchard, and Walter E. Natemeyer, "Situational Leadership, Perception, and the Impact of Power," *Group and Organizational Studies,* 4, No. 4 (December 1979), pp. 418–28.
3. Adapted from Paul Hersey, *The Situational Leader* (Escondido, Calif.: Center For Leadership Studies, 1985), p. 27.
4. This section on defining power and other concepts originated with Walter E. Natemeyer, *An Empirical Investigation of the Relationships Between Leader Behavior, Leader Power Bases, and Subordinate Performance and Satisfaction,* an unpublished dissertation, University of Houston, August 1975. See also J. J. Gibson, J. M. Ivancevich, and J. H. Donnelly, *Organizations* (Dallas: Business Publications, 1973). See also K. D. Mackenzie, "Virtual Position and Power," *Managerial Science,* 32 (May 1986), pp. 622–624.
5. B. Russell, *Power* (London: Allen and Unwin, 1938). See also Geoffrey Kemp, *Projection of Power: Perceptives, Perceptions, and Problems* (Hamden, Conn.: Archon Books, 1982).
6. R. Beirstedt, "An Analysis of Social Power," *American Sociological Review,* 15 (1950), pp. 730–36.
7. D. H. Wrong, "Some Problems in Defining Social Power," *American Journal of Sociology,* 73 (1968), pp. 673–81.
8. J. R. P. French, "A Formal Theory of Social Power," *Psychology Review,* 63 (1956), pp. 181–94. See also P. P. Poole, "Coalitions: The Web of Power," in D. J. Vredenburgh and R. S. Schuler (eds.), *Effective Management: Research and Application, Proceedings of the 20th Annual Eastern Academy of Management,* Pittsburgh, May 1983, pp. 79–82.
9. R. A. Dahl, "The Concept of Power," *Behavioral Science,* 2 (1957), pp. 201–15.
10. M. F. Rogers, "Instrumental and Infra-Resources: The Bases of Power," *American Journal of Sociology,* 79, 6 (1973), 1418–33. See also Rosabeth M. Kanter, "Power Failure in Management Circuits," *Harvard Business Review,* July–August 1979.
11. James A. Lee, "Leader Power and Managing Change," an unpublished paper written at the College of Business Administration, Ohio University, Athens, Ohio. See also J. Pfeffer, *Power In and Around Organizations* (Englewood Cliffs, N. J.: Prentice Hall, 1983).
12. Amitai Etzioni, *A Comparative Analysis of Complex Organizations* (New York: Free Press, 1961).
13. Niccolo Machiavelli, "Of Cruelty and Clemency, Whether It Is Better to Be Loved or Feared," *The Prince and the Discourses* (New York: Random House, 1950), Chap. 17.
14. This summary section adapted from Paul Hersey, *Situational Selling* (Escondido, Calif.: Center For Leadership Studies, 1985), pp. 14–15.
15. *Ibid.*
16. See note 4.
17. R. L. Peabody, "Perceptions of Organizational Authority: A Comparative Analysis," *Administrative Quarterly,* 6 (1962), pp. 463–82.
18. A. C. Filley and A. J. Grimes, "The Bases of Power in Decision Processes" (Industrial Relations Research Institute, University of Wisconsin, Reprint Series 104, 1967).
19. K. D. Beene, *A Conception of Authority* (New York: Teachers College, Columbia University, 1943); H. C. Kelman, "Compliance, Identification, and Internalization: Three Processes of Attitude Change," *Journal of Conflict Resolution,* 158, 2, pp. 51–60; and G. Gilman, "An Inquiry into the Nature and Use of Authority," in M. Haire, *Organization Theory in Industrial Practice* (New York: Wiley, 1962).
20. J. R. P. French and B. Raven, "The Bases of Social Power," in D. Cartwright, *Studies in Social Power* (Ann Arbor: University of Michigan, Institute for Social Research, 1959).
21. B. H. Raven and W. Kruglanski, "Conflict and Power," in P. G. Swingle, ed., *The Structure of Conflict* (New York: Academic Press, 1975), pp. 177–219.
22. Five of these descriptions of power bases (coercive, expert, legitimate, referent, and reward) have been adapted from the work of French and Raven, "The Bases of Social Power." One power base (information) was introduced by Raven and Kruglanski, "Conflict and Power." In addition to modifying some of these definitions, Paul Hersey and Marshall Goldsmith added a seventh power base: connection power.

23. This section adapted from Hersey, *The Situational Leader,* pp. 82–83.

24. *Ibid.,* pp. 222–23.

25. This section adapted from Hersey, *Situational Selling,* pp. 114–20.

26. Natemeyer, *An Empirical Investigation of the Relationships Between Leader Behavior.*

27. K. R. Student, "Supervisory Influence and Work-Group Performance, *Journal of Applied Psychology,* 52, 3 (1968), pp. 188–94.

28. J. G. Bachman, C. G. Smith, and J. A. Slesinger, "Control, Performance, and Satisfaction: An Analysis of Structural and Individual Effects," *Journal of Personality and Social Psychology,* 4, 2 (1966), pp. 127–36.

29. J. G. Bachman, D. G. Bowers and P. M. Marcus, "Bases of Supervisory Power: A Comparative Study in Five Organizational Settings," in Arnold S. Tannenbaum, *Control in Organizations* (New York: McGraw-Hill, 1968).

30. J. M. Ivancevich and J. H. Donnelly, "Leader Influence and Performance," *Personnel Psychology,* 23, 4 (1970), 539–49.

31. R. J. Burke and D. S. Wilcox, "Bases of Supervisory Power and Subordinate Job Satisfactions," *Canadian Journal of Behavioral Science* (1971).

32. D. W. Jamieson and K. W. Thomas, "Power and Conflict in the Student-Teacher Relationship," *Journal of Applied Behavioral Science,* 10, 3 (1974).

33. Natemeyer, *An Empirical Investigation of the Relationships Between Leader Behavior.*

34. Adapted from D. Kipnis, *The Powerholders* (Chicago: University of Chicago Press, 1976). See also J. Ivancevich, "An Analysis of Control, Bases of Control, and Satisfactional Setting," *Academy of Management Journal,* December 1970, pp. 427–36.

35. Hersey and Natemeyer, "Situational Leadership, Perception, and the Impact of Power."

36. Katherine Benzinger, "The Powerful Woman," *Hospital Forum* May–June 1982, pp. 15–20.

37. *Ibid.,* p. 15.

38. *Ibid.,* pp. 15–16.

39. *Ibid.,* p. 16.

40. *Ibid.,* pp. 16–17.

41. *Ibid.*

42. *Ibid.,* pp. 18–20.

43. *Ibid.,* p. 20. For a related discussion, see Jane Covey Brown and Rosabeth Moss Kanter, "Empowerment: Key To Effectiveness," *Hospital Forum,* May–June, 1982, pp. 6–12.

44. This instrument was developed by Paul Hersey and Walter E. Natemeyer. Published by the Center for Leadership Studies, Escondido, Calif.

10

Developing Human Resources

In chapter 4 we stated that in evaluating performance, a manager ought to consider both output (productivity) and intervening variables (the condition of the human resources). We urged that both these factors should be examined in light of short- and long-term organizational goals. If the importance of intervening variables is accepted, then one must assume that one of the responsibilities of managers, regardless of whether they are parents in the home or managers in a business setting, is developing the human resources for which they are responsible. Managers need to devote time to nurture the leadership potential, motivation, morale, climate, commitment to objectives, and the decision-making, communication, and problem-solving skills of their people. Thus, an important role for managers is the development of the task-relevant readiness of their followers.

We think it is vital to emphasize this developmental aspect of Situational Leadership. Without emphasizing this aspect, there is a danger that managers could use Situational Leadership to justify the use of any behavior they wanted. Since the concept contends that there is no "best" leadership style, the use of any style could be supported merely by saying "the individual or group was at such-and-such readiness level." Thus, while close supervision and direction might be necessary initially when working with individuals who have had little experience in directing their own behavior, it should be recognized that this style is only a first step. In fact, managers should be rewarded for helping their people develop and be able to assume more and more responsibility on their own. For example, in some progressive companies in which we have worked, we have been able to introduce a new policy, which essentially states: No managers will be promoted in this organization unless they do at least two things. First, they have to do a good job in what they are being asked to do; that is, good "bottom line" results (output variables). Second, they have to have a ready replacement who can take over their job tomorrow (intervening variables).

This means that if managers are using a leadership style with a high probability of success for working with a given level of readiness (as discussed in the last chapter), this is not really enough. These managers may be accomplishing their goals, but their responsibilities should not stop there. Besides achieving goals, managers must develop their human resources (their followers).

INCREASING EFFECTIVENESS

Likert found that employee-centered supervisors who use general supervision *tend* to have higher producing sections than job-centered supervisors who use close supervision.[1] We emphasize the word *tend* because there are exceptions to this tendency, which are even evident in Likert's data. What Likert found was that employees generally respond well to their supervisor's high expectations and genuine confidence in them and try to justify their expectations of them. Their resulting high performance will reinforce their supervisor's high trust for them; it is easy to trust and respect people who meet or exceed your expectations.

J. Sterling Livingston,[2] in discussing this phenomenon, refers to the words of Eliza Doolittle from George Bernard Shaw's play *Pygmalion* (the basis of the musical hit *My Fair Lady*):

> You see, really and truly, apart from the things anyone can pick up (the dressing and the proper way of speaking, and so on), the difference between a lady and a flower girl is not how she behaves but how she's treated. I shall always be a flower girl to Professor Higgins, because he always treats me as a flower girl, and always will; but I know I can be a lady to you, because you always treat me as a lady, and always will.

Livingston has found from his experience and research that:

> Some managers always treat their subordinates in a way that leads to superior performance. But most managers, like Professor Higgins, un-

intentionally treat their subordinates in a way that leads to lower performance than they are capable of achieving. The way managers treat their subordinates is subtly influenced by what they expect of them. If a manager's expectations are high, productivity is likely to be excellent. If his expectations are low, productivity is likely to be poor. It is as though there were a law that caused a subordinate's performance to rise or fall to meet his manager's expectations. . . .

Cases and other evidence available from scientific research now reveal:

- What a manager expects of his subordinates and the way he treats them largely determine their performance and career progress.
- A unique characteristic of superior managers is their ability to create high performance expectations that subordinates fulfill.
- Less effective managers fail to develop similar expectations, and, as a consequence, the productivity of their subordinates suffers.
- Subordinates, more often than not, appear to do what they believe they are expected to do.

When people respond to the high expectations of their managers with high performance, we call that the "effective cycle," as illustrated in Figure 10-1.

Yet, as we have pointed out earlier, the concentration on output variables as a means of evaluating effectiveness tends to lead to short-run task-oriented leader behavior. This style, in some cases, does not allow much room for a trusting relationship with employees. Instead, employees are told what to do and how to do it, with little consideration expressed for their ideas or feelings. After a while, the employees respond with minimal effort and resentment; low performance results in these instances. Reinforced by low expectations, it becomes a vicious cycle. We call this the "ineffective cycle." Many other examples could be given that result in this all-too-common problem in organizations, as shown in Figure 10-2.

These cycles are depicted as static, but in reality they are very dynamic. The situation tends to get better or worse. For example, high expectations result in high performance, which reinforces the high

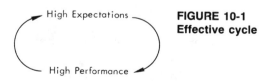

FIGURE 10-1
Effective cycle

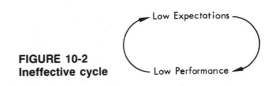

FIGURE 10-2
Ineffective cycle

expectations and produces even higher productivity. It almost becomes an upward-spiraling effect, as illustrated in Figure 10-3.

In many cases, this spiraling effect is caused by an increase in leverage created through the use of the motivators. As people perform, they are given more responsibility and opportunities for achievement, growth, and development.

This spiraling effect can also occur in a downward direction. Low expectations result in low performance, which reinforces the low expectations and produces even lower productivity. It becomes a downward-spiraling effect like a whirlpool, as shown in Figure 10-4.

If this downward spiraling continues long enough, the cycle may reach a point where it cannot be turned around in a short period of time because of the large reservoir of negative past experience that has built up in the organization. Much of the focus and energy is directed toward perceived problems in the environment such as interpersonal relations and respect for supervision rather than toward the work itself. Reaction to deteriorating hygiene factors takes such forms as hostility, undermining, and slowdown in work performance. When this happens, even if a manager actually changes behavior, the credibility gap based on long-term experience is such that the response is still distrust and skepticism rather than change.

One alternative that is sometimes necessary at this juncture is to bring in a new manager from the outside. The reason this has a higher probability of success is that the sum of the past experience of the people involved with the new manager is likened to a "clean slate"

FIGURE 10-3
Upward-spiraling effect of the effective cycle

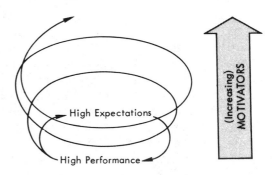

251

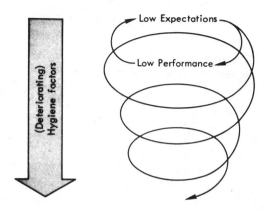

FIGURE 10-4
Downward-spiraling effect of the
ineffective cycle

and thus different behaviors are on a much more believable basis. This was evident in the case of Plant Y described by Guest, which was discussed in chapter 7. The ineffective cycle had been in a downward spiral far past the point where Stewart would have had an opportunity to make significant changes. But, with the introduction of a new manager, Cooley, significant changes were now possible.

Breaking the Ineffective Cycle

Although new managers may be in a better position to initiate change in a situation that has been spiraling downward, they still do not have an easy task. Essentially, they have to break the ineffective cycle. There are at least two alternatives available to managers in this situation. They can either fire the low-performing personnel and hire people whom they expect to perform well or they can respond to low performance with high expectations and trust.

The first choice is not always possible because competent replacements are not readily available or the people involved have some form of job security (civil service or union tenure), which means they cannot be fired without considerable cost in time, energy, and hassle.

The latter choice for managers is difficult. In effect, the attempt is to change the expectations or behavior of their people. It is especially difficult for managers to have high expectations about people who have shown no indication that they deserve to be trusted. The key, then, is to change appropriately.

From our work with Situational Leadership, we have identified two different cycles that managers can use for changing or maximizing the task-relevant readiness of their followers—the developmental cycle and the regressive cycle.

In this chapter we will discuss the developmental cycle. In chapter 11 we will present the regressive cycle.

DEVELOPMENTAL CYCLE

The role managers play in developing the readiness level of their people is extremely important. Too often managers do not take responsibility for the performance of their people, especially if they are not doing well. If they're having problems, often managers will say, "I have an example of a Peter Principle," and not take responsibility for the poor performance. It has been our experience that when managers have to fire someone or find a place to hide them (this is what Peter called a "lateral arabesque"), or when they are downright worried about someone's performance, these managers should look in the mirror. In most cases, the biggest cause of the performance problem is looking back at them. Managers are responsible for making their people "winners," and this is what the developmental cycle is all about. Managers are involved in the developmental cycle any time they attempt to increase the present readiness level of an individual or group in some aspect of their work. In other words, the developmental cycle is a growth cycle.

What's in It for the Manager?[3]

When followers are at low levels of readiness, the manager must take the responsibility for the "traditional" management functions such as planning, organizing, motivating, and controlling. The manager's role is that of supervisor of the group. However, when managers develop their people and have followers at high levels of readiness, the followers can take over much of the responsibility for these day-to-day traditional management functions. The manager's role can then change from supervisor to the group's representative in the next level of the organization.

Through the development of people, managers can invest their time in the "high payoff" management functions. These "linking pin" activities enhance the group's performance. When followers can take responsibility for their own tasks on a day-to-day basis, the manager can focus on these activities. These functions include acquiring resources necessary for maximizing the group's productivity, communicating both horizontally and vertically, and coordinating their group's efforts with that of other departments to improve overall productivity. The manager, instead of getting trapped in tunnel vision, has time for long-range strategic planning and creativity.

Initially, close supervision and direction are helpful when working with individuals who have little experience in directing their own behavior. The manager recognizes that this style is only a first step. In order to maximize their potential in the high-payoff functions, managers must change their style and take an *active* role in helping others grow. The development of followers depends not only on the manager's behavior, but also on values and expectations.

What Do We Want to Influence?

As we suggested in chapter 8, the first question managers have to ask themselves when they are thinking about the development of their people is: What area of my employees' work do I want to influence? In other words, what are their responsibilities or goals and objectives? A foreman, for example, might want to influence productivity, quality, waste, absenteeism, accident rate, and so on. A university department chairman might want to affect the faculty's writing and research, teaching, and community service.

Once the objectives or responsibilities are identified and understood, managers must clearly specify what constitutes good performance in each area, so that both know when their performance is approaching the desired level. What does a good sales record mean? Does it mean a number of sales made or volume of sales? What is meant by developing your people or being a good administrator? Managers have to specify what good performance *looks like*. Just telling a person, "I want you to make widgets" is not as helpful as saying, "I want you to make widgets at the rate of two hundred a day." For managers and staff members to know how well someone is doing, good performance has to be clearly specified. Managers cannot change and develop their followers' behavior in areas that are unclear.

How Is the Person Doing Now?

Before beginning the developmental cycle with an individual in a work situation, the manager must decide how well that person is doing right now. In other words, what is the person's readiness level right now in a specific aspect of the job? How able is the person to take responsibility for specific behavior? How willing or motivated is the person? As was discussed earlier, readiness is not a global concept. That is, people do not have a degree of readiness in any total sense. How can we know what a person's readiness level is in a given situation?

Determining Readiness

In assessing the readiness level of an individual, we will have to make judgments about that person's ability and willingness. Where do we get the information to make these judgments? We can either *ask the person* or *observe* the person's behavior. We could ask a person such questions as, "How well do you think you are doing at such and such?"

or "How do you feel about doing that?" or "Are you or are you not enthusiastic and excited about it?" Obviously, with some people, asking for their own assessment of their readiness won't be productive. However, it has been surprising how even young children are able to share that kind of information. Phil and Jane learned that when they used to ask their two-year-old daughter, Lee, to do something. Often Lee would reply, "I can't want to!" When translated, what Lee was really saying (in our terms) is, "I'm both unable and unwilling to do what you want me to do." If Lee's parents still wanted her to do it, they soon learned that they had to direct and closely supervise her behavior in this area (S1 – "telling"). As children get older, they can play an even more significant role in determining their own readiness level. That process will be discussed in much more detail in chapter 12.

You might be wondering whether people will always tell their managers the truth or just tell what is necessary to keep the manager off their backs. If managers doubt what their people tell them about their ability or willingness to do something, those managers can check out their opinion by observing staff members' behavior. Ability can be determined by examining past performance. Has the person done well in this area before or has performance been poor or nonexistent? Does the staff member have the necessary knowledge to perform well in the area or does that person not know how to do what needs to be done?

Willingness can be determined by watching a person's behavior in a particular case. What is the person's interest level? Does the person seem enthusiastic or interested? What is the person's commitment to this area? Does the person appear to enjoy doing things in this area or merely anxious to get them over with? Is the person's self-confidence secure in this area or does the person lack confidence and feel insecure? Remember that people can be at any of four levels of readiness in each of their various areas of responsibility. A person's readiness level gives us a good clue as to how to begin any further development of that individual. If a manager wants to influence a staff member in an area in which the person is both unable and unwilling (low readiness level), the manager must begin the developmental cycle by directing, controlling, and closely supervising ("telling") the staff member's behavior. If, however, the person is willing (motivated) to do something, but not able to do it (low to moderate readiness), the manager must begin the cycle by both directing and supporting ("selling") the desired behavior. If the person is able to do something without direction, but is unwilling to do it or is insecure (moderate to high readiness), the manager is faced with a motivational problem. Individuals reluctant to do what they are able to do are often insecure or lacking confidence. In this case, the manager should begin the developmental cycle by using a supportive style ("participating") to help the individual become secure enough to do what the individual already knows how to do. Finally, if staff members are both able and willing to direct their own behavior (high readiness), we can merely delegate responsibility to them and know that they will perform well. When that occurs, there is no need for beginning the development cycle. The person already has a high degree of readiness in that area.

Increasing Readiness

Managers are engaged in the developmental cycle any time they attempt to increase the task-relevant readiness of an individual or group beyond the level that individual or group has previously reached. In other words, the developmental cycle is a growth cycle.

To explain fully how the developmental cycle works, let us look at an example. Suppose a manager has been able to diagnose the environment and finds that the task-relevant readiness of a staff member is low (R1) in the area of developing a departmental budget. If the manager wants the staff member to perform well in this area without supervision, the manager must determine the appropriate leadership style for starting the developmental cycle. As can be seen in Figure 10-5, once this manager has diagnosed the readiness level of the follower as low, the appropriate style can be determined by constructing a right angle from a point on the readiness continuum to where it meets the curved line in the style-of-leader portion of the model. In this case, it would be appropriate to start the developmental cycle by using a directive "telling" style (S1). What would a "telling" style look like in this situation?

It would involve several things for the manager. First, the manager would have to tell the staff member exactly what was involved in developing a departmental budget—taking inventory, processing manpower and material requests, comparing present costs with last year's budget, and so on. Second, the manager would begin to show the staff member how to do each of the tasks involved. Thus, "telling" in a teaching situation involves "show and tell"; the staff member must be told what to do and then shown how to do it. Although this "telling" style is high on direction and low on support, this does not mean that the manager is not being friendly to the staff member. Low supportive behavior in this situation merely means that the manager is not patting the staff member on the back before the member has earned it. Till then, the manager emphasizes explaining the what, when, where, and how of the job.

If the manager uses an S1 "telling" style in this situation, the departmental budget will probably be done fairly well, since the

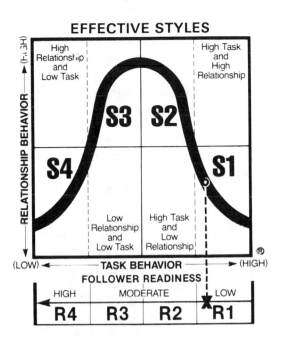

EFFECTIVE STYLES

High Relationship and Low Task

High Task and High Relationship

S3 S2

S4 S1

Low Relationship and Low Task

High Task and Low Relationship

RELATIONSHIP BEHAVIOR ——→ (HIGH)

(LOW) ◄—————— TASK BEHAVIOR —————→ (HIGH)

FOLLOWER READINESS

HIGH	MODERATE		LOW
R4	R3	R2	R1

FIGURE 10-5
Determining an appropriate leadership style

manager is working closely with the staff member. But if this same manager or leader assumes a responsibility to increase the task-relevant readiness of the follower(s), then the manager has to be willing to *take a risk* and begin to *delegate some responsibility* to the followers. This is particularly true when supervising an individual or group that has not assumed much responsibility in the past; and yet, if one is going to develop people—children in the home, employees on the job—one has to take that risk. While taking a risk is a reality in the developmental cycle, managers have to keep the degree of risk reasonable; it should not be too high. For example, suppose a mother wants to teach her eight-year-old daughter how to wash the dishes. The risk is a few broken dishes. It would be wise, then, to start the daughter off on old dishes, or even plastic dishes, rather than Grandma's priceless bone china. It's not a question of whether to take a risk or not; it's a matter of taking a calculated risk.

Successive Approximations

If a manager asks a staff member to do something the member has never been taught to do and expects good performance the first time, and doesn't offer any help to the staff member, the manager has set the person up for failure and punishment. This begins the widely used "tell, leave alone, and then 'zap' " approach to managing people. The manager tells the staff member what to do (without bothering to find out if the person knows how to do it), leaves the staff member alone (expecting immediate results), and then yells at and "zaps" the staff member when the desired behavior does not follow.

If the manager in our budget example used that approach, the events might look something like this. The manager might assume that anyone could prepare the departmental budget. So the manager tells the staff member to prepare the budget and have it within ten days. Not bothering to analyze whether the staff member is able or willing to prepare the budget alone, the manager gives the order and then goes about his own responsibilities. When the staff member produces the budget ten days later, the manager finds all kinds of mistakes and problems with it and screams and yells at the staff member about the poor quality of the work.

Managers should remember that no one (including themselves!) learns how to do anything all at once. We learn a little bit at a time. As a result, if a manager wants someone to do something completely new, the manager should reward the slightest progress the person makes in the desired direction.

Many parents use this process without really being aware of it. For example, how do you think we teach a child to walk? Imagine if we stood Eric up and said, "Walk," and then when he fell down we spanked him for not walking. Sound ridiculous? Of course. But it's not really any different from the manager's anger with the staff member about the poorly prepared budget. A child spanked for falling down will not try to walk because the child knows this leads to punishment. At this point Eric is not even sure what his legs are for. Therefore, parents usually first teach children how to stand up. If the child stays up even for a second or two, his parents get excited and hug and kiss him, call his grandmother, and the like. Next, when the child can stand and hold onto a table, his parents again hug and kiss him. The same happens when he takes his first step, even if he falls down. Whether or not his parents know it, they are positively rewarding the child for small accomplishments as he moves closer and closer to the desired behavior—walking.

Thus, in attempting to help an individual or group develop—to get them to take more and more responsibility for performing a specific task—a leader must first delegate *some* responsibility (not too much or failure might result); and second, reward as soon as possible any behavior in the desired direction. This process should continue as the individual's behavior comes closer and closer to the leader's expectations of good performance. What would relationship behavior look like in this situation?

Relationship behavior would involve providing "positive strokes" and reinforcement. Positive reinforcement strokes are anything that is desired or needed by an individual whose behavior is being rein-forced. While reducing task behavior precedes the desired behavior, relationship behavior or positive reinforcement follows the desired behavior and increases the likelihood of its recurring. It is important to remember that reinforcement must immediately follow any behav-ior in the desired direction. Reinforcement at a later time will be of less help in getting the individual or group to do something they've never done before on their own.

This two-step process of (1) reducing the amount of direction and supervision; and (2) after adequate performance follows, increasing socioemotional support (relationship behavior) is known as *positively reinforcing successive approximations.* This concept is associated with behavior modification and reinforcement theory,[4] and more recently, in industrial circles it has been called performance management.[5] This field will be discussed in more depth later in this chapter and in chapter 11. Let us look at an example to illustrate this concept.

Suppose a manager wanted to change leadership style with an individual from Point A to Point C along the curved line or cur-vilinear function of Situational Leadership, as illustrated in Figure 10-6. Step 1 would be to delegate some responsibility by decreasing task behavior to Point B. This is a risky step since the manager is turning over the direction and the supervision of some of the tasks to the follower. If the follower responds well to the increased respon-sibility, then it is appropriate to engage in Step 2—positively reinforc-

FIGURE 10-6 Two-step process of the developmental cycle

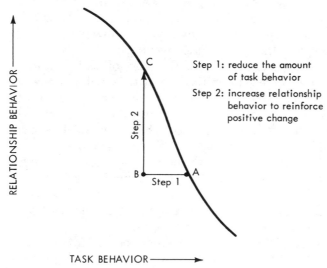

ing this behavior by increasing socioemotional support (relationship behavior) to the higher level Point C, as shown in Figure 10-6.

It is important to remember that a leader must be careful not to delegate too much responsibility too rapidly. This is a common error that many managers make. If this is done before the follower can handle it, the leader may be setting the follower up for failure and frustration that could prevent that person from wanting to take additional responsibility in the future. The process is often started off by good intentions. The manager provides direction and structure, but then moves too quickly to a "leave-alone" leadership style. This abrupt movement from "telling" to "delegating" often sets the person up for failure and punishment, since it assumes that telling is learning. The manager is likely to return to Style 1 rapidly in a punitive way if the job is not getting done.

In addition, a manager should be warned not to increase socioemotional support (relationship behavior) without first getting the desired performance. In positively reinforcing nonperformance, this manager may be viewed as a soft touch. That is why the manager in our example does not immediately move from Point A to Point C along the curved line in Figure 10-6. If the manager moved from Point A to Point C without some evidence that the individual could assume responsibility at Point B, it would be like giving the reward before the person has earned it. It would be like paying a person twenty dollars an hour right now who at present is worth only five dollars an hour. For many people, if you gave them twenty dollars an hour up front, there would be very little incentive to improve their performance. Thus, the leader should develop the readiness of followers slowly on each task that they must perform, using less task behavior and more relationship behavior as they become more willing and able to take responsibility. When an individual's performance is low on a specific task, one must not expect drastic changes overnight.

If the manager (in our example) finds that the follower is unable to handle that much added responsibility when task behavior is decreased to Point B, the manager might have to return to a moderate level of direction (where the follower is able to take responsibility) somewhere between Point A and Point B. This new level of task behavior is indicated by Point B' in Figure 10-7. If the subordinate is now able to be effective at that level, then the manager can appropriately increase socioemotional support (relationship behavior) to Point C'. Although this level of socioemotional support is less than depicted at Point C, it is appropriate to the amount of task behavior that the follower, at that time, is able to assume.

As shown in Figure 10-8, this two-step process—cutting back structure and then increasing socioemotional support if the follower

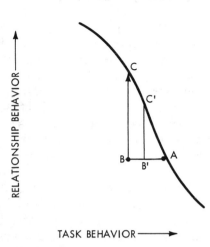

FIGURE 10-7
Adjustment when growth expectation is too high

RELATIONSHIP BEHAVIOR

TASK BEHAVIOR ——→

can respond to the additional responsibility–tends to continue in small increments until the individual is assuming moderate levels of readiness. This continual decreasing of task behavior does not mean the individual will have less structure, but that rather than being externally imposed by the leader, the structure can now be internally provided by the follower.

FIGURE 10-8
Development cycle as people develop over time

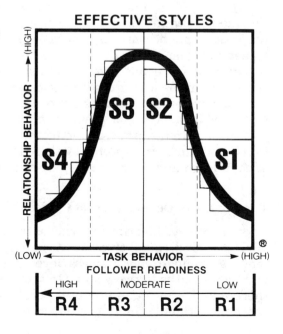

261

An interesting phenomenon occurs in the developmental cycle when the high point of the curvilinear function in the leadership style portion of the model is reached. This is where the function crosses the mean, or average, of task behavior. Past this point, a leader who is appropriately using leadership style 3 or style 4 is supervising people at moderate to high levels of readiness (R3 and R4). At that time, the process changes and becomes one whereby the leader not only reduces structure (task behavior), but, when the followers can handle their responsibility, reduces socioemotional support as well. This continuation of the successive approximation process is illustrated by the downward steps in Figure 10-8.

Sometimes the following question is raised: Doesn't the reduction of socioemotional support mean that there is a lack of confidence and trust between manager and follower(s)? In reality, when a manager reduces the amount of socioemotional support and structure appropriately, this indicates that there is more mutual trust and confidence between the leader and the follower(s). This suggests that as people change, their motives and needs hierarchy often change too. For example, people who have low levels of readiness tend to view increased socioemotional support and facilitating behavior as positive reinforcement. In fact, if the leader left them too much on their own, this behavior would create insecurities and help reinforce fear and anxiety on the part of the follower(s). As a result, this low relationship behavior could be perceived as punishment rather than reward.

On the other hand, as people move to high levels of readiness, they do not require as much encouragement or psychological "stroking." As people become high on task-relevant readiness, one way the leader can demonstrate confidence and trust in the follower(s) is to leave them more and more on their own. Just as socioemotional support from the leader tends to be positive reinforcement for persons with low levels of readiness, too much socioemotional support or relationship behavior for people at high levels of readiness is not seen as a reward. In fact, this supportive behavior is often seen as dysfunctional and can be interpreted by these high-readiness people as a lack of confidence and trust on the part of the leader.

Time and the Developmental Cycle

There is no set blueprint in terms of the amount of time necessary to develop an individual or group. A manager may be doing very well to move a group from readiness level 1 to level 2 over a period of eighteen months to two years. On the other hand, within that group there may be an individual or several individuals who will develop much more rapidly than the group as a whole. Thus, time is a function of the complexity of the job being performed and the performance potential of the individual or group. For example, one might take someone on a specific task through the total cycle—from low to high levels of readiness—in a matter of minutes. And yet, in other tasks with that same individual, the readiness development process may take a much greater amount of time. In fact, it could take weeks, months, or even years to move through the complete cycle in terms of appropriate leadership style from telling (S1) to delegating (S4). To illustrate a short development process, an example of teaching a child to tie her shoes may be helpful.

If the child has not made any attempt to learn to tie shoes, this fact may, in a sense, become a problem to the parent. In that case, the parent needs to provide some high task behavior for the child. Since the child has low readiness on this task, the parent should explain what to do, how to do it, and where to do it. In essence, the parent must move into the early stages of coaching and counseling by providing the child with a "hands-on experience." As the child begins to show the ability to do some of those functions, the parent reduces the amount of telling behavior and increases, to some extent, supportive behavior. "That's fine! Good! You're getting it!" And perhaps in a matter of minutes, the behavior of the parent may change from a "hands-on" highly structured style to just being in close proximity, where this adult can provide a moderate amount of structure, but also high levels of both verbal and nonverbal supportive and facilitative behavior. In another few minutes, the parent may leave the child to practice alone while staying close enough to make an intervention if there should be some regression. Thus, in a matter of ten to fifteen minutes, the parent has taken the child in that specific task of shoe tying from style 1 through styles 2 and 3 to almost a complete delegation of that function to the child in a manner characteristic of style 4. This does not mean that the parent's style with that child should now always be style 4. It just means that in that specific task (shoe tying), the most appropriate style to use with that child is style 4.

CHANGING READINESS THROUGH BEHAVIOR MODIFICATION

In our discussion of the developmental cycle, we made reference to behavior modification and, in particular, the concept of positively reinforcing successive approximations. This section will elaborate on some other concepts from this behavioral science field and attempt to show how these concepts provide guidelines for changing one's leadership style with shifts in readiness.[6]

Behavior modification is a useful tool for managers and leaders because it can be applied in almost all environments. Although it may involve a reassessment of customary methods for obtaining compliance and cooperation, it has relevance for persons interested in accomplishing objectives through other people. This may not be the case with some methods of psychotherapy.

For example, one form of psychotherapy is based on the assumption that to change behavior one must start with the feelings and attitudes within an individual. The problem with psychotherapy from a practitioner's viewpoint is that it tends to be too expensive and is appropriate for use only by professionals. One way of illustrating the main difference between these two approaches is to go back to a portion of the basic motivating situation model as illustrated in Figure 10-9.

Figure 10-9 shows that both psychotherapy and behavior modification are interested in affecting behavior. The emphasis in psychotherapy is on analyzing the reasons underlying behaviors that are often the result of early experiences in life. Behavior modification concentrates on observed behavior and uses goals or rewards outside the individual to modify and shape behavior toward the desired performance.

Behavior modification theory is based on observed behavior and not on internal unobserved emotions, attitudes, or feelings. Its basic premise is that *behavior is controlled by its immediate consequences.* Behavior can be increased, suppressed, or decreased by what happens immediately after it occurs. Because probabilities are difficult to work with, we use observations of the future frequency of the behavior as a measure of the effectiveness of a consequence. Five of the major concepts of reinforcement that help one to make behavioral changes are positive reinforcement, punishment, negative reinforcement, extinction, and schedule of reinforcement. In our discussions in this

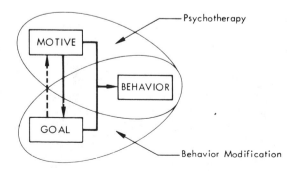

FIGURE 10-9
Comparison of psychotherapy and behavior modification

chapter we have and will continue to emphasize positive reinforcement and schedule of reinforcement. In the next chapter, "Constructive Discipline," we will examine punishment, negative reinforcement, and extinction.

Positive Reinforcement

Positive reinforcement, as mentioned earlier, can be anything that is desired or needed by the individual whose behavior is being reinforced. A positive reinforcer tends to strengthen the response it follows and make that response more likely to recur.

To increase the probability that desirable behavior will occur, reinforcement should *immediately* follow the response. Reinforcement at a later time may be of less help in making the desired behavioral change.

Individualizing Reinforcement

When thinking about this concept of positive reinforcement, managers should remember that reinforcement depends on the individual. What is reinforcing to one person may not be reinforcing to another. Money may motivate some people to work harder. But to others, money may not be a positive reinforcer; the challenge of the job might be the most rewarding aspect of the situation. In addition, the same individual at different times will be motivated by different things, depending on present need satisfaction. Thus, at one time an individual might respond to praise as a reinforcer, but at another time that same individual might not respond to praise, but be eager for more responsibility. Managers must recognize the dangers of over-generalizing and not only look for unique differences in their people, but also be aware of the various fluctuations in need satisfaction within a person.

For a desirable behavior to be obtained, the slightest appropriate behavior exhibited by the individual in that direction must be rewarded as soon as possible. This is the basic premise for the concept of *reinforcing positively successive approximations* of a certain response. For example, when an individual's performance is low, one cannot expect drastic changes overnight, regardless of changes in expectations for the individual or the type of reinforcers (rewards) used.

A child learning some new behavior is not expected to give a polished performance at the outset. So, as parent, teacher, or supervisor, we use positive reinforcement as the behavior approaches the desired level of performance. Managers must be aware of any progress of their employees so as to be in a position to reinforce this change appropriately.

This strategy is compatible with the concept of setting short-term goals rather than final performance criteria and then reinforcing appropriate progress toward the final goals as they are met. In setting goals it is important that they be programmed to be difficult, but obtainable so that the individual proceeds along a path of gradual and systematic development. Eventually this individual will reach the point of a polished performance.

The type of consequence individuals experience as a result of their behavior will determine the speed with which they approach the final performance. Behavior consequences can be either positive (money, praise, award, promotion); negative (scolding, fines, layoffs, embarrassment); or neutral. The difference between positive and negative consequences is important to reiterate. Positive consequences tend to result in an increase in the rewarded behavior in the future. Negative consequences, as you will discover in the discussion of punishment, merely disrupt and suppress on-going behavior. Negative consequences tend to have neither a lasting nor a sure effect on future behavior.

Schedule of Reinforcement

Once a manager has someone engaging in a new behavior, it is important that the new behavior is not extinguished over time. To ensure that this does not happen, reinforcement must be scheduled in an effective way. Most experts agree that there are two main reinforcement schedules: continuous and intermittent.[7] Continuous reinforcement means that the individuals being changed are reinforced each time they engage in the desired new pattern. With intermittent reinforcement, on the other hand, not every desired response is reinforced. Reinforcement either can be completely random or it can be scheduled. With continuous reinforcement, the individual learns the new behavior faster; but if the environment for that individual changes to one of nonreinforcement, extinction can be expected to take place relatively soon. With intermittent reinforcement, extinction is much slower because the individual has been conditioned to go for periods of time without any reinforcement. Thus, for fast learning, a continuous reinforcement schedule should be used. But once the individual has learned the new pattern, a switch to intermittent reinforcement should insure a long-lasting change.

How does the concept of reinforcement relate to Situational Leadership? In the early stages of a developmental cycle, whenever a manager delegates some responsibility to a person at a low level of readiness and that person responds well, the manager should provide reinforcement. That is, every time the manager cuts back on task behavior and the staff member responds well, the manager should immediately increase relationship behavior appropriately. This kind of reinforcement should continue until the manager's style is between "selling" and "participating" and the readiness of the person shifts toward readiness level 3. At that time, the manager should begin periodically to reinforce, so that the manager's decreased support and direction will not be seen by the staff member as punishment. When the style of a manager moves toward the "delegating" style, the person's behavior is self-reinforcing, and external "strokes" from the manager are significantly reduced. In sum, the developmental cycle moves from continual reinforcement to periodic reinforcement to self-reinforcement.

Consistency in Reinforcement

In chapter 5 consistency was defined as behaving the same way in similar circumstances. This is very important when it comes to reinforcement. Many managers are reinforcing or supportive of their people only when they feel like it. While that's probably more convenient for managers, it is not helpful if they want to have an impact on *other* people's behavior. Managers should know when they are being supportive and should be careful not to be supportive when their people are performing poorly. Be consistent! Only good behavior or improvement—not just any behavior—should be rewarded.

Isn't All This Reinforcement a Form of Bribery?

The ultimate goal of the developmental process discussed in this chapter is to shift people toward self-management so that they can eventually assume responsibility for motivating their own behavior. This ultimate goal is mentioned to reassure people who have some real doubts about the use of reinforcement. Some readers may say, "People should be motivated by a desire to succeed or the desire to please people around them, not by a hoped-for reward," or "This sounds like bribery to me," or "If I use positive reinforcement with people, won't they always expect rewards for every little thing they do?"

Although we have shared similar concerns in the past, our experience in observing people in organizations has been reassuring. It has been found that people who are reinforced when they are first learning new behaviors and performance areas and then gradually allowed to be more and more on their own turn out to be self-motivated people who can be left alone without productivity dropping significantly.

In this chapter we have discussed how managers increase the readiness level of their followers in a developmental process that emphasizes the use of positive reinforcement. In the next chapter we will discuss the regressive cycle and will consider what has to be done when followers begin, for whatever reason, to decrease in their task-relevant readiness.

NOTES

1. Rensis Likert, *New Patterns of Management* (New York: McGraw-Hill, 1961), p. 7.
2. J. Sterling Livingston, "Pygmalion in Management," *Harvard Business Review,* July–August 1969, pp. 81–82.
3. Adapted from Paul Hersey, *The Situational Leader* (Escondido, Calif.: Center for Leadership Studies, 1985), pp. 92–94.
4. The most classic discussions of behavior modification, reinforcement theory, or operant conditioning have been done by B. F. Skinner. See Skinner, *Science and Human Behavior* (New York: Macmillan, 1953). See also A. Bandura, *Principles of Behavior Modification* (New York: Holt, Rinehart & Winston, 1969) and C. M. Franks, *Behavior Therapy: Appraisal and Status* (New York: McGraw-Hill, 1969). B. F. Skinner, *Contingencies of Reinforcement: A Theoretical Analysis* (Englewood Cliffs, N. J.: Prentice Hall, 1969); B. F. Skinner, *About Behaviorism* (New York: Knopf, 1974).
5. One of the first applications of behavior modification and reinforcement theory to organizations was done by Fred Luthans and Robert Kreitner. See Luthans and Kreitner, *Organizational Behavior Modification* (Glenview, Ill.: Scott, Foresman, 1975). See also Thomas K. Connelian, *How to Improve Human Performance: Behaviorism in Business and in Industry* (New York: Harper & Row, 1978); Lawrence M. Miller, *Behavior Management: The New Science of Managing People at Work* (New York: Wiley, 1978); and Fred Luthans, *Introduction to Management: Organizational Behavior* (New York: McGraw-Hill, 1981).
6. Helpful resources in developing this section in addition to those mentioned above were provided by Glenna Holsinger, *Motivating the Reluctant Learner* (Lexington, Mass: Motivity, Inc., 1970); Madeline Hunter, *Reinforcement Theory for Teachers* (El Segundo, Calif., TIP Publications, 1967); and Lawrence M. Miller, *Behavior Management: New Skills for Business and Industry* (Atlanta: Behavioral Systems, Inc., 1976). Discussions with friend and colleague Bob Lorber, President, Lorber-Kamai, a performance improvement consulting company in Sacramento, CA, were also extremely helpful.
7. *Skinner for the Classroom: Selected Papers* (Champaign, Ill.: Research Press, 1982).

11

Constructive Discipline

In the last chapter we discussed how to develop readiness and independence in people through the use of positive reinforcement and changing leadership styles. However, you should be aware that for one reason or another, people's performance may begin to slip. And one of the most difficult challenges managers face is working with performance problems. That's because discipline is often viewed as a negative intervention. However, the origin of the word *discipline* is "disciple." A disciple is a learner.

Unfortunately in our culture many people interpret discipline as punishment. It is the problem-solving nature of *constructive discipline* that differentiates it from punitive discipline. As such, constructive discipline is designed to be a learning process that provides an opportunity for positive growth. Effective managers use constructive discipline when people slip in readiness.[1] In this chapter we will attempt to help managers determine what needs to be done when this happens.

THE REGRESSIVE CYCLE

Managers may need to make a regressive intervention when their followers begin to behave less willingly than they have in the past. Thus, in a developmental cycle, managers are attempting to increase the task-relevant readiness of an individual or group beyond where it has been in the past. The regressive cycle involves an intervention that leaders need to make when an individual or a group is becoming less effective. Thus, in a regressive cycle, managers must use a leadership style appropriate to the present level of readiness rather than the style that might have been effective when the individual or group was at a higher level of readiness.

Decreases in readiness are often the result of what might be called "high-strength competing responses" in the environment. Other things are competing with the goals of the leader or the organization and, therefore, have become higher strength needs to the followers in terms of their behavior.

Decreases in readiness occur for a variety of reasons. Followers can have problems with the supervisor, problems with co-workers, suffer burnout, boredom, and have other problems on or off the job. These are just a few of the things that can have a negative impact on people's performance. Let's take an example of a performance problem.[2]

While consulting with a large research and development laboratory, one of the authors worked with a manager who was responsible for supervising John, one of the most motivated scientists on the staff. John was so committed to his job that even if the manager went into the laboratory at eight o'clock in the evening, it was not unusual to see a light under his laboratory door. Even on weekends, John was often found working in the laboratory. He probably had more patents and made more contributions to the overall program than any other person in the laboratory.

From the author's observations, this manager was behaving appropriately in using a low relationship–low task style (S4) for John's high readiness level (R4). Thus, rather than operating as John's supervisor, the manager was behaving more as John's representative to higher levels in the organization. John's manager was attempting to maximize John's potential by engaging in such "linking pin" activities as acquiring necessary resources and coordinating his activities with the activities of other staff members.

Although John was at a high level of readiness in this organizational setting, we learned that John's behavior was seen in a different light in his interactions with another organization—his family. In that organizational setting, his wife saw his behavior of long hours and weekends at work as an indication that he no longer cared about her and their young daughter. So in his wife's eyes, John was behaving at a low readiness level. As a result, John went home one evening and found a note from his wife in which she told him that she had packed her bags and taken their daughter away to start a new life.

John was shocked by his wife's action since he had perceived his own behavior quite differently from the way she did. He felt that he was attempting to provide for his wife and child all those things he was not able to have as a youngster.

What happened on the job was that now, with these family problems on his mind, John's effectiveness began to decrease. It has been said many times that you should leave your family problems at home and your job problems at work, but in reality we tend to carry problems both ways. Problems at home affect our behavior in the work environment and problems at work affect our home environment. This was certainly true in John's case. As his concerns for his family began to take effect, his performance as a scientist began to shift from readiness level 4 into level 3, as shown in Figure 11-1. Although his work emphasized technical competency, his declining psychological readiness was now affecting his performance. John did not seem to be able to cope with his problems at home. This meant that to maximize performance, John's manager had to shift behavior from style 4 to style 3 to deal with this lowering readiness level (Figure 11-1). As a result, a moderate increase in direction and structure as well as significant increases in socioemotional support, two-way communication, and the willingness to listen actively and be supportive (relationship behavior) were necessary. At this point, the

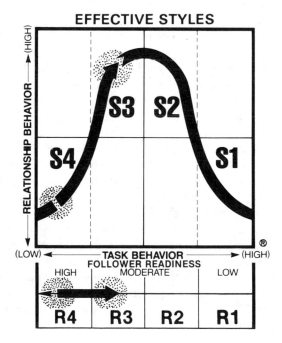

FIGURE 11-1
An example of a regressive cycle intervention

situation was still more of a problem to the follower than the leader. However, the high relationship intervention by the manager seemed to help the situation.

Once John was able to cope with his problem and put it in perspective, it was possible for his manager to move directly back to style 4. This illustrates one of the basic differences between a developmental cycle and a regressive cycle. In a regressive cycle, once an appropriate intervention has been made, the leader may often move back to the former leadership style without going through the process of positively reinforcing successive approximations. This is because the follower has previously demonstrated an ability to function at this level.

However, it should be pointed out in this example that if John's performance had continued to decline, the situation clearly would have become a problem to both leader and follower and would have demanded an eventual shift by the manager to a high task–high relationship style (S2).

In another example, Henry, a construction engineer, was operating as a project consultant; that is, he had a special expertise that was useful for a variety of projects. As a result, rather than being assigned to a specific project, he worked with a half-dozen projects at different construction sites. Since his readiness level was extremely high, his boss was also treating him appropriately in a style 4 manner. His supervisor was acting more as a linking pin with the rest of the organization than as his supervisor.

This style was effective until Henry began to take an active interest in golf. As a result of this new high-strength competing response, no longer was anybody able to get in touch with Henry after two o'clock in the afternoon. It took several months for his supervisor to make this discovery, since his co-workers just assumed that he was at one of the other construction sites. The supervisor finally became aware of Henry's behavior and discovered that his activity on the golf course was causing problems with the construction progress at some of the sites. As a result, Henry's readiness level as a project consultant in terms of the accomplishment of organizational goals had moved from readiness level 4 to readiness level 1, particularly between two and five in the afternoon. Thus, it became appropriate for the supervisor to shift his leadership style from S4 to S1 to deal with this drastic change in readiness. What might be called a disciplinary intervention was necessary to redefine roles and expectations for Henry. Once this was done, if the manager was able to unfreeze this new pattern of the employee, he might be able to shift his style back to S4. This is possible, once again, because Henry had been at a high readiness level before. Thus, it may not be necessary for the manager to positively reinforce successive approximations before he moves back to the previously appropriate style used with Henry. Often in a disciplinary intervention, all managers have to do is get the attention of their followers to get them moving back in the right direction.

The regressive cycle should be taken one step at a time. Thus, if we are letting individuals operate on their own ("delegating") and performance declines, we should move to "participating" and support their problem solving. If we are being supportive, but not directive with individuals (S3) and performance declines, we should move to "selling" and continue to engage in two-way communication, but we should also be more directive. If we are providing both task and relationship behavior (S2) and performance declines, we should move to "telling" and reduce some of our supportive behavior and increase direction and supervision. In both the regressive and developmental cycles, we should be careful not to jump from "delegating" (S4) to "selling" (S2) or "telling" (S1), or from "telling" to "participating" or "delegating." Making a drastic shift backward in leadership styles is one of the common mistakes managers make with their people. It sets up the "leave alone and 'zap'" (punish) style of management—an approach that is not only disruptive to the relationship a manager has with a staff member, but is also disruptive to that person's growth and development.

Relationship between Ability and Willingness in the Developmental and Regressive Cycles

Sometimes we are asked, "How can a person go from 'unable but willing or confident' (R2) to 'able but unwilling or insecure' (R3)?" Figure 11-2 answers this question. As people grow in their task specific readiness, the behaviors they need from the leader also change. Followers who are performing at readiness levels 1 and 2 need structure and guidance in order to perform well and grow. They also need increased supportive behavior as they move from R1 to R2 as reward and reinforcement for their efforts.

Often managers will observe followers moving from being unable and insecure, R1, to unable but confident, R2. They perform well as long as the leader is there providing direction. But as people grow and are given responsibility to accomplish tasks on their own, there is usually some apprehension with taking charge the first few times. Insecurity increases as the follower moves from R2 to R3. This is a new realm of *follower-directed* behavior versus *leader-directed* behavior.

Think about the first time you had to make a presentation in front of a group. Even though you practiced in front of a mirror and on

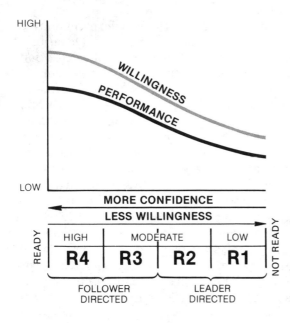

FIGURE 11-2
Relationship between ability and willingness in the developmental and regressive cycles

video tape, you probably had some "butterflies" and insecurity right before the moment of truth. But after you had a few wins under your belt, you became both able and confident about performing on your own. Your insecurity came about, in part, because the leader was not right there to bail you out when you got in trouble.

Figure 11-2 further clarifies the ability and willingness issues. Performance slippage in the short run is usually a willingness problem. It is not that an individual's or a group's ability has deteriorated significantly, but it is the *use* of ability that is causing the performance slippage. It is a motivation problem, not an ability problem. So if performance starts to slip, the person may be giving verbal and nonverbal clues about being upset with the boss, with a peer, with the organization about not getting an expected raise or promotion, or whatever it happens to be. The person's mental attitude is now focused on personal troubles rather than work requirements. If there are problems at home, you may have the same things occurring.

As illustrated in Figure 11-2, first comes the decline in willingness, as shown by the top gray line, followed by a decline in performance, shown by the bottom solid line. There is a lead-lag relationship. There is another related point. During the developmental cycle, issues of confidence or insecurity predominate psychological readiness; during the regressive cycle, it is issues of willingness and commitment.

Some Things to Remember When Disciplining an Individual

If a disciplinary intervention is called for, how can it be carried out effectively? Here are a few helpful guidelines.[3]

Timeliness

Problem solving needs to be done in a timely manner. The sooner the intervention, the better the chance of stopping the performance slippage. The longer a manager waits, the more directive the intervention will have to be. Therefore, a manager may risk a follower's becoming anxious, frustrated, or resentful. Even if the directive intervention is appropriate, this may lead to attempts to get out from under the manager or get the manager out.

For example, Mary, the office manager, expects all employees to maintain good attendance records. For the last three months, however, Susan, a data entry clerk has repeatedly arrived for work late and has failed to come to work twice. The other office staff have been complaining among themselves about Susan's behavior and have mentioned their complaints to Mary. Mary knows that Susan has had problems with child care and has decided to wait and see if Susan's behavior will improve. The weeks pass and Susan continues to arrive late for work. Mary has finally had enough and decides to let Susan really have it when Susan finally gets to the office today. Susan may then feel "zapped," feel bitter toward Mary, and not focus on her real problem of poor attendance.

If Mary had intervened earlier, a participative style would probably have been enough to turn the problem around. But now, the highly structured style is necessary and creates resentment in Susan. This is a trap that managers fall into when making disciplinary interventions. First they engage in "ostrich" leadership by sticking their heads in the sand and hoping the problem will go away. And then when it doesn't, they get angry and "zap" the follower.

By timing interventions appropriately and treating people at the level at which they are currently performing, managers can begin to take a proactive approach to problem solving, as opposed to just reacting to each new crisis.

Unless discipline occurs as close to the misbehavior or the poor performance as possible, it won't be helpful in influencing future behavior. Some managers are gunnysack discipliners. That is, they store up observations of poor behavior and then one day when the bag is full, they charge in and "dump everything on the table." Often, managers wait until the yearly performance review. That is why some people call an annual performance review program an "NIHYYSOB"–"Now I have you, you S.O.B." Managers using the "NIHYYSOB" performance review tell their people all the bad things they have done over the last months or year. Manager and employee usually end up arguing about the "facts," and the employee doesn't really hear what is wrong. This is a version of the "leave alone and 'zap'" form of discipline. If managers would only intervene early, they could calmly deal with one behavior at a time, and the person could "hear" the feedback.

Varying the Emotional Level

The emotional level of the intervention is different for constructive discipline than it is for developing people. When developing people, you are attempting to expand the present ability of the follower. Therefore, it helps to keep the emotional content of a development intervention at a low level. People often misinterpret Situational Leadership because they think a "telling" style is raising your voice, hollering, or blowing your cool. Actually, style 1 can be a very soft and caring approach by providing the needed demonstration of how to do things with some hands-on guidance. It would be inappropriate to shout at or raise the emotional level with people who are developing. It could tend to make them insecure about taking risks and continuing to learn in the future.

However, when followers choose not to use their present ability and constructive discipline is appropriate, you can raise the emotional content to a *moderate* level. This helps to get people's attention and lets them know that you are aware of the performance problem and that you care. It also helps to unfreeze the inappropriate behavior so that change can take place.

Focus on Performance

The next thing to consider in working with constructive discipline is *don't attack personality—focus on performance.*

If you attack personality and the person becomes angry, the probability of being able to successfully work with the person is much lower. So often a manager starts off a disciplinary intervention with, "I just told you that a week ago. Can't you remember to do anything, you dumb son of a gun? . . ." All this does is raise the emotional level of other people. It doesn't get them to focus on the problem. If the focus is on performance, not personality, both leader and follower can talk about it and problem solve.

Be Specific . . . Do Your Homework

Being specific about performance problems is important. When using constructive discipline, be careful of *glittering generalities*. So often managers on the job do all the other aspects of constructive discipline well; they treat people where they are, have good timing, keep a moderate emotional profile, and focus on performance. However, their intervention sounds like this, "Look, you're just not doing the kind of performance that we both know you're capable of; now let's get back on track." Then the manager is bewildered or gets angry when followers don't understand.

These kinds of glittering generalities don't get the job done. You have to do your homework before the intervention and gather specific details that may be useful in problem solving. With specific information the interventions might sound like, "Productivity is down fourteen and a half percent," "Scrap loss is up six and a half percent," or "Project Z is five days late and we've got three other departments depending on us for that component." This provides specificity so that the manager and followers together can work on developing a solution.

Keep It Private

The last thing to remember is to keep disciplinary interventions private. As a guideline, it's a good idea to praise people in public and problem solve in private. If you address followers about problems when others are around, you run the risk of having them more concerned about being seen "catching hell" than on solving the problem. Discussing problems in private tends to make it easier to get your points across and keep the other person focused on the problem-solving process.

The goal of constructive discipline is to make problem solving a positive growth-oriented opportunity instead of a punitive experience. It is important to:

- Treat people where they are presently performing
- Make the intervention timely
- Use an appropriate emotional level
- Focus on performance, not personality
- Be specific . . . do your homework
- Keep the intervention private

Managers find that by keeping these factors in mind when making disciplinary interventions, discipline is not seen as a destructive intervention, but as a helping relationship.

Punishment and Negative Reinforcement

Punishment, as we discussed earlier, is a negative consequence. A negative consequence tends to weaken the response it immediately follows; that is, it prevents the recurrence of that behavior. It is a stimulus that an individual "will reject, if given a choice between the punishment and no stimulus at all."[4] As punishment suppresses the behavior that brought it (the punishment) on, *negative reinforcement* strengthens the response(s) that eliminates the punishment.

An example of both punishment and negative reinforcement may be helpful. Suppose whenever a manager brings the work group together to share some new information with them, Bill, one of the employees, usually pays little attention and often talks to people around him. As a result, he is uninformed and his manager is irritated. The manager decides to punish Bill's whispering behavior by stopping in the middle of a sentence and looking at Bill whenever she sees him talk. The unexpected silence (a negative consequence) causes the whole work group to focus on what stopped the manager's sharing of information (Bill's talking). The silence from the manager and all eyes on him are uncomfortable to Bill (punishment). He stops talking and starts listening to his manager resume sharing information. His manager's use of a negative consequence or punishment (silence and look) has weakened and suppressed his whispering behavior. At the same time it has operated as negative reinforcement in strengthening his listening, the behavior that took the punishment away (his manager stops looking at him and starts talking).

It is important to remember that a manager has to be careful in using punishment because one does not always know what a person will do when punished. For example, suppose a manager reprimands Al, an employee, for sloppy work. If Al settles down, figures out what he has done wrong, and begins working carefully (negative reinforcement), the punishment has been helpful. After having this good experience in "shaping up," the manager might try the same technique with Mary, another employee who is doing sloppy work. But rather than the punishment (reprimand) getting Mary to behave more carefully, her work becomes worse, and she begins to become disruptive in other areas. Thus, while Al shaped up with a reprimand, Mary became more troublesome after the same intervention from the manager.

Another important point to keep in mind when using punishment is that punishment shows one what *not* to do, but does not show one what *to* do. This was vividly pointed out by John Huberman in a case study[5] about a Douglas fir plywood mill in which the management had continually used punitive measures to deal with sloppy workmanship and discipline problems. Although punishment seemed to stop the inappropriate behavior for the moment, it had little long-term effect. When top management finally analyzed the system during the preparation for the doubling of its capacity, they were amazed that:

... not a single desirable result could be detected.

The people who had been disciplined were generally still among the poorest workers; their attitude was sulky, if not openly hostile. And they seemed to be spreading this feeling among the rest of the crew.[6]

This reality and the findings that "85 percent of all those who entered the local prison returned there within three years of their release ..."[7] made management seriously question their system. Eventually they worked out a new and highly effective system, which Huberman called "discipline *without* punishment." One of the main ingredients of the new method was that rather than a punitive approach to unsatisfactory work or a discipline problem, a six-step process was initiated that clearly spelled out appropriate behavior and placed "on the employee the onus" of deciding whether the employee wished (or was able) "to conform to the requirements of a particular work situation."[8]

As this illustrates, it is essential when making a disciplinary intervention that task behavior follows immediately. That is, once an intervention has been made, the manager must identify the new behavior that is to replace the undesired behavior. Only when that occurs can positive reinforcement be used to increase the likelihood of the new behavior recurring.

Extinction

When reinforcement is withheld after a behavior occurs, the behavior is said to be on extinction. Punishment tends only to suppress behavior; extinction tends to make it disappear. To extinguish a response, nothing must happen as a result of behavior. For example, suppose a child finds that stomping up and down and crying gets the attention of the parents and usually receives something wanted, say a cookie. Now, if the parents don't want that kind of behavior, they could extinguish it by not responding to the child (either in a positive or negative way). After a while, when the child sees that stomping and crying do not get anything, this behavior will tend to decrease. People seldom continue to do things that do not provide positive reinforcement.

Although extinction can help to eliminate undesirable behavior, one should be careful not to use it when it is not intended. Let's look at our example of Al again.

Imagine that Al has adjusted pretty well to his setting. He works carefully and neatly because that is what pays off. But, suddenly, the manager stops rewarding Al for neat work. Al goes for perhaps a week or two weeks working neatly with no reward. He may not be able to tell us what is different, but gradually his behavior gives us a clue. He soon begins to try other behaviors. He becomes less careful and neat. If the former negative consequences (punishment) are also withheld, we see that within days he has reverted to his earlier behavior pattern. In essence, neatness and carefulness have been extinguished. As stated earlier, people seldom continue to do things that do not provide positive reinforcement, either through external reward or internal satisfaction. In Al's case, he does not yet find working carefully or neatly as rewarding in itself. The intervention by his manager helped his task readiness, but Al is not psychologically ready enough in this job (and he may never become so if it is a boring and unsatisfying job) to be left alone and not periodically reinforced for his neatness and carefulness.

In addition to its effect on the continuation of a particular behavior, extinction also can sometimes have an emotional impact on that behavior. We could predict, for example, with an excellent chance of being correct, that Al will likely become surly, may complain more than before, or may have problems getting along with his co-workers. Emotional behavior usually accompanies extinction in performance when expected reinforcement or former punishment is withheld.

Parents often have problems with extinction when they do not realize what they are doing and tend to pay attention to their children only when they are behaving poorly. When the children are behaving appropriately, they may pay little or no attention to them, which in a sense puts that behavior on extinction. If a child wants attention from the parents (it is rewarding to him), the child may be willing to endure what the parents think is punishment for that attention. So, in the long run, the parents might be reinforcing the very behavior they do not want and extinguishing more appropriate behavior.

Leaders in all kinds of settings must be careful of the possibility of positively reinforcing inappropriate behavior, and yet it happens all the time. Have you ever given a crying child a piece of candy? *"Don't cry, John. Here's some candy."* It works. The child eats the candy and stops crying. But does it really work? Behavior Modification Theory suggests that the next time the child wants a piece of candy (or your attention), he knows exactly how to get it—by crying. You have made the mistake of positively reinforcing inappropriate behavior.[9]

This phenomenon does not just happen at home, but is very common in the world of work. For example, a manager's work group had responded well to a high task–low relationship behavior of always spelling out tasks specifically and dealing firmly with anyone who did not demonstrate appropriate behavior. Now suddenly this behavior is not achieving results, and followers are being disruptive and making unreasonable demands. What should the manager do? The first impulse of most managers is to think "maybe I've been too hard on them" and begin to give in to their demands. Although perhaps the manager should have increased relationship behavior earlier and moved to a high task–high relationship leadership style, if the manager does it now it may be perceived as positively reinforcing inappropriate behavior—every time the work group wants something, they will become disruptive. Positively reinforcing inappropriate behavior generally results in more unwanted behavior.

When to Use Punishment or Extinction

In essence, what we are saying is that leaders must think before they behave because they never know what they may or may not be reinforcing. This is particularly true when it comes to using punishment and extinction. And yet, these can be useful concepts that managers can learn to use effectively for unfreezing inappropriate behavior so that they can begin to reinforce positively more desirable behavior. It should be remembered, however, in using punishment or extinction that it is important to know what behavior you want to change and communicate that in some way to the person(s) with whom you are working. To determine when to use punishment and when to ignore (extinguish by withholding reinforcement), managers need to estimate how long the undesirable behavior has been occurring. If the behavior is new, ignoring it (extinction) may get results and cause a person to abandon an inappropriate behavior. But if the behavior has been occurring for some time, it may be necessary to suppress this behavior through some form of punishment until some desirable behavior has a chance to become strong enough as a result of positive reinforcement to replace the undesirable behavior. As we discussed in chapter 2, the larger the reservoir of past experience that a person has in a particular behavior, the tendency is that the more difficult the behavior will be to change, and, thus, the harder the initial intervention may have to be before positive reinforcement can be used effectively to strengthen a new behavior.

An Example of Using Behavior Modification

Consider the behavior of Tony, a new employee right out of high school, who can be described as a very aggressive and competitive individual. During his first day on the job he argues over tools with another young employee. To make certain that a manager would not be unsure about what to do with Tony's behavior and to summarize our discussion of Behavior Modification, some steps that managers can use in attempting to change employee behavior are presented here.[10]

- *Step 1:* Identify (for yourself and then with Tony) the behavior to be changed and the new behavior that is to replace the old and discover what Tony would consider to be positive reinforcement and punishment. Devise a strategy to get the new behavior and determine the way you will positively reinforce it.
- *Step 2:* Attempt to find out whether the old behavior (arguing over tools) is such a strong behavior that you need to suppress it through punishment or whether it is a new enough behavior that a lack of any kind of reinforcement will extinguish it. If you decide to use punishment, determine what it will be. Remember, this punishment could operate as negative reinforcement and thus strengthen the behavior that removes the punishment. So be careful!
- *Step 3:* Develop a strategy to get Tony to practice the new behavior and positively reinforce it on a regular schedule. As soon as Tony has practiced the new behavior so that it is more likely to occur than the old behavior, change to an intermittent schedule of reinforcing the new behavior (make the intervals between reinforcement increasingly long) so that new behavior will resist extinction.

In examining these steps, one could get the impression that the manager is dominating the process with little if any involvement from Tony. According to Situational Leadership this may be appropriate in working with people at low levels of readiness, such as a new and inexperienced employee like Tony. But, as the readiness level of the people that a manager supervises begins to increase, this process of change becomes much more of a collaborative process. As we will discuss in chapter 12, the extent of involvement of people in the change process will vary from situation to situation.

PROBLEMS AND THEIR OWNERSHIP—WHO'S GOT THE MONKEY?

As we have been suggesting in this chapter, effective managers are not only able to develop the readiness of their people, they are also able to spot "slippage" in readiness and intervene early enough to turn the situation around. How can managers know when to intervene? What should they look for?

As a simple guideline, whenever managers receive feedback, either verbal (one of their people tells them) or nonverbal (they observe the performance of one of their people), indicating that that person is having a problem in some area, it's time to think about stepping in. A *problem* exists when there is a difference between what someone is doing and what that person's manager and (or) that individual believes is really happening. Thus, detecting problems is all-important in determining what areas of a person's job require attention.

Thomas Gordon, in his book *P.E.T., Parent Effectiveness Training,*[11] contends that one of the most important steps in becoming more effective in rearing responsible self-motivated children is determining whether their behavior is acceptable or unacceptable to their parents as well as to themselves. Once the acceptance question has been answered, then "who owns the problem" in terms of a child's behavior can be identified. Although the work of Gordon originated from observations of parents and teachers, the concepts behind the ownership of problems seem to apply to any organizational setting in which a leader is trying to influence the behavior of others.

Gordon's concept of "who owns the problem" can be combined with William Oncken's helpful "monkey-on-the-back" analogy.[12]

Monkey Management

Blanchard, Oncken, and Burrows ask, "Why is it that some managers are typically running out of time while their staffs are typically running out of work?"[13] This is a question many managers ask themselves while spending countless weekends at the office while followers are happily pursuing their nonwork activities. A key question the work-bound manager must ask is: "Whose work am I doing?" If the answer to this is not an unequivocal "mine," the manager may have a problem with *monkeys.*

Blanchard, Oncken, and Burrows define a monkey as "the next move."[14] If we state this definition in terms of a typical organizational situation, then a monkey is the "next move" on the path to solving a problem.

When a manager agrees to "think about" a follower's problem, then ownership of "the next move" shifts from the follower to the manager. Before the shift, responsibility for the action was on the follower. After the shift, when the manager takes ownership of the monkey, two responsibilities are assumed: (1) responsibility for the problem and; (2) responsibility for updating the follower on the progress of the problem.[15]

In this situation, the follower has effectively reversed the roles of leader and follower. The follower will now ask about the monkey daily and, of course, the manager will not have made much progress on the monkey because it is buried under all of the other monkeys accumulated from other followers. An accumulation of follower-imposed monkeys translates into less time for managers to attend to their monkeys.

Monkey Management and Situational Leadership

Looking at monkey management in the context of Situational Leadership, if managers can identify who has the monkey, then they are in a position to assess readiness level, determine the leadership style that has the best chance of success, and decide how to intervene with followers. The four problem situations described next combine these elements.

1. The manager has the monkey. In this situation the follower's behavior is a problem to the manager, but not to the follower. The follower's readiness level is R1 since the follower sees no problem. The appropriate leadership style for the manager is "telling" (S1). For managers to rid themselves of these monkeys, they must provide followers with structure in the form of direction regarding the task.

2. The manager and the follower have the monkey. This situation involves the follower's behavior when it is a problem for both the manager and the follower. The follower's readiness level is R2 since the follower needs some direction. Further, because the follower owns part of the problem, some relationship behavior in terms of two-way communication and facilitating behavior is also necessary. The appropriate leadership style is "selling" (S2) because the follower needs both direction and support to carry out the task.

3. The follower has the monkey. Here, the follower's behavior is a problem for the follower, but not for the manager. The follower's readiness level is R3 since the follower needs support and encouragement from the manager. The appropriate leadership style is S3, a "participating" style to facilitate two-way communication. The tragedy is that managers often treat this problem situation as if it were a problem to neither. If management intervention is not made somewhat soon, the monkey could become a serious problem for the follower, the manager, and the organization.

4. Neither the manager or the follower have the monkey. In this situation there are no monkeys requiring attention. Followers involved in this situation are R4, a high level of readiness. The most appropriate leadership style is "delegating" (S4), since the manager's job is to monitor the situation so no monkeys will form.

Let's look at some examples of how this concept might be used as a diagnostic tool. Ken, a commodities trader in a large exchange, has always executed trades and recorded exchanges according to the high standards developed by his company. Since he is operating within guidelines, his behavior is not a problem to his manager or his company. However, Ken's behavior may be a problem to himself since his best friends on the exchange floor have been involved in some questionable practices and are pressuring him to take part. If Ken's manager treats this situation as if it were a problem to neither and leaves Ken alone, the situation could quickly become a problem for both. Because of the competing pressures from his peers on the exchange floor, a lack of active listening and support by Ken's manager could move Ken toward the same behavior his peers are practicing. Thus, by not making a high relationship intervention at the appropriate time, Ken's manager could create a problem for his company that did not exist before.

If the situation is one in which the behavior of the employee is a problem to the manager, but not to the employee, the manager does not have to provide facilitating behaviors. For example, if the problem involves personal friends visiting the employee during working hours, the manager merely needs to provide the employee with an understanding of what the rules are (an S1 intervention). The employee wants to know what the rules are and what is expected of him or her. Since the situation is not a problem to the employee, the employee does not want to spend fifteen or twenty minutes discussing it.

Another example is a teacher who is making an assignment for the next day and asks the class to read fifteen, twenty, or twenty-five pages. That doesn't really matter to the students; any of those reading assignments are okay. All the students want to know is the expectations of the teacher; they don't want to sit around and talk about it. But if the teacher says the assignment is one hundred pages, the situation might quickly become a problem to both the students and the teacher. Now that the situation is also a problem to the students, the teacher has to engage in "selling" behavior rather than "telling." The teacher has to open up channels of communication and discussion, and engage in facilitating behaviors. The teacher has to get the students to understand the "why" of the large assignment and have them "buy in" psychologically to the decision. The teacher might say, "There is a top lecturer coming this week and, for that reason, a heavy assignment is being made for tomorrow; but later in the week we'll have no reading assignment." In other words, the teacher attempts to make some trades to facilitate interaction, but is still trying to get the students to buy into the decision.

As the discussion and examples suggest, it is felt that this integration of Situational Leadership with problem ownership (Gordon) and monkey business (Oncken) can be helpful in determining the appropriate leadership style in various situations. Remember, even if the follower's behavior is acceptable to the leader, the leader may still have to take action if the follower needs support and encouragement to keep up the good work. If the follower's behavior is unacceptable to the leader, a more directive intervention is needed to turn the situation around. How direct the intervention must be ("telling" or just "selling") depends on whether the follower also sees this behavior as a problem and "owns the monkey" too. If leaders are going to help their people grow and develop into self-motivated individuals, they must gradually let them think for themselves and solve their own problems.

POSITIVE DISCIPLINE

Another model of dealing with employees who fail to meet performance goals or who violate organizational rules is called *positive discipline*.[21] Developed by Eric L. Harvey, this approach to employee discipline follows three simple and direct steps:

1. Warn the employee orally.
2. Warn the employee in writing.
3. If steps 1 and 2 fail to resolve the problem, give the employee a day off, *with pay*.

The model removes punishment from the disciplinary process and places responsibility for appropriate performance on the employee. In the first two steps, the manager focuses on the specific discrepancy between the employee's actual and expected performance and the business reasons why the performance expectation must be met. The manager describes why meeting the performance standard is important and works to gain the employee's agreement to change behavior and meet the standard. The employee is reminded that proper performance and behavior is the individual's responsibility, not the manager's. Hostile or defensive employee reactions are met with mature and adult explanations of the specific discrepancy and the standard which needs to be met.

If the employee fails to change after the first two steps are taken, the manager moves to step three. During the day off with pay, which is referred to as a "decision-making leave," the employee is expected to be thinking about whether or not he or she wishes to remain in the organization. The leave communicates to the employee that, "Your job is on the line. What are *you* going to do about it?" The suspension from work highlights the seriousness of the situation; being paid for the day removes employee hostility and reinforces the organization's honest desire to help the individual take responsibility for his or her actions and meet organizational expectations. Upon returning to work, the employee tells the manager of his or her decision–to make the required changes and continue employment, or to quit. If the problems continue upon the employee's return, the employee is then terminated.

The model is based on the belief that an organization and its managers have the right to establish reasonable and appropriate standards; to point out discrepancies when they occur; and to let the individual decide whether or not to perform and meet these standards. Responsibility for performance is placed on the employee, not the manager or the organization.

The purpose of this chapter has been to help leaders develop strategies to assist them in disciplining followers constructively. Leaders must remove themselves from the traditional job of directing, controlling, and supervising their followers and assist them in learning to stand on their own and achieve individual effectiveness in the demanding work environment.

NOTES

1. Adapted from Paul Hersey, *The Situational Leader* (Escondido, Calif.: Center for Leadership Studies, 1985), p. 114.
2. *Ibid.*
3. Adapted from Paul Hersey, *Situational Selling* (Escondido, Calif.: Center for Leadership Studies, 1985), pp. 115–20.
4. R. L. Solomon, "Punishment," *American Psychologist*, 19 (1964), p. 239.
5. John Huberman, "Discipline Without Punishment," *Harvard Business Review*, May 1967, pp. 62–68.
6. *Ibid.*, pp. 64–65.
7. *Ibid.*, p. 65.
8. *Ibid.*
9. Taken from an enjoyable popular article on this subject by Alice Lake, "How to Teach Your Child Good Habits," *Redbook Magazine*, June 1971, pp. 74, 186, 188, 190.
10. These steps were adapted from seven steps identified by Madeline Hunter, *Reinforcement Theory for Teachers* (El Segundo, Calif., TIP Publications, 1967), pp. 47–48.
11. Thomas Gordon, *P.E.T., Parent Effectiveness Training* (New York: Peter H. Wyden, 1970). See also Muriel James and Louis Savary, *A New Self: Self Therapy with Transactional Analysis* (Reading, Mass.: Addison-Wesley, 1977); Abe Wagner, *The Transactional Manager: How to Solve Problems with Transactional Analysis* (Englewood Cliffs, N.J.: Prentice Hall, 1981).
12. William Oncken, Jr., and Donald L. Wass, "Management Time: Who's Got the Monkey?" *Harvard Business Review*, November–December 1974, pp. 75–80.
13. Kenneth H. Blanchard, William Oncken, Jr., and Hal Burrows, *The One Minute Manager and the Monkey*, New York: Morrow (1989), pg. 22.
14. *Ibid.*, p. 26.
15. "Time Management: Keeping the Monkey Off Your Back." Produced by the William Oncken Corporation and the Bureau of Business Practice (Division of Prentice-Hall), 24 Rope Ferry Road, Waterford, CT 06386, 1991.
16. Eric L. Harvey, "Discipline vs. Punishment," *Management Review*, March 1987, pp. 25–29.

12

Building Effective Relationships

In the last two chapters the emphasis was on helping leaders to develop people to their fullest potential. This involves shifting their leadership style forward and backward (according to Situational Leadership), thus utilizing various degrees of direction and support as followers increase or decrease in readiness or development levels. This shifting of leadership styles requires leaders to be flexible; that is, to be able to use a variety of leadership styles depending on the situation. That raises two questions: (1) Are most leaders able to be that flexible or do they tend to be limited only to one or two leadership styles? (2) If leaders change their leadership styles, how will that affect their followers' perception of their intentions?

The first question is something that has been examined at the Center for Leadership Studies for nearly two decades through the use of Leader Effectiveness and Adaptability Description (LEAD) instruments.[1] Answering the second question was an important impetus in the creation of the Contracting for Leadership Style[2] process developed to increase the effectiveness of management by objectives (MBO), a widely used formal leader-follower negotiation system.[3]

LEAD INSTRUMENTATION

The LEAD instrument developed at the Center for Leadership Studies was designed to measure three aspects of leader behavior: (1) style; (2) style range; and (3) style adaptability.

The *leadership style* of an individual is the behavior pattern that a person exhibits when attempting to influence the activities of others—as perceived by those others. This may be very different from the leader's perception, which we will define as *self-perception* rather than style. Comparing one's self-perception of leadership style with the perceptions of others can be very useful, particularly since one's self-perception may or may not reflect one's actual leadership style, depending on how close a person's perceptions are to the perceptions of others. For this reason, two LEAD instruments were developed: LEAD-Self and LEAD-Other. The LEAD-Self measures self-perception of how an individual behaves as a leader; the LEAD-Other reflects the perceptions of a leader's followers, supervisors, and peers or associates.[4]

Leadership Style

Our extensive research over many years has revealed that most leaders have a *primary* leadership style and a *secondary* leadership style. A leader's primary style is defined as the behavior pattern used most often when attempting to influence the activities of others. In other words, most leaders tend to have a favorite leadership style.

A leader's supporting style(s) is a leadership style that person tends to use on occasion. It is important to note that all leaders have a primary leadership style; that is, they tend to use one of the four basic leadership styles described in Situational Leadership more often than not in leadership situations. However, they may *not* have any secondary leadership styles. Therefore, a leader could have no secondary styles or up to three secondary styles, but a leader would always have at least one primary style.

Style Range or Flexibility

Leaders' *style range* is the extent to which leaders are able to vary their leadership style. Leaders differ in their ability to vary their style in different situations. Some leaders seem to be limited to one basic style: these rigid people tend to be effective only in situations in which their styles are compatible with the environment. Other leaders are able to modify their behavior to fit any of the four basic styles; still others can utilize two or three styles. Flexible leaders have the *potential* to be effective in a number of situations.

The style range of a leader can be illustrated in terms of task and relationship behavior, as shown in Figure 12-1. The area of the circle indicates the range of style. If the area is small, as in A, then the range of behavior of the leader is limit ᵓd; if the area is large, as in B, the leader has a wide range of behavior.

Leadership situations vary in the extent to which they make demands on flexibility. Reddin has cited some of the conditions that demand, in ᵓis terms, low and high flexibility. For example, conditions that demand low flexibility include low level managerial jobs, established tasks, and little environmental change. Conditions that demand high flexibility are the opposite, e.g. high-level managerial jobs, instructed tasks, and rapid environmental change.[5]

Style Adaptability

Style range indicates the extent to which leaders are able to vary their style; style *adaptability* is the degree to which they are able to vary their style appropriately to the demands of a given situation, according to Situational Leadership. Let's contrast style adaptability with style range. Style adaptability means that a leader, having diagnosed the appropriate style, can use that style appropriately in a given situation. The leader can *adapt* style to the situation. People who have a narrow style range can be effective over a long period of time if they remain in situations in which their style has a high

FIGURE 12-1   Style range in terms of task behavior and relationship behavior

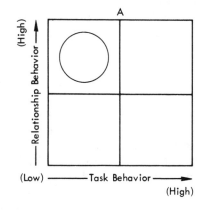
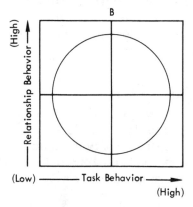

probability of success. Conversely, people who have a wide range of styles may be ineffective if these behaviors are not consistent with the demands of the situation.

Thus, style range is not as relevant to effectiveness as style adaptability; a wide style range will not guarantee effectiveness. For example, in A in Figure 12-1, the leader has a dominant relationship style with no flexibility; in B, the leader has a wide range of leadership styles because the leader is able to use all four leadership styles on various occasions. In this example, A may be effective in situations that demand a high relationship–low task style, such as in coaching or counseling situations. In B, however, the potential exists to be effective in a wide variety of instances. It should be remembered, however, that the B style range will not guarantee effectiveness. The B style will be effective only if the leader makes style changes appropriate to the situation.

Flexibility: A Question of Willingness

The importance of a leader's *diagnostic ability* cannot be over-emphasized. It is the key to adaptability. However, most leaders are more concerned about flexibility than when to use which leadership style. That gets us back to one of the questions raised at the beginning of the chapter: Are most leaders able to be that flexible or do they tend to be limited only to one or two leadership styles?

It has been our experience based on our research that there are few, if any, leaders who cannot learn to use all four basic leadership styles. In fact, people use those behaviors almost every day. At least once a day you probably tell somebody what to do and watch them closely (style S1), explain what you want somebody to do and permit them to ask clarifying questions (style S2), share ideas with people and support their efforts (style S3), and turn over responsibility to someone to "run with the ball" (style S4).

Learning to use the four basic styles is not the issue; the question is one of willingness. Anyone has the ability, but if the person does not want to learn, then there is not much that you can do. It is like the old saying, "You can lead a horse to water, but you can't make him drink."

When people are willing to learn to use all the leadership styles, we have found an interesting phenomenon. When people learn to use the leadership style that previously was not even considered a secondary style, the compensating styles often become their most effective styles. While these styles may never become comfortable, they can become the most effective, in many cases, because they've been learned. Therefore, such leaders know a lot more about these styles because they have practiced them consciously. People often use their comfortable or primary leadership styles by the "seat of their pants." This is true not only in terms of leadership styles, but also in many other areas of their lives.

For example, suppose you are a golfer who enjoys and excels at hitting a drive; yet you realize that the "drive is for show, but the putt is for the dough," so you decide to take lessons in putting. If you consciously make an effort and take lessons and practice to become a good putter, very often it is this part of the game that becomes your most effective weapon. You would still be more comfortable hitting the ball off the tee, but since you have practiced putting, it is now the strongest part of your game.

The same goes for leaders. Your primary style is often one that you do not have to think about using. But once you learn other styles through conscientious study and practice, these compensating styles can be your most effective. Thus, we find willingness—not ability—is the main issue in terms of style flexibility.

Is There Only One Appropriate Style?

The concept of adaptability implies that the effective leader is able to use the right style at the right time. What if a leader makes a good diagnosis and then is unwilling or is unable to use the "best" style? Is that leader doomed to failure? Situational Leadership not only suggests the high probability leadership styles for various readiness levels, but also indicates the probability of success of the other styles if the leader is unwilling or unable to use the "desired" style. The probability of success of each style for the four readiness levels is shown in Table 12-1.

As Table 12-1 indicates, the "desired" style always has a second "best" style choice; that is, a style that would probably be effective if the highest probability style could not be used. In attempting to influence people at the low to moderate (R2) and moderate to high (R3) readiness levels, you will notice that there are two second "best" style choices: which one should be used depends on whether the readiness of the individual is getting better, indicating that the leaders should be involved in a developmental cycle (chapter 10), or getting worse, revealing that a regressive cycle is occurring (chapter 11). If the situation is improving, "participating" and "delegating" would be the "best" second choices, but if things are deteriorating, "selling" and "telling" would be the most appropriate backup choices.

Table 12-1 also suggests that "telling" and "delegating" are the

TABLE 12-1 Matching Rediness Level with the Leadership Style Most Likely to Work Well

READINESS	"BEST" STYLE	SECOND "BEST" STYLE	THIRD "BEST" STYLE	LEAST EFFECTIVE STYLE
R1 Low	S1 Telling	S2 Selling	S3 Participating	S4 Delegating
R2 Low to Moderate	S2 Selling	S1 Telling or S3 Participating		S4 Delegating
R3 Moderate to High	S3 Participating	S2 Selling or S4 Delegating		S1 Telling
R4 High	S4 Delegating	S3 Participating	S2 Selling	S1 Telling

risky styles because one of them is always the lowest probability style. However, even though this appears to be true, later in this chapter we will discuss why it is so important for leaders to learn to use these styles effectively.

Use of LEAD Instrumentation

When staff members at the Center for Leadership Studies diagnose an organization, part of that diagnosis often involves use of the LEAD instruments. The process consists of having managers throughout the organization complete the LEAD-Self Instrument (how they perceive their own leadership style). At the same time, each of these managers' employees, supervisor, and several associates or peers fill out the LEAD-Other instrument. All the instruments are sent directly to the Center for Leadership Studies for analysis. Once the data have been analyzed, a LEAD-Profile is prepared for each individual manager. The profile gives managers an opportunity to see if there is any significant difference between how they perceive their own leadership style and how others in the environment perceive their style.

The purpose of distributing and analyzing the LEAD-Self and LEAD-Other data is to determine if there is any discrepancy between self-perception and the perception of others. In analyzing that data and feeding it back to participating managers, a useful framework developed by Joseph Luft and Harry Ingham[6] is used.

JOHARI WINDOW

The framework developed by Luft and Ingham is called the *Johari window* (taken from the first names of its authors). The Johari window is used in our consulting to depict leadership personality, not overall personality, as it is sometimes used. The difference between leadership personality and leadership style in this context is that leadership personality includes self-perception and the perception of others; leadership style consists only of an individual's leader behavior as perceived by others, that is, supervisor, employee(s), associates, and so on. Thus, leadership personality equals self-perception plus perception of others (style).

According to this framework, there are some attitudes or behaviors engaged in by leaders that they themselves know about. This *known-to-self* area includes their knowledge of the way they are coming across—the impact they are having with the people they are trying to influence. At the same time, part of the leader's personality is *unknown to self;* that is, in some areas leaders are unaware of how they are coming across to others. It may be that their followers have not given them feedback, or it may be that a leader has not been alert enough to pick up some of the verbal or nonverbal feedback that actually exists within the environment.

We can also look at leadership personality that includes behaviors and attitudes *known to others* in a leader's organizational setting, as well as areas *unknown to others.* In terms of what is known and unknown to self and known and unknown to others, we can create four areas that comprise the total window, as depicted in Figure 12-2.

The arena that is known to self and also known to others in any specific organizational setting is called the *public* arena—it is known to all (the leader and others; that is, supervisor, follower(s), and peer(s) within that organizational setting.

The arena that is unknown to self (the leader), but is known to others is referred to as the *blind* arena. It is unknown to the leader either because followers have been unwilling to share feedback with or communicate ("level") with that leader, or it may be that the data are there in terms of verbal and nonverbal behavior, but the leader is not able or does not care to "see" them.

The arena that is known to self, but unknown to others is referred to as the *private* arena since it is only known to the leader. Again, it may be private because the leader has been unwilling to share or disclose this to others in the organizational setting, or it may be private because the others in the system are not picking up the

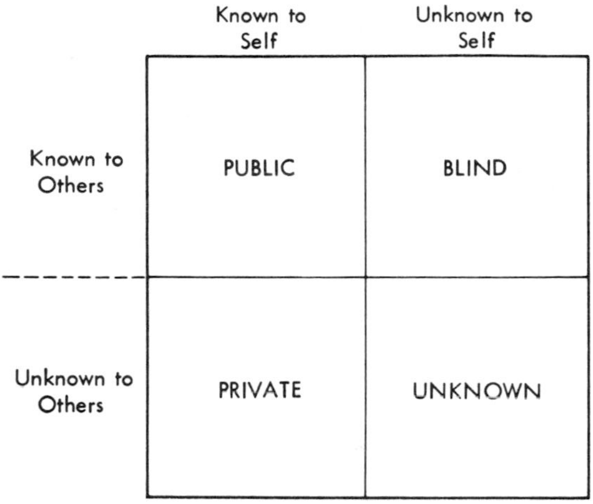

	Known to Self	Unknown to Self
Known to Others	PUBLIC	BLIND
Unknown to Others	PRIVATE	UNKNOWN

FIGURE 12-2
The Johari Window

nonverbal and verbal responses that are available from the leader in the system.

The last arena, unknown to self and unknown to others, is called the *unknown*. In Freudian psychology this would be referred to as the subconscious or unconscious.[7] As you will recall from chapter 2, Freud describes personality much like an iceberg. There is a certain portion of a leader's personality that is above the surface—that is, it is very graphic. Anyone who looks in that direction can hardly help but see the basic size, consistency, makeup, and configuration. But much of this iceberg exists beneath the surface, and unless we make conscious efforts to probe and understand, we will really never have any insight into its consistency. And yet, much of that part of a leader's personality referred to as unknown may be having a relevant impact in terms of the kinds of behaviors in which a leader engages when trying to influence the behavior of others.

Feedback

There are two processes that affect the shape of the Johari window (the configuration of the four arenas). The first, which operates in the direction illustrated in Figure 12-3, is called *feedback*. This is the extent to which others in the organizational setting are willing to share with the leader. It is the willingness of others to be open and level and to give relevant feedback to the leader. But again, you have to look at it from both perspectives. It is also the extent to which the leader is attempting to perceive the verbal and nonverbal feedback that exists in the system.

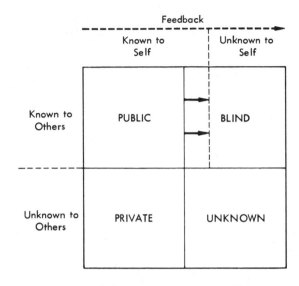

FIGURE 12-3
Effect of feedback on the Johari window

Many managers cut off and eventually stifle feedback from their people by arguing with them about their feelings and perceptions. The late Haim Ginott, author of the well-known book *Between Parent and Child*,[8] and his wife, Alice Ginott,[9] who has been carrying on some of his work, believe that people should be allowed to have any feelings they want. Feelings are to be heard and accepted; it's only behavior that should be limited. In other words, people are experts on their own feelings and perceptions. Managers should never say to their people, "You don't really feel that way" or "That's not true" because, obviously, these people do know how they feel about things.

To illustrate this point, let's look at an example. A mother is walking through a department store with her young son when the child notices a beautiful bicycle. He says, "Boy, would I like to have a bike like that!" His mother, rather than hearing his feelings, replies harshly, "You're such an ungrateful child. We just got you a new bike for Christmas and already you want a new one. I've had enough of your spoiled attitude. See if you get anything new again for a long time." Now, what exactly has this child learned from this experience? He has learned that he should never tell his mother how he feels about anything; he will only get punished. If this scene is repeated often enough, the mother may soon lose any chance of ever receiving feedback from her son again—which is certainly a high price to pay!

What should the mother do in this situation? Alice Ginott suggests that she should recognize her son's wish and rephrase it in simple words; for example, "I bet you wish you could get a new bike any time you wanted." The child undoubtedly would agree. Then the mother should follow up with a statement or question such as, "Why don't you think you can get that new bike?" The boy knows and will probably say, "Because I just got a new one for Christmas." After agreeing, the mother could conclude the conversation on a supportive note: "When you've gotten good use out of your bike and it starts to get too small for you, then you probably can get a new one." With this kind of interaction, the child won't be afraid to share his feelings with his mother again.

This same situation occurs day after day in every organization. For example, a staff member tells the manager, "Those staff meetings we have on Thursday run too long and I think generally are a waste of time." The manager, rather than listening to feelings and trying to find out why the staff member feels that way, responds quickly and harshly: "What do you mean those meetings are a waste of time? I'm sick and tired of your attitude around here. I think those meetings are the most productive sessions that we've had around here for a long time. And I'm sick and tired of this kind of ridiculous comment." Will this manager get much more feedback from the staff member? Probably not. The staff member has learned that with the manager "feelings are not allowed" unless they are "company line." That is unfortunate because in many ways "feedback is the breakfast of champions." Without feedback from their people, managers will develop significant blind areas that will eventually damage their effectiveness.

Another suggestion can give managers an additional clue to how they can encourage their people to share their feelings and perceptions with them. Why treat your people differently from the way you would treat a stranger, acquaintance, or friend? For example, Henry, a guest at a party in your home, forgets his hat and you discover it just after he has headed out to his car. Would you run out the door waving the hat and yelling, "How stupid can you be to leave your hat behind? How many times have I had to run after you with something you left? If your head wasn't glued on your shoulders, you'd probably forget that, too!" Of course you wouldn't. You would probably just say, "I'm glad I caught you. You left your hat!" And that's how staff members and family members deserve to be treated as well.

Treating staff members with respect will lead to a relationship in which they feel free to share and talk. As can be seen in Figure 12-3, the more relative feedback that takes place within an organization, the more the public arena of a leader begins to extend into and displace the blind arena and thus the smaller that leader's blind area becomes.

Disclosure

The other process that affects the shape of the Johari window is *disclosure*. This is the extent to which leaders are willing to share with others in their organizational setting data about themselves.

The way we use the term *disclosure* is different from the way others in the field often use it. First, the most relevant disclosure is not what people say about themselves but rather their behavior. It is not words that mean, it is people that mean. And if you want to understand people better, you really have to look at the behavior those people engage in to gain relevant insights into their values and what this behavior represents.

Second, we think disclosure is appropriate in organizations only when such disclosure is organizationally relevant. This is a different way of viewing disclosure than is urged by some people in the sensitivity training and personal growth field, who feel all disclosure is appropriate. In fact, some contend that it is appropriate for a leader or manager in an organizational setting to be open and disclose as much as possible and that the organization should process that data. Our experience from numerous organizational development interventions suggests that two of the scarcest resources in any organizational setting are time and energy. Therefore, if people disclosed almost everything about themselves within the organizational setting and others took time to process these various agendas, there would not be much time left to accomplish other organizational goals and objectives. We feel disclosure is important and helpful in organizations as long as it contributes to the operation of the organization.

In the process of disclosure, the more organizationally relevant the information that leaders disclose about the way they think or behave, the more the public arena opens into the private arena and the smaller that arena becomes, as shown in Figure 12-4. An interesting phenomenon occurs in settings where there is simultaneous feedback and disclosure between leaders and the people with whom they work. Not only does the public arena of these leaders begin to extend itself into the blind and the private arenas, but there is also a high probability that some of what was previously unknown (not known to either the leaders or other people in the organization) will begin to surface into the public arena.

A psychiatrist working with a patient in psychotherapy hopes to create an environment in which this process of simultaneous feedback and disclosure occurs. If that happens, the doctor can begin to release and understand some of the phenomena that have been evoking

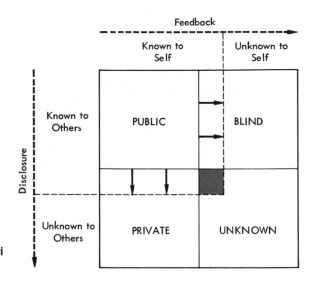

FIGURE 12-4
Effect of feedback and disclosure on the Johari window

behavior in the patient that was unknown to the patient as well as to the psychiatrist. This is also the same process that Carl Rogers[10] refers to in his work on coaching and counseling.

Self-perception versus Style

When we do an organizational diagnosis, the data from the LEAD-Self, as we explained, denote self-perception. In terms of the Johari window, the self-perception of leaders would represent what is known to them about their leadership style and would include both their public and private arenas. This self-perception of leadership style can be measured using the LEAD-Self. On the other hand, an individual's leadership style would represent what is known to others and would include on the Johari window both that person's public and blind arenas. Leadership style can be measured using the LEAD-Other. The relationship between self-perception, leadership style, and the Johari window is presented in Figure 12-5.

One of the interesting phenomena that we have discovered at the Center for Leadership Studies is that we can predict the shape of the public arena within the Johari framework. For instance, if there is a great discrepancy between self-perception and the way others perceive a manager (style), the public arena in that manager's Johari window would tend to be very small, as illustrated in Figure 12-6.

But if there is no significant difference between self-perception

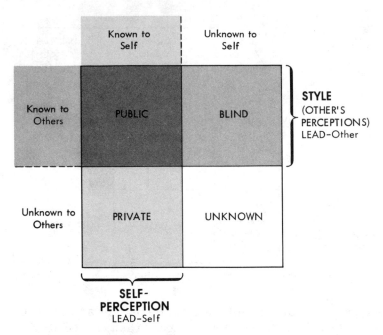

FIGURE 12-5   Self-perception and other perception (style)

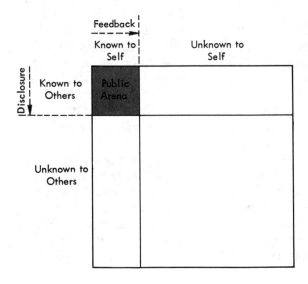

FIGURE 12-6
Public arena when there
is a large discrepancy
in perceptions

and the perception of others within a leader's organizational setting, the public arena in that person's leadership Johari window would be large, as illustrated in Figure 12-7. LEAD data can actually measure the shape of the arenas in a person's leadership Johari window in each of the organizational settings in which that person operates.

For example, a manager responsible for three departments may find that in Department A, where there is good feedback and disclosure, the public window is very open. In Department B, where there is very little contact, and thus infrequent feedback and disclosure, the public window might be small. And finally, in Department C, where there is average interaction, the public arena might be moderate in size.

Another interesting result of the work at the Center for Leadership Studies is a realization that there tends to be a high correlation between the openness of a leader's public arena and that person's effectiveness within that specific organizational setting. Since people often have different configurations for their leadership Johari window depending on the organizational setting in which they are operating, these people could vary in their effectiveness in these various settings. This is why some managers who have a very open public arena on the job and are very effective there are not as effective at home. It is often the case of managers coming home, picking up the paper, and having a drink. They are tired and don't want to be bothered by children or any problems of the home. Therefore, in their home environment there tends to exist far less feedback and disclosure. We could predict that these managers would not be as effective in their

FIGURE 12-7
Public arena when there is a small discrepancy in perceptions

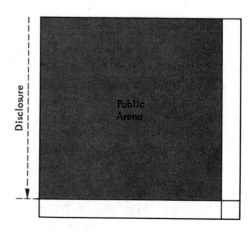

Disclosure

Public Arena

interactions at home as at work. And yet, they have trouble understanding why they are not having an effective impact on the development of their children because they see themselves as effective leaders in terms of the feedback they get on the job. On the other hand, there are individuals who are quite effective in the home and wonder why they are not effective on the job. We have to recognize that each organizational setting in which we are involved is unique, and if we want to have an impact on that setting, we have to be willing to engage in relevant feedback and disclosure.

Another thing managers must recognize is that within a given organizational setting they need to be effective on both individual and group levels, and both levels involve separate Johari windows. Thus, we have found it helpful in a family, for example, for the parents to get together with each of their children individually, as well as with all the children as a family. One might begin with something like taking each child out to dinner once a month, giving the child a chance to choose where and what to eat. The important thing is to create a situation in which the focus is on the child and the child's problems. You would be surprised how willing the child will be to open up and engage in feedback and disclosure when alone with the parent(s) than when brothers and sisters are there to create many competing responses in that environment. This process over time will help to develop an open public arena between children individually with their parents, as well as developing feedback and disclosure within the family as a total group. We need to build into our domestic environment, as well as our work setting, opportunities to work with groups as a whole, at the same time developing openness with individuals within that system.

Is It Too Late?

In reading about communication problems, managers might be feeling discouraged or even guilty. Maybe they have a problem employee or a child or two and are thinking they really have done a poor job as a manager or parent. Yet, as Wayne Dyer so aptly argues in his book *Your Erroneous Zones,*[11] guilt is a useless feeling.

> It is by far the greatest waste of emotional energy. Why? Because, by definition, you are feeling immobilized in the present over something that has already taken place, and no amount of guilt can ever change history.[12]

Managers can never redo what they should have done at an earlier time. Maybe you have made some mistakes. But that was yesterday; what are you going to do today? Today is the beginning of the rest of your life as a leader, manager, or parent. It is never too late to turn a situation around, as long as there is enough time. We mention time because it is a key factor. Why? Let us try to explain from a child-rearing point of view.

The earlier in a child's life a parent attempts to have an impact, the greater will be that parent's potential influence on the child's future behavior. During the early years, an intervention by a parent represents a substantial portion of the child's sum of experience in that area of the child's life; the same intervention later can never carry the same weight. In addition, the longer the behavior is reinforced, the more patterned it becomes, and the more difficult it is to change. That's why as a child gets older, it takes more time and more new experiences to bring about a change in behavior. Think of it this way: one drop of red food coloring in a half-pint bottle of clear liquid may be enough to change drastically the appearance of the total contents. But the same drop in a gallon jug may make little, if any, noticeable difference.

If our children are now teenagers—young adults—it is still possible, though difficult, to bring about some change in their behavior. Now it becomes a matter of economics: how much time are we willing to invest in implementing such a change.

Let's take an extreme case. Suppose a teenage son is discovered by his parents to be taking drugs and in trouble with the law. What can his parents do now? One choice is to feel guilty and try to make up for past mistakes by putting all kinds of time in with the son now. But the son might resent all this attention from his parents after having been left on his own for so long. If the son doesn't resent the sudden attention from his parents, then it becomes an economic question: our children have unlimited needs, but we have limited time. Where can we put in the most effective time with the biggest payoff?

If the parents have plenty of time and decide to attempt to change their son's behavior (even though it's an old pattern), the concepts presented in this book should provide some helpful hints as to where and how to begin. Probably they will have to do some "telling" (S1) and "selling" (S2), both of which are time-consuming styles. But with some concentrated effort, the parents can probably have an impact on this boy's behavior.

Before parents throw themselves into a change effort with one of their kids, it's a wise idea to consider what impact this attention will have on the other children in the family. By devoting all their time and energy to one problem, the parents may unwittingly create other problems. If all the parents' time is spent on this teenage son, the other children still at home may get the impression that the only way to get time with mom and dad is by getting into trouble (in effect, the parents have put all their good behavior on "extinction"). And soon one problem child has mushroomed into other problem children. Therefore, it's important always to look at the big picture and allot time accordingly.

The lesson to be learned in this example as a manager is to "get your shots in early" with your people. As we stated in chapter 11, loosening up is much easier than tightening up. Rescue and salvage work is tough and time consuming and often comes too late to do much good.

LEAD PROFILES

As was indicated earlier, LEAD data are gathered in organizations to give managers feedback on how they perceive their own leadership style as compared with how others see their style. Once a manager has learned that employees perceive that one style or another is used most of the time with them, what does it all mean?

Sample

In this section we will examine and interpret some of the common profiles that we have found from analysis of LEAD-Self and LEAD-Other data accumulated at the Center for Leadership Studies.[13] The information was generated from a LEAD sample of over twenty thousand leadership events from fourteen different cultures. A "leadership event" occurs when we have data not only in terms of self-perception (LEAD-Self), but also the perception of others (LEAD-Other) in that leadership environment. Of these respondents, we have interviewed some two thousand middle managers from industry and education; of that number, we have conducted more than five hundred in-depth interviews. The interviews have not only included the leaders in terms of self-perception, but also a sample of the leaders' followers and their perceptions of the leaders' style.

What Is a Two-Style Profile?

In our in-depth interviews, the emphasis has been on what we call "two-style profiles." A two-style profile includes either (1) a basic style that encompasses two of the four possible configuration styles or (2) a basic style and a supporting style.

It is suggested that as feedback is given on the specific two-style profiles, you keep in mind what you know about your own leadership style. If you think you have a one-style profile (you tend to use only one primary leadership style with little flexibility), then you need to remember that your profile represents only a portion of the two-style profile. If you think you have a three- or four-style profile (you have more than one supporting style in addition to your primary style), you may have to integrate the feedback that will be given to you into several of the two-style profiles. It must be pointed out that unless you have gathered specific data on how your leadership style is perceived by others, your perception of your own leadership style is only that— your perception.

Wide Flexibility

We have found that in working with people who have a wide range of styles, even though their effectiveness score may be low, a shorter period of time is needed to increase their effectiveness than is needed with people who have a smaller range of behavior. If people are engaging in a wide range of behavior, all you have to do to make a significant change in their effectiveness is to change their knowledge and attitude structure—in other words, teach them diagnostic skills. On the other hand, for people who have had no experience in using a variety of styles, much more time is necessary for them to become comfortable in using different styles.

Reference to Situational Leadership

Since we will be referring to Situational Leadership throughout the discussion of the two-style profiles, the basic framework is reproduced for your use in Figure 12-8.

Style Profile 1–3

People who are perceived as using predominately styles 1 and 3 (see Figure 12-9) fall into what is called the Theory X–Theory Y profile. What we have found is that people who have a style profile 1–3, with little flexibility to styles 2 and 4, generally view their followers with either Theory X or Theory Y assumptions about human nature. They see some people as lazy, unreliable, and irresponsible. The only way to get anything out of these people is to coerce, reward and punish, and closely supervise them. Other people they see very positively as creative and self-motivated; the only thing they have to do with these people is to provide socioemotional support. In fact, in interviewing managers with this profile, it has been found that they talk about individuals they supervise as "good people" or "bad people," "with me" or "against me." Their followers, when interviewed, tend to agree. They see their managers as labeling people, and thus being very

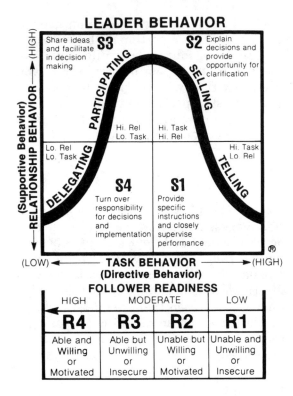

LEADER BEHAVIOR

(Supportive Behavior)
RELATIONSHIP BEHAVIOR
(HIGH)

S3 Share ideas and facilitate in decision making

PARTICIPATING

S2 Explain decisions and provide opportunity for clarification

SELLING

Hi. Rel
Lo. Task

Hi. Task
Hi. Rel

Lo. Rel
Lo. Task

Hi. Task
Lo. Rel

DELEGATING

TELLING

S4 Turn over responsibility for decisions and implementation

S1 Provide specific instructions and closely supervise performance

(LOW) ◄——— **TASK BEHAVIOR** ———► (HIGH)
(Directive Behavior)

FOLLOWER READINESS

HIGH	MODERATE		LOW
R4	**R3**	**R2**	**R1**
Able and Willing or Motivated	Able but Unwilling or Insecure	Unable but Willing or Motivated	Unable and Unwilling or Insecure

FIGURE 12-8
Situational Leadership model

supportive (S3) with people they see in their "camp," but closely supervising, controlling (S1), and even punishing people whom they perceive as against them.

One of the interesting things that occurs with this style profile is that it often becomes a self-fulfilling prophecy. A manager with this style takes people who are at moderate readiness levels (R2) and either moves them up to moderate to high (R3) or moves them down to low levels of readiness (R1). Thus, this manager tends to be effective working with low levels of readiness or moderate to high levels of readiness.

A problem with this style is that the leaders who adopt it often are doing little to develop the potential of the people they don't like; they keep them locked into low levels of readiness by always relying on S1 (high task–low relationship behavior) with them. They lack the interim behaviors between style 1 and style 3 to operate effectively in the developmental cycle. At the same time, their style 3 (high relationship–low task behavior) with people of moderate levels of readiness might keep these people psychologically dependent on them too long. These kinds of leaders do not seem to allow people to develop fully through delegation.

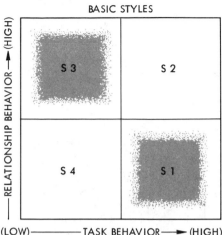

BASIC STYLES

RELATIONSHIP BEHAVIOR ——▲—(HIGH)

S 3   S 2

S 4   S 1

(LOW)——————TASK BEHAVIOR——►(HIGH)

FIGURE 12-9
Style Profile 1–3

It is also interesting that people who work for leaders with this style profile claim that if there is any change in their leader's style with them, it usually occurs in a movement from style 3 to style 1. In other words, it is very difficult if you are being treated in a style 1 fashion by these leaders ever to receive style 3 types of behavior from them. But it is not too difficult to move from receiving style 3 behaviors to receiving style 1 behaviors. All you have to do is make some mistakes and these leaders tend to respond with highly structured behavior.

Style Profile 1–4

People who are perceived as using mainly styles S1 and S4 (see Figure 12-10) have some similarity to the Theory X–Theory Y profile of style 1–3 leaders. But rather than assessing people on whether they are good or bad in terms of personal attachment to them, the sorting mechanism for this kind of leader often becomes competency. When interviewed, these managers suggest that if you are competent you will be left alone; but if you are incompetent, they will "ride you" and closely supervise your activities. Their style is either "telling" or "delegating." A leader with this style is effective at crisis interventions. This is the kind of style we might look for to make an intervention into an organization with severe problems where there are short-time restrictions to solve them. This kind of leader is quite capable of making disciplinary interventions, going in and turning around a situation, and hopefully moving people back to a higher level of readiness. But again, much like the style 1–3 profile, this type of leader lacks the developmental skills to take people from low levels of readiness and develop them into higher levels of readiness.

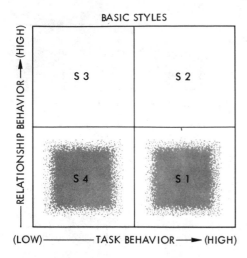

BASIC STYLES

RELATIONSHIP BEHAVIOR ⟶ (HIGH)

S 3　　　　S 2

S 4　　　　S 1

(LOW) ——————— TASK BEHAVIOR ⟶ (HIGH)

FIGURE 12-10
Style profile 1–4

An interesting thing occurs when leaders with this type of profile are introduced into a group with a normal distribution of readiness. What tends to happen is that the leader treats people in such a way that they either progress in their readiness or they regress, so that now, rather than a normal distribution of readiness levels, followers are clustered at the high end (R4) or low end (R1) of the readiness continuum. Once again, this becomes a self-fulfilling prophecy.

Style Profile 2–3

People who are perceived as using predominantly styles S2 and S3 (see Figure 12-11) tend to do well working with people of average levels of readiness. However, they find it difficult to handle discipline problems and work groups at low levels of readiness (R1), and also find it difficult to "delegate" with competent people to maximize their development. This style tends to be the most frequently identified style in the United States and other countries that have a high level of education and extensive industrial experience. Managers in some of the emerging cultures tend to have a more structured style profile (S1 and S2).

This style leader (S2 and S3) tends to be effective more often than not, because most people in work settings usually fall in readiness levels R2 and R3. We find far fewer people, on the whole, at readiness levels R1 and R4.

If styles S2 and S3 are considered "safe styles," then we would have to say that styles S1 and S4 are the "risky styles." We say "risky" because if they are used inappropriately, they can result in a great

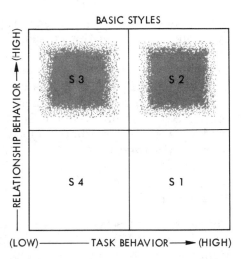

BASIC STYLES

RELATIONSHIP BEHAVIOR ——▶(HIGH)

S 3   S 2

S 4   S 1

FIGURE 12-11
Style profile 2–3   (LOW)————TASK BEHAVIOR——▶(HIGH)

deal of crisis. For instance, if someone is supervising a group at a very low level of readiness and uses style S4, leaving people on their own, there is a high probability that the environment is going to deteriorate and serious problems will result. On the other hand, if you have an extremely high level of readiness among your followers and you are attempting to use style S1 interventions, you are likely to generate much resentment, anxiety, and resistance, which may lead to what Machiavelli refers to as attempts to undermine, overthrow, or get out from under the leader; that is, hatred rather than fear. Although styles S1 and S4 are risky styles, if you are going to maximize your role as leader, you have to be willing to take the risk and use these styles when the situation is appropriate. One caution is that if you feel style 1 or style 4 is needed in a situation, you should be more careful in your diagnostic judgments before you make these kinds of interventions.

You need to learn to make style S1 interventions for the following reasons. First, they are effective interventions when beginning the process of developing the task-relevant readiness of people with low readiness levels. Second, this style is often necessary in making disciplinary interventions. On the other hand, S4 is often necessary if you are going to allow people to reach self-actualization by satisfying their need for achievement and desire to maximize their potential.

Learning to use style S4 is also important to leaders themselves. In any of the organizations for which we work, there are at least two prerequisites for promotion. The first is that managers have to do an outstanding job in their present position. In other words, their output in terms of that organization has to be high. The second prerequisite is that they have to have a ready replacement—someone who is ready and able to take over their responsibilities. To have this kind of ready replacement, managers must have at least one of several key followers with whom they are able to use style S4 and delegate significant responsibilities. If this is not so, the probability of these managers having a ready replacement is very low. In summary, the style profile S2–S3 is an excellent style for working with individuals at moderate levels of readiness, but if leaders with this profile are going to maximize their potential as leaders, they need to learn to use styles S1 and S4 when necessary.

Style Profile 1–2

People who are perceived as using predominantly styles S1 and S2 (see Figure 12-12) tend to be able to raise and lower their socioemotional support or relationship behavior, but they often feel uncomfortable unless they are "calling the shots"; that is, when they are providing the structure and direction. In our sample, we found that this style profile tends to be characteristic of engineers who have become supervisors of other engineers, but who tend to be reluctant to give up their engineering; salespersons who have become sales managers yet still love to sell; and teachers who have become administrators, but still want to be directing the activities of children. These leaders often project in interviews that "no one can do things as well as I can," and this often becomes a self-fulfilling prophecy.

The style profile S1–S2 tends to be effective with low to moderate levels of readiness. It is often an extremely effective style for people

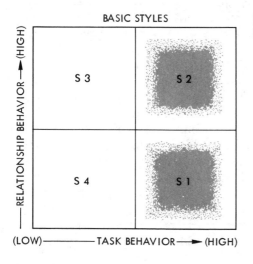

BASIC STYLES

RELATIONSHIP BEHAVIOR ——►(HIGH)

S 3

S 2

S 4

S 1

(LOW)———— TASK BEHAVIOR ——► (HIGH)

FIGURE 12-12
Style profile 1–2

engaged in manufacturing and production where managers have real pressures to produce, as well as with leaders in crisis situations where time is an extremely scarce resource. But when the crisis or time pressure is over, leaders with this style often are not able to develop people to their fullest potential. And this remains true until they learn to use styles S3 and S4 appropriately.

Style Profile 2–4

People who are perceived as using mainly styles S2 and S4 (see Figure 12-13) usually have a primary style of S2 and a secondary style of S4. This style seems to be characteristic of managers who do not feel secure unless they are providing much of the direction, as well as developing a personal relationship with people in an environment characterized by two-way communication and socioemotional support (high relationship behavior). Only occasionally do these people find a person to whom they feel comfortable delegating. And when they do delegate, their choice may not be able to handle the project. Thus, such a person may not be able to complete the task or may come to the manager for help because the person is used to the leader's providing direction and socioemotional support. The reason that style profile S2–S4 leaders tend not to be successful in delegating is that they generally move from style S2 to style S4 without moving through style S3. Let's look at an example.

Suppose Mac, a supervisor, usually directs and closely supervises (high task behavior) your activities, but you also have a good rapport with this supervisor and open communication and you receive socio-

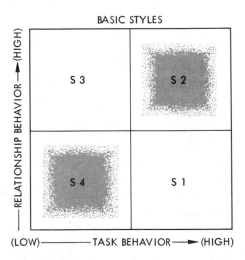

FIGURE 12-13
Style profile 2–4

BASIC STYLES

RELATIONSHIP BEHAVIOR ——→ (HIGH)

S 3

S 2

S 4

S 1

(LOW) ———— TASK BEHAVIOR ——► (HIGH)

emotional support from these interactions (high relationship behavior). One day Mac puts a couple of projects on your desk and tells you that they must be completed in a couple of weeks. You don't see Mac during that time. You would probably respond to that behavior from Mac as if it were a punishment rather than a reward. You might respond by saying, "What's Mac giving me all this work for?" and "Mac must not care about me much anymore because I never see him now!" So rather than suddenly shifting from style S2 to S4, managers with this style—if they are going to be effective in delegating—have to learn to move from "selling" (S2) through "participating" (S3) and then to "delegating" (S4).

In the previous example, if this strategy were followed by your supervisor, he should provide you with some socioemotional support, telling you that you have been doing a good job, that he has confidence in you, and that he feels that you will be able to take on some additional responsibility. Then he might give you a choice of several projects so that you could then participate in choosing which of the projects you would be interested in taking over. So your supervisor would be moving from style S2 into style S3 (participation and supportive behavior). Then he might say, "Look, I think you can run with this project on your own. If you get into some problems, give me a call." Now, because your supervisor has moved from style S2 through the supportive relationship behaviors (S3) to delegation (S4), you would tend to see this behavior as a reward rather than a punishment.

Style Profile 3–4

People who are perceived as using predominantly styles 3 and 4 (see Figure 12-14) tend to be able to raise and lower their socioemotional support or relationship, but they often feel uncomfortable if they have to initiate structure or provide direction for people. Thus, while this style profile is appropriate for working with moderate to high levels of readiness, it tends to create problems with people who are decreasing in readiness and need a regressive intervention or with inexperienced people who require more direction during the early phases of the developmental cycle.

We have found style profile S3–S4 to be characteristic of certain types of individuals or groups. It tends to be representative of very effective top managers in organizational settings where they have an experienced, competent staff that needs little direction from the top. It has also been found to be characteristic of managers who have been very deeply involved in sensitivity training, personal growth groups, or laboratory training. These managers sometimes become more interested in how people feel and the process of interpersonal relationships than what people do in terms of organizational goals. We also

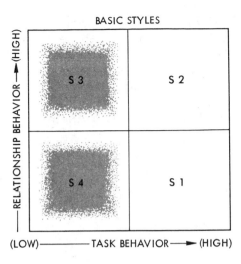

BASIC STYLES

RELATIONSHIP BEHAVIOR ──▶(HIGH)

S 3   S 2

S 4   S 1

FIGURE 12-14
Style profile 3-4   (LOW)──────── TASK BEHAVIOR ──▶ (HIGH)

have found this profile among people who have studied or are practicing in the area of humanistic education. For example, teachers with this kind of profile tend to be comfortable in "student-centered" environments where the norm is not for teachers to direct, control, and closely supervise the learning activities of children. However, because many youngsters are not yet ready to assume direction of their own learning, this style universally applied can lead to problems. In fact, some parents complain today that although youngsters seem to be much more willing to level, share, and be open about their feelings with adults—teachers in school and parents in the home—they often seem to lack the solid technical skills of reading, writing, and arithmetic, which tend to require more directive teacher behavior for development in the initial stage with an emphasis on the technical as well as the human skills.

Another group we have found, in several dozen cases, to have style profile 3 4 is women who have recently been promoted into significant middle-management positions. In interviewing these women, it has been noted that prior to their promotion, top management had not given them opportunities to engage in much "telling" (S1) or "selling" (S2) leader behavior; that is, they had little practice in initiating structure within the organizational setting. As a result, the only way they had an impact in the past was by raising or lowering socioemotional support. In terms of training experience, we found that with very little training these women respond quickly to trying on some of the other styles. It is just a matter of exposing them to concepts such as Situational Leadership to get them to feel comfortable trying these new behaviors. The tragedy is that women and other minorities restricted from management positions often have not received this training prior to promotion. And yet, they may find that they are dealing with people who need direction and supervision. When they initially use a high relationship (S3) style, it is much more difficult to use other styles later, even though they now understand that they are appropriate.

Implications for Growth and Development

If we look at an organizational hierarchy from very low levels of supervision to what we might call top management, we find that effective managers at each level tend to have a somewhat different *primary* style profile. Before looking at these general tendencies, we must caution that while managers at a given level may have a primary style profile, *effective* managers at *all levels* use all of the styles, as appropriate. We have discussed this point repeatedly, but it deserves special emphasis.

We have found that effective managers at the lower levels (see Figure 12-15) tend to have style profile S1–S2. The reason is that at these lower levels of management (in industry, the general foremen and first- and second-line supervisors), there is an emphasis on productivity—getting the work out. At the other end of the management hierarchy, however, effective top managers tend to engage in more "participating" and "delegating." The reason seems to be that as you move up in an organizational hierarchy, the greater the probability that the subordinates who report directly to you will have a high level of task-relevant readiness. So you can see that as you progress through an organization, you learn to engage in styles 3 and 4, as well as those styles that might be effective at lower ends of the hierarchy

FIGURE 12-15 Style profiles for different level of management

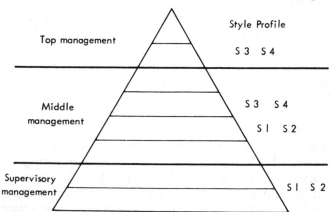

(styles S1 and S2). Thus, we have found in working with manufacturing organizations that while it may be appropriate for first-line supervisors to have a basic style of S1 and a supporting style of S2, when those people get promoted, it would be more appropriate if they had a basic style of S2 with supporting styles in S1 and S3. At this new supervisory level, they are no longer managers of hourly employees, but have now become managers of managers.

Another interesting observation in terms of the management hierarchy is that it is the middle managers who really have to wear "both hats"–they need the most flexibility. They have to be able to provide the structured style S1 and style S2 interventions when appropriate, but they also must be able to use "participating" and "delegating" styles when necessary. It is interesting to think of this phenomenon in terms of the Peter Principle.

As you will recall, the Peter Principle states: "In a hierarchy every employee tends to rise to his level of incompetence."[14] What we find in our work at the Center for Leadership Studies is that this is *not* a principle. In other words, it does not hold as a universal truth. In fact, as we suggested in chapter 7, one might think of the Anti–Peter Principle vaccine as being the appropriate training and development or experience prior to moving up to the next level of the hierarchy. Better than training and development *after* being appointed to the new position is having worked for a supervisor who is willing to delegate responsibilities and provide on-the-job experience for future higher level positions. Another interesting observation is that although the Peter Principle is not really a principle, it occurs often enough to merit some attention. There certainly is a tendency for people to reach their level of incompetency. So often when we interview people who are in a position they are having trouble handling, it turns out that they have the technical skills and conceptual skills required. In most cases, their incompetence is a result of not having the human skills. Many times they are not able to adapt their leadership style to the new environment.

Although this lack of flexibility does occur, we have found in working with managers in a variety of settings and cultures that given some training in Situational Leadership, they seem willing and able, almost without exception, to expand their adaptability. They are able to take on new leadership styles effectively. The most important criterion here is motivation–people have to want to do this. But if they want to, we feel strongly that most people have the capacity to increase their style range and adaptability provided they think through the appropriate leadership style needed and then seriously try to use a new style if it is appropriate for a particular situation. This assumption is an important difference between our approach and the thinking of some other people in the field, such as Fiedler.[15] Fiedler contends that if a leader's style is not appropriate to a given situation, what really needs to be done is either change the leader or change the job demands to fit the style of the leader. We feel that approach implies Theory X assumptions about human nature; and yet our work suggests strongly that the potential of people to operate under Theory Y assumptions is there to be tapped. Although this lack of flexibility does occur, as we indicated earlier, we found that managers in a variety of settings and cultures, once exposed to training in Situational Leadership, seem willing and able, almost without exception, to expand their adaptability.

One concluding thought before leaving this section. One of the major results of the current organizational resizing is compression of middle management. The result of this compression or reduction is expanding roles of both top management and supervisory management. We find that the *primary* roles of both top management and supervisory management are expanding toward styles 2 and 3. Once again, however, we must remind ourselves that *effective* managers at *all levels* use all of the styles, as appropriate.

Team Building

If managers have a narrow range of behavior, one way that they can expand their flexibility (without changing their own behavior) is by carefully choosing the people they gather around them. If leaders are careful to bring into the organization key followers who complement their leadership style rather than replicate it, the organization may develop a wider range of potential styles that can be brought to bear on the contingencies they face. As we cautioned in chapter 7, to avoid personality conflict and to increase the likelihood of building on the strength of others, it is important to select subordinates who understand each others' roles and have the same goals and objectives, even though their styles might be somewhat different.

Who Determines the Leadership Style of a Manager?

In the beginning of the chapter we raised the following question: If leaders continually change their leadership styles, how will that affect their followers' perception of their intentions?

From our experience, the sooner managers begin to share Situational Leadership with their key followers and clarify what is expected of them, this question no longer becomes an issue. When that occurs, managers no longer are the sole determiners of the style they use with their people. Their key staff now play a vital role. If their managers are not practicing situational leaders, they start to realize that it is *their behavior* (not their managers) that determines the leadership style to be used with them. Thus, if everyone in a management team knows Situational Leadership, the key staff realize how they can keep their manager off their backs. All they have to do is perform in responsible ways—ways that everyone has agreed are appropriate—and their manager will be supportive (S3) or leave them alone (S4). But if they do not produce and perform in responsible ways, they know their manager will be on them. They know why they are getting that kind of treatment from their manager and they know how they can get their manager to treat them in a more supportive way again—by getting back on track. It must be remembered though that this is effective only if managers are consistent (that is, that they treat their people the same way in similar circumstances) even when it is inconvenient and/or unpopular with their people.

Thus, Situational Leadership is a vehicle to help managers and their staff understand and share expectations in their organizational setting. If people know what is expected of them, they can gradually learn to supervise their own behavior and become responsible, self-motivated individuals.

CONTRACTING FOR LEADERSHIP STYLE

The process that was developed at the Center for Leadership Studies for sharing Situational Leadership with key staff and helping to open everyone's public window (in Johari window terms) is called "Contracting for Leadership Style." This process is a helpful addition to a management by objectives (MBO) program.

Of all the management concepts and techniques developed over the past several decades, few have received such widespread attention as management by objectives. Theoretically, MBO, discussed in chapter 6, offers tremendous potential as a participatory management approach, but problems have developed in implementation. Consequently, although many attempts have been made to utilize MBO, ineffective implementations have occurred. As a result, success stories do not occur as often as anticipated by theorists who have written about MBO or practitioners who have applied it. One reason is that often the role of the leader in helping followers accomplish objectives is not clearly defined in MBO.

What often happens in the MBO process is that once a leader and follower have negotiated and agreed upon goals and objectives for the follower, the leader may or may not engage in the appropriate leader behavior that will facilitate goal accomplishment for the follower. For example, if the leader leaves the follower completely alone, the leader will be unaware until the next interim performance evaluation period that this low relationship–low task leadership style is appropriate for accomplishing objectives in areas where the follower has had significant experience, but inappropriate when the follower lacks sufficient technical skill and know-how in a particular area. Conversely, if, after negotiating goals and objectives, a leader continually hovers over and directs the activities of the followers, this high task–low relationship style might alienate followers working in areas where they are competent and capable of working alone. Problems may occur when a leader uses too much of any one style.

Adding the Contracting Process

In terms of Situational Leadership, once a leader and follower have agreed upon and contracted certain goals and objectives for the follower, the next logical step would be negotiation and agreement about the appropriate leadership style that the leader should use in helping the follower accomplish each one of the objectives. For example, an individual and the leader may agree on five objectives for the year. After this agreement, the next step would be the negotiation of leadership style. In areas where the person is experienced and has been successful in accomplishing similar objectives over a period of time, the negotiated leadership contract might be for the leader to give the follower considerable freedom. In this case, rather than directing and closely supervising behavior, the role of the leader would be to make sure that the resources necessary for goal accomplishment are available and to coordinate the results of this project with other projects being supervised. With another goal, the follower might be working on a new project with little prior experience, while the leader does have some expertise in this area. In this case, the follower and leader might negotiate significant structure, direction, and supervision from the leader until the follower is familiar with the task. To accomplish all the goals, a variety of leadership styles may be appropriate at any given time, depending on the follower's readiness in relation to the specific task(s) involved.

Two things should be emphasized in discussing the negotiation of leadership style. First, it should be an open contract. Once style has been negotiated for accomplishing a particular goal, it can be opened for renegotiation by either party. For example, an individual may find on a particular task that working without supervision is not realistic. At this point, the follower may contact the leader and set up a meeting to negotiate for more direction. The leader, at the time, may gather some data that suggest the style being used with an individual on a particular task is not producing results. The leader in this case can ask for a renegotiation of style.

Second, when a negotiation over leadership style occurs, it implies a shared responsibility if goals are not met. For example, if a follower has not accomplished the agreed-upon goals and the leader has not provided the contracted leadership style or support, the data then become part of the evaluation of both people. This means that if a leader has contracted for close supervision, help cannot be withheld from a follower (even though the leader may be busy on another project) without the leader sharing some of the responsibility for lack of accomplishment of that goal.

MAKING THE PROCESS WORK

Initially, as people were exposed to Situational Leadership concepts and began to apply them in daily leader and follower interactions, they sought some general ways to judge similarities and differences between leadership styles and follower expectations.

An Example—Contracting for Leadership Styles in a School

Some interesting results of the Contracting for Leadership Style process occurred in an elementary school in eastern Massachusetts. In many school systems, the principal of a school is required by school policy to visit each classroom a certain number of times each year. This visitation policy is dysfunctional for principals who recognize that their teachers vary in their experience and competence and, therefore, have varying needs for supervision from the principal. If a principal decides to schedule visitations according to a perception of the competence of the teachers, problems often occur with teachers at either end of the extreme. As we discussed earlier, left alone, a highly experienced teacher may be confused by the lack of contact with the principal and may even interpret it as a lack of interest. At the same time, an inexperienced teacher may interpret the frequent visits of the principal as a sign of lack of trust and confidence. In both cases, what the principal does may be interpreted as negative by the teachers.

These problems were eliminated in this elementary school when the principal shared Situational Leadership with the staff and then attempted to negotiate what the principal's leadership style should be with each of the teachers. It was found that when low relationship– low task leadership style was negotiated between the principal and teachers because both agreed that these teachers were capable of working on their own, infrequent visits from the principal were perceived by the teachers as a reward rather than a punishment.

The same thing held true at the other end of the continuum. It was found that when negotiation for leadership style took place with inexperienced teachers (who realized that the system was designed to help teachers learn to work on their own) these teachers were less reluctant to share anxieties about certain aspects of their teaching. If the negotiation led to initial close supervision and direction, the teachers were able to view this interaction as positive not punitive, because it was a temporary style and demonstrated the principal's interest in helping them to operate on their own.

Using the Readiness Style Match

Since those early days, a useful instrument has been developed at the Center for Leadership Studies. The instrument formalizes the process of implementing Contracting for Leadership Style. It's called the Readiness Style Match. As discussed in chapter 8, the Readiness Style Match measures readiness using two dimensions: (1) *ability,* or job readiness; and (2) *willingness,* or psychological readiness. The rating form also describes precisely the four basic leadership styles. The description of those styles and the two readiness scales are depicted in Figure 12-16.

As indicated in Figure 12-16, a person's ability (knowledge and skill) is thought of as a matter of degree. That is, an individual's ability does not change drastically from one moment to the next. At any given moment, an individual has a little, some, quite a bit, or a great deal of ability. Willingness (confidence and commitment), however, is different. A person's psychological readiness can, and often does, fluctuate from one moment to another. Therefore, a person is seldom, on occasion, often, or usually willing to take responsibility in a particular area.

Combining establishing objectives and reaching consensus on performance criteria in a traditional MBO program with a similar process for negotiating the appropriate leadership style that a manager should use to facilitate goal accomplishment in a specific task area can be accomplished through the following steps.

1. Establish objectives and performance. Manager and staff member independently establish objectives and performance criteria for the staff member.

2. Reach agreement on objectives and performance criteria. Manager and staff member come together to reach agreement on objectives and performance criteria.

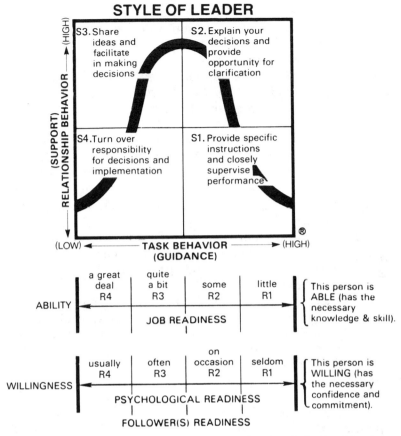

STYLE OF LEADER

S3. Share ideas and facilitate in making decisions	S2. Explain your decisions and provide opportunity for clarification
S4. Turn over responsibility for decisions and implementation	S1. Provide specific instructions and closely supervise performance

RELATIONSHIP BEHAVIOR (SUPPORT) — (HIGH)

(LOW) ◄——— TASK BEHAVIOR ———► (HIGH)
(GUIDANCE)

a great deal R4	quite a bit R3	some R2	little R1	This person is ABLE (has the necessary knowledge & skill).

ABILITY ◄——— JOB READINESS

usually R4	often R3	on occasion R2	seldom R1	This person is WILLING (has the necessary confidence and commitment).

WILLINGNESS ◄——— PSYCHOLOGICAL READINESS

FOLLOWER(S) READINESS

FIGURE 12-16   Defining readiness and the four basic leadership styles

3. Introduce Situational Leadership. Both manager and staff member are introduced to Situational Leadership, if they have not already been exposed to the concept (which can be accomplished by reading chapter 8 of this book).

4. Complete readiness style match. Manager and staff member independently complete a Readiness Style Match rating form. The staff member records the primary and secondary leadership styles that the manager has been using on each of the agreed upon goals and objectives. The manager does the same, indicating what leadership style has been used with the staff member on each of the agreed upon goals and objectives. If the staff member has never had a particular objective area before, no past leadership style can be diagnosed. After analyzing leadership style, both the staff member and manager make judgments on the ability and the willingness of the staff member to accomplish each of the goals and objectives established at the desired performance level without any supervision. In other words, the staff member participating in this process would analyze the leadership style that the manager has been using, as well as self-assessment judgments of the readiness level. At the same time, the manager would be analyzing the readiness level of the staff member as well as making leadership style self-assessment judgments.

5. Meet to share data from readiness style match. Manager and staff member meet together and share the data from their Readiness Style Match rating forms. It is recommended that they consider one objective or responsibility at a time. The purpose of sharing data is to agree upon the readiness level and appropriate leadership style that can be utilized with the staff member to maximize performance. During this process both manager and staff member should bring their calendars. Once they have determined the appropriate leadership style to make this commitment and turn it into behavior, they will require scheduled meetings.

For example, in a particular objective area, any one of the four leadership styles may have been agreed upon as appropriate. If the staff member is inexperienced and insecure about performing in a particular area, a "telling" (S1) style would be appropriate for the manager to use. If this is the case, they should schedule frequent meetings so that the manager can work closely with the staff member.

If the staff member is willing but inexperienced in a particular area, the manager should utilize a "selling" (S2) style. This would involve scheduling meetings to work with the staff member, but not as frequently as under S1 supervision.

If the staff member is able in a particular area, but is a little insecure about working completely alone, a participating (S3) leadership style would be appropriate. That may involve meeting periodically over lunch so that the staff member can show the manager what has been accomplished and the proper support and encouragement can be given.

If the staff member is able and willing to perform at the desired level in a particular objective area, no meetings are necessary unless called by the staff member. In this case, performance review can occur on an infrequent basis.

If the Contracting for Leadership Style process is utilized, the frequency of performance review will change depending on the ability and the willingness of the staff member to perform at the desired level without supervision. As stated earlier, if this process is used, the negotiation of leadership style should be an open contract and imply shared responsibility if goals are not met. In particular, if a staff member is improving in a particular area, there should be a renegotiation of leadership style to a less directive leadership style. At the same time, if a staff member's performance is not being maximized utilizing a particular leadership style, that will signal the need to move back to a more directive style. A give-and-take process should occur between leader and follower.

The Readiness Style Match Matrix, part of the Readiness Style Match, is useful in providing insight into whether or not your manager is using "overleadership"—you have high levels of readiness, but your manager is using "telling" and "selling" styles to a greater degree than necessary. "Underleadership" is where you have low levels of readiness, but your manager is using "participating" and "delegating" styles more than is appropriate. A high probability style match would be when the style(s) of your manager tends to correspond with the readiness level(s) you exhibit.

One warning should be given in using the Contracting for Leadership style process and the Readiness Style Match rating forms. When managers go through that process, their public arena in the Johari window becomes wide open. Very little about what these managers think and feel about the staff member is unknown to that staff member, and vice versa. Feedback and disclosure become an ongoing process. If managers do not want their people to know what they think and feel about them, then they should be careful about using the described process. With some people they might want to remain tight-lipped and aloof. When managers make that choice, they must remember that with those people, the blind and private arenas in their Johari window will be large. In some cases, that may very well be appropriate.

In summary, combining the establishment of goals and objectives and performance criteria with appropriate leadership style may help to make MBO more of a developmental process, which can be effective in working with all levels of readiness. Establishing such a program may be a significant change for an organization and its managers. In chapter 15 we will discuss how to implement change in an effective way.

NOTES

1. The development of LEAD (formerly known as the Leader Adaptability and Style Inventory—LASI) is based on Situational Leadership discussed earlier. The first publication on this LEAD instrument appeared as Paul Hersey and Kenneth H. Blanchard, "So You Want to Know Your Leadership Style?" *Training and Development Journal,* February 1974. Copies of the LEAD-Self and LEAD-Others can be ordered from the Center for Leadership Studies, Escondido, CA 92025.

2. This contracting process first appeared as Paul Hersey and Kenneth H. Blanchard, "What's Missing in MBO?" *Management Review,* October 1974. Much of the discussion that follows was taken from that article.

3. G. S. Odiorne, *The Human Side of Management* (San Diego, Calif.: University Associates, 1987).

4. The LEAD-Other is the same instrument as the LEAD-Self but written so a subordinate, superior, or peer could fill it out on a leader. Instruments are available from the Center for Leadership Studies, Escondido, CA 92025.

5. William J. Reddin, *The 3-D Management Style Theory,* Theory Paper #6–Style Flex (Fredericton, N.B., Canada: Social Science Systems, 1967), p. 6.

6. Joseph Luft and Harry Ingham, "The Johari Window, A Graphic Model of Interpersonal Awareness," *Proceedings of the Western Training Laboratory in Group Development* (Los Angeles: UCLA, Extension Office, 1955). A more up-to-date version of the framework is presented in Joseph Luft, *Group Process: An Introduction to Group Dynamics,* 2nd ed. (Palo Alto, Calif.: National Press Book, 1970).

7. Sigmund Freud, *The Ego and the Id* (London: Hogarth Press, 1927).

8. Haim Ginott, *Between Parent and Child: New Solution to Old Problems* (New York: Avon Books, 1965).

9. Kenneth Blanchard was a faculty resource with Alice Ginnott at the February 1977 YPO (Young Presidents' Organization) University of Honolulu, Hawaii. The discussions of what she said at a session entitled "Between Parent and Child" are taken from Blanchard's notes and do not represent her exact words.

10. Carl R. Rogers, *Client-centered Therapy* (Boston: Houghton Mifflin, 1951); see also *Freedom to Learn* (Columbus, Ohio: Merrill, 1969).

11. Wayne W. Dyer, *Your Erroneous Zones* (New York: Funk & Wagnalls, 1976).

12. This sentence is adapted from a quotation by Dorothy Canfield Fisher that Wayne Dyer referred to in *Your Erroneous Zones,* p. 195.

13. The analysis of LEAD data was first presented in Paul Hersey, *Situational Leadership: Some Aspects of Its Influence on Organizational Development,* an unpublished dissertation, University of Massachusetts, 1975.

14. Laurence J. Peter and Raymond Hull, *The Peter Principle: Why Things Always Go Wrong* (New York: Morrow, 1969). See also Laurence J. Peter, *The Peter Plan: A Proposal for Survival* (New York: Morrow, 1976); Laurence J. Peter, *Peter's Quotations: Ideas for Our Time* (New York: Morrow, 1977).

15. Fred E. Fiedler, "Engineer the Job to Fit the Manager," *Harvard Business Review,* 51 (1965), pp. 115–22. See also Fred E. Fiedler, *Leader Attitudes and Group Effectiveness* (Westport, Conn.: Greenwood, 1981); Fred E. Fiedler and Martin M. Chemers, *Improving Leadership Effectiveness: The Leader Match Concept* (New York: Wiley, 1984).

13

Communicating
with Rapport

Very early in this book we defined leadership as an attempt to influence, for whatever reason. We also noted that leadership and influence may be used interchangeably. You will also recall that we discussed the three basic competencies in influencing as (1) diagnosing—being able to understand the situation you are attempting to influence; (2) adapting—being able to adapt your behavior . . . and the other things that you have control over . . . to the contingencies of the situation; and (3) communicating—being able to put the message in a way that people can easily understand and accept. This chapter is about the third competency—communicating with rapport.[1]

HOW IMPORTANT IS
EFFECTIVE COMMUNICATION?

All of the evidence clearly shows that written and oral communication skills are critical not only in obtaining a job, but also in performing effectively on the job. For example, in a study reported in *Personnel,* a survey questionnaire was sent to the personnel managers of 175 of the largest companies in a western state.[2] One of the key questions in this study concerned the factors and skills most important in helping graduating business students obtain employment. The personnel managers' responses to this question are shown in Table 13-1. Written and oral communication skills were the two most important factors or skills in obtaining employment. But what about the relationship between these two skills and effective performance on the job?

Most Chief Operating Officers (COOs) rate employee communication skills as vital, using such phrases as "extremely important," "very important," or "tops."[3] Other COOs say that "There is a direct correlation between employee communication and profitability" and "I find that making good profits really goes hand in hand with having good communication." Perhaps the importance of good communication is best summarized by a senior executive who noted:

TABLE 13-1 Factors or Skills Considered Most Important by Personnel Managers in Helping Business School Graduates Obtain Employment

RANK/ SCORE	FACTOR/SKILL	SCORE
1	Oral communication skills	6.294
2	Written communication skills	6.176
3	Work experience	5.706
4	Energy level (enthusiasm)	5.706
5	Technical competence	5.647
6	Persistence/determination	5.529
7	Dress/grooming	5.235
8	Personality	5.118
9	Resumé	5.118
10	Appearance	5.000
11	Poise	4.882
12	Specific degree held (finance, marketing, accounting and so forth)	4.867
13	Grade point average	4.235
14	Letters of recommendation	4.059
15	Interview skills	4.059
16	Accreditation of the school/college	3.941
17	Social graces	3.824
18	Physical characteristics	3.647
19	School attended	2.941
20	Age	2.529
21	Marital status	2.000
22	Race	1.588
23	Sex	1.471
24	Religion	1.000

Source: Reprinted, by permission of the publisher, from "On the Campus: How Well Do Business Schools Prepare Graduates for the Business World?" by Gary L. Benson, *Personnel,* July–August 1983, p. 63, © 1983 American Management Association, New York. All rights reserved.

The best business plan is meaningless unless everyone is aware of it and pulling together to achieve its objectives. Good communications are the lifeblood of any enterprise, large or small. Communications are essential to keep our entire organization functioning at maximum levels and to make the most of our greatest management resource – our people.[4]

But how can we, as leaders and potential leaders, improve our communication competency? One way is to understand and use the process of communicating with rapport.

The Communication Process

When communicating with other people, the message passes through perceptual "filters," as shown in Figure 13-1, The Communications Process. And because of these filters, there is the potential for a communication breakdown at any point in the process. It is as if "I know you think you understood what I said, but I'm not sure that what you heard is what I meant."

The following descriptions relate to the three areas of Figure 13-1.

Leader

Leaders spend more time communicating than doing any other single activity; yet studies summarized in Table 13-2, Communication Skills Training, show that many need to develop their ability to communicate more effectively. This may result from the complexity of the interaction between leader and follower, as well as the nature of the training that the average person receives.

FIGURE 13-1 The communication process

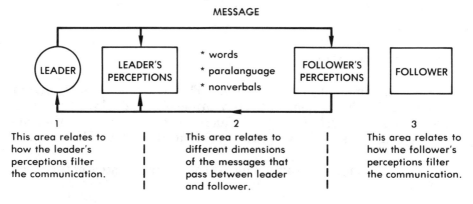

TABLE 13-2 Communication Skills Training (Average Person)

SKILLS	YEARS OF TRAINING	EXTENT USED IN ADULT LIFE
Writing	14	Little
Reading	8	Some
Speaking	1	Quite a bit
Listening	0	A great deal

Research also shows that people spend about 45 percent of their communication time listening. Despite this, the average listener understands and retains about half of what is said immediately after a presentation . . . and within 48 hours, this level drops off to 22 percent.

This data would suggest that listening is one of the most critical skills in the communication process.[5] It helps leaders to determine followers' needs, problems, moods, or levels of interest.

In order to become effective communicators, leaders need to tune in not only to words—and the way those words are expressed—but to nonverbal cues. Effective communication requires responses that demonstrate interest, understanding, and concern for the follower, as well as for the follower's needs and problems.

Message

Communication effectiveness is also dependent upon the following message forms:

Words. Words are the phrases that we select to express the thought that we intend to communicate, including:

- Vocabulary
- Language
- Phrases
- Sentence structure
- Sentence clarity

Words can insult, injure, or exalt. They can lead to costly errors, false hopes, or disillusionment. They can evoke pride, loyalty, action, or silence and are critical to the influence process. However, they are not the sole basis for how people represent and interpret reality.

Paralanguage. Paralanguage is the characteristics of the voice, such as:

- Rate of speech (speed)
- Diction
- Tone
- Rhythm
- Volume

Your voice is a highly versatile instrument. Through it you can convey enthusiasm, confidence, anxiety, urgency, serenity, and other states of mind and intent. The ability of the voice to affect how something is said is known as paralanguage. Timing when you speak, increasing or decreasing voice intensity, pausing, varying pitch, and other aspects of speech patterns can increase your ability to influence. By closely attending to the follower's paralanguage, you can pick up clues about your progress in influencing your followers.

Nonverbal behavior. Nonverbal behavior is anything that can be "seen" by the other person, such as:

- Gestures
- Facial expressions
- Eye contact
- Body language
- Positioning

How you enter an office, how you support your message through gestures and facial expressions, how you imply interest and vitality through eye contact and other nonverbal behaviors affect other people's reaction to you. In turn, the nonverbal cues of followers serve as windows to their emotions, desires, and attitudes.

Changes in a follower's body postures and gestures often signal a change in readiness. Movement toward the front of a chair may indicate interest. Relaxation of the body may reflect acceptance. Mirroring of your nods, smiles, and gestures could also indicate acceptance.

As a leader, it is also important to understand how followers view space and its relationship to you. It is important to monitor how you position yourself in relation to followers. People have levels of comfort when it comes to how close they want you to be. The general rule is, if you are making them uncomfortable, then change. This may involve moving closer or farther away.

When you first encounter a prospective follower, before you say your first word you have already made a statement about yourself. Part of this statement involves body language in terms of how confidently you carry yourself, how you walk, and your general manner.

Part of it involves the clothing you wear and your accessories. Grooming, neatness, hairstyle, and other personal features also enter into the equation.

Many of these nonverbals are under your direct control. You can make them what you want them to be. To the extent possible, your attire and general appearance should reflect a sense of personal dignity and self-worth. They should be appropriate to your followers' environment and should reflect your personal and your organization's values.[6]

Follower

In interpersonal communications, 7 percent of your meaning is from followers' interpretation or perception of your words—that is, *what* you say; 38 percent is conveyed by their perception of your voice—that is, *how* you say the words; and approximately 55 percent comes from their interpretation of your nonverbal signals.[7] As a leader, you need to monitor both the message you are sending—words, voice, and nonverbals—and follower feedback. It is also important to keep in mind that it is not the followers' perceptions that evoke behavior. It is their perceptions of the messages they receive from you that cause them to act.

Jay A. Conger, McGill University, reinforces the need for careful word selection, use of paralanguage, and nonverbal behavior to inspire others. Leadership, as we noted in chapter 1, is more than having technical and conceptual skills; leadership involves capturing the hearts and minds of followers.

Conger cites the well-known story of two stone masons to support his view of the motivational aspect of leadership. When one of the stone masons was asked what he was doing, the reply was: "I am cutting stone." When the other mason was asked, his reply was: "I am building a great cathedral." Leaders must build "great cathedrals" with their communications. Conger's guidelines for more expressive, inspirational leadership include:

1. Craft your organization's mission statement around the basic deeply-held values, beliefs, and societal purposes of the organization.
2. Use key elements of the organization's culture, e.g. stories, analogies, metaphors when you are communicating the mission in action.
3. Use rhetorical techniques such as paralanguage and nonverbal behavior.
4. Show your emotions to reflect your personal feelings and concern.[8]

Conger summarizes his views of the leader as a communicator by writing ". . . it is important that business leaders see their role as 'meaning makers.' They must pick from the rough materials of reality to construct pictures of great possibilities. . . . If you, as a leader, can make an appealing dream seem like tomorrow's reality, your [employees] will freely choose to follow you."[9]

Enhanced Model of the Communication Process

Communication does not always flow directly from the leader to the follower; feedback loops determine whether the message sent was accurately received and interpreted. The model shown in Figure 13-2 represents another model of the communication process.[10]

The *encoding* process refers to the forming of the message to be sent and is influenced by the knowledge, beliefs, biases, and feelings of the sender. An effective leader is aware of these influences and minimizes their effects in forming a message.

The *channel* is the medium for the message; for example, paper, television, radio, telephone, fax, voice mail, language, and many other forms. For effective transmission of the message, the sender needs to employ a channel the receiver uses.

In obtaining the message, the receiver *decodes* the message through assimilation and interpretation. During this process, the receiver's knowledge, beliefs, biases, and perceptions affect how well the message is understood and accepted.

Feedback is the process by which the receiver communicates to the sender an understanding of the message which was sent. Feedback can occur through words, paralanguage, and nonverbal communication. A question sent by the sender which is answered by a receiver's blank stare is an example of a nonverbal feedback loop.

FIGURE 13-2   Enhanced model of the communication process

Communication Model

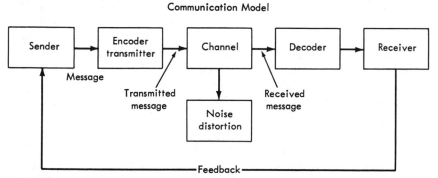

Reprinted, by permission of the publisher, from Management Systems: Conceptual Considerations, *4th Ed., 1990. ©Business Publications, Inc.*

Communication does not occur in a vacuum; *noise* can distort any part of the communication process. *Noise* is any activity, person, or thing that disrupts or impedes communication. Noise can occur if the sender and receiver do not have a common frame of reference for communication. The sender of the message should try to minimize the effects of noise.

The successful leader meets two goals in the communication process: influence and effectiveness. The leader can measure the influence of the communication through the amount of impact, action, or change in the receiver caused by the message. The fit between the message received and the readiness of the receiver to accept it will determine whether the leader exerted positive or negative influence. Effectiveness can be evaluated by how well the message is received by the sender; in other words, if the receiver is influenced in the manner intended by the leader. Effectiveness, therefore, is a measure of reception coupled with understanding.

Active Listening

Communication is not only a process of sending messages. A leader must also be skilled in receiving, or listening to, messages. A manager may spend as much as 75 percent of work time in face-to-face communication.[11] As much as half of this time may be spent listening.[12] Human physiology also influences our ability to listen accurately and actively. We speak at an average pace of 125 words per minute, but our brain is able to listen at a speed of 400 to 600 words per minute. Since the brain can listen faster than we can speak, a "listening gap" occurs for the average person. The "gap" allows the mind to wander to thoughts unrelated to those being expressed by the speaker and influences the ability of the receiver to accurately hear the message being sent.

Four types of listeners have been identified by Alessandra[13]: the nonlistener, the marginal listener, the evaluative listener, and the active listener. The nonlistener and the marginal listener hear the words being spoken, but are preoccupied, uninterested, or busy preparing their next statement. These listeners are neither concerned with the message nor the context in which it is being presented. The evaluative listener makes a sincere attempt to listen by paying attention to the speaker, but makes no effort to understand the intent of the speaker's message. This listener hears the words, but not the feelings and meaning of what is being said.

The active listener hears and understands the message. The active listener's full attention is on the content of the message and the intention of the speaker.

Active listening is a skill which can be learned through practice and use on a daily basis. Carl Rogers, who popularized the term *active listening,* has proposed five guidelines you can use to perfect your technique.

1. *Listen for the content of the message*—Make an effort to hear precisely what is being said.
2. *Listen for the feelings of the speaker*—Try to perceive the speaker's feelings about what is being said through the way the message is delivered.
3. *Respond to the feelings of the speaker*—Demonstrate to the speaker that you recognize and understand the feelings being expressed.
4. *Note the speaker's cues, both verbal and nonverbal*—Attempt to identify mixed messages and contradicting messages the speaker may be expressing.
5. *Reflect back to the speaker what you think you are hearing*—Restate to the speaker in your own words what you think the speaker said. Allow the speaker to respond to further clarify the message being sent.[14]

Becoming an effective, active listener takes much skill and practice. It must be achieved, not acquired. Through effective, active listening, the leader can develop better relationships between management and staff, can increase the establishment of clear and concise goals that are understood by all, and can decrease the chance of communication misunderstandings progressing to complex and costly problems.

Pacing, Then Leading

Leaders, as we have seen, influence from both personal power and position power. You can begin building personal power by establishing rapport. Part of establishing rapport is the ability to communicate effectively in a way that is comfortable with people you are attempting to influence. For people to feel comfortable, you have to get in step with them—pace with them.

In order to understand how to establish rapport, it is important to keep some key concepts in mind:

- *Rapport*—being in sync with other people verbally or nonverbally so that they are comfortable and have trust and confidence in you.
- *Pacing*—establishing rapport by reflecting what others do, know, or assume to be true (matching some part of their ongoing experience).
- *Leading*—getting other people to pace with *you* (attempting to influence them to consider other possibilities).

- *Behavioral adaptability*—having enough range in your own behavior to pace with the person or persons that you are interacting with.

The secret of establishing rapport with people is pacing. To pace with other people you need to adapt to match their behavior . . . to get in sync with them so that they feel comfortable with you. This means getting in alignment with their words, their voice characteristics, and their nonverbals.[15]

When you have established rapport with people, they are more apt to follow when you lead. The general pattern can be thought of in this way:

When you're interacting with other people, you're either pacing—doing something similar—or leading—having them pace with you. If your primary objective is to gain acceptance, then pacing may be enough. But if your objective is to influence them to consider other alternatives, then you must also lead.

Managers or parents can sometimes lead first and then pace to get results, since they often have access to position power.[16]

How to Test for Rapport

Sometimes, it is useful to test the level of rapport you have established. In the following example, the salesperson attempts to lead the customer to a buying decision after *pacing* with the customer through the early part of the sales process:

Salesperson attempts to lead customer: (leaning forward and showing interest) Tom, we've agreed that increasing sales is important. Our program has demonstrated a significant impact on that objective. You viewed turnover as the major problem your marketing group is presently facing. Our training program, through its emphasis on professionalism, can impact that directly.

Customer accepts lead: (leaning forward, partially mirroring the salesperson's posture) Yes, if we could cut down our turnover, this would be a positive step in cost containment.

> *Salesperson* (sensing that they now have rapport and are in agree-
> *continues leading:* ment and alignment at both the verbal and nonverbal
> levels) You might consider conducting some pilot pro-
> grams. Although our minimum order is two hundred
> units, training one hundred new hires with the five-day
> design and one hundred experienced representatives
> with a combination of the other designs would give you a
> chance to evaluate actual results.

If the customer continues to pace, then the salesperson can keep leading.

In the following example, the customer does not respond on a verbal or nonverbal basis, as the salesperson would like. The key here is to return to pacing to reestablish comfort and rapport.

> *Salesperson* (leaning forward and showing interest) Are we in agree-
> *attempts to* ment that turnover is the major problem your marketing
> *lead customer:* group is presently facing?
> *Customer* (remaining in the same posture) I'm not so sure. The real
> *resists lead:* issue might be our advertising program.
> *Salesperson* (mirroring customer's posture) I can understand how ad-
> *returns to pacing:* vertising can impact your sales . . .

In summary, the general rules of pacing, as shown in Figure 13-3 are (1) if your boss, associates, or followers go with your lead, continue to lead and (2) if your boss, associates, or followers resist your lead, go back to pacing—and look for new opportunities to lead.

FIGURE 13-3   Influencing from Personal Power: The Pace-Lead Process

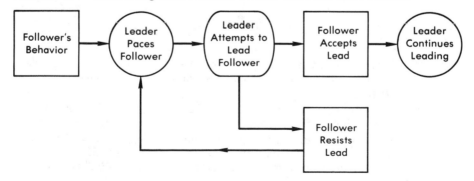

PREFERRED REPRESENTATIONAL SYSTEMS

People do not behave based on truth and reality. Their behavior is evoked from their *perception* and *interpretation* of truth and reality.

These perceptions and interpretations are the product of data taken in through the senses: sight, hearing, smell, taste, and touch. So much data come in that people cannot attend to it all. Through selective awareness, psychological maps are formed from only part of the data. Behavior is based upon these maps. And the maps affect what people perceive. Communication effectiveness is enhanced if you understand the way people map their psychological worlds.

People use their psychological maps to make decisions, to get around in life. However, the map is not the territory. It is based upon perceptions of that territory. And these perceptions differ from person to person.[17]

"Rep" Systems and Communication

People tend to perceive their worlds through the sensing systems they most prefer—the ones they're most comfortable with. It's like speaking five languages. You probably don't speak all of them with the same fluency. You prefer one over the other as your primary language. And that's the primary one you use to represent your psychological world.

These preferred sensory representational—or "Rep"—systems are important to you as a leader. You will have a higher probability of influencing people if you know how they map their psychological worlds through what they see, what they feel, or what they hear. They do not map exclusively in one of these modes, but tend to be more comfortable with the one they prefer.

- Some people are picture people, or "visuals." They are comfortable mapping their psychological worlds in *pictures*.
- Others are feelings people, or "kinesthetics." They are most comfortable mapping their psychological worlds from internal and external *feelings*.
- Some people are sounds people, or "auditories." Also referred to as "tonals," they tend to map their psychological worlds from *sounds*.
- Word people, or "digitals," are a hybrid of the other three. They have to make a transition from raw data sensing into a specific language—through *words* or numbers or computer symbols—before they can map their psychological worlds.

When attempting to communicate, you are in a better position if you know that person's primary Rep system. You may then be able to transmit your message in a way that that persr can better encode and decode . . . understand . . . and, therefore, 𝑎 ept.[18]

For example, auditories don't always "look people in the eye" because they're "tuning an ear." During a conversation or presentation, they may look elsewhere because they are listening and trying to take in data. Their intention is not to be rude or inattent⸲ e; they are trying to understand.

Children who are auditories often get in trouble with their parents because they look down when Mom or Dad talks to them. Parents make the mistake of telling the child, "You look at me when I talk to you!" because they feel the child isn't listening. The child looks up and has more difficulty understanding the data. The result often leads to further misunderstandings, anger, and frustration.

Picture people tend to like space. If you visit them in the office, they want you to sit across from them at the desk—back far enough to keep comfortably within their visual range. Feelings people prefer you to be closer. They often set up their office suites so that you can move closer and interact in a more personal way.

Digitals like written information presented to them in a logical fashion. Terms should be defined, and all spelling, punctuation, grammar, margins, and layout should be correct. Auditories, on the other hand, like short paragraphs, headings, italics, and indented areas. To get their attention, just underline or circle any parts of a message they shouldn't miss.

During group presentations, visuals tend to cluster to the rear of the room to keep all the data out in front of them, in their field of vision. The kinesthetics tend to cluster up front, close to the speaker; they want to feel they are part of the presentation. The auditories cluster to the side and, depending on their best ear (which ear they favor), sit to the left or right side of the room. For digitals, it's hard to predict where they will place themselves. Much of it depends on where they think they should be to filter data to the level of abstraction they are comfortable with. Because of these preferences, the message should be put in a variety of ways to increase the probability of communicating with all of those involved. This means when making a presentation, try to pace with the:

- Visuals by using diagrams, flow charts, and other graphics, particularly when presenting complex information.
- Digitals by defining terms and providing order and sequence to the information.

- Auditories by providing pizazz—moving around, energizing, varying voice speed and delivery.
- Kinesthetics by sitting down occasionally—talking to them from a relaxed, nonthreatening position. Whenever possible, try to get your eye level lower than the group's to help the kinesthetics feel more comfortable.[19]

Matching Predicates to Rep Systems

People will often provide you with direct cues to their preferred Rep system. One of the more frequent cues they provide are *words* or "predicates" that reflect their Rep systems. Visuals use picture words: "I can see that" or "Looks good to me." Auditories use words such as "Sounds good to me" or "I hear you." Kinesthetics use feelings words: "I sense that you're uncomfortable" or "How do you feel about that?" Digitals use expressions such as "That seems to be a reasonable approach" or "Have you verified the results?" Table 13-3 gives examples of preferred representational system predicates.

To build rapport, it is important to use predicates that are comfortable for the person you are attempting to influence.[20] If you do not match predicates, it is harder to communicate.

TABLE 13-3   Preferred Representational System Predicates

PICTURES (VISUAL)	SOUNDS (AUDITORY)	FEELINGS (KINESTHETIC)	WORDS (DIGITAL)
Clear	tune	touch	logical
focus	note	handle	data
perspective	accent	block	facts
see	ring	finger	information
outlook	shout	shock	results
spectacle	tone	stir	compute
preview	sing	strike	articulate
shortsighted	hear	impress	reasonable
illustrate	alarm	move	statistical
show	scream	hit	rational
reveal	click	grasp	conclude
hazy	static	impact	propose
glimpse	rattle	stroke	analyze
clarify	chord	tap	sequence
graphic	amplify	rub	verify
cloud	harmonize	sense	relevant
expose	key	tense	specific
bright	muffle	pressure	predict
flash	voice	irritate	objective
picture	sound	feel	word

Sales manager:	(visual) It appears problems are developing with our delivery service. Let's take a look at what's happening. Visualize a customer who has been waiting for our shipment that hasn't shown up.
Salesperson:	(auditory) I hear you, but I'm not tuning in.
Sales manager:	Imagine a concerned customer, loosening his tie, tapping his fingers, glancing up at the clock. Do you get the picture?
Salesperson:	OK, OK, so what are you trying to tell me?
Sales manager:	I'm trying to provide you with a picture of a good client examining other alternatives because they have a negative view of us.
Salesperson:	Before you sound the alarm, you ought to tune in to the other problems that are crying for attention.
Sales manager:	What other problems? I don't see what that has to do with following up on late orders.
Salesperson:	You haven't heard a word I've said. You're obviously not listening. I've got nothing more to say.

In the previous example, the predicates did not match and there was less opportunity for a positive consequence.

In the following example, predicates do match—and the probability of rapport, comfort, and positive action increases:

Sales manager:	(visual) It appears problems are developing with our delivery service. Let's take a look at what's happening. Visualize a customer who has been waiting weeks for our shipment that hasn't shown up.
Salesperson:	(visual) Yes, I see what you mean.
Sales manager:	Imagine a concerned customer, loosening his tie, tapping his fingers, glancing up at the clock. Do you get the picture?
Salesperson:	Mmmm! Clearly a potential problem. We can't afford to have our customers looking elsewhere for service. As I see it, clarifying our shipment policies with the transportation people might help. It is apparent that we need to develop a control system to ensure timely delivery. By keeping an eye on shipping dates, we can spot delays before they become a problem.
Sales manager:	Good idea. When you have something to show me, I'd like to look at it.

Pacing predicates is important. There are times when someone's preferred representational system may not be clear to you. That person may even switch among predicates during a discussion. The best thing to do in this circumstance is to pace the predicates you hear.

Matching predicates is crucial, particularly when summarizing, advocating, and asking for assistance. It is also important when you are managing the interface between your company and customers, suppliers, and other outside groups. Matching predicates with people in your own organization can also help in following through on special requirements and resolving problems.

ORGANIZATIONAL COMMUNICATION

Organizations have unique communication systems the leader can use to communicate effectively and efficiently. All members of an organization have an inherent desire to know what is occurring in their work place; information is gained through communication with others.

Organizations communicate externally with their environment and internally through specific systems. Researchers have identified five basic internal organizational communication systems: (1) *downward communication;* (2) *upward communication;* (3) *horizontal communication;* (4) *the grapevine;* and (5) *networks.*[21] These five systems can be further divided into formal and informal channels of communication. Formal communication channels are planned and established by the organization; informal channels allow information to be carried outside of the formal communication channels. The grapevine and networks are informal communication channels.

Downward communication is the most common communication system used in an organization. Communication flows from a manager to a follower. The communication channel most frequently used is writing; the following types of information are conveyed through this system.

1. *Specific task directives*—the best way to complete a task.
2. *Job rationale*—defines a job and relates it to organizational goals and objectives.
3. *Organizational policies and objectives*—as policies and objectives change, they need to be communicated to employees.
4. *Performance feedback*—rating of an employee's performance and ways to improve.
5. *Information of an ideological nature*—explanations of organizational goals.

Distortion of communication in this system can occur if a manager attempts to restrict or monitor the amount and type of information passed to employees. Monitoring is part of a manager's role and is not necessarily detrimental to the organization.

Upward communication is characterized by communication from the subordinate to the manager and occurs through verbal and written channels. Upward communication provides management with feedback about current issues and problems, with day-to-day information about progress toward meeting organizational goals, and with information about the effectiveness of downward communication. A sincere and trusting relationship between a manager and employees increases the accuracy of information passed in this system. Active listening can be used by the effective leader in this system to ensure honest and clear communication. Encouraging followers to discuss bad as well as good news will help build trust and confidence in the manager's ability.

Communication between a manager and peers or between co-workers is called *horizontal communication.* This system is less formal than the two vertical types of systems and usually involves problem solving and the coordination of work flow between peers or groups. Because horizontal communication is under limited control by managers, information can be widely spread and exchanged rapidly in times of crisis. Horizontal communication also forms a useful link in decision making for task coordination and provides emotional and social support to individual organizational members.

The *grapevine* communication system is often neglected by managers, but can be found in any organization. Grapevines grow primarily to meet organizational member's innate need for information. Although information is often incomplete, it is 70 percent to 90 percent accurate in content, and travels at an extremely rapid pace. The grapevine acts without conscious direction or thought; it will carry any information at any time, anywhere in the organization. Both managers and followers have links into the grapevine system.

The effective leader sees the positive and negative value of the grapevine system. It can let a manager gain insights into employee attitudes, provide a release valve for employee emotions, and help spread useful information. Negative aspects of the grapevine system include rumor carrying, untruths, and irresponsible communication. The grapevine grows most vigorously in organizations where secrecy, poor communication by management, and autocratic leadership behaviors are found. Adopting a proactive communication policy and integrating the grapevine into more formal communication systems can help decrease negative aspects of the grapevine system.[22]

Networks are the second informal communication system in an organization. Networks are patterned after regular interactions of organizational members and are composed of various groups of people. Networks link the other organizational communication systems. Members who take work breaks together and socialize outside of work form strong networks. Network characteristics and actions are reflective of small groups with members serving as opinion leaders, gatekeepers, and bridges to other networks. Networks can encourage strong identification with work and serve as essential socializing units.

The influential leader understands the communication systems inherent in an organization. Through the use of effective communication, including active listening, the leader can work with the systems to achieve organizational goals.

INTERNATIONAL BUSINESS COMMUNICATION

Computers, telephones, satellites, fax machines, and airplanes have eliminated the time and distance barriers once faced by business leaders in a global marketplace. Successful companies see the world, not their local area or nation, as the competitive arena. Exchanging ideas and information, leading, motivating, negotiating, and decision making are based on the ability of a manager from one culture to communicate effectively with managers and employees in other cultures.

Communication difficulties can occur when differences in culture and background lead to a misunderstanding of the message being sent. This section will highlight some of the issues involved in international communication.

Attribution, the judgments we make about the characteristics and behavior of others, plays an important role in cross-cultural communication. Three factors affect the attributions or judgments we make: perception, stereotyping, and ethnocentrism. Perception is the mental process we use to select, organize, and evaluate stimuli from the external environment to mold into a meaningful experience. We have more difficulty perceiving a person's behavior when we are unfamiliar with their language or their culture. Stereotyping is a mental form of organizing information about behavioral norms for members of a particular group. Effective stereotyping can assist you in understanding, communicating, and acting appropriately in new situations, but can lead to poor communication if the stereotypes we have are inaccurate. Ethnocentrism occurs when members of a particular group believe their cultural values, habits, beliefs, etc., are superior to those of all other groups. Ethnocentrism can lead to complete communication breakdowns.

Awareness of these three factors and active work to eliminate cultural biases facilitate effective international communication.

Nonverbal communication also varies between cultures. Gestures, the meaning of time and space, and facial expressions vary between cultural groups. For example, the American "OK" gesture with thumb and forefinger touching in a circle means money to the Japanese, zero to the French, and an obscenity to Brazilians.[23]

Cultures have unwritten rules, e.g. the distance one member stands or sits from another in a face-to-face interaction and how lines are formed and maintained.[24] The use of time also varies between cultures. Americans are clock watchers and punctual; an Indonesian business person does not place the same value on time and may be thirty minutes late for an appointment.

Differences in sentence structure, word meaning, and tense also create communication difficulties when translating messages from one language to another. Even within the same language, words can have different meanings; for example, what Americans call an *elevator* is called a *lift* in England.

Awareness of attributions we make about a person from another culture, understanding of cultural norms and behaviors, and the use of resources to bridge cultural and language gaps will aid the leader in achieving effective and influential international communication.

You need to practice and learn to become proficient in all of the communication systems. This kind of behavioral adaptability will help you to improve your communication ability, increase your effectiveness, and build ongoing relationships. Irving S. Shapiro thinks this is important as he has noted:

> One important day-to-day task for the CEO (Chief Executive Officer) is communication—digesting information and shaping ideas, yes, but even more centrally, the business of listening and explaining. Decisions and policies have no effect nor any real existence unless they are recognized and understood by those who must put them into effect. . . . It sounds banal to say that a CEO is first and foremost in the human relations and communication business—what else could the job be?—but the point is too important to leave to inference. No other item on the chief executive's duty list has more leverage on the organization's prospects.[25]

NOTES

1. This chapter has been generally adapted from Paul Hersey, *Situational Selling* (Escondido, Calif.: Center for Leadership Studies, 1985), pp. 123–38.
2. Gary L. Benson, "On the Campus: How Well Do Business Schools Prepare Graduates for the Business World?" *Personnel,* July–August 1983, pp. 63–65.

3. Louis C. Williams, Jr., "What 50 Presidents and Chief Executive Officers Think About Employee Communication," *Public Relations Quarterly,* Winter 1978, p. 7. See also "Information Mapping—The Fast Track to Better Business Communication," *Administrative Management,* 47 (May 1986), p. 6.
4. "Listening Your Way to the Top," *Graduating Engineer,* Winter 1980.
5. Anthony J. Allessandra, Phillip S. Wexler, and Jerry D. Deem, *Non-Manipulative Selling* (Reston, Virginia: Reston Publishing, 1979), pp. 81–118.
6. George Walter, "Communicating Clearly," *Profitable Telemarketing Audiocassette Program,* Tape No. 2 (Chicago: Nightengale-Conant Corporation, 1984).
7. Genie Z. LaBorde, *Influencing with Integrity,* (Palo Alto: Science and Behavior Books, 1983), pp. 27–74.
8. Jay A. Conger, "Inspiring Others: The Language of Leadership." *Academy of Management Executive,* 5 no. 1 (1991).
9. *Ibid.,* p. 44.
10. Peter P. Schoderbek, Charles G. Schoderbek, and Asterios G. Kefalas, *Management Systems: Conceptual Considerations,* 4th ed. (Homewood, Ill.: Business Publications, Inc., 1990), p. 162.
11. Tom W. Harris, "Listen Carefully," *Nation's Business,* 77 (1989) p. 78.
12. Donald W. Caudill and Regina Donaldson, "Effective Listening Tips for Managers," *Administration Management,* 47 (1986), pp. 22–24.
13. Anthony J. Alessandra, "How Do You Rate as a Listener?" *Data Management,* February 1986, pp. 20–21.
14. Carl Rogers, *Client Centered Therapy: Its Current Practice, Implications, and Theory* (Boston: Houghton Mifflin, 1951).
15. Jerry Richardson and Joel Margulis, *The Magic of Rapport* (San Francisco: Harbor Publishing, 1981), pp. 19–59.
16. John Grinder and Richard Bandler, *The Structure of Magic II* (Palto Alto: Science and Behavior Books, 1976), pp. 4–6.
17. Byron A. Lewis and R. Frank Pucelik, *Magic De-Mystified* (Lake Oswego: Metamorphous Press, 1982), pp. 11–49.
18. Hersey, *Situational Selling,* p. 135.
19. For a technical introduction to verbal and nonverbal predicate matching, see Robert Dilts, John Grinder, Richard Bandler, Leslie C. Bandler, and Judith DeLozier, *Neuro-Linguistic Programming: Volume I—The Study of the Structure of Subjective Experience* (Cupertino: Meta Publications, 1980), pp. 69–179.
20. Hersey, *Situational Selling,* p. 138.
21. J. L. DiGaetani, Ed., *The Handbook of Executive Communication,* (Homewood, Ill.: Dow-Jones Irwin, 1986). See also P. V. Lewis, *Organizational Communication: The Essence of Effective Management* (New York: John Wiley, 1987).
22. A. Zaremba, "Working with the Organizational Grapevine," *Personnel Journal,* July 1988, pp. 38–42.
23. Joseph H. Singer, "How to Work with Foreign Clients," *Public Relations Journal,* October 1987, pp. 35–37.
24. Rose Knotts, "Cross-Culture Management: Transformations and Adaptation," *Business Horizons,* January–February 1989, pp. 29–33.
25. Irving S. Shapiro, "Executive Forum: Managerial Communication: The View from Inside," *California Management Review,* Fall 1984, p. 157.

14

Group Dynamics:
Helping and Hindering Roles in Groups

One of the realities of organizational behavior is that we must work in and with problem-solving groups to accomplish our aspirations. No matter how much we value and protect our individuality, almost everything we value can only be achieved as a group member. Although the following description of this reality was presented by Krech, Crutchfield, and Ballachey more than three decades ago, it is probably even more true today.

> The paradox of modern man is that only as the individual joins with his fellows in groups and organizations can he hope to control the political, economic, and social forces which threaten his individual freedom. This is especially true now that massive social groupings—in nations and combinations of nations—are the order of the day. Only as the individual in society struggles to preserve his individuality in common cause with his fellows can he hope to remain an individual.[1]

It is, therefore, important to be able to apply behavioral science principles and concepts to make problem-solving groups more effective. In this chapter we will describe how Situational Leadership through an understanding of helping and hindering roles can accomplish this goal.

Is group effectiveness an operational problem? The answer is a resounding yes! For example, despite the rush to implement Quality Circles, studies by researchers such as Wayne, Griffin, and Bateman have shown very low success rates.[2] Other researchers, such as Hartenstein and Huddleston, have noted that the results, at best, are mixed.[3]

Why is this so? One reason is that labor and management lack shared values.[4] Another is because the structure and function of problem-solving groups was not established according to behavioral science concepts and techniques. Too often Quality Circles and other problem-solving groups are overly focused on participation as a single problem-solving mode, thus neglecting the potential richness of other possible modes. Where problem-solving groups have been effective — much as in the groups cited in the Plant Y Study by Guest, Hersey, and Blanchard[5] — it is because values were shared and the groups were structured to take advantage of all of the group problem-solving modes. Only then can groups reach their full potential payoff both in terms of goal achievement and in quality of life — the true components of productivity.[6]

Another important reason for problems in achieving group effectiveness is that skill is more critical in leading groups. By this we mean skill in the leadership role — the role of providing proactive influence and receiving feedback from group members. This is why much of the chapter is devoted to the understanding and use of helping and hindering roles in groups.

Peter Drucker summarizes this important point in his book, *The New Realities:* "Management is about human beings. Its task is to make people capable of *joint performance,* to make their strengths effective and their weaknesses irrelevant."[7]

Before we look at specific techniques, it is important that we review some fundamental group definitions and concepts.

INDIVIDUALS AND GROUPS

While much of the previous discussion has focused on one-on-one leadership, it is important to remember that the Situational Leadership model is equally applicable whether you are working with a group or organization or with an individual. Certainly there are some complicating factors when you are working with groups, but you still have to apply the three basic competencies in influencing — diagnosing, adapting, and communicating. It is also important to remember that you may have to deal with individual group members differently when you are in a one-on-one situation than when you are working with the entire group as a group. This is because individual group members may be at different levels of readiness from the entire group.

Just as individuals may be at different levels of readiness, so may groups. For example, most graduate classes are at a high level of readiness. Class members are there because they want to be, and they bring considerable academic and work experience to the class. There might be some insecurity due to some of the material being new or especially difficult, but on balance, most graduate classes are at an R3 to R4 readiness level.

A group consisting of managers attending a training seminar might be at a lower readiness level. They have made a considerable investment in time, transportation costs, and fees to attend the seminar, and are probably very willing. However, since they are attending the training seminar to learn new knowledge and skills, they are probably somewhat unable. It is also true that individuals in the group may be higher or lower than the entire group in readiness.

IMPORTANT DEFINITIONS

Before we continue, it is important that we define three key terms—group, organization, and collection.

There are, perhaps, as many definitions of groups as there are definitions of leadership. This lack of common definition creates problems in terms of communicating, diagnosing, and being able to think through strategies for change. To help reduce this confusion, we suggest this working definition of a group: *Group*–Two or more people interacting, in which the existence of all (the existence of the group as a group) is necessary for the needs of the individual group members to be satisfied.

An important point to keep in mind is that individual needs satisfaction may be quite different for each member of the group. This is the ingredient that is missing from most definitions of groups. One of the principal problems with most definitions is the assumption that group members have common goals and purposes. There are many examples of groups devoid of common goals or purposes. For example, you may have three people in a group who have very different needs. One person may have joined the group because of a need for power; another because of the need for interaction with other people, a social need; while a third may have joined because of a need for status, for esteem. While the individual group members do not necessarily have to have common needs, goals, or purposes, the key is that the satisfaction, at least in part, of these individual needs is dependent upon the accomplishment of group goals. The degree to which individual need satisfaction is achieved differentiates effective from ineffective groups. When the needs are harmonious, the group is probably effective. When they are not, the group is probably ineffective. Common goals or purposes are, therefore, not criteria of groups, but of *effective* groups.

A group without clear-cut objectives lacks guidelines for the behavior of its members. For the group to be productive, it must have goals that are understood by all participants. Progress toward these goals is the best way to measure effectiveness. Research has consistently shown that group productivity is highest in those groups in which techniques are used that simultaneously further the attainment of group goals and bring fulfillment of the needs of individual group members.

Figure 14-1 illustrates the goal alignment of group members at the four basic readiness levels of Situational Leadership. At readiness level 1, which we call "chaos," there is no alignment. Group members have widely differing and frequently opposing goals. Then, as the group develops through readiness levels 2 and 3, it becomes, in readiness level 4, a "self-managing group" that is both able and willing to work with little external supervision.[8]

The group leader's role changes throughout this developmental process. Consider Figure 14-2, which uses the leadership style or upper portion of the Situational Leadership model. Group members are depicted by the initial M. At readiness level 1, the leader's role is one of defining and structuring. The leader is outside the group. When

FIGURE 14-1 Goal alignment at different group readiness levels

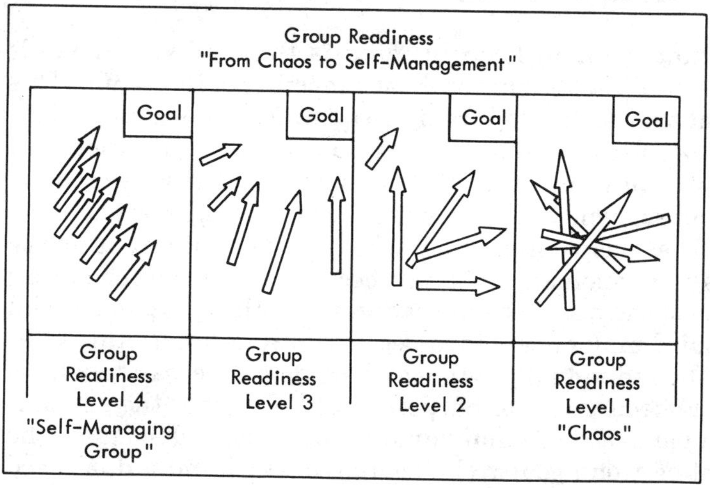

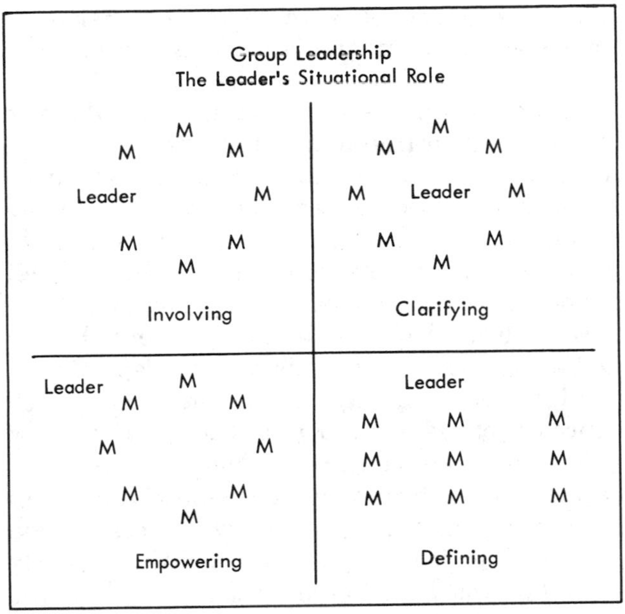

Group Leadership
The Leader's Situational Role

| | Involving | Clarifying | |

FIGURE 14-2 The leader's situational role in groups

the group is at readiness level 2, the leader's role becomes one of clarifying, as illustrated by the leader being in the center of the group. At readiness level 3, the leader's role is one of involving and providing support. This is depicted by the leader being part of the group circle. Lastly, at readiness level 4, the leader is outside the group, empowering it and providing needed resources.

Figures 14-1 and 14-2 illustrate that the fundamental concepts of Situational Leadership can be effectively applied at the group as well as at the individual level.

What is the difference between groups and organizations? Again, it is not commonality of goals or purposes. Do owners, managers, first-line supervisors, and line workers have the same goals? Not in very many organizations.

Our definition of an organization is one in which a group has stated and formal goals. Organizations exist for various reasons and have different organizational goals. Organizational goals are targets toward which input, process, and output are directed;[9] for example, make a 10 percent return on investment, help mankind conquer hunger, increase sales 20 percent during the current fiscal year.

Which of the three entities (group, organization, collection) has the best chance of having common goals? Not a group or an organization, but a collection. Twenty-seven people standing on a corner waiting for a bus have a common goal—everyone is waiting there for the bus. Interdependence of all of them is not necessary. Twenty-six people waiting for a bus would still be a collection, just like two hundred and fifty people waiting in line to see a movie.

Suppose you wanted to swim across San Francisco Bay from Oakland to San Francisco, a very difficult swim because of the severe tides and currents. You dive in and about halfway across you are in trouble. You feel a cramp coming on and you are beginning to get tired. Just then you see another swimmer coming alongside. What are the two of you now? A group? No, a *collection* because you only have a common goal—to get to San Francisco. There is no interdependence. If, however, you start to interact, give encouragement, support each other so that the existence of both is necessary for the satisfaction of individual member needs, then you have a *group*.[10] Once you both get to the other side, you decide to meet three times a week to swim to San Francisco to get in shape. Now you are an *organization* because you have stated or formal goals. Does it mean that you both necessarily share the same goal? No, but you both agree on the formal, stated goals.

GROUP PROBLEM-SOLVING MODES

Groups develop personalities—mores, customs, traditions—that tend to differentiate them from other groups and are characteristic of that group. It is the collective behavior of people within that group that gives it its special personality, its individuality as a group. Just as leaders have styles—patterns of behavior as perceived by the follower—so do groups have modes, or patterns of behavior as perceived by others. We can take a look at group modes in the same way that we can look at leadership styles. The different modes of group behavior, as shown in Figure 14-3, are helpful because we can use these different modes to help us recognize and organize patterns of group behavior.[11]

As in the Situational Leadership model, we place Task Behavior on the horizontal, or X axis, and Relationship Behavior on the vertical, or Y axis. When a group faces a situation that requires significant amounts of task behavior—lots of what, when, where, and how, but not a lot of time for dialogue and discussion—they may be heavily into high task behavior and low relationship behavior. When used appropriately for problem solving, this is the Crises Mode. The very nature of many crisis situations makes this the best approach for problem solving. The danger is that many organizations use this mode inap-

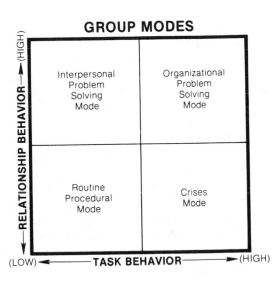

GROUP MODES

Interpersonal Problem Solving Mode	Organizational Problem Solving Mode
Routine Procedural Mode	Crises Mode

RELATIONSHIP BEHAVIOR → (HIGH)

(LOW) ◄——— TASK BEHAVIOR ———► (HIGH)

FIGURE 14-3
Group problem-solving modes

propriately and treat *every* situation as a crisis, just as some individuals treat every situation as a "telling" situation whether or not it is.

The Organizational Problem-Solving Mode when used appropriately requires high amounts of both task and relationship behavior. In this type of situation, considerable emphasis must be placed on structuring group activities, as well as motivating group members.

For example, eight teachers met with the principal and the superintendent of a school district. The job at hand was to revise the general curriculum. The curriculum has been neglected in the past because energies had been directed toward student disciplinary problems. The superintendent and principal both spelled out what needed to be done at the present meeting. The principal then elicited ideas from each group member and encouraged dialogue among the group members. By giving the group both content, structure, and a motivating process, the principal assured a productive group meeting.

In the Interpersonal Problem-Solving Mode, a high relationship, low task approach is appropriate. For example, if after a group is given a problem, cliques develop that serve to disrupt the group, relationship behaviors need to be used to increase interaction of all group members.

When appropriately used, the Routine Procedural Mode requires low task and low relationship behaviors. For example, a group of managers finds that they need to reassemble an important report before an early meeting the next day. The clerical staff has gone home. They quickly decide who is going to do what task and play what role. The emphasis is on getting the job done through performing the assigned roles with a minimum of structuring activities and socioemotional support.

In all of these modes, the focus must be on producing quality decisions in a timely manner. Quality decisions have no value if they are not timely. You may be highly skilled at picking the winners of Saturday's football games on Monday morning, but by then it's too late to do you any good.

A characteristic of effective groups is that they can move rapidly and easily from one mode to another without getting hung up on a normative mode. We enrich the ability of the group to respond to different situations and face different problems and contingencies if we build into them the ability and fluidity to move from one mode to another. Adaptability is very important. It is a product of growth and development. Mental receptiveness to the concept of change is the essence of adaptability. This is a positive virtue needed by persons in a group.[12]

HELPING AND HINDERING ROLES

Individuals within groups play roles—the individual behavior each member exhibits. It is not that a particular role by itself is helping or hindering to group performance, but that a high-performing group member plays a role that in a given situation contributes to maximizing the productivity of the group. This is the same principle that underlies leadership styles. A particular style is not intrinsically good or bad. The key is whether or not it is appropriate to the situation.

For some time the literature has given us lists of helping roles and lists of hindering roles. When these roles are researched, we find that the same roles are helping in some situations and hindering in others. So it is not that any combination of behavior *by itself* is a helping or hindering role, but it is the particular role in a particular contingency that makes the determination.

If we are to be effective in groups, all of us need to be able to adapt our roles to the needs of the group. We need to get rid of the idea that there are certain behaviors that are always good and certain behaviors that are always bad. There are behaviors that tend to be functional in some situations and dysfunctional in others.

In our extensive work with organizations in helping them improve their Quality Circles and other productivity programs, we have found that the material in Figure 14-4 has been particularly useful in giving people insights into roles they are and should be exhibiting in group settings. You will note that it is organized in much the same way as the Situational Leadership model, with the dimensions of Task Behavior and Relationship Behavior. It is a taxonomy of influence.

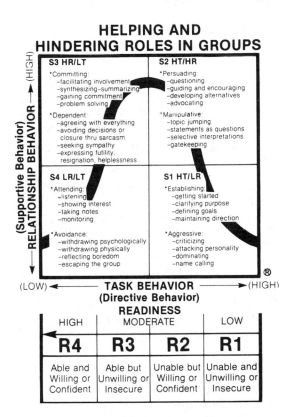

HELPING AND HINDERING ROLES IN GROUPS

S3 HR/LT

*Committing:
  –facilitating involvement
  –synthesizing–summarizing
  –gaining commitment
  –problem solving

*Dependent:
  –agreeing with everything
  –avoiding decisions or
    closure thru sarcasm
  –seeking sympathy
  –expressing futility,
    resignation, helplessness

S2 HT/HR

*Persuading:
  –questioning
  –guiding and encouraging
  –developing alternatives
  –advocating

*Manipulative:
  –topic jumping
  –statements as questions
  –selective interpretations
  –gatekeeping

S4 LR/LT

*Attending:
  –listening
  –showing interest
  –taking notes
  –monitoring

*Avoidance:
  –withdrawing psychologically
  –withdrawing physically
  –reflecting boredom
  –escaping the group

S1 HT/LR

*Establishing:
  –getting started
  –clarifying purpose
  –defining goals
  –maintaining direction

*Aggressive:
  –criticizing
  –attacking personality
  –dominating
  –name calling

(HIGH) ← **RELATIONSHIP BEHAVIOR** (Supportive Behavior)

(LOW) ←——— **TASK BEHAVIOR** ———→ (HIGH)
(Directive Behavior)

READINESS

HIGH	MODERATE		LOW
R4	**R3**	**R2**	**R1**
Able and Willing or Confident	Able but Unwilling or Insecure	Unable but Willing or Confident	Unable and Unwilling or Insecure

FIGURE 14-4
Helping and hindering roles in groups

Each style, S1 to S4, represents a *behavioral competency*. Within each *competency* there are two *categories* of behavior—one helping and one hindering. These *categories* are further divided into *indicators* of the types of behavior an individual could engage in under each *category*.

Some people seem to be fairly predictable in the roles that they play. They frequently enter into a series of transactions when interfacing with the group. In Transactional Analysis, this repetitive series of transactions is called a "psychological game." Because of their importance, we will include brief illustrations of some of the psychological games associated with hindering roles.

S1 (HT/LR) COMPETENCY

Helping Role Category

Establishing. Helps start the group along new paths. Proposes tasks and goals, defines problems, helps set rules, and contributes ideas. May suggest a plan of attack to handle a problem. Interprets issues and helps clear up ambiguous ideas or suggestions. Focuses attention on the alternatives and issues before the group.

Establishing Indicators

Getting started. Initiating action. Suggesting roles, structure, or procedures for the group to use. For example, "I suggest we go once around the table. Each of us will have an opportunity to give input."

Clarifying purpose. Stating why the group has been called together. Ensuring commonality of the intended result. "We are not here to play games. We have a responsibility to develop a workable strategic plan for our company."

Defining goals. Specifying what is needed to fulfill the group's purpose; the steps necessary for purpose attainment. For example, "To meet budget guidelines, we must submit our plan by December first and within the target of two and a half million. The first step is to agree on the line items."

Maintaining direction. Keeping the group on track; focusing on the stated goals and purpose. For example, "I think we're missing the point. We are not here to redefine the company's mission, we are here to agree on funding for each of the line items."

Hindering Role Category

Aggressive. Asserts personal dominance and attempts to get own way regardless of others. May react with hostility toward aspects of the problem of individuals who appear to be blocking progress. Criticism may be offered, either directly or through sarcasm and innuendo. May refuse to cooperate by rejecting all ideas or by interrupting, monopolizing the conversation, or by acting as an authority. May also engage in other aggressive behaviors such as bullying, discounting ideas, and boasting.

Aggressive Indicators

Criticizing. Downgrading, putting down, or otherwise finding fault with the suggestions or input of others. For example, "You keep coming up with these bright sayings. Why don't you try to sell them to the *Readers' Digest?*"

Attacking personality. Focusing on someone's personal attributes instead of the performance issue or problem the group is facing. For example, "That's one of the dumbest things I've heard. Why do you keep coming up with such stupid comments?"

Dominating. Taking "air time" and blocking other group members' opportunity to make suggestions. For example, "Just be quiet a minute. I've got something to say."

Name calling. Stereotyping. Using labels that generalize about a person or group in a demeaning manner. For example, "You staff types really don't know what is going on in this company."

Games Played by People in This Role

Uproar. Beginning with some form of critical statement that triggers an attack-defense series of transactions. The game ends with group members arguing in loud voices with any (or all) aggressive role category behaviors represented.

See what you made me do? and/or If it weren't for you. Using *blaming* games. The purpose is to transpose ownership or accountability for an error to another person, usually in a forceful, attacking manner. The message is: "My lack of influence, or the group's ineptness, is *your* fault."

S2 (HT/HR) COMPETENCY

Helping Role Category

Persuading. Requests the facts and relevant information on the problem. Seeks out expressions of feelings and values. Asks for suggestions, estimates, and ideas. Responds openly and freely to others. Encourages and accepts contributions of others, whether expressed orally or nonverbally.

Persuading Indicators

Questioning. Asking questions for the sake of clarity and shared understanding of a point. Productive questioning enhances group process and quality of content. For example, "Of your training objectives, which one do you consider to be the most important?"

Encouraging and guiding responses. It isn't sufficient to ask good questions. It is also people's willingness to respond that helps surface information and insights into their feelings and values. For example, "That is an excellent idea. Please tell us more about it."

Developing alternatives. Creating options. Coming up with various interpretations or multiple conclusions or strategies for consideration. For example, "Perhaps we should look at the financial plan from a 'best case'–'worst case' set of scenarios."

Advocating. Suggesting that the group pursue one suggestion or alternative over another. For example, "Since we seem to be stuck for a next step, I'd like to suggest that we talk about the Johnson Tool acquisition next."

Hindering Role Category

Manipulative. Responds to a problem rigidly and persists in using stereotypical responses. Makes repeated attempts to use solutions that are ineffective in achieving group goals. Selectively interprets data so as to validate personal opinions and censure nonsupportive input. Responds to personal motives, desires, and aspirations to the exclusion of the public agenda. Attempts to lure others into joining their position. Evaluates communication context. Judges remarks before they are understood and cross-examines the input of others.

Topic jumping. Getting off course, such as talking about X and suddenly discussing Y. Or, hairsplitting—overly focusing on and debating one detail so much that it is taken out of context and becomes a topic of its own. For example, "I agree that a business plan is important, but I think it is time that we rethink our company's mission statement."

Masking statements as questions. Saying something in question form or a one-liner that is actually a statement of justification or criticism. For example, "Don't you think it's time you got this meeting going again? We're not getting anything accomplished here."

Selective interpretation. Twisting what was said to discredit someone's point or taking a point out of context. For example, "That may be true, but we have never been successful in introducing a product without television advertising."

Gatekeeping. Hearing what you want to hear. Attempting to control the input to match one's own assessment of significance and responding accordingly. For example, "Thank you for your suggestion." (writes it down) "That is interesting." (does not write it down) "Worthwhile idea." (writes it down)

Games Played by People in This Role

Blemish. Becoming the group's nit-picker. Sifting through positive contributions looking for the chink in the armor and focusing on existing weak points.

Corner. Maneuvering other people through a series of seemingly plausible questions into a situation in which, no matter what they do, they never come out right.

"Now I've got you." Listening carefully to what is said, even questioning to get information, then once the ammunition is gathered, unloading on whoever makes the mistake or steps into the trap.

S3 (HR/LT) COMPETENCY

Helping Role Category

Committing. Helps to ensure that all members are part of the decision-making process. Shows relationships between ideas. May restate suggestions to pull them together. Summarizes and offers potential decisions for the group to accept or reject. Asks to see if the group is nearing a decision. Attempts to reconcile disagreements and facilitate the participation of everyone in the decision. Helps keep communication channels open by reducing tension and getting people to explore differences.

Committing Indicators

Facilitating involvement. Making sure that people are getting enough air time to provide input. Making efforts to tap into the resources that are available in the group. For example, "Come on, fella, you're doing a fine job. Nobody wants to cut into what you have to say."

Synthesizing/summarizing. Taking a variety of inputs and putting them into a new idea. Integrating what people say into a holistic framework. Summarizing existing ideas. For example, "If we take Joe's idea for a redesigned package and Mary's suggestion for in-store promotion, we may be able to launch the product introduction two months ahead of schedule."

Gaining commitment. Tapping into the group to ensure members are on board and buying into the group's progress or results. Securing a shared sense of ownership. For example, "How many of you are willing to sign on to our commitment to ship fifty thousand units by November first?"

Problem solving. Dealing with problems affecting group commitment near the point of implementation. If there is skepticism, offer proof; if there is misunderstanding, clarify; a drawback, be creative; procrastination, create a sense of urgency; a solution not within the group's scope of authority, identify who is in authority, ask for support, and make suggestions. For example, "We have not been making very good progress. If we are going to wind this up today, we have to reach agreement before lunch on this personnel evaluation system."

Hindering Role Category

Dependent. Reacts to people as authority figures. May acquiesce to anyone who is seen as an overt leader. Abdicates problem solving to others and expects someone else to lead to the solution. Unwilling to use leadership resources available within self or others. Attempts to escape tension through diversions or the inappropriate use of humor. Easily embarrassed and vulnerable to criticism. Often apologizes for given input. Requires constant encouragement to participate. Seeks sympathy.

Dependent Indicators

Agreeing with everything. Deferring to others. Suppressing one's feelings. Appears to be on board with all members on all issues. For example, "No, I guess you're right. I'm out of ideas."

Avoiding decisions or closure through sarcasm. Making an inappropriate attempt at humor that keeps issues open when the group could be making a decision. For example, "Did you hear the story about the . . ."

Seeking sympathy. Attempting to gain attention or concessions from other group members through sulking, looking dejected, or similar behaviors. Using such behaviors as manipulative ploys to gain influence. For example, "You always make my department take more than our share of the cuts. Why do we always have to give in? Why do we have to be punished?"

Expressing futility, resignation, or helplessness. Blowing smoke rings, drawing, playing paper-and-pencil games, and doing things that distract group members and demonstrate noninvolvement. Announcing all the reasons why something is wrong or will not work. The aim is to convince others that the group is powerless and lacks control. For example, "Management is never going to listen to our ideas anyway. It is just another waste of time."

Games Played by People in This Role

"Ain't it awful?" Presenting superficial concern and commitment to the group's efforts when really attempting to thwart those efforts through statements such as: "It will take too much work" or "There'll be no support" or "No one ever listens to us."

Wooden leg. Trying to avoid accomplishment, accountability, work, or to gain sympathy. Using some contrived or exaggerated handicap as an excuse for not being able to fulfill their good intentions.

"Poor Me." Behaving in a way that reinforces some form of self-pity and self-negation. The game is played to seek sympathy. Griping continues, but the person makes no real effort to change or improve the situation.

S4 (LR/LT) COMPETENCY

Helping Role Category

Attending. Listens as well as speaks. Easy to talk to. Encourages input from group members and tries to understand as well as be understood. Records input for use later. Demonstrates a willingness to become involved with other people. Takes time to listen and avoids interrupting.

Attending Indicators

Listening. Remaining silent, maintaining eye contact, and paying attention to what is being said with the purpose of *understanding;* not agreeing. For example, "I've been listening very carefully and it seems Tom has some very good points."

Showing interest. Communicating in a way that shows one is involved in the group's process and concerned with its workings. The communication is usually nonverbal and is a type of emotionally neutral reinforcement. For example, leaning forward, visibly concentrating on discussions.

Taking notes (for oneself) *or recording* (for the group). Keeping some form of registered evidence of the group's inputs, activities, and decisions that will make them accessible at a later point. For example, "I've made some notes and I'd like to say something . . ."

Monitoring or observing. Auditing or examining the group. Paying special attention to the impact things have on the group's process or performance. For example, showing alertness during discussions.

Hindering Role Category

Avoidance. Retreats emotionally in thought and/or physically. Daydreams, avoids the topics, or remains indifferent. Engages in individualistic activity that has little or nothing to do with group activity. May withdraw from the group. Scoffs at group effort, rolls eyes in disgust, or demonstrates aloofness nonverbally. Will occasionally preplan a means to leave the group early.

Avoidance Indicators

Withdrawing psychologically. Being unresponsive, withdrawn, seemingly checked out from the group's activities—preoccupied with thoughts other than the issues before the group. For example, trying not to be involved in the group's activities—looking intently at pictures and so on.

Withdrawing physically. Stationing oneself away from the group. Creating a physical distance between oneself and the group's activities. For example, getting up from the group discussion area and walking over to the windows, a few feet away.

Reflecting boredom. Pouting, physically conveying the message "I'd rather not be here." Being an active competing response for the group. For example, slouching in the chair and appearing disinterested.

Escaping the group. Physically leaving the environment, planning to be late, intentionally absenting oneself from the group. For example, phone rings as secretary makes prearranged call. "Sorry, folks, got to leave to take care of some important business."

Games Played by People in This Role

Harried. Appearing too overworked or busy to meet deadlines and commitments. To sustain the game and maintain this image the player will take on and even solicit added responsibilities to an already overfilled plate. This provides the basis for permission to be late, to leave meetings before the group comes to closure, and to turn over unfinished work with incomplete instructions to other group members — guilt-free and with justification.

Kick me. Making a mistake; that is, coming to work late or unprepared and hoping that someone in the group will provide the desired kick — criticism, questions, and so on. This kick provides the payoff the player seeks. An eventual result of this is that the person may withhold contributions or withdraw psychologically or physically from the group.

Withdrawing psychologically or physically from the group can be an outcome of any of these games. Although this may give the hinderer some short-term satisfaction, it undermines the group process.

SUMMARY

These are some of the behavioral indicators reflecting helping and hindering roles in each of the four competencies. They are illustrations of the types of activities that contribute to or detract from functional and constructive group problem solving. We want to emphasize again that these roles are not by themselves helping or hindering — there are no generic helping or hindering roles. A role may be helping or hindering depending upon the situation. Your awareness of these roles will make a very real contribution toward increasing your effectiveness in groups.

NOTES

1. David Krech, Richard S. Crutchfield, and Egerton L. Ballachey, *Individual in Society* (New York: McGraw-Hill, 1962), p. 529.
2. Sandy J. Wayne, Ricky W. Griffin, and Thomas S. Bateman, "Improving the Effectiveness of Quality Circles," *Personnel Administrator,* March 1986, pp. 79–88. See also Merle O'Don-

nel and Robert J. O'Donnel, "Quality Circles: Latest Fad or Real Winner?" *Business Horizons,* May–June 1984, pp. 48–52; Edward E. Lawler III and Susan A. Mohrman, "Quality Circles After the Fad," *Harvard Business Review,* January–February 1985, pp. 64–71.

3. Annette Hartenstein and Kenneth F. Huddleston, "Values: The Cornerstone of QWL," *Training and Development Journal,* October 1984, pp. 65–66. See also Shoichi Suzawa, "How The Japanese Achieve Excellence," *Training and Development Journal,* May 1985, pp. 110–17.

4. *Ibid.*

5. Robert H. Guest, Paul Hersey, and Kenneth H. Blanchard, *Organizational Change through Effective Leadership,* 2nd ed. (Englewood Cliffs, N.J.: Prentice Hall, 1986).

6. *Ibid.*

7. Peter F. Drucker, *The New Realities: In Government and Politics–In Economics and Business–In Society and World View* (New York: Harper Collins, 1990).

8. *Team Leadership, Executive Summary* (Escondido, Calif.: Leadership Studies International, Inc., 1991).

9. Sam Certo, *Principles of Modern Management: Functions and Systems* (Dubuque, Iowa: Brown, 1983).

10. Guest, Hersey, and Blanchard, *Organizational Change through Effective Leadership.*

11. The definition of leadership style in individuals we used in earlier chapters can also be applied to group behavior.

12. Guest, Hersey, and Blanchard, *Organizational Change through Effective Leadership.*

15

Planning and Implementing Change

In the dynamic society surrounding today's organizations, the question of whether change will occur is no longer relevant. Instead, the issue is, How do managers and leaders cope with the inevitable barrage of changes that confront them daily in attempting to keep their organizations viable and current? Although change is a fact of life, if managers are to be effective, they can no longer be content to let change occur as it will. They must be able to develop strategies to plan, direct, and control change.

To be effective managers of change, leaders must have more than good *diagnostic skills*. Once they have analyzed the demands of their environment, they must be able to *adapt* their leadership style to fit these demands and develop the means to *change* some or all of the other situational variables. Recognizing that sometimes the only avenue to effectiveness is through change, in this chapter we will concentrate on the processes and strategies for planning and implementing change.

GENERAL FRAMEWORK
FOR UNDERSTANDING CHANGE

Managers who are interested in implementing some change in their group or organization should have (or be able to obtain people with) skills, knowledge, and training in at least two areas:

1. *Diagnosis.* The first, and in some ways the most important, stage of any change effort is diagnosis. Broadly defined, the skills of diagnosis involve techniques for asking the right questions, sensing the environment of the organization, establishing effective patterns of observation and data collection, and developing ways to process and interpret data. In diagnosing for change, managers should attempt to find out: (a) what is *actually* happening now in a particular situation; (b) what is *likely* to be happening in the future if no change effort is made; (c) what would people *ideally* like to be happening in this situation; and (d) what are the *blocks*, or restraints, stopping movement from the actual to the ideal?

2. *Implementation.* This stage of the change process is the translation of diagnostic data into change goals and plans, strategies and procedures. Questions such as the following must be asked: How can change be effected in a work group or organization and how will it be received? What is adaptive and what is resistant to change within the environment?

Diagnosis

There are at least three steps in the diagnostic process: point of view, identification of problem(s), and analysis.

Point of View

Before beginning to diagnose in an organization, you should be clear through whose eyes you will be observing the situation—your own, those of your boss, your associates, your followers, an outside consultant, or others.

Ideally, to get the full picture you should look at the situation from the points of view of the people who will be affected by any changes. Reality, however, sometimes restricts such a broad perspective. At any rate, you should be clear about your frame of reference from the start.

Identification of Problem(s)

Any change effort begins with the identification of the problem(s). A problem in a situation exists when there is a discrepancy between what is actually happening (the *real*) and what you or someone who hired you (point of view) would like to be happening (the *ideal*). For example, in a given situation, there might be tremendous conflict occurring among individuals in a work group. If this kind of conflict is not detrimental, there may be no problem. Until you can explain precisely what you would like to be occurring and unless that set of conditions is different from the present situation, no problem exists.

On the other hand, if you would ideally like this work group to be harmonious and cooperative, then you have a problem—there is a discrepancy between the real and the ideal. *Change efforts involve attempting to reduce discrepancies between the real (actual) and the ideal.* It should be pointed out that change efforts may not always involve attempting to move the real closer to the ideal. Sometimes after diagnosis you might realize that your ideal is unrealistic and should be brought more in line with what is actually happening.

It is in problem identification that the concepts and theoretical frameworks presented in this book begin to come into play. For example, two important potential areas for discrepancy are, in Likert's terms, output–end-result variables and intervening variables.

In examining *end-result variables,* the question becomes: Is the organization, work group, or individual doing an effective job in what it was asked to do; that is, production, sales, teaching the 3 Rs, and so on? Are short-term goals being accomplished? How does the long-term picture look? If performance is not what it should be, there is an obvious discrepancy.

If performance is a problem, you might want to look for discrepancies in the *intervening variables* or condition of the human resources. For example, is there much turnover, absenteeism, or tardiness? How about grievances, accident rate, and such? The concepts that you have been studying in this book can generate diagnostic questions for the change situation you are examining, such as:

- What leadership, decision-making, and problem-solving skills are available? What is the motivation, communication, commitment to objectives, and climate (morale)? (Likert)
- What is the readiness level of the people involved? Are they willing and able to take significant responsibility for their own performance? (Hersey and Blanchard)
- What need level seems to be most important for people right now? (Maslow)
- How are the hygiene factors and motivators? Are people getting paid enough? How are the working conditions? Is job security an issue? How are interpersonal relations? Do people complain about the manger? Are people able to get recognition for their accomplishments? Is there much challenge in the work? Are there opportunities for growth and development? Are people given much responsibility? (Herzberg)

Good theory is just organized common sense. So use the theories and questions presented here to help you sort out what is happening in your situation and what might need to be changed.

Problem identification flows almost immediately into analysis. Once a discrepancy (problem) has been identified, the goal of analysis is to determine why the problem exists. The separation between problem identification and analysis is not always that clear, however, because identifying areas of discrepancy is often a part of analysis.

Once a discrepancy has been identified in the end-result variables or intervening variables, the most natural strategy is to begin to examine what Likert calls "causal variables"—the independent variables that can be altered or changed by the organization and its management, such as leadership or management style, organizational structure, organizational objectives. In other words, can you identify what in the environment might have caused the discrepancy? Again, different theorists come to mind and stimulate various questions.

- What is the dominant leadership style being used? How does it fit with the readiness level of the people involved? (Hersey and Blanchard)
- What are the prevailing assumptions about human nature adhered to by management? How well do those assumptions match the capabilities and potential of the people involved? (McGregor)
- Are people able to satisfy a variety of needs in this environment? How do the opportunities for need satisfaction compare with the high-strength needs of the people involved? (Maslow)
- How do the expectations of the various situational variables compare with the leadership style being used by management? (Hersey and Blanchard)

Again, these theories and questions are presented to suggest how the concepts studied can help you to analyze problems that exist in your environment and provide guidelines for developing strategies for implementing change.

Implementation

The implementation process involves the following: identifying alternative solutions and appropriate implementation strategies to use in attempting to reduce the discrepancy between what is actually happening and what you would like to be happening; anticipating the probable consequences of using each of the alternative strategies; and choosing a specific strategy and implementing it.

Once your analysis is completed, the next step is to determine alternative solutions to the problem(s). Hand in hand with developing alternative solutions is determining appropriate implementation strategies. Two theories seem helpful in designing change implementation strategies.

Force Field Analysis

In chapter 6, force field analysis was examined as a useful technique in looking at the variables involved in determining effectiveness. This technique for diagnosing situations, which was developed by Kurt Lewin,[1] also may be useful in analyzing the various change strategies that can be used in a particular situation.

Once you have determined that there is a discrepancy between what is actually happening and what you would like to be happening in a situation—and have done some analysis on why that discrepancy exists—then force field analysis becomes a helpful tool. Before embarking on any change strategy, it seems appropriate to determine what you have going for you in this change effort (driving forces) and what you have going against you (restraining forces). We have found from our experience that if managers start implementing a change strategy without doing that kind of analysis, they can get blown out of the water and not know why. An example might help.

In August, an enthusiastic superintendent of schools and his assistant took over a suburban school district outside a large urban area in the Midwest. Both men were committed to "humanizing" the schools. In particular, they wanted to change the predominant teaching approach used in the system from a teacher-centered approach in which the teachers always tell the students what to do, how to do it, when to do it, and where to do it (high task–low relationship style) to a child-centered approach in which students play a significant role in determining what they are to do (high relationship–low task or low relationship–low task style).

To implement the changes they wanted, the two administrators hired a business manager to handle the office and the paper work. They themselves essentially had no office. They put telephones in their cars and spent most of their time out in the schools with teachers and students. They spent fifteen to eighteen hours a day working with and supporting teachers and administrators who wanted to engage in new behavior. Then, suddenly, in January, only six months after they had been hired, the school board called a special meeting and fired the superintendent by a seven to two vote.

The administrators could not believe what had happened. They immediately started a court suit against the school board for due process. They charged that the board had served as both judge and jury. In addition to the court actions, the administrators became educational martyrs and began to hit the lecture tour to talk about the evils of schools. During one of their trips, the assistant superintendent was asked by one of the authors of this book to come to his graduate seminar on the management of change. The class at that time was discussing the usefulness of force field analysis. The administrator, who did not know Lewin's theory, was asked to think about the driving and restraining forces that had been present in the change situation. In thinking about the driving forces that were pushing for the change they wanted, the administrator was quick to name the enthusiasm and commitment of the top administrators, some teachers, and some students, but really could not think of any other driving forces. When asked about the number of teachers and students involved, the administrator suggested that they were a small but growing group.

In thinking about restraining forces, the assistant superintendent began to mention one thing after another. The assistant said that they had never really had a good relationship with the mayor, chief of police, or editor of the town paper. These people felt that the two administrators were encouraging permissiveness in the schools. In fact, the town paper printed several editorials against their efforts. In addition, the teachers' association had expressed concern that the programs being pushed were asking the teachers to assume responsibilities outside their contract. Even the Parent-Teachers Association (PTA) had held several meetings because of parent concerns about discipline in the schools. The administrator also reported the fact that the superintendent had been hired by a five to four vote of the board and that some of his supporters had been defeated in the November election. In general, he implied that the town had been traditionally very conservative in educational matters, and on and on.

Figure 15-1 suggests the relationship between driving and restraining forces in this change situation. As can be seen, even with adding some board members as driving forces and not mentioning some teachers and students as restraining forces, the restraining forces for changing this school system from a teacher-centered approach to a child-centered approach not only outnumbered, but easily outweighed the driving forces. As a result, the restraining forces eventually overpowered the driving forces and pushed the equilibrium even more in the direction of a teacher-centered approach.

In utilizing force field analysis for developing a change strategy, there are a few guidelines that can be used:

1. If the driving forces far outweigh the restraining forces in power and frequency in a change situation, managers interested in driving for change can often push on and overpower the restraining forces.

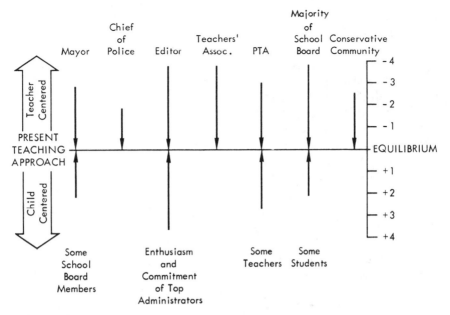

FIGURE 15-1 Driving and restraining forces in an educational change example

2. If the reverse is true and the restraining forces are much stronger than the driving forces, managers interested in driving for change have several choices. First, they can give up the change effort, realizing that it will be too difficult to implement. Second, they can pursue the change effort, but concentrate on maintaining the driving forces in the situation while attempting, one by one, to change each of the restraining forces into driving forces or somehow to immobilize each of the restraining forces so that they are no longer factors in the situation. The second choice is possible, but very time consuming.

3. If the driving forces and restraining forces are fairly equal in a change situation, managers probably will have to begin pushing the driving forces, while at the same time attempting to convert or immobilize some or all of the restraining forces.

In this school example, the situation obviously represented an imbalance in favor of restraining forces, yet the administrators acted as if the driving forces were clearly on their side. If they had used force field analysis to diagnose their situation, they would have seen that their change strategy was doomed until they took some time to try to work on the restraining forces.

Logical Incrementalism

Another theory that has received wide acceptance in designing change implementation strategies is James Brian Quinn's Logical Incrementalism. This theory recognizes that the process of implementing change in a large organization is complex and time consuming. Internal and external forces can exert significant pressure to resist the CEO and senior management team's plan for strategic reorganization of the company. James Brian Quinn, a professor of management, studied a number of large organizations undergoing significant changes and determined a pattern of planning that corporate leaders could use to facilitate effective implementation and acceptance of the change. Logical Incrementalism[2] describes the process and focuses on the evolution of the change as broad goals are more narrowly refined and adapted.

The stages of logical incrementalism are:

1. *General concern*—a vaguely felt awareness of an issue or opportunity.
2. *Broadcasting of a general idea without details*—the idea is floated for reactions pro and con, and for refinements.
3. *Formal development of a change plan.*
4. *Use of a crisis or opportunity to stimulate implementation of the change plan*—retirement of a senior manager or a sudden loss of market share can facilitate rapid acceptance and implementation of the change.
5. *Adaptation of the plan as implementation progresses.*

Logical incrementalism is viewed by many top-level managers as an accurate description of how change is successfully generated and implemented in a healthy organization. By floating an idea early on, a leader can improve the quality of information generated before decisions are made and can overcome political and emotional barriers to change. Early involvement by subordinate groups can create personal and organizational commitment to the change plan and facilitate effective implementation.

Conscious management of the change process and a clear, thoroughly analyzed vision and set of purposes are essential to using logical incrementalism successfully. Specific leadership actions can improve the likelihood of organizational acceptance of the strategic change. These actions include the following:

1. Use multiple information sources to refine and develop broad goals into specific objectives.
2. Build organizational awareness of the change.
3. Create credibility for the change.
4. Legitimize new viewpoints.
5. Use tactical shifts and partial solutions in refining the general idea.

6. Establish political support and overcome opposition.
7. Maintain flexibility.
8. Use trial balloons and systematic waiting.
9. Create pockets of commitment.
10. Crystalize organizational focus on the change at the right time.
11. Formalize commitments made to adopt the change.

Some critics have seen logical incrementalism as disjointed, a garbage-can approach, or as managerial muddling. These complaints are valid when logical incrementalism is used to implement an unclear or poorly formulated change plan. Logical incrementalism works most successfully when it is used as a process of integration of the change into the current organizational environment. Logical incrementalism works best when the manager uses it to concentrate on a few key change thrusts and is effective in building and managing coalitions of support.[3]

Now that two theories helpful in designing change implementation strategies–Force Field Analysis and Logical Incrementalism–have been reviewed, some understanding of the levels of change and the change cycles available might be useful.

First-Order and Second-Order Change

One way of approaching change for the purpose of diagnosis is to look at it from the perspective of two different frameworks. This is important because change does not always occur in a stable environment. Organizations have experienced revolutionary changes in technology, competition, and socioeconomic conditions; some changes have destroyed old industries and created new ones. Leaders need to recognize and understand the two frameworks in which change can occur.

The change process most managers are familiar with is continuous or *first-order change*—change that occurs in a stable system that itself remains unchanged. The change processes previously discussed in this chapter focus on managing first-order change. These changes are necessary for a business to grow and thrive in a competitive environment.

Discontinuous or *second-order change*[4] occurs when fundamental properties or states of the system are changed. The fall of communism and the introduction of democratic and free market principles in Eastern Europe and the former Soviet Union are examples of the cataclysmic upheaval of second-order change. Some industries currently experiencing the magnitude of second-order change include telecommunications, financial services, and health care, as discontinuous changes restructure the industry, relocate its boundaries, and change the bases of competition.

Figure 15-2 identifies current change theories and their relationship to first- and second-order change.[5] Adaptation theories maintain that organizations monitor their environments continuously and make purposeful adjustments to them. Incrementalism refers to organizational changes in new products, structures, and processes; resource dependence mechanisms see organizational change as a response to external dependencies such as suppliers, markets, or governmental policies.

Evolution theories describe the first-order changes that industries experience. Natural selection mechanisms view the entry and exit of firms in an industry as the primary method of evolution. Institutional isomorphism occurs when organizations change to conform to the norms of the industry environment.

As firms experience various stages of the organizational life cycle, they experience metamorphosis and second-order change. Metamorphosis differs from adaptation in that the entire firm goes through a transformation and emerges with a different configuration and strategic intent. An example of this type of change can be seen when a visionary inventor with a small business brings in a professional management team and the small business metamorphoses into a

FIGURE 15-2 Models of change within organizations and industries

	First-Order Change	Second-Order Change
	Adaptation	Metamorphosis
Firm Level	Focus: Incremental change within organizations Mechanisms: •Incrementalism •Resource dependence	Focus: Frame-breaking change within organizations Mechanisms: •Life cycle stages •Configuration transitions
	Evolution	Revolution
Industry Level	Focus: Incremental change within established industries Mechanisms: •Natural selection •Institutional isomorphism	Focus: Emergence, transformation, and decline of industries Mechanisms: •Punctuated equilibrium •Quantum speciation

Adapted, by permission of the publisher, from Strategic Management Journal, *1990.*

growing firm with a different organizational structure and competitive focus. The change is transforming for the members of the small business.

Revolutionary change occurs when an entire industry is restructured and reconstituted during a brief period of quantum change which is preceeded and followed by a long period of stability. Quantum speciation, a term from biology, has been proposed as a mechanism through which new organizational forms emerge during a revolution. The breakup of AT&T into "baby bells" and the introduction of new competitors into long distance telecommunications is an example of second-order revolutionary change in an industry.

As a leader, most organizational changes you initiate will occur on a level of first-order change. The visionary leader also understands the opportunities presented by second-order change, and can work to meet the challenges this type of change can create.

Change Cycles

Levels of change. In chapter 1, four levels of change were discussed: knowledge changes, attitudinal changes, individual behavior changes, and group or organizational performance changes.

Changes in knowledge tend to be the easiest to make; they can occur as a result of reading a book or an article or hearing something new from a respected person. Attitude structures differ from knowledge structures in that they are emotionally charged in a positive or negative way. The addition of emotion often makes attitudes more difficult to change than knowledge.

Changes in individual behavior seem to be significantly more difficult and time consuming than either of the two previous levels. For example, managers may have knowledge about the advantages of increased follower involvement and participation in decision making and may even feel that such participation would improve their performance, and, yet, they may be unable to delegate or share decision-making responsibilities significantly with followers. This discrepancy between knowledge, attitude, and behavior may be a result of their own authoritarian leader-follower upbringing. This past experience has led to a habit pattern that feels comfortable.

While individual behavior is difficult enough to change, it becomes even more complicated when you try to implement change within groups or organizations. The leadership styles of one or two managers might be effectively altered, but drastically changing the level of follower participation throughout an entire organization might be a very time-consuming process. At this level you are trying to alter customs, mores, and traditions that have developed over many years.

Levels of change become very significant when you examine two different change cycles—the participative change cycle and the directive change cycle.[6]

Participative change. A participative change cycle is implemented when new knowledge is made available to the individual or group. It is hoped that the group will accept the data and will develop a positive attitude and commitment in the direction of the desired change. At this level an effective strategy may be to involve the individual or group directly in helping to select or formalize the new methods for obtaining the desired goals. This is group participation in problem solving.

The next step will be to attempt to translate this commitment into actual behavior. This step is significantly more difficult to achieve. For example, it is one thing to be concerned about increased follower participation in decision making (attitude), but another thing to be willing actually to get involved in doing something (behavior) about the issue. An effective strategy may be to identify the informal and formal leaders among the work group(s) and concentrate on gaining their behavioral support for the desired change. Once this is accomplished, organizational change may be effected by getting other people to begin to pattern their behavior after those persons whom they respect and perceive in leadership roles. This participative change cycle is illustrated in Figure 15-3.

FIGURE 15-3 Participative change cycle

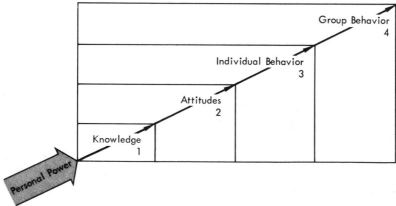

Directive change. We have all probably been faced with a situation similar to the one in which there is an announcement on Monday morning that "as of today all members of this organization will begin to operate in accordance with Form 10125." This is an example of a directive change cycle. It is through this change cycle that many managers in the past have attempted to implement such innovative ideas as management by objectives, job enrichment, and the like.

This change cycle begins by change being imposed on the total organization by some external force, such as higher management, the community, or new laws. This will tend to affect the interaction network system at the individual level. The new contacts and modes of behavior create new knowledge, which tends to develop predispositions toward or against the change. The directive change cycle is illustrated in Figure 15-4.

In some cases where change is forced, the new behavior engaged in creates the kind of knowledge that develops commitment to the change, and, therefore, begins to approximate a participative change as it reinforces the individual and group behavior. The hope is that "if people will only have a chance to see how the new system works, they will support it."

Is there a "best" strategy for change? Given a choice between the polarities of directive and participative change, most people would tend to prefer the participative change cycle. But just as we have argued that there is no "best" leadership style, there also is no best strategy for implementing change. Effective change agents are identified as those who can adapt their strategies to the demands of their

FIGURE 15-4   Directive change cycle

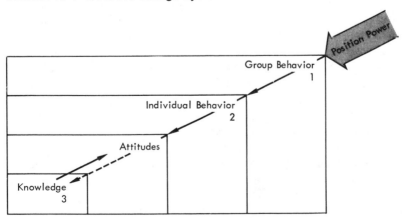

unique environment. Thus, the participative change cycle is not a better change strategy than the directive change cycle, and vice versa. The appropriate strategy depends on the situation, and there are advantages and disadvantages to each.

Advantages and disadvantages of change cycles. The participative change cycle tends to be more appropriate for working with individuals and groups who are achievement motivated, seek responsibility, and have a degree of knowledge and experience that may be useful in developing new ways of operating—in other words, people with moderate to high task-relevant readiness. Once the change starts, these people are much more capable of assuming responsibilities for implementation of the desired change. Although these people may welcome change and the need to improve, they may become very rigid and opposed to change if it is implemented in a directive (high task–low relationship) manner. A directive change style is inconsistent with their perceptions of themselves as responsible, self-motivated people who should be consulted throughout the change process. When they are not consulted and change is implemented in an authoritarian manner, conflict often results. Examples of this occur frequently in organizations in which a manager recruits or inherits a competent, creative staff that is willing to work hard to implement new programs and then proceeds to bypass the staff completely in the change process. This style results in resistance and is inappropriate to the situation.

A coercive, directive change style might be very appropriate and more productive with individuals and groups who are less ambitious, are often dependent, and who are not willing to take on new responsibilities unless forced to do so. In fact these people *might prefer* direction and structure from their leader to being faced with decisions they are not willing or experienced enough to make. Once again, diagnosis is all-important. It is just as inappropriate for a manager to attempt to implement change in a participative manner with a staff that has never been given the opportunity to take responsibility and has become dependent on its manager for direction as it is to implement change in a coercive manner with a staff that is ready to change and willing to take responsibility for implementing it.

There are other significant differences between these two change cycles. The participative change cycle tends to be effective when induced by leaders who have personal power; that is, they have referent, information, and expert power. On the other hand, the directive cycle necessitates that a leader have significant position power; that is, coercive, connection, reward, and legitimate power.

If managers decide to implement change in an authoritarian, coercive manner, they would be wise to have the support of their superiors and other sources of power or they may be effectively blocked by their staff.

With the participative change cycle, a significant advantage is that once the change is accepted, it tends to be long lasting. Since everyone has been involved in the development of the change, each person tends to be more highly committed to its implementation. The disadvantage of participative change is that it tends to be slow and evolutionary–it may take years to implement a significant change. An advantage of directive change, on the other hand, is speed. Using position power, leaders can often impose change immediately. A disadvantage of this change strategy is that it tends to be volatile. It can be maintained only as long as the leader has position power to make it stick. It often results in animosity, hostility, and, in some cases, overt and covert behavior to undermine and overthrow.

In terms of force field analysis, discussed earlier, the directive change cycle could be utilized if the power of the driving forces pushing for change far outweighed the restraining forces resisting change. On the other hand, a directive change cycle would be doomed to failure if the power of the restraining forces working against the change was greater than the power of the driving forces pushing for the change.

A participative change cycle that depends on personal power could be appropriate in either of the cases just described. With frequent and powerful driving forces pushing for change in a situation, a leader might not have to use a high task, directive change cycle since the driving forces are ready to run with the change already and do not have to be forced to engage in the new desired behavior. At the same time, when the restraining forces could easily overpower the driving forces, managers would be advised to begin with participative change techniques designed gradually to turn some of the restraining forces into driving forces or at least immobilize their influence in the situation. In other words, when things are stacked against you, it would seem to be more effective to try to moderate the forces against the change than to try to force change in a situation when little power is on the side of the change effort.

These two change cycles have been described as if they were either/or positions. The use of only one of these change cycles exclusively, however, could lead to problems. For example, if managers introduce change only in a directive, high task–low relationship manner without any movement toward participative change, members of their staff–if they decide to remain–may react in one of two ways. Some may fight the managers tooth and nail and organize efforts to undermine them. Others may buckle under to their authority and become very passive, dependent staff members, always needing the manager to tell them what to do and when to do it before doing anything. These kinds of people say yes to anything the manager wants and then moan and groan and drag their feet later. Neither of these responses ma̅ ̅es for a very healthy organization. At the other extreme, managers who will not make a move without checking with their staff and getting full approval also can immobilize themselves. They may establish such a complicated network of "participative" committees that significant change becomes almost impossible.

Thus, in reality, it is more a question of the proper blend of the directive and participative change cycles, depending on the situation, than a forced choice between one or the other.

Patterns of Communication

One of the most important considerations in determining whether to use a participative or directive change strategy or some combination of both is how communication patterns are structured within a group or organization prior to implementing a change.[7] Two of the most widely used ways of structuring communications, illustrated in Figure 15-5, are the star and the circle.

The arrowed lines represent two-way communication channels. In the circle each person can send messages in either direction to two colleagues on either side, and, thus, the group is free to communicate all around the circle. In other words, nothing in the structure of the communication pattern favors one group member over another as leader. In essence, this depicts an open, democratic organization in which there is participation in decision making by all members. In the star communication pattern, however, one individual (C) is definitely in a leadership position; C can communicate with the other four members of the group and they can communicate with C, but not with each other. This group represents an autocratic structure, with C acting as the manager. Either of these groups might be analogous to groups of department heads, each having a department, but all reporting eventually to the same manager. In both patterns, A, B, D, and E are department heads and C is the manager.

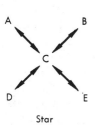

Star

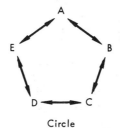

Circle

FIGURE 15-5
Two ways of structuring communications

Is there a "best" pattern of communication? Once these two patterns of communication have been identified, the usual question arises about which is the "best" pattern. Some classic experiments conducted by Alex Bavelas[8] attempted to answer that question. In particular, Bavelas was interested in determining how each of these communication patterns affected the efficiency of a group's performance as well as the group's morale.

In one experiment, the two groups were put to work in the star and circle patterns. Sets of five marbles were given to each of the five group members. The marbles of each set had different colors, but one color was common to all sets. Both groups were to discover the common color. When that had been accomplished, the task was completed. In essence, it was the star, or autocratic, pattern against the circle, or democratic, pattern.

The autocratic star pattern was much faster. Its four subordinate members simply had to describe their marbles to the leader. After noting the common color, the designated leader sent correct information back. In trial after trial, the star group arrived at correct answers in an average of about thirty to forty seconds. The circle group took sixty to ninety seconds. The star group was not only faster, but used fewer messages and developed more efficient ways of solving problems. In addition, group members respected their communication pattern.

The star pattern, although fast, tended to have a negative effect on morale. While group members had a high opinion of their communication pattern or organization, they had a low opinion of themselves except for the leader (C). With each ensuing trial they felt less important and more dissatisfied. In fact, on one occasion the leader received a message, "Enough of this game; let's play tic-tac-toe." On other occasions, messages were torn up or written in French and Spanish; yet, on the whole, the group still was faster and more productive than the circle group.

The circle could be described as "slow, inaccurate, but happy." It developed no system for working on problems and no one leader seemed to emerge. While members were openly critical of the organization's productivity, they seemed to enjoy the tasks. No one attempted to sabotage.

In terms of performance, everything seemed to be in favor of the autocratic groups, until Bavelas created a so-called emergency. He changed the marbles. Instead of simple solid colors, each group was given odd-colored marbles that were difficult to describe. The task, as before, was to find out which marble all members of the group had in common. The new marbles required close observation to tell one from another. In fact, two group members could be looking at identical marbles and describe them quite differently.

379

Since morale and the condition of the human resources were good in the circle group, members pulled together in the "emergency" and were able to solve the problem by utilizing all the available resources. On the other hand, the star pattern was a leader-dominated system; so group members looked to the leader in the emergency to solve the problem with little commitment from them.

The new task confused both groups. Errors mounted, and it took ten minutes or more to solve the problem. Yet, eventually, the circle seemed to adapt to the crisis, and after a number of trials had restored its efficiency completely. On the other hand, the star could not seem to cope with it, taking twice as much time and committing three to four times as many errors.

Why was the star communication pattern faster? Essentially, because it was a one-way communication system dominated by a single leader. With this communication pattern, an orderliness was imposed on the group that eliminated extra messages. In the circle, no such clear organization existed. Group members could communicate with two people. Since they had this kind of mobility, they seemed to get around more and thus spend more time. However, since the members of a circle group sent more messages, they could take advantage of more checkpoints and, thus, could locate and correct more of their errors.

Members of the circle group had more chance to participate and take responsibility. They were less dependent on one person since they could check with another member. Thus, they were more satisfied and happy. The leader (C) in the star also felt quite happy and satisfied, probably for the same reasons as the members of the circle pattern—C was given responsibility and had several sources of information and checkpoints. In essence, C was independent and powerful.

In summary, these experiments suggest that the mere structure of communication patterns can influence how people feel and act in terms of independence, security, and responsibility. This same structure also can influence the total operational efficiency of a group in terms of speed, accuracy, and adaptability. In essence, the structure seems to influence the way people feel in one direction and their speed and accuracy in another. Although the two communication patterns discussed have been described as if they were either/or structures, in reality, the design for an effective organization may need to incorporate both. For example, with an experienced staff, a manager might find it most appropriate to structure the communication pattern in a democratic, free-wheeling manner, as in the circle. However, with inexperienced personnel, the manager might find it appropriate to operate in a more autocratic manner, as in the star pattern. These groups may be at different levels of commitment, motivation, and ability to take responsibility, and, therefore, different kinds of communication patterns are needed.

Relationship between communication patterns and change strategies. The structure of communication patterns seems to have two significant relationships with the participative and directive change strategies discussed earlier. First, in implementing a change strategy, managers or leaders have to incorporate into the strategy the development of an appropriate communication pattern. In that sense, the unstructured democratic wheel pattern seems very compatible with the participative change cycle, while the structured, autocratic star pattern seems appropriate for the directive change cycle. In fact, the results of Bavelas's experiments with the circle and star patterns of communication seem to support the suggested advantages and disadvantages of the participative and directive change cycles; that is, the participative change cycle is slow, but tends to develop involvement and commitment; the directive change cycle is fast, but can create resentment and hostility.

Second, before implementing a change strategy in an organization or group, it is important for the change agent to know the present communication structure in operation. For example, if an organization has been run in a democratic manner in which the communication pattern did not favor the manager as a leader over any of the followers, a new manager should probably think twice before implementing a directive, coercive change. The structure of communication required of a directive change strategy would be alien to the already established communication pattern. The same warning applies to a manager attempting to implement change in a participative manner in an organization that for years has been organized with the manager in a strong leadership position. In such a situation, supervisors and staff members often learn to be more dependent and less responsible because the manager always seems to assume leadership. As a result, they may not be ready for a more open, democratic system at this time.

In conclusion, there is no one "best" strategy for implementing change in organizations. The strategy used—whether participative, directive, or some combination of both—depends on the situation. One variable that seems important to analyze in developing an appropriate change strategy is the present structure of communication patterns within the target group or organization.

Change Process

In examining change, Lewin identified three phases of the change process—unfreezing, changing, and refreezing.[9]

Unfreezing

The aim of unfreezing is to motivate and make the individual or the group ready to change. It is a thawing-out process in which the forces acting on individuals are rearranged so that now they see the need for change. According to Edgar H. Schein, when drastic unfreezing is necessary, the following common elements seem to be present: (1) the physical removal of the individuals being changed from the accustomed routines, sources of information, and social relationships; (2) the undermining and destruction of all social supports; (3) demeaning and humiliating experience to help individuals being changed to see their old attitudes or behavior as unworthy and thus to be motivated to change; (4) the consistent linking of reward with willingness to change and of punishment with unwillingness to change.[10]

In brief, unfreezing is the breaking down of the folkways, customs, and traditions of individuals—the old ways of doing things—so that they are ready to accept new alternatives. In terms of force field analysis, unfreezing may occur when either the driving forces are increased or the restraining forces that are resisting change are reduced.

Changing

Once individuals have become motivated to change, they are ready to be provided with new patterns of behavior. This process is most likely to occur by one of two mechanisms: identification and internalization.[11] *Identification* occurs when one or more models are provided in the environment—models from whom individuals can learn new behavior patterns by identifying with them and trying to become like them. *Internalization* occurs when individuals are placed in a situation in which new behaviors are demanded of them if they are to operate successfully in that situation. They learn these new behavior patterns not only because they are necessary for survival, but because of new high-strength needs induced by coping behavior.

> Internalization is a more common outcome in those influence settings where the direction of change is left more to the individual. The influence that occurs in programs such as Alcoholics Anonymous, in psychotherapy or counseling for hospitalized or incarcerated populations, in religious retreats, in human relations training of the kind pursued by the National Training Laboratories (1953), and in certain kinds of progressive education programs is more likely to occur through internalization or, at least, to lead ultimately to more internalization.[12]

Identification and internalization are not either/or courses of action, but effective change is often the result of combining the two into a strategy for change.

Force or compliance is sometimes discussed as another mechanism for inducing change.[13] It occurs when an individual is forced to change by the direct manipulation of rewards and punishment by someone in a power position. In this case, behavior appears to have changed when the change agent is present, but it is often dropped when supervision is removed. Thus, rather than discussing force as a mechanism of changing, we should think of it as a tool for unfreezing.

Refreezing

The process by which the newly acquired behavior comes to be integrated as patterned behavior into the individual's personality and/or ongoing significant emotional relationships is referred to as *refreezing*. As Schein contends, if the new behavior has been internalized while being learned, "this has automatically facilitated refreezing because it has been fitted naturally into the individual's personality. If it has been learned through identification, it will persist only so long as the target's relationship with the original influence model persists, unless new surrogate models are found or social support and reinforcement is obtained for expressions of the new attitudes."[14]

This highlights how important it is for an individual engaged in a change process to be in an environment that is continually reinforcing the desired change. The effect of many training programs has been short-lived when the person returns to an environment that does not reinforce the new patterns or, even worse, is hostile toward them.

What we are concerned about in refreezing is that the new behavior does not get extinguished over time. To keep this from happening, reinforcement must be scheduled in an effective way. There seem to be two main reinforcement schedules: continuous and intermittent.[15] As we discussed in chapter 10, with continuous reinforcement, the individuals learn the new behavior quickly, but if their environment changes to one of nonreinforcement, extinction can be expected to take place relatively soon. With intermittent reinforcement, extinction is much slower because the individuals have been conditioned to go for periods of time without any reinforcement. Thus, for fast learning, a continuous reinforcement schedule should be used. But once the individual has learned the new pattern, a switch to intermittent reinforcement should ensure a long-lasting change.

Updated Lewin Model of Change

Lynn A. Isabella, a professor of management at Southern Methodist University, developed a model of how managers interpret organizational events as change occurs and linked this model to Lewin's change process (see Figure 15-6). Isabella's model[16] describes four distinct stages; movement from one stage to another is initiated by a trigger event and the manager's personalization of that trigger.

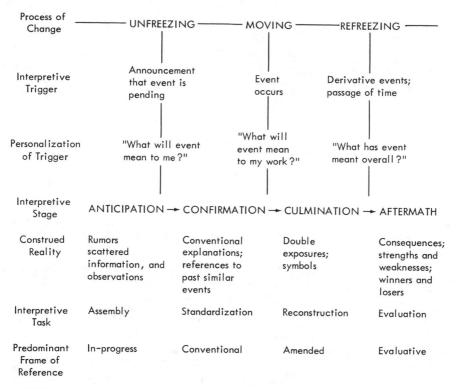

Process of Change	UNFREEZING ——————→ MOVING ——————→ REFREEZING ——————			
Interpretive Trigger	Announcement that event is pending	Event occurs	Derivative events; passage of time	
Personalization of Trigger	"What will event mean to me?"	"What will event mean to my work?"	"What has event meant overall?"	
Interpretive Stage	ANTICIPATION →	CONFIRMATION →	CULMINATION →	AFTERMATH
Construed Reality	Rumors scattered information, and observations	Conventional explanations; references to past similar events	Double exposures; symbols	Consequences; strengths and weaknesses; winners and losers
Interpretive Task	Assembly	Standardization	Reconstruction	Evaluation
Predominant Frame of Reference	In-progress	Conventional	Amended	Evaluative

FIGURE 15-6 Evolving interpretations of key events

During the stage of *anticipation,* managers collect rumors and scattered bits of information into a cohesive frame of reference. Fear and speculation run rampant. A definite announcement that the change event will occur acts as a trigger to move managers from anticipation to confirmation—*unfreezing.*

In *confirmation,* the change event is standardized and placed into a conventional frame of reference. Managers interpret events in this stage based on understandings of how things have worked in the past, and through analogies to similar events. As the change process is actually experienced, the second trigger, people are shifted into a state where change is necessary and required—*moving.*

Managers amend their view of an event during the stage of *culmination.* Individual understanding occurs as managers interpret changes by comparing before-and-after mental pictures of their organization or of other organizations which have undergone a similar type of change. Managers also refer frequently to the symbolism of certain actions, gestures, and decisions by the CEO and senior management team. As managers see small events that signal the change is permanent, they are triggered into the final stage of change—*refreezing*.

In the stage of *aftermath*, the change event is evaluated and winners and losers are identified. Positive and negative consequences of the change are discussed and become part of the managers' frame of reference.

The model suggests that leaders can view resistance to change not as an obstacle, but as a part of the mental process people experience as they undergo change and personalize the event. "In changing situations, perhaps it is not so much that people want to hold on to what they have as that they are simply questioning what the change will mean to them."[17] The effective leader can assist followers through the change process by managing rumors, communicating concrete information, and providing symbols to demonstrate what is important to the organization.

Change Process—Some Examples

To see the change process in operation, several examples can be cited.

In 1981, partial deregulation of the banking industry led to major changes at BankAmerica Corporation.[18] Alterations in banking regulations, fierce competition in the industry, and an unstable world economy led to serious problems in the company. In 1986, BankAmerica was losing money (net loss, $1.8 billion from 1985 to 1987); payment of dividends on common stock had been suspended after November 1985; First Interstate Bankcorp was threatening a hostile takeover; and regulators were insisting that BankAmerica's deteriorating capital situation be rapidly corrected.

In the years since 1986, BankAmerica has made a dramatic turnaround and has returned to profitability through a planned program of management-led change. The five fundamental steps BankAmerica Corporation took are:

1. Selected a management team of proven winners and spread the message that corporate survival depended on how well each job was done.
2. Reassessed the entire business and restructured the organization of the bank and its approach to banking.
3. Focused on generating maximum value for shareholders.
4. Managed the business to produce immediate and positive results.
5. "Communicated—credibly, constantly, consistently, and confidently—both inside and outside the organization."[19]

In addition, BankAmerica developed two strategic business objectives to guide the corporate restructuring. The company focused on becoming the major provider of retail and wholesale banking services in the western United States. This goal required the company to concentrate on one area of the nation and on specific banking services. The second objective focused on becoming a top-tier global wholesale bank serving multinational corporations, governments, and other global financial institutions. Global retail banking services were eliminated.

Through careful planning and implementation of a corporate-wide plan for change and through careful attention to goals and objectives, BankAmerica was able to successfully reverse a deteriorating situation and retake a leadership position in the banking industry.

Another example of the change process in operation follows.

A college basketball coach recruited Bob Anderson, a six-foot seven-inch center, from a small town in a rural area where six feet seven inches was a good height for a center. This fact, combined with his deadly turnaround jump shot, made Anderson the rage of his league and enabled him to average close to thirty points a game.

Recognizing that six feet seven inches is small for a college center, the coach hoped that he could make Anderson a forward, moving him inside only when they were playing a double pivot. One of the things the coach was concerned about, however, was how Anderson, when used in the pivot, could get his jump shot off when he came up against other players ranging in height from six feet ten inches to seven feet. He felt that Anderson would have to learn to shoot a hook shot, which is much harder to block, if he were going to have scoring potential against this kind of competition. The approach that many coaches would use to solve this problem would probably be as follows: On the first day of practice the coach would welcome Anderson and then explain the problem to him as he had analyzed it. As a solution, he would probably ask Anderson to start to work with the varsity center, Steve Cram, who was six feet ten inches tall and had an excellent hook. "Steve can help you start working on that new shot, Bob," the coach would say. Anderson's reaction to this interchange might be one of resentment, and he would go over and work with Cram only because of the coach's position power. After all, he might think to himself, "Who does he think he is? I've been averaging close to thirty points a game for three years now and the first day I show up here the coach wants me to learn a new shot." So he may start to work with Cram reluctantly, concentrating on the hook shot only when the coach is looking, but taking his favorite jump shot when not being observed. Anderson is by no means unfrozen, or ready to learn to shoot another way.

Let us look at another approach the coach might use to solve this problem. Suppose that on the first day of practice he sets up a scrimmage between the varsity and the freshmen. Before he starts the scrimmage he takes big Steve Cram, the varsity center, aside and tells him, "Steve, we have this new freshman named Anderson who has real potential to be a fine ball player. What I'd like you to do today, though, is not to worry about scoring or rebounding—just make sure every time Anderson goes up for a shot you make him eat it. I want him to see that he will have to learn to shoot some other shots if he is to survive against guys like you." So when the scrimmage starts, the first time Anderson gets the ball and turns around to shoot, Cram leaps up and stuffs the ball right down his throat. Time after time this occurs. Soon Anderson starts to engage in some coping behavior, trying to fall away from the basket, shooting from the side of his head rather than from the front in an attempt to get his shot off. After the scrimmage, Anderson comes off the court dejected. The coach says, "What's wrong, Bob?" Bob replies, "I don't know, coach, I just can't seem to get my shot off against a man as big as Cram. What do you think I should do, Coach?" he asks. "Well, Bob, why don't you go over and start working with Steve on a hook shot. I think you'll find it much harder to block. And with your shooting eye I don't think it will take long for you to learn." How do you think Anderson would feel about working with Cram now? He'd probably be enthusiastic and ready to learn. Being placed in a situation in which he learns for himself that he has a problem will go a long way in unfreezing Anderson from his past patterns of behavior and preparing him for making the attempt at identification. Now he'll be ready for identification. He has had an opportunity to internalize his problem and is ready to work with Steve Cram.

So often the leader who has knowledge of an existing problem forgets that until the people involved recognize the problem as their own, it is going to be much more difficult to produce a change in their behavior. Internalization and identification are not either/or alternatives, but they can be parts of developing specific change strategies appropriate to the situation.

Another example of the change process in operation can be seen in the military, particularly in the induction phase. In a few short months they are able to mold these soldiers into an effective combat team. This is not an accident. Let us look at some of the processes that help accomplish this.

The most dramatic and harsh aspect of the training is the unfreezing phase. All of Schein's four elements are present. Let us look at some specific examples of these elements in operation.

1. The soldiers are *physically removed from their accustomed routines, sources of information, and social relationships.*
2. *The undermining and destruction of social supports* is one of the DI's (drill instructor's) tasks. "Using their voices and the threat of extra PT (physical training), the DI . . . must shock the recruit out of the emotional stability of home, . . . girl friend, or school."[20]
3. *Demeaning and humiliating experiences* are commonplace during the first two weeks of the training as the DIs help the soldiers *see themselves as unworthy and thus motivated to change* into what the DIs want a soldier to be.
4. Throughout the training there is *consistent linking of reward with willingness to change and of punishment with unwillingness to change.*

While the soldiers go through a severe unfreezing process, they quickly move to the changing phase, first identifying with the DI and then emulating informal leaders as they develop. "Toward the end of the third week a break occurs. What one DI calls 'that five percent— the slow, fat, dumb, or difficult' have been dropped. The remaining [soldiers] have emerged from their first week vacuum with one passionate desire—to stay with their platoon at all costs."[21]

Internalization takes place when the recruits, through their forced interactions, develop different high-strength needs. "Fear of the DI gives way to respect, and survival evolves into achievement toward the end of training. 'I learned I had more guts than I imagined' is a typical comment."[22]

Since the group tends to stay together throughout the entire program, it serves as a positive reinforcer, which can help to refreeze the new behavior.

The theories discussed should help a person interested in change determine some alternative solutions to the identified problem(s) and suggest appropriate implementation strategies. For example, let us reexamine the case of our enthusiastic school administrators who wanted to humanize the schools in their system and change the predominant teaching approach from teacher-centered to child-centered. As we suggested, if they had done a force field analysis, they would have realized that the restraining forces working against this change far outweighed the driving forces in power and frequency. The analysis would have suggested that a directive, coercive change strategy would have been ineffective for implementing change since significant unfreezing had to occur before the restraining forces against the change could have been immobilized or turned into driving forces. Thus, a participative change effort probably would have been appropriately aimed at reeducating the restraining forces by exposing them in a nonthreatening way (through two-way communication patterns) to new knowledge directed at changing their attitudes and eventually their behavior.

While this participative reeducative approach might be appropriate, it also must be recognized that it will be time consuming (four to seven years). The superintendent and his assistant just might not be willing to devote that kind of time and effort to this change project. If they are not, then they could decide not to enter that school system, or, to charge on in a coercive, directive manner and be ready for the consequences. Or they could choose their action from a number of other alternatives that may have been generated at this time.

Change Process—Recommended Action

After suggesting various alternative solutions and appropriate implementation strategies, a leader or manager interested in change should anticipate the probable consequences (both positive and negative) of taking each of the alternative actions. *Remember* (1) Unless there is a high probability that a desired consequence will occur and that consequence will be the same as the conditions that would exist if the problem were not present, then you have not solved the problem or changed the situation. (2) The ultimate solution to a problem (the change effort) may not be possible overnight, and, therefore, interim goals must be set along the path to the final goal (the solving of the problem).

The end result of analysis (which includes determining alternative solutions) should be some recommended action that hopefully will decrease the discrepancy between the actual and the ideal. Although action is the end result, you must remember that action based on superficial analysis may be worse than taking no action at all. Too frequently, people want to hurry on to the action phase of a problem before they have adequately analyzed the situation. The importance of the analysis part cannot be given too much emphasis—a good analysis frequently makes the action obvious.

The "A Victory" Model

The influential leader does not initiate and implement the change process in a vacuum. Change is accomplished through the careful choreography of many parts. Thorough consideration and review of the factors influencing successful change can have a positive impact on whether the proposed change will occur. The acronym "A Victory"[23] focuses attention on the factors important to successful implementation of change and serves as a review of the ideas presented in this chapter.

A = Ability

What are the abilities and inabilities of the organization and its members with respect to change? Are the necessary resources and capabilities available?

V = Values

How compatible are management's attitudes and practices with the values, cultural norms, and attitudes required by the change?

I = Idea/Information

Complex information about the proposed change should be provided as simply as possible. The reason and need for the change should be readily understood by all.

C = Circumstances

What factors in the organization affect the acceptance and implementation of the change?

T = Timing

How ready is the organization to implement the proposed change? Are current circumstances to your advantage?

O = Obligation

Do relevant decision makers and "champions" perceive the need for change? Are they ready and committed?

R = Resistance

What is the level of resistance to change? How can you overcome or manage this resistance?

Y = Yield

What are the benefits of the change for those who are asked to approve it or implement it? Do measurable benefits facilitate the implementation of the change process?

MANAGING INTERGROUP CONFLICT

One of the problems that often occurs during a change effort is intergroup conflict. A total organization is really a composite of its various working units or groups. The important thing for organizational accomplishment—whether these groups be formal or informal—is that these groups either perceive their goals as being the same as the goals of the organization or, although different, see their own goals being satisfied as a direct result of working for the goals of the organization.

On occasion, groups or parts of an organization come into conflict. The atmosphere *between* groups can affect the total productivity of the organization. According to Schein,

> this problem exists because as groups become more committed to their own goals and norms, they are likely to become competitive with one another and seek to undermine their rivals' activities, thereby becoming a liability to the organization as a whole. The overall problem, then, is how to establish high-productive, *collaborative* intergroup relations.[24]

Consequences of Group Competition

Sherif was the first to study systematically the consequences of intergroup conflict.[25] His original studies and more recent replications have found the effects of competition on individuals consistent to the extent that they can readily be described.[26] As Schein reports, some interesting phenomena occur both *within* and *between* each competing group.[27]

During competition, each group becomes more cohesive; internal differences are forgotten for the moment as increased loyalty takes over. The group atmosphere becomes more task-oriented as group accomplishment becomes paramount. The leadership shifts more toward an autocratic style as the group becomes more tolerant of some one's taking the lead. The group becomes more organized and highly structured, and with this demands more loyalty and conformity from its members in order to present a "solid front."

At the same time that these phenomena are occurring *within* the group, the relationship *between* the groups has some common characteristic. Each group starts to see the other as the enemy and distorts perceptions of reality—recognizing only their own strengths and the weaknesses of the other group. Hostility toward the other group increases, while communication decreases. This makes it easier to maintain negative feelings and more difficult to correct false perceptions. If the groups are forced to interact, as at a bargaining table, neither one really listens to the other, but only listens for cues that support its arguments.

Schein stresses that while competition and the responses it generates may be very useful to a group in making it more effective and achievement motivated, "the same factors which improve intragroup effectiveness may have negative consequences for intergroup effectiveness."[28] Labor-management disputes are cases in point because the more these parties perceive themselves as competitors, the more difficult they find it to resolve their differences.

When win-lose confrontations occur between two groups or teams, even though there eventually is a winner, the loser (if it is not a clear-cut win) is not convinced that it lost, and intergroup tension is higher than before the competition began. If the win is clear-cut, the winner often loses its edge, becomes complacent, and is less interested in goal accomplishment. This loser in this case often develops internal conflict while trying to discover the cause of the loss or someone to blame. If reevaluation takes place, however, the group may reorganize and become more cohesive and effective.[29]

When the negative consequences of intergroup conflict outweigh the gains, management seeks ways to reduce this intergroup tension. As Schein suggests, "the basic strategy of reducing conflict, therefore, is to find goals upon which groups can agree and to reestablish valid communication between the groups."[30] He contends that this strategy can be implemented by any combination of the following: *locating a common enemy, inventing a negotiation strategy which brings subgroups of the competing groups into interaction with each other,* and *locating a superordinate goal.*

Preventing Intergroup Conflict

Since it is difficult to reduce intergroup conflict once it has developed, it is desirable to prevent its occurrence in the first place. This might be done in several ways. First of all, management should emphasize the contributions to total goals rather than the accomplishment of subgroup goals. Second, an attempt should be made to increase the frequency of communication and interaction between groups and develop a reward system for groups who help each other. Third, whenever possible individuals should be given experiences in a wide range of departments to broaden their base for empathy and understanding of intergroup problems.[31]

Collaborative organizations often appear to have an abundance of task-relevant conflict, which improves overall effectiveness. This may occur because under these conditions individuals trust each other and are frank and open in sharing information and ideas. In competitive situations characterized by win-lose confrontations, observations may suggest lower levels of open conflict, since total interaction is significantly less and each group is committed to withholding its resources and information from the other groups, thus lowering the potential for overall organizational effectiveness.

Blake, Shepard, and Mouton Model

According to Blake, Shepard, and Mouton,[32] there are three attitudinal sets or basic assumptions that people can have toward intergroup conflict: (1) conflict is inevitable, agreement is impossible; (2) conflict is not inevitable, yet agreement is impossible; and (3) although there is conflict, agreement is possible. These attitudinal sets will lead to predictable behavior depending on the way the people involved see the "stakes"; that is, the extent to which they see the conflict as important or having value.

As illustrated in Figure 15-7,[33] if people think that conflict is inevitable and agreement is impossible, their behavior will range from being passive to very active. When the stakes are low, they will tend to be passive and willing to let fate (like a flip of a coin) decide the conflict. When the stakes are moderate, they will permit a third-party judgment to decide the conflict. And, finally, when the stakes are high, they will actively engage in a win-lose confrontation or power struggle.

FIGURE 15-7 **The three basic assumptions toward intergroup disagreement and their management.**

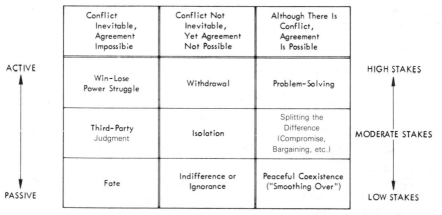

Source: By Robert R. Blake, Herbert A. Shepard & Jane S. Mouton. Houston: Gulf Publishing Company, p. 13. Copyright © 1964 by Scientific Methods, Inc. Reproduced by permission of the owners.

If people think that conflict is not inevitable, yet if it does occur then agreement is impossible, they will be passive and indifferent if the stakes are low. When the stakes are moderate, they will isolate themselves from such a conflict situation. And when the stakes are high and they find themselves actively involved, they will eventually withdraw.

If people think that although there is conflict, agreement is possible, they will be passive and attempt to smooth over the situation when the stakes are low. When the stakes are moderate, they will engage in bargaining or some form of negotiation. And if the stakes are high, they will actively engage in problem solving.

In using this model in consulting, we contend that if you have some knowledge of the attitudes people have about a potential conflict and what the stakes are for them, you can predict their behavior, and vice versa. If you observe the behavior of people during a conflict, you can usually predict their assumptions about conflict in this situation. For example, if you see people actively engaging in a win-lose power struggle, you can predict that the stakes in this conflict are high and that they think agreement is impossible. At the same time, if you learn that people think that a certain conflict is inevitable but agreement is impossible and the stakes are high in this situation, you can predict that if the conflict occurs the situation will deteriorate to a win-lose power struggle. If such a win-lose power struggle occurs, one possible intervention might be to attempt initially to lower the stakes so that the conflicting parties will at least permit a third-party intervention. When that intervention is made, efforts can be directed toward changing the assumptions of the people involved to "although there is conflict, agreement is possible." When that is done, an attempt to increase commitment again will tend to move them into an active problem-solving mode.

ORGANIZATIONAL GROWTH

Our discussions in this chapter have focused on changing or working on problems in organizations that are already established. How different are the issues in new or emerging organizations? A developmental theory developed by Larry E. Greiner[34] is helpful in examining growing organizations.

Greiner argues that growing organizations move through five relatively calm periods of *evolution*, each of which ends with a period of crisis and revolution. According to Greiner, "each evolutionary period is characterized by the dominant *management* style used to achieve growth, while each revolutionary period is characterized by the dominant *management* problem that must be solved before growth will continue."[35]

As illustrated in Figure 15-8, the first stage of organizational growth is called *creativity*. This stage is dominated by the founders of the organization, and the emphasis is on creating both a product and a market. These "founders are usually technically or entrepreneurially oriented, and they disdain management activities; their physical and mental energies are absorbed entirely in making and selling a new product."[36] But as the organization grows, management problems occur that cannot be handled through informal communication and dedication. "Thus the founders find themselves burdened with unwanted management responsibilities . . . and conflicts between the harried leaders grow more intense."[37]

FIGURE 15-8   Greiner's five stages of growth

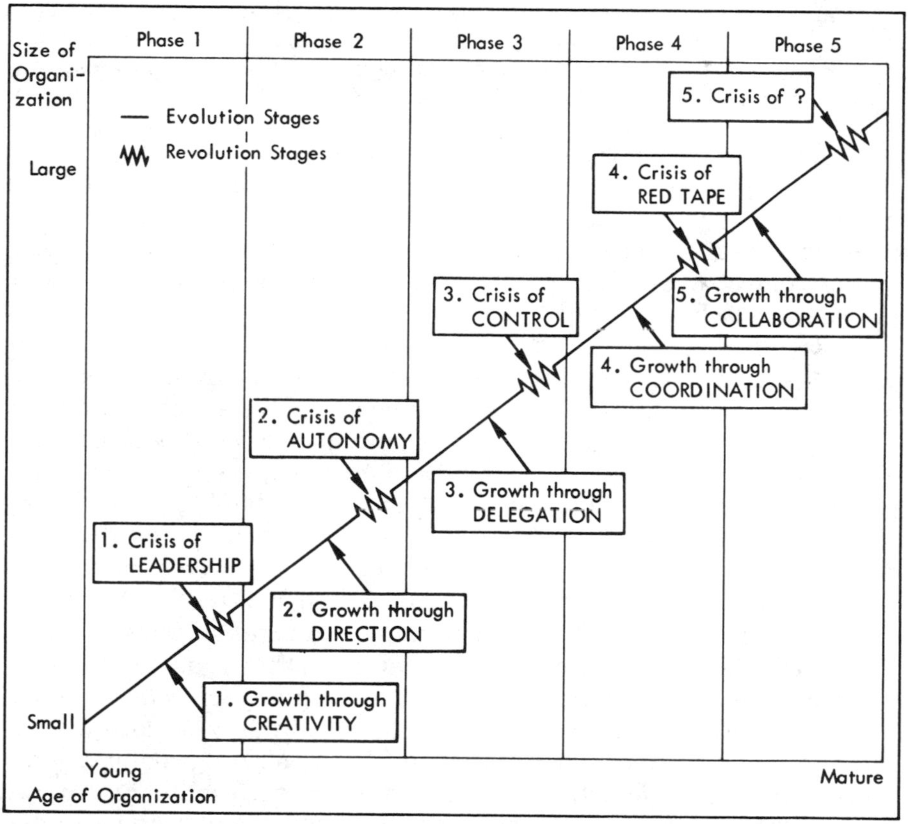

Source: Larry E. Greiner, *"Evolution and Revolution as Organizations Grow,"* Harvard Business Review, July–August 1972, p. 41.

It is at this point that the *crisis of leadership* occurs and the first revolutionary period begins. "Who is going to lead the organization out of confusion and solve the management problems confronting the organization?" The solution is to locate and install a strong manager "who is acceptable to the founders and who can pull the organization together."[38] This leads to the next evolutionary period—growth through *direction.*

During this phase the new manager and key staff "take most of the responsibility for instituting direction, while lower level supervisors are treated more as functional specialists than autonomous decision-making managers."[39] As lower level managers demand more autonomy, this eventually leads to the next revolutionary period—the *crisis of autonomy.* The solution to this crisis is usually greater delegation.

> Yet it is difficult for top managers who were previously successful at being directive to give up responsibility. Moreover, lower level managers are not accustomed to making decisions for themselves. As a result numerous [organizations] flounder during this revolutionary period, adhering to centralized methods, while lower level employees grow more disenchanted and leave the organization.[40]

When an organization gets to the growth stage of *delegation,* it usually begins to develop a decentralized organizational structure, which heightens motivation at the lower levels. Yet, eventually, the next crisis begins to evolve as the top managers "sense that they are losing control over a highly diversified field operation . . . freedom breeds a parochial attitude."[41]

The *crisis of control* often results in a return to centralization, which is now inappropriate and creates resentment and hostility among those who had been given freedom. A more effective solution tends to initiate the next evolutionary period—the *coordination* stage. This period is characterized by the use of formal systems for achieving greater coordination with top management as the "watchdog." Yet most coordination systems eventually get carried away and result in the next revolutionary period—the *crisis of red tape.* This crisis most often occurs when "the organization has become too large and complex to be managed through formal programs and rigid systems."[42]

If the crisis of red tape is to be overcome, the organization must move to the next evolutionary period—the phase of *collaboration.* While the coordination phase was managed through formal systems and procedures, the collaboration phase "emphasizes greater spontaneity in management action through teams and the skillful confrontation of interpersonal differences. Social control and self-discipline take over from formal control."[43]

Greiner is not certain what the next revolution will be, but he anticipates that it will "center around the 'psychological saturation' of employees who grow emotionally and physically exhausted by the intensity of teamwork and the heavy pressure for innovative solutions."[44]

It is felt that to overcome and even avoid the various crises, managers could attempt to move through the evolutionary periods more consistently with the sequencing that Situational Leadership would suggest–direction to coordination to collaboration to delegation–rather than the ordering depicted by Greiner.

ORGANIZATIONAL DEVELOPMENT

Throughout this chapter we have been discussing various frameworks that managers may find useful in helping them initiate change in their organizations. The need for managers to be able to plan and implement change in the future is a given, particularly as people begin to demand that organizations be more than just a place to "pick up a pay check." As Richard Beckhard views it, the challenge of change facing managers is:

> How can we optimally mobilize human resources and energy to achieve the organization's mission and, at the same time, maintain a viable, growing organization of people whose personal needs for self-worth, growth and satisfaction are significantly met at work?[45]

An attempted response to this dilemma and the corresponding need for changes in the way organizations operate has been the growing field of organizational development (O.D.).

Organizational Effectiveness and O.D.

In defining O.D. from our perspective, it is important to remember, as we discussed in Chapter 6, that the effectiveness of a particular organization depends on its goals and objectives. Thus, we do not accept a set of normative goals that are right for all organizations, as many O.D. theorists and practitioners seem to do.[46] As Bennis suggests, the philosophy and values of O.D. change agents provide the "guidelines and directions for *what* will be undertaken in an [O.D.] effort and *how* the program will evolve and be sustained."[47] With the humanistic values that are communicated by O.D. practitioners and theorists, it is not hard to understand why the goals of organizational development are generally reported as aiming toward an open, trusting type of organization and O.D. interventions seem to stress the use of collaborative or interpersonal strategies for change. As Bennis argues:

I have yet to see an organization development program that uses an intervention strategy other than an interpersonal one, and this is serious when one considers that the most pivotal strategies of change in our society are political, legal and technological.[48]

A Problem with Organizational Development

If it is true that most O.D. consultants and practitioners use collaborative or interpersonal strategies of change and, thus, almost always concentrate on the "people variable" in helping organizations, it becomes clear why there are more O.D. intervention failures than successes. First, as we have suggested throughout this chapter, using the same strategy for change all the time will lead to effective change in some situations, but in many others might be ineffective. Thus, there is no one best strategy of change. Effective O.D. interventions depend on diagnosing the situation and determining the highest probability success approach for the particular environment.

Second, if one analyzes the interpersonal change strategy so often used in O.D. interventions, one can see that it tends to be related to high relationship–low task (S3). According to Situational Leadership, this interpersonal change strategy would be most appropriate in organizations in which members tend to have moderate to high levels of readiness; that is, they are able to take responsibility for implementing the desired change, but just need someone to help facilitate it. Such an organization, as we discussed in Chapter 3, would probably be classified by Argyris as a YB organization. And yet as Argyris[49] contends, most organizations are not operating in YB patterns, but are more typically XA organizations. These organizations, in terms of Situational Leadership, would be at low levels of readiness since they are not only unable to direct their own change, but are often even unwilling. Thus, one of the greatest challenges facing the field of O.D. is developing strategies to move organizations from XA to YB and from low levels of readiness (in terms of implementing their own change) to higher levels. As a result, O.D. practitioners and change agents need to develop their skills in structured, directive change strategies, as well as to maintain their skills in interpersonal, participative change strategies so that the movement toward "self-renewing" organizations can begin with some hope of success.

IMPACT OF CHANGE ON THE TOTAL SYSTEM

In Chapter 1, the importance of combining the social and the technical into a unified social systems concept was stressed. As Robert H. Guest argues:

> On his part the social scientist often makes the error of concentrating on human motivation and group behavior without fully accounting for the technical environment which circumscribes, even determines, the role which the actors play. Motivation, group structure, interaction processes, authority — none of these abstractions of behavior takes place in a technological vacuum.[50]

A dramatic example of the consequences of introducing technical change and ignoring its consequences on the social system is the case of the introduction of the steel axe to a group of Australian aborigines.[51]

This tribe remained considerably isolated, both geographically and socially, from influence of Western cultures. In fact, their only contact was an Anglican mission established in the adjacent territory. The polished stone axe was traditionally a basic part of the tribe's technology. Used by men, women, and children, the stone axe was vital to the subsistence economy. But more than that, it was actually a key to the smooth running of the social system; it defined interpersonal relationships and was a symbol of masculinity and male superiority. "Only an adult male could make and own a stone axe; a woman or a child had to ask his permission to obtain one."[52]

The Anglican mission, in an effort to help improve the situation of the aborigines, introduced the steel axe, a product of European technology. It was given indiscriminately to men, women, and children. Because the tool was more efficient than the stone axe, it was readily accepted; but it produced severe repercussions unforeseen by the missionaries or the tribe. As Stephen R. Cain reports:

> The adult male was unable to make the steel axe and no longer had to make the stone axe. Consequently, his exclusive axe-making ability was no longer a necessary or desirable skill, and his status as sole possessor and dispenser of a vital element of technology was lost. The most drastic overall result was that traditional values, beliefs, and attitudes were unintentionally undermined.[53]

The focus in this book has been on the management of human resources, and, as a result, we have spent little time on how technical change can have an impact on the total system. Our attempt in this example was to reiterate that an organization is an "open social system"; that is, all aspects of an organization are interrelated; a change in any part of an organization may have an impact on other parts or on the organization itself. Thus, a proposed change in any part of an organization must be carefully assessed in terms of its likely impact on the rest of the organization.

NOTES

1. Kurt Lewin, *Field Theory in Social Science,* D. Cartwright, ed. (New York: Harper & Brothers, 1951).
2. James Brian Quinn, *Strategies for Change: Logical Incrementalism,* (Homewood, Ill.; Irwin, 1980).
3. James Brian Quinn, "Strategic Change: 'Logical Incrementalism,' " *Sloan Management Review,* 30, no. 4 (Summer 1989), pp. 45–59.
4. Paul Watzlawick, John Weakland, and Richard Fisch, *Change: Principles of Problem Formation and Problem Resolution* (New York: Norton, 1974).
5. Alan D. Meyer, Geoffrey R. Brooks, and James B. Goes, "Environmental Jolts and Industry Revolutions: Organizational Responses to Discontinuous Change," *Strategic Management Journal,* 11 (1990), pp. 93–110.
6. Paul Hersey and Kenneth H. Blanchard, "Change and the Use of Power," *Training and Development Journal,* January 1972. See also Chris Argyris, *Strategy, Change and Defensive Routines* (Cambridge: Ballenger Publishing, 1985).
7. Kenneth H. Blanchard and Paul Hersey, "The Importance of Communication Patterns in Implementing Change Strategies," *Journal of Research and Development in Education,* 6, no. 4 (Summer 1973), pp. 66–75.
8. Alex Bavelas, "Communication Patterns in Task-Oriented Groups" in Dorwin Cartwright and Alvin Zander, eds., *Group Dynamics: Research and Theory* (Evanston, Ill.: Row, Peterson, 1953).
9. Kurt Lewin, "Frontiers in Group Dynamics: Concept, Method, and Reality in Social Science; Social Equilibria and Social Change," *Human Relations,* I, No. 1 (June 1974), pp. 5–41. See also Kenneth D. Beene et al., eds. *Laboratory Method of Changing and Learning Theory and Application* (Palo Alto, Calif.: Science and Behavior Books, 1975); Amitai Etzioni and Richard Remp, *Technological Shortcuts to Social Change* (New York: Russell Sage Foundation, 1973).
10. Edgar H. Schein, "Management Development as a Process of Influence," in David R. Hampton, *Behavioral Concepts in Management* (Belmont, Calif.: Dickinson Publishing, 1968), p. 110. Reprinted from *Industrial Management Review,* II, No. 2 (May 1961) pp. 59–77.
11. The mechanisms are taken from H. C. Kelman, "Compliance, Identification and Internalization: Three Processes of Attitude Change," *Conflict Resolution,* (1958), pp. 51–60.
12. Schein, "Management Development," p. 112.
13. Kelman discussed compliance as a third mechanism for attitude change.
14. Schein, "Management Development," p. 112.
15. See C. B. Ferster and B. F. Skinner, *Schedules of Reinforcement* (New York: Appleton-Century-Crofts, 1957).
16. Lynn A. Isabella, "Evolving Interpretations as a Change Unfolds: How Managers Construe Key Organizational Events," *Academy of Management Journal,* 33, no. 1 (1990), pp. 7–41.
17. *Ibid.,* p. 34.
18. A. W. Clausen, "Strategic Issues in Managing Change: The Turnaround at BankAmerica Corporation," *California Management Review,* Winter 1990, pp. 98–105.
19. *Ibid.,* p. 100.
20. "Marine Machine," *Look Magazine,* August 12, 1969.
21. *Ibid.*
22. *Ibid.*

23. Vincent P. Barabba and Gerald Zaltman, "The Inquiry Center," *Planning Review,* 19, no. 2 (March–April 1991), pp. 4–9, 47–48.
24. Edgar H. Schein, *Organizational Psychology* (Englewood Cliffs, N. J.: Prentice Hall, 1965), p. 80.
25. M. Sherif, O. J. Harvey, B. J. White, W. R. Hood, and Carolyn Sherif, *Intergroup Conflict and Cooperation: The Robbers Cave Experiment* (Norman, Okla.: Book Exchange, 1961).
26. Robert R. Blake and Jane S. Mouton, "Reactions to Intergroup Competition under Win-Lose Conditions," *Management Science,* 7 (1961), pp. 420–35.
27. Schein, *Organizational Psychology,* p. 81.
28. *Ibid.*
29. *Ibid.,* p. 82.
30. *Ibid.,* p. 83.
31. *Ibid.,* p. 85.
32. Robert R. Blake, Herbert Shepard, and Jane S. Mouton, *Managing Intergroup Conflict in Industry* (Houston: Gulf Publishing, 1964). See also Robert R. Blake and Jane S. Mouton, *Solving Costly Organizational Conflicts: Achieving Intergroup Trust, Cooperation, and Teamwork* (San Francisco: Jossey-Bass, 1984); Alan C. Filley, *Interpersonal Conflict Resolution* (Glenview, Ill.: Scott, Foresman, 1975); Rensis Likert and Jane G. Likert, *New Ways of Managing Conflict* (New York: McGraw-Hill, 1976).
33. *Ibid.,* p. 13. Minor changes made in the figure but major change in the figure title so it is more consistent with the way we use the model in consulting.
34. Larry E. Greiner, "Evolution and Revolution as Organizations Grow," *Harvard Business Review,* July–August 1972, pp. 37–46. See also Larry E. Greiner and Robert O. Metzger, *Consulting to Management* (Englewood Cliffs, N. J.: Prentice Hall, 1983); Jack R. Gibb, *A New View of Personal and Organizational Development* (La Jolla, Calif.: Omicron Press, 1978).
35. *Ibid.,* p. 40.
36. *Ibid.,* p. 42.
37. *Ibid.*
38. *Ibid.*
39. *Ibid.*
40. *Ibid.,* p. 43.
41. *Ibid.*
42. *Ibid.*
43. *Ibid.*
44. *Ibid.,* p. 44
45. Richard Beckhard, *Organization Development: Strategies and Models* (Reading, Mass.: Addison-Wesley, 1969), p. 3.
46. Warren G. Bennis, *Organization Development: Its Nature, Origins, and Prospects* (Reading, Mass.: Addison-Wesley, 1969) p. 13. See also Warren G. Bennis, *The Planning of Change* (New York: Harper & Row, 1985); Warren G. Bennis, *Beyond Bureaucracy: Essays on the Development and Evolution of Human Organization* (New York: McGraw-Hill, 1973).
47. *Ibid.*
48. Bennis, "Editorial," *Journal of Applied Behavioral Science,* 4, No. 2 (1968), p. 228.
49. Chris Argyris, *Management and Organization Development: The Path From XA to YB* (New York: McGraw-Hill, 1971).
50. Robert H. Guest, *Organizational Change: The Effect of Successful Leadership* (Homewood, Ill.: Irwin, Dorsey Press, 1964), p. 4. See also Robert H. Guest, Paul Hersey, and Kenneth Blanchard, *Organizational Change through Effective Leadership,* 2nd ed. (Englewood Cliffs, N. J.: Prentice Hall, 1986); Stanley E. Seashore, ed., *Assessing Organizational Change: A Guide to Methods, Measures, and Practices* (New York: Wiley, 1983).
51. Lauriston Sharp, "Steel Axes for Stone Age Australians," in *Human Problems in Technology Changes,* ed. Edward H. Spicer (New York: Russell Sage Foundation, 1952), pp. 69–94.
52. Stephen R. Cain, "Anthropology and Change," taken from *Growth and Change,* University of Kentucky, I, No. 3 (July 1970).
53. *Ibid.*

16

Implementing Situational Leadership:
Managing People to Perform

This is the first in a series of chapters that builds upon or uses significant aspects of Situational Leadership together with One Minute Management in bottom-line approaches to managing people to perform. We emphasize bottom line because regardless of how a leadership or management concept might appear to be initially, the most fundamental issue is *does it contribute to organizational productivity*. This is what we mean by effective management.

Our approach in these chapters is to draw upon some of the most significant contributions to effective management in recent years, using as the key points of focus Situational Leadership and One Minute Management. In this chapter, we will begin with a strategic model, the Satellite Model of Organizational Performance, and then follow up with several tactical or operational approaches to management. The first, the ACHIEVE model, will be presented in this chapter. The next two chapters, 17 and 18, will use the powerful insights of One Minute Management. Chapter 19 will focus on important contributions to decision making and building commitments. While the approaches in these chapters may differ in terminology and in specific areas of emphasis, they all are related to Situational Leadership and the achievement of organizational productivity through effective leadership and management.

ORGANIZATIONAL PERFORMANCE

We need to remind ourselves again through a strategic model that organizational performance is the product of many factors, as shown in Figure 16-1, Satellite Model of Organizational Performance.[1] This model identifies several of the most important factors, including organizational structure, knowledge, nonhuman resources, strategic positioning, and human process. A strategy is a broad integrated plan of action to accomplish organizational goals; in our frame of reference, the goal of improving human productivity. Because a strategy is an integrated plan, you will note that all of the factors or variables are interrelated. You should also note that all of the factors contribute to performance, which is defined in the model as achieving or surpassing business and social objectives and responsibilities from the perspective of the judging party. Integration is not only essential to meeting current business and social needs but, as Figure 16-2[2] suggests, it is essential to the change process necessary to meet future business and social needs of the organization.

While all of these factors are important and are certainly worthy

FIGURE 16-1   Satellite model of organizational performance

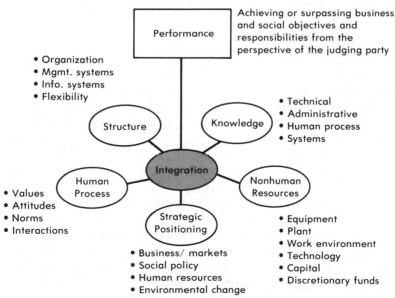

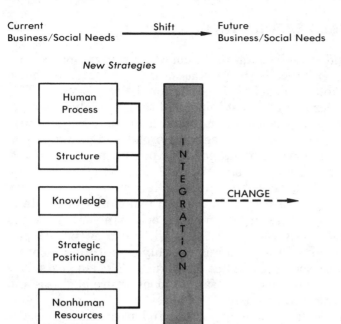

Current
Business/Social Needs — Shift → Future
Business/Social Needs

FIGURE 16-2 Positioning for future performance

of study, our primary emphasis in this book is on human resources. This emphasis is justified because increasing attention is being directed toward human resources, not only in their traditional roles, but also in their influence on the other key performance factors.[3] For example, MacMillan and Schuler suggest that "focusing on a firm's human resources could provide a significant opportunity to secure a sustained edge over competitors.[4] Let's take a brief look at this interesting idea. Using superior human resources as a competitive weapon in improving organizational performance is certainly a new dimension in the management of organizational behavior. But how can organizations use human resources as strategic weapons?

MacMillan and Schuler have found that companies have gained an edge by either capturing or developing greater shares of critically needed human resource skills or by leveraging existing human resources to gain a competitive advantage. This cannot be done in isolation. There must be very close coordination between human resources planning and the other performance factors.

Increasingly, human resources managers will come under pressure to anticipate the major gaps in key skills needed for the firm. . . . The role of human resources management (HRM) in developing strategy will become critical. Clearly these managers are best equipped to identify the key skills that can be applied to create the competitive edge, and clearly they can play a major role in managing any transfer of skills to the strategic target, as well as assure the quality and quantity and continuity of the existing in-house skills. So it becomes vital for the HRM staff to become involved in the strategic process—not only in the traditional sense as a support function that assures the availability of human resources to support the strategic effort, but also as an aggressive participant that helps identify significant strategic advantages based on the corporation's existing human resources or to identify areas in which emerging skill needs can be preempted ahead of competitors.[5]

Questions MacMillan and Schuler recommend be asked include:

1. Which human resources in the company are unequivocally excellent?
2. How must HRM practices be applied to motivate the employees who possess the key skills?
3. What strategic targets could be pursued?
4. What strategic thrusts will be critical in the industry chain in the future?[6]

Their main argument that "Companies can gain a competitive advantage through their human resources by making sure that employees both have the appropriate skills and are suitably motivated"[7] is the same argument that we have been using for more than twenty-five years. Managing people to perform can make a very significant difference. We hope that the ACHIEVE model that follows and the other tactical approaches discussed in the subsequent chapters will give you useful ideas in your own human resources management.

Background of the ACHIEVE Model[8]

A common problem that occurs in the management process is that many managers tend to be effective in letting followers know *what* performance problems exist, but they are not as effective in helping followers determine *why* these problems exist. In other words, many managers are strong in problem identification, but are much weaker in problem analysis or diagnosis.

In order to be most effective in evaluating and solving performance problems, managers need to determine why problems have occurred. The ACHIEVE model was designed by Hersey and Goldsmith to help managers determine why performance problems may have occurred and then develop change strategies aimed at solving these problems.[9]

In developing a model for analyzing human performance problems, Hersey and Goldsmith had two primary goals in mind: to determine the key factors that can influence staff members' performance and to present these factors in a way that can be used and remembered by practicing managers.

The first step in the development of the ACHIEVE model was to isolate the key factors that influence performance management. Earlier work by Atkinson[10] indicated that performance is a function of motivation and ability. Put in simple terms, the follower has to have a certain degree of willingness to do the job and the necessary skills for task completion. Porter and Lawler[11] expanded this idea by including role perception or job understanding, noting that followers can have all the willingness and skills needed to do the job, but will not be effective unless there is a clear understanding of what to do and how to do it.

Lorsch and Lawrence[12] approached the topic from a different perspective and concluded that performance was not merely a function of attributes possessed by the individual, but also depends on the organization and the environment. Individuals can be highly motivated and have all the skills to do the job, but will not be effective unless they get needed organizational support and direction and unless their work fits the needs of their organizational environment.

The ACHIEVE model uses two more factors in the performance management equation. The first factor is feedback, which means that the followers need to know not just what to do, but also how well they are doing it on an ongoing basis. Feedback includes day-to-day coaching and formal performance evaluation. The other performance management factor is validity. In today's environment managers need to be able to document and justify decisions that affect people's careers. Valid personnel practices have become a legal necessity in the United States. In analyzing performance, managers need to continually check for validity in all personnel practices, such as job analyses, recruitment, appraisal, training, promotion, and dismissal.

Hersey and Goldsmith isolated seven variables related to effective performance management: (1) motivation; (2) ability; (3) understanding; (4) organizational support; (5) environmental fit; (6) feedback; and (7) validity. Their next step was to put these factors together in a manner that managers could easily remember and use. One technique for making items on a list easy to remember is to make their first letter form a common word, an acronym. A seven-letter word that is synonymous with "to perform" is *achieve.* By substituting *incentive* for the motivation factor; *clarity* for understanding; *help* for organizational support; and *evaluation* for performance feedback, the ACHIEVE model was developed. The seven factors in the model are as follows: Ability, Clarity, Help, Incentive, Evaluation, Validity, and Environment.

Using the ACHIEVE Model

In using the ACHIEVE model the manager evaluates how each factor will affect the present or potential performance of followers for a given task. Then the manager should take the steps that "fit" the unique cause(s) of the performance problem. The seven factors in the ACHIEVE model, along with typical problem-solving alternatives are listed next.

A—Ability (knowledge and skills). In the ACHIEVE model the term *ability* refers to the follower's knowledge, experience, and skill— the ability to complete the specific task successfully. It is important to remember that individuals are not universally competent. Key components of ability include task-relevant education (formal and informal training that facilitates the successful completion of the specific task); task-relevant experience (prior work experience that contributes to the successful completion of the task); and task-relevant skills (proficiencies that enhance the successful completion of the task). In analyzing follower performance, the manager should ask, Does this follower have the knowledge, skill, and experience to complete this task successfully?

If the person has an ability problem, solutions may include specific training, coaching, formal educational courses, or reassignment of specific duties or responsibilities. These alternatives should be considered from the viewpoint of cost effectiveness.

C—Clarity (understanding or role perception). Clarity refers to an understanding and acceptance of what to do, when to do it, and how to do it. To have a thorough understanding of the job, the follower needs to be clear on the major goals and objectives, how these goals and objectives should be accomplished, and the priority of goals and objectives (which objectives are most important at what times).

If the follower has a problem in clarity or understanding, there may well be a problem in the performance-planning phase. In many cases, oral agreement on objectives is insufficient. The manager should assure that all objectives are formally recorded. The follower should be encouraged to ask questions for further clarification.

H—Help (organizational support). The term *help* refers to the organizational help, or support, that the follower needs for effective task completion. Some organizational support factors might include adequate budget, equipment, and facilities that are suitable for task completion; necessary support from other departments; product availability and quality; and an adequate supply of human resources.

If there is a lack of help or organizational support, managers should clearly identify where the problem exists. If the problem is lack of money, human resources, equipment, or facilities, the manager should see whether the necessary resources can be acquired in a cost-effective manner. If the resources cannot be acquired, the manager may have to revise objectives to avoid holding followers responsible for circumstances beyond their control.

I—Incentive (motivation or willingness). The term *incentive* refers to the follower's task-relevant incentive—the motivation to complete the specific task under analysis in a successful manner. In evaluating incentive it is important to remember that most people are not equally motivated to complete all tasks. Followers tend to be more motivated toward the successful completion of tasks that will bring them either intrinsic or extrinsic rewards.

If the follower has an incentive problem, the first step is to check the use of rewards and punishments. The follower should clearly understand that performance on this task is related to pay, promotion, recognition, and job security. Research indicates that managers sometimes hope followers will engage in certain behaviors without rewarding these behaviors.[13] People have a natural tendency to pursue tasks that are rewarded and to avoid tasks that are not. Rewards can be tangible or intangible; feedback on performance, such as recognition or a pat on the back, can be an important part of the overall incentive system.

E—Evaluation (coaching and performance feedback). *Evaluation* refers to informal day-to-day performance feedback as well as formal periodic reviews. An effective feedback process lets followers know, on a regular basis, how well they are doing the job. It is unrealistic to expect followers to improve performance if they are unaware that performance problems exist. People should know how they are being evaluated on a regular basis before their formal periodic evaluation occurs. Many performance problems can be caused by a lack of necessary coaching and performance feedback.

If there is an evaluation problem, it may be caused by the lack of day-to-day feedback on both effective and ineffective performance.

Many managers tend to focus on the bad news and forget to recognize when things are going well. Recognition for a job well done can be a vital part of the ongoing evaluation process. It can increase motivation and cost the organization very little.

One method that helps to highlight extremes in performance is the "significant incident" process, which includes formally documenting highly positive or negative performance. This ensures that the follower receives feedback that is part of the formal record.

V—Validity (valid and legal personnel practices). The term *validity* refers to the appropriateness and legality of human resources decisions made by the manager. Managers need to make sure that decisions about people are appropriate in light of laws, court decisions, and company policies. The manager should make sure that personnel practices do not discriminate against any specific group or individual and should be aware that organizations need valid and legal performance evaluations, training and promotion criteria selection techniques, and so on.

In there is a validity problem, the manager should know that the trend of the law in management is clear: personnel decisions need to be documented and justified on the basis of performance-oriented criteria. Managers uncertain about validity issues should discuss them with the personnel department or the organization's legal office.

E—Environment (environmental fit). The term *environment* refers to the external factors that can influence performance even if the individual has all the ability, clarity, help, and incentive needed to do the job. Key elements of the environmental factors include competition, changing market conditions, government regulations, suppliers, and so on.

If there is an environmental problem beyond their control, followers should not be rewarded or reprimanded for performance. In short, followers should be expected to perform at a level consistent with the limitations of their environment.

As stated earlier, performance management integrates the widely used Situational Leadership concept and the ACHIEVE model. In explaining how to implement performance management, the major steps required in performance planning will be outlined, including the coaching process that can be used to reinforce performance plans and develop followers. Finally, guidelines on conducting the formal performance review, which completes the performance management cycle, will be provided.

THE THREE FUNCTIONS
OF PERFORMANCE MANAGEMENT

Performance management includes three major functions:

1. *Performance planning*—setting objectives and directions for followers at the beginning of a planning period and developing plans for achieving these objectives.
2. *Coaching*—day-to-day feedback and development activities aimed at the enhancement of performance plans.
3. *Performance review*—overall evaluation of performance for the specific planning period.

The situational approach to performance management enables managers to individualize performance planning, coaching, and review by choosing managerial techniques that fit the unique situation faced by each of their followers.

PERFORMANCE PLANNING

Many traditional MBO approaches indicate that managers and followers should always develop objectives in a joint decision-making process. Situational Leadership suggests that degrees of joint decision making may be appropriate for followers at moderate readiness levels (R2 or R3), but not as appropriate with followers who have very high or very low readiness levels (R1 or R4).

In cases where followers have low readiness levels for setting certain goals, managers may be better off setting the goals and communicating them to the low-readiness-level follower. In cases where follower readiness is extremely high, followers may take the key role in the goal-setting process due to their readiness regarding a particular task. If the follower is at a very high readiness level it may be acceptable (and even desirable) for the follower to take the major leadership responsibility in setting more specific objectives. In summary, Situational Leadership suggests that managers should involve followers in the performance-planning process at a level consistent with the follower's readiness concerning the task under discussion.

Another use of Situational Leadership in the performance-planning process involves the idea of contracting for leadership style.[14] In setting objectives it is not enough for the manager and follower to determine what objectives should be achieved; it is also useful for them to agree upon their respective roles in the achievement of objectives. Managers and followers should agree up front on the degree of managerial involvement expected for each specific task. Managers should let followers know where structure and direction can be expected and where delegation may be appropriate. By clarifying their roles in the performance-planning process, both managers and followers can help avoid unnecessary stress and surprises in the implementation phase.

One weakness of many MBO-type systems is that the manager and follower negotiate only for what the follower is going to contribute. The ACHIEVE system suggests that the manager and follower also need to get a clear idea of what needed support the organization is going to contribute. Using the ACHIEVE model in performance planning, the manager can deal with questions such as, Does the follower have the ability to do the job? Does the follower clearly understand what to do and how to do it? What degree of support is needed from the organization? Is there a process for ongoing coaching and feedback?

The ACHIEVE model gives the manager a clear analysis of performance potential. If any problems appear to exist, the manager should address these problems before the individual is assigned specific objectives. For example, if the manager feels the follower lacks ability, necessary training should occur before the follower starts unsuccessfully trying to achieve the objective.

An analysis of each performance factor in the ACHIEVE model before the follower starts to work increases the probability of setting challenging, realistic objectives. Special attention should be paid to the validity factor. If performance objectives have been set in a way that may unfairly discriminate against any individual or group, the company personnel staff may be contacted and the objectives changed.

Coaching

Managers can develop a situational approach to coaching by actually using the leadership styles contracted for during the performance-planning process.

In coaching, Situational Leadership helps managers make clear connections between their leadership styles, the objectives set in the performance-planning process, and the follower's readiness level for achieving each specific objective.

One serious problem managers have in coaching is the lack of sufficient analysis before making a coaching intervention.[15] Managers can use the ACHIEVE model to analyze performance problems quickly before deciding what remedial actions to take.

Performance problems need to be faced as early as possible— before they turn into disasters. Managers observing a problem in its early stages often refrain from taking action because they hope the problems will go away. Very seldom does this happen. With the ACHIEVE model, the manager has a quick mental checklist for day-to-day problem solving that can be used without formal meetings, documents, or office appointments. After using the ACHIEVE model to diagnose a unique problem, the manager can dramatically increase the probability of making a problem-solving intervention that fits the situation faced by the follower.

Performance Review

In the final performance appraisal meeting between manager and follower there should be no surprises. If the manager has done a thorough job of performance planning and day-to-day coaching, both parties should see this meeting as a review of what happened during the planning period. The manager can use Situational Leadership to determine the degree of follower involvement in the formal review process.

Managers may want followers at high readiness levels to complete self-evaluations, which can be discussed before final managerial ratings. Followers at moderate readiness levels may require a joint decision-making process, with the degree of follower direction depending on readiness level for each specific goal. Followers at low readiness levels may require a directive review, with most of the information going from the manager to the follower. Managers can use a situational approach to avoid the issue of determining what levels of follower participation in reviews are "good" or "bad." The Situational Leadership framework allows followers to engage in the degree of participation that works for their particular review.

In the final performance review managers can use the ACHIEVE model to analyze why performance results did or did not meet the standards set in the performance-planning process. After the causes of performance problems have been determined by the manager and follower, developmental strategies can be designed to fit the specific performance problems that have occurred. The ACHIEVE model can help the manager attain specific performance-related data that can be used in future training, transfer, and personnel decisions. The ACHIEVE model also helps managers decide whether failure to meet performance standards was due to a lack of follower performance or to managerial, organizational, or environmental problems.

Performance management builds upon the basic philosophy of Situational Leadership. There is no one best way to solve human resource problems. The manager should use the problem-solving strategy that best fits the needs of followers in their unique situations. Performance management provides managers with easy-to-use guidelines for analyzing work situations, determining why performance problems may exist, and choosing solution strategies to fit the problems faced by their followers.

Also, a significant benefit of the situational approach to performance management is that it provides an effective framework that trainers can use for developing managers in performance planning, coaching, and performance review.

The next two chapters will present one of the most important concepts in the behavioral sciences in recent years, One Minute Management. Chapter 17 will introduce One Minute Management, while Chapter 18 will discuss the concepts of putting One Minute Management to work, including the interrelation of Situational Leadership and One Minute Management.

NOTES

1. Alan A. Yelsey, "Strategies and Actions for Improving Organizational Performance," *Academy of Management Review,* June 1984, p. 25.
2. *Ibid.,* p. 26.
3. See, for example, the increasing importance of human resources in "Human Resources Managers Aren't Corporate Nobodies Anymore," *Business Week,* December 2, 1987, pp. 58–59. See also William A. Medlin, "Managing People to Perform," *The Bureaucrat,* Spring 1985, pp. 52–55; Jac Fritz Enz, "Human Resource: Formulas for Success," *Personnel Journal,* 64, No. 10 (October 1985), pp. 52–60; Philip H. Mirvis, "Formulating and Implementating Human Resource Strategy," *Human Resource Management,* 24, no. 4 (Winter 1985), pp. 385–412.
4. Ian C. MacMillan and Randall S. Schuler, "Gaining a Competitive Edge through Human Resources," *Personnel,* April 1985, p. 24. See also Dave Ulrich, "Human Resource Planning as a Competitive Edge," *Human Resource Planning,* 9, no. 2 (1986), pp. 41–49.
5. *Ibid.,* p. 27.
6. *Ibid.,* p. 28.
7. *Ibid.,* p. 28–29.
8. This section on the ACHIEVE model is adapted from Paul Hersey and Marshall Goldsmith, "A Situational Approach to Performance Planning," *Training and Development,* 34 (November 1980), pp. 38–40.
9. This has been a primary research objective at the Center for Leadership Studies.
10. J. W. Atkinson, *An Introduction to Motivation* (New York: Van Nostrand, 1958).
11. Lyman Porter and Edward Lawler, *Managerial Attitudes and Performance* (Homewood, Ill.: Irwin, 1968. See also G. Miller, "Management Guidelines: The Right Perspective," *Supervisory Management,* 26 (March 1981), pp. 22–28; Charles R. Gowen, "Managing Work Group Performance by Individual Goals and Group Goals for an Interdependent Group Task," *Journal of Organizational Behavior,* 7, no. 3 (Winter 1986), pp. 5–27.
12. Jay Lorsch and Paul Lawrence, "The Diagnosis of Organizational Problems" in Newton Margulies and Anthony P. Raia, *Organizational Development: Values, Processes, and Technology* (New York: McGraw-Hill, 1972).
13. Steven Kerr, "On the Folly of Hoping for A While Rewarding B," *Academy of Management Journal,* 4 (1975), pp. 76–79. See also Thomas Kemper, "Motivation and Behavior, A Personal View," *Journal of General Management,* 9, no. 3 (Fall 1983), pp. 51–57; Martin Gevans, "Organizational Behavior: The Central Role of Motivation," *Journal of Management,* 12, no. 2 (Summer 1986), pp. 203–22.
14. See discussion in Chapter 12.
15. Ferdinand Fournies, *Coaching for Improved Work Performance* (New York: Van Nostrand, 1978).

17

Implementing Situational Leadership: *One Minute Management*

The previous chapters have introduced and elaborated upon the Situational Leadership model, including a discussion of the behavioral science foundations of modern leadership theory. These chapters, and the ones that follow, illustrate adaptations and extensions of Situational Leadership that have been developed by the Center for Leadership Studies and other internationally recognized management development organizations with extensive experience in working with managers, administrators, teachers, parents, and other leaders concerned with improving human performance.

Several of the concepts presented in this chapter were more academically discussed in previous chapters, especially chapter 10, Developing Human Resources; and chapter 11, Constructive Discipline. In this chapter, however, the concepts are presented with more of an eye toward implementation. For example, a previous discussion of behavior modification and reinforcement theory focused on its importance in shaping human performance. While the concepts associated with those two theories are powerful, they have not been used widely in organizations per se for two reasons. First, the terminology—*reinforcement, extinction, successive approximations* and the like—is not palatable to most managers. The terms are too academic. Second, the concepts have been associated with animal research and have a connotation of controlled manipulation; that is, getting people to do what *you* want them to do, not necessarily what *they* want to do. In this chapter managers are shown how the theories discussed earlier in this book can be applied to day-to-day management situations. For example, we translate the theory of behavior modification into the more memorable technique of "catching people doing things right."

Spencer Johnson and Kenneth Blanchard attempted to overcome some of the objections to the academic nature of behavior modification in their best-selling book, *The One Minute Manager*.[1] The book focused on three powerful concepts derived from behavior modification principles: One Minute Goal Setting, One Minute Praisings, and One Minute Reprimands. The notion of a "One Minute Manager" was developed to encourage managers to take an extra minute to make sure they are focusing on those things that have the most impact in obtaining desired performance from workers. Managers need to concentrate on setting clear goals with their people, praising good performance, and reprimanding or redirecting poor performance when necessary.

This chapter is primarily based on the work of Blanchard and his colleagues at Blanchard Training and Development Inc., a human resources organization based in Escondido, California. Since 1981, associates at BTD have been implementing and refining the One Minute Management concepts with their version of Situational Leadership (SLII®)[2] into the management systems of organizations throughout the United States and abroad.

ONE MINUTE GOAL SETTING

The first key to being a One Minute Manager is One Minute Goal Setting. All good performance starts with clear goals. This involves making sure that all employees are clear about two things: what they are being asked to do (their areas of accountability) and what good performance looks like (performance standards by which they will be evaluated). While these two stipulations may seem simple, they are often lacking in organizations.

Areas of Accountability

To obtain desired performance from its employees, an organization must first have a well-defined accountability system. For example, when employees are asked what they do and their managers are asked what their people do, widely divergent answers typically are given. This is particularly so if each group is asked to prioritize their list of responsibilities. As a consequence, individuals in organizations often get punished for not doing what they didn't know they were supposed to do in the first place.

One of the biggest obstacles to productivity improvement stems from this problem of unclear organizational expectations and accountability. At times those individuals whom management deems most responsible for a specific activity may be unaware of their role altogether. For example, a group of restaurant managers concerned about sales were asked: "Who is responsible for generating sales in your organization?" The almost unanimous reply was: "The waiters and waitresses." But when the waiters and waitresses were asked what the primary responsibilities of their jobs were, their reply was consistently: "Serving food and taking orders." No reference was made to selling. So although it may seem very basic, managers need to make sure their people know what is expected of them.

Performance Standards

Employees must also know what good performance looks like. This is accomplished through *performance standards*. Performance standards help managers and employees more easily monitor performance and serve as a basis for evaluation. To determine whether an organization has clear performance standards, employees can be asked: "Are you doing a good job?" Most people will respond to this question by saying: "Yes, I think so." A revealing follow-up question would then be: "How do you know?" The typical response: "I haven't been criticized by my manager lately." Such an answer implies that employees receive very little encouragement concerning mistakes or delays. This is a sad state of affairs. A habitual practice by managers leads to the most commonly used management style in America: the "leave alone then zap," S4–S1 style of management, discussed in chapter 11 Constructive Discipline. This style of managing can also be called "seagull management." A seagull manager flies in, makes a lot of noise, dumps on everyone, and flies out. Since this is the predominant style of management in most organizations, it is no wonder that the motivation of people is a major organizational behavior problem today.

Scott Meyers,[3] a long-time consultant in the field of motivation, makes the same point with a novel analogy. Meyers was struck by the contrast between workers when they worked and the same individuals when they were involved in a social or recreational activity, such as bowling. While bowling, it was common to see someone get excited after throwing a strike—perhaps the person would jump up and down or yell. The same individual would seldom if ever get as excited at work. Meyers wondered why they didn't. He posed the questions:

"Why aren't people jumping up and down and yelling in most organizations?" and "What can be done to make work a more exciting environment and workers more highly motivated?"

Goals Need to Be Clear

The reasons people are not yelling in organizations, Meyers contends, is in part because it is not clear what is expected of them. To continue his bowling analogy, when they approach the alley, they notice there are no pins at the other end; that is, they don't know what their goals are. How long would you want to bowl without any pins? Yet every day in the world of work, people are bowling without any pins, and as a result cannot tell how well they are doing.

Reaching Goals Requires Feedback

A second obstacle to obtaining good performance involves feedback to employees on how they are doing. It's as if when an employee goes to bowl, a sheet is covering the pins. When the ball is rolled down the alley, it goes through the sheet and a crack is heard. When asked, "How did you do?" an employee might reply: "I don't know, but I thought it was OK." To move toward goals, employees need feedback on their performance.

This feedback can serve to motivate employees. There seems to be adequate evidence that the number one motivator of people is feedback on results. Another way of emphasizing this is with the slogan: "Feedback is the Breakfast of Champions."[4] Can you imagine training for the Olympics with no one telling you how fast you had run or how high you had jumped? The idea seems ludicrous, yet many employees operate in a vacuum, without knowing essential information to do their jobs well—if at all.

Money is only a motivator of people if it's feedback on results. Have you ever gotten a raise that you were pleased with only to find out that somebody else who you don't think works as hard as you got the same or even a better raise? Not only is that increase in money *not motivating,* it became *demotivating* once you knew it had nothing to do with results. Suddenly, it didn't seem to matter how hard you worked at all.

Once managers are convinced that the number one motivator of people is feedback on results, they usually start giving feedback—but not always the right type. Back to our analogy: When employees go to the line to roll the ball, they notice that the boss is standing on the other side of the sheet. When the ball is rolled down the alley, it goes through the sheet, they hear a crack, and then the boss holds up two fingers and says, "You knocked down two." In fact, most bosses would not phrase the feedback so positively, but would say, "You missed eight." Thus we come to a central point that will be elaborated upon later in this chapter as well as in the next chapter: Positive feedback is more effective at shaping desired performance than negative feedback.

Performance Review Can Undermine Performance

Why don't managers lift the sheet so everyone can see the pins? Because there is a strong tradition in organizations known as the performance review. We called it NIHYYSOB, and it stands for: "Now I have you, you S.O.B." Sadly, many managers use the performance review as a once-a-year opportunity to get even with an employee.

The performance review process is also used to spread people over a distribution curve, thus categorizing employees and distorting their performance. In most organizations, if you have six or seven people reporting to you, the practice of rating them all high—even if they all deserve it—is discouraged. For example, it doesn't take managers very long to realize that if they rate all of their people high, then they subsequently will get rated low by *their* managers. The only way they can get rated high is if they rate some of their people low. This practice is often encouraged by having a set budget or percentage for a group's salary increases.

One of the toughest jobs a manager can have is to decide who gets the low ratings. Most Americans grew up with this win-lose mentality in which some people in every group must lose. It pervades our educational system. For example, a fifth grade teacher giving a test on state capitals to her class would never consider making atlases available during the test to allow the class to get up and look up the answers. Why not? Because all the children would get 100. Can you imagine what would happen to American education if kids who had to take vocabulary tests were allowed dictionaries on their desks? There would be an uproar!

As we discussed in the last chapter, Hersey and Goldsmith[5] have identified three parts of a performance review: (1) performance planning, in which you set the goals and objectives; (2) day-to-day coaching, in which you work with your people to help them reach their goals; and (3) performance evaluation, in which you evaluate progress toward goals. Of these three steps, most organizations tend to start with performance evaluation. The personnel department comes up with some form to be filled out once a year on every employee. Then somebody might say that some goals ought to be set. Notebooks are filled with goals and job descriptions—many of which are never looked at until someone decides a year or more later that they should be revised. The only part of the performance-review process that is seldom done on a systematic basis is the most important of the three steps: day-to-day coaching. The primary value of Situational Leadership is obtained in working daily with people at different levels of readiness to help them win.

Limit the Number of Goals

All the research on high performance shows that three to five goals are the ideal number of goals peak performers concentrate on. Remember Pareto's 80/20 rule: 80 percent of the results you want to obtain from people comes from 20 percent of their activities. Therefore, you want to limit the number of goals employees have and attempt to identify the few key activities that will have the highest impact and yield the greatest results. Once these goals are established, they should be written down so they can be frequently used to compare actual behavior against targeted behavior.

Often goal setting is considered a paper-work activity—a necessary evil of organizational life—but one that seemingly has little value in getting the job done. When this is the case, goals are filed and people go off and do whatever they want until a performance review draws near. In One Minute Goal Setting the philosophy is that you should keep your goals close at hand. Goals should be able to be read in a minute and be written in no more than 250 words.

Although most managers we've worked with agree with the importance of setting goals, many do not take the time to clearly develop their own goals and to write them down. They tend to get caught in the "activity trap," in which they become busy doing things, but not necessarily the right things—that is, those activities they would deem most important. To help out with this problem, Kelsey Tyson and Drea Zigarmi have developed two instruments[6] managers can use to set goals for both themselves and those with whom they work. These instruments systematically guide the user through nine steps for establishing goals in a way that increases the probability for their successful achievement. We will briefly discuss each of these steps.

Step 1: Setting Goals "What is the person's job?" Specifically list the most important activities you want a person to accomplish in the next three to six months.

Step 2: Setting Priorities "Which goals are most important?" Rank the priority of achieving the goals, with a specific deadline for each goal.

Step 3: Measurable Indicators "How will you know if the person is doing the job well?" This should include two or three specific variables within the person's control that need to be tracked for changes and improvement.

Step 4: Standards of Performance "What does outstanding performance look like?" There should be minimal, acceptable, and outstanding levels of performance determined for each goal. For example, different amounts of time or different degrees of quality, quantity, and cost.

Step 5: Incentives and Benefits "What will the person gain by doing a good job?" These can include such items as increased autonomy, flextime, increased responsibilities, or additional money.

Step 6: Obstacles to Goal Accomplishment "What could get in the way of accomplishing the person's goals?" Consider both factors within the person's control and likely factors beyond personal control.

Step 7: Action Steps "What steps will the person take to accomplish the goals?" Determine what is the most feasible plan for success, including the help and support that will be needed from others. Most goals can be successfully accomplished in a variety of ways.

Step 8: Praising and Rewards "What happens if the goal is accomplished?" Recognition should be planned for both final completion and progress toward final completion. Don't overlook one of the simplest yet important and powerful forms of recognition: sincere appreciation.

Step 9: Reprimands and Redirection "What happens if the goal is not accomplished?" If the person has the necessary skills to complete a task but doesn't, the person should be reprimanded. If the person lacks the necessary skills, redirection is more appropriate. When redirecting, goals and action steps are redetermined and the person tries again.

Diagnosing Blocks to Goal Setting

If the goal-setting process is unsuccessful, check the goals you have set for clarity, feasibility, and unanticipated problems, using the following questions, also taken from Tyson and Zigarmi's instruments:

Are the time lines you have established realistic? Will other competing demands cause delay? Will the person be able to overcome those demands to accomplish the goals you have agreed on, on time?

How central to the long-range goals of your department are the goals that you have established?

Will the goals you have established have the impact you want for the effort needed to achieve them?

How will these goals help move the company ahead? Are the goals in keeping with the prevailing thrust of the organization?

How will these goals help the person develop new skills? How will these goals help him or her to build confidence? What is the likely reaction if the employee fails to achieve the predetermined goals? Will the person be able to accept a reprimand if necessary or redirection to get back on track?[7]

Good Goals are SMART Goals

SMART is an acronym for the most important factors in setting quality goals.

S—Specific. You don't say to somebody, "I want you to improve." The area and method of improving must be specifically defined.

M—Measurable. An important thing to remember is, "If you can't measure it, you can't manage it." Therefore, the goals have to be observable and measurable. If somebody says, "That leaves my job out—you can't measure my job," offer to eliminate it to see if it will be missed.

A—Attainable. You need to be able to reach your goals and stretch yourself in the process. This relates back to the research conducted by David McClelland on achievement motivation, presented in Chapter 2. He found that high achievers like to set moderately difficult but obtainable goals: that is, goals that stretch the individual.

R—Relevant. You want to set goals in areas that are important to the job.

T—Trackable. You need to set interim goals so that people's progress can be praised along the way. If a goal consists of completing a report due June 1, the chances of receiving an acceptable report will increase if interim reports are required. Remember, good performance is a journey, not a destination. The goal is the destination. What managers have to do is manage the journey. This is best done through One Minute Praisings.

THE ONE MINUTE PRAISING

Once your people are clear on what you are asking them to do and what good behavior looks like, you are ready for the second key to obtaining desired performance: One Minute Praising. Praising is the most powerful activity a manager can do. In fact, it is the key to training people and making winners of everyone working for you. The

One Minute Praising focuses on reinforcing behavior that is moving an employee closer to the goals. While all the keys of the One Minute Manager—Goal Setting, Praising, Reprimanding—are important, One Minute Praising is the most important. Look around your organization and see if you can "catch people doing something right." When you do, give them a One Minute Praising that is immediate and specific, and state your feelings.

Be Immediate and Specific

In order for praising to be effective, it must be *immediate and specific.* Tell people exactly what they did right as soon as possible. For example, "You submitted your report on time Friday and it was well written; in fact, I used it in a meeting today and that report made you and me and our whole department look good." Use examples such as, "I see productivity in your department is up 10 percent" or "Your report helped us win the contract with the Jones Company." If comments are too general, such as "Appreciate your efforts," "Thank you very much," "I don't know what I'd do without you," or "Keep up the good work," they are less likely to seem sincere and thus are not likely to be effective. Instead of praising people at random, first find out what they have done right. A manager should schedule time to observe employees' behavior and specifically praise improvements that are noticed.

State Your Feelings

After you praise employees, tell them how you *feel* about what they did. Don't intellectualize. State your gut feelings: "Let me tell you how I feel. I was so proud after hearing your financial report presentation at the Board of Director's meeting that I want you to know I really feel good about your being on our team. Thanks a lot." Although praisings do not take very long, they can have lasting effects. To help managers master the important skill of praising, Tyson and Zigarmi developed The One Minute Manager Praising Planning Guide.[8] This instrument systematically takes the user through the steps for a quality praising on a specific person who works for or with the manager. It lists sample items, questions for consideration in planning specific praisings, and a means for evaluating the effectiveness of praisings after they are delivered. Following are some sample questions from the instrument.

Pre-Planning Analysis

Are you considering a praising because you feel good today or because you feel the person deserves the praise?

Is the praising related to performance demonstrated in accomplishing a new task or assignment or to the improved performance of previously performed tasks or assignments?

Have you praised this person before for the same behavior?

Is there a chance that the person will feel manipulated by the praising?

Were any other people involved whom you should praise?

Post-Planning Analysis

Did the praising result in increased commitment and motivation for you and the person being praised?

Did you deliver any "bad news" or assign additional work as part of the praising? If so, why?

Did you add a "but" and give some critical feedback?

Praisings drive all effective human interaction. These same concepts apply to any relationship, not only making people better managers, but also better parents, spouses, friends, and customers. Consider marriage, for example. A recent study reported that second marriages are breaking up at a higher rate than first marriages. This is grimly amusing because some people argue that success in marriage is merely a matter of selection—that if you could only get a second chance, you could do much better. What this study confirmed was that, "if you are a jerk in one relationship, you'll probably be a jerk in your next relationship as well"—*unless* you learn the basics of human interaction.

Just trace the demise of a love relationship. When people fall in love, they seldom see the faults or limitations of the loved one. Have you ever seen a couple in love, in a restaurant? When one is talking, the other is very attentive—listening, smiling, and supporting. They don't seem to care if their meal ever comes.

In contrast, have you ever seen a couple in a restaurant who are not really happy together? They may look as if they have nothing to say to each other. They may not say four sentences to each other in two-and-a-half hours. Perhaps the man finally says, "How is your meal?" And the woman counters with, "Fine! How's yours?" That is the extent of their conversation. Their marriage is dead, but nobody has buried it!

How do two people go from being excited over each other's words to having nothing to say? It's really quite simple. Good relationships are all about the frequency with which you catch each other doing something right!

When you first fall in love, everything is right. Then when you decide to get married or commit to some permanency in your relationship, you often start to see things wrong with each other. You begin to say things such as, "I didn't know that!" or "That's strange you should do something like that!" After awhile you might become critical, and your emphasis is on what's wrong with the other person, rather than what's right. In fact, the final demise of a loving relationship is when you do something right and you get yelled at because you didn't do it *exactly* right—"You had to ask" or "You should have done it earlier."

Being Close Counts

This brings up one of the most important points to remember about praising. Don't wait for exactly the right behavior before praising; catch people doing things *approximately* right. What we expect from each other is exactly right behavior. And yet, if you wait for exactly right behavior before you recognize it, you'll probably never get it. What we have to remember is that *exactly right* behavior is made up of a whole series of *approximately right* behaviors.

Bob Davis, president of Chevron Chemical, has as one of his favorite mottos: "Praise progress—it's at least a moving target." What a powe. ful statement! What we need to do in all of our interactions at work and at home is to reward or praise people for performing.

Another example is childrearing. Teenagers are a problem for many parents. Why? Before kids become teenagers, their parents think they are "cute," and when "cute" kids do something wrong they are usually forgiven. Cute kids are caught doing things approximately right. But the minute teenagers walk in the house, they get yelled at, "Where have you been?" or "Why didn't you do this?" or "That sure was a stupid mistake." It doesn't take teenagers long to figure out that they don't like hanging around at home. Parents lose influence with their children because they catch them doing things wrong more frequently than they catch them doing things right.

Think about this in relation to your children. Parents tell us they can't understand why their children are so different. For example, "Mary is a model child. She does well in school, helps around the house, is polite and friendly to adults. But Harry and Alice—my other children—are nothing but trouble." In every case we find that Mary is caught doing things right, while Harry and Alice are caught doing things wrong.

If you are having difficulty with a spouse, a child, an employee, your boss, or friends, ask yourself, "Do I want this relationship to work?" When you are looking for an answer, go to your gut feelings. If deep down you don't want to make the relationship work, you won't. Why? Because you have control of the qualifier—the "yes, but." If you want to make the relationship work, you will catch the other person doing things right. But if you don't want to make it work, for whatever reason, you can easily undermine another person's best efforts to please you. No matter what that person does right, you will say, "Yes, but . . . you didn't do this or that right."

Make Time for Praisings

You should set aside at least two hours a week for "praisings." Write it on your calendar just like your appointments. Then use the Hewlett-Packard philosophy of MBWA—Management by Wandering Around—made famous by Peters and Waterman in their book *In Search of Excellence.*[9] Wander around your operation and catch people doing things right—and tell them about it. Do the same with your spouse, children, friends. At home you may not need two hours per week—but ten minutes surely wouldn't hurt. Are you doing that much?

Try it. You'll like catching people doing things right. It will put a spring in your step and a sparkle in your eye. And just imagine what it will do for the people you catch!

THE ONE MINUTE REPRIMAND

People often comment about One Minute Management, as they do of other research-based behavioral science approaches, "It just isn't tough enough." They say, "In the real world you have to be tough." The third key to One Minute Management focuses on reprimanding others.

There are four keys to remember about a reprimand. First, as with One Minute Praising, reprimand as *soon as possible* after an incident. Do not save up your feelings. If you "gunnysack" and store up your feelings, when you finally let go of them, they are apt to be out of proportion to the event that triggered your emotional release. This will make the mistake—and the situation—seem much worse than it really is. Such is often the case with personality attacks. The longer you wait to give someone negative feedback, the more emotional it becomes. So give negative feedback as soon as possible—it causes fewer problems.

Second, *be specific.* Tell people specifically what they did wrong. For example, "John, you didn't get your report in on time on Friday" or "I notice your sales were down 20 percent this quarter" or whatever. Be specific with people.

Third, *share your feelings* about what was done. "Let me tell you how I feel about the late report, John. I'm angry because everyone else got their report in on time and not having your report delayed my

analysis of our market position. It really frustrated me!" Don't intellectualize about what the person did wrong—it is more important to just
focus on how you feel. Describe your feelings sincerely and honestly.

Fourth—and this is probably the most important of the steps—
reaffirm the person. In the late report example, you might say: "Let
me tell you one other thing. You're good. You're one of my best people.
That's why I was angry about your late report. It's so unlike you. I
count on you to set an example for others. That's why I'm not going to
let you get away with that late report behavior. You're better than
that."

To help managers integrate these steps into their own behavior,
Tyson and Zigarmi developed The One Minute Manager Reprimand
Planning Guide,[10] which—like the Praising Planning Guide—can be
used to focus on actual people and situations with which a manager
works. Following are some of the questions from the instrument.

Pre-Reprimand Analysis

Is this person a learner or has he or she previously demonstrated
expertise in the area of responsibility?

What are the specific behaviors that you want discontinued? What
behavior or performance do you want increased?

Are you convinced that this poor performance is within the control of
the person you are about to reprimand?

Why do you feel you should reprimand rather than redirect?

What are the possible positive and negative outcomes of this
reprimand?

Post-Reprimand Analysis

Was the reprimand given as soon after the behavior as possible?

Did you affirm their past performance in this area?

Did you threaten or attack the person personally?

Did you pause in order to let the reprimand sink in and to let go of your
feelings?

Reprimand Behavior, Not the Person

Many people can't understand why you would praise someone just
after you have reprimanded them. You do it for two very important
reasons. First, you want to separate people's behavior from them as
individuals. That is, you want to keep the people, but get rid of their
poor behavior. By reaffirming people after you have reprimanded
them, you focus on their behavior without attacking them personally.

Second, when you walk away after reprimanding, you want

people thinking about what they did wrong, not about how you treated them. If no reaffirmation is done, people who are reprimanded tend to direct their energy back to you, the reprimander. Why? Because of the way they are treated. For example, many reprimands not only don't end with a praising, but with a comment such as, "And let me tell you one other thing . . ." and then the individual is given one last shot—". . . if you think you're going to get that promotion, you have another thing coming."

Then when you walk away, the person who has been reprimanded often turns to a co-worker and instead of discussing the poor performance, talks about the incident and the manager's poor performance. That person is psychologically off the hook with the poor behavior, and the manager becomes the villain.

If, however, you end a reprimand with a praising, the person you reprimand is less likely to turn to a co-worker and complain about you after you walk away because you just told that individual how good the person was. Now that person has to think about what was wrong, not about your leadership style.

Many problems in life stem not from making mistakes, but from not *learning from* our mistakes. Whenever we do not learn from our mistakes, it is often because we are attacked personally for those mistakes. We are called names such as idiot or stupid and generally downgraded by other people who discover our mistakes.

When our self-concept is under attack, we feel the need to defend ourselves and our actions, even to the extent of distorting the facts. When people become defensive, they never hear the feedback they are getting. As a result, little learning takes place. The effective use of the One Minute Reprimand with someone who makes a mistake will hopefully eliminate this defensive behavior.

Remember, people are OK. It is just their behavior that is sometimes a problem. The proper use of the One Minute Reprimand will help to communicate important information necessary to get poor performance back on track. How the One Minute Management skills are used together to achieve better performance is discussed in greater detail in *The One Minute Manager* and graphically presented in The One Minute Manager Gameplan.[11]

THE ONE MINUTE APOLOGY

Since everyone makes mistakes, the ability to apologize is a valuable addition to the three original One Minute Management skills. The One Minute Apology has the same first three steps as the One Minute Praising and the One Minute Reprimand. In apologizing to someone, it is important to do it as soon as possible. The longer you wait, the harder it is to say you are sorry. When you apologize, you also need to be specific with people; otherwise, you are like the little boy who hears his dad yell for him and enters the room saying "I'm sorry, I'm sorry, I'm sorry," trying to cover the possibility that he might have done something wrong. You also need to tell the other person how you feel about what you did wrong; that is, embarrassment, disappointment, remorse, or whatever.

The fourth step of the One Minute Apology is, however, slightly different from the final step of the One Minute Reprimand. Instead of reaffirming the other person by saying how the person is better than that, in the One Minute Apology you reaffirm *yourself* and say, for example, how the behavior you are apologizing for is unlike you or, "That isn't my typical behavior, and if I had thought about it more first, I wouldn't have done it." So often when people do something wrong, not only do they not apologize, but they also may feel guilty for something they have done. By apologizing and reaffirming yourself, you can release the guilt for the inappropriate behavior and move forward with a stronger, more productive relationship.

Managers may be hesitant to use the One Minute Apology because (1) it might appear as a weakness and (2) there is a fear that others might use the apology against them. Both concerns are unfounded. Apologies need to be thought of as a legitimate behavioral alternative in organizations, so that managers and employees can stop expending so much energy trying to "be right" and instead more quickly pinpoint and correct problems as they arise.

Contrary to the popular phrase from Erich Segal's book *Love Story*, "Love means never having to say you're sorry,"[12] we believe that in organizations and families alike, "Love is being able to say you're sorry." The One Minute Apology can help to make saying you are sorry easier and more productive.

ADDITIONS TO ONE MINUTE MANAGEMENT FOR THE 1990s[13]

A frequently asked question is: "What changes would you make to One Minute Management for the 1990s?" After reflecting on this question, we feel that the "secrets" of *The One Minute Manager* are just as relevant today as when the book was published in the early 1980s. There are, however, three additional basic skills that every manager should practice to be effective on the job. These skills are: (1) being specific; (2) enhancing self-esteem; and (3) listening effectively. Let's look at each of these skills.

Talk Specifics

Being specific means *conveying directions that are precise and clear* about what needs to be done and what results are to be achieved. It means describing the behaviors of people instead of just labeling them. Being specific includes positive feedback that tells people what to repeat; it also includes corrective feedback that is firm, but noncritical. It is not saying, "Don't leave callers on hold for so long," but rather saying, "Please don't leave customers on hold for more than fifteen seconds without getting back to them—they like to know we think they are important."

Build Them Up

It is no secret that the way people feel about themselves affects their work. We have long believed that people who feel good about themselves produce better results.

Self-esteem is a private, individual matter. It isn't fixed; it can change from day to day or even hour to hour. As a supervisor, you can't just "make" people feel good about themselves. Self-esteem is basically like a door that is locked from the inside.

If people are in charge of their own self-esteem, what can managers do to make an impact? They can help create a work environment that invites people to feel good about themselves and the work they do. The first step is to avoid damaging or lowering the self-esteem of others. This means eliminating what we call *eroders*—something said or done to someone that wears away feelings of self-worth. For example, it would be eroding to greet a tardy employee, "Late again! You win the prize for being the least reliable in the department!"

Instead, supervisors must develop ways of communicating genuine respect and concern for their people, actively helping them enhance self-image. A comment like, "I knew you could do an exceptional job on that new assignment—and you proved me right," will make anyone's day.

Going back to our first point, the best praise is specific, not general. You can't go around saying to people, "I really appreciate your work" or "Thanks for all of your efforts." Your people will think that you are running for public office.

A comment like, "That report you did for me on Thursday was just what I needed for my marketing meeting," states the action *and* its positive consequences.

Hear Them Out

We don't think it can be stressed enough that listening is a skill we all need to improve. This was the essence of our discussion on active listening in Chapter 13. Many managers still think of listening as a commonplace skill, but we have found that it is not valued—or practiced nearly as often as it needs to be today. Our experience is that people tend to focus more on formulating a rebuttal to what someone else is saying rather than on listening to what the other person is saying.

Let us emphasize again that as you listen to someone else speaking, show that you are listening. One effective way, as Carl Rogers has suggested, is to paraphrase what has just been said when the speaker stops talking, *before* you state your own ideas. This way you improve understanding and minimize miscommunication.

Leaders and followers are more interdependent than ever in today's workplace. You need to be able to gather information from your people: how their work is going, what problems they are having, what resources they need. Listening helps people feel understood and supported, which, in turn, helps them do better work. In addition, good listening skills strengthen mutual respect between managers and their people. When you listen to others, they'll be more likely to listen to you.

New Skills, New Roles

To be effective today, managers must enhance their people skills—and the most important way of doing this is to improve their communication skills. The changing role of management requires that supervisors make a greater use of influence through their personal power rather than their position power. As we discussed before, personal power is having power *with* people, not *over* people.

INTEGRATION WITH
SITUATIONAL LEADERSHIP

The keys of the One Minute Manager integrate well into Situational Leadership and enhance several very important aspects of that model. For example, One Minute Goal Setting starts the Contracting for the Leadership Style process, as discussed in Chapter 12, Building Effective Relationships, and elsewhere in this book. Without clear goals, people don't know where they are going. If you don't know where you are going, any road will get you there or get you lost! Once goals are clear between a manager and the employees, they will be prepared to contract for a leadership style according to their level of readiness for each of the goals. Goal setting thus fits closely with an analysis of employee readiness.

The One Minute Praising plays a key role in the *developmental cycle* of the Situational Leadership model used with employees, as discussed in Chapter 10, Developing Human Resources, when you are trying to increase an employee's level of readiness. When you attempt to develop somebody, remember the three key steps are to (1) provide direction; (2) let them try; and (3) reinforce good behavior. Praising comes into play when you observe performance and catch employees doing the right things. Praising is thus crucial in the reinforcement process. Praising is one of the driving forces moving a manager from the more directive leadership styles to the participating and delegating styles. Praising is thus a very important part of the developmental process.

The One Minute Reprimand comes into play in the *regressive cycle* of the Situational Leadership model as discussed in Chapter 11, Constructive Discipline, when an employee declines in level of readiness. For example, when you have delegated to someone and something goes wrong so that task is not completed properly, you should return to a participating style to find out what went wrong. After you know what went wrong, you can decide whether the performance failure was due to a lack of ability or a lack of motivation. If there is an ability problem, then you move back to an S2 style and redirect, using both direction and support. If there is a motivation problem, the reprimand can be effective. Reprimanding is also a selling style, in that you are directing the person – being honest about what the person has done wrong – but also providing supportive behavior with the use of the reaffirmation.

In summary, three of the secrets of The One Minute Manager – One Minute Goal Setting, Praisings, and Reprimands – describe three management behaviors that are key to making Situational Leadership come alive for managers. Goal setting is a key part of Contracting for Leadership Style – it permits a manager to analyze task-specific aspects of an employee's level of readiness. One Minute Praising is an important part of the developmental process, and the One Minute Reprimand is a potentially useful strategy for dealing with regressions when and if they occur.

In Chapter 18, Implementing Situational Leadership: Effective Follow-Up, we discuss other methods for successfully implementing the behavioral science concepts discussed earlier in this book.

NOTES

1. Kenneth Blanchard and Spencer Johnson, *The One Minute Manager* (New York: Morrow, 1982).
2. The version of the Situational Leadership Model (SLII®) advocated by Blanchard Training and Development consists of the four styles of Directing (S1), Coaching (S2), Supporting (S3), and Delegating (S4). The first publication of this version appeared in a series of three

articles by Kenneth Blanchard in *Executive Excellence* during January–March 1985: "A Situational Approach to Managing People," "Situational Leadership II: A Dynamic Model for Managers and Subordinates," and "Contracting for Leadership Style: The Key to Effective Communications."

3. Scott Meyers, *Every Employee a Manager* (New York: McGraw-Hill, 1970).

4. The slogan "Feedback is the Breakfast of Champions" was coined by Rick Tate, a BTD associate, when he was conducting leadership training for the U.S. Coast Guard.

5. Paul Hersey and Marshall Goldsmith, "A Situational Approach to Performance Planning," *Training and Development,* 34 (November 1980).

6. These instruments, Goal Setting–Self and Goal Setting–Other, are available from Blanchard Training and Development, Escondido, CA 92029.

7. *Ibid.*

8. Available from Blanchard Training and Development, Escondido, CA 92029.

9. Thomas J. Peters and Robert H. Waterman, Jr., *In Search of Excellence* (New York: Harper & Row, 1982).

10. Available from Blanchard Training and Development, Excondido, CA 92029.

11. *Ibid.*

12. Erich Segal, *Love Story* (New York: Harper & Row, 1970), p. 131.

13. Adapted, by permission, from The Blanchard Management Report, 125 State Place, Escondido, CA 92029 and from Kenneth Blanchard, "New Communication Skills, New Roles in the '90s," *Supervisory Management,* July, 1991, pp. 1–2. ©American Management Association. All rights reserved. These skills are described and taught in Leadership Training for Supervisors developed for Blanchard Training and Development, Inc. by Fred Finch, Pat Stewart and Ken Blanchard. For further information, contact Blanchard Training and Development, Escondido, CA 92029.

18

Implementing Situational Leadership: *Effective Follow-Up*

We have repeatedly emphasized the difficulty organizations face in implementing applied behavioral science concepts and techniques. Research has shown that implementation is both problem laden and time consuming. This chapter addresses one of the primary reasons why most companies fail to implement their plans *most* of the time: the lack of follow-up. The problem of little or no follow-up was summarized in Kenneth Blanchard and Robert Lorber's *Putting the One Minute Manager to Work*[1] when they noted, "Most companies spend all their time looking for another management concept and very little time following up the one they have just taught their managers." It seems to be human nature to always look for the next quick fix rather than to use the knowledge and skills that already exist.

Why is this so? We believe it is because top management views training as a fringe benefit—a nice frill that can be given employees as the budget permits. Management often doesn't seem to really believe that what their people learn can make a significant and lasting difference in individual and organizational performance. It is important to overcome this false belief about training and instead become committed to making a difference with training. The veteran manager in the parable presented in *Putting the One Minute Manager to Work* said it well:

I'm enthusiastic right now and so are they, but that has happened before when a new management system has been introduced. My question is, how do you put One Minute Management to work in a way that makes a difference where it really counts–in performance?[2]

Suppose a manager was really committed to effectively implementing One Minute Management? What would that manager have to do? Two practical approaches, which we will discuss in depth in this chapter, are the ABCs of Management and the PRICE system.

THE ABCs OF MANAGEMENT

In *Putting the One Minute Manger to Work,* Lorber and Blanchard discussed the "ABCs of Management," which stands for *Activators, Behavior,* and *Consequences.*

Activators are things you have to do before you can expect good performance. The ACHIEVE model presented in chapter 16 is a good checklist of what managers should be doing ahead of time to ensure that desired performance is obtained. Activators are essential to good performance planning.

Goal setting clearly is an activator. Before people can be expected to perform well, they need to know what they are being asked to do and what good behavior looks like. These principles were discussed in greater depth in the last chapter. If done after performance, goal setting usually comes across to people as punitive and unfair. For example, if you ask, "Why didn't you turn in a report on the Johnson situation?" and that is the first the employee heard of the need or desire for a report, the employee might rightfully wonder: "What report?"

Behavior is the performance you want. In most of their activities, managers try to influence the performance behavior of others. This can be done primarily with activators, as was just discussed, or with consequences; that is, anything that happens after behavior.

Consequences are what follow behavior. While goal setting can set the stage for good performance, it does little to ensure the desired performance will continue. That's where managing consequences comes into play. As we discussed in chapter 10, Developing Human Resources, there are three main consequences that can follow someone's performance: something positive, something negative, or nothing at all. If you do something and that performance is followed by a *positive consequence,* you will want to repeat that performance. Positive consequences tend to increase the frequency of a particular behavior. If you do something and that behavior is followed by a *negative* consequence, you will probably not do it again. Negative consequences tend to decrease the frequency of a particular behavior.

Figure 18-1, the ABCs of Management, summarizes these above ideas and relates these ABCs to the three "keys" of One Minute Management.

What happens when you work hard on a project but no one seems to notice or say anything about it? You might work harder the next time to see if you get any attention. But after a while, when your hard work gets no response, motivation and subsequent performance drop. Thus, *no consequence* at all also tends to decrease the frequency of a particular behavior.

The only consequence that tends to increase the frequency of behavior is a positive consequence. And yet, the two most frequent responses people consistently get to their performance are negative responses and no responses. This leads to the "leave alone/then zap" style of management, mentioned in chapter 17, that has come to be the predominant management style in most organizations.

Once managers know their ABCs, they usually want to know

FIGURE 18-1   The ABCs of Management

The term:

A	B	C
ACTIVATOR	BEHAVIOR	CONSEQUENCE

What it means:

What a manager does before performance	Performance: What someone says or does	What a manager does after performance

Examples:

One Minute Goal Setting • Areas of accountability • Performance standards • Instructions	• Writes report • Sells product • Comes to work on time • Misses deadline • Types letter • Makes mistake • Fills order	*One Minute Praising* • Immediate, specific • Shares feelings *One Minute Reprimand* • Immediate, specific • Shares feelings • Supports individual *No Response*

Source: Blanchard and Lorber, **Putting the One Minute Manager to Work**
(New York: Morrow, 1984).

what impacts behavior more – activators or consequences. Most managers tend to think that activators like goal setting have more of an impact than consequences on obtaining desired behavior. We have found the reverse to be true. While activators are important, only about 20 percent of what influences people's performance come from these factors – the other 80 percent come from consequences. As we have said before, behavior is primarily controlled by its consequences.

The power of the ABC model for managers is that whenever somebody is not performing at the level you want, you can attribute the behavior to either an activator problem or a consequence problem. An *activator problem* could stem from a number of factors. An employee could lack training or clarity as to what to do. Also, the person may not have known what help and support were available to complete an assigned task. As mentioned, the ACHIEVE model presented in chapter 16, is a good activator checklist of things that should be done beforehand to obtain the desired performance.

The most common *consequence problem* occurs when employees do something and nobody says anything. The only time many employees are approached is when they do something wrong. As a result, people's performance deteriorates because they spend all of their time trying to avoid being punished or, rather, trying to avoid the punisher. It can be helpful then for managers to ask: "Why is this person not performing? Did I not provide adequate activators or am I not adequately managing consequences?" Sometimes managers do not do either, and obtaining desired performance becomes almost a random activity. The following is an example of the use of the ABC model to manager employee behavior.

Bob Lorber and his staff worked on a productivity improvement project in a manufacturing plant where there was a very high noise density. People working in the plant were expected to wear hearing protection during working hours to conform to legal requirements and to avoid hearing loss. While everyone was issued hearing protection, few people wore the apparatus in the plant with any consistency. When Bob's staff was asked to see if they could improve the frequency and use of hearing protection in the plant, they immediately wondered whether this contrary behavior was a result of poor goal setting and training (activators) or inappropriate responses to performance (consequences).

They found that hearing protection was discussed and demonstrated in orientation meetings for new employees, so Lorber's staff eliminated the possibility that the low use was an activator problem. They turned their attention to an examination of consequences; that is, what happened when employees wore or did not wear their hearing protection.

They found that most new employees started wearing their hearing protection because of what they learned at their orientation session; however, they soon stopped wearing the protection once on the job. Why was this?

When supervisors noticed a new employee wearing hearing protection, they reported "feeling pleased," yet they seldom communicated any of their thoughts to the new employee. As a result, new employees who conformed to the safety guidelines received no positive supervisory response as a consequence of their behavior. This highlights a point all managers (and parents and spouses, for that matter) should remember: unless good feelings and kind thoughts are expressed, they mean nothing.

So new employees received no positive feedback from their supervisors. But they did get a clear message from other co-workers: they got kidded and called names for being so soft and willing to "butter up to the boss." In other words, a negative consequence. New employees quickly found themselves in a dilemma. If they wore the hearing protection, they got zapped by co-workers; if they did not wear the hearing protection, they got zapped by supervisors. They spent all their time putting the headphones on and off and dodging supervisors to avoid reprimands! It was a wonder they were able to do their jobs at all!

The only way out of this lose-lose dilemma was for supervisors to start to provide a positive consequence. The moment a new employee was seen wearing hearing protection, the supervisor needed to praise the employee: "I see you're wearing your hearing protection. I really appreciate that—it's important. I appreciate your cooperation and feel good about having you on my team." Now the new employee has a positive consequence to match up against a negative one received from co-workers. The positive consequence will tend to influence behavior more strongly over time.

When self-assessment instruments are given to managers, they usually evaluate themselves as supportive, caring people. And yet often when these same managers are evaluated on the same instrument by the people who work for them, they are not seen as supportive, caring people. The reality is that unless you express your good feelings, people often do not know they exist. People are not mind readers.

This point is humorously illustrated by a story of a Swedish couple, Olaf and Anna, who had been married for more than thirty years. Anna said, "Olaf, you never say you love me." Olaf was quick to reply, "Anna, I told you I loved you the day we got married. If I change my mind, you'll be the first to know."

Communication once every thirty years is not enough. Nor is once-a-year feedback delivered during a performance review adequate. Most people need to know how they are performing on a daily basis. You can do this by making use of the ABCs of Management, another simple yet powerful management technique. Putting this concept into practice can make your job as a manager easier and more fulfilling.

THE PRICE SYSTEM

Although learning the ABCs of management and recognizing that any performance problem is either an activator problem or a consequence problem is important, applied behavioral science concepts also come alive when they are integrated into the PRICE system. The PRICE system is a five-step productivity improvement system developed by Robert Lorber and his associates.[3] Lorber and Blanchard Training and Development have been using the PRICE system to improve companies' performance for almost a decade. Both firms have a long list of clients, who have achieved significant bottom-line results in using the principles discussed here. Examples will be discussed later in this chapter.

The PRICE acronym stands for Pinpoint, Record, Involve, Coach, and Evaluate. We will discuss each of these factors, in turn, along with general advice for establishing and implementing a performance-improvement plan.

P—Pinpoint

Pinpoint refers to identifying one or more key performance areas that a manager wants to improve. Remember the 80/20 rule. Most of the performance you want from people—80 percent—comes from 20 percent of their activities. You want to pinpoint performance-improvement areas that will focus on the 20 percent that have the biggest impact. Pinpointing involves a tentative analysis of the problem which will be refined and changed as the PRICE process unfolds.

The areas for improvement may vary quite a bit, depending on you, your unit, and your company. During pinpointing ask yourself: Where is current performance not meeting expectations? Where is the biggest discrepancy between the *real* and the *ideal* level of performance as I see it? Some areas that companies have focused on include:

- Enhanced customer satisfaction
- Improved employee productivity
- Improved return on equipment
- Improved return on capital investment
- Creation of better inventory procedures

- More timely receipt of accounts receivable
- Stimulated innovation
- Expanded managerial training and development
- Increased organizational accountability

If You Can't Measure It, You Can't Manage It

It is important to remember in pinpointing a performance-improvement area that you must be able to measure progress in that area. In other words, you have to be able to observe and quantify performance. There is very little room for vagueness in a successful performance-improvement plan. You must be able to specifically describe the current and desired level of performance and how you will measure improvement as it is made. The five key measurement areas used in many companies are quantity (how many); quality (how good); cost (amount of money); timeliness (on or off schedule); and amount of change (the difference between past and present performance).

You must also establish what you think might be reasonable levels of improvement. Ask how much, how often, by when, and what is an outstanding level of improvement? What is acceptable or minimal? For example, the closure of half of the sales presentations made by a sales staff would most likely be considered outstanding, a closure rate of 10 percent might be considered minimal.

Measurement Formats

Measurements can be made through observations, surveys, interviews, or analyses of reports and records. Which format you use depends on a number of factors, including available time and staff, ease of data collection, and the method that gives you the information you most need. There are several other points to keep in mind regarding measurements:

1. Select measurements that are simple and easy to understand by those who will be held accountable for the measures.
2. Select measurements that are reliable. A measure is reliable if it measures what you say it measures. For example, the number of cold calls made may not measure an increase in the number of divisionwide sales. Cold calls are related to the number of divisionwide sales, but are not a reliable predictor of increased sales. You could have an increase in cold calls, but not a corresponding increase in division sales.
3. Use measures that are fair and unbiased. Measurements become unfair or biased when those collecting the information have a vested interest in the outcome or when the measure involves a great deal of subjectivity. If the outcomes are observable and verifiable by any-

one who cares to examine the results, the measurements are fair and unbiased. In the sales example, the measurements would most likely be unbiased if the accounting office confirms or verifies the sales and forwards the figures to you.

4. Organize measurements so that they can reflect the performance of the smallest work unit. In the sales example, the division may be divided into four regions. You might want to measure and compare regionwide sales figures for each region. These figures would allow you to place greater focus on those regions that require more of your time and expertise to improve performance.

5. Choose measurements that are stable and not subject to too many outside influences and contingencies. In the sales example, if the price for the product changes randomly due to the availability of raw materials, this product might not be an effective outcome area on which to focus—too many variables are outside of one's control.

Although it may not initially seem so, almost anything can be measured. For example, we were asked to increase the "friendliness" of the tellers in a bank that we were working with. When we asked the top manager what was meant by "friendliness," the manager was stumped and finally said: "If you're so smart, why don't you find out for me?" So we set out to find out what a friendly teller was. We asked customers, since they were in the best position to evaluate teller friendliness.

We found there were three ways that people determined whether or not a teller was friendly, and these three ways apply in any situation where people are dealing with customers.

The first thing that was mentioned about a friendly teller was that the teller was good at *name-face recognition*. It is very important to people that they be recognized for who they are. If you don't know their name at first, it is desirable to use it as soon as you do learn it. Customers reported very little name and face recognition on the part of the tellers in this bank. In fact, the typical teller used the customer's name only once or less per interaction.

The second thing that people talked about when they talked about a friendly teller was that the teller had a *friendly face*. How would you measure a friendly face? Again, we asked customers to show us a friendly face versus a very businesslike face. They identified distinctions that we were able to describe to a cartoonist who consequently was able to sketch five faces, from very businesslike to very friendly. After the drawings were prepared, we were able to show them to customers in the bank and ask people to rate the face of each of the tellers on a scale of 1 (very unfriendly) to 5 (very friendly). We found that the average teller's face in this bank was rated 1.5. If any of these tellers were in a good mood, they sure weren't letting their faces know about it!

The third factor that determined friendliness was whether tellers *discussed nonbusiness topics*. A business-related topic would be, "Would you please sign here?" or "Would you like it all in twenties?" A friendly topic would be, "Isn't the weather lovely today?"

Once we knew about the difference between friendly and unfriendly conversation, we were able to specifically observe tellers' interaction and track the instances of "friendly" and "unfriendly" conversation. Every time the teller changed the topic, it would be indicated whether the teller had gone from a business to business topic, or business to friendly, or friendly to friendly, and the like. We found out that the tellers were engaging in less than 10 percent nonbusiness-related conversation. All in all, the tellers communicated professionalism, but not all that much warmth and friendliness toward customers. Since friendliness was an important factor to customers, this was a worthwhile area in which to improve the bank's performance and perceptions.

Prioritize Areas for Improvement

When pinpointing, you will probably identify more than one or two areas to improve. You might want to list several areas to be worked on. Then separate those areas into two groups: those that demand your immediate attention (top priority) and those that aren't quite as pressing (lower priority). Your criteria for separation might be cost, impact on the company's human resources, degree of difficulty for change, centrality to the company mission, or the time the change will take. Initially, with a first or second productivity effort, you might want to choose an area in which you can have a significant impact and where the chances of success are high. Do not try to impact more than three or four areas at once.

To summarize, benefits of the pinpoint step include:

1. Enables managers to see and understand where unit performance improvement is most needed.
2. Helps managers to determine effective measurements for evaluating improvement.
3. Assists managers in selecting priorities for performance improvement.

R—Record

Once you have identified a performance area that you want to improve, the next step is to record present performance in that area. You want to do this for several reasons. First, you don't want to "fix what isn't broken." So many managers tend to generalize from a population of one. To illustrate, we once worked with a manger who owned more than twenty restaurants. When we asked him in what areas he would like to improve performance, he said, "One of the things that really bugs me is that a machine will break down in a restaurant and employees will take their 'own sweet time' to report the broken machine to the central office so we can get it fixed." We asked him, "How many times has that occurred in the last three months?" He said, "What do you mean?" We answered, "Just what we said. How many times has it occurred in the last three months?" The manager said, "I don't know, but yesterday I saw a broken machine that had not been reported." Based on a single incident he was ready to launch an organizationwide performance improvement program!

Start with a Base Line of Data

Make sure you have base-line data before implementing strategies to improve performance. Base-line data are developed by tracking and recording performance or behavior in the area you want to improve so that it can be compared with future data. If you have no base line, it is difficult to assess improvements or changes. Make sure your base line is based on the most recent information.

Record Systematically on an Ongoing Basis

Once data have been collected for problem diagnosis and strategies have been decided upon, tracking data must continue through to the point where you evaluate and decide to de-emphasize this particular productivity improvement effort. Recording data also allows you to identify trends that will give you greater problem definition and clarity and possibly will help to suggest ideas for solutions. There needs to be enough information to show a trend. Trends are influenced by many factors, such as client needs or even, in some instances, the weather. Data gathered over several months or even years, might be appropriate. For example, if you were tracking sales by region and it was found that one sales region out of four had abnormally good performance, you might begin to examine what this region is doing that the other regions are not. The recording is done on an ongoing basis to track progress against performance goals.

In order to increase your effectiveness and collect data most consistently, keep the following points in mind as measurements are recorded:

1. Collect your data regularly and at short intervals. Don't allow lengthy amounts of time to go between data collection points. Opportunities for on-line corrections may be lost, or your people may be

waiting for the positive feedback that comes with productivity improvement. It may also be hard to retrieve the data if they are not collected at short, regular intervals.

2. Collect data in a consistent fashion. If the same person collects data at the same time of the week or month in the same way, the incidence or error in the data will be minimized. Otherwise, collection errors can be misleading and frustrating to those trying to improve.

3. Collect data that cover all relevant aspects of the productivity improvement effort. In the sales example, the number of divisionwide sales of a product may be the only outcome measure that will effectively evaluate the program's value.

4. Make sure your data are accurate. Continuously be on the lookout for inaccuracies in your data. Check your figures with data recorded in the past. Use some measures to validate other measures.

Prominently Display Progress

Another crucial factor we have found in tracking progress involves data display procedures. Data that are tracked should be graphically depicted in a prominent place for those individuals who can most impact and benefit from the productivity improvement effort. This becomes an automatic feedback mechanism that can help motivate employees. When progress is being made, the graph can be a source of pride to workers and managers.

To return to our teller example, performance could be tracked on a graph (see Figure 18-2). The horizontal axis represents time—when and how often performance will be observed. The vertical axis is used to track performance improvement. So if you are going to measure friendliness once a week for ten weeks, each of the weeks (one through ten) would be indicated at the bottom of the graph. If the person was initially identified as engaging in 8-percent friendly conversation and the goal was to get that teller up to 35 percent, that measure would appear on the vertical axis. The same with sales, profits, or any other area you have decided to track.

To summarize, benefits derived from recording present performance include the following:

1. Prevents managers from "fixing what is not broken."
2. Gives managers a clear starting point for improvement.
3. Sets up opportunities for managers to praise future progress.
4. Enables managers to track performance and to make decisions about how to improve performance.
5. Allows managers to check on the validity and reliability of outcome measures.

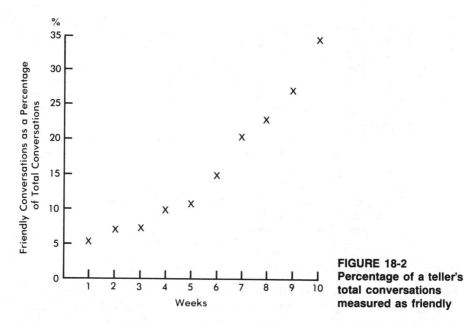

FIGURE 18-2
**Percentage of a teller's
total conversations
measured as friendly**

6. Results in a clear graphic representation of past and ongoing performance.
7. Provides managers with an opportunity to reevaluate the pinpoint stage and refine their perceptions of the problem.

I—Involve

Once you have recorded in order to present performance in a pinpointed area, you are now ready to involve others. A manager can personally do the pinpoint and record stage, but to effectively implement a performance-improvement project, the people who can most influence that area must be involved.

This stage requires you to work in two different ways with your people. First, you need to work with the *group* as a group or team to build consensus around goals, standards, and strategies. Then you need to work with *individuals* in the group to set personal performance goals that correspond with the group goals. Individual involvement provides an opportunity to identify the people who can influence the problem and get them squarely behind the effort to improve unit performance.

You need to engage your people in dialogue that may refine or redefine the area of improvement, based on the perceptions and contributions of the group members. Involving is a mutual process of setting standards to which your people can be committed, as well as brainstorming strategies and incentives for reaching the desired performance outcomes. The most important thing to realize is that for any productivity improvement program to succeed, this step must be a group effort. The involve stage consists of four steps: (1) inform; (2) agree on standards and strategy formulation; (3) set goals with individuals that correspond with unit goals; and (4) establish rewards and incentives.

Inform the Group

In this step you share the information gathered in the record stage. In presenting the results of your investigation, you focus on the performance of the unit as a whole, rather than evaluating the problem on an individual performance basis. To be effective, informing should allow for an exchange of data wherein you can ask your group's opinion of the accuracy of the problem and the feasibility and appropriateness of different solutions. Remember that your view of the problem may change, depending on the data and the perceptions of others.

Agree on Standards and Strategies

After you have passed on the data, your group must focus on setting performance standards. Share with your group the tentative performance standards you established in the pinpoint stage. Even though you have developed your own ideas, the group should agree on the standards, since they will be required to maintain them. That's why it is important to develop reasonable standards with the group. Standards should be determined for three levels of performance: minimal, acceptable, and outstanding. To gain perspective and help determine reasonable ranges for each of these three levels, look to past performance, industry averages, and the capabilities of those involved.

The group must then develop strategies for achieving the levels of expected improvement in the targeted areas. The group must reach some agreement as to how the improvement will occur. The means of doing this may depend upon such factors as cost, manpower, time, and customer or client reaction. How the group goes about arriving at suitable strategies will depend on the group's history and patterns of working together and the manager's management style. The manager should facilitate an open exploration of all alternatives. Strategies that you come up with as a group may lead to further data collection or to the establishment of strategy measures to be collected during the productivity improvement effort. At the end of this step, a group action plan should be in place that will facilitate a group effort toward the intended change. It should no longer be your plan, but the group's plan—one they have generated and one to which they can be committed.

Set Individual Goals

Much has already been said about goal setting, and the point that is to be emphasized here is that individual goals need to mesh well with those of the overall group. Because different employees perform different functions in the organization, the goals will vary quite a bit. A person in sales uses different skills from one in training or advertising, yet each will contribute to the overall effort of improvement. The variation in function becomes more diverse as the unit involved in the project increases in size or the goal itself becomes more complex.

Determine Rewards and Feedback

If productivity is to be sustained, it will be necessary to set up a system of feedback for performance at each level and for each phase of the performance-improvement project. As mentioned in the record step, managers should use the ongoing posting of information in graphs as an opportunity to celebrate the progress being made. People take pride in their own performance and like to see and be recognized for a job well done. As the members of the group reinforce each other's performance, group pride develops. Managers can have an enormous impact on shaping the work atmosphere. It is useful to explore specific ways to create a climate of appreciation. For instance, incentives can help increase the chances of performance improvement. At the very least, healthy amounts of praise and encouragement are important, and sincere appreciation for work well done is a must!

To summarize, the benefits of the involve step include the following:

1. Allows for employee commitment as to how the performance is improved.
2. Allows for employee input into the standards and levels of performance. How much can be done by when is as important to the employee as it is to you.
3. Allows for employee understanding as to how their individual goals fit into the overall unit goal.
4. Emphasizes informal and formal incentives to reinforce outstanding performance.

C—Coach

In many ways the pinpoint, record, and involve steps are all activators. They are all things that need to be done *before* you can expect performance improvement. It is in the fourth step—coaching—that managers begin to deal with consequences. Coaching involves the management of consequences by praising progress, reprimanding poor performance, and redirecting the errors of inexperienced people. As such, this step is closely associated with some of the principles discussed in the last chapter involving One Minute Management. People need to be praised for good performance. When performance is not measuring up, you may need to restate what you want and how it is to be done. When good performance drops off, a reprimand may be necessary. In Situational Leadership, coaching occurs when you deliver and use the agreed-upon leadership style.

Coaching Requires
Constant Communication

Sometimes managers monitor the performance of individuals, but fail to give them feedback on their efforts until they make a mistake. Even worse, some managers do not even monitor the job being done until a problem arises. In addition, many managers do not think of showing sincere appreciation for a job well done when the goal is accomplished. Nor do they think about reinforcing "successive approximations" of goal accomplishments when the task is new or difficult. Too often performance is regarded as "what we pay them for."

Consequences Must Be Clear

As described earlier in this chapter in the ABCs of Management, it can't be emphasized enough that good performance is managed by its consequences. You must notice your people's efforts and apply consequences to their behavior. When you ignore performance, your people may initially try harder so as to receive some kind of recognition. But if that recognition does not come, they usually stop trying as hard because, from what they've seen where they work, good performance makes no difference. As a manager, you must use consequences to separate good performers from poor performers. If you do not treat the two differently, there is little motivation to be a good performer (except for self-pride), and you will demotivate your good performers or lose them to another company.

Poor performers also need to know of the consequences, the available assistance, and the feedback that you will provide them in order to help them to succeed. When working with a new person or a new task, the employee is in a training mode. Training takes time, and the learner needs to know that you will be there to support and encourage and to apply consequences as learning and performance occur.

Types of Consequences

There are four types of consequences that make a difference when working with people: praise, redirection, renegotiation of goals and/or standards, and reprimands.

Praise. Praise is showing sincere appreciation for a job well done. It should follow the accomplishment of a goal or the successful completion of interim steps toward a goal.

Redirection. Redirection is the restatement of what is to be accomplished and how. Simply stated, redirection involves returning to the beginning and restating with greater clarity the goals and a revised plan for reaching those goals.

Renegotiation. In this case, you change a person's goals, strategies, or standards because existing ones are inappropriate for some reason. The standard might be too low or too high, the strategies no longer suitable, or the goal no longer relevant or feasible.

Reprimand. A reprimand is stating your displeasure with performance. It should follow instances of poor performance or times when a person who has demonstrated ability should be doing better. Reprimands should not be used with learners or before all the facts concerning performance have been gathered.

To summarize, the benefits of the coaching step include the following:

1. Employees get immediate feedback on performance.
2. Feedback is specific and concerned with behavior.
3. Employees feel appreciated and recognized for their efforts.
4. Learners are not punished while they learn.
5. Renegotiation is built in as the situation changes.

E—Evaluate

Since data is constantly being collected and you are continually coaching, it could be asked why evaluation is a separate step in the PRICE system. Evaluation allows a formal way to recognize progress and evaluate future strategies and directions. It sets a date in the future with enough time allowed for trends to develop. Month-by-month coaching and evaluation of individual performance may not allow for total project evaluation, so the evaluation is of value for its overall analysis for the group.

At predetermined, periodic intervals, managers and their people need to sit down and evaluate performance. At this time, there should be no surprises. Interaction between the manager and employees will be reviewed and progress toward goals assessed. In this step, you might also find that you obtained the results you wanted and are ready to put your efforts elsewhere. If the project shows positive impact, you should celebrate the improvement.

Or you might determine that strategies are not working and that you must create some alternatives. If the data reveal little or no progress, then you must return to the involve stage and get your people to generate different strategies, assuming the incentives and standards were initially valid. Go back and restrategize, set standards, and apply consequences to individual goals with the knowledge gained from this overall evaluation of the project. If you choose to discontinue the effort, leave the tracking mechanisms in place to review the data at a future date.

In the event there is little or no progress, avoid punishing the group. When you evaluate, try to focus on results and reasons why they weren't realized, as well as new strategies that can be generated to obtain the desired results. There can be many reasons for lack of progress since performance can break down at every stage of the PRICE system. You might have pinpointed an irrelevant area, or you could have been recording data ineffectively. In the involve stage, your people might have agreed to too high or too low a goal. Your feedback may have been erratic or your consequences not sufficiently motivating.

In many ways, responsibility for the success of the project rests on the shoulders of the manager, who must take significant responsibility for ensuring that employees perform well. If proper results are not obtained, try to learn why and attack the problem again, this time armed with new knowledge and experience. The evaluation stage also includes an examination of a manager's own leadership behavior. Did you continually emphasize and reinforce the change you requested? Did you use consequences effectively? Did you allow enough time for the desired improvement to occur? Were there unexpected internal or external conditions that might have influenced the data?

To summarize, the benefits of the evaluation step include the following:

1. Formalizes the examination of project results and the group effort.
2. Allows for further group strategy generation and problem solving.
3. Requires alternative actions if little or no progress has resulted.

Many of the principles of the PRICE system that we have elaborated here are taken from the Blanchard Trucking and Distribution Case, by Zigarmi, Blanchard, and Lorber.[4]

The principles of the PRICE system and the ABCs of Management are both discussed in *Putting the One Minute Manager to Work*. They are graphically illustrated and explained in the Putting the One Minute Manager to Work Gameplan.[5]

PRINCIPLES IN PRACTICE

We have presented some very powerful principles in this chapter. To demonstrate the impact they can have, we'd like to share the experiences we've had with three companies that incorporated these principles into their organizations. We believe that the results obtained by these organizations are both realistic and typical of any organization that makes a firm commitment to install and maintain a system in which the principles of Situational Leadership and One Minute Management are practiced. Following are the results of application at Transco, Canadian Pacific, and Fairweather.

Transco Energizes

Transco Energy Company became committed to learning and applying the principles discussed in this chapter and, working with Blanchard Training and Development, implemented a three-phase approach that involved:

- *Phase Ia*—Five one-day training sessions over a two-month period for the top one hundred managers, which focused on developing the three skills of the One Minute Manager.
- *Phase Ib*—The training of eight in-house trainers on the One Minute Manager skills. These trainers later provided workshops for the lower level management down through the supervisory management level over an eight-month period (this overlapped with the training in Phase Ia).
- *Phase II*—Five two-day sessions focused on Leadership and Group Development for the top one hundred managers of Transco over a two-month period.
- *Phase III*—The development of Productivity Improvement Projects and Teams focused on increasing productivity by improving operations and cutting costs. BTD's goals were the creation of eight to fifteen projects within six months.

As a result of this effort, the company closely tracked its cost and savings that could be directly attributed to the extensive training and were able to document savings of more than $2 million in a nine-month period. Based on a $159,000 training investment, that's a ten-to-one return. Some twenty-four performance improvement projects were initiated within six months that involved sixty-four core team members.

Says George Slocum, president of Transco:

> We project $18 million in savings over the next two and one-half to three years. In addition, there has been a noticeable movement toward collaborative and participative management styles at Transco as a result of our managers learning the secrets of One Minute Management, developing the flexibility of a Situational Leader, functioning more effectively in teams, and mastering the PRICE Model for productivity improvement. . . . I couldn't be more positive about the ability of these principles to make a difference in the companies in which they are applied.

Canadian Pacific Keeps Trucking

The scenario was repeated at Canadian Pacific Trucking, where fuel costs were reduced by 10 percent in four months; claims were reduced by 50 percent in eight months; and accounts receivable dropped from an average collection period of forty-nine days to forty-one days in a nine-month period.

Training at Canadian Pacific also involved a three-stage approach: unfreezing and initial training, skill training and ongoing consultation, and refreezing and evaluation. Prior to the start of any training, an "implementation team" was established to help monitor the project, several days of confidential interviews were conducted with selected top- and mid-level managers, and an extensive survey of all employees was taken that covered the topics of leadership, communication patterns, decision-making patterns, meeting effectiveness, performance appraisal practice, training opportunities, role clarity and standards, role conflict and overload, feedback and rewards on performance, and equal employment opportunity practice.

Phase I: Unfreezing and initial training. After the initial data collection and planning, a two-and-one-half day Situational Leadership–One Minute Management seminar was conducted for the company's senior management staff. During the workshop, each senior manager planned how he intended to implement Situational Leadership back on the job. Each manager was also encouraged to begin a performance- and productivity-improvement project. Five one-day videotape workshops were conducted on the same material for mid-level managers at various company sites.

Phase II: Skill training and ongoing consultation. More specific skill training was then conducted with senior management staff during two two-day workshops given a month apart. In these sessions, management was taught to determine the development level, needs for direction, and support needs of each of their employees. Managers were taught how to be more flexible with their management styles as the situation warranted. The skills of effective performance planning, performance monitoring, and performance evaluation were also taught. Individual coaching and counseling were provided to managers as they implemented these skills and their performance- and productivity-improvement plans.

Phase III: Refreezing and evaluation. At this stage specific work was done with the company's performance review system, including new performance planning, monitoring, and evaluation policies and procedures, and record-keeping forms, based on Situational Leadership and One Minute Management. New positions were designed as needed to maintain ongoing progress of the initial work that had been done. Once the new system was developed, consultants worked with the implementation team and in-house trainers to assure that managers were adequately trained on how to use the system. Additional follow-up training using a variety of diagnostic instruments focused on management styles during crisis situations.

The final impact of the training and development efforts was made and provided to top management and the implementation team. The president of the company, Karl Wahl, claims:

> The PRICE Model has been a major tool in improving results in the key accountability areas of safety and cargo claims prevention, and has resulted in significant savings to our company.

A Fairweather Forecast

What happened at the Fairweather stores—a moderately priced women's fashion chain with 150 stores in Canada—also serves as a good example. As part of our training sessions, we have initially explained to managers at Fairweather how most businesses are organized like a pyramid, with hourly employees at the bottom and the chairman at the top. There is nothing wrong with pyramid organizations unless people *think* in terms of the pyramid. When that happens, they work for the person above them. When this occurs, managers think they are responsible, and the people who report to them must be responsive to them. People think they are at the mercy of their boss's whims.

At our suggestion, they turned the pyramid upside down, so that the customers were placed at the top of the organization and given greater service. With the inverted triangle philosophy, managers work for their people and are thus responsive to their people's needs.

In the summer of 1985, we heard seven Fairweather store managers and Rick Colbear, the company's director of training, share with top management of the division how they had implemented the PRICE system and the inverted triangle philosophy. By implementing the PRICE model throughout key stores in the Toronto area and adopting the "inverted triangle" philosophy, Fairweather made tremendous gains in performance. The difference between 1984–1985 earnings and those of 1983–1984 was almost a million dollars in terms of productivity improvement.

One of the more exciting aspects about the implementation of One Minute Management concepts at Fairweather is that they did it by themselves. For a long time, we knew that organizations didn't need consultants if they were really committed to implementing and using concepts they had learned. Managers at Fairweather proved this was true by showing the initiative and follow-through necessary to stick with implementing management techniques they believed in.

In the final analysis, the most important thing about any management concept is whether or not it works on a day-to-day basis. The proof is in the application. And at the three sample companies discussed in this chapter – Transco, Canadian Pacific, and Fairweather – the application became proof.

Applications of the principles discussed in this chapter are further discussed in Chapter 19, Implementing Situational Leadership: Making Decisions That Stick. As is the case in learning about leadership concepts and techniques and *not* applying them, that chapter will show how making decisions and not following up on them leads to an ineffective decision-making process.

NOTES

1. This chapter is adapted from Kenneth Blanchard and Robert Lorber, *Putting the One Minute Manager to Work* (New York: Morrow, 1984).
2. *Ibid.*, p. 17.
3. For further information, contact Blanchard Training and Development, Escondido, CA 92029.
4. This case study with worksheets and exercises for classroom or individual use is available from Blanchard Training and Development.
5. Available from Blanchard Training and Development, Escondido, Calif.

19

Implementing
Situational Leadership:
Making Decisions That Stick

Making decisions that stick and building commitments are two of the most important activities a manager can perform. Both are essential to managerial success. In this chapter we will first look at an application of Situational Leadership to making good decisions, an indispensable skill at every level of management. We will then examine a major contribution of the management consulting firm of Keilty, Goldsmith, and Boone[1]—building commitments, which uses Situational Leadership as an important aspect of their approach.

MAKING EFFECTIVE DECISIONS

Managers spend much of their time reviewing and acting on the proposals of associates, upper management, and nonmanagement personnel. As such, it is common to hear some managers spoken of as "decisive" or as "having business sense." Unfortunately, it is also common to hear other managers spoken of as "wishy-washy" or as "lacking prudent judgment." That's why your chances for present success and future career advancement are helped if you can (1) make the right decisions in areas you control and (2) submit sound recommendations when requested by your supervisor.[2]

Viewed in a vacuum, decision making seems like a fairly straightforward process. There appear to be simple steps for collecting and analyzing data, weighing alternatives, testing possible solutions, and arriving at a course of action.

But the world rarely rotates so conveniently. Real-life decisions are usually called for in a pressure-packed environment of inadequate input, conflicting information, budget restraints, time squeezes, scarce resources, and many other elements that cloud the issues and threaten the quality of decisions. Despite all this, poor decision making is not likely to be excused because of the complexities of the manager's workload. The manager needs a simple and logical framework for making decisions that stick.

Situational Leadership can serve as the framework. Just as your diagnosis of follower readiness can determine the high-probability leadership style, it can also indicate which style of decision making is most apt to succeed in a given situation.

Figure 19-1, Problem-solving and decision-making styles, not only describes four problem-solving situations, but also suggests four basic decision-making styles—authoritative, consultative, facilitative, and delegative. Each decision-making style has a high probability of

FIGURE 19-1
Problem-solving and decision-making styles

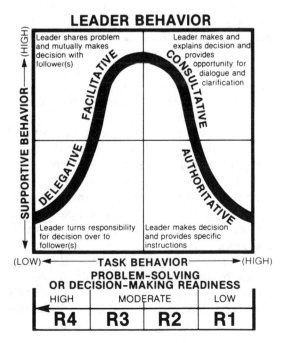

getting results depending on the readiness of the followers and the situation.

Decision Style

Authoritative decision making applies in situations where the manager has the necessary experience and information to reach a conclusion and followers do not possess the ability, willingness, or confidence to help. In this case the manager should make the decision without seeking assistance.[3]

The authoritative style requires directive leader behavior. Followers are usually not actively involved in determining the course of action. Therefore, they hear little about the decision until the manager announces it. Authoritative decisions are commonly communicated with phrases such as "I've decided that . . . " and "Here's what we're going to do. . . ."

What kinds of circumstances require leader-made authoritative decisions? Suppose that your background in product development is all that is needed to set the budget for next year's research program. You've managed your department for four years. You know the goals set for your work group. You are aware of all budgeting policies governing staff, supplies, travel, and so on. Further, your followers know little about budgeting and are new to your department (R1 for most tasks). They are still learning the basics and just are not ready to assist you in making this decision. Therefore, you need to make this decision yourself. Your experience in this area assures you that (1) your conclusion has a high probability of being correct and (2) your proposed budget has a high probability of being accepted by your supervisor.

Authoritative decisions are also required in cases where you are the *only* source of information or expertise. If a co-worker suddenly begins choking—even though your knowledge of first aid is limited—you may be the *only* available resource. While your experience may not provide all the answers you need, there are no other alternatives.

Consultative decision making is a valuable strategy when the manager recognizes that the followers also possess *some* experience or knowledge of the subject and are willing, but not yet able to help. In this case the best strategy is to obtain their input before making the decision.

When using the consultative approach, the manager selects those followers who can help to reach a decision and asks their assistance with phrases such as "What do you know about . . ." and "I'd like some information on . . ." The manager may or may not share all aspects of the problem. After hearing from the followers, *the manager makes the final decision.*

Suppose you are a marketing manager and are considering a new ad campaign for one of your company's products. Two members of your staff have some experience in this area, so you ask their assistance in determining the product market strategy.

Your consultative strategy has two immediate benefits. First, by enlisting the cooperation of your somewhat knowledgeable resources, you increase the likelihood that your decision will be correct. Second, by giving your followers a chance to contribute, you reinforce their motivation and help them identify more closely with the goals of your department.

A word of caution: Whenever you bring others into the decision-making process, you must make the ground rules very clear. Followers low to moderate in readiness, (R2), can be included in the process, but are not ready to run the ball on their own. A consultative decision is still leader-made. To avoid misunderstandings you should let your people know you'll weigh their input carefully but may not follow their advice in reaching a final conclusion.[4]

Facilitative decision making is a cooperative effort in which manager and follower(s) work together to reach a shared decision. In situations where followers are moderate to high in readiness, (R3), the manager can enlist their help with phrases such as: "Let's pool our thoughts and decide on . . ." or "We've got a problem and I'd like your opinion . . ." The implication is that these followers are capable of sharing the authority to decide what should be done.

For example, let us assume that both you and your assistant have been through project management situations before. You know how the scheduling and work assignments should be handled. Your assistant can administer "process" items such as communications, record keeping, reporting procedures, and so forth. Your best approach is to work together in deciding how the new project should be set up. In this case you are effectively committing yourself to a shared decision-making process—a perfectly good leadership style when dealing with an able, but not yet confident follower.[5]

Finally, *delegative* decision making is used with followers high in readiness, (R4), who have the experience and information needed to make the proper decision or recommendation.

In situations where delegation is appropriate, the manager can look forward to a high level of performance simply by saying: "You know this subject . . . work on it and let me know what you come up with."

For example, your plant supervisors are old pros who know how to schedule their swing shifts so that all your requirements are met. Although you could accomplish this task yourself, you recognize that your people are self-motivated and capable of self-direction in this specific situation. Therefore, your high-probability strategy is to delegate this task to them and await their decision.[6]

As a general rule, you can select the appropriate decision-making style by using Situational Leadership to determine "who owns the decision."

- If none of your followers have experience or information in the specific area, they cannot own any part of the decision. You should make the *authoritative* decision by yourself and tell them what to do.
- If your followers have some knowledge of the subject, they may be capable of contributing to (but not making) the final decision. You should seek their help in a *consultative* manner and make your decision after considering their input.
- If your followers have quite a bit of experience, they can take some of the responsibility for making the decisions. You should use a *facilitative* strategy to share the decision-making process with them.
- If your followers have a thorough understanding of the subject and a willingness to deal with it, you should use a *delegative* style. Give them the ball and let them run with it.

It is important to remember that although you may choose to give others a degree of authority in making decisions, the ultimate responsibility is yours alone. However, that's usually no problem for the manager who uses a logical approach to guide the decision maker's process. Followers are usually more likely to approve, follow, and support the decisions of someone who knows not only where to go, but also the best way to get there!

DECISION MAKING AND LEADER LATITUDE

The LaJolla-based management consulting firm of Keilty, Goldsmith, and Boone has adapted the Situational Leadership model to an approach to decision making that combines the leader's decision-making latitude with follower readiness.[7] As illustrated in Figure 19-2, Selecting your decision-making style, the basic decision-making styles of directing (high task–low relationship), guiding (high task–low relationship), supporting (high relationship–low task) and delegating (low task–low relationship) are combined with four degrees of decision-making latitude. These are L1 (little or no latitude), L2 (low to moderate latitude), L3 (moderate to high latitude), L4 (high latitude), L3

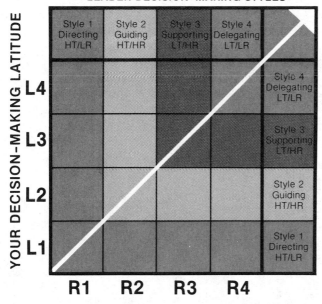

LEADER DECISION-MAKING STYLES

	Style 1 Directing HT/LR	Style 2 Guiding HT/HR	Style 3 Supporting LT/HR	Style 4 Delegating LT/LR	
L4					Style 4 Delegating LT/LR
L3					Style 3 Supporting LT/HR
L2					Style 2 Guiding HT/HR
L1					Style 1 Directing HT/LR

(YOUR DECISION-MAKING LATITUDE)

R1　R2　R3　R4

THEIR DECISION-MAKING READINESS

FIGURE 19-2　Selecting your decision-making style

(moderate to high altitude), and L4 (high latitude). And, as in Figure 19-1, follower readiness is a key variable.

Keilty, Goldsmith, and Boone illustrate the relationships in Table 19-1, Decision-Making Characteristics. This table integrates your decision-making style, characteristics of the decision, your decision-making latitude, follower decision-making readiness, and the characteristics of effective design makers. Working through this table in much the same way as a decision-logic table will help you improve your decision-making skills.

BUILDING COMMITMENTS

Keilty, Goldsmith, and Boone have performed extensive research in identifying and defining the qualities that make managers successful and helping their clients apply these qualities within their own corporation or organization. As frequently happens, some individuals are admired and respected for the way that they manage others, but the reasons for their success are not always apparent. Building on the work of McKinsey and Company, the internationally respected

TABLE 19-1 Decision-Making Characteristics

Your Decision-Making Style	Characteristics of the Decision	Your Decision-Making Latitude	Their Decision-Making Readiness	Characteristics of Effective Decision Makers
Style 1 Directing		L1	R1	
High Task and Low Relationship HT/LR	The decision is made by you or from top down with little input from them	Little or no latitude Decision is already made Decision is nonnegotiable Examples: rules, regulations, clearly defined procedures	They lack the motivation, ability, or understanding to make the decision	Makes the rules clearly understood Levels with people on what is not negotiable Gives specific direction when it is needed Maintains tight controls when necessary
Style 2 Guiding		L2	R2	
High Task and High Relationship HT/HR	The decision is primarily made by you or with high input from them	Low to moderate latitude Decision can be changed but will be made top down Examples: decisions on strategy implementation	They want to be involved, but lack the ability and understanding to make the decision	Gives orientation to people in new assignments Build's people's understanding and ability Takes time to answer questions and explain decisions Provides coaching and guidance when needed

TABLE 19-1 *(continued)*

Your Decision-Making Style	Characteristics of the Decision	Your Decision-Making Latitude	Their Decision-Making Readiness	Characteristics of Effective Decision Makers
Style 3 Supporting		L3	R3	
Low Task and High Relationship LT/HR	The decision is primarily their responsibility with high input from you	Moderate to high latitude Decision must involve you but need not be controlled by you Examples: decisions requiring your feedback to higher management	They have the ability and understanding to make the decision with high input from you	Colloborates appropriately in setting objectives Encourages participation in decision making when appropriate Provides support when needed Builds and maintains people's confidence
Style 4 Delegating		L4	R4	
Low Relationship and Low Task LR/LT	The decision is their responsibility with little input from you	High latitude Decision can legitimately be made by them Examples: their defined job responsibilities	They are willing and have the ability to make the decision with little input from you	Delegates when possible Lets others make decisions when appropriate Encourages others to take as much responsibility as they can handle Gives people the freedom to do their job well

461

management consulting firm, and through their experience with many excellent companies and managers, they have developed valuable insights and a very useful model concerning managerial excellence, The Five Key Commitments model, shown in Figure 19-3.[8]

The essential qualities and relationships necessary for successful management can be explained and understood. Managerial excellence stems from *commitment,* a characteristic common to all individuals recognized for successful management.

Managers carry out their tasks in an interpersonal world. Other people continually view the manager's manner, bearing, and conduct. From their observations, they form impressions of the manager's values, beliefs, and attitudes. Excellent managers make a powerful and positive impression on others because they blend a set of positive beliefs with an equally appropriate set of positive behaviors. These beliefs and actions form "commitments." The most effective managers share a fundamentally similar set of five commitments. These are

- Commitment to the customer
- Commitment to the organization
- Commitment to self
- Commitment to people
- Commitment to task

FIGURE 19-3 The Five Key Commitments model

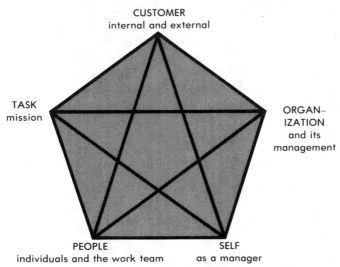

Louis Boone and James C. Johnson, "Profiles of the 801 Men and 1 Woman at the Top," Business Horizons, 23, no. 1 (February 1980).

Separately, each commitment is extremely important to effective management. Together, these commitments form the essential framework for long-term achievement of managerial excellence. True excellence seems to result from genuine dedication and positive service in all five areas of commitment. Figure 19-3 shows the five key commitments and their interrelationships.

Commitment to the Customer

The first and probably most important management commitment focuses on the customer. Excellent managers strive to provide useful service to customers. A customer is defined as anyone who rightly should benefit from the work of a manager's unit. For some managers, their work directly affects the external customer. For other managers, the essential customer is internal. For example, employees in one unit often serve members of another unit in the same organization. Whether the customer is primarily external or internal, the key to this commitment is service. The two primary ways in which an excellent manager demonstrates strong commitment to the customer are serving the customer and building customer importance.

Serving the customer boils down to consistent, conscientious dedication to customer needs. This requires responsiveness to customers through continually encouraging and listening to input from the people who use the manager's services or products. Clear, current identification of customer needs is necessary to genuinely serve the customer. In addition to knowing the customer and the needs of the customer, the excellent manager acts to solve customer problems in a timely manner.[9]

Building customer importance means presenting the customer in a positive manner to those who actually provide service to the customer. The customer is not always appreciated by others within an organization. In fact, some employees view the customer as a necessary evil. To these employees, the customer is the source of most problems and often is viewed as someone to be tolerated. Excellent managers build customer importance by (1) clearly communicating the importance of the customer to employees; (2) treating the customer as a top priority; and (3) prohibiting destructive comments about the people who use their work group's products or services.

Commitment to the Organization

The second management commitment focuses on the organization. Effective managers personally project pride in their organizations. They also instill the same pride in others. A manager positively demonstrates this commitment in three ways: building the organization, supporting higher management, and operating by the basic organizational values.

Building the organization is achieved by constantly presenting the organization in a positive way. Most people lose their motivation if they are ashamed of where they work or embarrassed by what they do. They want to be part of something positive. The excellent manager builds support for what the organization does and effectively prevents destructive comments.

Supporting higher management is essential to the loyalty any organization needs in order to function. Excellent managers add value to the organization by showing and inspiring this necessary loyalty. These managers view their position in the organization as involving a dual responsibility (see Figure 19-4). The first responsibility is to actively challenge and lead "up" in the organization. The excellent manager takes decisions from above in the organization, makes them work, and expects others to do likewise. This manager does not blame higher management or pass the buck. The excellent manager's behavior strengthens the organization's ability to implement decisions and achieve objectives.

Operating by the basic organizational values clearly communicates the importance of what the organization stands for. A difficult aspect of managerial excellence is living the values of the organization, especially when those values are challenged during trying times. If an organization has a clearly defined and communicated set of basic beliefs, it is the manager's responsibility to function in a manner consistent with those fundamental beliefs. Managers are the clearest models of what the organization stands for. The excellent manager lives up to this challenge and this commitment.[10]

FIGURE 19-4   The roles of the manager

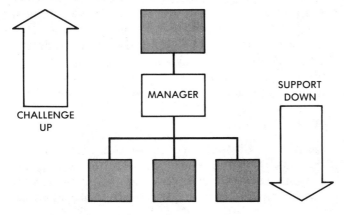

Commitment to Self[11]

The third management commitment focuses on the manager personally. Excellent managers present a strong, positive image of others. They act as a positive force in all situations. This is not to be mistaken as self-serving or selfish. Excellent managers are seen as individuals who combine strength with a sense of humility. Commitment to self is evidenced in three specific activities: demonstrating autonomy, building self as a manager, and accepting constructive criticism.

Demonstrating autonomy is an important dimension for an effective manager. Within their own organizational units, excellent managers act as though they are running their own business. They take responsibility and ownership for decisions. They stand up for personal beliefs. When taking risks, they are reasonable and more concerned with achieving excellence than "playing it safe."

Building self as a manager deals with the self-image a manager projects to others. Excellent managers appear confident and self-assured. They act on the basis of total integrity. They do not belittle or overplay their own accomplishments. It becomes obvious to others that these managers belong in their jobs. Excellent managers live up to the faith others place in them. They act on the basis of honesty and expressly behave with exceptional integrity.

Accepting constructive criticism forms a balance with the first two aspects of a positive commitment to self. Many people act autonomously and worthy of their positions. It is the truly excellent manager who remains receptive to criticism or comment in order to become even better. Excellent managers demonstrate long-term ability to admit mistakes, encourage and accept constructive criticism, and avoid recrimination and adverse reaction. In other words, after receiving personal feedback, excellent managers do not "shoot the messenger" or discount the message. It is not easy to graciously accept criticism. However, the ability to listen and act positively to improve oneself is essential to sustain personal excellence over time.

Commitment to People

The fourth management commitment focuses on the work team and individual group members. Excellent managers display a dedication to the people who work for them. This denotes the manager's use of the proper style of leadership to help individuals succeed in their tasks. Figure 19-5 reinforces the developmental process of matching leadership style to the ability and motivation of individuals. Positive commitment to people is demonstrated daily by a manager's willingness to spend the necessary time and energy working with people. Specifically, three vital activities comprise this commitment: showing

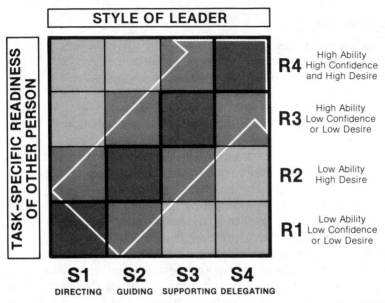

STYLE OF LEADER

TASK-SPECIFIC READINESS OF OTHER PERSON

R4 High Ability
High Confidence
and High Desire

R3 High Ability
Low Confidence
or Low Desire

R2 Low Ability
High Desire

R1 Low Ability
Low Confidence
or Low Desire

S1 **S2** **S3** **S4**
DIRECTING   GUIDING   SUPPORTING   DELEGATING

FIGURE 19-5   Using the leadership style that fits

positive concern and recognition, giving developmental feedback, and encouraging innovative ideas.

Showing positive concern and recognition focuses on the positive aspects of making people feel and act like winners. This is accomplished through rewarding and reinforcing others' performance. It also involves the creation of an environment in which people treat each other with courtesy and respect. For example, destructive comments concerning other people are not acceptable.

Giving developmental feedback is a realistic method of dealing with individual performance failure or setback. People sometimes fail to live up to positive expectations. The excellent manager is willing to intervene when performance does not meet established standards. Using honest feedback, the excellent manager works with the individual to reestablish realistic performance goals. Also, the manager is willing to take the time to guide and coach the individual to improve performance.

Encouraging innovative ideas demonstrates interest in others and stimulates individual and group progress. This positive action is often the difference between successful work teams and those that stagnate or disintegrate. The excellent manager taps into the full capacity of people through such common-sense actions as listening to others' ideas, providing opportunities to test ideas, and directing the credit for a successful idea to its originator. These actions tend to create a desirable atmosphere of confidence, accomplishment, and trust.

Commitment to the Task

The fifth management commitment concentrates on the tasks that need to be done. Successful managers give meaning and relevance to the tasks people perform. They provide focus and direction, assuring successful completion of tasks. The durability of a manager's excellence is demonstrated through the sustained high performance of the organizational unit managed. This commitment is achieved by keeping the right focus, keeping it simple, being action-oriented, and building task importance.

Keeping the right focus refers to maintaining the proper perspective on tasks. The excellent manager concentrates everyone's attention on what is most important. This is determined through knowledge and support of the organization's overall mission. The manager consistently ties individual objectives into larger organizational goals.

Keeping it simple entails breaking work down into achievable components while avoiding unnecessary complications and procedures. The excellent manager fully considers objectives, tasks, and human capabilities, thus restraining the natural tendency to try to accomplish too much. Focus is clearly centered on major objectives within organizational priorities.

Being action-oriented is simply described as accomplishing. Excellent managers get things done. They execute. They maintain positive momentum. Realistic deadlines are set and met. People are encouraged to take action, and a sense of positive direction and accomplishment results.

Building task importance is the element that completes the fabric of managerial excellence. The excellent manager plays up the importance of the work. Excellence in task achievement is an expected result. Continuous excellence becomes the hallmark of the manager and the group.

Consistently applied, the five commitments are the keys to effective management. The manager is the critical link among each of the commitments. The excellent manager takes a personal perspective with regard to the five commitments (see Figure 19-6).

The excellent manager is central to the process of developing and sustaining commitments. By taking personal responsibility and acting as a positive force, the manager can strongly influence the organization and its people, tasks, and customers. The active involvement and personal integrity of excellent managers flow to others. Excellent companies have long realized that "they are their people." What

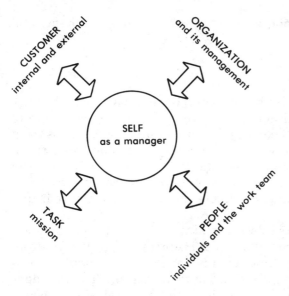

CUSTOMER
internal and external

ORGANIZATION
and its management

SELF
as a manager

TASK
mission

PEOPLE
individuals and the work team

FIGURE 19-6
The central perspective of the manager

separates the excellent companies from the rest appears to be that they simply are made up of a greater number of individual managers acting as models of excellence.

These excellent managers recognize that their own task is to build specific commitments to the customer, organization, key tasks, people, and themselves. For each commitment, this means building proper attitudes and demonstrating positive caring and concern. This becomes the responsibility of every employee, not just the manager. The excellent manager lives by the five commitments and works in concert with others to build commitments. Table 19-2, What Does the Excellent Manager Do? outlines specific behaviors characteristic of the excellent manager in each of the five commitments. Sustaining and replicating excellence is a reinforcing cyclical process based on the five key commitments (see Figure 19-7).

Fundamentally, these commitments are built through dedication and service. When the excellent manager demonstrates genuine dedication and service to employees, they demonstrate a dedication and commitment to their tasks. This dedication to task excellence forms the basis for a strong dedication and service to the customer. The net result is that the customer benefits. As the customer profits, so does the organization. Customers maintain the organization's health and vitality through the same kind of dedication and loyalty to the organization. An organization experiencing continued customer loyalty is then in a position to build loyalty and dedication to its management by providing the tools for management's continued

TABLE 19-2 What Does the Excellent Manager Do?

COMMITMENT TO THE CUSTOMER
internal and external
THE EXCELLENT MANAGER:
Serves the Customer
Knows who the customers are.
Is dedicated to meeting the needs of people who use the organization's services or products.
Encourages and listens to input from the people who use the organization's services or products.
Acts to solve customers' problems in a timely manner.
Builds Customer Importance
Consistently treats the users of the organization's products or services as a top priority.
Clearly communicates the importance of the pople who use the organization's products or services.
Does not allow destructive comments about the people who use the organization's products or services.
Is more committed to customers' long-term satisfaction than the organization's short-term gain.

COMMITMENT TO THE ORGANIZATION
and its management
THE EXCELLENT MANAGER:
Builds the organization
Knows and supports the mission of the overall organization.
Discourages destructive comments about the organization.
Is honest and positive in describing organizational benefits.
Inspires pride in organization.
Supports Higher Management
Describes higher level managers in a positive way.
Avoids destructive comments about higher level managers.
Personally supports higher level management decisions.
Does not pass the buck or blame higher level management.
Operates by the Basic Values
Understands the basic values of the organization.
Manages using the basic values of the organization.
Encourages others to operate using the basic values of the organization.
Takes corrective action when basic organizational values are compromised.

COMMITMENT TO SELF
as a manager
THE EXCELLENT MANAGER:
Demonstrates Autonomy
Stands up for personal beliefs.
Takes responsibility and ownership for decisions.
Takes reasonable risks in trying out new ideas.
Is more concerned with achieving excellence than playing it safe.
Builds Self as a Manager
Shows a high degree of personal integrity in dealing with others.
Presents self in a positive manner.

(Continued)

TABLE 19-2   *(Continued)*

Demonstrates confidence as a manager.
Avoids destructive self-criticism.
Accepts Constructive Criticism
Is willing to admit mistakes.
Encourages and accepts constructive criticism.
Acts on constructive advice in a timely manner.
Does not discourage people from giving constructive criticism.

COMMITMENT TO PEOPLE
individuals and the work team
THE EXCELLENT MANAGER:
Shows Positive Concern and Recognition
Consistently shows respect and concern for people as individuals.
Gives positive recognition for achievement without discomfort to either party.
Adequately rewards and reinforces top performance.
Makes people feel like winners.
Avoids destructive comments about people at work.
Gives Developmental Feedback
Effectively analyzes performance.
Develops specific plans when performance needs improving.
Strives to improve people's performance from acceptable to excellent.
Gives developmental performance feedback in a timely manner.
Encourages Innovative Ideas
Encourages suggestions for improving productivity.
Provides opportunities for others to try out new ideas.
Acts on ideas and suggestions from others in a timely manner.
Avoids taking credit for the ideas of others.

COMMITMENT TO THE TASK
mission
THE EXCELLENT MANAGER:
Keeps the Right Focus
Knows and supports the mission of the overall organization.
Ties individual objectives to larger organizational goals.
Concentrates on achieving what is most important.
Places greater emphasis on accomplishing the mission than following procedures.
Keeps It Simple
Keeps the work simple enough to be understood and implemented.
Breaks work into achievable components.
Encourages efforts to simplify procedures.
Avoids unnecessary complications.
Is Action-Oriented
Communicates a positive sense of urgency about getting the job done.
Emphasizes the importance of day-to-day progress.
Encourages taking action to get things done.
Concentrates on meeting deadlines.
Builds Task Importance
Is committed to excellence in task achievement.
Makes the task meaningful and relevant.
Encourages suggestions for improving productivity.
Does not downplay the importance of the work.

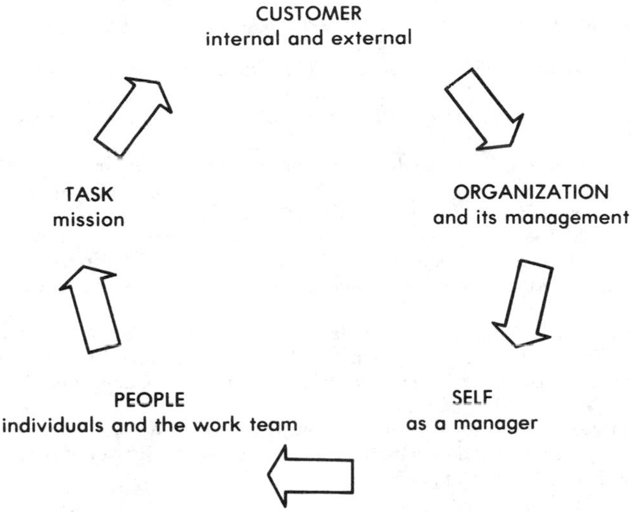

CUSTOMER
internal and external

TASK
mission

ORGANIZATION
and its management

PEOPLE
individuals and the work team

SELF
as a manager

FIGURE 19-7 The commitments as a reinforcing cycle

success. Long-term excellence is not a mystery. It is the result of building commitments.

This concludes the four chapters focusing on implementing Situational Leadership. We have attempted to give you several specific examples of how Situational Leadership and One Minute Management interrelate and how these powerful behavioral science techniques can make measurable improvements in productivity. In chapter 20 we will illustrate how several of the motivational and organizational theories we have discussed can be directly related to the Situational Leadership model.

NOTES

1. Louis E. Boone, C. Patrick Fleenor, and David L. Kurtz, "The Changing Profile of Business Leadership," *Business Horizons,* 26, no. 4, pp. 43–46.
2. Mohammad A. Yaghi, "The Behavioral Model: A New Approach to Decision Making," *Pakistan Management Review,* 23, no. 2 (Fall 1982), pp. 39–49.
3. Joseph Steger, George Manners, and Thomas Zimmerer, "Following the Leader: How to Link Management Styles to Subordinate Personality," *Management Review,* 71, no. 10 (October 1982), pp. 22–28.
4. Waldon Berry, "Group Problem Solving: How to Be Efficient Participants," *Supervisory Management* 28, no. 6 (June 1983), pp. 13–19. See also Edwin A. Locke, David M. Schweiger, and Gary P. Latham, "Participation in Decision Making," *Organizational Dynamics,* 14, no. 3 (Winter 1986), pp. 65–79.
5. Col Eden and John Harris, *Management Decision and Decision Analysis* (New York: Wiley, 1975). See also Robert Hollmann and Maureen F. Ulrich, "Participative and Flexible

Decision Making," *Journal of Small Business Management,* 21, no. 1 (January 1983), pp. 1–7.

6. Patrick J. Montana and Deborah F. Nash, "Delegation: The Art of Managing," *Personnel Journal,* 60, no. 10 (October 1981), pp. 784–87. See also Charles D. Pringle, "Seven Reasons Why Managers Don't Delegate," *Management Solutions,* 31, no. 11 (November 1986), pp. 26–30.

7. Robert R. Blake, Jane S. Mouton, and Mian A. Ghani, "Situationalism vs. One Best Style: A Brief Study of Two Controversial Styles of Managerial Leadership in Pakistan and U.S.A.," *Pakistan Management Review,* 23, no. 2 (Fall 1982), pp. 70–91.

8. Louis Boone and James C. Johnson, "Profiles of the 801 Men and 1 Woman at the Top," *Business Horizons,* 23, no. 1 (February 1980), pp. 47–52. See also Robard Y. Hughes, "A Realistic Look at Decision Making," *Supervisory Management,* 25, no. 1 (January 1980), pp. 2–8.

9. Saul W. Gellerman, *Managers and Subordinates* (Hinsdale, Ill: Dryden Press, 1976). See also Loretta M. Church and Raymond E. Alie, "Relationships between Managers' Personality Characteristics and Their Management Levels and Job Foci," *Akron Business and Economic Review,* 17, no. 4 (Winter 1986), pp. 29–45.

10. Andrew M. McCosh, *Management Decision Support Systems* (New York: Wiley, 1978).

11. J. Keith Murnighan, "Group Decision Making: What Strategies Should You Use? *Management Review,* 70, no. 2 (February 1981), pp. 55–62.

Synthesizing
Management Theory:
A Holistic Approach

All the theories, concepts, and empirical research presented in earlier chapters have made a contribution to the field of management. They seem to have some relevance in diagnosing an environment, in making some predictions, and in planning for changes in behavior. These viewpoints have often appeared to be like threads, each thread unique to itself.

Our attempt in this book has been to weave these independent viewpoints into a holistic fabric to increase significantly the usefulness of each in diagnosis and prediction. In this last chapter we will attempt to integrate these theories, using Situational Leadership (discussed in chapter 8) as a synthesizing framework to portray their compatibilities rather than their differences.

SITUATIONAL LEADERSHIP AND MASLOW'S
AND HERZBERG'S THEORIES OF MOTIVATION

In developing the model of the motivating situation (chapter 2), it was contended that motives directed toward goals result in behavior. One way of classifying high-strength motives is Maslow's hierarchy of needs[1] (chapter 2). Goals that tend to satisfy these needs can be described by Herzberg's hygiene factors and motivators[2] (chapter 3). Both these frameworks can be integrated into Situational Leadership in terms of their relation to various readiness levels and the appropriate leadership styles that have a high probability of satisfying these needs or providing the corresponding goals, as illustrated in Figure 20-1.

It should be stressed that the relationship of Maslow's theory to the readiness levels in Situational Leadership is not necessarily a direct correlation; it is an integrative bench mark to use in attempting to make better decisions for managing human resources. As a result, styles suggested as appropriate for one concept might not be exclusively for that concept; other styles may also satisfy these needs or goals to some degree. This caution will hold true throughout our discussions in this chapter.

Upon examining Figure 20-1, one can begin to plot the styles that tend to be appropriate for working with people motivated by the

FIGURE 20-1 Relationship between Situational Leadership and Maslow's hierarchy of needs and Herzberg's motivation-hygiene theory

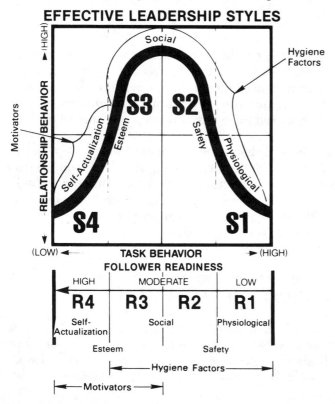

various high-strength needs described by Maslow. At the same time, leadership styles S1, S2, and S3 tend to provide goals consistent with satisfying hygiene factors, whereas styles S3 and S4 seem to facilitate the occurrence of the motivators.

SITUATIONAL LEADERSHIP AND McGREGOR'S, LIKERT'S, AND ARGYRIS' THEORIES

McGregor's Theory X and Theory Y,[3] Likert's management systems,[4] and Argyris' immaturity-maturity[5] continuum (Chapter 3) blend easily into Situational Leadership, as illustrated in Figure 20-2.

In essence, Likert's System 1 describes behaviors that have often been associated with Theory X assumptions. According to these assumptions, most people prefer to be directed, are not interested in

FIGURE 20-2 **Relationship between Situational Leadership and McGregor's Theory X and Theory Y, Argyris' maturity-immaturity continuum, and Likert's management systems**

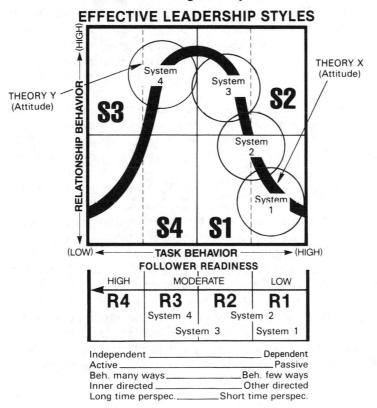

assuming responsibility, and want security above all. The assumptions and the corresponding System 1 behaviors seem to be consistent with the immature end of Argyris' continuum. System 4 illustrates behaviors that have often been associated with Theory Y assumptions. A Theory Y manager assumes that people are *not* lazy and unreliable by nature, and thus can be self-directed and creative at work if properly motivated. These assumptions and the corresponding System 4 behaviors seem to relate to the mature end of Argyris's continuum. System 1 is a task-oriented, highly structured authoritarian management style. System 4 is based on teamwork, mutual trust, and confidence. Systems 2 and 3 are intermediate stages between these two extremes.

In general, the tendency among people is to consider Theory X managers as engaging primarily with task behaviors in highly structured ways and Theory Y managers primarily as using relationship behaviors. This is not always accurate. Theory X and Theory Y are managers' *assumptions* about the nature of people and do not necessarily translate directly into leader *behaviors*. There are examples of both Theory X and Theory Y managers who use all of the four leadership styles.

In one example, Jim, a Theory X manager, calls a staff meeting and asks for participative (S3) solutions to a problem. In reality, Jim may keep everyone at the meeting until they agree with his own *predetermined* ideas for a solution. Jim's behavior is participative in nature, but his assumptions are that only his own answer is acceptable.

In another instance, Sharon, a Theory X manager with a wide span of control, does not have sufficient time to closely supervise all of the people who report to her. Therefore, she uses close supervision (S1) with those people she perceives as major problems and, by necessity, leaves the others on their own (S4).

In a third example, Mike, a Theory Y manager, may demonstrate support (S2) behaviors in explaining his decisions to his employees. However, his behavior may be manipulative rather than "selling" and may be more closely related to his personal objectives than to the goals of the organization or his people.

On the other hand, Mary, a Theory Y manager who has learned to diagnose employee levels of readiness, may be found to use all four leadership styles effectively. With people at below-average levels of readiness, she provides the necessary guidance and close supervision (S1). She gives direction to people whose abilities are improving (S2), and encouragement to those whose confidence is growing (S3). And she delegates appropriately to motivated and competent employees who are capable of functioning on their own (S4).

SITUATIONAL LEADERSHIP AND ARGYRIS', SCHEIN'S, McCLELLAND'S, AND McGREGOR'S THEORIES

As illustrated in Figure 20-3, Argyris' concept of examining A behavior (structured) and B behavior (unstructured) patterns with Theory X and Theory Y;[6] Schein's four assumptions about human nature and their implied managerial styles;[7] and McClelland's achievement motive[8] can also be integrated into Situational Leadership. Argyris contends that most often structured, controlling, A behavior patterns are associated with Theory X assumptions about human nature; and that unstructured, nondirective, B behavior patterns are associated with Theory Y assumptions. But, as discussed in Chapter 3, there is an important difference between attitude and behavior. The relationship between Theory X and Theory Y assumptions and A behavior and B behavior patterns is not necessarily a one-to-one relationship. Thus, as Argyris points out, you can find a number of managers who have the predictable XA combination, but there are also some YA

FIGURE 20-3
Relationship between Situational Leadership and Argyris' A and B behavior patterns, McGregor's Theory X and Theory Y, Schein's four assumptions about people and their implied managerial strategies, and McClelland's achievement motive

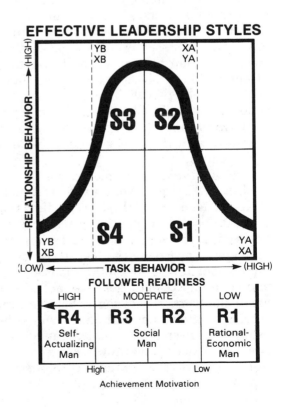

managers. Although both types of managers will tend to use styles S1 and S2, their assumptions or attitudes are not the same. The same holds true for YB and XB managers. Their behavior is similar (S3 and S4), but their assumptions are different.

In his book *Organizational Psychology,* Schein discusses four assumptions about people and their implied managerial styles: (1) rational-economic man; (2) social man; (3) self-actualizing man; and (4) complex man. These assumptions can help us further to integrate the work of Argyris, Likert, and McGregor into Situational Leadership, as seen in Figure 20-3.

The assumptions underlying *rational-economic* people are very similar to those depicted by McGregor's Theory X. In essence, people are seen as primarily motivated by economic incentives: passive beings to be manipulated, motivated, and controlled by the organization, and irrational beings whose feelings must be neutralized and controlled. These assumptions imply a managerial strategy that places emphasis on efficient task performance and would be consistent with styles S1 and S2.

With *social* people come the assumptions that human beings are basically motivated by social needs; they seek meaning in the social relationships on the job and are more responsive to these than to the incentives and the controls of the organization. The managerial strategy implied for social people suggests that managers should not limit their attention to the task to be performed, but should give more attention to the needs of the people. Managers should be concerned with the feelings of their people, and in doing so, must often act as the communication link between the employees and higher management. In this situation, the initiative for work begins to shift from leader to follower, with the leader tending to engage in behaviors related to styles S2 and S3.

Self-actualizing people are seen as seeking meaning and accomplishment in their work as their other needs become fairly well satisfied. As a result, these people tend to be primarily self-motivated, capable of being very self-directed, and willing to integrate their own goals with those of the organization. With self-actualizing people, managers need to worry less about being considerate to them and more about how to enrich their jobs and make them more challenging and meaningful. Managers attempt to determine what will challenge particular workers—managers become catalysts and facilitators rather than motivators and controllers. They delegate as much responsibility as they feel people can handle. Managers are now able to leave people alone to structure their own jobs and to provide their own socioemotional support through task accomplishment. This strategy is consistent with an S4 style appropriate for working with people of high levels of readiness (R4).

According to Schein, people are really more complex than rational-economic, social, or self-actualizing. In fact, people are highly viable, are capable of learning new motives, are motivated on the basis of many different kinds of needs, and can respond to numerous different leadership styles. Complex individuals tax the diagnostic skills of managers, and as Situational Leadership implies, effective managers must change their style appropriately to meet various contingencies.

According to McClelland, achievement-motivated people have certain characteristics in common. They like to set their own goals, especially moderately difficult, but potentially achievable ("stretching") goals. In addition, they seem to be more concerned with personal achievement than with the rewards of success. As a result, they like concrete task-relevant feedback. They want to know the score. As illustrated in Figure 20-3, low achievement motivation tends to be associated with readiness levels R1 and R2, and high achievement motivation tends to be associated with readiness levels R3 and R4.

SITUATIONAL LEADERSHIP AND TRANSACTIONAL ANALYSIS

As discussed in Chapter 3, two concepts from transactional analysis (TA) and the work of Berne[9] and Harris[10] are ego states and life positions. As illustrated in Figure 20-4, these concepts can be integrated into Situational Leadership.

The three ego states in TA are Parent, Adult, and Child. An individual whose behavior is being evoked from the Child ego state can be either a destructive Child or a happy Child. The destructive Child seems to be associated with readiness level R1 and, therefore, the leadership style that is necessary with that Child ego state is S1. Low "strokes" are appropriate because too much socioemotional support along with high structure may be viewed as permissiveness and support for the destructive behavior. If you are interacting with a happy Child, movement is toward readiness level R2, and thus the style that seems to be more effective is S2. Now there is a need for more two-way communication, socioemotional support, and facilitating behavior along with the structure.

An individual whose behavior is being evoked from the Parent ego state can be either a nurturing Parent or critical Parent. The nurturing Parent seems to be associated with R2, and, therefore, the leadership style that is necessary with that Parent ego state, as illustrated in Figure 20-4 is S2. Any role defining or structuring has to be done in a supportive way. Too much task behavior without corresponding relationship behavior might suggest to nurturing Par-

EFFECTIVE LEADERSHIP STYLES

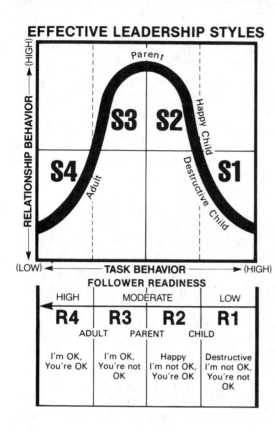

FIGURE 20-4
Relationships between Situational Leadership and ego states and life positions associated with transactional analysis

ents that the person trying to influence them does not care for them and this might move their ego state more toward critical Parent. That form of Parent ego state tends to be associated with readiness level R3 because style S3 tends to work best when trying to work with a critical Parent ego state. If leaders use a high task style with critical Parents, it just tends to evoke more critical Parent "tapes," and soon these leaders may find themselves in a win-lose, Parent-Parent power struggle. To work with individuals with a critical Parent, leaders first must try to develop a good personal relationship with them before being able to use either of the high task styles (S1 and S2) effectively.

In working with people whose behavior is being evoked from their Adult ego state, leaders can use an S4 style and leave them alone. These people are already thinking in rational, problem-solving ways, and provided they have the competence to do their jobs, tend to prefer to be left alone.

As illustrated in Figure 20-4, individuals with an "I'm not OK, you're not OK" life position tend to be associated with readiness level R1 and thus need high direction and close supervision. People who feel "I'm not OK, you're OK" are related to readiness level R2 and thus need both direction and socioemotional support. They will appreciate direction from leaders because they think these people are "OK" but also need high relationship behavior to help increase their "OK" feelings about themselves. People who feel "I'm OK, you're not OK" tend to be associated with readiness level R3. (Remember we are talking about normal people with this ego state and not mentally disturbed people, to whom psychiatrists like Berne would be referring in their discussion of transactional analysis). Since people with this life position are often covering up "not OK" feelings about themselves, they tend to require high relationship behavior from others before feeling "OK" about them or themselves. People with life positions of "I'm OK, you're OK" seem to relate to readiness level R4 because they can be given responsibility and left alone and still feel good about themselves and other people.

SITUATIONAL LEADERSHIP AND CONTROL SYSTEMS

In Chapter 7 we discussed three fundamental control systems: Type I is the most structured and like an assembly line; Type II involves job enlargement, but still requires manager control; and Type III is the least structured and involves job enrichment and little manager control. The impact that these various control systems have on leadership style is illustrated in Figure 20-5.

As evident in Figure 20-5, the appropriate style to use with Type I control system is high task–low relationship; Type II needs a high task–high relationship or high relationship–low task style; and Type III requires a low relationship–low task style. Relationships between control systems and appropriate leadership style are supported by the research of Stinson and Johnson.[11]

SITUATIONAL LEADERSHIP AND POWER BASES

In Chapter 9 we discussed seven power bases: coercive, connection, reward, legitimate, referent, information, and expert. As illustrated in Figure 20-6 and supported by the work of Hersey, Blanchard, and Natemeyer,[12] Situational Leadership can provide the basis for understanding the potential impact of each power base. In fact, in Chapter 9 it was argued that the readiness of the follower not only dictates which style of leadership will have the highest probability of success, but that the readiness of the follower also determines the power base

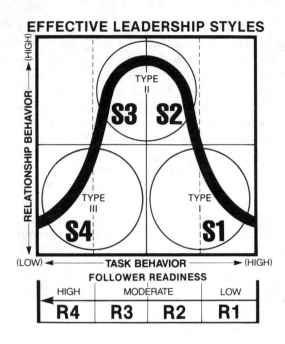

FIGURE 20-5
Structural impact of control system on leadership style

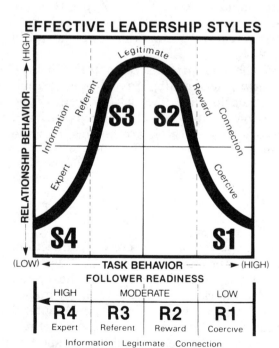

FIGURE 20-6
Relationship between Situational Leadership and power bases

that the leader should have in order to induce compliance or influence behavior.

As is suggested in Figure 20-6, a follower low in readiness (R1) generally needs strong directive behavior in order to become productive. To engage effectively in this S1 style, coercive power is often needed. As a follower begins to move from readiness level R1 to R2, directive behavior is still needed and increases in supportive behavior are also important. The S1 and S2 leadership styles appropriate for these levels of readiness may become more effective if the leader has connection power and reward power. Legitimate power seems to be helpful to the S2 and S3 leadership styles that tend to influence moderate levels of readiness (R2 and R3). Referent power enhances the high supportive, but low directive S3 style required to influence a moderate to high level of readiness. Information and expert power seem to be helpful in using the S3 and S4 styles that tend to motivate followers effectively at above-average readiness levels (R3 and R4).

SITUATIONAL LEADERSHIP, PARENT EFFECTIVENESS TRAINING (P.E.T.), AND MONKEY MANAGEMENT

As discussed in chapter 11, the work of Thomas Gordon[13] on parent effectiveness training (translated into leader-follower terminology) and the Oncken "Monkey Management" analogy[14] integrate well into Situational Leadership. (See Figure 20-7.)

In working with people, Gordon suggests that people's behavior can either be acceptable or unacceptable to leaders. If the behavior of the follower is acceptable to the leader, the leader can use an S3 or S4 style. If the behavior of the follower is unacceptable to the leader, an S1 or S2 leadership style is appropriate. To differentiate further among S1 and S2, and S3 and S4 styles, a leader needs to determine who owns the problem, or "who owns the monkey." As Figure 20-7 illustrates, if the behavior of the follower is acceptable and not a problem to either the leader or the follower (no monkey exists), then an S4 style is appropriate. If that same acceptable behavior is a problem to the follower—that is, the follower lacks understanding or motivation to continue the acceptable behavior for long periods of time—but not to the leader (the follower owns the monkey), the appropriate leadership style to be used with that follower is S3. If a follower's behavior is unacceptable and a monkey to both follower and leader, then an S2 style should be used. And, finally, when the follower's behavior is unacceptable and a problem to the leader, but

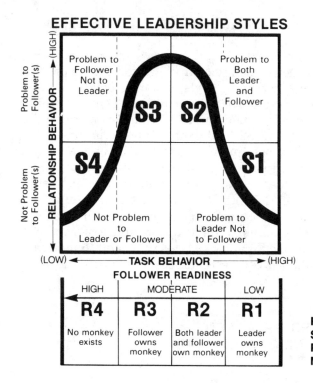

EFFECTIVE LEADERSHIP STYLES

FIGURE 20-7
Situational Leadership,
P.E.T., and Monkey
Management

not a problem to the follower (the leader owns the monkey), an S1 leadership has the highest probability of changing that behavior.

SITUATIONAL LEADERSHIP AND ORGANIZATIONAL GROWTH

As suggested in Chapter 15, organizations might be able to grow and develop over time without the crisis or revolutionary phases discussed by Greiner.[15] This could occur if, after the phase of creativity, managers moved their organization through the growth phases in an order consistent with Situational Leadership.

As illustrated in Figure 20-8, the crisis of leadership might be averted by moving from the phase of creativity right into the phase of direction; the crises of autonomy, control, and red tape might be averted by moving from the direction phase right into the coordination phases, then into the collaboration phase, and finally into delegation.

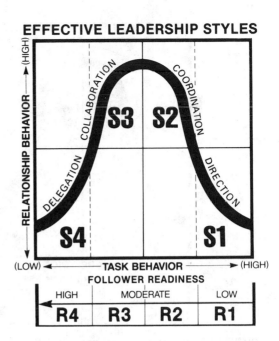

EFFECTIVE LEADERSHIP STYLES

FIGURE 20-8
Situational Leadership and the
evolutionary and growth
phases of organizations
discussed by Greiner

SITUATIONAL LEADERSHIP AND CHANGE

Whenever you talk about initiating change (Chapter 15), a first step is determining the readiness level of the people with whom you are working. If they are low in readiness—dependent and unwilling to take responsibility for the change—they will tend to require more unfreezing (Lewin[16]) than if you are working with people who are moderate or high in their readiness levels. As illustrated in Figure 20-9, leadership styles S1 and S2 tend to play a major role in terms of unfreezing; the emphasis in S2 and S3 styles is on the change process; and S3 and S4 stress the refreezing process.

   One of the techniques used to increase readiness is behavior modification[17] (chapter 10), as illustrated in Figure 20-10. When working with people at low readiness levels, at first leaders tend to cut back on structure, giving individuals an opportunity to take some responsibility. When leaders get the smallest approximation of higher levels of readiness, they must immediately increase their socioemotional support as positive reinforcement. This stairlike process (cut back on structure and then increase socioemotional support) continues until the change or changes start to become a habit as the people develop. At that point, leaders tend also to cut back on rein-

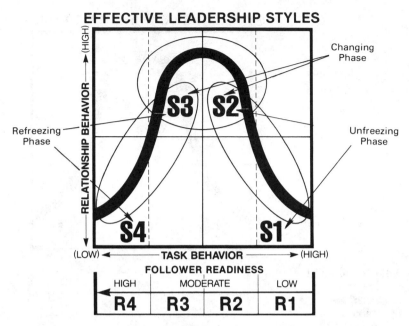

EFFECTIVE LEADERSHIP STYLES

FIGURE 20-9 **Relationship between Situational Leadership and the process of change**

forcement as they move toward S4 and a low relationship–low task style. If done earlier, this cutback on socioemotional support would have appeared as punishment to people at low or moderate levels of readiness. But to people of high readiness, the fact that their leader tends to leave them alone is positive reinforcement, not only in terms of the task, but also in terms of socioemotional support. As depicted in Figure 20-10, Homme's concept of contingency contracting[18] illustrates the gradual development movement (associated with behavior modification) from leader control (S1) to partial control by follower (S2) to equal control (S2 and S3) to partial control by leader (S3) and finally to follower control (S4).

As illustrated in Figure 20-11, S1 and S2 styles seem to be consistent with the behaviors associated with a directive change cycle, while S3 and S4 are more representative of a participative change cycle.[19] In a participative change cycle, the change begins at the knowledge level and eventually moves to the organizational level, while the directive change cycle starts with changes in the organization and gradually moves toward changes in knowledge and attitudes.

As also shown in Figure 20-11, S1 and S2 styles tend to be appropriate for building on strong driving forces; S3 and S4 styles

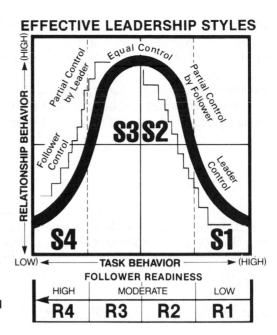

FIGURE 20-10
Situational Leadership and behavior modification

FIGURE 20-11 **Relationship between Situational Leadership, change cycles, and force field analysis**

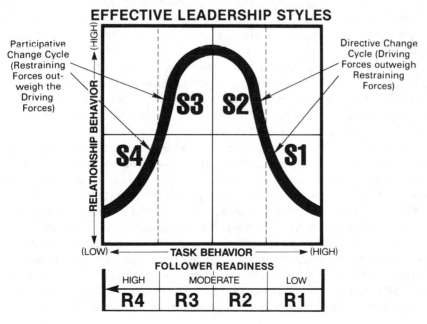

seem appropriate for attempting to overcome restraining forces (chapters 6 and 15).[20] In increasing the driving forces, the emphasis seems to be on short-term output; when attempting to eliminate restraining forces, the concern is more with building intervening variables and concentrating on long-term goals. It should be emphasized that these are only tendencies and bench marks, and it should be recognized that under certain conditions other styles might be appropriate.

SUMMARY

Table 20-1 integrates the summary material presented in this chapter. The table indicates how many of the theories discussed throughout this book are related to the various readiness levels and their corresponding appropriate leadership style.

CONCLUSIONS AND REFLECTIONS

There is still much that is unknown about human behavior. Unanswered questions remain and further research is necessary. Knowledge about motivation, leader behavior, and change will continue to be of great concern to practitioners of management for several reasons: it can help improve the effective utilization of human resources; it can help in preventing resistance to change, restriction to output, and personnel disputes; and often it can lead to a more productive organization.

Our intention has been to provide a conceptual framework that may be useful to the reader in applying the conclusions of the behavior sciences. The value that a framework of this kind has is *not* in changing one's knowledge, but in changing one's behavior in working with people.

We have discussed three basic competencies in influencing: *Diagnosing*—being able to understand and interpret the situation you are attempting to influence; *Adapting*—being able to adapt your behavior and the resources you control to the contingencies of the situation; and *communicating*—being able to put the message in such a way that people can easily understand and accept it. Each of these competencies is different and requires a different developmental approach. For example, *diagnosing* is cognitive in nature and requires thinking skills; *adapting* is behavioral in nature and requires behavioral practice; and *communicating* is process-oriented and requires learning and interrelating the key steps in the process. Since these

TABLE 20-1 Relationship Between Leadership Styles, Readiness Levels, and Other Organizational Behavior Theory, Concepts, and Research

READINESS OF FOLLOWERS (THEREFORE HIGH PROBABILITY)	STYLE OF LEADER
(R1) Low Readiness "Unable and insecure or unwilling . . ." Physiological–safety hygiene factors Rational-economic man Low achievement motivation Child (destructive) ego state I'm not OK, you're not OK Unacceptable behavior Leader "owns the monkey"	(S1) HT/LR Telling "Provide specific instructions and closely supervise . . ." Theory X (attitude) XA/YA System 1/System 2 Coercive and connection power Type 1 control system Leader control contracting Direction growth stage Unfreezing, changing (coercion) Directive change cycle
(R2) Low to Moderate Readiness "Unable but confident or willing . . ." Safety–social hygiene factor Rational-economic man/social man Low achievement motivation Child (happy) or Parent ego state I'm not OK, you're OK Unacceptable behavior Both leader and follower "own the monkey"	(S2) HT/HR Selling "Explain your decision and provide opportunity for clarification . . ." XA/YA System 2/System 3 Connection, reward, and legitimate power Type 2 control by follower–equal control contractor Coordination growth stage Unfreezing, changing (identification) Directive or participative change cycles
(R3) Moderate to High Readiness "Able but insecure or unwilling . . ." Social–esteem hygiene factors and motivators Social or self-actualizing man High achievement motivation Parent and Adult ego states I'm OK, you're not OK Acceptable behavior Follower "owns the monkey"	(S3) HR/LT Participating "Share ideas and facilitate decision making . . ." Theory Y (attitude) YB/XB System 3/System 4 Legitimate, referent, information power Type 2 control system Equal control or partial control by leader contracting Collaborative growth stage Changing–refreezing (internalization) Participative or directive change cycles *(continued)*

TABLE 20-1 *(Continued)*

READINESS OF FOLLOWERS (THEREFORE HIGH PROBABILITY)	STYLE OF LEADER
(R4) High Readiness 　　"Able and confident or willing . . ." 　　Esteem–self-actualization motivators 　　Self-actualizing person 　　High achievement motivation 　　Audlt ego state 　　I'm OK, you're OK 　　Acceptable behavior 　　No monkey exists	(S4) LR/LT Delegating 　　"Turn over responsibility for 　　　decisions and 　　　implementation . . ." 　　Theory Y (attitude) 　　YB/XB 　　System 4 　　Information, expert power 　　Type 3 control system 　　Follower control contracting 　　Delegation growth stage 　　Refreezing 　　Participative change cycle

three competencies require different knowledge and skills, how do we continue the process that we started with this book?

The key to starting the process of changing behavior is sharing the theories that you have read about in this book with other people in your own organization. Two things occur when people who work together all have a common language. First, they are able to give each other feedback and help in a very rational, unemotional way that affects behavior. For example, we once worked with an autocratic manager, "Bill," who was noted for his Theory X memos, such as, "it has come to my attention, and, therefore, as of Monday all personnel will be required to . . ." Shortly after exposing this manager and his staff from two levels below him on the management hierarchy to Situational Leadership, the manager sent out one of his "famous" Theory X memos. Several days later when we talked to him, he related that he had received a number of written (unsigned) comments on the memo. The comments included such remarks as "A little Theory X today, don't you think?" "Do you have anything else in your repertoire beside S1 style?" "Are we really that unwilling?" This feedback had a real impact on the manager as he reexamined his memo and his approach. It was difficult for him to rationalize away the feedback, because like R. D. Laing's *Knots*[21] "he knew that they knew that he knew the theory" and "they knew that they knew that he knew the theory." As some of the managers suggested, this was one of the first times he had really "heard" feedback. As a result of this incident and use of the language in meetings, everyone started helping each other (not just the manager) make changes in their behavior so they could become a more effective working team.

Second, followers start to realize that if their manager is using Situational Leadership it is not the manager, but *their* behavior that determines the leadership style to be used with them. For example, if everyone knows the theory in a family, the children (especially teenagers) realize how they can keep their parents off their backs. All they have to do is behave in solid, responsible ways, which everyone has agreed are appropriate, and their parents will be supportive (S3) or leave them alone (S4). But if they want to get hassled and closely supervised by their parents, all they have to do is misbehave and be irresponsible. Thus, theory is a vehicle to help people understand and share expectations in their environment so that they can gradually learn to supervise their own behavior and become responsible, self-motivated individuals. An observation on leadership by the Chinese philosopher Lao-Tse[22] sums it up well: "Of the best leaders, when their task is accomplished, the people will remark, 'We have done it ourselves.' "

We have provided many examples and illustrations throughout this book showing how the behavioral sciences can make a positive difference in the performance of both individuals and organizations. But perhaps our primary objective in writing this book is to make a contribution to world peace. We believe that significant contributions to human well-being will *not* come primarily through economic, military, political, or technological decisions. If we are going to achieve our long-sought goal of world peace, it must come through utilization of our human resources — toward helping people become more productive and to have a greater share of the benefits that human productivity can achieve. Our outlook is a world outlook for practical applied behavioral science — an outlook that sees all peoples sharing in the benefits that technology can bring, a world of people living and working in an environment that contributes to their personal well-being, a world of peace. We invite you to join us in working toward this goal.

NOTES

1. Abraham Maslow, *Motivation and Personality* (New York: Harper & Row, 1954).
2. Frederick Herzberg, *Work and the Nature of Man* (New York: World Publishing, 1966).
3. Douglas McGregor, *The Human Side of Enterprise* (New York: McGraw-Hill, 1960).
4. Rensis Likert, *The Human Organization* (New York: McGraw-Hill, 1967).
5. Chris Argyris, *Personality and Organization* (New York: Harper & Row, 1957). See also Chris Argyris, Robert Putnam, and Diana M. Smith, *Action Science* (San Francisco: Jossey-Bass, 1985).
6. Chris Argyris, *Management and Organizational Development: The Path From XA to YB* (New York: McGraw-Hill, 1971). See also Chris Argyris and Donald A. Schon, *Organizational Learning: A Theory of Action Perspective* (Reading, Mass.: Addison-Wesley, 1978); Chris Argyris, *Reasoning, Learning, and Action: Individual and Organization* (San Francisco: Jossey-Bass, 1982).

7. Edgar H. Schein, *Organizational Psychology,* 2nd ed. (Englewood Cliffs, N.J.: Prentice Hall, 1970), pp. 50–72. See also Edgar H. Schein, *Organizational Culture and Leadership* (San Francisco: Jossey-Bass, 1985); Edgar H. Schein, *Career Dynamics: Matching Individual and Organizational Needs* (Reading, Mass.: Addison-Wesley, 1978).

8. David C. McClelland, J. W. Atkinson, R. A. Clark, and E. L. Lowell, *The Achievement Motive* (New York: Appleton-Century-Crofts, 1953); and *The Achieving Society* (Princeton, N.J.: D. Van Nostrand, 1961). See also David C. McClelland, *Motivation and Society* (San Francisco: Jossey-Bass, 1982); David C. McClelland, *Motives, Personality, and Society: Selected Papers* (New York: Praeger, 1984).

9. Eric Berne, *Games People Play* (New York: Grove Press, 1964). See also Eric Berne, *Beyond Games and Scripts* (New York: Grove Press, 1976); Eric Berne, *Transactional Analysis in Psychotherapy* (New York: Grove Press, 1961).

10. Thomas Harris, *I'm OK – You're OK: A Practical Guide To Transactional Analysis* (New York: Harper & Row, 1969). See also Thomas A. Harris and Amy Bjork, *Staying OK* (New York: Harper & Row, 1985).

11. John E. Stinson and Thomas W. Johnson "The Path-Goal Theory of Leadership: A Partial Test and Suggested Refinement," *Academy of Management Journal,* 18, no. 2 (June 1975), pp. 242–52.

12. Paul Hersey, Kenneth H. Blanchard, and Walter E. Natemeyer, "Situational Leadership, Perception, and the Impact of Power" *Group and Organizational Studies,* 4, no. 4 (December 1979), pp. 418–28.

13. Thomas Gordon, *P.E.T. (Parent Effectiveness Training)* (New York: Peter H. Wyden, 1970). See also Thomas Gordon, *T.E.T. (Teacher Effectiveness Training)* (New York: Peter H. Wyden, 1974).

14. William Oncken, Jr. and Donald L. Wass, "Management Time: Who's Got the Monkey?" *Harvard Business Review,* November–December 1974, pp. 75–80. See also Kenneth H. Blanchard, William Oncken, Jr., and Hal Burrows, *The One Minute Manager Meets the Monkey,* New York: Morrow (1989).

15. Larry E. Greiner, "Evolution and Revolution as Organizations Grow," *Harvard Business Review,* July–August 1972, pp. 37–46.

16. Kurt Lewin, "Frontiers in Group Dynamics: Concept Methods, and Reality in Social Science; Social Equilibria and Social Change," *Human Relations,* 1, no. 1 (June 1947), pp. 5–41.

17. B. F. Skinner, *Science and Human Behavior* (New York: Macmillan, 1953). See also A. Bandura, *Principles of Behavior Modification* (New York: Holt, Rinehart & Winston, 1969); B. F. Skinner, *About Behaviorism* (New York: Knopf, 1974); A. Bandura and D. Cervone, "Self-evaluative and Self-efficacy Mechanisms Governing the Motivational Effects of Goal Systems," *Journal of Personality and Social Psychology,* 1983.

18. Lloyd Homme, *How to Use Contingency Contracting in the Classroom* (Champaign, Ill.: Research Press, 1970).

19. Paul Hersey and Kenneth H. Blanchard, "Change and the Use of Power," *Training and Development Journal,* January 1972.

20. Lewin, "Frontiers in Group Dynamics."

21. R. D. Laing, *Knots* (New York: Pantheon Books, 1970).

22. Lao-tsu, *The Way of the Ways: Lao-tsu, Translated and with a Commentary by Herrymon Maurer* (New York: Schocken Books, 1985), p. 52.

Recommended
Supplementary Reading

ACKERMAN, LEONARD, and JOSEPH P. GRUENWALD. "Help Employees Motivate Themselves," *Personnel Journal*, 63 (July 1984).

ALBRECHT, KARL. *Service Within: Solving the Middle Management Leadership Crisis*. Homewood, Ill.: Dow Jones-Irwin, 1990.

ALDEFER, C. P. *Existence, Relatedness, and Growth: Human Needs in Organizational Settings*. New York: Free Press, 1972.

ALESSANDRA, ANTHONY J., PHILLIP S. WEXLER, and JERRY D. DEEM. *Non-Manipulative Selling*, 2nd ed. Englewood Cliffs, N.J.: Prentice Hall, 1987.

ALEXANDER, JOHN W. "Sharing the Vision," *Business Horizons*, 32 (May–June 1989), 56–59.

ALLCORN, SETH. "Leadership Styles: The Psychological Picture," *Personnel*, 65 (April 1988), 46–48.

ALTANY, DAVID. "Lead Now, or Forever Rest in Peace," *Industry Week*, 238 (April 17, 1989), 16–17.

ARGYRIS, CHRIS. *Management and Organizational Development: The Path from XA to YB*. New York: McGraw-Hill, 1971.

ARGYRIS, CHRIS. *Organization and Innovation*. Homewood Ill.: Dorsey Press and Richard D. Irwin, 1965.

ARGYRIS, CHRIS. *Personality and Organization*. New York: Harper & Row, Pub., 1957.

ARGYRIS, CHRIS. *Reasoning, Learning, and Action: Individual & Organizational*. San Francisco: Jossey-Bass, 1982.

ARGYRIS, CHRIS. *Strategy, Change and Defensive Routines.* Belmont, Calif.: Pitman Pub., 1985.

ARGYRIS, CHRIS. "Teaching Smart People How to Learn," *Harvard Business Review,* 69 (May–June 1991), 99–109.

ARGYRIS, CHRIS, and RICHARD M. CYERT. *Leadership in the Eighties: Essays on Higher Education.* Management, 1980.

ARGYRIS, CHRIS, and ROGER HARRISON. *Interpersonal Competence and Organizational Effectiveness.* Homewood, Ill.: Dorsey Press and Richard D. Irwin, 1962.

ARGYRIS, CHRIS, and DONALD A. SCHON. *Organizational Learning: A Theory of Action Perspective.* Reading Mass.: Addison-Wesley, 1978.

ASCH, S. E. "Effects of Group Pressure upon the Modification and Distortion of Judgments," in *Group Dynamics* (2nd ed.), pp. 189–200, eds. Dorwin Cartwright and Alvin Zander. Evanston, Ill.: Row, Peterson & Company, 1960.

ASCH, S. E. *Social Psychology.* Englewood Cliffs, N.J.: Prentice Hall, 1987.

AUSTIN, N., and T. PETERS. "A Passion for Excellence," *Fortune,* May 13, 1985, pp. 20–30.

AXLEY, STEPHEN R. "The Practical Qualities of Effective Leaders," *Industrial Management,* 32 (September–October 1990), 29–31.

AXLINE, LARRY L. "TQM: A Look in the Mirror," *Management Review,* 80 (July 1991), 64.

BACHMAN, J. G., D. G. BOWERS, and P. M. MARCUS. "Bases of Supervisory Power: A Comparative Study in Five Organizational Settings," in *Control in Organizations,* ed. Arnold S. Tannenbaum. New York: McGraw-Hill, 1968.

BACLARACCO, JOSEPH L., JR. *The Knowledge Link: How Firms Compete Through Strategic Alliances.* Boston, Mass.: Harvard Business School Press, 1990.

BAILEY, GERALD D., and WILLIAM F. ADAMS. "Leadership Strategies for Non-bureaucratic Leadership," *NASSP Bulletin,* 74 (March 1990), 6–12.

BAILEY, RONALD. "Not Power But Empower," *Forbes,* 141 (May 30, 1988) 119–23.

BAILYN, L., and E. H. SCHEIN. "Life/Career Considerations as Indicators of Quality of Employment," in *Measuring Work Quality for Social Reporting,* eds. A. D. Biderman and T. F. Drury. New York: Wiley (Sage Publications), 1976.

BAILYN, L., and E. H. SCHEIN. *Living with Technology: Issues at Midcareers.* Cambridge: MIT Press, 1980.

BALES, R. F. "Task Roles and Social Roles in Problem-Solving Groups," in *Readings in Social Psychology* (3rd ed.) ed. N. Maccoby et al. New York: Holt, Rinehart & Winston, 1958.

BANDLER, RICHARD and JOHN GRINDER. *Frogs into Princes: Neuro-Linguistic Programming.* Moab, Utah: Real People Press, 1979.

BANDROWSKI, JAMES F. *Corporate Imagination Plus: 5 Steps into Translating Innovative Strategies into Action.* New York: Free Press, 1990.

BARNARD, CHESTER I. *Functions of the Executive.* (30th Anniversary ed.). Cambridge: Harvard University Press, 1968.

BARNETT, TIMOTHY R., and DANNY R. ARNOLD. "Justification and Application of Path-Goal Contingency Leadership Theory to Marketing Channel Leadership," *Journal of Business Research,* 19 (December 1989), 283–92.

BASS, BERNARD M. "From Transactional to Transformational Leadership: Learning to Share the Vision," *Organizational Dynamics,* 18 (Winter 1990), 19–31.

BASS, BERNARD M. *Leadership and Performance Beyond Expectations.* New York: Free Press, 1985.

BASS, BERNARD M. "Leadership Good Better and Best," *Organizational Dynamics,* Winter 1985.

BASS, BERNARD M., *Leadership, Psychology, and Organizational Behavior.* New York: Harper & Row Pub., 1973.

BASS, BERNARD M. *Organizational Decision Making.* Homewood, Ill.: Richard D. Irwin, 1983.

BASS, BERNARD, M. *Organizational Psychology.* Boston: Allyn & Bacon, 1965.

BASS, BERNARD M., and RALPH M. STOGDILL. *Stogdill's Handbook of Leadership* (3rd ed.) New York: Free Press, 1990.

BASS, BERNARD M., et al. *Assessment of Managers: An International Comparison.* Free Press, 1979.

BATTEN, JOE D. "Leading By Expectation," *Management World,* 17 (January–February 1988) 35–36.

BATTEN, JOE D. *Tough-Minded Leadership.* New York: American Management Association, 1989.

BAVELAS, A. "Communication Patterns in Task-Oriented Groups," in Dorwin Cartwright and Alvin Zander, eds. *Group Dynamics,* 2nd ed. Evanston, Ill.: Row, Peterson, & Company, 1953.

BAVELAS, A., and R. T. HARRIS. *Organizational Transitions: Managing Complex Change.* Reading, Mass.: Addison-Wesley, 1977.

BAVELAS, A., and G. STRAUSS. "Group Dynamics and Intergroup Relations," in K. Benne and R. Chin, eds. *The Planning of Change.* New York: Holt, Rinehart & Winston, 1962.

BECK, DON EDWARD. "Beyond the Grid and Situationalism: A Living Systems View," *Training and Development Journal,* August 1982, p. 76.

BELL, GRAHAM B., and ROBERT L. FRENCH. "Consistency of Individual Leadership Position in Small Groups of Varying Membership," *Journal of Abnormal and Social Psychology,* 45 (1950), 764–67.

BELLMAN, GEOFFREY M. "The Staff Manager as Leader," *Training,* 25 (February 1988), 39–40.

BENFIELD, CLIFFORD J. "Problem Performers: The Third-Party Solution," *Personnel Journal,* August 1985, pp. 96–101.

BENNIS, WARREN. "The 4 Competencies of Leadership," *Training and Development Journal,* August 1984, p. 15.

BENNIS, WARREN. "How to Be the Leader They'll Follow," *Working Woman,* 15 (March 1990), 75–79.

BENNIS, WARREN. "Managing the Dream: Leadership in the 21st. Century," *Training,* 27 (May 1990), 43–46.

BENNIS, WARREN. *On Becoming a Leader.* Reading, Mass.: Addison-Wesley, 1989.

BENNIS, WARREN. *The Unconscious Conspiracy: Why Leaders Can't Lead.* New York: AMACON, 1976.

BENNIS, WARREN. *Why Leaders Can't Lead: The Unconscious Conspiracy Continues.* San Francisco: Jossey-Bass, 1989.

BENNIS, WARREN, and BURT NANUS. *Leaders: The Strategies for Taking Charge.* New York: HarperCollins, 1986.

BENNIS, WARREN, et al, eds. *The Planning of Change* (4th ed.). New York: Harper & Row, Pub., 1985.

BENZIGER, KATHERINE. "The Powerful Woman," *Hospital Forum,* May–June 1982, pp. 15–20.

BERNE, ERIC. *Games People Play.* New York: Grove Press, 1964.

BERRY, LEONARD L., and GEORGE A. RIEDER. "Industry Must Band Together to Promote Leadership Programs," *American Banker,* 153 (November 25, 1988), 4

BISSELL, CHARLES BEN. "Diffusing the Difficult Employee," *Management World,* February 1985, pp. 30–31.

BLAIR, JOHN D., and CARLTON J. WHITEHEAD. "Can Quality Circles Survive in the United States?" *Business Horizons,* 27 (September–October 1984), 17–23.

BLAKE, ROBERT R., and JANE S. MOUTON. *The Managerial Grid III* (3rd ed.). Houston, Texas: Gulf Pub., 1984.

BLAKE, ROBERT R., and JANE S. MOUTON. *The Versatile Manager: A Grid Profile.* Homewood, Ill.: Richard D. Irwin, 1982.

BLANCHARD, KENNETH H. "College Board of Trustees: A Need for Directive Leadership," *Academy of Management Journal,* 10 (December 1967).

BLANCHARD, KENNETH H., and SPENCER JOHNSON. *The One Minute Manager.* New York: Morrow, 1982.

BLANCHARD, KENNETH H., and ROBERT LORBER. *Putting the One Minute Manager to Work.* New York: Berkley Publishing Corp., 1987.

BLANCHARD, KENNETH H., and ROBERT LORBER. *Putting the One Minute Manager to Work: How to Turn the Three Secrets into Skills.* New York: Morrow, 1984.

BLANCHARD, KENNETH H., WILLIAM ONCKEN, JR., and HAL BURROWS. *The One Minute Manager Meets the Monkey.* (One Minute Manager Library), New York: Morrow (1989).

BLANCHARD, KENNETH H., PATRICIA ZIGARMI, and DREA ZIGARMI. *Leadership and the One Minute Manager.* New York: Morrow, 1985.

BLANK, WARREN, JOHN R. WEITZEL, and STEPHEN G. GREEN. "A Test of the Situational Leadership Theory," *Personnel Psychology,* 43 (Autumn 1990), 579–97.

BOLMAN, LEE G., and TERRENCE E. DEAL. *Modern Approaches to Understanding and Managing Organizations.* San Francisco: Jossey-Bass, 1984.

BORGATTA, EDGAR F., ROBERT F. BALES, and ARTHUR S. COUCH. "Some Findings Relevant to the Great Man Theory of Leadership," *American Sociological Review,* 19 (1954), 755–59.

BOWERS, D. G., and S. E. SEASHORE. "Predicting Organizational Effectiveness with a Four-Factor Theory of Leadership," *Administrative Science Quarterly,* XI, no. 2 (1966), 238–63.

BRAID, ROBERT W. "Seven Rules for Disciplining Problem Employees," *Supervisory Management*, 28 (May 1983), 2–8.

BRASS, DANIEL J. "Being in the Right Place: A Structural Analysis of Individual Influence in an Organization," *Administrative Science Quarterly*, 29 (1984), 518.

BROWN, JANE COVEY, and ROSABETH MOSS KANTER. "Empowerment: Key to Effectiveness," *Hospital Forum*, May–June 1982, pp. 6–12.

BROWN, STEPHEN W. "Managers Are Not Necessarily Leaders," *Marketing News*, 23 (October 23, 1989), 16.

BROWN, THOMAS L. "Leaders for the '90s: What Key Traits are Called for?" *Industry Week*, 239 (March 5, 1990), 34.

BROWN, THOMAS L. "Putting Vision into Perspective," *Industry Week*, 237 (July 4, 1988), 11.

BUCKMAN, STEVE. "Finding Out Why a Good Performer Went Bad," *Supervisory Management*, August 1984, pp. 39–42.

BUHLER, PATRICIA M. "What Kind of Leader Are You, Anyway?" *Supervision*, 49 (October 1988), 3–5.

BURNS, T., and G. M. STALKER. *The Management of Innovation.* London: Tavistock Publications, 1961.

BURTON, JOHN. *Conflict: Resolution and Prevention.* New York: St. Martin's Press, 1990.

BUTLER, MELVIN L. "Quality Leadership Equals Quality Service," *Bureaucrat*, 19 (Summer 1990), 44–46.

CALANO, JAMES and JEFF SALZMAN. "Move from Management to Leadership," *Women in Business*, 42 (November–December 1990), 11–12.

CAMPBELL, DAVID N., R. L. FLEMING, and RICHARD C. GROTE. "Discipline Without Punishment—At Last," *Harvard Business Review*, July–August 1985, pp. 162–64.

CARTWRIGHT, D., and A. ZANDER, eds. *Group Dynamics: Research and Theory* (2nd ed.). Evanston, Ill.: Row, Peterson & Company, 1960.

CARUTH, DON, and ROBERT M. NOE. "How Not to Motivate," *Management World*, October 1985, pp. 19–20.

CHAMPAGNE, PAUL J., and R. BRUCE McAFEE. *Motivation Strategies for Performance and Productivity: A Guide to HRD.* New York: Quorum Books, 1989.

CHRISTNER, CHARLOTTE A., and JOHN K. HEMPHILL. "Leader Behavior of B-29 Commanders and Changes in Crew Members' Attitudes toward the Crew," *Sociometry*, 18 (1955), 82–87.

CLARKE, CHRISTOPHER, and SIMON PRATT. "Leadership's Four-Part Progress," *Management Today*, March 1985, pp. 84–86.

COCH, L., and J. R. P. FRENCH, JR. "Overcoming Resistance to Change," *Human Relations*, 1, no. 4 (1948), 512–32.

COHEN, SHERRY SUIB. "How to Be a Leader," *Reader's Digest*, 135 (August 1989), 98–100.

COHEN, WILLIAM A. *The Art of a Leader.* Englewood Cliffs, N.J.: Prentice Hall, 1991.

CONGER, JAY A. *The Charismatic Leader: Behind the Mystique of Exceptional Leadership.* San Francisco: Jossey-Bass, 1989.

CONGER, JAY A. "The Dark Side of Leadership," *Organizational Dynamics,* 19 (Autumn 1990), 44–55.

CONGER, JAY A. "Inspiring Others: The Language of Leadership," *Academy of Management Executive,* 5 (February 1991), 31–45.

COOPER, WILLIAM W., HAROLD J. LEAVITT, and MAYNARD W. SHELLY II, eds. *New Perspectives in Organization Research.* New York: John Wiley, 1964.

CORNELL, RICHARD D. "The 'Age of Entrepreneurialism'–What It Means to You," *Supervisory Management,* January 1985, pp. 22–24.

CROSBY, PHILLIP B. *Leading: The Art of Becoming an Executive.* New York: McGraw-Hill, 1990.

CROWE, SANDY. "Leadership Lore," *Executive Female,* 14 (January–February 1991), 10.

CULLINAN, TERRENCE. "Women's Needs Will Continue Job Impact," *California Business,* August 1985, pp. 100–101.

CULPAN, REFIK. "Leadership Styles and Human Resources Management: A Content Analysis of Popular Management Writings," *Management Decision,* 27, no. 4 (1989), 10–16.

CYERT, RICHARD M., and JAMES G. MARCH. *A Behavioral Theory of the Firm.* Englewood Cliffs, N.J.: Prentice Hall, 1963.

DALTON, GENE and PAUL H. THOMPSON. *Novations: Strategies for Career Management.* Glenview, Ill.: Scott, Foresman, 1986.

DALZIEL, MURRAY M., and STEPHEN C. SCHOONOVER. *Changing Ways: A Practical Tool for Implementing Change.* New York: American Management Association, 1988.

DE BOARD, ROBERT. "Bridging the Culture Chasm," *Management Today,* March 1985, pp. 88–92.

DePREE, MAX. "What is Leadership?," *Planning Review,* 18 (July–August 1990), 14–15.

DIBOLD, JOHN. *Making the Future Work.* New York: Simon and Schuster, 1984.

DILTS, ROBERT, et al. *Neuro-Linguistic Programming: Volume I–The Study of the Structure of Subjective Experience.* Cupertino, Calif.: Meta Publications, 1980.

DIMMA, WILLIAM A. "On Leadership," *Business Quarterly,* 53 (Winter 1989), 17–20.

DOLL, BILL. "Avoiding Culture Conflict: Dangers Threaten Long-term Client-Firm Relationships," *Public Relations Journal,* 47 (May 1991), 22–25.

DRUCKER, PETER F. *The Changing World of the Executive.* New York: Times Books, 1985.

DRUCKER, PETER F. *Innovation & Entrepreneurship: Practice & Principles.* New York: Harper & Row, 1986.

DRUCKER, PETER F. *Management.* New York: Harper & Row, 1985.

DRUCKER, PETER F. *Managing for Results.* New York: Harper & Row, 1986.

DRUCKER, PETER F. *Managing in Turbulent Times.* New York: Harper & Row, 1985.

DRUCKER, PETER F. *The New Realities: In Government and Politics–In Economics and Business–In Society and World View.* New York: Harper & Row, 1990.

DRUCKER, PETER F. *The Practice of Management.* New York: Harper & Row, 1986.

DUBLIN, R., et al. *Leadership and Productivity.* San Francisco, Calif.: Chandler Publishing Co., 1965.

DUMAINE, BRIAN. "What the Leaders of Tomorrow See," *Fortune,* 120 (July 3, 1989), 40–51.

EDWARDS, MARK R., and S. RUTH SPROULL. "Making Performance Appraisal Perform: The Use of Team Evaluations," *Personnel,* 62, no. 3 (March 1985), 28–32.

EMERY F. E., and E. L. TRIST. "The Casual Texture of Organizational Environments," *Human Relations,* 18 (1965), 21–32.

ENDERLE, GEORGES. "Some Perspectives of Managerial Ethical Leadership," *Journal of Business Ethics,* 7 (April 1988), 283–94.

ERTEL, DANNY. "How to Design a Conflict Management Procedure that Fits Your Dispute," *Sloan Management Review,* 32 (Summer 1991), 29–42.

EUSTER, JOANNE R. "The New Hierarchy: Where's the Boss?" *Library Journal,* 115 (May 1, 1990), 40–44.

EVAN, W. M., ed. *Interorganizational Relations.* Philadelphia: University of Pennsylvania Press, 1978.

FARRANT, DON. "The Simple Math of Leadership," *Supervision,* 50 (March 1989), 11–12.

FAYOL, HENRI. *Industrial and General Administration.* Paris: Dunod, 1925.

FERSTER, C. B., and B. F. SKINNER. *Schedules of Reinforcement.* New York: Appleton-Century-Crofts, 1957.

FESTINGER, LEON. *The Human Legacy.* New York: Columbia University Press, 1983.

FESTINGER, LEON. *A Theory of Cognitive Dissonance.* Stanford, Calif.: Stanford University Press, 1957.

FESTINGER, LEON, STANLEY SCHACTER, and KURT BACK. *Social Pressures in Informal Groups: A Study of Human Factors in Housing.* Stanford, Calif: Stanford University Press, 1950.

FIEDLER, FRED E. "Engineer the Job to Fit the Manager," *Harvard Business Review,* 51 (1965), 115–22.

FIEDLER, FRED E. *A Theory of Leadership Effectiveness.* New York: McGraw-Hill, 1967.

FIEDLER, FRED E. "Validation and Extension of the Contingency Model of Leadership Effectiveness: A Review of Empirical Findings," *Psychological Bulletin,* 76 (1971), 128–48.

FIEDLER, FRED E., and MARTIN M. CHEMERS. *Improving Leadership Effectiveness: The Leader Match Concept* (2nd ed.). Wiley Press, 1984.

FIELD, RICHARD H. G. "Leaders as Stars, Pulsars, Quasars, and Black Holes," *Business Horizons,* 32 (May–June 1989), 60–64.

FILLEY, ALAN C. *The Compleat Manager: What Works When.* Green Briar Press, 1985.

FINKEL LEE M. "Just-in-Time Principles Can Strengthen Dispute Resolution Processes," *Employment Relations Today,* 18 (Summer 1991), 167–73.

FINKEL, LEE M. and HARRY KAMINSKY. "Teaching Managers to Mediate Win-Win Solutions," *Employment Relations Today,* 18 (Spring 1991), 71–78.

FLEISHMAN, E. A. "Twenty Years of Consideration and Structure," in *Current Developments in the Study of Leadership.* eds. E. A. Fleishman and J. G. Hunt. Carbondale, Ill.: Southern Illinois University Press, 1973.

FLEISHMAN, EDWIN A. "Leadership Climate, Human Relations Training, and Supervisory Behavior," *Personnel Psychology,* 6 (1953), 205–22.

FRENCH, J. R. P., JR., JOACHIM ISRAEL, and DAGFINN ÅS. "An Experiment on Participation in a Norwegian Factory," *Human Relations,* XIII, no. 1 (1960), 3–19.

FRENCH, J. R. P., and B. RAVEN. "The Bases of Social Power," in *Studies in Social Power,* ed. D. Cartwright. Ann Arbor: University of Michigan, Institute for Social Research, 1959.

FRENCH, WENDELL L., and CECIL H. BELL, JR. *Organizational Development: Behavior Science Intervention for Organizational Improvement* (4th ed.). Englewood Cliffs, N.J.: Prentice Hall, 1990.

FREUD, SIGMUND. *The Ego and the Id.* London: Hogarth Press, 1927.

FRIANT, RAY J. "Leadership Training for Long-Term Results," *Management Review,* 80 (July 1991), 50–53.

FROMM, ERICH. *The Sane Society.* New York: Holt, Rinehart & Winston, 1990.

FULK, JANET, and ERIC R. WENDLER. "Dimensionality of Leader-Subordinate Interactions: A Path-Goal Investigation," *Organizational and Human Performance,* November 1982, pp. 241–64.

GALAGAN, PATRICIA A. "Execs Go Global, Literally," *Training and Development Journal,* 44 (June 1990), 58–63.

GALBRAITH, JOHN KENNETH. *The Anatomy of Power.* Boston: Houghton Mifflin Co., 1985.

GARDNER, JOHN W. "The Antileadership Vaccine," reprinted from the *1965 Annual Report, Carnegie Corporation of New York.*

GARDNER, JOHN W. "Leadership and the Future: Leaders Help People to Believe in Themselves and in the Possibilities of the Future," *The Futurist,* 24 (May–June), 8–12.

GARDNER, JOHN W. "Mastering the Fine Art of Leadership," *Business Month,* 133 (May 1989), 77–78.

GARDNER, JOHN W. "The Moral Aspects of Leadership," *NAASP Bulletin,* 73 (January 1989), 43.

GARDNER, JOHN W. "Executive Trends Beat the Management Shortage," *Nation's Business,* LII, no. 9 (September 1964).

GEARY, DAVID L. "Are You a Leader or a Manager?" *Public Relations Journal,* 46 (August 1990), 16.

GELLERMAN, SAUL W. *Management by Motivation.* New York: American Management Association, 1968.

GHISELLI, EDWIN E. *Measurement Theory for the Behavioral Sciences.* New York: W. H. Freeman & Company Publishers, 1981.

GIBB, CECIL A. "Leadership," in *Handbook of Social Psychology,* Gardner Lindzey, ed. Cambridge, Mass.: Addison-Wesley, 1954.

GILMORE, THOMAS NORTH. *Making a Leadership Change: How Organi-*

zations and Leaders Can Handle Leadership Transitions Successfully. San Francisco: Jossey-Bass, 1988.

GINSBURG, SUSAN G. "Diagnosing and Treating Managerial Malaise," *Personnel,* July–August 1984, pp. 34–46.

GLASSMAN, MYRON, and BRUCE R. MCAFEE. "Enthusiasm: The Missing Link in Leadership," *Advanced Management Journal,* 55 (Summer 1990), 4–6.

GODDARD, ROBERT W. "Creative Leaders: Can Supply Meet Demand?" *Personnel Journal,* 69 (February 1990), 92.

GOLDSTEIN, IRWIN L. *Training and Development in Organizations.* San Francisco: Jossey-Bass, 1989.

GOODKIN, SANFORD R. "Can You Be Both a Leader and a Manager?" *Professional Builder and Remodeler,* 56 (March 1, 1991), 56.

GORDON, THOMAS. *Leader Effectiveness Training.* New York: Bantam, 1984.

GORDON, THOMAS. *P.E.T. Parent Effectiveness Training.* New York: McKay, 1970.

GORDON, THOMAS. *Teacher Effectiveness Training.* New York: McKay, 1974.

GRASSELL, MILT. "Supervisory Leadership Skills for Supervisors," *Supervision,* 51 (January 1990), 3–4.

GRENIER, LARRY E. "Evolution and Revolution as Organizations Grow," *Harvard Business Review,*" July–August 1972, pp. 37–46.

GRIFFIN, RICKY. *Management* (2nd ed.). Boston: Houghton Mifflin Company, 1987.

GROSS, N., W. S. MASON, and A. McEACHERN. *Explorations in Role Analysis.* New York: John Wiley, 1958.

GROVE, ANDREW S. "Taking the Hype Out of Leadership," *Fortune,* 117 (March 28, 1988), 187–88.

GROVER, MARY BETH. "Letting Both Sides Win," *Forbes,* 148 (September 80, 1991), 178.

GUEST, ROBERT H. *Innovative Work Practices.* Elmsford, N.Y.: Pergamon, 1982.

GUEST, ROBERT H. *Organizational Change: The Effect of Successful Leadership.* Homewood, Ill.: Dorsey Press and Richard D. Irwin, Inc., 1964.

GUEST, R., et al. *Organizational Change Through Effective Leadership* (2nd ed.). Englewood Cliffs, N.J.: Prentice Hall, 1986.

GULICK, LUTHER, and L. URWICK, eds. *Papers on the Science of Administration.* New York: Institute of Public Administration, 1937.

HACKETT, MICHAEL E. "A Worm's Eye View of Leadership," *Supervisory Management,* 35 (September 1990), 8–9.

HACKMAN, J. R., and E. E. LAWLER. "Employee Reactions to Job Characteristics," *Journal of Applied Psychology Monograph,* (1971), pp. 259–86.

HACKMAN, J. R., and G. R. OLDHAM. *Work Design.* Reading, Mass.: Addison-Wesley, 1980.

HAGBERG, JANET. "The Good, the Bad and the Ugly, Understanding Power Styles," *Working Women,* 12 (1984), 124–78.

HAIRE, M. *Psychology in Management.* New York: McGraw-Hill, 1956.

HAIRE, M. "Psychological Problems Relevant to Business and Industry," *Psychological Bulletin,* 56 (1959), 169–94.

HALL, E. *The Hidden Dimension.* New York: Doubleday, 1992.

HALL, E. *The Silent Language.* New York: Doubleday, 1973.

HALPERT, JANE A. "The Dimensionality of Charisma," *Journal of Business and Psychology,* 4 (Summer 1990), 399–410.

HALPIN, ANDREW W. *The Leadership Behavior of School Superintendents.* Chicago: Midwest Administration Center, University of Chicago, 1959.

HALPIN, ANDREW W., and BEN J. WINER. *The Leadership Behavior of Airplane Commanders.* Columbus: Ohio State University Research Foundation, 1952.

HAMBLIN, ROBERT L. "Leadership and Crises," in *Group Dynamics: Research and Theory* (2nd. ed.). eds. Dorwin Cartwright and Alvin Zander. Evanston, Ill.: Row, Peterson, & Company, 1960. Also in *Sociometry,* 21 (1958), 322–35.

HANEY, WILLIAM V. *Communication and Interpersonal Relations* (5th ed.). Homewood, Ill.: Richard D. Irwin, 1985.

HANNEMAN, GERHARD J., and WILLIAM J. McEWEN. *Communication and Behavior.* Reading, Mass.: Addison-Wesley, 1975.

HARRIS, T. *I'm OK – You're OK: A Practical Guide To Transactional Analysis.* New York: Harper & Row, Pub., 1969.

HARRISON, EDWARD L. "Why Supervisors Fail to Discipline," *Supervisory Management,* April 1985, pp. 18–22.

HAYAKAWA, S. I., ed. *The Use and Misuse of Language.* New York: Fawcett New World Library, 1962.

HELM, LESLIE, and KYOKO TAKAHASHI. "Japan's Secret Economic Weapon: Exploited Women," *Business Week,* March 4, 1985, pp. 54–55.

HEMPHILL, JOHN K. *Leader Behavior Description.* Columbus: Ohio State University, 1950.

HEMPHILL, JOHN K. "Relations Between the Size of the Group and the Behavior of the 'Superior' Leaders," *Journal of Social Psychology,* 32 (1950), 11–32.

HEMPHILL, JOHN K. *Situational Factors in Leadership,* Monograph no. 32. Columbus: Bureau of Educational Research, Ohio State University, 1949.

HERMAN, JERRY J. "Action Plans to Make Your Vision a Reality," *NASSP Bulletin,* 74 (February 1990), 14–17.

HERSEY, PAUL. *The Situational Leader.* Escondido, Calif.: Center for Leadership Studies, 1984.

HERSEY, PAUL. *Situational Selling: An Approach for Increasing Sales Effectiveness.* Escondido, Calif.: Center for Leadership Studies, 1985.

HERSEY, PAUL, and KENNETH H. BLANCHARD. "Cultural Changes: Their Influence on Organizational Structure and Management Behavior," *Training and Development Journal,* (October 1970).

HERSEY, PAUL, and KENNETH H. BLANCHARD. "Life Cycle Theory of Leadership," *Training and Development Journal,* 23 (May 1969).

HERSEY, PAUL, and KENNETH H. BLANCHARD. "What's Missing in MBO?" *Management Review,* October 1974.

HERSEY, P., BLANCHARD K. H., and W. E. NATEMEYER. "Situational

Leadership, Perception, and the Impact of Power," *Group and Organizational Studies,* 4, no. 5 (December 1979), 418–28.

HERSEY, PAUL, and DOUGLAS SCOTT. "A Systems Approach to Educational Organizations: Do We Manage or Administer?" *OCLEA, Publication of the Ontario Council for Leadership in Educational Administration,* Toronto, Canada, pp. 3–5.

HERSEY, PAUL, and JOHN E. STINSON. *Perspectives in Leader Effectiveness.* Oxford, Ohio: Ohio University Press, 1980.

HERZBERG, FREDERICK. "One More Time: How Do You Motivate Employees?" *Harvard Business Review,* 65 (September–October 1987), 109–21.

HERZBERG, FREDERICK. *Work and the Nature of Man.* New York: World Publishing Co., 1966.

HESHIZER, BRIAN. "An MBO Approach to Discipline," *Supervisory Management,* March 1984, pp. 2–7.

HICKMAN, CRAIG R. *A Manager's Mind, Soul of A Leader: Hickman's Lessons for World Class Performers.* New York: Wiley, 1990.

HILL, NORMAN C. "The Need for Positive Reinforcement in Corrective Counseling," *Supervisory Management,* 29 (December 1984), 10–11.

HITT, WILLIAM D. *Ethics and Leadership: Putting Theory into Practice.* Columbus: Battelle Press, 1990.

HOBSON, C. J., R. B. HOBSON, and J. J. HOBSON. "Why Managers Use Criticism Instead of Praise," *Supervisory Management,* 30 no.3 (1985), 24–31.

HODGSON, RICHARD C. "Learning From Leaders," *Business Quarterly,* 54 (Summer 1989), 15–18.

HOGAN, ROBERT, DAN FAZZINI, and ROBERT RASKIN. "How Charisma Cloaks Incomptence," *Personnel Journal,* May 1990, pp. 72–76.

HOLLANDER, E. P. "Emergent Leadership and Social Influence," in *Leadership and Interpersonal Behavior,* eds. Luigi Petrullo and Bernard M. Bass. New York: Holt, Rinehart & Winston, 1961.

HOMANS, G. C. *The Human Group.* New York: Harcourt Brace Jovanovich, Inc., 1950.

HORTON, THOMAS R. "Beyond Charisma," *Supervisory Management,* 34 (April 1989), 16–17.

HOSKING, DIAN MARIE, "Organizing, Leadership, and Skillful Process," *Journal of Management Studies,* 25 (March 1988), 147–66.

HOSKING, D., and C., SCHRIESHEIM. "Review of Fiedler et al., Improving Leadership Effectiveness: The Leader Match Concept," *Administrative Science Quarterly,* 23 (1978), 496–504.

HOUSE, ROBERT J. "A Path-Goal Theory of Leader Effectiveness," *Administrative Science Quarterly,* 16 (1971), 321–38.

HOUSE, ROBERT J., and TERENCE R. MITCHELL. "Path-Goal Theory of Leadership," *Journal of Contemporary Businesss,* Autumn 1974, pp. 81–98.

HOWELL, JANE M., and CHRISTOPHER A. HIGGINS. "Champions of Change: Identifying, Understanding, and Supporting Champions of Technological Innovations," *Organizational Dynamics,* 19 (Summer 1990), 40–55.

HOWELL, JOHN P., DAVID E. BOWEN, and PETER W. DORFMAN.

"Substitutes for Leadership: Effective Alternatives to Ineffective Leadership," *Organizational Dynamics,* 19 (Summer 1990), 20–38.

HUNT, J. G. "Personal Factors Associated with Leadership: A Survey of the Literature," *Journal of Psychology,* 25 (January 1982), 35–71.

HUNT, J. G., and L. L. LARSON, eds. *Contingency Approaches to Leadership.* Carbondale: Southern Illinois University Press, 1974.

HUSSEIN, RAEF T. "Understanding and Managing Informal Groups," *Management Decision,* 28, no. 8 (1990), 35–41.

INDIK, BERNARD P., BASIL S. GEORGOPOULOS, and STANLEY E. SEASHORE. "Superior Subordinate Relationships and Performance," *Personnel Psychology,* 14 (1961), 357–74.

IVANCEVICH, J. M., and J. H. DONNELLY. "Leader Influence and Performance," *Personnel Psychology,* 23, no. 4 (1970), 539–49.

JANOWITZ, MORRIS. "Changing Patterns of Organizational Authority: The Military Establishment," *Administrative Science Quarterly,* 3 (March 1959), 473–93.

JASINSKI, F. J. and R. H. GUEST. "Redesigning the Supervisor's Job," *Factory Management and Maintenance,* 115, no. 12 (December 1957).

JAVIDAN, MANSOUR. "Leading a High-commitment High-performance Organization," *Long Range Planning,* 24 (April 1991), 28–36.

JEANNOT, THOMAS M. "Moral Leadership and Practical Wisdom," *International Journal of Social Economics,* 16 (June 1989), 14–28.

JENNINGS, EUGENE E. "The Anatomy of Leadership," *Management of Personnel Quarterly,* 1, no. 1 (Autumn 1961).

JENSEN, THOMAS D., DONALD D. WHITE, and RAGHAVENDRA SINGH. "Impact of Gender, Hierarchical Position, and Leadership Styles on Work-related Values," *Journal of Business Research,* 20 (March 1990), 145–52.

JESSUP, HARLAN R. "New Roles in Team Leadership," *Training and Development Journal,* 44 (November 1990), 79–83.

JOHNSON, DEWEY E. *Concepts of Air Force Leadership.* Washington, D.C.: Air Force ROTC, 1970.

JOHNSON, WILLIAM L., PAUL N. DIXON, and LINDA L. McDONALD. "Organizational Leadership: Is There One Best Way?" *Bureaucrat,* 18 (Summer 1989), 37–40.

JONGEWARD, D., and P. C. SEYER. *Choosing Success: Transactional Analysis on the Job.* New York: John Wiley, 1978.

JOSEFOWITZ, NATASHA. *You're the Boss!: A Guide to Managing People with Understanding and Effectiveness.* New York: Warner Books, 1985.

KAHN, R. L., and D. KATZ. "Leadership Practices in Relation to Productivity and Morale," in *Group Dynamics: Research and Theory,* (2nd ed.), eds. Dorwin Cartwright and Alvin Zander. Evanston, Ill.: Row, Peterson & Company, 1960.

KAHN, R. L. et al. *Organizational Stress: Studies in Role Conflict and Ambiguity.* New York: John Wiley, 1964.

KANTER, ROSABETH MOSS. *The Changemasters: Innovations for Production in American Corporations.* New York: Simon & Schuster, 1983.

KANTER, ROSABETH MOSS. "The New Managerial Work," *Harvard Business Review,* 67 (November–December 1989), 85.

KATZ, DANIEL, and ROBERT L. KAHN. *The Social Psychology of Organization* (2nd ed.). New York: John Wiley, 1978.

KEPNER, C. H. and B. B. TREGOE. *The Rational Manager.* New York: Princeton Research Press, 1976.

KERLINS, MARVIN, and EDYTH HARGIS. "Beyond Leadership: The Human Factor in Leadership," *Management Solutions,* 33 (August 1988), 18–21.

KEYS, BERNARD, and THOMAS CASE. "How to Become an Influential Manager," *Academy of Management Executive,* 4 (November 1990), 38–51.

KIECHEL, WALTER. "A Hard Look at Executive Vision," *Fortune,* 120 (October 23, 1989), 207.

KIRBY, DONALD. "Situating the Employee Rights Debate," *Journal of Business Ethics,* 4, no. 4 (August 1985), 269–76.

KIRKLAND, RICHARD I. "What Makes Business Leaders," *Fortunc,* 122 (September 24, 1990), 215.

KIRKPATRICK, SHELLY A., and EDWIN A. LOCKE. "Leadership: Do Traits Matter," *Academy of Management Executive,* 5 (May 1991), 48–60.

KISER, GLENN A., TERRY HUMPHRIES, and CHIP BELL. "Breaking Through Rational Leadership," *Training and Development Journal,* 44 (January 1990), 42–43.

KLIEN, J., and W. CONRAD. "The Right Approach to Participative Management," *Working Woman,* May 1985, pp. 29–29.

KNAPP, MARK. *Nonverbal Communications in Human Interacting,* (2nd ed.). New York: Holt, Rinehart & Winston, 1978.

KOESTENBAUM, PETER. *The Heart of Business: Ethics, Power, and Philosophy.* San Francisco: Saybrook Pub. Co., 1987.

KOLB, DAVID A., IRWIN M. RUBIN, and JAMES M. McINTYRE. *Organizational Psychology: A Book of Readings,* Englewood Cliffs, N.J.: Prentice Hall, 1979.

KOLZOW, DAVID R. "Communication and Leadership: The Critical Foundation for an Effective Economic Development Program," *Economic Development Review,* 8 (Summer 1990), 19–23.

KOONTZ, HAROLD, and CYRIL O'DONNELL. *Principles of Management,* (8th ed.). New York: McGraw-Hill, 1984.

KORMAN, A. K. "Consideration, Initiating Structure, and Organizational Criteria–A Review," *Personnel Psychology: A Journal of Applied Research,* 19, no. 4 (1966), 349–61.

KOTTER, JOHN P. *A Force for Change: How Leadership Differs from Management.* New York: Free Press, 1990.

KOTTER, JOHN P. *The Leadership Factor.* New York: Free Press, 1988.

KOTTER, JOHN P. "What Leaders Really Do," *Harvard Business Review,* 68, (May–June), 103–5.

KOUZES, JAMES M., and BARRY Z. POSNER. "The Credibility Factor: What Followers Expect from Their Leaders," *Management Review,* 79 (January 1990), 29–33.

KOVACH, KENNETH A. "Tracking Motivation: Surveys Help Gauge Employee Needs," *Management World,* January 1983.

KRANTZ, JAMES, and THOMAS N. GILMORE. "The Splitting of Leadership and Management as a Social Defense," *Human Relations,* 43 (February 1990), 183–204.

KUHNERT, KARL W., and PHILIP LEWIS. "Transactional and Transformational Leadership: A Constructive/Development Analysis," *The Academy of Management Review,* 12 (October 1987), 648–57.

LABICH, KENNETH. "The Seven Keys to Business Leadership," *Fortune,* 118 (October 24, 1988), 58–62.

LARSON, L. L., J. G. HUNT, and R. N. OSBORN. "The Great Leader Behavior Myth," *Proceedings of the Academy of Management,* 1975, pp. 170–72.

LAWLER, E. E., III. *High Involvement Management,* San Francisco: Jossey-Bass, 1990.

LAWLER, E. E., III. *Pay and Organizational Effectiveness.* New York: McGraw-Hill, 1971.

LAWLER, E. E., III. "Paying, Participation, and Organizational Change," in *Man and Work in Society,* eds. E. L. Cass and F. G. Zimmer. New York: Van Nostrand Reinhold, 1975.

LAWLER III, EDWARD E., and SUSAN A. MOHRMAN. "Quality Circles After the Fad," *Harvard Business Review,* 63 (January–February 1985), 64–71.

LAWRENCE, P. R. and J. W. LORSH. *Organization and Environment: Managing Differentiation and Integration.* Boston: Harvard Graduate School of Business Administration, 1967.

LAWRIE, JOHN. "The Differences Between Effective and Ineffective Change Managers," *Supervisory Management,* 36 (June 1991), 9–10.

LEAVITT, H. J. *Managerial Psychology: Managing Behavior in Organizations.* Chicago: University of Chicago Press, 1958.

LEAVITT, H. J. "Suppose We Took Groups Seriously?" in *Man and Work in Society,* eds. E. L. Cass and F. G. Zimmer. New York: Van Nostrand Reinhold, 1975.

LEE, CHRIS. "Can Leadership Be Taught?" *Training,* 26 (July 1989), 19–26.

LEE, CHRIS. "Followership: The Essence of Leadership," *Training,* 28, (January 1991), 27–35.

LEE, CYNTHIA. "Increasing Performance Appraisal Effectiveness: Matching Task Types, Appraisal Process, and Rater Training," *Academy of Management Review,* 10, no. 2 (April 1985), 222–31.

LEVINSON, H. *The Exceptional Executive: A Psychological Conception.* Cambridge, Mass.: Harvard University Press, 1968.

LEVINSON, H. *Men, Management, and Mental Health.* Cambridge, Mass.: Harvard University Press, 1968.

LEWAN, LLOYD S. "Diversity in the Workplace," *Human Relations,* 35 (June 1990), 42–45.

LEWIN, K. "Group Decision and Social Change," in *Readings in Social Psychology* (3rd ed.), eds. E. E. Maccoby, T. M. Newcomb, and E. L. Hartley. New York: Holt, Rinehart & Winston, 1958.

LEWIN, K., R. LIPPETT, and R. WHITE. "Leader Behavior and Member Reaction in Three Social Climates," in *Group Dynamics: Research and Theory* (2nd ed.), eds. D. Cartwright and A. Zander. Evanston, Ill.: Row, Peterson & Company, 1960.

LIEBERMAN, S. "The Effects of Changes in Roles on the Attitudes of Role Occupations," *Human Relations,* IX, no. 4 (1956), 385–402.

LIKERT, RENSIS. *Human Organization: Its Management and Values.* New York: McGraw-Hill, 1967.

LIKERT, RENSIS. *New Patterns of Management.* New York: McGraw-Hill, 1961.

LILEY, WILLIAM. "Leadership Beyond the Obvious," *Fortune,* 120 (October 9, 1989), 193–94.

LINDHOLM, C. E. *The Intelligence of Democracy.* New York: Free Press, 1965.

LINDHOLM, C. E. "The Science of Muddling Through," *Public Administration Review,* 19 (1959), 79–99.

LINDHOLM, R., and J. NORSTEDT. *The Volvo Report.* Stockholm: Swedish Employers' Confederation, 1975.

LIPPETT, GORDON. *Organizational Renewal.* New York: Appleton-Century-Crofts, 1969.

LIPPETT, GORDON, JEANNE WATSON, and B. WESTLEY. *The Dynamics of Planned Change: A Comparative Study of Principles and Techniques.* New York: Harcourt Brace Jovanovich, 1958.

LITTERER, J. A. *Analysis of Organzations.* New York: John Wiley, 1965.

LIVINGSTON, J. STERLING. "Pygmalion in Management," *Harvard Business Review,* July–August 1969, pp. 81–89.

LOMBARDO, MICHAEL. "The Intolerable Boss," *Psychology Today,* January 1984, pp. 44–48.

LUKASZEWSKI, JAMES E. "How to Coach Executives," *Communication World,* 6 (June 1989), 38–41.

LUTHANS, F. *Introduction to Management: A Contingency Approach.* New York: McGraw-Hill Book, 1976.

MACCOBY, MICHAEL. "How to Be a Quality Leader," *Research Technology Management,* 33 (September–October 1990), 51–52.

MACHIAVELLI, NICCOLO. *The Prince.* New York: Mentor Classic–New American Library, 1952.

MAIER, NORMAN R. F. *Frustration: The Study of Behavior Without a Goal.* Ann Arbor: The University of Michigan Press, 1961.

MAIER, NORMAN R. F. *Psychology in Industry* (2nd ed.). Boston: Houghton Mifflin Company, 1955.

MAIN, JEREMY. "The Trouble with Managing Japanese-Style," *Fortune,* 109 (April 2, 1984), 50–52.

MANN, CARL P. "Transformational Leadership in the Executive Office," *Public Relations Quarterly,* 33 (Spring 1988), 19–23.

MANN, F. C. "Putting Human Relations Findings to Work," *Michigan Business Review,* II, no. 2 (1950), 16–20.

MANZ, CHARLES C., and HENRY P. SIMS. "SuperLeadership: Beyond the Myth of Heroic Leadership," *Organizational Dynamics,* 19 (Spring 1991), 18–35.

MANZ, CHARLES C., HENRY P. SIMS, JR. *Superleadership: Leading Others to Lead Themselves.* New York: Prentice Hall Press, 1989.

MARCH, J. G. and H. A. SIMON. *Organizations.* New York: John Wiley, 1958.

MARIN, NED. "Team Managers as Creative Heroes," *Managers Magazine,* 62 (October 1987), 12–14.

MARROW, A. J., D. G. BOWERS, and S. E. SEASHORE. *Management by Participation.* New York: Harper & Row, Pub., 1967.

MARSICK, VICTORIA J., and KAREN E. WATKINS. *Informal and Incidental Learning in the Workplace.* New York: Routledge, 1990.

MARTEL, MYLES. *Before You Say a Word: The Executive to Effective Communication.* Englewood Cliffs, N.J.: Prentice Hall, 1984.

MARTIN, PETER, and JOHN NICHOLLI. "How to Manage Commitment," *Management Today,* April 1985, pp. 56–57.

MASCARI, PATRICIA A. "Leading with a Vision," *Association Management,* 42 (September 1990), 34–36.

MASLOW, ABRAHAM H. *Eupsychian Management.* Homewood, Ill.: Richard D. Irwin, and The Dorsey Press, 1965.

MASLOW, ABRAHAM H. *Motivation and Personality.* New York: Harper & Row, 1954.

MASLOW, ABRAHAM H. *Toward a Psychology of Being* (2nd ed.). Princeton, N.J.: D. Van Nostrand Co., Inc., 1968.

MAYO, ELTON. *The Human Problems of an Industrial Civilization.* New York: MacMillan, 1977.

MAYO, ELTON. *The Social Problems of an Industrial Civilization.* Boston: Harvard Business School, 1977.

McCLELLAND, DAVID C. *The Achieving Society.* Princeton, N.J.: D. Van Nostrand Co., Inc., 1967.

McCLELLAND, D., and D. H. BURNHAM. "Power Is the Great Motivator," *Harvard Business Review,* March–April 1976, pp. 100–110.

McCLELLAND, DAVID C., et al. *The Achievement Motive.* New York: Appleton-Century-Crofts, 1953.

McCONKEY, DALE D. "Are You an Administrator, a Manager, or a Leader?" *Business Horizons,* 32 (September–October 1989), 15–21.

McGREGOR, DOUGLAS. *The Human Side of Enterprise* (35th Anniversary ed.). New York: McGraw-Hill, 1985.

McGREGOR, DOUGLAS. *Professional Manager.* New York: McGraw-Hill, 1967.

McKELVEY, B., and R. H. KILMANN. "Organization Design: A Participative Multi-value Approach," *Administrative Science Quarterly,* 20 (1975), 24–36.

McMASTER, MICHAEL, and JOHN GRINDER. *Precision: A New Approach to Communication.* Beverly Hills: Precision Models, 1980.

McPHERSON, R. "The People Principle," *Leaders,* January–March 1982, p. 52.

McTHOMAS, DAVID W. "Leadership and the Attribute of Managing Partners," *The CPA Journal,* 57 (October 1987), 120–23.

MENKUS, BELDEN. "Leadership and Professional Performance," *Journal of Systems Management,* 42 (July 1991), 19.

MERCHANT, KENNETH A. *Rewarding Results: Motivating Profit Center Managers.* Boston: Harvard Business School Press, 1989.

MEYERS, SCOTT M. "Who Are Your Motivated Workers," *Harvard Business Review,* January–February 1964, pp. 73–88.

MIENDL, JAMES R. "Managing to Be Fair: An Exploration of Values, Motives, and Leadership," *Administrative Science Quarterly,* 34 (June 1989), 252–75.

MILES, M. *Learning to Work in Groups.* New York: Teachers College, Columbia University, 1959.

MILES, RAYMOND E. "Human Relations or Human Resources," *Harvard Business Review,* July–August 1965.

MINER, JOHN B., and JOHN E. CULVER. "Some Aspects of the Executive Personality," *Journal of Applied Psychology,* 39 (1955), 348–53.
MINTZBERG, H. *The Nature of Managerial Work.* New York: Harper & Row, Pub., 1973.
MOLZ, RICH. "How Leaders Use Goals," *Long Range Planning,* 20 (October 1987), 91–101.
MORAND, JOHN D. "The Role of Practitioner Leadership," *Economic Development Review,* 8 (Summer 1990), 3.
MORTENSEN, C. DAVID. *Basic Readings in Communications Theory* (2nd ed.). New York: Harper & Row, Pub., 1979.
MORTON, T. BALLARD. "Leadership," *Business Horizons,* 33 (November–December 1990), 3–7.
MOSKAL, BRIAN S. "Tomorrow's Best Managers: Where Are They Now," *Industry Week,* 237 (July 18, 1988), 32–34.
MUSSELWHITE, W. CHRISTOPHER, and LINDA S. DILLON. "Timing for Leadership Training Is Everything," *Personnel Journal,* 66 (May 1987), 103–7.
MYERS, OLGA. "Supervisors Don't Have Job Conflicts?" *Supervision,* 52 (June 1991), 14–16.
NADLER, DAVID A., and MICHAEL L. TUSHMAN. "Beyond the Charismatic Leader: Leadership and Organizational Change," *California Management Review,* 32 (Winter 1990), 77–79.
NADLER, DAVID A., and MICHAEL L. TUSHMAN. "What Makes for Magic Leadership," *Fortune,* 117 (June 6, 1988), 261–62.
NAISBITT, JOHN. *Megatrends.* New York: Warner Books, 1982.
NAISBITT, JOHN. "Megatrends for Women," *Ladies Home Journal,* January 1985, pp. 80–85.
NATEMEYER, W. E. *An Empirical Investigation of the Relationships Between Leader Behavior, Leader Power Bases, and Subordinate Performance and Satisfaction,* an unpublished dissertation, University of Houston, August 1975.
NELTON, SHARON. "Look for Leaders on the Job," *Nation's Business,* 76 (October 1988), 67.
NELTON, SHARON. "Men, Women, and Leadership," *Nation's Business,* 79 (May 1991), 16–22.
NICHOLLS, JOHN. "Nearly All There Is to Know About Leadership," *International Management,* 43 (April 1988), 65–66.
NICHOLLS, JOHN. "Rescuing Leadership from Humpty Dumpty," *Journal of General Management,* 16 (Winter 1990), 76–90.
NIEHOUSE, OLIVER. "Controlling Burnout: A Leadership Guide for Managers," *Business Horizons,* July–August 1984, pp. 81–85.
NIEHOUSE, OLIVER. "Measuring Your Burnout Potential," *Supervisory Management,* July 1984, pp. 27–30.
ODIORNE, GEORGE S. *Management Decisions by Objectives.* New York: Pitman Publishing Corp., 1968.
O'DONNEL, MERLE, and ROBERT J. O'DONNEL. "Quality Circles: Latest Fad or Real Winner?" *Business Horizons,* 27 (June 1984), 48–52.
OUCHI, W. G., and A. M. JAEGER. "Social Structure and Organizational Type," in *Environments and Organizations,* eds. M. W. Meyer and Associates. San Francisco: Jossey-Bass, 1978.

OVERMAN, STEPHENIE. "Conflict? Act Out a Solution," *Executive Female,* 14 (September–October 1991), 14–15.

OWENS, ELIZABETH A. "The Art of Winning at Business Games," *Data Management,* 25 (March 1987), 31.

OWENS, ROBERT G. *Organizational Behavior in Schools.* Englewood Cliffs, N.J.: Prentice Hall, 1970.

PACKARD, VANCE. *The Status Seekers.* New York: D. McKay, 1959.

PARKINSON, C. NORTHCOTE. *Parkinson's Law.* Boston: Houghton Mifflin Company, 1957.

PASCARELLA, PERRY. "Visionary Leadership Will Design the Future," *Industry Week,* 238 (August 21, 1989), 48–49.

PATRELLIS, A. J. "Producing Results: Using Power with Your Employees," *Supervisory Management,* March 1985, pp. 32–37.

PATRELLIS, A. J. "Using Power in Interactions with Peers," *Supervisory Management,* February 1985, pp. 18–24.

PATRELLIS, A. J. "Your Power as an Employee," *Supervisory Management,* April 1985, pp. 37–41.

PATTON, BOBBY R., and KIM GIFFIN. *Interpersonal Communication in Action: Basic Text and Readings* (3rd ed.). New York: Harper & Row, Pub., 1980.

PAVETT, C. M. "Evaluation of the Impact of Feedback on Performance and Motivation," *Human Relations,* 15, no. 2 (1983), 58–63.

PEAK, MARTHA H. "Crisis in Supervision," *Personnel,* 67 (November 1990), 1–2.

PENNAR, KAREN, and EDWARD MERVOSH. "Women at Work," *Business Week,* January 28, 1985, pp. 80–85.

PERROW, CHARLES. "The Analysis of Goals in Complex Organizations," *American Sociological Review,* 26 (December 1961), 854–66.

PERROW, CHARLES. *Organizational Analysis: A Sociological View.* Belmont, Calif.: Wadsworth, 1970.

PETER, LAWRENCE J., and RAYMOND HULL. *The Peter Principle: Why Things Always Go Wrong.* New York: Morrow, 1971.

PETERS, THOMAS. "The New Builders," *Industry Week,* 239 (March 5, 1990), 27–28.

PETERS, THOMAS J., and N. AUSTIN. *A Passion for Excellence: The Leadership Difference.* New York: Random House, 1985.

PETERS, THOMAS, J., and ROBERT H. WATERMAN, JR. *In Search of Excellence: Lessons from America's Best-Run Companies.* New York: Warner Books, 1982.

PETROCK, FRANK. "Planning the Leadership Transition," *Journal of Business Strategy,* 11 (November–December 1990), 14–16.

PFEFFER, JEFFREY. *Power in Organizations.* Marshfield, Mass.: Pittman Publishing, Inc., 1986.

PHILLIPS, JACK J. *Improving Supervisors' Effectiveness.* San Francisco: Jossey-Bass, 1985.

PITMAN, BEN. "How Do I Motivate and Lead My People?" *Journal of Systems Management,* 42 (March 1991), 32–34.

POLLOCK, TED. "A Personal File of Stimulating Ideas and Problem Solvers," *Supervision,* May 1985, pp. 25–26.

POR, JOHN, and CERI EVANS. "Taking Charge as a New Executive," *Business Quarterly*, 55 (Spring 1991), 44–48.

PORTER, LYMAN W. "A Study of Perceived Need Satisfactions in Bottom and Middle Management Jobs," *Journal of Applied Psychology*, 45 (1961), 1–10.

PREMACK, DAVID. "Toward Empirical Behavioral Laws: 1. Positive Reinforcement," *Psychological Review*, 66 (1959), 219–33.

PRICE, FRANK. "Out of Bedlam: Management by Quality Leadership," *Management Decision*, 27 (May 1989), 15–21.

PRYER, MARGARET W., AUSTIN W. FLINT, and BERNARD M. BASS. "Group Effectiveness and Consistency of Leadership," *Sociometry*, 25 (1962), 391–97.

PULICH, MARCIA ANN. "Train First-Line Supervisors to Handle Discipline," *Personnel Journal*, December 1983, pp. 980–85.

PULICH, MARCIA ANN. "What Supervisors Should Know About Discipline," *Supervisory Management*, October 1983, pp. 20–24.

QUEYSSAC, DANIEL. "U.S. Managers No Longer No. 1: Better Leadership Is the Reason for Japanese Dominance," *Industry Week*, 238 (April 17, 1989), 34.

QUICKEL, STEPHEN W. "Forget Managers: What We Need Are Leaders," *Business Month*, 233 (January 1989), 69–70.

QUINN, JAMES BRIAN. "Managing Innovation: Controlled Chaos," *Harvard Business Review*, no. 3 (May–June 1985), 73–84.

REDDIN, WILLIAM J. *Managerial Effectiveness*. New York: McGraw-Hill, 1970.

REDDIN, WILLIAM J. "The 3-D Management Style Theory," *Training and Development Journal*, April 1967, pp. 8–17.

REYNOLDS, PAUL D. "Leaders Never Quit," *Small Group Behavior*, 15, no. 3 (August 1984), 404–13.

RHINESMITH, STEPHEN H., et al. "Developing Leaders for Global Enterprises," *Training and Development Journal*, 43 (April 1989), 24–34.

RICE, B. "Evaluating Employees," *Venture, The Magazine for Entrepreneurs*, 7 (September 1985), 33–34.

RICHARDSON, JERRY, and JOEL MARGULIS. *The Magic of Rapport: How You Can Gain Personal Power in Any Situation*. San Francisco: Harbor Publishing Company, 1981.

RICHARDSON, PETER R. "Courting Greater Employee Involvement Through Participative Management," *Sloan Management Review*, Winter 1985.

ROBBINS, STEPHEN P. *The Essentials of Organizational Behaviors*, (2nd ed.). Englewood Cliffs, N.J.: Prentice Hall, 1988.

ROBBINS, S. P. *Organizational Behavior: Concepts, Controversies, and Applications*, (2nd ed.). Englewood Cliffs, N.J.: Prentice Hall, 1988.

ROBINSON, DANA GAINES. "The 1990s: From Managing to Leading," *Supervisory Management*, 34 (June 1989), 5–10.

ROETHLISBERGER, F. J. *Management and Morale*. Cambridge: Harvard University Press, 1941.

ROETHLISBERGER, F. J., and W. J. DICKSON. *Management and the Worker: An Account of A Research Program Conducted by the Western*

Electric Company Hawthorne Workers. Cambridge: Harvard University Press, 1939.

ROGERS, C. *On Becoming a Person.* Boston: Houghton-Mifflin Company, 1961

ROGERS, M. F. "Instrumental and Infra-Resources: The Base of Power," *American Journal of Sociology,* 79, no. 6 (1973), 1418–33.

ROGUS, JOSEPH F. "Developing a Vision Statement—Some Considerations for Principals," *NASSP Bulletin,* February 1990, pp. 1–4.

ROSENBAUM, BERNARD L. "Leading Today's Professional," *Research Technology Managemenat,* 34 (March–April 1991), 30–35.

ROSENER, JUDY B. "The Valued Ways Men and Women Lead," *Human Resources,* 36 (June 1991), 147.

ROSKIN, RICK. "Management Style and Achievement: A Model Synthesis," *Management Decision,* 27 (July 1989), 17–22.

ROSS, I. C., and A. ZANDER. "Need Satisfactions and Employee Turnover," *Personnel Psychology,* X, no. 3 (1957), 327–38.

ROWNEY, J. I. A., and A. R. CAHOON. "Individual and Organizational Characteristics of Women in Managerial Leadership," *Journal of Business Ethics,* 9 (April–May 1990), 293–316.

ST. JOHN, WALDET D. "You Are What You Communicate," *Personnel Journal,* October 1985.

SANDEMAN, HUGH. "The U.S. Management Evolution," *World Press Review,* March 1985, pp. 27–28.

SANFORD, FILLMORE H. *Authoritarianism and Leadership.* Philadelphia: Institute for Research in Human Relations, 1950.

SANFORD, FILLMORE H. "Leadership Identification and Acceptance," in *Groups, Leadership and Men,* ed. Harold Guentzkow, Pittsburgh: Carnegie Press, 1951.

SASHKIN, MARSHALL. "Participative Management Is an Ethical Imperative," *Organizational Dynamics,* 12 (Spring 1984), 5–22.

SCHACHTER, STANLEY. *The Psychology of Affiliation.* Stanford, Calif.: Stanford University Press, 1959.

SCHAFFER, R. H. "Job Satisfaction as Related to Need Satisfaction in Work," *Psychological Monographs,* 67, no. 14 (1953).

SCHEIN, EDGAR. *Organizational Culture and Leadership.* San Francisco: Jossey-Bass, 1985.

SCHEIN, E. H., and WARREN G. BENNIS. *Personal and Organizational Change through Group Methods.* New York: John Wiley, 1965

SCHRIESHEIM, C. "The Great High Consideration–High Initiating Structure Myth," *Journal of Social Psychology,* April 1982.

SCHROEDER, PATRICIA K. "The Other Side of Leadership: Strengthening the Support Base," *Economic Development Review,* 8 (Summer 1990), 16–18.

SEARS, DAVID L. "Situational Performance Appraisal," *Supervisory Management,* 29, no. 5 (May 1985), 6–11.

SEASHORE, S. E. *Group Cohesiveness in the Industrial Work Group.* Ann Arbor: Survey Research Center, University of Michigan, 1954.

SELTZER JOSEPH, and BERNARD M. BASS. "Transformational Leadership: Beyond Initiation and Consideration," *Journal of Management,* 16 (December 1990), 693–703.

SELTZER, JOSEPH, and RITA E. NUMEROF. "Supervisory Leadership and Subordinate Burnout," *Academy of Management Journal,* 31 (June 1988), 439–46.

SENGE, PETER M. "The Leaders New Work: Building Learning Organizations," *Sloan Management Review,"* 32 (Fall 1990), 7–19.

SERGIOVANNI, THOMAS J. "Adding Value to Leadership Gets Extraordinary Results," *Educational Leadership,* 47 (May 1990), 23–27.

SHANKS, DAVID C. "The Role of Leadership in Strategy Development," *Journal of Business Strategy,* 10 (January–February 1989), 32–36.

SHARTLE, C. L. *Effective Performance and Leadership.* Englewood Cliffs, N.J.: Prentice Hall, 1956.

SHERIF, M., et al. *Intergroup Conflict and Cooperation: The Robbers' Cave Experiment.* Norman, Okla.: University Book Exchange, 1961.

SHERIF, M., and C. SHERIF. *Social Psychology.* New York: Harper & Row, 1969.

SHIRLEY, STEVE. "The Change Managers," *Management Today,* July 1989, p. 5.

SHULTZ, G. P. "Worker Participation on Production Problems," *Personnel,* XXVIII, no. 3 (1951), 202–11.

SIMON, H. A. *The New Science of Management Directions.* New York: Harper & Row, Pub., 1960.

SIMS, RONALD R. *An Experimental Learning Approach to Employee Training Systems.* New York: Quorum Books, 1990.

SINETAR, MARSHA. "SMR Forum: Entrepeneurs, Chaos, and Creativity – Can Creative People Really Survive Large Company Structure?" *Sloan Management Review,* Winter 1985, pp. 57–62.

SKILLMAN, KEITH C. "Leadership Close-up," *Association Management,* 43 (September 1991), 57–61.

SKINNER, B. F. *Analysis of Behavior.* New York: McGraw-Hill, 1961.

SKINNER, B. F. *Science and Human Behavior.* New York: Macmillan, 1953.

SKRZYCKI, CINDY. "Shaking Up Old Ways of Training Managers," *Bureaucrat,* 19 (Summer 1990), 52–54.

SLATER, STANLEY F. "The Influence of Managerial Style on Business Unit Performance," *Journal of Management,* 15 (September 1989), 441–55.

SMITH, FRANCES B. "Changing Leadership: Meeting the Challenges of a Competitive Environment," *Credit,* November–December 1987, pp. 12–13.

SMITH, GEOFFREY. "The Leap of Leadership," *Financial World,* 158 (July 25, 1989), 4.

SMITH, JONATHAN E., KENNETH P. CARSON, and RALPH A. ALEXANDER. "Leadership: It Can Make a Difference," *Academy of Management Journal,* December 1984, pp. 765–76.

SMITH, GLEN R., and BRIAN H. KLEINER. "Differences in Corporate Culture and Their Relationship to Organizational Effectiveness," *Leadership and Organizational Development Journal,* 8 (Winter 1987), 10–12.

SMITH, PERRY M. "Twenty Guidelines for Leaderships," *Nation's Business,* 77 (September 1989), 60–61.

SNYDER, NEIL H., BERNARD A. MORIN, and MARILYN A. MOR-
GAN. "Motivating People to Build Excellent Enterprises," *Business,*
38 (April–May–June 1988), 14–19.
SOLOMON, R. L. "Punishment," *American Psychologist,* 19 (1964), 239.
SONNENBERG, FRANK K. "A Vision for the 1990s," *Journal of Business
Strategy,* 11 (September–October 1990), 52–55.
SPECK, BRUCE W. "The Manager as Writing Mentor," *Training and De-
velopment Journal,* 44 (April 1990), 78–81.
STANTON, ERWIN S. "A Critical Revaluation of Motivation, Manage-
ment, and Productivity," *Personnel Journal,* March 1985.
STARR, MARTIN. "The Adaptability of Management: Winners and
Losers," *Government Executive,* NASA Special Report, September 1985.
STEERS, R. M. *Organizational Effectiveness: A Behavioral View.* Santa
Monica, Calif.: Goodyear, 1977.
STEIL, LYMAN K. "On Listening and Not Listening," *Executive Health,*
December 1981, pp. 30–35.
STEINER, IVAN D., and HOMER H. JOHNSON. "Authoritarianism and
Conformity, *Sociometry,* 26 (1963), 21–34.
STEVENSON, HOWARD H., and DAVID E. GUMPERT. "The Heart of
Entrepreneurship," *Harvard Business Review,* no. 2 (March–April
1985), 85–94.
STOGDILL, R. M., *Handbook of Leadership.* New York: The Free Press,
1974.
STOGDILL, R. M. *Individual Behavior and Group Achievement.* New York:
Oxford University Press, 1959.
STOGDILL, R. M. "Personal Factors Associated with Leadership: A Survey
of the Literature," *Journal of Psychology,* 25 (1948), 35–71.
STOGDILL, R. M., and ALVIN E. COONS, eds. *Leader Behavior: Its De-
scription and Measurement, Research Monograph No. 88.* Columbus:
Bureau of Business Research, The Ohio State University, 1957.
STONER, J. A. "Risky and Cautious Shifts in Group Decisions: The Influ-
ence of Widely Held Values," *Journal of Experimental Social Psychology,* 4 (1968), 442–59.
STRANG, T. S. "Positive Reinforcement: How Often and How Much," *Supervisory Management,* 30, no. 1 (1985), 7–9.
STRAUSS, GEORGE. "Tactics of Lateral Relationship: The Purchasing
Agent," *Administrative Science Quarterly,* no. 2 (September 1962), 161–
86.
STRAUSS, GEORGE. "Workers: Attitudes and Adjustments," in *The Work-
er and the Job,* ed. J. M. Rosow. Englewood Cliffs, N.J.: Prentice Hall,
1974.
STRENSKI, JAMES B. "Quality and Communication: Keys to Leadership
in the Service Industry," *Public Relations Quarterly,* 34 (Winter 1989),
17–18.
STUMPF, STEPHEN A., and THOMAS P. MULLEN. "Strategic Leader-
ship: Concepts, Skills, Style, and Process," *Journal of Management
Development,* 10 (Winter 1991), 42–53.
STUTZ, F. H., R. G. MORROW, and K. H. BLANCHARD. "Report of a
Survey," in *College and University Trustees and Trusteeship: Recom-
mendations and Report of a Survey.* Ithaca: New York State Regents
Advisory Committee on Educational Leadership, 1966.

SUTTON, CHARLOTTE DECKER, and KRIS K. MOORE. "Public Opinions" *Harvard Business Review,* 5 (1985), 42–66.

SZILAGYI, ANDREW D., JR., and MARC J. WALLACE. *Organizational Behavior and Performance* (5th ed.). Glenview, Ill.: Scott, Foresman, 1990.

TAIT, GRANT. "Managing by Psychology," *Management Today,* July 1985, pp. 64–65.

TANNENBAUM, ROBERT, and WARREN H. SCHMIDT. "How to Choose a Leadership Pattern," *Harvard Business Review,* March–April, 1958, pp. 95–102.

TAYLOR, FREDERICK W. *The Principles of Scientific Management.* New York: Harper & Brothers, 1991.

TELL, TERRY VAN. "Communicating with Your Employees and Boss," *Supervisory Management,* 34 (October 1989), 5–10.

TERKEL, S. *Working.* New York: Random House, 1974.

TERRY, GEORGE R. *Principles of Management* (3rd ed.) Homewood, Ill.: Richard D. Irwin, 1960.

THARENOU, PHYLLIS, and JOHN T. LYNDON. "The Effect of a Supervisory Development Program on Leadership Style," *Journal of Business and Psychology,* 4 (Spring 1990), 365–73.

THOMAS, ALAN BERKELEY. "Does Leadership Make a Difference to Organizational Performance?" *Administrative Science Quarterly,* 33 (September 1988), 388–400.

THORNE, PAUL. "Visions That Transform," *International Management,* 44 (October 1989), 74.

THORNTON, SCOTT J. "Leadership Traits That Work Worldwide," *Association Management,* 42 (August 1990), 22.

TJOSVOLD, DEAN. "Interdependence and Power Between Managers and Employees: A Study of the Leader Relationship," *Journal of Management,* 15 (March 1989), 49–62.

TOWNSEND, ROBERT C. *Up the Organization.* New York: Knopf, 1970.

TRICE, HARRISON M., and JANICE M. BEYER. "Studying Organizational Cultures Through Rites and Ceremonials," *Academy of Management Review,* 9, no. 4 (1984).

TRIST, E. L., et al. *Organizational Choice.* London: Tavistock Publications, 1963.

TUBBS, STEWART L. *A Systems Approach to Small Group Interaction* (2nd ed.). Reading Mass.: Addison-Wesley, 1984.

TUSTIN, TIM. "Follow My Leader," *Management Today,* December 1989, p. 5.

URWICK, LYNDALL F. *The Theory of Organization.* New York: American Management Association, 1952.

VALENZANO, JOSEPH M. "New Leadership for a Changing Workforce," *Journal of Business Strategy,* 11 (March–April 1990), 62–63.

VICERE, ALBERT A. "The Changing Paradigm for Executive Development," *Journal of Management Development,* 10 (Summer 1991), 44–47.

VROMM, V. H. "Can Leaders Learn to Lead?" *Organizational Dynamics,* Winter 1976, pp. 17–28.

VROOM, V. H. *Some Personality Determinants of the Effects of Participation.* Englewood Cliffs, N.J.: Prentice Hall, 1960.

VROOM, VICTOR H., and ARTHUR G. JAGO. *The New Leadership: Man-*

aging Participation in Organizations. Englewood Cliffs, N.J.: Prentice Hall, 1988.

VROOM, V. H., and PHILIP YETTON. *Leadership and Decision Making.* Pittsburgh, Pa.: University of Pittsburgh Press, 1976.

WAGEL, WILLIAM H. "Leadership Training for a New Way of Managing," *Personnel,* 64 (December 1987), 4–8.

WALTHER, GEORGE. *Profitable Telemarketing* (Audiocassette Program), Tape 2: "Communicating Clearly," Chicago: Nightingale–Conant Corporation, 1984.

WALTON, RICHARD E. "From Control to Commitment in the Workplace," *Harvard Business Review,* March–April 1985.

WANT, JEROME H. "Managing Change in a Turbulent Business Climate," *Management Review,* 79 (November 1990), 38–41.

WEBER, MAX. *The Theory of Social and Economic Organization,* trans. A. H. Henderson and ed. Talcott Parsons. New York: Oxford University Press, 1946.

WEISS, W. H. "Being Innovative Pays Off," *Supervision.* February 1985, pp. 3–6.

WERTHER, WILLIAM B. "Loyalty at Work," *Business Horizons,* 31 (March–April 1988), 20–24.

WESTHAVER, MARIE. "Scoring the Business Touchdown," *Business Credit,* 91 (October 1989), 26–27.

WEX, SAMUEL. "Leadership and Change in the 1990s," *Optimum,* 21 (Spring 1990), 25–30.

WHEELAN, SUSAN A. *Facilitating Training Groups: A Guide to Leadership and Verbal Intervention Skills.* New York: Praeger, 1990.

WHITE, CHARLES S. "Managing Worker Competition–Hints and Pitfalls," *Industrial Management,* 29 (November–December 1987), 28–31.

WHITE, E. "Trust–A Prerequisite for Motivation," *Supervisory Management,* 29 (February 1984), 22–25.

WHITE, ROBERT W. "Motivation Reconsidered: The Concept of Competence," *Psychological Review,* LXVI, 5 (1959).

WHITE, ROBERT W., and R. LIPPITT. *Autocracy and Democracy: An Experimental Inquiry.* New York: Harper & Row, Pub., 1960.

WHITEHEAD, T. N. *The Industrial Worker: Human Relations in a Group of Manual Workers.* Cambridge: Harvard University Press, 1977.

WHITMIRE, MARSHALL, and PHILIP R. NIENSTEDT. "Lead Leaders into the '90s," *Personnel Journal,* 70 (May 1991), 80–81.

WHYTE, W. F. *Man and Organization.* Homewood, Ill.: Richard D. Irwin, 1959.

WHYTE, W. F., ed. *Money and Motivation.* New York: Harper & Row, Pub., 1955.

WIEBERG, LARS-ERIK. "Should You Change Your Leadership Style?," *Management Solutions,* 33 (January 1988), 5–12.

WILHITE, JIM O. "A Point of View: Toughness and True Leadership in the 1990s," *National Productivity Review,* 8 (Summer 1989), 219–22.

WILLIAMS, MALCOLM "Leadership–The Key to Economic Development," *Economic Development Review,* 8 (Summer 1990), 4–6.

WLODKOWSKI, RAYMOND J. *Enhancing Adult Motivation to Learn: A Guide to Improving Instruction and Increasing Learner Achievement.* San Francisco: Jossey-Bass, 1985.

WOLFF, MICHAEL F. "Exercising Leadership in Corporation," *Research-Technology Management,* 31 (May–June 1988), 9–11.

WOODRUFF, DAVIS M. "Seven Steps to Better Employee Relations," *Supervisory Management,* 34 (January 1989), 35–38.

WOODWARD, J. *Industrial Organizations: Theory and Practice.* London: Oxford University Press, 1965.

WRIGHT, N. "Leadership Styles–Which Are Best When," *Business Quarterly,* Winter 1984.

WYNNE, BERNARD. "Leadership and Excellence," *Management Decision,* 28, (January 1990), 15–19.

YANKELOVICH, D. "The Meaning of Work," in *The Worker and the Job,* ed. J. M. Rosow, Englewood Cliffs, N.J.: Prentice Hall, 1974.

ZALEZNIK, ABRAHAM. "The Leadership Gap," *Academy of Management Executive,* 4 (February 1990), 7–22.

ZANDER, A., E. J. THOMAS, and T. NATSOULAS. "Personal Goals and the Group's Goals for the Member," *Human Relations,* XIII, no. 4 (1960), 333–44.

Index